D1425213

Guenther Roth and Claus Wittich. New York: Bedminster Press, 3 vols.

WHITEFORD, ANDREW
1964   *Two Cities of Latin America.* Garden City: Anchor Books.

WHITEFORD, MICHAEL
1976   *The Forgotten Ones: Colombian Countrymen in an Urban Setting.* Gaines-ville: University of Florida Press.

WHYTE, WILLIAM FOOTE
1943   *Street Corner Society: The Social Structure of an Italian Slum.* Chicago: University of Chicago Press.

WIRTH, LOUIS
1938   "Urbanism as a Way of Life." *American Journal of Sociology,* 44:1-24.

YOUNG, M., and P. WILMOTT
1957   *Family and Kinship in East London.* London: Routledge and Kegan Paul.

URBAN PLACE

A N D

Process:

Readings in the Anthropology of Cities

IRWIN PRESS / M. ESTELLIE SMITH

MACMILLAN PUBLISHING CO., INC.

NEW YORK

COLLIER MACMILLAN PUBLISHERS

LONDON

Macmillan Publishing Co., Inc.
866 Third Avenue, New York, New York 10022

Collier Macmillan Canada, Ltd.

Library of Congress Cataloging in Publication Data

Main entry under title:

Urban place and process.

Bibliography: p.
Includes index.
1. Urban anthropology—Addresses, essays, lectures.
2. Cities and towns—Addresses, essays, lectures.
I. Press, Irwin.   II. Smith, M. Estellie (date)
GN395.U73   301.36   79-13355
ISBN 0-02-396540-1

Printing: 1 2 3 4 5 6 7 8   Year: 0 1 2 3 4 5 6

Preface

Although this is basically a reader in urban anthropology, we have attempted to take a broad perspective. Influential and insightful works from other disciplines are utilized where possible. Overall, it was decided to aim for a maximum of selections and representative sub-areas. In so doing, we have had to shorten a number of contributions and extract some brief excerpts from larger books and monographs. We are most grateful to our authors for their permission to so edit. We believe we have not done damage to the basic sense and contribution of their work.

The selection process was most difficult. Each of the co-editors initially made an independent choice of some 50 "critical" works. We were surprised to note that a number of our picks did not coincide—a reflection of both the breadth and still-unclear direction of the growing discipline of urban anthropology. The first cut, the next, and the next were increasingly agonizing; for in each instance, absolutely "indispensable" articles and excerpts had to be dropped. The final draft is a result of heated negotiation between two personal professional orientations, and in no way reflects a lack of quality in the material we decided to omit. Indeed, the selections omitted could constitute a top-notch reader in their own right. Overall, we have attempted to strike some balance between "classical" works and variant approaches, between the development of cities and contemporary urban dynamics, between urban theory and description of actual towns and peoples.

We wish to offer special thanks to our research assistants—Jane Ball, Sheila Muldoon, Terry O'Nell, and Maria Choca for their hard work and for the valuable student perspective they contributed. Thanks also to George Carr and Ken Scott of Macmillan for a thoroughly professional job.

Irwin Press
University of Notre Dame
M. Estellie Smith
SUNY College, Oswego

Contents

PART FIVE
Units of Urban Organization

PART SIX
Urban Places

PART SEVEN
Economic and Cultural Differentiation in the City

The Urban Future

Editors' Bibliography

Introduction

IRWIN PRESS AND M. ESTELLIE SMITH

Why Cities?

The study of urban places has been a concern of many disciplines over the past century. Cities have attracted attention because everywhere, and with astonishing speed, they continually increase in number, size, population, and sensory impact. Indeed, it has been suggested that there will soon be little that is not urban. Kingsley Davis predicts that by the year 2031, all the world's population will be living in "urban places" (however that is defined—and we will return to this point), *if* urban growth continues at the 1950–1970 rate (1972:52). Admittedly, some of those places will be small, but Davis maintains that by 2009, half the world's population will reside in cities of 100,000 or larger, and *all* humans will be in cities of that size by the year 2045 (Davis, 1972:52).

Cities attract study because, for one thing, they offer social scientists seemingly unlimited data on the nature of various kinds of institutional complexities and change. As locus and ultimate concentrator of powerful elites, of capital, wage labor, esoteric skills, constituencies, product markets, and services, the city is also the context in which many material, social, and ideological trends reach climax—the most elaborate architecture, the most complex economic structures, the most pervasive poverty, the most intricate and cumbersome bureaucracies, and the most varied and dynamic population conglomerations. Architects, historians, sociologists, economists, and political scientists have all contributed significantly to our knowledge of urban places and processes.

We are interested not only in the city as place, but are also concerned with the dynamics of urbanization. At its base, urbanization is a process that involves the transfer of tribal, peasant, and other rural populations to urban life-styles. As Philip Mayer shows so clearly (reprinted on pages 223–240 of this text), the mere fact of migrancy to cities does not imply automatic urbanization. *Urbanization* is a process of culture change and implies shifts in values, attitudes, and behaviors toward compatibility with local urban patterns.

Anthropology, Sociology, and the Development of Urban Study

Such a process falls naturally within the realm of anthropology, as does description and analysis of the origins and varieties of the more basic urban cultural patterns.

Although archaeologists have maintained a long and consistent interest in the origins and development of cities, ethnologists have only recently begun to develop a significant body of data from which to draw generalizations about the contemporary functions and variations of urban life. Traditionally, anthropology's focus has been directed almost exclusively to the study of isolated primitive societies with exotic customs and obscure pasts. This interest arose in the nineteenth century as contrast between the rapidly industrializing/urbanizing nations and the world's remote and primitive peoples came into increasingly sharp perspective. It solidified in response to extravagances concerning the nature of man and the origins and relative abilities of different cultures and races. As steamships, railroads, autos, and airplanes quickly shrunk the world, anthropologists intensified their interest in primitives as a means of salvaging a record of customs seemingly doomed to disappear beneath the onslaught of cash, colonialism, modernization, and tourism. If anthropologists of the early twentieth century touted the charms of lusty and innocent primitives, while decrying the decadence of modern urban society, they were doing no more than joining sociologists and philosophers influenced by Rousseau, Toënnies, Simmel, Cooly, Durkheim, and others, who viewed the good, simple (and ostensibly better) life as having been despoiled by the unique and dubious qualities of urban society. Such a stance was most forcefully proclaimed by a group of sociologists based at the University of Chicago in the early decades of the twentieth century. Foremost among them were Robert Park, E. W. Burgess, R. D. McKenzie, and Louis Wirth. The "Chicago School" attempted to clarify and codify some of the concepts concerning urban places and the nature of urban life. In so doing, they significantly influenced the goals and methods of later generations of social scientists.

Their contributions were twofold. First, they depicted the city (any city, all cities) as a natural ecological system, consisting of "natural areas" or subareas (such as slums, ethnic and residential neighborhoods, central business district, industrial zones) in dynamic interaction. Each had specific functions, but all contributed to the maintenance of the whole community (Park and McKenzie, 1925). Cities were to be identified, in the first place, as communities that were *larger, denser,* and more socioculturally *heterogeneous* than other community types (Wirth, 1938, reprinted in this volume).

The implications for values and behavior within such communities constituted the second major contribution of the Chicago School. Park depicted the city as a place that put a premium upon rationality, upon the use of technical devices, and upon the development of unusual skills (1915:585). City dwelling called for role specialization, competition, and the ability to accommodate rapid change. Urban social groups were based not upon kinship but upon common jobs or interests. Urban social interaction involved "the substitution of indirect, 'secondary,' for direct, face-to-face 'primary' " relationships (Park, 1915:593). Park's views were thoroughly compatible with those of Georg Simmel (Park had studied with him for a short time), whose own depiction of urban social organization was based upon experience with German cities of the late nineteenth century. Park and Simmel, in turn, were echoed later by Louis Wirth, perhaps the most well-known advocate of this particular view of urban life.

Wirth (1938, reprinted on pages 30–48) stressed the impersonality and heterogeneity of urban life. He saw cities as housing a variety of economic classes, ethnics, interest groups, and elites. Interaction in such a milieu would "naturally" tend to be more impersonal, superficial, and transitory (Park's "secondary relationships"). Having many roles and playing each in a different arena (job, church, family, street, social club, and so on), the urban individual has many *segmentalized* relationships, no one of which requires the exhibition of his full identity or personality. Urbanites thus have less intensive knowledge of one another and less control over one another's behavior.

Such a view was closely reflected in anthropology. Anthropologist Robert Redfield (also at the University of Chicago, and Robert Park's son-in-law) saw cities not only as disorganized, heterogeneous, impersonal, and secular but capable as well of influencing and tainting the hinterlands. Redfield suggested that primitive life (or "folk" life, as he put it) would continue in pure form unless contaminated by contact with urban forces. As a means of typing societies according to degree of purity or urban contamination, he proposed a *folk-urban continuum*, ranging from pure "folk societies" at one ideal pole, to equally "pure" cities at the other. Supposedly, all societies would fall somewhere along the continuum (Redfield, 1941; 1947). Those towards the folk end were characterized by (among other things) homogeneity, personal interaction, religious significance of mundane behaviors, and concern for group opinion and welfare. Societies towards the urban end exhibited the "opposite" characteristics. Redfield was never very clear about them.

Redfield's scheme was significant for several reasons. First and foremost, it brought the city (or at least urban influence) under anthropological consideration by suggesting that contemporary rural social disorganization and modernization resulted in large measure from urban contact. Second, by selecting Mexican peasant villages as examples of both folk and modernizing communities, he stimulated the study of peasantry by anthropologists who had long disdained fieldwork among any but primitive or tribal peoples. There was yet another dividend. When anthropologists began studying peasant towns, they found them to be one of the major sources of migrants to the world's growing cities. The necessity of having to follow up on the fate of these migrants was perhaps the major impetus for anthropologists to leave the isolated hinterlands and migrate to the contemporary urban setting. What they looked for, what they found, and how they found it was strongly influenced by the urban paradigm of Simmel, Park, Wirth, Redfield, and others.

This overall paradigm essentially depicted the city as a pathological milieu, difficult for resident and scholar alike, especially anthropologists who stressed the normative rather than the deviant. This meant research would be difficult if one wished to make a general statement about behavior or values. If each urban individual was unique and his behavior fragmented, if each social class, economic category, neighborhood, or ethnic group had its own values, integration patterns, and social control mechanisms, how could one select typical or representative urban individuals or groups and make generalizations about them, let alone about the city as a whole?

Anthropologists were readily intimidated by this view of the city. Their methodological stock-in-trade—"participant observation"—had developed as a response to research in relatively small, isolated, and homogeneous communities. This method includes meticulous observation (census taking, map making, minute behavioral descriptions, and so on), directed, intense interviews (as well as casual conversation), and participation in as many life-events as possible (and permissible) over a long period of time, generally a year or more. Because anthropologists usually go into the field as individuals, rather than as members of large research teams, they do not have the time or resources to observe and interview all persons and events in the target community. Therefore, under the assumptions that the community is more or less homogeneous and that any one member is fairly representative of all others, traditional anthropological field research usually involves intensive work with a limited number of informants judged to be maximally representative of the whole. Of course, no community is truly homogeneous. In the end, it is the anthropologist's prolonged residence in and intimate personal involvement with the community that make it possible for him to catch the discrepancies and note the variant behavior patterns, which then flesh out his description and analysis.

But would such an approach work in cities? And what would anthropologists find when they got there? The Chicago School had depicted urban and rural as social phenomena of quite different orders. And anthropologist Ralph Beals proposed that "rural-urban acculturation and cross-cultural acculturation differ only in degree and do not represent substantially different processes of change" (1951:7). In short, expect substantial cultural breakdown.

Anthropology in the City

When anthropologists followed their tribal peoples and peasants to the cities, they were surprised to find that the picture was apparently not so grim. Generally, rural migrants were discovered to be still fairly well integrated into a cohesive group of friends and kin. Further, they frequently exhibited a significant number of rural behaviors and values, sufficient to label their transition to city life as "urbanization without breakdown" (the title of Oscar Lewis' early study of migrants from Tepoztlan to Mexico City, 1952). It was found that migrants rarely moved to, lived in, or interacted with "the city at large." Rather, they tended to concentrate in, and deal predominantly with, enclaves of other migrants having similar cultural and economic background. Often they lived with kin during their initial period in the city.

Such findings did not directly contradict the Chicago urban paradigm but did stress the easily forgotten point that cities were far more heterogeneous *across* neighborhoods, classes, or subgroups than *within* them. Furthermore, although Lewis ignored the point, subsequent anthropologists (particularly Africanists) showed that urban centers differ in the migrant pools from which they draw. Cities that attract migrants from nearby hinterlands are much more likely to house urbanites with significant rural characteristics than are cities (Chicago, for example) whose migrant population comes from a distance too great to allow continuing rural (particularly tribal or peasant) influence.

By and large, the Chicago urban paradigm at best has been modified rather than disproven. In the early 1940s, Horace Miner attempted to test it by studying a whole non-Western urban community. He selected the small African city of Timbuctoo (population 6,000) and concluded that despite its size it fit the paradigm in general terms. That is, the heterogeneous tribal makeup, the markets, the cash economy, and the ties with outside cultures mark Timbuctoo as classically urban. At the same time, Miner noted that various segments and levels of the population differed greatly from one another in urbanity or folklike characteristics (1965:286). Thus, the Chicago paradigm holds at the larger, macro-city level of organization, yet does not necessarily describe life at lower (more prescribed) tribal, neighborhood, or family levels. Herbert Gans (1962) reflected similar conclusions in characterizing an Italian neighborhood of Boston as an "urban village"—a homogeneous, well-

organized, and integrated unit of what is assumed to be a generally heterogeneous, impersonal large city (his description of the neighborhood
appears on pages 352–362 of this volume).

On the other hand, William Bascom (1955) and Gideon Sjoberg (1960)
suggest that the Chicago paradigm applies only to Western industrial cities and not necessarily to cities of other times or places. Bascom (see
pages 48–60) demonstrated the antiquity of native African cities, noted
their tribal origins, and showed how they reflect patterns of land use
and population makeup quite distinct from Western urban stereotypes.
Sjoberg (pages 167–182) suggested that the Chicago urban paradigm describes only modern industrial cities, not earlier or non-Western urban
forms that he calls "pre-industrial." In other words, the Wirthian city (if
it existed at all) was but one form of city. There were various others.
And heterogeneity may be characteristic of whole city structures but not
necessarily at lower levels of organization.

When anthropologists found there were units within cities that were
relatively small, homogeneous, and susceptible to study with traditional
concepts and methods, they began to approach urban research in increasing numbers. Still clearly influenced by the Chicago paradigm, the
majority of anthropologists dealt (and still do) with "peasants in cities"
(or tribesmen in cities). They concerned themselves with describing the
effects of city residence upon rurally derived kinship, family, economic
behavior, interpersonal control mechanisms, and other "familiar"
aspects of social organization. A number of significant studies were
produced. There emerged a picture of urbanization as a complex, multifaceted process, dependent upon city type, rural culture, urban and
rural economic bases, residence forms, stratification systems, and a host
of other variables. The focus on urbanization led naturally to the discovery of adaptive mechanisms unique to cities. Squatter settlements and
voluntary associations (including tribal, caste, clan, and family organizations) were shown to play potentially significant roles in certain stages of
the urbanization process (see pages 309–333 and 362–369). Subsequent
studies expanded the interests of anthropology to include an array of new
problems not traditionally associated with small, rural communities—neighborhoods, buildings, social networks, urban relocation, poverty, racism, ethnicity, specialized occupations, and unemployment, to
name only a few. Urban research has produced a further dividend of
tool sharpening. Methods and theories generated by urban work are
being fruitfully applied to research in peasant and tribal communities. At
the same time, many traditional methods and theories are being
strengthened by successful application in this nontraditional milieu.

The Question of Holism

Regardless of problem orientation, however, most of these studies had one thing in common: they were narrowly focused upon small target portions of the total urban population. Not only clearly bounded migrant, tribal, or ethnic enclaves and neighborhoods, but also street corner peer groups (Rubel, 1966; Liebow, 1967), single families (Lewis, 1959; Bott, 1957), gangs (Whyte, 1943; Keiser, 1969), individuals (Plotnicov, 1967), bums (Spradley, 1970) and other rather isolated or limited population segments were the most consistent units of study for urban anthropologists. Each study focused upon one "manageable" element of the urban milieu to the exclusion of most others.*

Anthony Leeds suggests that overall there has been a "thorough failure to justify the units of study used and failure to show mutual effects between the asserted units of study and the city in which they are immersed" (1968:32). The narrow focus of most urban studies, adds Richard Fox (reprinted on pages 105–121 of this volume), places the emphasis "on the city as a research locale rather than as the object of investigation . . ." and this "has given much urban anthropology a limited theoretical perspective" (Fox, 1972:218).

This is not to say that urban investigators lacked the crucial *holistic* orientation of anthropology. Rather, they applied their holism within the confines of bounded population or behavioral segments of the city. Today, therefore, the relationship of these segments to the wider city—its structure, ecology, function, and history—and the relationship between the city, its environment, and wider societal (cultural, political) context is still incompletely known.

Studies of entire urban communities ("urban ethnographies") are few in number. There has been a slow trickle of them since William Lloyd Warner and his students began their "Yankee City" study in the early 1930s (published 1941 on). Warner, an anthropologist who had worked among Australian aborigines, attempted to dissect the economic and social structure of a New England town by combining the painstaking participant observation of traditional ethnography with formal interviews, census materials, and other more "sociological" methods. His work demonstrated complex interrelationships between economic status, social stratification, and political power in an American town. Miner's study of Timbuctoo produced one of the earliest descriptions of urban ethnic complexity. The important relationship between national

---

* If the manageable enclave, street corner, or network study became the magic bullet with which anthropology attacked the big, bad, analytically ungainly urban mega-unit, sociology's weapon was the "sample" which "guaranteed" the representativeness of results obtained through questionnaires or surveys among limited numbers of individuals in a large population. The invention of the computer also allowed sociology to coax extremely subtle correlations from often seemingly disparate variables whose relationship is invisible to human actors or observers and becomes apparent only through the magic of complex electronic and statistical manipulations.

culture, historical development of cities, and contemporary urban structure (particularly social stratification) has been brilliantly demonstrated
by Andrew Whiteford in his comparative studies of Popayan, Colombia
and Queretero, Mexico (1964). More recent works such as those of
Gulick on Tripoli (1967), de Blij on Mombasa (1968), and Press on Seville
(1979) offer broad overviews of specific cities and show the interrelationship of city ecology, services, economic sectors, ethnicity, and other
factors. A number of ethnographic accounts of towns appear to be of
wide scope on the surface, yet actually deal with specific problems
(such as housing relocation, social stratification, unionization, and industrialization) rather than the broader urban context and its effects.

A growing body of studies has also dealt more or less holistically with
neighborhoods, treating them as economic, ethnic, and social wholes
while indicating their dependence upon elements of the broader urban
context. Carolyn Ware's pioneer investigation of Greenwich Village
(1935), Dore's Tokyo neighborhood study (1968), Marris' contrast between city center and housing estate in Lagos, Nigeria (1971), Kenny's elegant treatment of a Madrid parish (1962), Gans' work on an Italian
neighborhood in Boston (1962), Whiteford's investigation of a Popayan
(Colombia) barrio (1976), and the slum studies of Roberts (Guatemala
City, 1973), Leeds (Rio and São Paulo favelas, 1968), Safa (Puerto Rican
shanty town, 1974), and Peattie (a Venezuelan new town barrio, 1968)
are examples of such holistic subcity works, which also attempt to relate neighborhood to wider city and national cultural patterns.

More broadly holistic studies have begun leading to an anthropology
of cities, rather than simply *in* cities. Today, the notion that one can understand roles, groups, or institutions without understanding their connections to the wider urban context is becoming passé. This wider context includes all ethnic groups, social classes, neighborhoods,
organizations, and institutions within the city that compete for resources and with which any single unit must ultimately contend. The
context also includes the *history* of the city, both actual and remembered or assumed, because the historical development of the city significantly conditions local attitudes toward change and outside influence.
Thus, for example, a city's long tradition of elitism, based upon control
of ritual, rural landholdings, and patronage can work against industrialization and social mobility (see pp. 121–128 for Press' discussion of
historical influence upon development in Seville). The nature of the particular city's *economic system* (degree of mechanization, labor and skill
requirements, availability of capital, and so forth) and *power base* (for
example, rural-oriented versus urban-oriented, hereditary versus achieved) determines avenues or barriers to migrancy, social mobility, and
general well-being. The economic base also affects residential patterns
and the operation and function of kin groups. Small-scale craft opera-

tions plus the importance of patronage, nepotism, and ascribed status can encourage maintenance of strong kin and family ties, whereas wage labor, skill differentiation, and universalism can make the need for kin group dependencies minimal. The nature and effectiveness of *services* offered by and within the city along with pervasiveness of the local bureaucracy can have significant modifying influence upon the form and operation of family and kin group. Publicly offered education, health, and welfare benefits can effectively rob families of traditional functions, thus creating special pressure upon sex role and marriage stability. Such benefits also serve as a basis for attracting migrants from the hinterlands and even from other societies. The immediate *natural environment* of the city, such as its geographic features or resources, can influence its size, shape, and visual impact, the location of transportation and service centers, and certain general functions of the city (communication versus manufacturing versus bureaucratic control). The nature of the wider *societal government* can influence city function and power, particularly if the seat of government lies elsewhere. External policy decisions readily affect such elements as city capital availability, credit, public housing, and indigent support. Finally, the wider *sociocultural patterns* constitute the base upon which any and all urban behaviors are laid; cities that develop in tribal-based "kinship societies," for example, will be different from those that emerge from a peasant base.

Obviously, there are different levels of holistic concern, reflection of the fact that larger systems usually contain subsystems, which may contain smaller systems, and so on. No single study can marshal the time or funds to permit adequate investigation of all urban levels (including outside influences). A truly holistic study would have to involve the perspectives not only of anthropology but of many related disciplines as well. If complete holism is an unattainable goal, it is nonetheless an essential guideline to urban research. Awareness of the potentially complex interrelationships between urban segments or cities and hinterlands serves to increase the sophistication with which we identify, investigate, and analyze our urban units of study.

What Is a City?

An important factor contributing to the weakness of holistic orientation in urban studies is the ambiguity that characterizes definitions of the city. *City* and *urban* are generally used interchangeably, although as Halley noted (1971:8), urban more correctly "refers to a quality of life that is typically found" in cities. At any rate, most of the definitions of city or urban place can be subsumed under a half-dozen or so general orientations:

1. *Nature of the Economic Base.*
   Cities as defined by presence of trade, middlemen, commerce, cash, and markets (Weber, 1958:81; Pirenne, 1956:39; Park, 1915:584; Childe, 1950).
2. *Special Functions vis-a-vis the Wider Society.*
   Cities have nodal functions, controlling and linking hinterlands, areas and communities (Arensberg, 1968:6, 13; Smith, 1976).
3. *Degree of Structural Independence.*
   City is a legal entity with control over its own matters and self-government (Pirenne, 1956:39; Hawley, 1971:6).
4. *Intellectual and Esoteric Characteristics.*
   City as seat of the societal "great tradition" (Redfield, 1956:70).
   City as place of ultimate self-consciousness, a place of news, questioning, and discussion (Friedman, 1961:88).
   City as locus of literacy (Sjoberg, 1960:11).
5. *The Quality of Interpersonal Relationships.*
   City as locus of individual freedom, compartmentalization, and competition (Park, 1915:585; Simmel, 1950).
   City as place whose size prevents the "reciprocal personal acquaintance of its inhabitants" (Weber in Roth and Wittich, 1968:1213).
6. *Social Structural Characteristics.*
   City as place with a middle class (Pirenne, 1956:39).
   City as open social system—a meeting place for nonresidents as well as locals (Mumford, 1961:9–10).
   City as level of "sociocultural integration" characterized by roles, groups, and institutions (Steward, 1951; Moore, 1975).
   City as place of association of unrelated families and kin groups (Fustel de Coulanges, 1956:134).
   City as locus of greatest concentration of diversely based pressures and controls upon individual behavior (Press, 1979).
   City as place where contract replaces kinship (Maine, 1894; Martindale, 1958:48).
7. *Demographic Characteristics.*
   City as larger, denser, more heterogeneous than other community types (Wirth, 1938). The difficulty in specifying the size of communities to be designated as urban is clearly seen in Table 1. Note that some countries view as urban any community with as few as 100, others with a minimum of 30,000 residents. Some nations avoid the issue entirely, "urban" being simply any community labeled as such.

By and large, all of these views and definitions fall within, or straddle, two overall approaches. One depicts the city as a "real" place, with defi-

TABLE 1   Official Definitions of Urban (Selected countries, latest year reported)

Country	Definition
Ethiopia	Localities of 2,000 or more inhabitants.
Ghana	Localities of 5,000 or more inhabitants.
Senegal	Agglomerations of 10,000 or more inhabitants.
Canada	Incorporated cities, towns, and villages of 1,000 or more inhabitants, and their urbanized fringes; unincorporated places of 1,000 or more inhabitants, having a population density of at least 1,000 per square mile or 390 per square kilometer, and their urbanized fringes.
Greenland	Localities proclaimed as urban.
Mexico	Localities of 2,500 or more inhabitants.
United States	Places of 2,500 inhabitants or more incorporated as cities.
Ecuador	Capitals of provinces and cantons.
Peru	Populated centers with 100 or more occupied dwellings.
Indonesia	Municipalities, regency capitals, and other places with urban characteristics.
Japan	City (*shi*) having 30,000 or more inhabitants with 60% or more of the houses located in the main built-up areas and 60% or more of the population (including their dependants) engaged in manufacturing, trade, or other urban types of business. Alternatively, a *shi* having urban facilities and conditions as defined by the prefectural order is considered as urban.
West Malaysia	Gazetted areas with population of 10,000 or more.
Sweden	Built-up areas with at least 200 inhabitants and usually not more than 200 meters between houses.
U.S.S.R.	Cities are urban-type localities, officially designated as such by each of the constituent Republics, usually according to the criteria of number of inhabitants and predominance of agricultural, or number of nonagricultural workers and their families.

SOURCE: *U.N. Demographic Yearbook 1975.* 27th issue. New York, 1976.

nite physical boundaries, specific population size, clearly visible social groups and economic institutions. Cities have names and histories, hinterlands, and environments. The other approach deals less with *city as place* than with *urban as process*—a concept with several interpretations. One use of *process* refers to a special quality of social relations *generated,* though not limited to operating exclusively in, cities (Smith, 1976). By this view, it is possible to speak of urban phenomena (values, behaviors) in places other than cities (suburbs, pipeline and boom-towns, even peasant villages), which otherwise do not meet the demographic or institutional criteria for city status.

Another interpretation of urban as process focuses upon the complex interactions generated by the close juxtaposition of diverse groups, institutions, and, in Julian Steward's terms, "levels of socio-cultural integration" that all typically coexist in cities. This "diversity in proximity" (Moore, 1975) reflects the concentration in cities of not only complex, impersonal institutions, but also highly personal family groups, ethnic enclaves, and associations. The special processes of interaction between these varied and multilevel sectors are viewed as the elements that define *urban*. By such a definition, however, it is virtually impossible to describe as urban certain behavioral, particularly interactional, processes that may operate in nonurban places.

In truth, urban must be viewed as *both place and process* (Smith, 1976). After all, without certain resources, population minima, and economic bases, urban processes are not likely to be *generated*. This is true whether urban is defined in terms of processes qualitatively distinct from rural phenomena, or in terms of quantity (heterogeneity) of processes. Even if urban processes can operate in communities other than cities, they are unlikely to *originate* in such milieus and, indeed, can scarcely *continue* to function in the absence of outside, city-generated reinforcement (urban values, status systems, role structures, exchange mechanisms, and so forth).

Regardless of whether the focus is upon urban as place, urban as process, or both, definitions largely consist of threshold criteria that describe minimal levels of demographic, institutional, or structural complexity beneath which city or urban labels cannot be applied. The problem with threshold definitions lies in the differentiation of cities from one another once they exhibit the key urban characteristics. Gulick, in 1962, lamented the inability of existing urban definitions and typologies (theory) to meaningfully differentiate two cities such as Greensboro, North Carolina, and Manhattan (1962:446). They are both industry-fed, cash-based, socially heterogeneous, and democratically organized. However, the many subtle cultural differences between them are difficult to fit into a ready scheme.

The problem of how (upon what basis) to differentiate cities is still with us today. Certainly, typological schemes exist. There are a number of them, and most were available when Gulick made his complaint. By and large, city typologies fall into four general categories:

1. City organization.
2. City function.
3. Cultural identity.
4. National impact.

The first is represented by Max Weber's and Gideon Sjoberg's distinction of types based upon interaction of the organizational and institutional sectors of cities. Weber's (1927) dichotomy of occidental and oriental city types focuses upon the presence or absence of city autonomy from outside control and the independence of population or economic sectors from one another (if such autonomy exists, the city is occidental). Sjoberg dichotomized cities as industrial and pre-industrial (1960). The closer the integration of economic, political, religious institutions, and elites, the greater the control of these elites over the labor sector, the greater the degree of family control over economic roles and resources—the more pre-industrial the city (Sjoberg's typology is more fully developed on pages 167–182 of this volume).

The second typology is based upon functions attributed to cities. Pirenne's early dichotomy between *political/intellectual* and *economic* cities (1925:55 ff) was a precursor to Nutini's Latin American-based typology of cities as (a) administrative-bureaucratic, (b) trading-agricultural, (c) mining-manufacturing, and (d) military-religious. A recent refinement by Richard Fox (1977; see pages 205–209 of this volume) presents cities as reflecting the broader society types in which they arise. Fox sees all cities as fulfilling in varying degrees (a) ideological, (b) administrative, (c) mercantile, and (d) industrial functions for their societies (1977:3). However, the dominant function and thus predominant type of the city depends upon the society. Thus, for example, "in weak, or segmentary states, the ideological function of urban places is primary and defines the external adaptation of the city to the wider society" (1977:34).

The third typology was proposed by Redfield and Singer (1954, reprinted in this volume (pp. 183–205), whose *orthogenetic* and *heterogenetic* cities reflect "local" versus "outside" cultural origins and influences, respectively. The *native* cities of which some scholars speak, to distinguish them from colonial or other outside-influenced towns, could easily be viewed as orthogenetic, whereas *colonial* cities fall somewhere between orthogenetic and heterogenetic (McGee, however, would place them in the industrial/pre-industrial continuum; 1964:173).

The national impact typology was suggested by Hoselitz (1955:279), who distinguishes between *generative* cities, which exert a favorable impact upon national economic growth, and *parasitic* cities, which exert an opposite impact. Hoselitz (as well as Jefferson before him, 1939) also views other urban centers in a given nation or region as distinct from a single *primate* city, which monopolizes most nationally or regionally oriented decisions and activities.

Certainly, these typologies have utility. Each deals with a different aspect of the urban phenomenon—cultural identity, function, organization, or influence of the city. Each is a valid, if limited view. In one way or another, all shed light on the evolution and development of specific city types. The problem lies in the diversity of focus. The typologies have no common theoretical base; they reflect no common paradigm of urban growth, form, organization, or structure (equivalent, say, to the "part society" model of peasantry), which could make any and all cities or any and all urban studies directly amenable to comparison, contrast, and further theory building.

Looking for Urban Anthropology

Gulick, in a recent book review, expressed the opinion that we are "still searching for urban anthropology" (1974). The range of studies is dizzying, running the gamut from archaeological investigation of ancient irrigation systems to descriptions of swinging as an alternative style of modern marriage. The criticism is valid insofar as urban anthropology has yet to develop an explicit, commonly agreed-upon urban research focus and a "theory of cities." Of course, no other discipline has produced these either. While the topics of urban anthropological research vary greatly, the questions asked and analyses undertaken are derived from a solid core of anthropological concerns. This core represents a century of accumulated insights into past and present community formation, interpersonal relationships, and human strategies for adaptation to a wide array of societies and ecosystems.

No other social or humanistic science exhibits the special combination of historical, contemporary, ecological, and comparative concerns that characterizes anthropology. This broad perspective ensures that each urban anthropologist, regardless of his research focus, brings to the study of the city a fundamental grounding in the variety of human experience and cultural manifestations, an eclecticism born of awareness of alternative solutions in other times and places, a built-in skepticism of so-called universals or natural behavior, and a penchant for withholding judgment.

Thus, although anthropology is a relative newcomer to the city (most of the work in it has been done within the past two decades), it contributes significant insight and generalizations to the overall field of urban studies. These understandings complement and build upon the contributions of sociology, psychology, economics, political science, and history—disciplines that have traditionally focused upon Western, industrial cities and urban processes.

Cities are not easy to understand or study. They are the most complex of human communities, often seeming to concentrate the cumulative social and cultural creations of the species. Small wonder, therefore, that no single discipline can have a lock on urban studies.

The chapters that follow offer a cross section of anthropological contributions toward an urban science. At the same time, we also include from related disciplines a number of selections by scholars whose work has influenced and complemented anthropological thought, or whose views add significantly to the teaching function of this text.

Bibliography for references cited in this introduction and in editorial remarks throughout the remaining chapters can be found at the end of this volume.

A Note on Research and Term Paper Topics

Following each part of the text, you will find several suggested topics for student research and term papers. These are offered merely as examples of topics you can use. Some are strictly library topics to be researched in the literature of anthropology and other disciplines. Others require some form of fieldwork or archival investigation in the community. Remember that fieldwork, too, requires that you justify your selection of problem and final analysis by appropriate reference to the literature.

Many possible field research problems require observation only and do not involve direct intervention with people. Others may require direct dealings. Remember that in the United States federal guidelines now regulate research on human subjects, and most campuses have committees that must clear any such research. Be sure to contact the appropriate individual(s) and have your research approved, if such clearance is required for the type of investigation you propose.

PART

*Urbs and
Urbanism*

ONE

What is a town? As you have seen in the introduction, there are many ways in which you can define urban places and urban phenomena. By and large, size, function, and sociopsychological characteristics are the most commonly used criteria. In truth, there must be an interrelation between them. Size permits the development and maintenance of certain functions (communication, trade center, administrative control, and so on), which, in turn, encourages further increase in size. Both size and function condition the life-style of the community through creation of a milieu in which certain kinds of values and social behaviors are most adaptive. Most of the questions about cities and urban life are now known, but the answers are still coming in.

The following section offers up some of the more important questions and attempts at meaningful answers. The classic statements of Georg Simmel and Louis Wirth present a paradigm of impersonality, heterogeneity, and individuality of urban life. That such characteristics may be only partially relevent to the definition of an urban place, is reflected in the critical look Bascom takes at indigenous West African city development. And that the problem of an urban definition is still not resolved is indicated in the selection by Gulick who, almost forty years after Wirth, gives clear evidence that we are "still looking for Urban Anthropology" (Gulick 1974).

If the reader remains still unsure of whether urban is place or process, it will indicate a successful comprehension of the material.

The Metropolis and Mental Life

GEORG SIMMEL

Georg Simmel (1858–1918), a German sociologist, made a major impact on Park, Wirth, and other members of the Chicago School. Much of the Chicago School's concern with urban impersonality, individual freedom, and behavioral compartmentalization is clearly presaged in Simmel's work.

In this classic paper (written around 1903), Simmel is especially concerned with the psychosociological concomitants of urbanism. He contrasts the intense sensory stimulation of urban dwellers with the slower, more habitual, even-paced rhythm of life found in small towns and rural areas. The picture of urban life that he draws leaves no doubt where he stands: Urban associations are ruled by the head, not the heart; relations—as befits life in a money-dominated, commercial milieu—are calculating, objective, impersonally hard, and dominated by self-interest of "an unmerciful matter-of-factness." "An urban dweller's self-preservation," Simmel maintains, must be ". . . bought at the price of devaluating the whole objective world . . . which unavoidably drags one's own personality down into a feeling of the same worthlessness."

Still, when Simmel views "the struggle between objective and individual culture" (which he describes as "the two ways of allocating roles to men"), he states that it is "the function of the metropolis to provide the arena for this struggle and its reconciliation" [our italics]. Is there, because of this reconciliation, some positive good in cities?

The deepest problems of modern life derive from the claim of the individual to preserve the autonomy and individuality of his existence in the face of overwhelming social forces, of historical heritage, of external culture, and of the technique of life. The fight with nature which primitive man has to wage for his *bodily* existence attains in this modern form its latest transformation. The eighteenth century called upon man to free himself of all the historical bonds in the state and in religion, in morals and in economics. Man's nature, originally good and common to all, should develop unhampered. In addition to more liberty, the nineteenth century demanded the functional specialization of man and his work; this specialization makes one individual incomparable to another, and each of them indispensable to the highest possible extent. However, this specialization makes each man the more directly dependent upon the supplementary activities of all others. Nietzsche sees the full development of the individual conditioned by the most ruthless struggle of individuals; socialism believes in the suppression of all competition for the same reason. Be that as it may, in all these positions the same basic motive is at work: the person resists to being leveled down and worn out by a social-technological mechanism. An inquiry into the inner meaning of specifically modern life and its products, into the soul of the cultural body, so to speak, must seek to solve the equation which structures like the metropolis set up between the individual and the super-individual contents of life. Such an inquiry must answer the question of how the personality accommodates itself in the adjustments to external forces. This will be my task today.

The psychological basis of the metropolitan type of individuality consists in the *intensification of nervous stimulation* which results from the swift and uninterrupted change of outer and inner stimuli. Man is a differentiating creature. His mind is stimulated by the difference between a momentary impression and the one which preceded it. Lasting impressions, impressions which differ only slightly from one another, impressions which take a regular and habitual course and show regular and habitual contrasts—all these use up, so to speak, less consciousness than does the rapid crowding of changing images, the sharp discontinuity in the grasp of a single glance, and the unexpectedness of onrushing impressions. These are the psychological conditions which the metropolis creates. With each crossing of the street, with the tempo and multiplicity of economic, occupational and social life, the city sets up a deep contrast with small town and rural life with reference to the sensory foundations of psychic life. The metropolis exacts from man as a discriminating creature a different amount of consciousness than does rural life. Here the rhythm of life and sensory mental imagery flows more slowly, more habitually, and more evenly. Precisely in this connection the sophisticated character of metropolitan psychic life becomes understandable—as over against small town life which rests more upon deeply felt and emotional relationships. These latter are rooted in the more unconscious layers of the psyche and grow most readily in the steady rhythm of uninterrupted habituations. The intellect, however, has its locus in the transparent, conscious, higher layers of the psyche; it is the most adaptable of our inner forces. In order to accommodate to change and to the contrast of phenomena, the intellect does not require any shocks and inner upheavals; it is only through such upheavals that the more conservative mind could accommodate to the metropolitan rhythm of events. Thus the metropolitan type of man—which, of course, exists in a thousand individual variants—develops an organ protecting him against the threatening currents and discrepancies of his external environment which would uproot him. He reacts with his head instead of his heart. In this an increased awareness assumes the psychic prerogative. Metropolitan life, thus, underlies a heightened awareness and a predominance of intelligence in metropolitan man. The reaction to metropolitan phenomena is shifted to that organ which is least sensitive and quite remote from the depth of the personality. Intellectuality is thus seen to preserve subjective life against the overwhelming power of metropolitan life, and intellectuality branches out in many directions and is integrated with numerous discrete phenomena.

The metropolis has always been the seat of the money economy. Here the multiplicity and concentration of economic exchange gives an importance to the means of exchange which the scantiness of rural commerce would not have allowed. Money economy and the dominance of the intellect are intrinsically connected. They share a matter-of-fact attitude in dealing with men and with things; and, in this attitude, a formal justice is often coupled with an inconsiderate hardness. The intellectually sophisticated person is indifferent to all genuine individuality, because relationships and reactions result from it which cannot be exhausted with logical operations. In the same manner, the individuality of phenomena is not commensurate with the pecuniary principle. Money is concerned only with what is common to all: it asks for the exchange value, it reduces all quality and individuality to the question: How much? All intimate emotional relations between persons are founded in their individuality, whereas in rational relations man is reckoned with like a number, like an element which is in itself indifferent. Only the objective measurable achievement is of interest. Thus metropolitan man reckons with his merchants and customers, his domestic servants and often even with persons with whom he is obliged to have social intercourse. These features of intellectuality contrast with the nature of the small circle in which the inevitable knowledge of individuality as inevitably produces a warmer tone of behavior, a behavior which is beyond a mere objective balancing of service and return. In the sphere of the economic psychology of the small group it is of importance that under primitive conditions production serves the customer who orders the good, so that the producer and the consumer are acquainted. The modern metropolis, however, is supplied almost entirely by production for the market, that is, for entirely unknown purchasers who never personally enter the producer's actual field of vision. Through this anonymity the interests of each party acquire an unmerciful matter-of-factness; and the intellectually calculating economic egoisms of both parties need not fear any deflection because of the imponderables of personal relationships. The money economy dominates the metropolis; it has displaced the last survivals of domestic production and the direct barter of goods; it minimizes, from day to day, the amount of work ordered by customers. The matter-of-fact attitude is obviously so intimately interrelated with the money economy, which is dominant in the metropolis that nobody can say whether the intellectualistic mentality first promoted the money economy or whether the latter determined the former. The metropolitan way of life is certainly the most fertile soil for this reciprocity, a point which I shall document merely by citing the dictum of the most eminent English constitutional historian: throughout the whole course of English history, London has never acted as England's heart but often as England's intellect and always as her moneybag!

In certain seemingly insignificant traits, which lie upon the surface of life, the same psychic currents characteristically unite. Modern mind has become more and more calculating. The calculative exactness of practical life which the money economy has brought about corresponds to the ideal of natural science: to transform the world into an arithmetic problem, to fix every part of the world by mathematical formulas. Only money economy has filled the days of so many people with weighing, calculating, with numerical determinations, with a reduction of qualitative values to quantitative ones. Through the calculative nature of money a new precision, a certainty in the definition of identities and differences, an unambiguousness in agreements and arrangements has been brought about in the relations of life-elements—just as externally this precision has been effected by the universal diffusion of pocket watches. However the conditions of metropolitan life are at once cause and effect of this trait. The relationships and affairs of the typical metropolitan usually are so varied and complex that without the strictest punctuality in promises and services the whole structure would break down into an inextricable chaos. Above all, this necessity is brought about by the aggregation of so many people with such differentiated interests, who must integrate their relations and activities into a highly complex organism. If all clocks and watches in Berlin would suddenly go wrong in different ways, even if only by one hour, all economic life and communication of the city would be disrupted for a long time. In addition an apparently mere external factor, long distances, would make all waiting and broken appointments result in an ill-afforded waste of time. Thus, the technique of metropolitan life is unimaginable without the most punctual integration of all activities and mutual relations into a stable and impersonal time schedule. Here again the general conclusions of this entire task of reflection become obvious, namely, that from each point on the surface of existence—however closely attached to the surface alone—one may drop a sounding into the depth of the psyche so that all the most banal externalities of life finally are connected with the ultimate decisions concerning the meaning and style of life. Punctuality, calculability, exactness are forced upon life by the complexity and extension of metropolitan existence and are not only most intimately connected with its money economy and intellectualistic character. These traits must also color the contents of life and favor the exclusion of those irrational, instinctive, sovereign traits and impulses which aim at determining the mode of life from within, instead of receiving the general and precisely schematized form of life from without. Even though sovereign types of personality, characterized by irrational impulses, are by no means impossible in the city, they are, nevertheless, opposed to typical city life. The passionate hatred of men like Ruskin and Nietzsche for the metropolis is understandable in these terms. Their natures discovered the value of life alone in the unschematized existence which cannot be defined with precision for all alike. From the same source of this hatred of the metropolis surged their hatred of money economy and the intellectualism of modern existence.

The same factors which have thus coalesced into the exactness and minute precision of the form of life have coalesced into a structure of the highest impersonality; on the other hand, they have promoted a highly personal subjectivity. There is perhaps no psychic phenomenon which has been so unconditionally reserved to the metropolis as has the blasé attitude. The blasé attitude results first from the rapidly changing and closely compressed contrasting stimulations of the nerves. From this, the enhancement of metropolitan intellectuality, also, seems originally to stem. Therefore, stupid people who are not intellectually alive in the first place usually are not exactly blasé. A life in boundless pursuit of pleasure makes one blasé because it agitates the nerves to their strongest reactivity for such a long time that they finally cease to react at all. In the same way, through the rapidity and contradictoriness of their changes, more harmless impressions force such violent responses, tearing the nerves so brutally hither and thither that their last reserves of strength are spent; and if one remains in the same milieu they have no time to gather new strength. An incapacity thus emerges to react to new sensations with the appropriate energy. This constitutes that blasé attitude which, in fact, every metropolitan child shows when compared with children of quieter and less changeable milieus.

This physiological source of the metropolitan blasé attitude is joined by another source which flows from the money economy. The essence of the blasé attitude consists in the blunting of discrimination. This does not mean that the objects are not perceived, as is the case with the half-wit, but rather that the meaning and differing values of things, and thereby the things themselves, are experienced as insubstantial. They appear to the blasé person in an evenly flat and gray tone; no one object deserves preference over any other. This mood is the faithful subjective reflection of the completely internalized money economy. By being the equivalent to all the manifold things in one and the same way, money becomes the most frightful leveler. For money expresses all qualitative differences of things in terms of "how much?" Money, with all its colorlessness and indifference, becomes the common denominator of all values; irreparably it hollows out the core of things, their individuality, their specific value, and their incomparability. All things float with equal specific gravity in the constantly moving stream of money. All things lie on the same level and differ from one another only in the size of the area which they cover. In the individual case this coloration, or rather discoloration, of things through their money equivalence may be unnoticeably minute. However, through the relations of the rich to the objects to be had for money, perhaps even through the total character which the mentality of the contemporary public everywhere imparts to these objects, the exclusively pecuniary evaluation of objects has become quite considerable. The large cities, the main seats of the money exchange, bring the purchasability of things to the fore much more impressively than do smaller localities. That is why cities are also the genuine locale of the blasé attitude. In the blasé attitude the concentration of men and things stimulate the nervous system of the individual to its highest achievement so that it attains its peak. Through the mere quantitative intensification of the same conditioning factors this achievement is transformed into its opposite and appears in the peculiar adjustment of the blasé attitude. In this phenomenon the nerves find in the refusal to react to their stimulation the last possibility of accommodating to the contents and forms of metropolitan life. The self-preservation of certain personalities is bought at the price of devaluating the whole objective world, a devaluation which in the end unavoidably drags one's own personality down into a feeling of the same worthlessness.

Whereas the subject of this form of existence has to come to terms with it entirely for himself, his self-preservation in the face of the large city demands from him a no less negative behavior of a social nature. This mental attitude of metropolitans toward one another we may designate, from a formal point of view, as reserve. If so many inner reactions were responses to the continuous external contacts with innumerable people as are those in the small town, where one knows almost everybody one meets and where one has a positive relation to almost everyone, one would be completely atomized internally and come to an unimaginable psychic state. Partly this psychological fact, partly the right to distrust which men have in the face of the touch-and-go elements of metropolitan life, necessitates our reserve. As a result of this reserve we frequently do not even know by sight those who have been our neighbors for years. And it is this reserve which in the eyes of the small-town people makes us appear to be cold and heartless. Indeed, if I do not deceive myself, the inner aspect of this outer reserve is not only indifference but, more often than we are aware, it is a slight aversion, a mutual strangeness and repulsion, which will break into hatred and fight at the moment of a closer contact, however caused. The whole inner organization of such an extensive communicative life rests upon an extremely varied hierarchy of sympathies, indifferences, and aversions of the briefest as well as of the most permanent nature. The sphere of indifference in this hierarchy is not as large as might appear on the surface. Our psychic activity still responds to almost every impression of somebody else with a somewhat distinct feeling. The unconscious, fluid and changing character of this impression seems to result in a state of indifference. Actually this indifference would be just as unnatural as the diffusion of indiscriminate mutual suggestion would be unbearable. From both these typical dangers of the metropolis, indifference and indiscriminate suggestibility, antipathy protects us. A latent antipathy and the preparatory stage of practical antagonism effect the distances and aversions without which this mode of life could not at all be led. The extent and the mixture of this style of life, the rhythm of its emergence and disappearance, the forms in which it is satisfied—all these, with the unifying motives in the narrower sense, form the inseparable whole of the metropolitan style of life. What appears in the metropolitan style of life directly as dissociation is in reality only one of its elemental forms of socialization.

This reserve with its overtone of hidden aversion appears in turn as the form or the cloak of a more general mental phenomenon of the metropolis: it grants to the individual a kind and an amount of personal freedom which has no analogy whatsoever under other conditions. The metropolis goes back to one of the large developmental tendencies of social life as such, to one of the few tendencies for which an approximately universal formula can be discovered. The earliest phase of social formations found in historical as well as in contemporary social structures is this: a relatively small circle firmly closed against neighboring, strange, or in some way antagonistic circles. However, this circle is closely coherent and allows its individual members only a narrow field for the development of unique qualities and free, self-responsible movements. Political and kinship groups, parties and religious associations begin in this way. The self-preservation of very young associations requires the establishment of strict boundaries and centripetal unity. Therefore they cannot allow the individual freedom and unique inner and outer development. From this stage social development proceeds at once in two different, yet corresponding, directions. To the extent to which the group grows—numerically, spatially, in significance and in content of life—to the same degree the group's direct, inner unity loosens, and the rigidity of the original demarcation against others is softened through mutual relations and connections. At the same time, the individual gains freedom of movement, far beyond the first jealous delimitation. The individual also gains a specific individuality to which the division of labor in the enlarged group gives both occasion and necessity. The state and Christianity, guilds and political parties, and innumerable other groups have developed according to this formula, however much, of course, the special conditions and forces of the respective groups have modified the general scheme. This scheme seems to me distinctly recognizable also in the evolution of individuality within urban life. The small-town life in Antiquity and in the Middle Ages set barriers against movement and relations of the individual toward the outside, and it set up barriers against individual independence and differentiation within the individual self. These barriers were such that under them modern man could not have breathed. Even today a metropolitan man who is placed in a small town feels a restriction similar, at least, in kind. The smaller the circle which forms our milieu is, and the more restricted those relations to others are which dissolve the boundaries of the individual, the more anxiously the circle guards the achievements, the conduct of life, and the outlook of the individual, and the more readily a quantitative and qualitative specialization would break up the framework of the whole little circle.

The ancient *polis* in this respect seems to have had the very character of a small town. The constant threat to its existence at the hands of enemies from near and afar effected strict coherence in political and military respects, a supervision of the citizen by the citizen, a jealousy of the whole against the individual whose particular life was suppressed to such a degree that he could compensate only by acting as a despot in his own household. The tremendous agitation and excitement, the unique colorfulness of Athenian life, can perhaps be understood in terms of the fact that a people of incomparably individualized personalities struggled against the constant inner and outer pressure of the de-individualizing small town. This produced a tense atmosphere in which the weaker individuals were suppressed and those of stronger natures were incited to prove themselves in the most passionate manner. This is precisely why it was that there blossomed in Athens what must be called, without defining it exactly, "the general human character" in the intellectual development of our species. For we maintain factual as well as historical validity for the following connection: the most extensive and the most general contents and forms of life are most intimately connected with the most individual ones. They have a preparatory stage in common, that is, they find their enemy in narrow formations and groupings, the maintenance of which places both of them into a state of defense against expanse and generality lying without and the freely moving individuality within. Just as in the feudal age, the "free" man was the one who stood under the law of the land, that is, under the law of the largest social orbit, and the unfree man was the one who derived his right merely from the narrow circle of a feudal association and was excluded from the larger social orbit—so today metropolitan man is "free" in a spiritualized and refined sense, in contrast to the pettiness and prejudices which hem in the small-town man. For the reciprocal reserve and indifference and the intellectual life conditions of large circles are never felt more strongly by the individual in their impact upon his independence than in the thickest crowd of the big city. This is because the bodily proximity and narrowness of space makes the mental distance only the more visible. It is obviously only the obverse of this freedom if, under certain circumstances, one nowhere feels as lonely and lost as in the metropolitan crowd. For here as elsewhere it is by no means necessary that the freedom of man be reflected in his emotional life as comfort.

It is not only the immediate size of the area and the number of persons which, because of the universal historical correlation between the enlargement of the circle and the personal inner and outer freedom, has made the metropolis the locale of freedom. It is rather in transcending this visible expanse that any given city becomes the seat of cosmopolitanism. The horizon of the city expands in a manner comparable to the way in which wealth develops; a certain amount of property increases in a quasi-automatical way in ever more rapid progression. As soon as a certain limit has been passed, the economic, personal, and intellectual relations of the citizenry, the sphere of intellectual predominance of the city over its hinterland, grow as in geometrical progression. Every gain in dynamic extension becomes a step, not for an equal, but for a new and larger extension. From every thread spinning out of the city, ever new threads grow as if by themselves, just as within the city the unearned increment of ground rent, through the mere increase in communication, brings the owner automatically increasing profits. At this point, the quantitative aspect of life is transformed directly into qualitative traits of character. The sphere of life of the small town is, in the main, self-contained and autarchic. For it is the decisive nature of the metropolis that its inner life overflows by waves into a far-flung national or international area. Weimar is not an example to the contrary, since its significance was hinged upon individual personalities and died with them; whereas the metropolis is indeed characterized by its essential independence even from the most eminent individual personalities. This is the counterpart to the independence, and it is the price the individual pays for the independence, which he enjoys in the metropolis. The most significant characteristic of the metropolis is this functional extension beyond its physical boundaries. And this efficacy reacts in turn and gives weight, importance, and responsibility to metropolitan life. Man does not end with the limits of his body or the area comprising his immediate activity. Rather is the range of the person constituted by the sum of effects emanating from him temporally and spatially. In the same way, a city consists of its total effects which extend beyond its immediate confines. Only this range is the city's actual extent in which its existence is expressed. This fact makes it obvious that individual freedom, the logical and historical complement of such extension, is not to be understood only in the negative sense of mere freedom of mobility and elimination of prejudices and petty philistinism. The essential point is that the particularity and incomparability, which ultimately every human being possesses, be somehow expressed in the working-out of a way of life. That we follow the laws of our own nature—and this after all is freedom—becomes obvious and convincing to ourselves and to others only if the expressions of this nature differ from the expressions of others. Only our unmistakability proves that our way of life has not been superimposed by others.

Cities are, first of all, seats of the highest economic division of labor. They produce thereby such extreme phenomena as in Paris the renumerative occupation of the *quatorzième*. They are persons who identify themselves by signs on their residences and who are ready at the dinner hour in correct attire, so that they can be quickly called upon if a dinner party should consist of thirteen persons. In the measure of its expansion, the city offers more and more the decisive conditions of the division of labor. It offers a circle which through its size can absorb a highly diverse variety of services. At the same time, the concentration of individuals and their struggle for customers compel the individual to specialize in a function from which he cannot be readily displaced by another. It is decisive that city life has transformed the struggle with nature for livelihood into an inter-human struggle for gain, which here is not granted by nature but by other men. For specialization does not flow only from the competition for gain but also from the underlying fact that the seller must always seek to call forth new and differentiated needs of the lured customer. In order to find a source of income which is not yet exhausted, and to find a function which cannot readily be displaced, it is necessary to specialize in one's services. This process promotes differentiation, refinement, and the enrichment of the public's needs, which obviously must lead to growing personal differences within this public.

All this forms the transition to the individualization of mental and psychic traits which the city occasions in proportion to its size. There is a whole series of obvious causes underlying this process. First, one must meet the difficulty of asserting his own personality within the dimensions of metropolitan life. Where the quantitative increase in importance and the expense of energy reach their limits, one seizes upon qualitative differentiation in order somehow to attract the attention of the social circle by playing upon its sensitivity for differences. Finally man is tempted to adopt the most tendentious peculiarities, that is, the specifically metropolitan extravagances of mannerism, caprice, and preciousness. Now, the meaning of these extravagances does not at all lie in the contents of such behavior, but rather in its form of "being different," of standing out in a striking manner and thereby attracting attention. For many character types, ultimately the only means of saving for themselves some modicum of self-esteem and the sense of filling a position is indirect, through the awareness of others. In the same sense a seemingly insignificant factor is operating, the cumulative effects of which are, however, still noticeable. I refer to the brevity and scarcity of the inter-human contacts granted to the metropolitan man, as compared with social intercourse in the small town. The temptation to appear "to the point," to appear concentrated and strikingly characteristic, lies much closer to the individual in brief metropolitan contacts than in an atmosphere in which frequent and prolonged association assures the personality of an unambiguous image of himself in the eyes of the other.

The most profound reason, however, why the metropolis conduces to the urge for the most individual personal existence—no matter whether justified and successful—appears to me to be the following: the development of modern culture is characterized by the preponderance of what one may call the "objective spirit" over the "subjective spirit." This is to say, in language as well as in law, in the technique of production as well as in art, in science as well as in the objects of the domestic environment, there is embodied a sum of spirit. The individual in his intellectual development follows the growth of this spirit very imperfectly and at an ever increasing distance. If, for instance, we view the immense culture which for the last hundred years has been embodied in things and in knowledge, in institutions and in comforts, and if we compare all this with the cultural progress of the individual during the same period—at least in high status groups—a frightful disproportion in growth between the two becomes evident. Indeed, at some points we notice a retrogression in the culture of the individual with reference to spirituality, delicacy, and idealism. This discrepancy results essentially from the growing division of labor. For the division of labor demands from the individual an ever more one-sided accomplishment, and the greatest advance in a one-sided pursuit only too frequently means dearth to the personality of the individual. In any case, he can cope less and less with the overgrowth of objective culture. The individual is reduced to a negligible quantity, perhaps less in his consciousness than in his practice and in the totality of his obscure emotional states that are derived from this practice. The individual has become a mere cog in an enormous organization of things and powers which tear from his hands all progress, spirituality, and value in order to transform them from their subjective form into the form of a purely objective life. It needs merely to be pointed out that the metropolis is the genuine arena of this culture which outgrows all personal life. Here in buildings and educational institutions, in the wonders and comforts of space-conquering technology, in the formations of community life, and in the visible institutions of the state, is offered such an overwhelming fullness of crystallized and impersonalized spirit that the personality, so to speak, cannot maintain itself under its impact. On the one hand, life is made infinitely easy for the personality in that stimulations, interests, uses of time and consciousness are offered to it from all sides. They carry the person as if in a stream, and one needs hardly to swim for oneself. On the other hand, however, life is composed more and more of these impersonal contents and offerings which tend to displace the genuine personal colorations and incomparabilities. This results in the individual's summoning the utmost in uniqueness and particularization, in order to preserve his most personal core. He has to exaggerate this personal element in order to remain audible even to himself. The atrophy of individual culture through the hypertrophy of objective culture is one reason for the bitter hatred which the preachers of the most extreme individualism, above all Nietzsche, harbor against the metropolis. But it is, indeed, also a reason why these preachers are so passionately loved in the metropolis and why they appear to the metropolitan man as the prophets and saviors of his most unsatisfied yearnings.

If one asks for the historical position of these two forms of individualism which are nourished by the quantitative relation of the metropolis, namely, individual independence and the elaboration of individuality itself, then the metropolis assumes an entirely new rank order in the world history of the spirit. The eighteenth century found the individual in oppressive bonds which had become meaningless—bonds of a political, agrarian, guild, and religious character. They were restraints which, so to speak, forced upon man an unnatural form and outmoded, unjust inequalities. In this situation the cry for liberty and equality arose, the belief in the individual's full freedom of movement in all social and intellectual relationships. Freedom would at once permit the noble substance common to all to come to the fore, a substance which nature had deposited in every man and which society and history had only deformed. Besides this eighteenth-century ideal of liberalism, in the nineteenth century, through Goethe and Romanticism, on the one hand, and through the economic division of labor, on the other hand, another ideal arose: individuals liberated from historical bonds now wished to distinguish themselves from one another. The carrier of man's values is no longer the "general human being" in every individual, but rather man's qualitative uniqueness and irreplaceability. The external and internal history of our time takes its course within the struggle and in the changing entanglements of these two ways of defining the individual's role in the whole of society. It is the function of the metropolis to provide the arena for this struggle and its reconciliation. For the metropolis presents the peculiar conditions which are revealed to us as the opportunities and the stimuli for the development of both these ways of allocating roles to men. Therewith these conditions gain a unique place, pregnant with inestimable meanings for the development of psychic existence. The metropolis reveals itself as one of those great historical

formations in which opposing streams which enclose life unfold, as well as join
one another with equal right. However, in this process the currents of life,
whether their individual phenomena touch us sympathe:ically or antipathe-
tically, entirely transcend the sphere for which the judge's attitude is appropriate. Since such forces of life have grown into the roots and into the crown
of the whole of the historical life in which we, in our fleeting existence, as a
cell, belong only as a part, it is not our task either to accuse or to pardon, but
only to understand.*

Urbanism As a Way of Life

LOUIS WIRTH

*Louis Wirth, a leading member of the influential Chicago School, wrote his
best known works after he departed from the then common armchair approach
to sociological research and went out to walk the city streets. There, he explored, talked, and, in general, did what is now considered a standard type of
ethnographic field study.*

*The following article is the now classic statement of urbanism as a product of
population size, density, and heterogeneity. It created a stir when it first appeared in the* American Journal of Sociology *(1938). Wirth suggests that it is not
so much the city per se that creates urban problems as those particular cities that
are rapidly mushrooming conglomerates of peoples. In fact, the urban mode of
life is not reserved solely for city folk but can be a life-style followed by anyone.
This being the case, Wirth attempts to deal with certain fundamental aspects of
urban analysis. How does one define or identify* urban *and* urbanism? *What are
the empirically available attributes of the city? What are the psychological and
sociocultural dynamics of urban segmentalization, specialization, and heterogeneity? What kind(s) of model(s) can best be used to deal with "the complicated
phenomena of urbanism"?*

*Wirth makes it clear that the aim of his essay is to serve as a point of departure
for urban scholars who, if they use the theory of urbanism that he presents, will
be well on the way to developing "a unified body of reliable knowledge." They
should then be able to contribute to solving such problems as "poverty, housing, city planning, sanitation, municipal administration, policing, marketing,
transportation, and other technical issues." One wonders if Wirth would be satis-*

---

* The content of this lecture by its very nature does not derive from a citable literature. Argument and
elaboration of its major cultural-historical ideas are contained in my *Philosophie des Geldes* [The Philosophy of Money; München und Leipzig: Duncker und Humblot, 1900].

"Urbanism As a Way of Life," *The American Journal of Sociology,* Vol. XLIV, #1, 1938, pp. 1–24, University of Chicago Press.

fied with the progress of his colleagues in the more than 40 years since he presented his programmatic paper.

I. The City and Contemporary Civilization

Just as the beginning of Western civilization is marked by the permanent settlement of formerly nomadic peoples in the Mediterranean basin, so the beginning of what is distinctively modern in our civilization is best signaled by the growth of great cities. Nowhere has mankind been farther removed from organic nature than under the conditions of life characteristic of great cities. The contemporary world no longer presents a picture of small isolated groups of human beings scattered over a vast territory, as Sumner described primitive society.[1] The distinctive feature of the mode of living of man in the modern age is his concentration into gigantic aggregations around which cluster lesser centers and from which radiate the ideas and practices that we call civilization.

The degree to which the contemporary world may be said to be "urban" is not fully or accurately measured by the proportion of the total population living in cities. The influences which cities exert upon the social life of man are greater than the ratio of the urban population would indicate, for the city is not only in ever larger degrees the dwelling-place and the workshop of modern man, but it is the initiating and controlling center of economic, political, and cultural life that has drawn the most remote parts of the world into its orbit and woven diverse areas, peoples, and activities into a cosmos.

The growth of cities and the urbanization of the world [are among] the most impressive facts of modern times. Although it is impossible to state precisely what proportion of the estimated total world population of approximately 1,800,000,000 is urban, 69.2 per cent of the total population of those countries that do distinguish between urban and rural areas is urban.[2] Considering the fact, moreover, that the world's population is very unevenly distributed and that the growth of cities is not very far advanced in some of the countries that have only recently been touched by industrialism, this average understates the extent to which urban concentration has proceeded in those countries where the impact of the industrial revolution has been more forceful and of less recent date. This shift from a rural to a predominantly urban society, which has taken place within the span of a single generation in such industrialized areas as the United States and Japan, has been accompanied by profound changes in virtually every phase of social life. It is these changes and their ramifications that invite the attention of the sociologist to the study of the differences between the rural and the urban mode of living. The pursuit of this interest is an indispensable prerequisite for the comprehension and

[1] William Graham Sumner, *Folkways* (Boston, 1906), p. 12.
[2] S. V. Pearson, *The Growth and Distribution of Population* (New York, 1935), p. 211.

possible mastery of some of the most crucial contemporary problems of social life since it is likely to furnish one of the most revealing perspectives for the understanding of the ongoing changes in human nature and the social order.[3]

Since the city is the product of growth rather than of instantaneous creation, it is to be expected that the influences which it exerts upon the modes of life should not be able to wipe out completely the previously dominant modes of human association. To a greater or lesser degree, therefore, our social life bears the imprint of an earlier folk society, the characteristic modes of settlement of which were the farm, the manor, and the village. This historic influence is reinforced by the circumstance that the population of the city itself is in large measure recruited from the countryside, where a mode of life reminiscent of this earlier form of existence persists. Hence we should not expect to find abrupt and discontinuous variation between urban and rural types of personality. The city and the country may be regarded as two poles in reference to one or the other of which all human settlements tend to arrange themselves. In viewing urban-industrial and rural-folk society as ideal types of communities, we may obtain a perspective for the analysis of the basic models of human association as they appear in contemporary civilization.

II. A Sociological Definition of the City

Despite the preponderant significance of the city in our civilization, however, our knowledge of the nature of urbanism and the process of urbanization is meager. Many attempts have indeed been made to isolate the distinguishing characteristics of urban life. Geographers, historians, economists, and political scientists have incorporated the points of view of their respective disciplines into diverse definitions of the city. While in no sense intended to supersede these, the formulation of a sociological approach to the city may incidentally serve to call attention to the interrelations between them by emphasizing the peculiar characteristics of the city as a particular form of human association. A sociologically significant definition of the city seeks to select those elements of urbanism which mark it as a distinctive mode of human group life.

The characterization of a community as urban on the basis of size alone is obviously arbitrary. It is difficult to defend the present census definition which designates a community of 2,500 and above as urban and all others as rural. The situation would be the same if the criterion were 4,000, 8,000, 10,000, 25,000, or 100,000 population, for although in the latter case we might feel that we were more nearly dealing with an urban aggregate than would be the case in communities of lesser size, no definition of urbanism can

---

[3] Whereas rural life in the United States has for a long time been a subject of considerable interest on the part of governmental bureaus, the most notable case of a comprehensive report being that submitted by the Country Life Commission to President Theodore Roosevelt in 1909, it is worthy of note that no equally comprehensive official inquiry into urban life was undertaken until the establishment of a Research Committee on Urbanism of the National Resources Committee. (See *Our Cities: Their Role in the National Economy* [Washington: Government Printing Office, 1937].)

hope to be completely satisfying as long as numbers are regarded as the sole criterion. Moreover, it is not difficult to demonstrate that communities of less than the arbitrarily set number of inhabitants lying within the range of influence of metropolitan centers have greater claim to recognition as urban communities than do larger ones leading a more isolated existence in a predominantly rural area. Finally, it should be recognized that census definitions are unduly influenced by the fact that the city, statistically speaking, is always an administrative concept in that the corporate limits play a decisive role in delineating the urban area. Nowhere is this more clearly apparent than in the concentrations of population of the peripheries of great metropolitan centers which cross arbitrary administrative boundaries of city, county, state, and nation.

As long as we identify urbanism with the physical entity of the city, viewing it merely as rigidly delimited in space, and proceed as if urban attributes abruptly cease to be manifested beyond an arbitrary boundary line, we are not likely to arrive at any adequate conception of urbanism as a mode of life. The technological developments in transportation and communication which virtually mark a new epoch in human history have accentuated the role of cities as dominant elements in our civilization and have enormously extended the urban mode of living beyond the confines of the city itself. The dominance of the city, especially of the great city, may be regarded as a consequence of the concentration in cities of industrial and commercial, financial and administrative facilities and activities, transportation and communication lines, and cultural and recreational equipment such as the press, radio stations, theaters, libraries, museums, concert halls, operas, hospitals, higher educational institutions, research and publishing centers, professional organizations, and religious and welfare institutions. Were it not for the attraction and suggestions that the city exerts through these instrumentalities upon the rural population, the differences between the rural and the urban modes of life would be even greater than they are. Urbanization no longer denotes merely the process by which persons are attracted to a place called the city and incorporated into its system of life. It refers also to that cumulative accentuation of the characteristics distinctive of the mode of life which is associated with the growth of cities, and finally to the changes in the direction of modes of life recognized as urban which are apparent among people, wherever they may be, who have come under the spell of the influences which the city exerts by virtue of the power of its institutions and personalities operating through the means of communication and transportation.

The shortcomings which attach to number of inhabitants as a criterion of urbanism apply for the most part to density of population as well. Whether we accept the density of 10,000 persons per square mile as Mark Jefferson[4] proposed, or 1,000, which Willcox[5] preferred to regard as the criterion of

---

[4] "The Anthropology of Some Great Cities," *Bull. American Geographical Society,* XLI (1909), 537–66.
[5] Walter F. Willcox, "A Definition of 'City' in Terms of Density," in E. W. Burgess, *The Urban Community* (Chicago, 1926), p. 119.

urban settlements, it is clear that unless density is correlated with significant social characteristics it can furnish only an arbitrary basis for differentiating urban from rural communities. Since our census enumerates the night rather than the day population of an area, the locale of the most intensive urban life—the city center—generally has low population density, and the industrial and commercial areas of the city, which contain the most characteristic economic activities underlying urban society, would scarcely anywhere be truly urban if density were literally interpreted as a mark of urbanism. Nevertheless, the fact that the urban community is distinguished by a large aggregation and relatively dense concentration of population can scarcely be left out of account in a definition of the city. But these criteria must be seen as relative to the general cultural context in which cities arise and exist and are sociologically relevant only in so far as they operate as conditioning factors in social life.

The same criticisms apply to such criteria as the occupation of the inhabitants, the existence of certain physical facilities, institutions, and forms of political organization. The question is not whether cities in our civilization or in others do exhibit these distinctive traits, but how potent they are in molding the character of social life into its specifically urban form. Nor in formulating a fertile definition can we afford to overlook the great variations between cities. By means of a typology of cities based upon size, location, age, and function, such as we have undertaken to establish in our recent report to the National Resources Committee,[6] we have found it feasible to array and classify urban communities ranging from struggling small towns to thriving world-metropolitan centers; from isolated trading-centers in the midst of agricultural regions to thriving world-ports and commercial and industrial conurbations. Such differences as these appear crucial because the social characteristics and influences of these different "cities" vary widely.

A serviceable definition of urbanism should not only denote the essential characteristics which all cities—at least those in our culture—have in common, but should lend itself to the discovery of their variations. An industrial city will differ significantly in social respects from a commercial, mining, fishing, resort, university, and capital city. A one-industry city will present different sets of social characteristics from a multi-industry city, as will an industrially balanced from an imbalanced city, a suburb from a satellite, a residential suburb from an industrial suburb, a city within a metropolitan region from one lying outside, an old city from a new one, a southern city from a New England, a middle-western from a Pacific Coast city, a growing from a stable and from a dying city.

A sociological definition must obviously be inclusive enough to comprise whatever essential characteristics these different types of cities have in common as social entities, but it obviously cannot be so detailed as to take account of all the variations implicit in the manifold classes sketched above. Presum-

[6] Op. cit., p. 8.

ably some of the characteristics of cities are more significant in conditioning the nature of urban life than others, and we may expect the outstanding features of the urban-social scene to vary in accordance with size, density, and differences in the functional type of cities. Moreover, we may infer that rural life will bear the imprint of urbanism in the measure that through contact and communication it comes under the influence of cities. It may contribute to the clarity of the statements that follow to repeat that while the locus of urbanism as a mode of life is, of course, to be found characteristically in places which fulfil the requirements we shall set up as a definition of the city, urbanism is not confined to such localities but is manifest in varying degrees wherever the influences of the city reach.

While urbanism, or that complex of traits which makes up the characteristic mode of life in cities, and urbanization, which denotes the development and extensions of these factors, are thus not exclusively found in settlements which are cities in the physical and demographic sense, they do, nevertheless, find their most pronounced expression in such areas, especially in metropolitan cities. In formulating a definition of the city it is necessary to exercise caution in order to avoid identifying urbanism as a way of life with any specific locally or historically conditioned cultural influences which, while they may significantly affect the specific character of the community, are not the essential determinants of its character as a city.

It is particularly important to call attention to the danger of confusing urbanism with industrialism and modern capitalism. The rise of cities in the modern world is undoubtedly not independent of the emergence of modern power-driven machine technology, mass production, and capitalistic enterprise. But different as the cities of earlier epochs may have been by virtue of their development in a preindustrial and precapitalistic order from the great cities of today, they were, nevertheless, cities.

For sociological purposes a city may be defined as a relatively large, dense, and permanent settlement of socially heterogeneous individuals. On the basis of the postulates which this minimal definition suggests, a theory of urbanism may be formulated in the light of existing knowledge concerning social groups.

III. A Theory of Urbanism

In the rich literature on the city we look in vain for a theory of urbanism presenting in a systematic fashion the available knowledge concerning the city as a social entity. We do indeed have excellent formulations of theories on such special problems as the growth of the city viewed as a historical trend and as a recurrent process,[7] and we have a wealth of literature presenting in-

---

[7] See Robert E. Park, Ernest W. Burgess, et al., *The City* (Chicago, 1925), esp. chaps. ii and iii; Werner Sombart, "Städtische Siedlung, Stadt," *Handwörterbuch der Soziologie*, ed. Alfred Vierkandt (Stuttgart, 1931); see also bibliography.

sights of sociological relevance and empirical studies offering detailed information on a variety of particular aspects of urban life. But despite the multiplication of research and textbooks on the city, we do not as yet have a
comprehensive body of compendent hypotheses which may be derived from a
set of postulates implicitly contained in a sociological definition of·the city,
and from our general sociological knowledge which may be substantiated
through empirical research. The closest approximations to a systematic theory
of urbanism that we have are to be found in a penetrating essay, "Die Stadt,"
by Max Weber,[8] and a memorable paper by Robert E. Park on "The City:
Suggestions for the Investigation of Human Behavior in the Urban Environment."[9] But even these excellent contributions are far from constituting an ordered and coherent framework of theory upon which research might profitably proceed.

   In the pages that follow we shall seek to set forth a limited number of identifying characteristics of the city. Given these characteristics we shall then indicate what consequences or further characteristics follow from them in the
light of general sociological theory and empirical research. We hope in this
manner to arrive at the essential propositions comprising a theory of urbanism. Some of these propositions can be supported by a considerable body
of already available research materials; others may be accepted as hypotheses
for which a certain amount of presumptive evidence exists, but for which
more ample and exact verification would be required. At least such a procedure will, it is hoped, show what in the way of systematic knowledge of the
city we now have and what are the crucial and fruitful hypotheses for future
research.

   The central problem of the sociologist of the city is to discover the forms of
social action and organization that typically emerge in relatively permanent,
compact settlements of large numbers of heterogeneous individuals. We must
also infer that urbanism will assume its most characteristic and extreme form
in the measure in which the conditions with which it is congruent are present.
Thus the larger, the more densely populated, and the more heterogeneous a
community, the more accentuated the characteristics associated with urbanism will be. It should be recognized, however, that in the social world institutions and practices may be accepted and continued for reasons other than
those that originally brought them into existence, and that accordingly the
urban mode of life may be perpetuated under conditions quite foreign to
those necessary for its origin.

   Some justification may be in order for the choice of the principal terms
comprising our definition of the city. The attempt has been made to make it
as inclusive and at the same time as denotative as possible without loading it
with unnecessary assumptions. To say that large numbers are necessary to
constitute a city means, of course, large numbers in relation to a restricted
area or high density of settlement. There are, nevertheless, good reasons for

   [8] *Wirtschaft und Gesellschaft* (Tübingen, 1925), Part II, chap. viii, pp. 514–601.
   [9] Park, Burgess, et al., op. cit., chap. i.

treating large numbers and density as separate factors, since each may be connected with significantly different social consequences. Similarly the need for adding heterogeneity to numbers of population as a necessary and distinct criterion of urbanism might be questioned, since we should expect the range of differences to increase with numbers. In defense, it may be said that the city shows a kind and degree of heterogeneity of population which cannot be wholly accounted for by the law of large numbers or adequately represented by means of a normal distribution curve. Since the population of the city does not reproduce itself, it must recruit its migrants from other cities, the countryside, and—in this country until recently—from other countries. The city has thus historically been the melting-pot of races, peoples, and cultures, and a most favorable breeding-ground of new biological and cultural hybrids. It has not only tolerated but rewarded individual differences. It has brought together people from the ends of the earth *because* they are different and thus useful to one another, rather than because they are homogeneous and like-minded.[10]

There are a number of sociological propositions concerning the relationship between (a) numbers of population, (b) density of settlement, (c) heterogeneity of inhabitants and group life, which can be formulated on the basis of observation and research.

Size of the Population Aggregate

Ever since Aristotle's *Politics*,[11] it has been recognized that increasing the number of inhabitants in a settlement beyond a certain limit will affect the relationships between them and the character of the city. Large numbers involve, as has been pointed out, a greater range of individual variation. Furthermore, the greater the number of individuals participating in a process of

[10] The justification for including the term "permanent" in the definition may appear necessary. Our failure to give an extensive justification for this qualifying mark of the urban rests on the obvious fact that unless human settlements take a fairly permanent root in a locality the characteristics of urban life cannot arise, and conversely the living together of large numbers of heterogeneous individuals under dense conditions is not possible without the development of a more or less technological structure.

[11] See esp. vii. 4. 4–14. Translated by B. Jowett, from which the following may be quoted:

"To the size of states there is a limit, as there is to other things, plants, animals, implements; for none of these retain their natural power when they are too large or too small, but they either wholly lose their nature, or are spoiled. . . . . . [A] state when composed of too few is not as a state ought to be, self-sufficing; when of too many, though self-sufficing in all mere necessaries, it is a nation and not a state, being almost incapable of constitutional government. For who can be the general of such a vast multitude, or who the herald, unless he have the voice of a Stentor?

"A state then only begins to exist when it has attained a population sufficient for a good life in the political community: it may indeed somewhat exceed this number. But, as I was saying, there must be a limit. What should be the limit will be easily ascertained by experience. For both governors and governed have duties to perform; the special functions of a governor are to command and to judge. But if the citizens of a state are to judge and to distribute offices according to merit, then they must know each other's characters; where they do not possess this knowledge, both the election to offices and the decision of lawsuits will go wrong. When the population is very large they are manifestly settled at haphazard, which clearly ought to be. Besides, in an overpopulous state foreigners and metics will readily acquire the rights of citizens, for who will find them out? Clearly, then, the best limit of the population of a state is the largest number which suffices for the purposes of life, and can be taken in at a single view. Enough concerning the size of a city."

interaction, the greater is the *potential* differentiation between them. The personal traits, the occupations, the cultural life, and the ideas of the members of an urban community may, therefore, be expected to range between more widely separated poles than those of rural inhabitants.

That such variations should give rise to the spatial segregation of individuals according to color, ethnic heritage, economic and social status, tastes and preferences, may readily be inferred. The bonds of kinship, of neighborliness, and the sentiments arising out of living together for generations under a common folk tradition are likely to be absent or, at best, relatively weak in an aggregate the members of which have such diverse origins and backgrounds. Under such circumstances competition and formal control mechanisms furnish the substitutes for the bonds of solidarity that are relied upon to hold a folk society together.

Increase in the number of inhabitants of a community beyond a few hundred is bound to limit the possibility of each member of the community knowing all the others personally. Max Weber, in recognizing the social significance of this fact, pointed out that from a sociological point of view large numbers of inhabitants and density of settlement mean that the personal mutual acquaintanceship between the inhabitants which ordinarily inheres in a neighborhood is lacking.[12] The increase in numbers thus involves a changed character of the social relationships. As Simmel points out:

> [If] the unceasing external contact of numbers of persons in the city should be met by the same number of inner reactions as in the small town, in which one knows almost every person he meets and to each of whom he has a positive relationship, one would be completely atomized internally and would fall into an unthinkable mental condition.[13]

The multiplication of persons in a state of interaction under conditions which make their contact as full personalities impossible produces that segmentalization of human relationships which has sometimes been seized upon by students of the mental life of the cities as an explanation for the "schizoid" character of urban personality. This is not to say that the urban inhabitants have fewer acquaintances than rural inhabitants, for the reverse may actually be true; it means rather that in relation to the number of people whom they see and with whom they rub elbows in the course of daily life, they know a smaller proportion, and of these they have less intensive knowledge.

Characteristically, urbanites meet one another in highly segmental roles. They are, to be sure, dependent upon more people for the satisfactions of their life-needs than are rural people and thus are associated with a greater number of organized groups, but they are less dependent upon particular persons, and their dependence upon others is confined to a highly fractionalized aspect of the other's round of activity. This is essentially what is meant by say-

---

[12] Op. cit., p. 514.

[13] Georg Simmel, "Die Grossstädte und das Geistesleben," *Die Grossstadt*, ed. Theodoro Petermann (Dresden, 1903), pp. 187–206.

ing that the city is characterized by secondary rather than primary contacts. The contacts of the city may indeed be face to face, but they are nevertheless impersonal, superficial, transitory, and segmental. The reserve, the indifference, and the blasé outlook which urbanites manifest in their relationships may thus be regarded as devices for immunizing themselves against the personal claims and expectations of others.

The superficiality, the anonymity, and the transitory character of urban-social relations make intelligble, also, the sophistication and the rationality generally ascribed to city-dwellers. Our acquaintances tend to stand in a relationship of utility to us in the sense that the role which each one plays in our life is overwhelmingly regarded as a means for the achievement of our own ends. Whereas, therefore, the individual gains, on the one hand, a certain degree of emancipation or freedom from the personal and emotional controls of intimate groups, he loses, on the other hand, the spontaneous self-expression, the morale, and the sense of participation that comes with living in an integrated society. This consitutes essentially the state of *anomie* or the social void to which Durkheim alludes in attempting to account for the various forms of social disorganization in technological society.

The segmental character and utilitarian accent of interpersonal relations in the city find their institutional expression in the proliferation of specialized tasks which we see in their most developed form in the professions. The operations of the pecuniary nexus leads to predatory relationships, which tend to obstruct the efficient functioning of the social order unless checked by professional codes and occupational etiquette. The premium put upon utility and efficiency suggests the adaptability of the corporate device for the organization of enterprises in which individuals can engage only in groups. The advantage that the corporation has over the individual entrepreneur and the partnership in the urban-industrial world derives not only from the possibility it affords of centralizing the resources of thousands of individuals or from the legal privilege of limited liability and perpetual succession, but from the fact that the corporation has no soul.

The specialization of individuals, particularly in their occupations, can proceed only, as Adam Smith pointed out, upon the basis of an enlarged market, which in turn accentuates the division of labor. This enlarged market is only in part supplied by the city's hinterland; in large measure it is found among the large numbers that the city itself contains. The dominance of the city over the surrounding hinterland becomes explicable in terms of the division of labor which urban life occcasions and promotes. The extreme degree of interdependence and the unstable equilibrium of urban life are closely associated with the division of labor and the specialization of occupations. This interdependence and instability is increased by the tendency of each city to specialize in those functions in which it has the greatest advantage.

In a community composed of a larger number of individuals than can know one another intimately and can be assembled in one spot, it becomes necessary to communicate through indirect mediums and to articulate individual interests by a process of delegation. Typically in the city, interests are made effective through representation. The individual counts for little, but the voice of the representative is heard with a deference roughly proportional to the numbers for whom he speaks.

While this characterization of urbanism, in so far as it derives from large numbers, does not by any means exhaust the sociological inferences that might be drawn from our knowledge of the relationship of the size of a group to the characteristic behavior of the members, for the sake of brevity the assertions made may serve to exemplify the sort of propositions that might be developed.

Density

As in the case of numbers, so in the case of concentration in limited space, certain consequences of relevance in sociological analysis of the city emerge. Of these only a few can be indicated.

As Darwin pointed out for flora and fauna and as Durkheim[14] noted in the case of human societies, an increase in numbers when area is held constant (i.e., an increase in density) tends to produce differentiation and specialization, since only in this way can the area support increased numbers. Density thus reinforces the effect of numbers in diversifying men and their activities and in increasing the complexity of the social structure.

On the subjective side, as Simmel has suggested, the close physical contact of numerous individuals necessarily produces a shift in the mediums through which we orient ourselves to the urban milieu, especially to our fellow-men. Typically, our physical contacts are close but our social contacts are distant. The urban world puts a premium on visual recognition. We see the uniform which denotes the role of the functionaries and are oblivious to the personal eccentricities that are hidden behind the uniform. We tend to acquire and develop a sensitivity to a world of artifacts and become progressively farther removed from the world of nature.

We are exposed to glaring contrasts between splendor and squalor, between riches and poverty, intelligence and ignorance, order and chaos. The competition for space is great, so that each area generally tends to be put to the use which yields the greatest economic return. Place of work tends to become dissociated from place of residence, for the proximity of industrial and commercial establishments makes an area both economically and socially undesirable for residential purposes.

Density, land values, rentals, accessibility, healthfulness, prestige, aesthetic consideration, absence of nuisances such as noise, smoke, and dirt determine the desirability of various areas of the city as places of settlement for

[14] E. Durkheim, *De la division du travail social* (Paris, 1932), p. 248.

different sections of the population. Place and nature of work, income, racial and ethnic characteristics, social status, custom, habit, taste, preference, and prejudice are among the significant factors in accordance with which the urban population is selected and distributed into more or less distinct settlements. Diverse population elements inhabiting a compact settlement thus tend to become segregated from one another in the degree in which their requirements and modes of life are incompatible with one another and in the measure in which they are antagonistic to one another. Similarly, persons of homogeneous status and needs unwittingly drift into, consciously select, or are forced by circumstances into, the same area. The different parts of the city thus acquire specialized functions. The city consequently tends to resemble a mosaic of social worlds in which the transition from one to the other is abrupt. The juxtaposition of divergent personalities and modes of life tends to produce a relativistic perspective and a sense of toleration of differences which may be regarded as prerequisites for rationality and which lead toward the secularization of life.[15]

The close living together and working together of individuals who have no sentimental and emotional ties foster a spirit of competition, aggrandizement, and mutual exploitation. To counteract irresponsibility and potential disorder, formal controls tend to be resorted to. Without rigid adherence to predictable routines a large compact society would scarcely be able to maintain itself. The clock and the traffic signal are symbolic of the basis of our social order in the urban world. Frequent close physical contact, coupled with great social distance, accentuates the reserve of unattached individuals toward one another and, unless compensated for by other opportunities for response, gives rise to loneliness. The necessary frequent movement of great numbers of individuals in a congested habitat gives occasion to friction and irritation. Nervous tensions which derive from such personal frustrations are accentuated by the rapid tempo and the complicated technology under which life in dense areas must be lived.

Heterogeneity

The social interaction among such a variety of personality types in the urban milieu tends to break down the rigidity of caste lines and to complicate the class structure, and thus induces a more ramified and differentiated framework of social stratification than is found in more integrated societies. The heightened mobility of the individual, which brings him within the range of stimulation by a great number of diverse individuals and subjects him to

---

[15] The extent to which the segregation of the population into distinct ecological and cultural areas and the resulting social attitude of tolerance, rationality, and secular mentality are functions of density as distinguished from heterogeneity is difficult to determine. Most likely we are dealing here with phenomena which are consequences of the simultaneous operation of both factors.

fluctuating status in the differentiated social groups that compose the social structure of the city, tends toward the acceptance of instability and insecurity in the world at large as a norm. This fact helps to account, too, for the sophistication and cosmopolitanism of the urbanite. No single group has the undivided allegiance of the individual. The groups with which he is affiliated do not lend themselves readily to a simple hierarchical arrangement. By virtue of his different interests arising out of different aspects of social life, the individual acquires membership in widely divergent groups, each of which functions only with reference to a single segment of his personality. Nor do these groups easily permit of a concentric arrangement so that the narrower ones fall within the circumference of the more inclusive ones, as is more likely to be the case in the rural community or in primitive societies. Rather the groups with which the person typically is affiliated are tangential to each other or intersect in highly variable fashion.

Partly as a result of the physical footlooseness of the population and partly as a result of their social mobility, the turnover in group membership generally is rapid. Place of residence, place and character of employment, income and interests fluctuate, and the task of holding organizations together and maintaining and promoting intimate and lasting acquaintanceship between the members is difficult. This applies strikingly to the local areas within the city into which persons become segregated more by virtue of differences in race, language, income, and social status, than through choice or positive attraction to people like themselves. Overwhelmingly the city-dweller is not a home-owner, and since a transitory habitat does not generate binding traditions and sentiments, only rarely is he truly a neighbor. There is little opportunity for the individual to obtain a conception of the city as a whole or to survey his place in the total scheme. Consequently he finds it difficult to determine what is to his own "best interests" and to decide between the issues and leaders presented to him by the agencies of mass suggestion. Individuals who are thus detached from the organized bodies which integrate society comprise the fluid masses that make collective behavior in the urban community so unpredictable and hence so problematical.

Although the city, through the recruitment of variant types to perform its diverse tasks and the accentuation of their uniqueness through competition and the premium upon eccentricity, novelty, efficient performance, and inventiveness, produces a highly differentiated population, it also exercises a leveling influence. Wherever large numbers of differently constituted individuals congregate, the process of depersonalization also enters. This leveling tendency inheres in part in the economic basis of the city. The development of large cities, at least in the modern age, was largely dependent upon the concentrative force of steam. The rise of the factory made possible mass production for an impersonal market. The fullest exploitation of the possibilities of the division of labor and mass production, however, is possible only with standardization of processes and products. A money economy goes hand in hand with such a system of production. Progressively as cities have developed upon a background of this system of production, the pecuniary nexus which implies the purchasability of services and things has displaced personal relations as the basis of association. Individuality under these circumstances must be replaced by categories. When large numbers have to make common use of facilities and institutions, an arrangement must be made to adjust the facilities and institutions to the needs of the average person rather than to those of particular individuals. The services of the public utilities, of the recreational, educational, and cultural institutions must be adjusted to mass requirements. Similarly, the cultural institutions, such as the schools, the movies, the radio, and the newspapers, by virtue of their mass clientele, must necessarily operate as leveling influences. The political process as it appears in urban life could not be understood without taking account of the mass appeals made through modern propaganda techniques. If the individual would participate at all in the social, political, and economic life of the city, he must subordinate some of his individuality to the demands of the larger community and in that measure immerse himself in mass movements.

IV. The Relation Between a Theory of Urbanism and Sociological Research

By means of a body of theory such as that illustratively sketched above, the complicated and many-sided phenomena of urbanism may be analyzed in terms of a limited number of basic categories. The sociological approach to the city thus acquires an essential unity and coherence enabling the empirical investigator not merely to focus more distinctly upon the problems and processes that properly fall in his province but also to treat his subject matter in a more integrated and systematic fashion. A few typical findings of empirical research in the field of urbanism, with special reference to the United States, may be indicated to substantiate the theoretical propositions set forth in the preceding pages, and some of the crucial problems for further study may be outlined.

On the basis of the three variables, number, density of settlement, and degree of heterogeneity, of the urban population, it appears possible to explain the characteristics of urban life and to account for the differences between cities of various sizes and types.

Urbanism as a characteristic mode of life may be approached empirically from three interrelated perspectives: (1) as a physical structure comprising a population base, a technology, and an ecological order; (2) as a system of social organization involving a characteristic social structure, a series of social institutions, and a typical pattern of social relationships; and (3) as a set of attitudes and ideas, and a constellation of personalities engaging in typical forms of collective behavior and subject to characteristic mechanisms of social control.

Urbanism in Ecological Perspective

Since in the case of physical structure and ecological processes we are able to operate with fairly objective indices, it becomes possible to arrive at quite precise and generally quantitative results. The dominance of the city over its hinterland becomes explicable through the functional characteristics of the city which derive in large measure from the effect of numbers and density. Many of the technical facilities and the skills and organizations to which urban life gives rise can grow and prosper only in cities where the demand is sufficiently great. The nature and scope of the services rendered by these organizations and institutions and the advantage which they enjoy over the less developed facilities of smaller towns enhances the dominance of the city and the dependence of ever wider regions upon the central metropolis.

The urban-population composition shows the operation of selective and differentiating factors. Cities contain a larger proportion of persons in the prime of life than rural areas which contain more old and very young people. In this, as in so many other respects, the larger the city the more this specific characteristic of urbanism is apparent. With the exception of the largest cities, which have attracted the bulk of the foreign-born males, and a few other special types of cities, women predominate numerically over men. The heterogeneity of the urban population is further indicated along racial and ethnic lines. The foreign born and their children constitute nearly two-thirds of all the inhabitants of cities of one million and over. Their proportion in the urban population declines as the size of the city decreases, until in the rural areas they comprise only about one-sixth of the total population. The larger cities similarly have attracted more Negroes and other racial groups than have the smaller communities. Considering that age, sex, race, and ethnic origin are associated with other factors such as occupation and interest, it becomes clear that one major characteristic of the urban-dweller is his dissimilarity from his fellows. Never before have such large masses of people of diverse traits as we find in our cities been thrown together into such close physical contact as in the great cities of America. Cities generally, and American cities in particular, comprise a motley of peoples and cultures, of highly differentiated modes of life between which there often is only the faintest communication, the greatest indifference and the broadest tolerance, occasionally bitter strife, but always the sharpest contrast.

The failure of the urban population to reproduce itself appears to be a biological consequence of a combination of factors in the complex of urban life, and the decline in the birth-rate generally may be regarded as one of the most significant signs of the urbanization of the Western world. While the proportion of deaths in cities is slightly greater than in the country, the outstanding difference between the failure of present-day cities to maintain their population and that of cities of the past is that in former times it was due to the exceedingly high death-rates in cities, whereas today, since cities have become more livable from a health standpoint, it is due to low birth-rates. These biological characteristics of the urban population are significant sociologically, not merely because they reflect the urban mode of existence but also because they condition the growth and future dominance of cities and their basic social organization. Since cities are the consumers rather than the producers of men, the value of human life and the social estimation of the personality will not be unaffected by the balance between births and deaths. The pattern of land use, of land values, rentals, and ownership, the nature and functioning of the physical structures, of housing, of transportation and communication facilities, of public utilities—these and many other phases of the physical mechanism of the city are not isolated phenomena unrelated to the city as a social entity, but are affected by and affect the urban mode of life.

Urbanism As a Form of Social Organization

The distinctive features of the urban mode of life have often been described sociologically as consisting of the substitution of secondary for primary contacts, the weakening of bonds of kinship, and the declining social significance of the family, the disappearance of the neighborhood, and the undermining of the traditional basis of social solidarity. All these phenomena can be substantially verified through objective indices. Thus, for instance, the low and declining urban-reproduction rates suggest that the city is not conducive to the traditional type of family life, including the rearing of children and the maintenance of the home as the locus of a whole round of vital activities. The transfer of industrial, educational, and recreational activities to specialized institutions outside the home has deprived the family of some of its most characteristic historical functions. In cities mothers are more likely to be employed, lodgers are more frequently part of the household, marriage tends to be postponed, and the proportion of single and unattached people is greater. Families are smaller and more frequently without children than in the country. The family as a unit of social life is emancipated from the larger kinship group characteristic of the country, and the individual members pursue their own diverging interests in their vocational, educational, religious, recreational, and political life.

Such functions as the maintenance of health, the methods of alleviating the hardships associated with personal and social insecurity, the provisions for education, recreation, and cultural advancement have given rise to highly specialized institutions on a community-wide, statewide, or even national basis. The same factors which have brought about greater personal insecurity also underlie the wider contrasts between individuals to be found in the urban world. While the city has broken down the rigid caste lines of preindustrial society, it has sharpened and differentiated income and status groups. Generally, a larger proportion of the adult-urban population is gainfully employed than is the case with the adult-rural population. The white-collar class, comprising those employed in trade, in clerical, and in professional work, are proportionately more numerous in large cities and in metropolitan centers and in smaller towns than in the country.

On the whole, the city discourages an economic life in which the individual in time of crisis has a basis of subsistence to fall back upon, and it discourages self-employment. While incomes of city people are on the average higher than those of country people, the cost of living seems to be higher in the larger cities. Home ownership involves greater burdens and is rarer. Rents are higher and absorb a larger proportion of the income. Although the urban-dweller has the benefit of many communal services, he spends a large proportion of his income for such items as recreation and advancement and a smaller proportion for food. What the communal services do not furnish the urbanite must purchase, and there is virtually no human need which has remained unexploited by commercialism. Catering to thrills and furnishing means of escape from drudgery, monotony, and routine thus become one of the major functions of urban recreation, which at its best furnishes means for creative self-expression and spontaneous group association, but which more typically in the urban world results in passive spectatorism on the one hand, or sensational record-smashing feats on the other.

Being reduced to a stage of virtual impotence as an individual, the urbanite is bound to exert himself by joining with others of similar interest into organized groups to obtain his ends. This results in the enormous multiplication of voluntary organizations directed toward as great a variety of objectives as there are human needs and interests. While on the one hand the traditional ties of human association are weakened, urban existence involves a much greater degree of interdependence between man and man and a more complicated, fragile, and volatile form of mutual interrelations over many phases of which the individual as such can exert scarcely any control. Frequently there is only the most tenuous relationship between the economic position or other basic factors that determine the individual's existence in the urban world and the voluntary groups with which he is affiliated. While in a primitive and in a rural society it is generally possible to predict on the basis of a few known factors who will belong to what and who will associate with whom in almost every relationship of life, in the city we can only project the general pattern of group formation and affiliation, and this pattern will display many incongruities and contradictions.

Urban Personality and Collective Behavior

It is largely through the activities of the voluntary groups, be their objectives economic, political, educational, religious, recreational, or cultural, that the urbanite expresses and develops his personality, acquires status, and is able to carry on the round of activities that constitute his life-career. It may easily be inferred, however, that the organizational framework which these highly differentiated functions call into being does not of itself insure the consistency and integrity of the personalities whose interests it enlists. Personal disorganization, mental breakdown, suicide, delinquency, crime, corruption, and disorder might be expected under these circumstances to be more prevalent in the urban than in the rural community. This has been confirmed in so far as comparable indices are available; but the mechanisms underlying these phenomena require further analysis.

Since for most group purposes it is impossible in the city to appeal individually to the large number of discrete and differentiated individuals, and since it is only through the organizations to which men belong that their interests and resources can be enlisted for a collective cause, it may be inferred that social control in the city should typically proceed through formally organized groups. It follows, too, that the masses of men in the city are subject to manipulation by symbols and stereotypes managed by individuals working from afar or operating invisibly behind the scenes through their control of the instruments of communication. Self-government either in the economic, the political, or the cultural realm is under these circumstances reduced to a mere figure of speech or, at best, is subject to the unstable equilibrium of pressure groups. In view of the ineffectiveness of actual kinship ties we create fictional kinship groups. In the face of the disappearance of the territorial unit as a basis of social solidarity we create interest units. Meanwhile the city as a community resolves itself into a series of tenuous segmental relationships superimposed upon a territorial base with a definite center but without a definite periphery and upon a division of labor which far transcends the immediate locality and is world-wide in scope. The larger the number of persons in a state of interaction with one another the lower is the level of communication and the greater is the tendency for communication to proceed on an elementary level, i.e., on the basis of those things which are assumed to be common or to be of interest to all.

It is obviously, therefore, to the emerging trends in the communication system and to the production and distribution technology that has come into existence with modern civilization that we must look for the symptoms which will indicate the probable future development of urbanism as a mode of social life. The direction of the ongoing changes in urbanism will for good or ill transform not only the city but the world. Some of the more basic of these factors and processes and the possibilities of their direction and control invite further detailed study.

It is only in so far as the sociologist has a clear conception of the city as a social entity and a workable theory of urbanism that he can hope to develop a unified body of reliable knowledge, which what passes as "urban sociology" is certainly not at the present time. By taking his point of departure from a theory of urbanism such as that sketched in the foregoing pages to be elaborated, tested, and revised in the light of further analysis and empirical research, it is to be hoped that the criteria of relevance and validity of factual data can be determined. The miscellaneous assortment of disconnected information which has hitherto found its way into sociological treatises on the city may thus be sifted and incorporated into a coherent body of knowledge. Incidentally, only by means of some such theory will the sociologist escape the futile practice of voicing in the name of sociological science a variety of often unsupportable judgments concerning such problems as poverty, housing, city-planning, sanitation, municipal administration, policing, marketing, transportation, and other technical issues. While the sociologist cannot solve any of these practical problems—at least not by himself—he may, if he discovers his proper function, have an important contribution to make to their comprehension and solution. The prospects for doing this are brightest through a general, theoretical, rather than through an *ad hoc* approach.

Urbanization Among the Yoruba

WILLIAM BASCOM

Wirth's seminal paper provided one possible set of distinguishing criteria for students of urban life. It, and others like it, led to a number of studies designed to test the hypotheses generated.

William Bascom was one of the first to apply Wirth's paradigm to non-Western communities. He was disturbed by the difficulties in utilizing Wirth's concepts because of the lack of precision in such aspects as the homogeneous/-heterogeneous dichotomy. Bascom felt much of the existing work on cities was too narrowly based on Euro-American urban data; African cities would thus introduce some necessary comparative and contrastive cross-cultural data.

He maintained that large-scale Yoruba settlements were cities in every sense of the word. This, in spite of the fact that a major portion of the population engaged in farming for a primary livelihood, and in spite of sociocultural homogeneity among city dwellers. Bascom then argued that one must distinguish between those of Wirth's criteria that were primary and those that were only secondary. However, as Bascom stresses, work such as his is only a first step. It demonstrates the need to refine a typology of cities, distinguishing, for example, between industrial/nonindustrial and cosmopolitan/noncosmopolitan communities.

Wirth has defined a city as "a relatively large, dense, and permanent settlement of socially heterogeneous individuals."[1] His final criterion is not clearly defined; and, in the absence of specific standards which can be applied cross-

"Urbanization Among the Yoruba," *The American Journal of Sociology*, Vol. 60, 1955, pp. 446–454, University of Chicago Press ©.
    [1] L. Wirth, "Urbanism as a Way of Life," *American Journal of Sociology*, XLIV (1938), 8.

culturally, it is difficult to distinguish between heterogeneity and homogeneity. Miner has recently commented on "the lack of any concise benchmark
from which to appraise the degree of homogeneity"[2] in his study of Timbuctoo, although he concludes that "Timbuctoo is a city. It has a stable population of over six thousand persons, living in a community roughly a square mile
in area and patterning their lives after three distinct cultural heritages. The
size, density, and heterogeneity of the city are all evident."[3] Miner admittedly rests his case for heterogeneity on the ethnic diversity of the Songhai,
Tuareg, and Arabs who inhabit it, but neither he nor Wirth suggests that ethnic diversity is essential to the definition of the city. Many Western cities
include groups of different racial, linguistic, and cultural backgrounds, but
this can be regarded as a secondary feature of the process of urbanization and
a basis for distinguishing cosmopolitan from noncosmopolitan cities.

The shortcomings of Wirth's criterion of social heterogeneity are suggested
by the equivocal conclusions of those who have attempted to apply it to traditional African communities. Miner describes Timbuctoo as a "primitive city"
and its inhabitants as a "city-folk." Schwab, in a study of a Yoruba city,
concludes that "if Oshogbo was viewed on the level of form, it was an urban
community; if viewed in terms of social organization and process, it was
folk."[4] If the concepts of "folk" and "urban" are useful, it should at least be
possible to distinguish between them.

Contrasted to Timbuctoo's 6,000 inhabitants, the Yoruba have six cities of
more than 100,000, including Ibadan, the largest Negro city in Africa (Table
1). Only Lagos, which is both the principal port and the capital of Nigeria, is
ethnically heterogeneous and follows the familiar African pattern of the
growth of cities at mining and trading centers, ports, and colonial administrative headquarters.

Nine out of the ten largest cities in Nigeria in 1931 were Yoruba, excepting
only Kano, with 97,031 inhabitants. In these nine cities of over 45,000 lived
901,262, or 28.4 per cent, of the 3,166,164 Yoruba recorded in the *Census of
Nigeria, 1931*, while 1,077,691, or 34 per cent, lived in sixteen cities of over
20,000 (including, in addition to those listed in Table 1, Ijebu-Ode, 27,909;
Ikirun, 23,874; Ikire, 20,920; and Ondo, 20,859). In addition, there were 27
other Yoruba centers with populations between 10,000 and 19,999; 55 with
populations between 5,000 and 9,999; and 180 with populations between
2,000 and 4,999.[5]

Taking the average populations of the last three groups as 15,000, 7,500,
and 3,500 and counting only the 77 per cent of the population of Lagos who
were Yoruba, we arrive at the distribution of urban Yoruba in 1931 given in
Table 2. For comparison, the figures for European and North American countries cited by Davis and Casis are included, and, following these authors, the

[2] H. Miner, *The Primitive City of Timbuctoo* (Princeton: Princeton University Press, for the American Philosophical Society, 1953), p. 268.
[3] Ibid., p. 267.
[4] W. Schwab, "Urbanization and Acculturation" (MS).
[5] There were also 7,338 communities with populations under 2,000.

TABLE 1 Yoruba Cities with Populations over 40,000 *

	1952 (Census)	1931 (Census)	1931 (Non-natives)	1921 (Census)	1911 (Census)	Estimates by		
						Millson (1890)	Bowen (1856)	Tucker (1853)
Ibadan	459,196	387,133	226	238,094	175,000	200,000	70,000	60,000
Lagos	267,407	126,108	1,443	99,690	73,766		20,000	
Ogbomosho	139,535	86,744	0	84,860	80,000	60,000	25,000	45,000
Oshogbo	122,698	49,599	31	51,418	59,821	35,000– 40,000		
Ife	110,790	24,170	5	22,184	36,231			
Iwo	100,006	57,191	4	53,588	60,000	60,000	20,000	
Abeokuta	84,451	45,763	66	28,941	51,255		60,000	80,000
Oyo	72,133	48,733	19	40,356	45,438	40,000	25,000	
Ilesha	72,029	21,892	7					
Iseyin	49,680	36,805	0	28,601	33,362	40,000– 60,000	20,000	70,000
Ede	44,808	52,392	0	48,360	26,577	30,000– 40,000	20,000	
Ilorin	41,000	47,412	27	38,668	36,342		70,000	

* Other estimates, not included above, are as follows: Ogbomosho: 50,000 (1860, Campbell); Abeokuta: 45,000 (1842, Freeman), 50,000 (1843, Townsend), 100,000 (1852, Irving), twice the usual figures of 60,000–100,000 (1855, Consul Campbell), 80,000 (1858, Bowen), 100,000 (1874, Chause and Holley); Iseyin: 20,000 (1860, Campbell); Ilorin: 100,000 (1858, Bowen). The 1952 figures were kindly made available by the Nigerian government in advance of publication.

TABLE 2 Percentage of Population in Cities by Size Class

	Over 2,000	Over 5,000	Over 10,000	Over 25,000	Over 100,000	Index of urbanization
Yoruba (1931)	78.8	58.9	45.9	29.6	15.3	37.4
Great Britain (1931)		81.7	73.6	63.1	45.2	65.9
Germany (1939)		57.4	51.7	43.5	31.8	46.1
United States (1940)		52.7	47.6	40.1	28.8	42.3
Canada (1941)		43.0	38.5	32.7	23.0	34.3
France (1936)		41.7	37.5	29.8	16.0	31.2
Sweden (1935)		37.1	33.4	27.0	17.5	28.7
Greece (1937)		33.1	29.8	23.1	14.8	25.2
Poland (1931)		22.8	20.5	15.8	10.7	17.4

index of urbanization has been computed as the average of the previous four columns.[6] The estimated index of urbanization of Yoruba cities falls between that of the United States and Canada, and the distribution of population in urban centers is remarkably similar to that in France.

Official figures on population density are lacking except for Lagos Island (25,000 in 1901, 50,000 in 1921, 58,000 in 1931, and 87,000 in 1950; in 1950 the three wards of Lagos Island had densities of 67,000, 111,000, and 141,000 per square mile). It has been possible to calculate approximate densities for three other cities, using 1931 census figures and official maps[7] for that period. Abeokuta's area is calculated roughly as 8 square miles, giving a density of 5,720; Oyo's area is about 3½ square miles, giving a density of 13,914; Ogbomosho's area is calculated, probably more accurately than the others, at 2 square miles, giving a density of 43,372 per square mile. Because of the higher ratio of inhabitants per room and per square foot and the greater compactness of the traditional Yoruba housing, the size of the older Yoruba cities is easily underestimated by outsiders. Abeokuta, for example, appears much larger than Ogbomosho, which is actually something like half again as large and eight times as dense.

The permanency of Yoruba cities is partially documented in Table 1. Bowen's estimates of a century ago are conservative but incomplete; he visited Ogbomosho but does not estimate its size, and he states: "The eastern parts of Yoruba, and the countries of Ifeh (Ife), Ijesha (Ilesha), Igbona (Igbomina), and Effong (Effon-Alaive) have not been visited by the missionaries. We are assured that there are many large towns in that region."[8] The interior of Yoruba country was first reached in 1825 by Clapperton and Lander, who visited

[6] K. Davis and A. Casis, "Urbanization in Latin America," *Milbank Memorial Fund Quarterly*, XXIV (1946), 186–207.

[7] Abeokuta: Scale 1:12,500; drawn and reproduced by Land and Survey Department, Lagos, 1947; surveyed in 1930. Oyo: 300/723/3–50; scale 1:12,500; drawn and reproduced by Land and Survey Department, Lagos, Ogbomosho Town: 300/684/1.50; scale 400 feet to 1 inch; surveyed in 1938 and reproduced by Land and Survey Department, Lagos, 1939; reprinted in 1950.

[8] The principal historical sources are listed in the Bibliography.

Katunga (Old Oyo) and other large cities, some of which were obliterated before Bowen's arrival in 1849. The wars of the last century destroyed or reduced many Yoruba cities and resulted in a very considerable depopulation of the entire area.

Earlier historical materials can be found in the accounts of Benin, to the east, and Dahomey, to the west, which indicate that both were subject to some measure of political control by Yoruba cities as early as 200–500 years ago. When the Portuguese explorer d'Aveiro first visited the city of Benin in 1485, it was learned that the sanction of the Ogane, a powerful king in the interior, was required when the king of Benin was crowned; the Ogane has been identified by Talbot as the King of Ife. In 1505–8 Pereira mentions "a very large city called Geebuu," which is unquestionably Ijebu-Ode. In 1668 Dapper mentions the kingdom of Oedebo, and D'Anville's map of 1729 locates Oudobo in the region of the province and city of Ondo. Dapper also mentions the kingdom of Ulkami, which Talbot identifies as Old Oyo; Old Oyo may also be referred to in Bosman's account of the invasion of Arder in Dahomey in 1698. Old Oyo was certainly an important and powerful center by 1724, if not earlier, and was able to collect annual tribute from Dahomey for almost a century (1747–1837). Between 1830 and 1841 Old Oyo was evacuated and the present city of Oyo was founded.

Urbanization can therefore be considered a traditional Yoruba pattern and not the outgrowth of European acculturation. It cannot be explained in terms of the development of colonial administrative centers, ports, mines, or industry. The real basis of the Yoruba economy is, and was, farming. Yet the farmers are city dwellers, and the city is not really a "nonfarm area" as we view it. A belt of peripheral farms which are visited regularly surrounds the city, extending as much as fifteen miles or more ouside it. Families whose farms are more distant may have farm huts, where they spend several days at a time during the height of the farming activity, but they maintain a residence in the city and regard it as their real home. Some Yoruba, of course, live on farms or in very small villages.

Nearly all Yoruba engage in farming, but the production of many other goods is specialized. Weaving, dyeing, ironworking, brass-casting, wood-carving, ivory-carving, calabash-carving, beadworking, and leather-working, as well as drumming, divining, the compounding of charms and medicines, and certain other activities, are crafts, whose techniques are known only to a small group of specialists. These specialists, who are organized into guilds, supply all other members of the community with their particular goods and services. Formerly these occupations tended to be more hereditary within the clan or lineage, but the apprenticeship system provided a method by which individuals from outside the kinship unit could be taught a craft. Specialization, however, was only on a craft basis and never reached the extent to which it is found in industrialized societies with the adaptation of labor to the machine.

Trading in local produce within the community is a necessary outgrowth of craft specialization, and both intercommunity and intertribal trade are apparently traditional. The Landers met one hundred wives of the king of Old Oyo trading for him at "Jadoo," north of Ilaro and "Egga." Clapperton and Lander met Hausa and Nupe caravans at "Coosoo" and "Jaguta" between Shaki and Old Oyo and at Kiama, north of Yoruba country, who traded with Yoruba and Dahomeans, with Gonja, Ashantee, and Accra in the Gold Coast, and with Bornu in northeastern Nigeria. In at least Ife, Abeokuta, and Ijebu-Ode, guilds of male traders held monopolies on imported goods from other Yoruba towns and from Europe, buying them in wholesale lots and letting them out to women traders for retail in the markets. Tolls levied on all trade, which provided an important source of income for Yoruba chiefs and kings, are mentioned by Lander on his first visit to Old Oyo. These, and the monopolies on imported goods held by the guilds of male traders, were actively opposed and eventually broken by the British in their efforts to extend trade in Nigeria. The desire to control trade routes to the sea and insure a supply of European imports, including arms, and an outlet for slaves led Ibadan, Abeokuta, and other inland cities to attack coastal enemy towns and defend those of their allies.

Trading is the third basis of the Yoruba economy, and the size and importance of Yoruba markets impress the visitor today as they did the early explorers. Retail trade in the markets is primarily in the hands of women, who also tend to specialize in yams, corn, chickens, cloth, and other commodities, as they become successful, and who are organized into guilds. Trade does not involve a simple exchange of goods between the producer and the consumer but is carried on by middlemen whose role and motivation are similar to those in our own society. In the simplest case a trader buys from the producer and sells at a higher price for a monetary profit; but in some cases goods are sold and resold through a chain of middlemen which has so many links that it becomes difficult to distinguish between wholesaler and retailer. True money in the form of the cowrie shell was used by the Yoruba probably even before European contact, and early European officials received their pay in cowries. Barbot (1732) mentions that "cauries" or "boejies" were being imported from the Maldive Islands in the East Indies as ballast, "no other people in the universe putting such a value on them as the Guineans," but their use as money at Benin is mentioned as early as 1589. Some Yoruba traditions speak of the insititution of barter, but others suggest that cowrie shells were used as money before even the Portuguese arrived and that the pecuniary economy of the Yoruba is of long standing. To say the least, it is difficult to imagine how the European traders would have hit upon cowrie shells as an importable commodity which the Africans would accept in exchange for goods if the shells had not been already known and valued. One may conclude that the traditional Yoruba pattern of trade involved large markets, true middlemen, and true money.

The earliest available evidence indicates an important and well-developed trade between Yoruba cities and with other tribes but does not suggest that these cities developed as trading centers of the type represented by Timbuctoo, Kano, and other Sudanese cities. Under British rule, trade in European goods has increased tremendously, as has trade in local produce, owing to the development of new occupations such as those of clerk, carpenter, and mechanic and to the increasing amounts of farm land devoted to cocoa. The typical pre-British markets, however, excluding those which specialized in the buying and selling of slaves, dealt mainly with local produce rather than with goods from abroad, from other tribes, or from other Yoruba cities. In other words, trade was based upon specialization within the city rather than the city itself being based upon trade growing out of extensive regional or tribal specialization.

It is important to distinguish between industrial and nonindustrial cities. Industrialization, where it has occurred, has produced a kind and degree of specialization that are unknown in nonindustrialized societies. Industrialization has given rise to urbanization in Western societies, but this is not to say that it is its prerequisite or its only cause. On this point, Wirth has stated specifically: "It is particularly important to call attention to the danger of confusing urbanism with industrialism and modern capitalism. The rise of cities in the modern world is undoubtedly not independent of modern power-driven machine technology, mass production, and capitalistic enterprise. But different as the cities of earlier epochs may have been by virtue of their development in a preindustrial and precapitalistic order from the great cities of today, they were, nevertheless, cities."[9]

The Yoruba cities were nonindustrial and lacked the degree of specialization based upon the machine. Nevertheless, the craft form of specialization made each individual economically dependent upon the society as a whole. The weaver depended upon the blacksmith for tools and upon the farmer, the hunter, and the trader for his food; the blacksmith depended upon others for his food and upon the weaver for his clothes; the farmer depended upon the hunter and the trader for his meat, the smith for his cutlass and hoe, and the weaver for his clothing. Each of these, moreover, had to rely upon the diviner, the herbalist, the priest, the drummer, the potter, the wood-carver, and other specialists for goods and services which they could not provide for themselves.

Aside from craft specialization, the Yoruba cities were heterogeneous only in terms of their social stratification and their social and political segmentation. Nine social strata can be distinguished in the Yoruba city of Ife. Over-simplifying for the sake of brevity, the five lowest strata, comprising perhaps 95 per cent of the population, may be described as positions which are ascribed on the basis of clan or lineage, while the four highest strata are primarily achieved, although often only within specified clans or lineages.[10] The patrilineal lineage or clan is basic to Yoruba society, rural or urban. The large cities are composed of many such segments based on kinship, organized

[9] Wirth, op. cit., pp. 7–8.
[10] W. Bascom, "Social Status, Wealth and Individual Differences among the Yoruba," *American Anthropologist*, LIII (1951), 490–505.

politically into permanent, clearly defined wards or "quarters" and precincts or subquarters, while the small villages may contain only a few or even only a single lineage. In Ife heads of each lineage constitute the precinct council, one of their number serving as its chief. Precinct chiefs constitute the ward council, headed by a ward chief. The five ward chiefs and three other city chiefs represent the interests of the townspeople and, with eight chiefs chosen from the palace retinue, serve as the king's council and in former times served as a chief tribunal. The king, whose position is hereditary within the related lineages of the royal clan, is responsible for the affairs of the capital and of the outlying towns and villagers within the kingdom.

Within the lineage, individual relationships are dependent upon such circumstances as seniority, sex, wealth, personal qualities, and status as slave, pawn, or free; but between lineages individual relationships are dependent upon the relative rank of the lineage.[11] The individual counts for little except as a member of the lineage. Further, in Wirth's words, "interests are made effective through representation."[12] Representation or delegation is clearly illustrated in the system of lineage heads, precinct councils and precinct chiefs, ward councils and ward chiefs, city council with its city chiefs, representatives of the palace officials, and the king himself.

The city is a secondary group, while the lineage is primary. Wirth says: "The contacts of the city may indeed be face to face, but they are nevertheless impersonal, superficial, transitory and segmental." All these characteristics are exemplified in Yoruba market transactions. As in our own urban communities, one may have regular customers with whom relations are not impersonal, but one also must deal with casual customers of whom one must always beware in either buying or selling. Miner notes the cheating of a gullible buyer or seller in Timbuctoo. Among the Yoruba the principle of *caveat emptor* is also well established, as is illustrated by an edict of the king of Ife prohibiting the "hawking" or peddling of palm wine through the streets so as to restrict the possibility of its being watered down. Furthermore, the counterfeiting of government currency was so perfected by one Yoruba subgroup that counterfeit coins became known throughout Nigeria as "Ijebu money." Another new kind of cheating was made possible by the "money doubling" machines of the early thirties. Into these Westernized gadgets the up-country dupe would put shillings and pounds in increasing amounts and have double value returned, until he became greedy for the big kill and put in all the cash he could; at this point the operator explained that the machine had stuck and would take overnight to digest such a large amount, and skipped out of town under the cover of darkness.

Wirth emphasizes that urbanization refers to a distinctive mode of life. This is evident among the Yoruba in clothing, food habits, manners, and attitudes toward each other of even the non-Europeanized city dweller and the people

---

[11] Ibid.; W. Bascom, "The Principle of Seniority in the Social Structure of the Yoruba," *American Anthropologist*, XLIV (1942), 37–46.

[12] Wirth, op. cit., p. 14.

from the small village, the rural farm area, and the hinterland. The city dwellers ridicule the unsophisticated "bush" people; their attitudes, as expressed in conversation and proverbs,[13] closely parallel our concepts of "rube" or "hick." The attitudes of the rural Yoruba toward the city dweller also seem to resemble those in our society. On the other hand, the anomie stressed by Durkheim and later sociologists does not seem to be apparent, unless it is to be found among the rural Yoruba who find themselves in the city. Since the lineage is the residential unit and involves reciprocal social and economic obligations, the city dweller need not feel lonely or insecure. Competitiveness is strong, and economic failure can lead to frustration or suicide but not to starvation.

There is no evidence that the old pattern of city life tended to weaken the lineage, or produce the increased mobility, instability, and insecurity which Wirth suggests are the results of heterogeneity. To the extent that the lineage has been weakened, the causes have been other conditions, such as the increased ease of travel with the ending of warfare and the development of Western forms of transportation, the introduction of a valuable permanent crop in cocoa, the superimposition of British control and European ethics over the traditional Yoruba authorities and mores, and the emphasis on the individual in the teaching of Christian missions, which have affected the Yoruba over the last fifty to a hundred years.[14] All these things are today producing changes in Yoruba cities similar to those in the newer African cities and to the Western cities of which Wirth speaks; kinship bonds, traditionally a basic element in the structure of the city, are weakening.

Wirth states that "the bonds of kinship, of neighborliness, and the sentiments arising out of living together for generations under a common folk tradition are likely to be absent or, at best, relatively weak in an aggregate the members of which have such diverse origins and backgrounds. Under such circumstances competition and formal control mechanisms furnish the substitutes for the bonds of solidarity that are relied upon to hold a folk society together." This statement is undoubtedly true of the cosmopolitan cities in the United States and perhaps elsewhere, but in the Yoruba cities the bonds of kinship and living together which unite the lineage were strong, and the elements of competition and formal control mechanisms were not developed as *substitutes* for kinship control mechanisms but, rather, as mechanisms of control on a suprakinship, secondary level, transcending the primary groups, such as lineages, which were very much alive and functional.

Although Wirth dismisses forms of political organization as an arbitrary and therefore unsatisfactory criterion for urbanism, the presence or absence of a formalized city government which exercises authority over neighboring pri-

---

[13] E.g., "They don't call a man a man; they don't call a human a human; therefore the farm people [ara oko] wear a breechclout to town," meaning that they do not have enough respect for others to dress properly in public.

[14] The effects of these factors cannot be analyzed here. They are touched on partially in W. Bascom, "African Culture and the Missionary," *Civilisations* (Brussels), III (1953), 491–504.

mary groups and incorporates them into a community seems, on the contrary, no less arbitrary and certainly far less subjective than social heterogeneity. When coupled with size, density, and permanency, formalized community government would seem to be a useful criterion of urbanism for cross-cultural comparisons. It is this factor which differentiates the urban Yoruba from the Ibo of eastern Nigeria, whose total population is comparable and whose over-all population densities are about double [15] but the growth of whose cities has been recent. We do not know why the Yoruba developed cities and city government while the Ibo did not, but city life is definitely a part of the Yoruba tradition.

Some Yoruba cities, such as Oyo, Ife, Ilesha, Ijebu-Ode, Ondo, and Ketu, were metropolitan in that, as capitals, they served as centers of the entire kingdom and can be considered metropolitan. The capital city maintained regular communication with the outlying towns over which they ruled, and representatives of the king were stationed in them. Taxes of several kinds were collected throughout the kingdom and brought to the capital for the king. Death sentences had to be referred to the capital, where executions were performed and where each case could be reviewed by the king's court. Other large cities, such as Iseyin, Ogbomosho, and Ibadan, were not metropolitan except as they served as centers of trade or warfare, but these also had formalized city government. Each was ruled by a "town" chief (*bale*) under the authority of the king (*oba*), who lived elsewhere and to whom allegiance was owed. Ibadan became so powerful as a military center that it achieved a measure of independence from Oyo and could command the allegiance of many surrounding towns, but its ruler is still a *bale*, not an *oba*.

Ethnically the Yoruba cities were homogeneous. With the end of the wars of the last century, individuals from the Hausa, Ibo, Jekri, and other cultural and liguistic groups have settled in them, but in relatively small numbers except for Lagos. One may assume that in earlier times the non-Yoruba consisted mainly of slaves and transient traders. The wars of the last century flooded some cities with refugees, including those from other Yoruba kingdoms and subcultures; but one may also assume that even on the level of subcultural and dialectical variation Yoruba cities were previously noncosmopolitan.

Despite the absence of industrialization and ethnic heterogeneity and despite the continued importance of kinship units, the Yoruba had cities even before European penetration. They had cities because they had large, dense, permanent communities whose inhabitants were economically independent, socially stratified, and politically unified. These cities were based on farming, craft specialization, and trading. Only Lagos represents the common type of recent growth of African cities as ports, mining and trading centers, and colonial administrative headquarters. Some Yoruba cities were metropolitan, serv-

---

[15] Population densities in 1931 for the Yoruba provinces in Southern Nigeria run as follows: Ondo, 56; Abeokuta, 74; Oyo, 94; Ijebu, 125; and the Colony, 153; for the Ibo provinces: Ogoj, 94; Owerri, 268; and Onitsha, 306. In 1931 the Ibo numbered 3,184,585, as against 3,166,164 Yoruba in Nigeria.

ing as capitals and centers of the Yoruba kingdoms; others were nonmetropolitan. Some were founded as defensive or predatory centers during the wars of the last century; others undoubtedly existed when the Portuguese arrived and before the beginning of the slave wars. Although the cause of their growth is still not fully known, they were definitely a part of the traditional Yoruba pattern, providing permanent residence for farmers and markets for trade within, as well as beyond, the city's boundaries.

It is difficult to decide whether or not the Yoruba cities were heterogeneous in Wirth's sense, because social heterogeneity is not clearly defined. At best, it is a relative criterion which is difficult to apply cross-culturally. Perhaps the answer may be to define it in terms of specialization to the extent that each individual is economically dependent on the production and the special skills of the other members of his community. It is necessary at least to distinguish between industrial and nonindustrial cities and between cosmopolitan and noncosmopolitan cities. It is also suggested that the existence of a formalized government which exercises authority over the primary groups and incorporates them into a political community may be more useful than heterogeneity when applied cross-culturally, since it is less subjective. It is hoped that these points may broaden the concept of urbanization so that it is less dependent upon the historical conditions of Western urbanization and so that it can be applied more profitably to the study of the urban centers of India and Southeast Asia.

Bibliography

ADAMS, J.
   1823   *Remarks on the Country Extending from Cape Palmas to the River Congo.* London: G. & B. W. Whittaker.
ADAMS, J.
   1821   *Sketches Taken during Ten Voyages to Africa, between the Years 1786 and 1800.* London: Hurst, Robinson & Co.
BARBOT, J.
   1732   *Description of the Coasts of North and South Guinea.* London (no publisher listed).
BARROS, JOÃO DE
   1945   *Ásia de João de Barros: Dos feitos que os portugueses fizeram no descobrimento e conquista dos mares e terras do Oriente.* 4 vols. 6th ed. Lisboa: Divisáo de Publiçacões e Biblioteca, Agência Geral das Colónias, Ministério das Colónias, República Portuguesa. First published in 1553. Extracts translated in G. R. CRONE, *The Voyages of Cadamosto and Other Documents on Western Africa in the Second Half of the Fifteenth Century.* London: Hakluyt Society, 1937.
BOSMAN, W.
   1721   *A New and Accurate Description of Guinea.* 2d ed. London: J. Knapton,

D. Midwinter, B. Lintot, G. Strahan, J. Round, and E. Bell. First published in 1705.

BOWEN, T. J.
1857 Central Africa: Adventures and Missionary Labors in Several Countries in the Interior of Africa, from 1849 to 1856. Charleston, S.C.: Southern Baptist Publication Society.

BOWEN, T. J.
1858 Grammar and Dictionary of Yoruba Language. ("Smithsonian Contributions to Knowledge," Vol. X.) Washington: Smithsonian Institution.

BURTON, R. F.
1893 A Mission to Gelele, King of Dahomey. 2 vols. London: Tylston & Edwards.

CAMPBELL, R.
1860 A Pilgrimage to My Motherland: An Account of a Journey among the Egbas and Yorubas of Central Africa in 1859–1860. London: W. J. Johnson.

CENSUS OF NIGERIA, 1931
1932– 6 vols. London: Crown Agents for the Colonies for the Government of
1933   Nigeria.

CHAUSE, H., AND HOLLEY
1885 "Voyage dans le Yoruba," Les Missions catholiques, Vol. XVII (1855), Nos. 814–21.

CLAPPERTON, H.
1829 Journal of a Second Expedition into the Interior of Africa, from the Bight of Benin to Soccatoo. Philadelphia: Carey, Lea & Carey.

DALZELL, A.
1793 The History of Dahomy, an Inland Kingdom of Africa. London: for the author, by T. Spilsbury.

DAPPER, O.
1670 Umständliche und eigentliche Beschreibung von Africa. Amsterdam: Jacob von Meurs. First published in Flemish in 1668.

DUNGLAS, E.
1948 "La première attaque des Dahoméens contre Abéokuta (3 mars 1851)," Études dahomeennes, I, 7–19.

FOA, E.
1895 Le Dahomey. Paris: A. Hennuyer.

HERMON-HODGE, H. B.
1929 Gazetteer of Ilorin Province. London: George Allen & Unwin.

HERSKOVITS, M. J.
1938 Dahomey: An Ancient West African Kingdom. 2 vols. New York: J. J. Augustin.

HINDERER, A.
n.d. Seventeen Years in the Yoruba Country. London: Religious Tract Society. First published ca. 1872.

LABAT, (J. B.)
1731 Voyage du Chevalier des Marchais en Guinee, isles voisines, et à Cayenne, fait en 1725, 1726 & 1727. 4 vols. Amsterdam: La Compagnie.

LAGOS
  1951   Population Census, 1950. Kuduna: Government Printer.
LANDER, R.
  1830   Records of Captain Clapperton's Last Expedition to Africa. 2 vols. London: Henry Colburn & Richard Bentley.
LANDER, R. AND J.
  1854   Journal of an Expedition To Explore the Course and Termination of the Niger. New York: Harper & Bros. First published in 1832.
MEEK, C. K.
  1925   The Northern Tribes of Nigeria. 2 vols. London: Oxford University Press.
MILLSON, A. W.
  1891   "The Yoruba Country, West Africa," Proceedings of the Royal Geographical Society, Vol. XIII (2d ser.)
NIGERIA
  1932–   Census, 1931. London: Crown Agents. . . .
  1933
NORRIS, R.
  1789   Memoirs of the Reign of Bossa Ahadee, King of Dahomy. London: W. Lowndes.
PEREIRA, DUARTE PACHECHO
  1937   Esmeraldo de situ orbis. Translated and edited by G. H. T. KIMBLE. London: Hakluyt Society. First published in 1892. Written in two parts in 1505 and 1507–8.
SCHÖN, J. F., and CROWTHER, S. A.
  1842   Journals of the Rev. James Frederick Schön and Mr. Samuel Crowther, Who, with the Sanction of Her Majesty's Government, Accompanied the Expedition up the Niger in 1841, in Behalf of the Church Missionary Society. London: Hatchard & Son, Nisbet & Co., Seeleys.
SNELGRAVE, W.
  1734   A New Account of Some Parts of Guinea, and the Slave Trade. London: James, John & Paul Knapton.
TALBOT, P. A.
  1926   The Peoples of Southern Nigeria. 4 vols. London: Oxford University Press.
TUCKER, MISS.
  1853   Abbeokuta; or, Sunrise within the Tropics: An Outline of the Origin and Progress of the Yoruba Mission. London: James Nisbet & Co.

Urban Domains: Environments That Defy Close Definition

JOHN GULICK

That the problem of definitions has not yet been resolved is evidenced in the many definitions and conceptual treatments of "urban" here reviewed and discussed by John Gulick.

Gulick carefully considers past work and subsequently offers his own model of the "urban domain". He appears to see urban as describable quantitatively and urbanism as best approached in qualitative terms, a position that is rather pervasive among urban anthropologists. Among the more interesting aspects of his analysis are a rejection of the technique of looking at cities per se and an unusual focus, instead, upon "some of the smallest settlements with which the words 'city' and 'urban' have been associated, either by the inhabitants or by observers." In this way he is able to draw our attention to the process of becoming urban, as well as to the minimal criteria for defining a place as urban.

Because the basis of anthropological research is the use of cross-cultural data, six ethnographic studies are employed. Target populations are drawn from Brazil, Guatemala, Baffin Island (Canada), Ecuador, Afghanistan, and Iran. To these that Gulick uses others could be added, such as Silverman's Three Bells of Civilization (1975); Miner's St. Denis, A French Canadian Parish (1939); Powdermaker's Copper Town: Changing Africa (1962); and Geertz's The Social History of an Indonesian Town (1965), to mention only a handful of available studies. From these six ministudies, Gulick abstracts seven characteristics of urbanism. It is interesting to note how these seven encompass or summarize a great many items of his bipolar model, in which locales can be placed on a rural/urban continuum.

Gulick's paper (of which only an excerpt appears here) is a major contribution to the understanding of urbanism. Its importance lies less in what it tells us than in what he asks us to consider.

Biases

No one, it seems, is indifferent to cities. There are city-lovers and city-haters, and there are those whose feelings about cities are ambivalent and contradictory—but not indifferent. One reason for this lack of indifference is, I think, that cities are, to a large extent, manmade environments. City life therefore involves not only constant interactions with other human beings, but also constant coping with other human beings' physical designs, arrangements, and artifacts. This kind of coping is not wholly absent from village life,

Reprinted as an excerpt from John Gulick's "Urban Anthropology," in *Handbook of Social and Cultural Anthropology* (John J. Honigmann, ed.), pp. 979–1029, 1973, Rand McNally & Company.

but in a village the natural environment constitutes an ever present coun-
terelement to the manmade one. For many people the natural environment
provides an escape or release from the impingements on their lives of other
human beings. It is difficult to be indifferent to such impingements, and the
larger a city is, the more intense they are, either through other people directly or through the manmade physical environment or both. It would be interesting to establish at what points in the range of size of human settlements
and under what conditions the manmade environment begins to be predominant in the inhabitants' perceptions, but no one, to my knowledge, has done
so.

And yet for at least two thousand years people have been trying to define
just what the urban environment is, as distinct from other environments.
Many have convinced themselves or others that they had the answer, but all
of the answers so far have been found wanting. Lack of objectivity—often
unrecognized or unacknowledged—seems to have been one factor in this lack
of agreement. Another is the vast variety, in size and other features, of settlements that have been considered urban.

Qualitative Models

Many people feel intuitively that a relatively large population is an important factor in determining whether a settlement can be considered urban.
Since population size can be measured with fair accuracy, it should be a valuable objective index of urbanism. But it is not, and the reason is that there is
no agreement on what the minimum size of an urban place is. The United
States Bureau of the Census says 2,500; the United Nations says 20,000
(Breese, ed., 1969:23); and Kingsley Davis, the renowned demographer, says
100,000 (Breese, ed., 1969:5f). Since there is no agreement on a minimum
population size that will qualify a settlement as urban, there cannot, objectively speaking, be agreement on any qualitative phenomena that might be
variables dependent on size. However, this lack of objective criteria of judgment has never stopped people from inventing qualitative characteristics of
urban life.

In fact, a traditional model of urban life has accumulated. Contributed to by
many people, it has had its systematizers, Robert Redfield among them. The
model is bipolar and primarily moralistic, reflecting the partisan feelings that
apparently dominate most people's thinking about cities.

Items 12 through 15 will be recognized as the core elements in the folk/ur-
ban distinction of Redfield. Redfield has been credited with refining this distinction from a crude dichotomy into a more sophisticated continuum; but this
was really a minor modification, for the distinction is that of polar opposites in
either case. Louis Wirth, who was himself a major contributor to this model,
in one of his last papers (1964:223) expressed chagrin at the way in which
these arbitrary, ideal-typical polar concepts have so often been taken for es-

The Moralistic Bipolar Model

	Rural		Urban
0r	Country (village)	0u	Town (city)
1r	Community (*Gemeinschaft*)	1u	Noncommunity (*Gesellschaft*)
2r	Folk	2u	Urban
3r	Primitive	3u	Civilized
4r	Natural ("true")	4u	Spurious, super-ficial, artificial
5r	Simple	5u	Sophisticated
6r	Provincial	6u	Cosmopolitan
7r	Tribal society	7u	Mass society
8r	Moral	8u	Corrupt
9r	Inherently stable	9u	Inherently changing
10r	Human in scale	10u	Dehumanized
11r	Particularistic	11u	Universalistic
12r	Homogeneous	12u	Heterogeneous
12rx	Few alternative modes of behavior	12ux	Many alternative modes of behavior
13r	Personal	13u	Impersonal (anonymous)
13rx	Constrained	13ux	Free
14r	Integrated	14u	Disintegrated (anomic)
14rx	Conformist	14ux	Nonconformist
15r	Sacred	15u	Secular
15rx	Superstitious, myth-oriented	15ux	Rational

tablished facts, rather than for what they are, merely bases for hypotheses to be tested.

On the whole, this model is anti-urban. Items 1*u*, 4*u*, 7*u*, 8*u*, 10*u*, and 13*u*-15*u* have usually been employed in pejorative contexts, whereas their opposite numbers in the rural series have been used as positive terms. Items 3*u*, 5*u*, 6*u*, 9*u*, and 12*u* are ambiguous as far as moralistic import is concerned, but they are not neutral terms, any more than are 3*r*, 5*r*, 6*r*, 9*r*, and 12*r*.

Many observers have discerned distinctions among the phenomena represented by the 12–15 series besides those implied in the polar pairs. I have made an attempt to identify these distinctions by items labeled *x*. Thus an aspect of impersonal relationships (13*u*) is freedom (13*ux*) from various kinds of interference. This freedom contrasts with the constraints (13*rx*) that are inherent in many personal relationships (13*r*). Items 13*ux*, 14*ux*, and 15*ux* seem most often to be used in positive terms and their opposite numbers in pejorative ones, resulting in a reversal of the generally predominant preference for the rural items. (That urban life lacks constraining personal relationships is one of the many easily refutable implications of the model.)

Some social scientists continue to think explicitly in terms of this model or some version of it. Kahl's (1959) is a good example, one that puts relative stress on the pro-urban interpretation to which I have just alluded. Frankenberg's (1966) review of communities in Britain is a more extended exposition that generally expresses the traditional anti-urban point of view. So, too, is a very recent anthropological textbook (Oswalt, 1970) that idealizes man the noble hunter (p. 121) and refers to urbanites as "enslaved by an artificial environment" (p. 121), to Timbuctoo as similar to American urban culture in its money emphasis, crime, cheating, and dishonesty (p. 127), and to the "dehumanized and unnatural city" (p. 144). Many others assume the validity of the model but express this assumption implicitly.

The bipolar model has been thoroughly criticized, but I am not sure how effective these attacks really have been, at least so far, in discrediting it. For one thing, the critics have not yet been able to work out a sufficiently comprehensive substitute model that has equal appeal.

And the appeal of the bipolar moralistic model is great, for it is a system of stereotypes that encapsulates a great number of prejudices that camouflage the oversimplifications and inconsistencies of the system. A major fallacy of the model is its assumption that "rural" represents a single, uniform type of settlement, and that "urban" does also.

Another fallacy is the glaring internal inconsistency among the urban traits. Cultural heterogeneity is one of the few traits (perhaps the only one) that all observers agree is characteristic of cities. (Whether and to what extent city dwellers are able to participate in this heterogeneity in their individual experiences is an interesting question but one that need not be pursued at this point.) If heterogeneity is in fact characteristic of cities, it should follow by logic alone that the other traits—for example, anonymity and anomie—cannot be assumed to characterize all city-dwellers. This and related points have been made very effectively by Oscar Lewis (1965:496) in a short paper that is one of the most succinct and comprehensive critiques of the moralistic bipolar approach in print. It is paired with a paper by Philip Hauser (1965) that demonstrates that when the moralistic bipolar traits are taken at face value and applied to cross-cultural data, a very poor fit is revealed between the stereotype and known facts.

Gideon Sjoberg's *The Preindustrial City* (1960:13–16) criticizes the bipolar moralistic model in general and finds particular fault with its failure to apply to preindustrial and nonindustrial cities. Sjoberg's own model of preindustrial cities is based on an assumption of various cross-cultural uniformities. This model should be taken as the basis of hypotheses to be tested by fieldwork where possible.

Since some of Sjoberg's data pertain to past conditions that no longer exist, it is now impossible to test these hypotheses in some cases, but it is still possible in others. For example, Windle and Sabagh (1963:436), using a census of 19,000 employees of the Iranian National Oil Company, set about to test Sjoberg's generalization that preindustrial urban upper-class parents have more children who reach adulthood than do lower-class parents, not because of higher fertility but because of lower mortality. They discovered that the professional and staff employees did indeed have more children than the skilled and unskilled workers, but that the foremen had even more children than the professional and staff employees. They concluded (1963:441–42):

While the findings of this study do not contradict Sjoberg's generalization, they suggest that it may no longer be sufficient to describe the situation when the preindustrial city is beginning to experience industrialization and modernization. One should consider the possible effect of this new process on the willingness or desire to adopt fertility control practices. A white collar upper status class . . . may be most ready to accept such practices. If they do, then this is likely to counteract the effect of declining infant and child mortality. Other classes and groups more imbued with tradition but benefiting also from the quickening tempo of economic growth [e.g., the foremen] may use their newly acquired wealth to maximize the size of their families.

Windle and Sabagh, demographers, thus conclude their hypothesis-testing by in effect proposing another hypothesis, one to which urban anthropologists could well address themselves. Inadvertently, perhaps, they also point up the dangers inherent in so many publications about the process of industrial urbanization in the world, which assume the established factual truth of the bipolar model (e.g., having a small number of children is automatically the *rational* pattern item 15*ux* of all urbanites).

It is because of such persistent and pervasive thinking that the bipolar moralistic model cannot be ignored. If, as Sjoberg claims, most of its elements are not applicable to the preindustrial city, we are still left with the question of what the central qualities of industrial cities are, and therefore what the effects of urban industrialization are, and the only available answer so far is the bipolar moralistic model. Yet its inadequacies have been demonstrated in the most highly industrialized cities as well as in preindustrial ones. The problem is not that the human characteristics itemized in the model are imaginary, for they are real enough. But the model expresses them in an overly abstract fashion and asserts a pattern of distribution that does not fit reality.

The question remains: What are the essential characteristics of urban environments that distinguish them from nonurban environments? If, in search of answers, we look only at the largest cities in the world, we may succeed only in begging the question. In 1960 there were twenty-five cities in the world that had more than 2.5 million inhabitants each (Breese, ed., 1969:33). Surely the sheer immensity of these cities must result in consequences that are similar in all and could be identified as essentially urban? Perhaps, but there are also differences despite size, though sometimes related to it. Let us consider three similarly sized pairs of these cities. Moscow is relatively free of smog: Los Angeles is choking on it. Cairo has no suburbs to speak of and therefore no suburbia-related commuter problem: Detroit has both. Rio de Janeiro, despite its enormous size (four to five million), is famous for its spirit of relaxation, gaiety, and traditional charm: São Paulo, just as big and just as surely Brazilian, is known for its competitiveness and its emphasis on modernity and hardheaded business (Leeds, 1968:37). The differences between these pairs of cities can be accounted for by amount and type of industrialization, size of gross national product, and history; but this is just another way of saying that the effects of size alone are themselves affected by other factors.

As for any demonstration of the validity of the bipolar model that the world's largest cities can offer, one needs only to consider three studies done in Tokyo (Dore, 1958, Norbeck, 1965, and Vogel, 1967) to see that in the heterogeneity of big cities one can discover *all* of the elements in the model, both "rural" and "urban."

This statement also holds true when one considers smaller cities like Ibadan, Nigeria, population about 900,000, whose inhabitants include (1) Westernized office workers living in single-family suburban houses and dependent upon the private automobile for the maintenance of their social life, (2) various "ethnic" groups living in circumscribed quarters, and (3) "inner city" residents who live in lineage compounds and commute to the countryside each week for farmwork (Lloyd et al., eds., 1967). Or Oshogbo, Nigeria, population about 120,000, whose cultural patterns range from "universalism and achievement" to the traditional kinship system (Schwab, 1965:109). Or Timbuctoo, Mali, population 7,000, whose combination of "folk" and "urban" patterns was Miner's major discovery (Miner, 1965). Largely on the basis of African materials, Bascom (1968:91) seems to despair of associating any behavioral traits definitively with urbanism; "cities should be defined strictly in terms of demographic factors: relative size, density and permanence." Since relative size is such a demonstrably elastic concept, I do not see that such reductionism can be very helpful in either the building or the testing of hypotheses.

Urban Essentials in Six Small Towns

If the "essential urban" characteristics elude us in the complexities of the largest and some of the not so large cities, perhaps we can make greater progress if we consider some of the smallest settlements with which the words "city" and "urban" have been associated, either by the inhabitants or by observers.

Charles Wagley's (1953) study of Itá, a Brazilian community on the Amazon River, is not concerned with definitions of the city but with the problems of underdevelopment in the tropics. Itá's status as an urban community must be deduced from scattered remarks that Wagley makes on the subject.

Itá was founded as a community early in the seventeenth century. By the middle of the nineteenth century it had a population of about seven hundred people and was divided into two sections, one called the "village" (inhabited by the Indians and their descendants), the other called the "city" (inhabited by Europeans and *mestiços*—merchants, government officials, landowners, and artisans) (Wagley, 1953:45). Growing up around a fort, it became an important river port and government control station. From about 1890 to 1912 it shared in the prosperity of the rubber boom that affected the whole Amazon valley, but from 1912 to 1942, during the collapse of the rubber market, its population declined to only three hundred. At the time of Wagley's study it had begun to recover.

Itá has a gridiron street plan, with the town hall (which would have been a monumental structure if the rubber boom had not suddenly ended) and the new public health post fronting on the main square. The public health post serves a large area for which Itá is an excellent center of communication. Itá is the administrative center of a "municipality" consisting of jungle and small hamlets situated on subsidiary streams flowing into the Amazon.

Wagley refers to Itá variously as a "city" (p. 23), a "backward, decadent, and isolated community" (p. 58), a "rural" community (p. 148), and "essentially" a "farming" community (p. 276). These designations are quite contradictory in terms of the standard rural-urban model, but Wagley is not concerned with that. He devotes much attention, however, to the social class structure of Itá and its hinterland, identifying four classes in ranked order: first class (local upper class), second class (lower-class town dwellers), farmers, and collectors (mostly of rubber) (p. 105). Of a sample of ninety-eight men in Itá town whom he interviewed systematically, Wagley classified fourteen as first class, forty-six as second class, twenty-nine as farmers, and nine as collectors, categorizing the first class as upper class and the other three as lower class (p. 132). Wagley's comments are significant (1953:104–105).

To the outsider . . . Itá may appear to be a homogeneous society of rural peasants, of people who differ little from one another in social rank. In Belém upper class people are apt to classify the people of Itá, with the exception of a few government officials stationed there, as caboclos. . . . Yet, as one lives and participates in Itá social life, it soon becomes apparent that people, within the confines of the community itself, are quite sensitive to differences in social rank. . . .

Such present-day distinctions . . . result from the class system of colonial Amazon society, from the former servitude of Indians and imported African slaves, and from the social ascendancy of the Portuguese colonials. They also reflect the economic and social position of the various groups who inhabit Itá today. . . .

As the city folk tend to view Itá as a homogeneous society of small-town peasants, the First Class people of Itá are apt to view the people below them in the social hierarchy as simply "the people," or as "caboclos." In turn, the town-dwelling Second Class indicate their superiority to all the rural population by speaking of them as "caboclos," and the farmers reserve this term for the Island collectors, to whom they feel superior. And finally, the Island collectors would be slightly offended if they were called "caboclos," for they make little distinction between themselves and the farmers.

With a population of six hundred, Itá is no larger than hundreds of thousands of farmers' settlements throughout the world that no one (native or foreign observer) would be tempted to call cities or urban or urbanized. In fact, it is smaller than many of them. Since Wagley does not discuss the matter, we can only infer the reasons for Itá's being considered, by some people at least, to be a city. My inferences are that Itá, small as it is, is larger than surrounding settlements over which certain inhabitants of Itá have political

and economic control; that Itá as a community is the location of linkages between different segments and levels of a national society; that the localization
of these linkage functions is an important factor in the social status heterogeneity of its population; that Itá is considered urban only in relative terms by
its inhabitants, yes, but not by people in much larger coastal cities of Brazil.
If, by at least some people's standards, Itá is urban, this does not mean that it
exhibits all of the supposedly definitive urban characteristics. For instance,
the natural environment is of overwhelming importance in daily life, and
Wagley's chapter "From Magic to Science" makes it clear that items 13*r*, 15*r*,
and 15*rx* in the bipolar moralistic model are at least as important in the life of
the place as are their opposite numbers. Perhaps there is a gradient of characteristics that define "urban" that we should seek to discover and describe in
detail, and then test.

Unlike Wagley, Rubén Reina, in his study of Flores, Guatemala (1964), is
primarily interested in the definition of urbanism. Flores appears to be similar
to Itá in a number of respects. Though its population is more than twice that
of Itá (1,500), it is nevertheless very small. It is located on an island in Lake
Petén-Itzá, and one can walk around the island's perimeter in half an hour
(Reina, 1964:268). Like Itá, Flores has a colonial-Iberian-Indian ethnic history; is the economic, administrative, and communications center of a district
that is remote from the big urban centers of its society; subsists on the extrac-
tive economy of its region (rubber, lumber, chicle), which links it with the
world market; and has a clearly distinct structure of social classes.

> Upon first acquaintance with Flores, it is rather difficult to recognize social differ-
> ences. . . . Differences in terms of wealth, leadership, intellectualism, or 'cultura'
> acquire very particular social meanings. But all these attributes are not apparent at
> first because of the even degree of sophistication across all social groups which is con-
> sciously upheld]Reina, 1964:269].

People of every social class in Flores apparently share a pride in their collectively heterogeneous background and in their city's "civilization" in the midst
of the forest.

The social classes are (Reina, 1964:270):

1. Upper: about half a dozen families of wealth, owning property in Guatemala City and interacting largely with each other.
2. Upper middle: politically active professional people who aspire to
   greater affluence and intellectualism.
3. Middle: artisans, shopkeepers, and minor officials extremely intent on
   upward mobility, especially through the education of their children.
4. Poor: wage laborers, including chicle collectors, with a low level of education; interested in but fearful of upward mobility through the education of their children.

Reina proceeds to describe the "city style" of festivals and ceremonies, and
the "impersonalization" of the Florentinos' business behavior. He ascribes

this impersonalization to the precariousness of the market and the exploi-
tiveness that it generates, rather than to any lack of personal familiarity among
the inhabitants, for "everyone knows the biographical details of everyone
else's life." Reina concludes (1964:274–75):

The important point emerging from this material is the strong urban world view held
by only a handful of people who know each other intimately. It presents us with a large
number of the elements of the city discussed by Redfield, Wirth . . . namely, individualization, emotional atomization, secularization, blasé attitudes, rationalism, cosmopolitanism, differentiation, and self-criticism. . . . But the most important fact . . . is
that this image appears . . . in an environment largely dominated by the forces of nature. The outstanding social feature of Flores is the exaggerated degree to which the
ideal of living in a "city" and being urban has become the core of their general cultural
orientation.

The idea that urbanism is a set of attitudes, values, and behavioral patterns
that is not necessarily a direct adaptation to an immediate city environment
was not originated by Reina, but he has pursued it further than others. A cor-
ollary idea, which I did not originate either, is that "nonurban" behavior can
exist in the midst of a city environment. Perhaps *some* of the stereotypic
urban characteristics are dependent upon the city environment while others
are not, and one of the tasks of urban anthropology should be to factor out
which ones are which. However, we are still begging the question of what a
city is, and therefore general assertions about the "process of urbanization"
remain ambiguous and meaningless.

Frobisher Bay is a settlement of 1,600 people located about a hundred
miles north of the Arctic Circle on Baffin Island, Canada. Except for its size
and the fact that it is an administrative center for a sparsely settled region, a
remote outpost of a national society, it has little in common with Flores. The
forces of nature are overwhelming in both places, but in one they are tropical
and in the other arctic.

Unlike Flores (and Itá), Frobisher Bay has a very short history, which
began in 1942 with the construction of a U.S. Air Force airstrip. In 1955
Frobisher Bay became a transshipment point for supplies and personnel to
the eastern end of the U.S.-Canada Distant Early Warning Radar Defense
Line (DEW Line). Flores and Itá were originally creatures of Spanish and
Portuguese preindustrial imperialism; Frobisher Bay is a creature of the twentieth-century North American military-industrial complex.

John and Irma Honigmann (1965) studied Frobisher Bay in 1963, by which
time its population consisted of about nine hundred Eskimos and about seven
hundred "Eurocanadians." The Honigmanns' basic aim was to study the adap-
tations of the aborigines of the area—the Eskimos—to life in this "instant
town" (my phrase, not theirs), much of that life being the Eskimos' own.
Since all the inhabitants of Frobisher Bay are recent immigrants, this is not an
urban-migrant adaptation study so much as it is a study of Eskimos' adaptation
to Eurocanadian material culture, work patterns, and sociopolitical organization. The Honigmanns consistently refer to Frobisher Bay as a "town" (never,

I believe, as a "city") and do not concern themselves explicitly with urbanism as a concept. They refer to it as an "urban setting" (p. 100) but without specifying what is meant. The relatively large number of organized groups is said to be consistent with its "urban character" (p. 118), and the "urban impersonality" of the Eurocanadians is mentioned (p. 5).

Implicitly, however, this study is concerned with the definition of urbanism. In the first place, it was very much stimulated by reports that social disorganization (a classic stereotypic trait of urbanism) was conspicuous in the life of the town (Honigmann and Honigmann, 1965:3). This stereotype is refuted in the study (p. 152). The Eskimos' shyness and "the town's impersonality" were facts with which the Honigmanns had to cope (p. 5). They also refer to its "large" population (p. 6) in comparison with other Eskimo settlements, a relative statement comparable to the idea that Itá is large in comparison with hamlets in its administrative district. However, Frobisher Bay is not a dense settlement, even relatively speaking, for it consists of at least three widely separated subsettlements. Transportation between these subsettlements consists of bus and taxi service, which is essential for the daily life of the inhabitants and bears all the earmarks of urban, "impersonal" transportation (pp. 49–51). One of the uses to which these buses and taxis is put is visiting among the members of relatively restricted circles of kinsmen whose members' homes are often scattered in different subsettlements, rather than concentrated in one place (p. 102). Although the Honigmanns do not say so, such nonlocalized networks are often considered to be characteristically "urban."

Other facilities in Frobisher Bay are clearly characteristic of North American industrial cities (though not of preindustrial ones). Electricity, fuel oil, gasoline, and water are delivered to the consumer. Most of the food and beverages are imported from afar and sold in packaged form. Housing is prefabricated and standardized in a limited number of styles. Having been totally self-sufficient before the town existed, Eskimos frequently find an adjustment problem in all this provision of necessities (p. 153), particularly with regard to identity formation and self-esteem (p. 170).

The Honigmanns point out, however, that many Eskimos came to Frobisher Bay voluntarily and have remained there by their own choice (p. 161), and that the typical Eskimo, "while not reared for routine and repetition" (p. 231), is "venturesome, optimistic, independent and resourceful . . . eager to try and able to change" (p. 234). Such a person obviously has advantages as a migrant to a town, or in any new situation.

This introduces the topic of predispositions for urban adjustment, which will be discussed later; it is an important corrective to the widespread idea that the urban environment inevitably simply imposes itself on the hapless newcomer.

The Honigmanns make much of the fact that the Eskimos in Frobisher Bay are under the tutelage of the Eurocanadians and their institutions. Among other things, this situation involves the maintenance of clear social distance between the two populations. The Honigmanns insist, however, that among the Eskimos there is nothing more than an incipient social class differentiation (p. 248), if that (p. 101).

Though it is a new town, characterized by "incessant built-in change" (p. 231), and with an uncertain future, Frobisher Bay cannot be dismissed as an aberrant case. Many now long-established cities began in similar fashion, and its lines of dependent communication with the parent culture to the south are really no longer than those of Flores and Itá with their parent cultures. Missing from Frobisher Bay, apparently, is a strong sense that the town is a carrier of cultivation and civilization, a sense that is very strong in Flores and in the Latin and Islamic Mediterranean urban traditions in general. Perhaps this is because Frobisher Bay is a carrier of twentieth-century industrialism. This would, I think, be the reaction of urban theorists like Lewis Mumford. Some people might argue that the school curriculum, as directed toward the Eskimo children (pp. 173–74), is evidence of such a tradition in Frobisher Bay, though I am doubtful about that.

In any case, what is clearly remarkable about Frobisher Bay, from the viewpoint of current notions of cultural evolution, is that in it are juxtaposed one group of people inured to twentieth-century industrial technology and another group of people many of whom were enculturated in a preneolithic technology. Yet the stresses being undergone by the Eskimos do not appear to be excessive, and they are not so great as those experienced by many nonurban groups in the world who are adapting to urban situations to which they are much closer, as far as cultural history is concerned, than are the Eskimos and the Eurocanadians in Frobisher Bay. This should, once again, alert us to the existence of predispositions toward urban adaptation and to the fact that "urban situations" are many and varied.

San Lorenzo is a port town on the northern coast of Ecuador. It was founded in the nineteenth century when the Ecuadorian government granted exploitation rights in the region, chiefly exploitation of forest products, to two foreign companies, one English and the other German (Whitten, 1965:25). Negroes, who now constitute most of the population of the town, were from the beginning the major source of labor in the region. Linked as it was to national policies first by commercial exploitation and then literally by a railroad connecting it with Quito, the national capital, San Lorenzo has continually been subject to changes originating in the larger society of which it is a part:

San Lorenzo has an upper class of forty-eight white or *mestizo* persons, whose wage-earners are professional people none of whom is native to the town. There is a middle class of about three hundred persons, somewhat less than half of whom are *mestizos* and the majority Negroes. All the rest of the population are lower class and almost entirely Negro (Whitten, 1965:45).

Whitten (1965:195) points out that between 1942 and 1963 San Lorenzo changed from being a "predominantly Negro village with a population of between 500 and 700 into an ethnically and culturally heterogeneous town with a population approaching 3,000."

Aq Kupruk is a settlement in Afghanistan that had about 300 households in 1965 (Dupree, 1966:11). Estimating an average of 6 persons per household, the place should have a population of about 1,800, but this figure would evidently be too small, in view of Dupree's remark that about 70 percent of the 1,500 men are landowners (p. 18). Dupree categorizes Aq Kupruk as intermediate between a "true village" and a "true town" (p. 51), for which, together with "city," he provides some very handy (somewhat too handy, in my opinion) definitions (p. 10).

Dupree's main point about Aq Kupruk is that it is becoming "de-urbanized," owing to two recent events outside the control of anyone in the settlement: (1) a major trade route that had gone through it was diverted and (2) it was made the administrative center of a less significant region than the one of which it had previously been the center.

Nevertheless, at the time of study it had many features that are associated with urbanness: it was still an administrative and trading center with a bazaar of almost a hundred shops (p. 44); it was ethnically heterogeneous (p. 24) and the ethnic groups were rank-ordered hierarchically (p. 48); gangs of youths and young men were recruited on a multiethnic basis, growing out of work groups, suggesting "incipient unionism" (p. 49); and little sense of loyalty to Aq Kupruk or identification with the town as a whole was felt by its inhabitants (p. 50) because, as an organized settlement, it largely represented the government (that is to say, the police, tax collection, and conscription), whose locale is characteristically thought of in the Middle East as being urban. Thus elements of urbanism are clearly present in Aq Kupruk, despite the facts that most of its inhabitants are farmers and that it is a small place compared to what most Middle Eastern people would call a city.

The same statement can be made about the sixth and last example I shall present. Daghara, a town in southern Iraq, has a population of about 3,000 and serves as the administrative center of a district with a population of about 26,000 (Fernea, 1970:17). It has a bazaar whose specialists attract customers from the surrounding hamlets of farmers; it adjoins a main road that connects it with two of the major cities of the country; and it has government facilities (police station, irrigation office, infirmary, schools, and general administrative offices). Many of the functionaries connected with these offices are outsiders whose residence is temporary, but there are also resident merchants and farmers who are native to Daghara, Also living there is a tribal chief to whom many townsmen and farmers in the hamlets owe allegiance, and whose guesthouse is an important institution in the town (Fernea, 1970:18–20).

Fernea sometimes refers to Daghara as a village and sometimes as a town, but never as a city. In a footnote (p. 198) he writes the following, which is of some interest:

I have reserved the use of the term "hamlet" to refer to the many small settlements of cultivators scattered throughout the countryside. These settlements contain no specialized buildings other than those associated with a household, or mudhifs which are meeting places for men and where male guests are entertained. Daghara village could, because of its size and local importance, be as well called "Daghara town." I have heard local people call it both *qariya* (village) and *madina* (city). I am unaware of a term in Arabic for a collectivity of intermediate size such as is usually meant by the term "town" in English. By long tradition "madina" has usually been reserved to refer to a center which has a market place, a mosque, and a public bath. Daghara lacks a public bath. Except for these minor considerations, the use of the term "village" to refer to Daghara is entirely arbitrary and probably reflects the urban background of the writer. As an administrative and market center, Daghara village might be similar to county seats in some sections of rural America.

Urban Essentials Generalized

It is my impression that these six small and in many respects very different settlements have certain characteristics in common which led each of the anthropologists who studied them, and some of the inhabitants as well, to perceive them as urban. The common characteristics are these:

1. There are local residents and institutions that serve as brokers between the larger society of which the settlement is a part and the immediate region that the settlement dominates by reason of the brokerage functions located in it. The brokerage functions are concerned primarily with governmental administration, transportation, communication, and commerce.

2. In connection with these brokerage functions, persons considered to be strangers or outsiders to the settlement regularly visit it. The presence of these strangers and outsiders is a normal condition of life in the settlement.

3. There is a distinct system of social classes among the inhabitants. Members of the different classes tend to behave toward each other in terms of a categorical order of social relationships. In other words, they tend to treat each other in terms of stereotypes (Mitchell, ed., 1969:10).

4. Members of the uppermost class, in particular, have various personal connections and associations in other, larger cities. These connections impart prestige and probably usually imply power. They may also be accompanied by behavior and attitudes that are, in the context of the particular culture, sophisticated, cosmopolitan, cultivated, universalistic, and urbane. However, the fact that the majority of lower-class city dwellers do not exhibit such traits has, often mistakenly, been seen as a reason for considering these people's life style as separate and different from the urban way of life (Richardson and Bode, 1969:2).

5. Impersonal, rationalistic, goal-oriented, or single-stranded interpersonal relationships characterize much, though not all, of the behavior involved in items 1, 2, and 3. However, the same people who are involved in such relationships are also involved in intensely personal, multiplex, or many-stranded relationships with friends, relatives, neighbors, and others.

6. Many aspects of life in the settlement are subject to change as a consequence of changes in the larger society over which the inhabitants have no control. This tendency to change can intensify the impersonal aspect of social interaction in some instances. It also tends to make the inhabitants change-

oriented. Though change orientation may be actively negative or passive, as well as actively positive, it nevertheless is conscious (see King, 1967:513). Drastic vicissitudes have been the lot of many cities and their inhabitants (for just one example, see Gulick, 1967a:36).

7. Cultural heterogeneity, in various forms, is a factor in all of the above six characteristics.

That these characteristics can be present in very small settlements, that their presence is not dependent on large size alone, has been demonstrated. I believe it could also be demonstrated that in the vast number of small rural tribal or peasant villages in the world—villages that no one would think of calling urban—these characteristics are not present at all or are present in only rudimentary form, and that it is for this very reason that they are excluded from the urban category by their inhabitants and outsiders alike. When I speak of characteristics that may be present in rudimentary form, I have in mind a situation that is common in Middle Eastern peasant villages, for example, where absentee landlords' agents or school-teachers—outsiders—may be resident and where there are status differences between landowning farmers and landless laborers. Though these characteristics are suggestive of urban characteristics 1 and 3, they do not by any stretch of the imagination make such villages urban.

On the other hand, it is not true that the urbanness of Itá, Flores, Frobisher Bay, San Lorenzo, Aq Kupruk, and Daghara is purely a state of mind that has no causal connection with large cities. Though none of them is itself a large city, each one exhibits urbanness by reason of its linkages with at least one city that *is* large. None of these six little towns would exist in its present form, and some of them would not exist at all, if there were no large city somewhere within the larger society of which it is a part.

In general terms, any city of any size "is a behavioral product of a larger socio-cultural system," and the larger system must be understood if the city itself is to be fully understood (Richardson and Bode, 1969:3).

The urban elements that have been abstracted from the cultures of these six small settlements are also present, of course, in larger settlements. There are exceptions, notably some of the peasant villages in very densely populated areas such as the Nile Delta and Java, which may have populations as large as 25,000, but the likelihood is that settlements of more than a few thousand will have at least some urban elements. An important reason is that some institutions of regional political and economic power are likely to be located in them. The localization of such institutions of power, even on a very small scale, may, it has been suggested, be the crucial determining element of urbanism (Miner, ed., 1967:6). At the smallest scale level, as illustrated by each of the six cases reviewed above, regional political power is most likely to be discerned in formal administrative structures and personnel. There are hierarchies of such formal administrative localizations that are useful as indices of urbanism, especially in preindustrial societies, but less so in industrial ones.

At what point in the size and industrialization scales do the manmade-en-

vironment aspects of urban life become significant? For reasons already discussed, these aspects of urbanism were not accounted for in my analysis of the
six small towns, and for the present I believe the question must remain
open—a serious problem unresolved.

For the time being, I propose that the seven characteristics that I have abstracted from the work of seven other anthropologists be considered phenomena that constitute the urban human environment in which urban anthropologists do their research. The idea is similar to that of the "external" factors of
which Mitchell has written (1966:48–49):

> The factors that determine the context in which town-dwellers interact we call external
> because . . . we are able to take them for granted and to examine instead the behav-
> iour of individuals within the social matrix created by these factors. These are what
> Southall . . . . refers to as "extrinsic factors" and what I earlier called "external impera-
> tives."

Mitchell goes on to list six factors, four of which, though phrased differently,
coincide with mine, while the other two are chiefly relevant only to African
cities.

The aim of all this is not to split hairs, but to see to what extent urban anthropological work so far enables us to reach agreement on what our common
subject of interest is. Unless we can reach such agreement, we shall not be
able to develop any very powerful hypotheses concerning the effects of urbanization or to test them very convincingly.

Bibliography

BASCOM, WILLIAM
    1968   "The Urban African and his World." In *Urbanism in World Perspective*,
           (S. F. Fava, ed.), pp. 81–93. Originally published 1963.
BREESE, GERALD, ed.
    1969   *The City in Newly Developing Countires.* Englewood Cliffs, N.J.: Pren-
           tice-Hall, Inc.
DORE, R. P.
    1958   *City Life in Japan: A Study of a Tokyo Ward.* Berkeley: University of Cali-
           fornia Press.
DUPREE, LOUIS
    1966   Aq Kupruk: A Town in North Afghanistan." In *City and Nation in the
           Developing World.* AUFS Readings, Vol. 2, pp. 9–61. New York: Ameri-
           can University Field Staff.
FERNEA, ROBERT A.
    1970   *Shaykh and Effendi: Changing Patterns of Authority Among the El Sha-
           bana of Southern Iraq.* Cambridge: Harvard University Press.
FRANKENBERG, RONALD
    1966   *Communities in Britain: Social Life in Town and Country.* Baltimore:
           Penguin Books.

GULICK, JOHN
    1967   *Tripoli: A Modern Arab City.* Cambridge: Harvard University Press.
HAUSER, PHILIP
    1965   "Observations on the Urban-Folk and Urban-Rural Dichotomies as
           Forms of Western Ethnocentrism." In *The Study of Urbanization* (P.M.
           Hauser & L. F. Schnore, eds.), pp. 503–517. New York: John Wiley &
           Sons, Inc.
HONIGMANN, JOHN J. and IRMA HONIGMANN
    1965   *Eskimo Townsmen.* Ottawa: Canadian Research Centre for Anthropol-
           ogy, University of Ottawa.
KAHL, JOSEPH A.
    1959   "Some Social Concomitants of Industrialization and Urbanization."
           Human Organization **18:** 53–74.
KING, ARDEN R.
    1967   "Urbanization and Industrialization." In *Handbook of Middle American
           Indians* **6:** 512–36.
LEEDS, ANTHONY
    1968   "The Anthropology of Cities: Some Methodological Issues." In *Urban
           Anthropology,* (E. Eddy, ed.), pp. 31–47. Athens: University of Georgia
           Press.
LEWIS, OSCAR
    1965   "Further Observations on the Folk-Urban Continuum and Urbanization
           with Special Reference to Mexico City." In *The Study of Urbanization*
           (P. M. Hauser and L. F. Schnore eds.), pp. 491–503. New York: John
           Wiley & Sons, Inc.
LLOYD, P. C., A. L. MABOGUNJE, and B. AWE, eds.
    1967   *The City of Ibadan.* Cambridge: University Press.
MINER, HORACE
    1965   *The Primitive City of Timbuctoo* (Rev. Ed.), Garden City, N.Y.: Anchor
           Books, Doubleday & Company, Inc.
MINER, HORACE, ed.
    1967   *The City in Modern Africa.* New York: Praeger Publishers, Inc.
MITCHELL, J. CLYDE
    1966   "Theoretical Orientations in African Urban Studies." In *The Social An-
           thropology of Complex Societies* (M. Banton, ed.), pp. 37–68. London:
           Tavistock.
MITCHELL, J. CLYDE, ed.
    1969   *Social Networks in Urban Situations.* Manchester, England: University
           of Manchester Press.
NORBECK, EDWARD
    1965   *Changing Japan.* New York: Holt, Rinehart and Winston.
OSWALT, WENDELL H.
    1970   *Understanding Our Culture: An Anthropological View.* New York: Holt,
           Rinehart and Winston.
REINA, RUBEN E.
    1964   "The Urban World View of a Tropical Forest Community in the Absence
           of a City: Peten, Guatemala." *Human Organization,* **23:** 265–77.
RICHARDSON, MILES, and BARBARA BODE
    1969   *Urban and Societal Features of Popular Medicine in Puntarenas, Costa*

Rica. Working paper No. 3, Ser. 1. Latin American Studies Institute, Louisiana State University.

SCHWAB, WILLIAM B.
1965 "Oshogbo—an Urban Community?" In *Urbanization and Migration in West Africa* (H. Kuper, ed.), pp. 85–109.

SJOBERG, GIDEON
1960 *The Pre-Industrial City, Past and Present*. New York: Free Press.

VOGEL, EZRA F.
1967 *Japan's New Middle Class: The Salary Man and His Family in a Tokyo Suburb*. Berkeley: University of California Press.

WAGLEY, CHARLES
1953 *Amazon Town: A Study of Man in the Tropics*. New York: Macmillan Publishing Co., Inc.

WHITTEN, NORMAN E., JR.
1965 *Class, Kinship, and Power in an Ecuadorian Town*. Stanford: Stanford University Press.

WINDLE, CHARLES, and GEORGES SABAGH
1963 "Social Status and Family Size of Iranian Industrial Employees." *Milbank Memorial Fund Quarterly*, **41**: 436–43.

WIRTH, LOUIS
1964 "Rural-Urban Differences." In *On Cities and Social Life* (A. J. Reiss, ed.), pp. 221–225. Chicago: University of Chicago Press.

Part I: Research/Term Paper Topics

1. "The Chicago School and the African City."
   Dig into the literature on urban anthropology in Africa. Analyze the effect of the Chicago School upon it, and the way in which material from African cities might modify the Chicago paradigm.

2. "Patterns of City Definition by Urban Residents."
   There may be little consensus among social scientists on the definition of the city, but residents have patterned perceptions of the city. These patterns, however, are dependent upon age, occupation, sex, residence, education, leisure activities, and other phenomena that affect one's interaction with the city. Select some of these variables, draw a sample (random or selective), and conduct a survey on views of the city. Attempt to draw conclusions about the factors that influence one's perception and definition of the city. Remember that in research such as this, the questions one asks are at least as important as the answers one receives.

3. "The City in Literature: Perspective and Definition."
   Using literature as a source, make a list of definitions of the city. Categorize the definitions and offer some analytical commentary concerning the problems of reaching agreement on a definition. Select your definitions from fic-

tion, nursery rhymes, popular songs, poetry, dictionaries, and encyclopedias; texts in different academic disciplines; ancient historians and philosophers. Don't forget official sources—the Bureaus of Census and Land Management, Congressional Record, and others. Also include definitions by other governments.

4. "City Organization and Physical Layout."

Using informant data and/or archival material (such as census tracts, parish and police precinct maps, public transit routes and schedules, school district boundaries, zoning laws), draw a map of your city. Through the use of overlays, compare and contrast the various institutional and cultural boundaries. What does this tell you about the city?

5. "An Urban Diary."

Keep a diary for one week of the things you do that would occur only in the urban milieu.

PART

The Study of the Urban Milieu

TWO

Anthropology brings to its study of the city a special humanistic approach, based on firsthand observation and intensive interaction with the population under investigation. This is coupled with a concern for behavior as culturally patterned and thus ostensibly observable, repeatable, and shared events. Such activities and concerns shape anthropology's special contribution to the study of urban places.

Does anthropology in the city differ significantly from anthropology in the primitive or peasant community? Some suggest it does. At the same time, it can be argued that most anthropological methods (excepting survey research and perhaps network analysis, both of which are no less useful in rural settings) were originally developed in nonurban research. Mental maps, town maps, censuses, archival investigations, networks (the urban version of geneologies?), sociometry, as well as old standby participant observation, are as common to rural as to urban research. So, too, for that matter, are the typical fieldwork traumas of culture shock, subject selection, establishing rapport, and finding a house that doesn't afflict one's spirit, budget, or health. And urban bureaucrats are no more or less candid or accessible than rural alcaldes, big men, head men, and chiefs. Some obvious differences offer a mix of advantages and disadvantages. Urban anthropologists usually do not live with the people they study. Housing is often unavailable (and sometimes undesirable) in the building or neighborhood under investigation. This can require much commuting and long, irregular hours for coverage of unplanned events and for observation of all significant time periods. The question of boundary may also be a problem in the city. The physical and membership limits of villages, tribes, and lineages are usually clearly demarcated. Urban groupings are rarely so. Units of study in cities thus require more deliberate selection, with more concern for representativeness. On the positive side, urban research can mitigate some of the shock-related traumas of fieldwork by offering ready escape from the field—familiar entertainment, new faces, and temporary invisibility.

The question of holism in urban research has become a major concern in the past decade. It is not that anthropology in cities has avoided a holistic approach. The enclaves, families, gangs, ethnics, and street corner groups have always been treated holistically—within themselves. More recently, the call for holism is a response to the need to relate these specific units of study to the wider context of the city and its hinterlands. The call reflects the growing ease of anthropologists with research in the urban milieu. It also recognizes that every group, regardless of its homogeneity, in the act of adapting to a wider community becomes part of it.

A Perspective on Anthropological Fieldwork in Cities

GEORGE M. FOSTER and ROBERT V. KEMPER

The urbanization process is one of the most significant social phenomena of the twentieth century. Individuals whose ancestors, for millenia, lived in tribal or rural peasant settings are now migrating to the city, leaving depleted hinterlands and even whole villages abandoned as emigration increases.

George M. Foster and Robert V. Kemper emphasize how the growing interest in urban studies by anthropologists is part of an evolutionary process. Thus, because we began studying these isolated societies, we must migrate with their members to the city as more and more turn to the metropolis to seek a livelihood. In some cases, cities even come to the hinterland—as when they expand spacially and engulf villages, or when new urban places are constructed where once there was only countryside (the creation of new towns such as Brasilia, carved out of the jungle). Finally, cities have expanded their spheres of influence. They are exporting goods and ideas, making increased demands on the land, imposing administrative controls (taxes), and providing services (health, education, transportation, entertainment), which affect the traditional target populations of anthropological research.

Anthropologists cannot ignore the urban impact. The growth of this disciplinary focus, the transformations in research techniques and methods required of anthropologists, and the new directions that have emerged are the subjects of this review article

Anthropologists are latecomers to urban research. More than fifty years ago sociologists began systematic research in American cities, especially through the efforts of the "Chicago" school, and since that time most sociological research has dealt with urban phenomena. In contrast, the earliest anthropological research on city life took place scarcely a generation ago, and widespread interest in urbanization has developed only in the past decade. Whereas urban sociology is a mature discipline, urban anthropology is still in its infancy.[1] We have yet to define the parameters of the field, identify the topics to be studied, settle upon the most appropriate research strategies, and come to grips with new problems of ethics and relevance.

This recent interest in cities is the third—and probably the final—major revolution in anthropology's definition of its subject matter. When anthropol-

"A Perspective on Anthropological Fieldwork in Cities" in *Anthropologists in Cities*, (George M. Foster and Robert V. Kemper, eds.), pp. 1–17, 1974. Boston: Little, Brown and Company, by permission of the authors. (Abridged by the editors, with additional changes by the authors.)

[1] A journal, *Urban Anthropology*, and its companion, *Urban Anthropology Newsletter*, the first anthropological publications devoted to urban research, began only in 1972.

ogy emerged as a formal science at the end of the nineteenth century it was concerned exclusively with "primitive" (i.e., nonliterate) peoples. Then, about 1940, interest began to shift to peasant societies, the rural dimension of traditional cultures. Now, as we turn to cities, we are again on the threshold of a major change. During these transformations the research goals, the definitions of problems, and the kinds of hypotheses that intrigued anthropologists have varied greatly. One principle, however, has remained constant: the anthropologist's dedication to fieldwork as his primary data-gathering strategy. Whether interested in tribal peoples, peasant villagers, or city-dwellers, anthropologists believe that the richest, most complete information on how people live comes from direct, personal participation in gathering this information.

In the Beginning

Anthropologists have not always insisted that fieldwork is their basic data-gathering technique. With rare exceptions nineteenth-century anthropologists relied upon the descriptions of native life published by missionaries, colonial administrators, and travelers for the data on which they based their theories and hypotheses. Only when anthropology became a legitimate academic discipline at the turn of the century, with formal Ph.D. graduate programs, was field research accepted as essential to professional preparation and practice. In America, Franz Boas was the teacher most influential in standardizing this new approach to data gathering.

In some ways research methods have changed very little since those early days. Most anthropologists still draw the greater part of their data from first-hand contact with relatively small numbers of people. In other ways, though, the changes have been great. New research goals have been formulated, and field trips have grown longer. When Boas, Clark Wissler, A. L. Kroeber, Robert Lowie, and others of their generation began their research, anthropology was assumed to be an historical discipline rather than a social science. Faced with a bewildering array of languages, cultures, and physical types, anthropologists saw as their task the discovery of the origins and migrations of the world's peoples, especially "primitive" societies lacking written histories. In the United States, most indigenous cultures had already changed greatly as a consequence of white contact. Because even greater changes seemed inevitable, a related goal of field research here was to draw upon the memories of the oldest surviving Indians to reconstruct as completely as possible the "untouched" precontact situation.

Since most data gathering consisted of sitting with elderly Indians (who were usually paid for their help) and writing down what they remembered of earlier years, anthropologists needed little field equipment. As late as 1937, when Foster was preparing for his first research among the Yuki Indians of California, the only advice he received from his professor, A. L. Kroeber, was to "buy a pencil and a stenographer's notebook." In the United States prior to World War II, field trips were usually short, often limited to a summer's vacation. Even the largest departments of anthropology had only three or four staff members, and long leaves were difficult to arrange. Moreover, the research goals of ethnographers led them to see little advantage in spending twelve or more continuous months in the field; instead, they worked over several summers, beginning again each year where they had stopped the summer before. In the first quarter of this century, most American Indian tribes were disrupted and acculturated. This fact, plus the "memory culture" orientation of fieldworkers, combined to convince authropologists that no single group needed or justified more than a few months' study. Because native peoples appeared to be dying out, anthropologists felt it their scientific responsibility to survey all groups, rather than to study intensively a few and neglect the rest.

Even in these relatively short, early field trips the distinctive methodological characteristic of anthropology was apparent. From the beginning anthropologists formed close personal ties with the people they studied, and almost all anthropologists of that period have written affectionately about their key informants, some of whom became lifelong friends. Anthropologists quickly realized that the best and most accurate data come from persons who like and trust them. Hence, "establishing rapport" came to be an anthropologist's first assignment upon arriving in the field: to search out the most knowledgeable individuals, present oneself to them in a plausible and empathetic role, and make friends. Without fully realizing it, these early anthropologists were inventing the "depth" interview—the ability to talk with, to probe, to "pump" an informant, day after day, in order to extract from him maximum information about his people and their history. Today, in cities as in rural areas, most anthropologists retain this basic philosophy: good rapport with good friends, trust and confidence, and abundant conversation over long periods of time.

Fieldwork in the United States during the first third of the century was strongly conditioned by restrictions of time, distance, and money. Research in the West involved train trips of from three to six days in each direction, often followed by stage coach, river boat, or horseback rides to the final destination. Sources of financial support were limited, and long and costly trips of the type now routinely undertaken would have been difficult indeed. When, in the late 1920's and 1930's, American anthropologists began to embark on research in more distant areas, it was not unusual to spend six weeks in merely reaching the field site. Now that the most distant parts of the earth are rarely more than twenty-four hours away, young anthropologists often forget how huge the world was only a little over a generation ago.

As long as the emphasis of American anthropology was on the disappearing tribe, field research methods, including "scientific" equipment, changed very little. The first bulky portable typewriters, the Kodak camera, and primitive cylinder recording machines were occasionally carted to the reservation, but the pencil (or fountain pen) and the stenographer's notebook continued to be the only indispensable items of equipment.

The British Revolution

In England, meanwhile, a revolution in the concept of field research was occurring: long-term analysis of a viable community, emphasizing form and function in their synchronic rather than their diachronic dimensions. Tribal origins, it was assumed, were lost in dim antiquity; they could never be known. What *could* be known was the structure of the contemporary group, its form and content, and the way this system functioned. Anthropology was thus converted into a social science. Although he was not the first anthropologist to live for a long period with a single people, the Polish-born, British-naturalized Bronislaw Malinowski justly receives credit for introducing this new approach to fieldwork. Beginning in the early 1920's at the London School of Economics, he taught his students what he had discovered a few years earlier on the Trobriand Islands: live with the people, learn their language, observe their activities, question, speculate, theorize.

Malinowski and his students were favored in their revolutionary endeavors by conditions in the British Empire. Most of the Commonwealth's "native" peoples belonged to viable societies which functioned with much of their precontact vigor; they certainly were not disappearing. There was little need to press for "salvage" ethnography, to record while there was still time. Consequently, young anthropologists with enough financial support could afford to spend as much time as needed with a single group, untroubled by the nagging thought that they should turn their attention to disappearing groups elsewhere. Wherever they worked, field researchers were not foreigners, they were simply in parts of the Commonwealth where the societies were more exotic than at home. The British colonial service encouraged anthropological research, and the Union Jack flying at the District Officer's headquarters symbolized the special privileges that anthropologists could expect from government and native peoples alike. Under Malinowski's tutelage, and favored by the colonial setting—especially in Africa—a new generation of British social anthropologists produced superb monographs on a wide variety of topics which even today are required reading in most doctoral programs.

In the United States, research sophistication lagged behind that of England for a number of years; we lacked a Malinowski, and we were still committed to recording the ways of disappearing societies. The first American anthropologist to adopt the new approach, ten years after Malinowski's pioneering efforts, was Margaret Mead who, in 1925, set out for nine months' research in American Samoa. She was soon followed by Robert Redfield, who spent eight months in Tepoztlán, Mexico during 1926–1927, and by Hortense Powdermaker, who went to Lesu, in New Ireland, for ten months during 1929–1930. (Although American-born, Powdermaker was a student of Malinowski, so she is perhaps best thought of as carrying on a British tradition in the United States rather than beginning an American style of fieldwork.)

In spite of the demonstrable advantages of long-term fieldwork, quickly brought to the attention of American anthropologists in *Coming of Age in Samoa* (Mead, 1928), *Tepoztlán* (Redfield, 1930), and *Life in Lesu* (Powdermaker, 1933), extended field trips did not become commonplace until after World War II. Although a growing number of American anthropologists made long trips to India and Africa shortly before the war, most doctoral candidates (and their professors as well) continued the old tradition of short trips.

After the war, however, American researchers rapidly adopted the British research pattern, for several reasons. First, we had just about run out of Indians. The fairly exhaustive product of fifty years of North American research, coupled with the accelerating rate of acculturation of native North Americans, meant that these tribes looked much less attractive as research subjects than they had a generation earlier. Second, transportation to distant parts of the world had vastly improved; even in 300-mph piston planes, most places were no more than forty-eight hours from the United States. Research support, too, was becoming more abundant than in earlier years, and for the first time anthropologists could seriously contemplate prolonged research in foreign countries.

The Discovery of Peasants

In growing numbers American anthropologists now traveled to Latin America, Europe, Africa, and Asia. Some—particularly in Africa—studied tribal peoples, but a majority chose to work in small rural communities in modern or developing nations, for it was soon discovered that these peasant villages made ideal research sites. During the 1950's and 1960's, half or more of American anthropological fieldwork was carried out in such communities.

With the study of peasants came greatly improved data-gathering techniques. Now fully aware of the importance of observing as much as possible, of being present when significant events occurred, anthropologists tried to be as close as we could to the people we studied. Under ideal circumstances we were able to live with village families, to sleep and work in a spare room, and to share meals with them. When this was not feasible, we rented a house near the center of the village, usually hiring local women to cook, clean, wash clothes, baby sit—and simultaneously to serve as informants to explain the meaning of what we saw. Now we had opportunities to attend weddings, funerals, baptisms, and other family and community rites on a scale that had never before been possible. For the first time that familiar, but much abused, phrase "participant observation" really came alive. We did not simply ask informants how people behaved; we saw with our own eyes what happened, so that our notes took on a richness, a depth, a detail rarely if ever achieved by earlier researchers.

Because we were observing real people acting out real roles, we needed to know more about them as individuals than in the earlier days of salvage ethnography: where they lived, who their relatives were, their occupation, their incomes and socioeconomic statuses, and the like. To gather this data we adopted the census as a basic technique to provide a factual and statistical framework for our observations and interviews. We also buckled down and learned the local language. Prior to this time relatively few American anthropologists had mastered the language of the people they studied, preferring to use bilingual informants or interpreters. Now we realized that language competence was essential to good fieldwork, and intensive language training became a basic part of every well-planned field trip.

In the post-World War II era more elaborate recording and coding techniques to control and retrieve ever greater quantities of data came into common use. For many anthropologists, the $5'' \times 8''$ card or sheet, filed according to the Human Relations Area File code, replaced the stenographer's notebook (Murdock, et al., 1961). Technological advances likewise vastly facilitated fieldwork: portable typewriters became truly lightweight, miniature cameras replaced the old Kodaks, and flash equipment was perfected. Transistors made possible small tape recorders, which greatly simplified recording linguistic texts, folklore, and other data such as dreams and projective tests (e.g., the Rorschach and Thematic Apperception Tests), where textual accuracy is essential. Antibiotics reduced the apprehension of serious illness in the field, and with radios and telephones, anthropologists were usually less isolated even in remote countries than their professional ancestors had been among Indian tribes in Canada and Western United States. For those who had known the conceptual limitations and technological handicaps of earlier field research, the fifties and sixties were a great time to be a practicing anthropologist.

Urban Anthropology

After about a generation of intensive fieldwork in peasant communities, anthropologists realized that significant changes were occurring in the research situation. For one thing, we felt that we had defined rather completely the parameters of peasant societies and had constructed models to explain much of their cross-cultural variation. So, as with the Indians a generation earlier, we appeared to be approaching a point of diminishing returns. At the same time, many of our peasant friends were ceasing to be peasants. Influenced by radio and television, work experiences in foreign countries, and the modernity that follows new roads, many of them gave up their folk costumes and their fiestas; they adopted tractors, fertilizers, and insecticides in farming; and they sent their children to secondary schools and universities. Others simply packed up and moved to cities, where they found work in factories or service fields and after a few years became townsmen themselves.

To a large extent the transformation of traditional peasant societies and the mass exodus to the city explain the new interest of anthropologists in urban research. Beyond this, many of us are genuinely concerned with the social, ethnic, and economic problems so clearly seen in cities; we believe that anthropology, along with the other social sciences, can help to ameliorate these problems. Together these events and convictions have created a new field, *Urban Anthropology.*

From the beginning, the urban research of anthropologists has differed significantly from that of other social scientists and historians. While they have been concerned primarily with the technologically developed countries of Europe and North America, we have been especially interested in the growing cities of Latin America, Africa, and Asia. Our theoretical orientation, too, is different. Because the first people we knew well in these countries were peasants and tribesmen, who today are moving to the cities in increasing numbers, we have been curious about what happens to them in urban environments. As a result, anthropological urban studies have dealt largely with *urbanization,* the process by which rural emigrants settle in and adjust to urban life, rather than with the way of life in cities, which is commonly referred to as *urbanism* (cf. Wirth, 1938). In addition, because we have been interested primarily in how people adjust to urban life, we have paid much less attention than have other social scientists to broader issues involving the operation of the urban *system* (i.e., the network of cities within a nation, the ways in which these cities are interrelated, and how the lives of urbanites and rural residents are influenced by large-scale demographic, political, economic, and sociological processes). And finally, although anthropologists have occasionally utilized the results of comparative statistical studies, which have become so important in political science, economics, and sociology, we have continued to offer theories about urbanization on the basis of first-hand field research.

The anthropological urban studies that have appeared since World War II, and especially during the past ten years, make it possible for us to trace common patterns in the urbanization process and to discern fruitful directions for future work. But with few exceptions (e.g., Whyte, 1943; Liebow, 1967; Leeds, 1968) these reports tell us little or nothing about the urban fieldwork experience. For the anthropologist, how does this research compare with that undertaken in peasant villages and tribal groups? What research techniques are equally valuable in both settings? What new methodologies must be developed (or borrowed from other disciplines) to investigate urbanites? Is the anthropologist working in a city a new breed of scientist, an "urban anthropologist," or does he differ from his rural-based colleagues only by his choice of field site? That is, is the urban anthropologist simply the mirror image of the rural sociologist?

In the following paragraphs we attempt to answer some of these questions, drawing particularly on the experiences of the nine authors in *Anthropologists in Cities.*

Urbanites As Rural People

Accustomed as we are to working in small, "bounded" rural communities, anthropologists are often disconcerted by the amorphous and heterogeneous populations of large cities. How are the boundaries of the urban sample to be determined, and how should the fieldworker proceed with his study? As Anthony Leeds has pointed out (1968:31), we often try to solve this problem by concentrating on slums, squatter settlements, or ethnic minorities, on the assumption that they are analogous to the small rural villages we know, and that they can be investigated in similar fashion. This tendency to see urban peoples in the light of our rural experiences may have serious consequences, as Peter Gutkind has pointed out for Africa:

The methodological traditions brought to this [urban] field of research are mostly those acquired by social anthropologists working in rural areas. It is this background which for long fostered the view that we were studying tribesmen in town and not townsmen in town (1967:136).

As a consequence, he continues, "Far less attention has been paid to those Africans who have been resident in urban areas for a considerable length of time . . . than to migrants and those less committed to urban life" (1967: 143–144). A number of contemporary studies reemphasize Gutkind's point, since they stress the theme of migration. We believe that he is correct in noting that anthropologists have been shortsighted in ignoring long-settled urbanites.

In urban research the anthropologist faces one insumountable problem: defining a population in the holistic context taken for granted in rural fieldwork. He may investigate a group of migrants from a single village, migrants from many regions, or a group composed of migrants and urban natives. The group may be dispersed throughout the metropolitan zone, clustered in a few neighborhoods, or restricted to a single spatial unit as small as an apartment house (as in Oscar Lewis' well-known studies of *vecindades* in Mexico City). Alternatively, the population may be defined in social terms, as members of a religious sect, a voluntary association, a professional or occupational category. Selecting and delineating the urban population segment to be investigated is *the* critical first step in urban anthropological research.

Once this decision is made, another issue emerges: should the anthropologist concentrate on the internal structure of the group or on the relations of its members to the rest of the urban population? Most anthropologists, following the community study approach, have chosen the former. But, as Leeds argues, this "has led to a thorough failure to justify the units of study used and the failure to show mutual effects between the asserted 'units' of study and the city in which they are immersed" (1968:31–32).

Getting Settled

Although the fieldworker faces different problems in defining the group to be studied in rural and urban settings, the difficulties of settling in—of finding a place to live, experiencing culture shock, establishing a plausible role, and finding informants—remain much the same. As we have seen, in village fieldwork the anthropologist usually lives with a family or maintains quarters in the middle of town; in either case he resides among the people he is studying and constantly observes their daily life. In cities, arrangements of this kind are more difficult; families studied by anthropologists almost always live in crowded quarters with barely enough room for themselves, much less for a researcher and his or her family. Rented rooms, too, are usually less attractive in urban slums than in peasant villages. Moreover, unless the anthropologist decides to study a compact population—a suburban neighborhood, an inner-city slum, or a peripheral squatter settlement—he almost literally cannot live "with" his informants. As a result, when an anthropologist studies a general social institution or a group of people spread throughout the city, he nearly always finds an apartment or house in a convenient area, then commutes to visit informants.

This arrangement has advantages and disadvantages. On the one hand, the anthropologist gains privacy, a comfort often denied him in tribal or village areas where he is a constant object of curiosity. When tired and irritated, and on those days when he hopes never to see another informant, he can retire to his comfortable lodgings to rest and recuperate. On the other hand, many anthropologists who have lived like this feel both guilty and cheated. Conditioned by his colleagues to expect a close emotional identification with the people he studies, even the most conscientious researcher may come to ask himself whether he is doing a good job and whether he is in fact a true anthropologist, if he must carry out fieldwork in circumstances where he is isolated much of the time from the target population.

Culture Shock

Culture shock is often a major occupational hazard for anthropologists. Although anthropologists working in urban areas are just as susceptible to culture shock as those in villages, cities do offer more "escape hatches" than the countryside. If the fieldworker makes contact with local scholars, he can discuss his problems—real and imagined—with them, and they often can reassure him that seemingly enormous barriers are actually quite trivial. In the city, too, the anthropologist can see a movie, splurge at an elegant restaurant, visit tourist sights, and in many other ways free himself from the need to be always on his best behavior, friendly and amiable with all the world.

Meeting Informants

When he begins research in a village, the anthropologist sometimes has letters to a few people, who in turn can introduce him to others. More often, though, for the first few days he simply wanders the streets, talks to as many people as he can, leans over fences to chat and make friends, gives candy and balloons to children, cigarettes to men, and in other encounters tries to explain why he is in the village and what he hopes to accomplish. In this informal way, he develops friendships. Often the anthropologist "scouts" several communities, then chooses the one where he feels most accepted. All of the people he meets in these early contacts are potential informants.

In contrast, only a few of the people the urban anthropologist meets in the course of a day are potential informants. Although casual encounters . . . may offer insights into city life, the researcher must work at building a network of informants. As intermediaries he may use members of the group itself (e.g., a migrant whom he already knows), local officials, or other social scientists who are known to the people the anthropologist has selected for study.

Just as rapport-building techniques vary from one fieldworker to another, finding a suitable role depends as much on circumstances as on planning. . . . For doctoral candidates, the role of students preparing themselves for teaching careers and required by their professors to learn about another way of life is usually satisfactory. For older anthropologists, the reverse role of professor seems to work best, at least outside of the United States. Sometimes it is as difficult to avoid a negative role as to establish a positive one; most anthropologists have at one time or another been accused of being a CIA agent, a Protestant missionary (if working in a Catholic community), a social worker, a tax collector, or even a misguided tourist.

Official and Professional Ties

Whether an anthropologist undertakes research in a foreign country or in the United States, it is considered proper—and usually it is essential—to notify the appropriate governmental and anthropological authorities of the research plan and to obtain their permission *before* beginning work. These formalities sometimes seem a nuisance, but for the urban anthropologist they often provide an introduction to potential associates in his fieldwork. Precisely because cities are centers for universities and government agencies, urban fieldworkers need not be isolated from professional and official assistance.

Relationships with government officials are extremely important to all anthropologists, for an unsympathetic person in a position of power can make research impossible, while a helpful official can open otherwise closed doors. Ties with local anthropologists can be especially rewarding. As experts in residence, they can point out possible problems in the research design, suggest alternate groups for investigation, and introduce the newcomer to potential informants. Of course, local social scientists may not always be helpful, but taking them into one's confidence at the outset may prevent subsequent misunderstandings and usually makes for good relationships in the future. This is especially important if the anthropologist plans to return later to continue the research project or wishes to carry out related fieldwork in other cities in the same country.

The urban anthropologist is more fortunate than his rural counterpart in that he can easily repay professional and social obligations to his local colleagues by attending their professional meetings, joining their societies, teaching part-time in their institutions, and (if he maintains a separate residence during fieldwork) bringing them into his home. In addition, he may be able to include local scholars and students in the research project, an important advantage in equalizing anthropological skills and training throughout the world. Urban fieldwork also offers young anthropologists an opportunity to meet the community of scholars they will know and cooperate with throughout their careers: another reason to stress mutual support and reciprocity during initial fieldwork.

Changes in Research Design

Chance often plays a major role in an anthropologist's decision to select a particular city for fieldwork, or even to engage in urban research. Until very recently, at least, graduate training in field research methods has emphasized the rural community. With increasing frequency, however, visa difficulties, fellowship problems, or family responsibilities lead anthropologists to make last-minute changes in their plans, which may include the shift from a rural to an urban site. Sometimes this means that the researcher does not have sufficient time to become acquainted with the literature on the new location, or with the data-gathering techniques that urban research requires. Not a few graduate students have reported that they have felt poorly prepared for their urban research experiences and that a longer tradition of urban anthropology in doctoral programs would have better equipped them to work in cities. Although anthropologists customarily read the materials available on the areas where they plan to do fieldwork, this can be exceedingly time-consuming for urban studies because of the vast documentation available on cities. A related problem is that while nearly all urban theory is the product of other social sciences, anthropologists seldom spend enough time on urban sociology, urban geography, urban history, urban economics, and urban politics to familiarize themselves with this theory. For a variety of reasons, then, anthropologists working in urban settings almost always find that they must reformulate their research plans *after* reaching the field.

Rural Research Models in the City

We have already seen that anthropologists tend to view urban populations from a rural perspective, to look upon them as transplanted villagers. Not surprisingly, then, research design and problem definitions are often based on rural models, on the assumption that what works well in the country will also work well in the city. This rural bias is apparent in the nine experiences . . . [described in *Anthropologists in Cities:*] all studies were made by a single anthropologist or by a husband and wife, the traditional method for village fieldwork. This "jack-of-all-trades" approach stands in sharp contrast to most other social science models for urban research, where team members are chosen to provide interdisciplinary and interethnic perspectives. Although rich data and valuable theoretical insights have emerged from these anthropological studies, the size and complexity of urban environments clearly places limits on what can be accomplished by a lone fieldworker, even when aided by a trained spouse. Paid assistants are a partial solution to this problem, especially in taking a census and conducting social surveys, but they are no substitute for a genuine team approach, whose advantages have been summarized by John Price:

The team represents a wide variety of academic skills and personalities that together produce a wider variety of ethnography than an individual does over a long period of time. Through formal and informal discussions, the team is able to create a productive information exchange. It also accelerates the generation and testing of hypotheses much more rapidly than individuals working alone (1927:27).

Although the lone researcher will continue to make important contributions to urban studies, we believe that anthropologists working in cities will increasingly do so as members of social science teams. At the same time it seems likely that many anthropologists working in cities will continue—as they have done in the country—to form close personal friendships with urban informants.

Although they do not provide a full picture of city life, friendship and the depth interview, with contact over a long period of time between anthropologist and respondent, should continue to be a major research technique in the city. When combined with the statistical survey approaches favored in the other social sciences, it may well prove to be the single most important contribution anthropologists can make to urban studies.

But despite the benefits of deep and continuing relationships, the . . . need for census and questionnaire data beyond the limits common in rural research [is obvious.] Chance contacts alone are insufficient to provide the balance that marks first-class research. The conclusion we draw is that anthropologists contemplating urban fieldwork will need to devote much more attention than they have in the past to sociological research techniques such as survey research and the design and pretesting of interview schedules. Familiarity with computers, too, . . . will be essential if anthropologists are to make the best use of census and questionnaire materials.

Whether the urban anthropologist carries out fieldwork alone or as a team member, he must strike a balance between "total immersion" and dependence on the more formal techniques of the other social sciences. Andrew Whiteford has described the dilemma we face:

Such approaches as sampling techniques, the use of census data, and statistical analysis of masses of data would appear to be absolutely necessary for understanding [urban phenomena], but their use also tends to impersonalize the research and deprive the worker of his most satisfying experience, the personal identification with the people being studied (1960:2).

Anthropologists become easily disenchanted when close friendships with informants are replaced by limited, impersonal contacts with "subjects" or "respondents." But, however we might wish it were not so, we must recognize that in cities we can neither observe our informants with the same ease as in villages, nor expect as many contact hours with factory workers as with craftsmen who labor at home. Thus, unless we are content to limit ourselves to the "street corner" variety of urban research (e.g., Whyte, 1943; Liebow, 1967), we must learn to combine the most valuable features of traditional research models with the quantitative methods common in the other social sciences.

Ethics and Relevance

Urban research introduces many new ethical problems to anthropology. For example, . . . we are not dealing with nameless faces in the crowd when describing and commenting on important people in cities. Their roles are distinctive enough to make them easily identifiable no matter how we try to disguise them in our reports. And when . . . the attitudes and life styles of the urban elite strike the anthropologist as unattractive, and when our analyses are constantly unflattering, what are we to do? Like tribesmen or peasants, these upper-class urbanites have great power over us, to the point of making our research impossible.

Even the least visible city-dwellers we study often are literate. They are more interested than villagers in the end product of our research, and they are anxious to see what we say about them. Increasingly, anthropological publications are translated into the languages of the people studied, and they can read about themselves. As anthropologists, we must become more concerned about their privacy, and about the harm that careless revelations might cause them.

Although . . . [most anthropologists have] carried into their urban research the traditional anthropological stance of objectivity—the desire to find out about what life was like in the community in question, without major concern for resolving social problems—it seems inevitable that future urban research will be more concerned with "relevance," that it will be more "applied" than earlier work. Already we see signs of this. During her two years of fieldwork in the Ciudad Guayana project in Venezuela, Lisa Peattie found herself becoming an advocate of the poor people she studied and lived among, defending them against the "system" represented by the project coordinators and their elite clientele. Her description of the role of "The Social Anthropologist in Planning" (1967) and her "Reflections on Advocacy Planning" (1968) make thought-provoking reading for urban anthropologists concerned with the relevancy of their work. In the same way, the Valentines have argued convincingly that the urban fieldworker owes a debt to the people he studies, the people who make his job possible. This debt can best be repaid, they believe, when the anthropologist becomes attentive to community needs and attempts to help his informants to cope with the urban system (Valentine and Valentine, 1970).

This combined emphasis on ethics and applied urban anthropology has led to a reevaluation of the anthroplogist's "prime directive"—his commitment not to interfere with "native" life unless it is absolutely necessary. This in turn has raised an even more fundamental question: Is the best fieldwork performed by "outsiders" or "insiders"? For instance, can Anglo anthropologists understand the life styles of urban blacks, Chicanos, or native Americans—or, for that matter, any group outside the white middle class—without falling prey to unconscious prejudices? Anthropologists have assumed that on many points insiders are less perceptive observers than outsiders, just as a fish is unaware of the water it lives in until the tank is drained. As the literate, predominantly urban, ethnic minorities in the United States strive to establish their identities, and similar forces are at work in developing nations, this fundamental bias of anthropological research is being put to the test. And more often than not, it is the urban anthropologist rather than his rural colleague who must withstand these pressures.

The net result of these transformations is still unclear, but it seems unlikely that future anthropologists will be allowed to carry out their research without some regard to contemporary social problems or to the needs and feelings of their informants. Just as the peasant migrant to the metropolis faces a new world, so anthropologists moving from the "bush" to the city must adapt their ideas regarding fieldwork to fit a new environment.

The future of anthropology, we believe, lies largely in urban research. Yet the evidence . . . indicates that urban fieldwork is more difficult than rural, and that it is often emotionally less satisfying, because of the problems of maintaining close affective ties with informants. At the same time urban research presents anthropology with challenges and opportunities that cannot be ignored if the profession is to increase its contributions to social science theory and the resolution of society's problems.

And if, as Morris Freilich suggests, "the critical tool in anthropological research is the researcher himself" (1970:33), then the ingenuity anthropologists have shown in working in tribal and peasant communities will serve in equal measure to master the problems of urban fieldwork. Just as in rural areas, urban anthropologists will find adequate housing, establish good rapport, define a suitable social role, overcome culture shock, deal successfully with government officials and anthropological colleagues, and ultimately combine the best in traditional research methods with the new techniques required for sound urban research.

Bibliography

FREILICH, MORRIS (ed.)
   1970   *Marginal Natives: Anthropologists at Work.* New York: Harper & Row, Publishers.
GUTKIND, P. C. W.
   1967   "Orientation and Research methods in African Urban Studies" in D. G. Longmans and P. C. W. Gutkind (eds.), *Anthropologists in the Field,* pp. 133–169. Assen: Van Gorcum.
LEEDS, ANTHONY
   1968   "The Anthropology of Cities: Some Methodological Issues" in E. M. Eddy (ed.), *Urban Anthropology: Research Perspectives and Strategies,* pp. 31–47. Athens, Georgia: Southern Anthropological Society, Proceedings, No. 2.
LIEBOW, ELLIOT
   1967   *Tally's Corner: A Study of Negro Streetcorner Men.* Boston: Little, Brown and Company.
MEAD, MARGARET
   1928   *Coming of Age in Samoa.* New York: William Morrow & Co., Inc.
MURDOCK, GEORGE P., CLELLAN S. FORD, ALFRED E. HUDSON, RAYMOND KENNEDY, LEO W. SIMMONS, and JOHN W. M. WHITING
   1961   *Outline of Cultural Materials.* New Haven, Conn.: Human Relations Area Files, Inc. (4th revised edition).
PEATTIE, LISA R.
   1967   "The Social Anthropologist in Planning." *Journal of the American Institute of Planners,* 33:266–268.
   1968   "Reflections on Advocacy Planning." *Journal of the American Institute of Planners,* 34:80–88.
POWDERMAKER, HORTENSE
   1933   *Life in Lesu, The Study of a Melanesian Society in New Ireland.* New York: W. W. Norton & Company, Inc.
PRICE, JOHN A.
   1972   "Reno, Nevada: The City as a Unit of Study." *Urban Anthropology,* 1:14–28.
REDFIELD, ROBERT
   1930   *Tepoztlan: A Mexican Village.* Chicago: The University of Chicago Press.
VALENTINE, CHARLES A., and BETTY LOU VALENTINE
   1970   "Making the Scene, Digging the Action, and Telling it Like It Is: An-

thropologists at Work in a Dark Ghetto," in N. E. Written and J. F. Szwed (eds.), *Afro-American Anthropology: Contemporary Perspectives*, pp. 403–418. New York: The Free Press.

WHITEFORD, ANDREW H.
1960   *Two Cities of Latin America: A Comparative Description of Social Classes.* Logan Museum Publications in Anthropology, No. 9. Beloit, Wis.: Beloit College.

WHYTE, WILLIAM FOOTE
1943   *Street Corner Society: The Social Structure of an Italian Slum.* Chicago: The University of Chicago Press.

WIRTH, LOUIS
1938   "Urbanism As a Way of Life." *The American Journal of Sociology,* **44**:1–24.

Mental Maps

PETER GOULD
RODNEY WHITE

Social scientists have long known that there is a systemic interface between humans and their environment. We all see our environment selectively, and it forms our view of "what is out there." Thus, it is of great importance that social scientists understand what is cognitively "there" for the people with whom they work. This not only helps the investigator see beneath the surface to the underlying logic of daily activities and long-range goals; it also aids in working out the processes that go on in our informant's heads—how they make decisions, what information about their world is not available, or how other factors influence what they perceive in their community environment.

Like many data-gathering techniques, the construction of mental maps is not unique to urban researchers. The complexity and compartmentalization of the metropolis has made the use of such a tool particularly exciting and insightful. We have found that age, sex, occupation, income, ethnicity, residential locale, and education all influence our mental construct of the city.

This excerpt illustrates many of the points just made and also demonstrates how one map can save many hours of fieldwork and how "one picture may be worth a thousand words."

Although we knew very little about people's preferences for places until quite recently, and while much remains to be done, a number of people have

Excerpt from *Mental Maps*, P. Gould and R. White, 1974, pp. 28–37. Penguin Books © with abridgements.

thought about the images that men have of their local environments. Usually these environments are urban areas, and interest has focused on the way in which people perceive certain landmarks, routes, boundaries, and neighborhoods. One of the first people to comment upon such things was Charles Trowbridge in 1913, when he noted that some people in a city always seemed to have a good sense of orientation, while others '. . . are usually subject to confusion as to direction when emerging from theaters, subways, etc.' Some people, he thought, had informal, imaginary maps in their heads centered upon the locations of their homes. They were able to move around the urban landscape as long as they remained on familiar ground, but they quickly become disoriented in unfamiliar areas. Others appeared to be egocentric, and see directions in relation to their own position at the moment. These people seemed to be able to navigate much more surely, and Trowbridge even went so far as to recommend directional training for children in schools.

For some reason few people followed up the early anecdotal leads of Trowbridge, but in the 1950s Kevin Lynch raised the question of environmental perception once again with his book, *Image of the City*. By asking a group of people about their feelings for prominent landmarks in Boston, Jersey City and Los Angeles, and questioning them about major routes and areas they used in driving around, he was able to build up a general image of the city that pulled out the basic elements of the urban landscape. Interestingly, Lynch's concern for the information people have about the city of Boston has been translated into practical planning terms in Birmingham [England]. Brian Goodey, with the help of the *Birmingham Post*, asked people to cooperate in a study investigating their perception of the city center. He asked readers to send in maps that conveyed the major impression they had of the area. Accuracy for its own sake was not required, and no published maps were to be used by readers in drawing the sketches. What was wanted was a quick, unaided impression to give the basic pieces of information that people had in their heads, and which they used in moving around the center of Birmingham. The response was very large; people seemed to like the idea of helping planners and being involved in some small way with the planning process going on in *their* town. By combining many hundreds of responses (Figure 1), the planners were able to build up a weighted mental image that seemed to emphasize a marked preference for things at a human scale. Some of the tall, skyline features were not nearly as prominent as expected, while others such as the Cathedral Yard and the Bull Ring were singled out as desirable 'oases' in the bustling urban scene. Many specific shops were mentioned because of their street-level interest, while other areas were virtual blanks. Such a map, and the large number of comments about the area, proved very valuable to planners trying to think through the future appearance of this city.

Cities are not always pleasant places to live in, and the information that goes into building a mental image of a particular area may reflect much more than just the knowledge of landmarks and routes. In America many urban

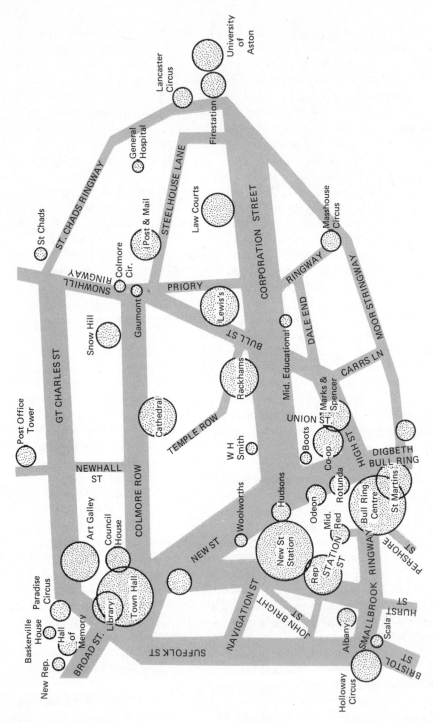

FIGURE 1. The people's preferences for features in Birmingham's urban landscape.

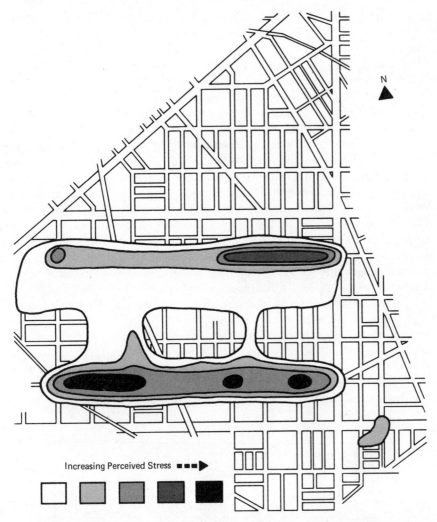

FIGURE 2. The perceived environmental stress surface for a portion of Philadelphia.

places are highly stressful, even dangerous environments, and we can think of invisible surfaces lying over these areas, whose peaks represent places of high psychic stress, while the valleys are safer channels through the urban jungle. In a predominantly black area of northern Philadelphia, for example, David Ley mapped a large sample of the local people's fears as an environmental stress surface (Figure 2). There is an invisible, mental topography of psychic stress in this neighborhood, where the peaks are places to be avoided, while the lower areas and valleys are areas of greater safety. The peaks generally coincide with the headquarters of gangs close to the center of their turfs, areas of abandoned buildings, and places where drugs are peddled. For an adult or child living in the area, information about this invisible topography literally lets them survive in a physically dangerous environment that is solely the creation of man.

People's information about a particular area in one of America's cities may vary considerably, and the mental images they build up may reflect not only their surroundings but many other aspects of themselves and their lives. In the Mission Hill area of Boston, for example, Florence Ladd asked a number of black children to draw a map of their area, and then she tape-recorded her conversation with them. On Dave's map (Figure 3a), the Mission Hill project is where the white children live, and he has drawn it as the largest, completely blank area on his map. From his taped conversation it is clear that he is physically afraid of the area and has never ventured near it. On his map the white residential area is literally *terra incognita,* while all the detail on the map is immediately around his home and school on the other side of Parker Street. Ernest also puts in Parker Street dividing his area from the white Mission Hill project (Figure 3b), and uses about a quarter of his sheet of paper to emphasize, quite unconsciously, the width of this psychological barrier. Both of these boys going to the local neighborhood schools have never ventured across this barrier to the unknown area beyond. However, another black youth, Ralph, who attends the well-known Boston Latin School, draws a completely different map (Figure 3c). The white Mission Hill project is greatly reduced in scale, and he puts in five educational institutions in the area, indicative of his perception of education as an escape route from the segregated life he leads. Similar pieces of information are given quite different emphasis in the mental images these boys have, and the patterns of informa-

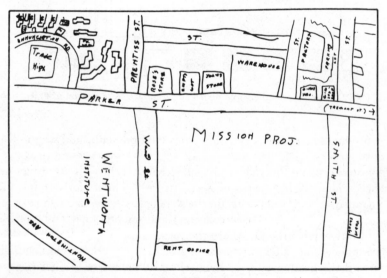

FIGURE 3a. Dave's map.

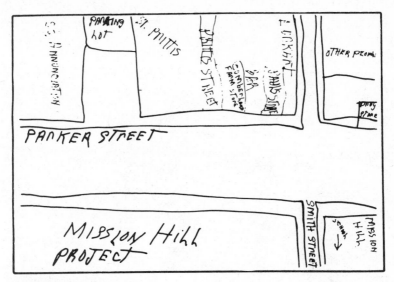

FIGURE 3b.   Ernest's map.

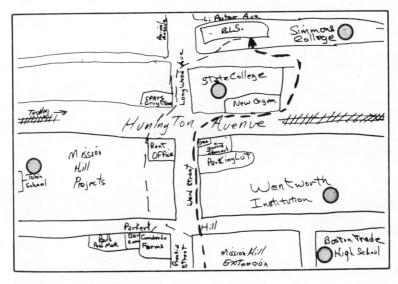

FIGURE 3c.   Ralph's map.

tion even begin to define their neighborhoods. Dave and Ernest obviously feel at home only in a quite restricted area which they know well, while Ralph has a much wider view and allocates his information evenly across the map.

The concept of a neighborhood is an important mental image, both to the town planner and the rest of us who are subject to planning. We have much

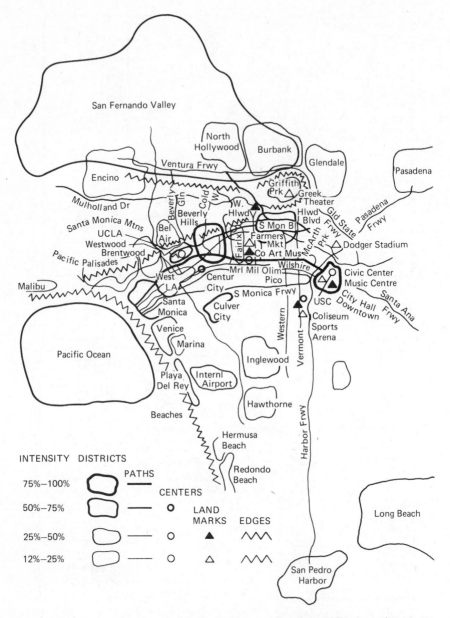

FIGURE 4a. Los Angeles perceived through the eyes of upper middle class whites in West-wood.

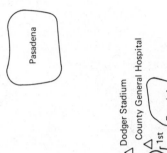

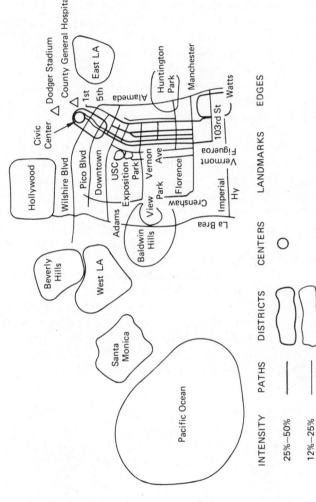

INTENSITY   PATHS   DISTRICTS   CENTERS   LANDMARKS   EDGES

25%–50%

12%–25%

FIGURE 4b. Los Angeles through the eyes of black residents in Avalon.

evidence today, from many of the world's cities, that breaking up a cohesive neighborhood can have many detrimental social and psychological effects. The question of measuring this social space, which has such an important degree of familiarity for a particular group of people, has been examined in some detail by Terrence Lee in England. He wanted to see if the town-planning concept of a basic neighborhood unit was really an appropriate one for modern urban living. What he discovered was that social space and physical space are so tightly linked that most people simply do not distinguish between the two. On the average, people tend to define their neighborhoods as an area whose size seems to be quite independent of the density of the people living in it. Neighborhoods in outer middle-class suburbs and high-density slums are perceived as about the same size. In other words, people do not think of their neighborhoods in terms of the number of people, as planners often do, but only as a comfortable and familiar space around them.

On the other hand, the wider knowledge that a group of people possess of their city may vary very markedly with both their social class and location. In Los Angeles, for example, Peter Orleans questioned a wide range of groups in the city, and from their responses constructed composite maps showing how the intensity of their knowledge varied over the urban space. Upperclass, white respondents from Westwood had a very rich and detailed knowledge of the sprawling city and the wide and interesting areas around it (Figure 4a), while black residents in Avalon near Watts had a much more restricted view (Figure 4b). For the latter, only the main streets leading to the city center were prominent, and other districts were vaguely 'out-there-somewhere', with no interstitial information to connect them with the area of detailed knowledge. Most distressing of all was the viewpoint of a small Spanish-speaking minority in the neighborhood of Boyle Heights (Figure 4c). Their collective map includes only the immediate area, the City Hall, and, pathetically, the bus depot—the major entrance and exit to their tiny urban world.

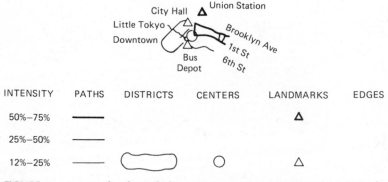

FIGURE 4c. Los Angeles through the eyes of Spanish-speaking residents in Boyle Heights.

Rationale and Romance in Urban Anthropology

RICHARD G. FOX

In a wide-ranging (and, some would say, scathing) review of the accomplishments—or lack of them—of urban anthropologists, Richard Fox claims that much of anthropology in the city is simply a transplanted variant of the small-scale community studies that have been a trademark of the discipline. He argues that we emphasize the exotic—underclasses, the culture of poverty, ghettos, and ethnic enclaves—the networks of a handful of often atypical individuals. Such "romantic" excursions have made of urban anthropology "something less than it could be," for they tell us little, if anything, about the city as the context for such behavior.

Listing "four major conceptual limitations" that such research has produced, Fox attempts to demonstrate how urban studies could proceed. *

"The community with which this volume is concerned is nondescript; it is a place of unusual interest."—ROBERT PARK, Introduction to *The Gold Coast and the Slum*, by Harvey Zorbaugh (1929).

"Romance—[a prose tale] dealing with the remote in time or place, the heroic, the adventurous, and often the mysterious."—*Webster's Third New International Dictionary of the English Language, Unabridged.*

Whether urban anthropology will ever provide significant insights into urban society and city man ultimately depends on how it defines its purpose. In much contemporary urban anthropology, the city only appears as a difficult, even hostile environment for impoverished, culturally distinctive and historyless populations. Great emphasis is also placed on newly arrived urban settlers and the process by which individuals accommodate to the urban locale. Little of the city as urban community and less of the interactional or ideological fit of the city to the larger society emerge from such studies. Justification for this approach usually comes from the supposed difficulty of transforming traditional anthropological methodology to meet the complexities of the urban sphere, as though methodology rather than conceptual framework should determine the proper arena for anthropology. What in fact often restricts the scope of urban anthropology is its pursuit of the exotic and marginal within urban locales rather than any necessary limitations of ethnographic method or ethnological theory. Gaining an insider's view of the outsider to

* This is an abridged version of a paper that included an example of the desired approach, drawing upon Fox's ethnographic data from Newport, Rhode Island, and Charleston, South Carolina.
"Rationale and Romance in Urban Anthropology," *Urban Anthropology*, 1:205–233 (1972).

the city, knowing what it means to be an urban man cultured in poverty
recreates the traditional anthropological vision of the strange, the exotic, the
bypassed in a modern world of industrialism, mass culture, and high-rise existence. Although pursuit of the exotic has been the basis of anthropology's
strength in the past, the form it takes in contemporary urban anthropology
often means that little can be said about city and society or urban organization
and national culture. The primary objective of this paper[1] is a critical examination of current research and conception in urban anthropology with the aim
of indicating the limited approach to cities often adopted in such studies. But
rather than purely negative scholarship, the paper also proposes a remedy for
some of the ills which beset the study of urban peoples and places in anthropology.

Cities and Societies

To see the city and its behavioral and ideological links to the larger society
should be a major goal of urban anthropology (cf. Miner, 1965:6 and Arensberg, 1968:3.) The emphasis on the urban world as a separate social realm,
with its own dynamic, and its special features of umland, heterogeneity, ecological zones, and architectural form may be appropriate to other disciplines;
it may also be an ethnocentrism derived from modern times when the city
creates the political order for the society and when the urban center origi-
nates and transmits its mass culture (cf. Keyfitz, 1967:275–276.) For the anthropologist interested in cross-cultural comparison or analysis or urban development, the city becomes only one of many institutions such as kinship,
value systems, and subsistence activity which he has always treated as parts of
a socio-cultural whole. This "super-organic" approach to urbanism absolves
the anthropologist of the psychological and sociological reductionism implicit
in studying city men, families, and associations or urban streets and corners.

I wish to suggest two ways in which the urban anthropologist may perceive
the city in the context of the larger society. Both require a diachronic approach and a wider viewpoint than the single urban center or one of its component class or ethnic populations. One way is to focus on the ideological ties
which bind the city to the countryside and vice versa, to measure how the
ideological motifs of the larger society are embedded in the culture of its cities, to recognize how the urban sphere projects self-generated beliefs onto its
hinterland. This approach is no great departure for anthropology. Is there any
difference between studying belief systems as they effect carvings on a totem
pole or as they arrange urban space and condition urban values? The other
viewpoint is interactional: the city is a socio-economic and political factor in
the organization of the society; it is both product and producer of particular
political alignments, economic sectors, and social structures. Just as kinship
organization stands in functional relationship to ecological factors, just as the

---

[1] This paper is a revision of one read at the 70th annual meeting of the American Anthropological Association, November 19, 1971.

form of the family reflects political and economic institutions, so the city relates to the political and economic order in which it exists.[2]

These two ways to a macroscopic urban anthropology are not revolutionary. They have been already partially marked out, although in many areas the road is very rough and other places are not yet reached. Studies such as those of Miner (1965), Banton (1957), Van der Berghe (1964) and Gulick (1967), which take the entire city as the unit of description pave the way for cross-cultural comparison and necessarily do away with psychological and sociological reductionism. In one of the first essays into the ideological links of city and society, Singer and Redfield distinguished "heterogenetic" and "orthogenetic" urbanism (Singer, 1960:261). Whether or not the distinction is valid, the approach is an important step which few have followed. Continuing this interest in the ideological links of city and society, Harris (1956:279–280) described the "urban ethos" of a small country town in Brasil: the passion for city life, the contempt for the country and agricultural labor. This urban ethos exists in spite of the town's isolation and lack of great population. For Harris, it derives from a historical tradition of the Mediterranean and Latin America reinforced by the town's continuous involvement in an industrial economy. Leeds (1968:37) has recently sketched the difference in ethos between Rio and São Paolo and discusses how it helps explain the condition of urban migrants in either city. Another urban ethos appears in pre-British northern India, where local lineage leaders living in what were little more than mud huts emulated the image of the urban as they perceived it from the king's court (Fox, 1971:170–182). Elliot Liebow's concept of a "shadow system of values" among street corner Negroes in Washington most clearly indicates what the anthropologist may come to see of city and society even from the confines of ghetto streets when he views them in relation to the larger society:

> . . . the stretched or alternative value systems [of the ghetto] are not the same order of values, either phenomenologically or operationally, as the parent or general system of values [in the larger society]: they are derivative, subsidiary in nature . . . less completely internalized, and seem to be value images reflected by forced or adaptive behavior rather than real values with a positive determining influence on behavior. . . . a shadow cast by the common value system in the distorting lower-class setting" (1967:213).

The interactional study of city and society is even less well developed. Pocock (1960) and Lynch (1967) indicate the continued role of caste and kin institutions of Indian society in an urban context. Another study of a North Indian market town traces the town's political and economic development and relates it to preindustrial and postcolonial types of urbanism (Fox, 1969b). Although he does not believe in specifically urban studies, Cohen's work (1969) on the Hausa merchants of Nigeria indicates how economic conditions in the larger society and spatial allocations in the city "retribalized" and ghettoized

---

[2] Cf. Arensberg's comment (1968:13) that ". . . as we come to identify new forms of the city, perhaps we shall also identify new forms of the state;" and Miner's contention (1967:9) that ". . . societal dominance is the city's raison d'etre . . . ."

this people. Geertz (1965) shows how the process of involutional change which he delineates for Java conditions the social history of a special Indonesian town. Tiger (1967) analyses the role of bureaucracy and the mass media in the organization of modern towns.

An ideological and interactional approach to the city is not automatically a dynamic one. The concept of "adaptation" must be added to introduce a perspective on urban development and social change in the city. Cities are and have been in a continual (and often long-standing) process of adjustment to their external socio-cultural environments and their internal economic and political conditions. To perceive the city in the setting of a society, the anthropologist must study the enduring pattern of relations between the urban sphere and the external socio-cultural fabric which conditions its existence. A similar position is articulated in Lampard's call for a "multilineal" analysis of cities:

The great variety of urbanizing experience underlines the fact that population concentration is everywhere an *adaptive* process. Each urban tradition, like each city, represents a continuing accommodation of general societal tendencies to particular sets of demographic and environmental exigencies (1967:538–539).

"Environment" for the anthropologist need not directly involve physical circumstances affecting the city, such as water supply, soil type, or rainfall average. Rather, a city's external environment represents the sum of all social and cultural factors impinging on the city (some of which may ultimately derive from the physical environment because of those cultural rules which are technologically and ecologically determined). These social and cultural factors include political pressure, economic conditions, communication and transportation channels, and rural values which condition a city's "foreign" relations with the part of society external to it (including other urban places) and which necessarily affect the course of urban development and internal urban social arrangements. Adaptation to an external environment thus refers to the changing pattern of ideological and interactional links between city and society over time. The adjustments of cities to their external environments can be discussed as their pattern of relationship with their "hinterlands."

Another process of adaptation congruent with the pattern of hinterland relations goes on within the city. The organization of urban government, class structure, and residential arrangements reflect the city's economic functions, political power, and communication lines as they develop over time and in conjunction with or apart from those of the hinterland. This internal adaptation of cities in terms of their interactional links with the hinterland can be discussed as the "functional organization" of the city or "urban (functional) organization." . . . Hinterland relations also condition urban spatial arrangements and physical layout through the ideological links between city and larger society. The ideological arrangement of urban space as determined by the city's adaptation and its effects on urban organization and form convey the conceptual base for investigating the interactional and ideological settings of cities in their societies through time.

Urbanization Studies and the Anthropology of City Streets

Not all anthropology done in cities is urban anthropology, at least as it has been defined in this paper. Many studies take the urban environment as a given, a mere location, a site selected for small-scale investigation of what are assumed to be (on the basis of their residence in the city) urbanized tribals or poverty-stricken industrials. This emphasis on urbanization and slum denizens has made of urban anthropology something less than it could be. It has promoted at least four major conceptual limitations: 1. Failure to undertake research which aims to define the city or cities, and in the absence of such an overview, concentration on the city as merely a location for research rather than the conceptual object of research; 2. Implicit assumption of the Western or industrial city as the model of urbanism, and lack of a cross-cultural investigation of urban adaptive patterns; 3. Absence of a holistic view of the city and its cultural and behavioral links with the larger society; and 4. Preservation of a synchronic approach originated in the ethnography of primitive society.

1. The emphasis on the city as a research locale rather than as the object of investigation has given much urban anthropology a limited theoretic perspective. This defect characterizes the two major currents of urban work in anthropology: urbanization research in Africa and slum studies in the United States and Latin America.

According to Epstein, ". . . urbanization refers to a social process involving people in social relationships within a new kind of *physical environment*" (1967:293, italics added). Mitchell similarly believes

> . . . the focus of sociological interest in African urban studies must be on the way in which the behavior of town-dwellers fits into, and is adjusted to, the social matrix created by the commercial, industrial, and administrative framework of a modern metropolis—having regard to the fact that most African town-dwellers have been born and brought up in the rural hinterland of the city in which the cultural background is markedly dissimilar from that in the city itself (1966:38).

This focus on urbanization may clarify how individuals adapt to new social environments, including urban ones, but it has only obscured anthropological investigation of the city and urban life. In the African material, the city is rarely described as such (beyond introductory demographic data and a smattering of chronological history); it only enters the study parenthetically as the unanalysed "something" which requires acculturative behavior patterns from recent migrants or as an unexplained "ether" through which situational structures and person networks channel.

Epstein, for example, describes the political urbanization of former tribals in a Copperbelt mining town without ever indicating why he regards the community as urban or what attributes distinguish it from what he refers to as the "rural" area. He makes occasional reference to an "urban" or "industrial milieu" (1958:236) as if all urban places were industrial or all industrial centers were urban. The appeal is to the reader's intuition. In any case, the author need not be more specific since the "urban" designation is only a convenient peg upon which to hang an analysis which deals neither with the city nor urban man, but only native locations filled with dislocated men.

Mitchell builds this nonconception of the urban into an analytic virtue. He believes that treatment of African towns as single social systems has no heuristic value. He also negatively evaluates comparative studies of African urban types, and treats investigations of processive or historical change as "of limited interest" to African urban sociology.[3] Instead, Mitchell suggests, urban studies must concentrate on social relationships and personal networks as conditioned within any particular urban location (or "framework") by external determinants. The latter (called "external imperatives" by Mitchell and "extrinsic factors" by Southall) include density of settlement, mobility, heterogeneity, demographic disproportion, economic differentiation, and administrative and political limitations. These external imperatives form as much of a view of urbanism as Mitchell and his colleagues ever propound. Yet, characteristically, Mitchell (1966:48–51) believes this external backdrop needs no analysis by the anthropologist. It is a structural given upon which the ethnographer builds up his network and situational analysis.

Plotnicov continues this limited use of the city. The object of his study "is to describe and analyse the adjustments individuals make to modern conditions of urban development . . ." (1967:3). He utilizes the technique of "situational analysis" as developed by Gluckman, Mitchell, and Epstein. This methodology delimits

> . . . the urban field of inquiry—the totality of which can appear as an incomprehensible jumble of contrasts and contradictions—in order to concentrate on, and thereby to abstract, the normative patterns of behavior that associate with role and group identification (1967:10)

In this form of situational analysis or in the "network" approach favored by other British urban anthropologists (cf. the articles in Mitchell, 1969) the city appears neither as an object nor a goal of research (cf. Leeds, 1968:31). Can we put all normative patterns of role and group identity together, can we trace out the many-stranded networks which link urban individuals and see the reflection of city and society? That Plotnicov could not accomplish this will become clear below.

The pitfalls in the urbanization approach are especially transparent when its

---

[3] Mitchell (1966:38 ff.) distinguishes between "situational" or adaptive change by individuals or groups newly come to the urban area and "processive" or evolutionary change of the urban area and its population in response to such phenomena as modernization.

advocates leave their native locations and discuss cities in general. In a review of African town studies, Epstein recognizes that a valuable urban anthropology must address other questions besides urbanization, among them, the integration of town and country and the role of urban institutions in national integration. Yet his subsequent discussion mainly concerns the effects of town *residence* on the countryside. Epstein describes the physical or demographic interaction of town and rural areas as if they stood apart from a national political order (1967:282–283). Concentration on urbanization means the scholar sees the city in its physical aspect as a receptacle of population, and leads him to overlook its position in an urban hierarchy or a chain of political power leading from rural community to state. As Bruner indicates, "Epstein's major weakness is that he . . . sees urbanization processes almost entirely as a function of factors intrinsic to the city itself" (Bruner, 1967:297).

Excessive emphasis on urbanization in African studies often leads to narrow visions of the city. Sometimes the city disappears altogether from the anthropologist's enterprise—in this case, purposely defined away as a construct of limited significance. Southall differentiates type A towns which are "old, established, slowly growing" from those of type B containing "new populations of mushroom growth" (1961:6). Cities are thus distinguished solely by different sorts of acculturative space and differential quantities of migrants. Cohen values urban locales only as anthropological supermarkets that bring together divergent groups and social processes which in tribal society are too dispersed for easy study. Urban research is not significant, according to Cohen, for what it may say about urbanism or urbanization since he does not believe special principles govern urban life. He concludes that much urban social anthropology is nothing more than human ecology, and that when an urban study is indeed sociological, it is "no longer necessarily urban" (1969:214).

Urban anthropology in the New World has often evolved little from its African genesis. Some American research duplicates the limited perspective of African urbanization studies. Mangin, Leeds, and others have described the accommodation of rural peasant to urban "tin can" cities. Such shanty towns are often viewed as communities with an internal cohesion which justifies their study as isolates within the city (cf. Leeds, 1968:31 ff.). None of these studies attempts to define the city as an outgrowth of shanty town research, or primarily focuses on the involvement of tin can settlements in the larger urban sphere. Other studies go beyond the assumption of community in shanty town, and reify cultures or subcultures of poverty or homeless and migratory urban alcoholics. Spradley writes of the latter "urban nomads," "The distance between most Americans and urban nomads cannot be measured in miles; they are separated from us by cultural distance" (1970:6). Oscar Lewis has identified another urban "culture of poverty," comprehension of which is hindered by analysing the city as a totality. In a critical summary of the work of Louis Wirth and the folk-urban concept, Lewis writes,

The city is not the proper unit of comparison or discussion for the study of social life because the variables of number, density, and heterogeneity as used by Wirth are not the crucial determinants of social life or personality. There are many intervening variables. Social life is not a mass phenomenon. It occurs for the most part in small groups, within the family, within households, within neighborhoods, within the church, formal and informal groups, and so on. Any generalizations about the nature of social life in the city must be based on careful studies of these smaller universes rather than on a priori statements about the city as a whole (1967:497).

Lewis provides an outline of the priorities in urban research which accentuates such small-scale study of communities within the city and the collection of data on urban personality (1967:502–503). Yet, if the anthropology of tribal societies had concentrated only on family and household, on neighborhood and church, would the concept of cultures and societies as organized systems of social life have arisen? Have Lewis' descriptions of family life in Mexico, Puerto Rico, and the United States clarified the nature of the city or even elucidated his own concept of the culture of poverty? (cf. Valentine, 1968:48–77.) Lewis' concentration on individual psychology, on family life is an attractive step for the anthropologist confronted with the complexities of urban society. But it is a great retreat from the traditional holistic approach of anthroplogy to society and culture (cf. Beals and Hoijer, 647–648). Lewis absolves the anthropologist of any concern with analysis of the city; he replaces Wirth's urbanism as a way of life with the altogether different concentration on the urban way of individual lives.

Even Valentine who convincingly argues against the assumption of distinctive poverty cultures within the city, who questions whether it is "not equally important to understand how the affluent and the powerful threaten the poor," nevertheless suggests "neighborhoods and districts of the poor in our cities" as the locale for ethnographic fieldwork (1968:90, 175). Although Valentine recognizes that the "units of study and boundaries of inquiry" should be determined by research, he seems to view their discernment as an empirical matter rather than as the result of a theoretical orientation towards the study of urban places. Mitchell (1966:60) also sees the tactics of urban research as initially an exploration of networks and fields of activity, and only afterward an "attempt to see their connection at a higher level of abstraction." This "cargo cult" view of theory-building suggests that accumulating enough powerful facts inevitably brings the anthropologist to high-level abstraction. Such beliefs rationalize the present limited horizon of urban anthropology more effectively than they hold out a future promise of theoretical rewards. Without an approach based on a conception of the city or cities, will the observer ever generate it from slum localities, improverished families or formerly tribal peoples?

In one way the city is always visible, even to the anthropologist deep down in the ghetto. In their most material form, modern cities are always locations of concrete and glass, they comprise streets on which men live or try to live. Only in this ecological sense does the city appear in the work of many American urban anthropologists as a *zone* of misery and penury, as an *area* "across the tracks," as a harsh *environment* which demands, as do the African towns, accommodation. In America, the equivalent of the African tribal (that is, of the stranger to the city) is fabricated from outcaste populations, culturally foreign to mainstream American life. Spradley writes, "The problems and vicissitudes of urban nomads differ from those encountered by other categories of urban dwellers and [the nomad learns] varied strategies for satisfying biological needs, achieving his goals, and adjusting to his environment" (1970:98).

To see city and society, is it not more important to know what in American (urban) culture produces urban nomads, rather than describing their conception of and coping behavior in a hostile environment? How might American, Hindu, or perhaps pan-urban notions of alcohol consumption alter or determine the circumstances of urban nomads? Although Spradley provides some very interesting data on how American courts promote the mobility of urban nomads, on how they are economically exploited as trustees in prisons, his primary concern is with delimiting the nomad's "culture" rather than analysing that of the larger society.

For Spradley, Lewis, Mangin and many of the African social anthropologists, the urban area is only a locale for research on men. In the case of urban nomads, this environment is summed up in the term, Skid Road. The city as a sociological or cultural institution remains unstated. Its cultural identity or qualities do not appear clearly or in central focus. We learn of city streets and city men but not about urban society or urban man.

2. The Western city is the often assumed but rarely analysed version of urbanism which appears in the literature of urban anthropology. This view of the city clearly lies behind Epstein's conjunction of "urban" and "industrial" citied earlier. Mitchell recognizes urbanism outside the Western model but finds the great majority of African towns to be colonial in origin. He regards traditional Yoruba urbanism as not really constituting city forms and cites the difficulty of distinguishing what was truly urban structure from what was determined by Yoruba culture. Mitchell is, therefore, content to make the colonially derived African town the single avenue for sociological research, acceptance of which neatly avoids the definitional problems inherent in a cross-cultural approach to urbanism (1966:75–150 *passim*). In urbanization studies, then, rural and (industrial) urban are treated as synchronic evolutionary levels similar to those found in a former (diachronic) evolutionary anthropology. The task of the anthropologist is to chart the passage from tribal rung to city level. That the sequence from rural or tribal to urban always requires family breakdown or secularization has been contested; that these distinctive types or stages are universally meaningful constructs is generally assumed. Following Gluckman, Mitchell argues that "an urban social institution is not a changed rural institution: it is a separate social phenomenon existing as part of a separate social system . . ." (1966:48; also see P. Gutkind, 1969:217).

Other scholars have contested this view of rural and urban as separate social systems, at least in some areas of the world (cf. Pocock, 1960:63–81, and Lynch, 1967:142–158). Resolution of this problem requires a cross-cultural view of city and society much wider than the Western model implied by American urban studies. In the African case and to a smaller degree in Latin America, the assumption of a single (industrial) urban type to which migrants must accommodate is reinforced by the historical nature of the assimilation pattern. Lacking a well-developed indigenous urbanism, such societies inherit a European and industrial or capitalist form of the city as a heritage of conquest. The familiarity of such city types to the Western or capitalist anthropologist perhaps explains why he fails to analyse what he means by "urban." In this sense, even those studies fail which only wish to talk about small group social life in the city, unless they see the urban research location as purely a sociological accident (cf. Marris, 1962 and Rubel, 1966). Yet, most such studies at least in their titles proclaim an involvement with *urban* studies. Perhaps that is not their message, and what the author really means by politics or family or burial societies "in Urban Africa" is really merely a geographical designation, a more specific version of the "Todas of the Nilgiris" or "The Trobrianders of Melanesia." Yet some urban social anthropologists wish to be more than just geographically precise. Epstein (1969:117) notes an increasing tendency to see all urban areas as sharing common characteristics, but he does not say of what this similarity consists or how studies of urbanizing Africans pertain to this assertion of universality. Similar preconceptions of the city (or more precisely, a willingness to accept it as given) exist in American urban anthropology. Spradley hopes that increasing tolerance will root out "the separateness which now permeates *our* cities" (1970:262, italics added). What is the reference of "our" cities: American cities, industrial cities, all cities? In a geographical sense, the statement clearly refers to American cities, but in an anthropological sense, the dominain of its applicability remains unspecified. Until the anthropology of the city is added to the anthropology of urban streets and migrant men, such statements will only communicate the sentiments and implicit beliefs of the urbanist, but not his knowledge.

3. The populations which urban anthropologists study often impede a recognition of the links between city and society or a holistic approach to urban organization and form. To see the city through recently detribalized peoples or newly arrived peasants is extremely difficult. Urban nomads and ghetto men also participate minimally in the city. (This may also be a reflection of the community study methods: cf. Valentine and Valentine, 1970). Residentially, economically, and politically, they are often strangers to the city. Even were it true that traditional ethnographic techniques require study of small-scale urban localities or communities, what explains the lack of research on middle-class Americans or European elites in Africa? In his analysis of such influential or powerful social categories, the anthropologist could not so readily ignore the city and larger society. By choosing urbanization and ghetto men instead, anthropologists only confirm their inadequacies in the description of urban

life. They thus practice a strange empiricism in which the research universe is defined by the observer's sensibilities (more on this . . . follows).

Although he recognizes the restricted scope of an urban community study, Epstein takes the "embracing politico-economic system and its events" as given. He writes ". . . the community, as conceived here, is not a microcosm, but a field of social relations the limits of which have been arbitrarily set for convenience of study" (1958:xiii–xiv). That convenience of study may be at the price of conceptual vigor is illustrated by Plotnicov's work which also arbitrarily demarcates a field of social relations in the city. From his intensive analysis of eight individuals in Jos, Nigeria, Plotnicov concludes that urban life is not disorganized: ". . . the people of Jos make up a stable urban population and the community itself continues to develop its own vitality" (1967:60). Plotnicov's approach may indicate that selected urban lives show little disorganization, in this case lives selected for high status. It cannot, however, say much about urban life which is a generalization of a rather different order. Yet Plotnicov offers more than psychological generalizations. He concludes "[the city's] institutions are viable and durable and integrate the various ethnic components" (1967:290). In an earlier footnote, the author indicates that this statement, based on fieldwork in the early 1960's, is no longer valid because of the clashes between Ibo and Hausa in Nigeria during the mid-1960's. Situational analysis based on urban lives or urban networks does not allow even short-term prediction of urban events which are a reflex of national happenings. More reliable judgments of urban viability can only be achieved by noting the relationship of tribal region to central polity and the intermediary role of the city in the larger society.[4]

4. A slice of the present is perhaps an inevitable modus operandi in societies without pasts. The anthropologist duplicates the ahistory of the primitive world by a careful selection of urban populations without pasts. But he pays dearly for this gratuitous continuity of approach. Urban anthropology cannot engage cross-cultural comparison of city development or cultural patterns of urban migration. It cannot address the problems of ethnocentric approaches to city research as raised by Sjoberg (1960), or even legitimately criticize the concept of the preindustrial city which Sjoberg proposes as a cure. (For an historian's criticism, see Thrupp, 1961:60–63).[5] The anthropology of contemporary urban communities says little to those archaeologists who adopt holistic views of the city and urban development in the past (Adams, 1960:153–172 *passim*, and the historian, Lampard, 1967:519 ff.), and even less to historians interested in the cross-cultural validity of Weber's distinction (1927:318) between oriental and occidental patterns of urbanism.

In what is for many urban anthropologists the most important aspect of their work (in the analysis of contemporary urban problems and in prediction

---

[4] Plotnicov argues that his analysis will again hold true when national political stability returns. But if this factor is so determinative, why exclude it from the initial formulation and prediction?

[5] An exception is Arensberg's (1968) criticism of Sjoberg and Wittfogel, and his contrast between traditional "stone" and "green" cities.

and prescription for their future course) the urban anthropologist often seems as impoverished as the peoples he studies. A diachronic viewpoint coupled with a holistic approach to city and society might more analyse the malaise of American cities and the nature of an urban society which is "multicultural" and in crisis. But how do we explain the emergence of this presumed multicultural American city instead of the expected or hoped-for melting pot urbanism? And what do we, as theoreticians of the city, offer as cure, beyond the palliatives of social welfare or a respect for the urban outsider which leaves him still outcaste? These fundamental problems of society and culture the urban anthropologist must evidently leave to a historian like Warner, who adopts a holistic and diachronic view of the city. In his study of Philadelphia over three centuries, Warner (1968:x) describes an American (urban) cultural tradition of "privatism" which fixes the nature of urban polity and through its limitations creates the urban crisis which Spradley, Lewis, and Valentine see in the city's poor. Whether or not Warner's analysis proves viable, it is significant as a statement of what can be done in urban research and as a reflection of what has not yet been done in urban anthropology.

Why have city streets and urban men formed the main concentration of urban anthropology? Traditional ethnographic methodology and an antiurban bias have been suggested as contributing factors (Gulick, 1968:93–95). The selection and training of the anthropologist is perhaps another determinant. Gulick believes that ". . . anthropology . . . tends to attract individuals who by temperament are inspired to live among and study people about whom no one else cares" (1963:560–561). In urban areas, the poverty-stricken, often ethnically distinct slum dweller is the equivalent of the primitive about whom none care. Training in anthropology fosters a highly individual scholarly experience, and anthropologists, also individualized and isolated by their research style, perhaps overemphasize similar qualities in peasant and urban societies.

Still another factor—or perhaps a summation of all previous ones—is the anthropological quest for the romantic and foreign. Although most introductory texts proclaim an anthropology larger than the primitive world, students quickly learn that anthropologists are specialists in the arcane, the outre, and the exotic. Very early in the development of anthropology, the Seligmanns viewed with the disdain proper to ethnographers seeking the "true" culture those Veddas who donned loin cloth and hefted spears in a British-inspired image of the primitive. Such "professional primitives" garnered tips from the less sophisticated British colonial officers who only wanted photographs of the exotic, rather than a scholarly description of it (Fox, 1969a:13–27). Like the Seligmanns, other anthropologists figuratively turn off the radios and phonographs which bring new waves to peasant villages and tribal settlements. Their eyes close to the cinema which etches on celluloid a different culture from the acceptably exotic sort carved on monuments or shaped into temple dieties.[6] Such problems attending the pursuit of the romantic have always

---

[6] Tiger (1967) is one of the few anthropologists doing research in cities to discuss the role of the mass media.

hampered anthropology, but even in most modern guise, as Whitten and Szwed (1970:17) recognize in their preface to *Afro-American Anthropology*, "Anthropologists are people who specialize in the study of the culturally exotic."

Pursuit of the romantic in anthropology is no discredit, for it has given the field a breadth and involvement with humanity which other disciplines rarely achieve. Only when the exotic is narrowly defined, as it must to be rediscovered in modern urban environments, only when the romantic grows beyond a frame of mind and materializes into city streets and urbanising men does the problem of limited perspective arise. Gutkind notes how hesitantly African ethnographers turned to urban places. Most cities were of recent origin and populated by non-Africans, and " . . . anthropologists were not particularly interested in studying Europeans or Asians" (1969:216). A similar distaste for the unromantic and familiar explains the lack of middle class or elite studies in urban America. But pursuit of the exotic in urban anthropology has produced greater disabilities than mere avoidance of mainstream economic and ethnic categories. Ethnographers of the tribal world studied the romantic customs of family, religion, or war as reflections of the variety of human cultural experience. Only incidentally to this purpose and in recognition of world political realities did they investigate uncared for peoples in out of the way places. Yet contemporary urban anthropology gives its whole attention to fulfilling only the latter geographical or physical criterion of the exotic in its selection of what and whom to study in the urban sphere. By embracing the exotica of poverty populations, slum environments, and native locations, much urban anthropology falls into an inappropriate ahistoricism, accepts the absence of a holistic viewpoint, denies the city as the goal of research—and thus factors out what cities can say about the nature of man and his societies. A cross-cultural reflection of the varieties of urban experience, an analysis of urban familial, religious, or political institutions as aspects of the larger society, in sum, a theoretical as apart from a locational interest in the exotic remains undefined in urban anthropology.

If such is to be the approach in urban anthropology, the field has been misnamed. It would more properly earn the title of "street" anthropology from its involvement with social life found on cement sidewalks, at the bottom of highrise buildings, or in housing clusters at the periphery of the urban core. Unfortunately, this field's comparability would be narrowly defined, for other anthropologists have yet to institute an equivalent "mountain," "rice-paddy," or "ice-float" anthropology.

Is the only defense of this urban anthropology to be that we study those for whom no other scholarly fraternity cares? Is an impoverished urban anthropology behind the "culture of poverty?" This paper has attempted to define urban anthropology as something more than the left-overs of other disciplines. It suggests a holistic approach to city and society and an investigation of patterns of adaptation by cities—thus a view of their changing ideological and behavioral linkage to the societies in which they occur.

Many questions of the city and urban society are not resolved in the current literature of urban anthropology; many have not yet been asked. Until urban anthropologists adopt a larger view of their work, many questions will not even be recognized, and the research of other disciplines which might help both ask and answer anthropology's questions will remain unused. Such is the case for Warner's historical study of Philadelphia and the American urban ethos of privatism, previously mentioned. An urban anthropology interested in the ideological fit of city and society would benefit greatly from the work of city planners and architects, such as E. A. Gutkind's monumental *International History of City Development* (1964). An interactional urban anthropology could follow many leads in the sociology of Vidich and Bensman's *Small Town in Mass Society* (1968), or in English's (1966) geographical analyses of Kirman and its hinterland, or in the historical sociology of Muslim cities as undertaken by Lapidus (1967). Urban anthropology may justifiably plead backwardness because of the present paucity of comparative material or juniority as a field. It is quite another matter if it defaults due to conceptual poverty and thus pursuit of limited research goals.

Bibliography

ADAMS, ROBERT M.
  1960   "The Origin of Cities." *Scientific American,* **2033**: 153–172.
ARENSBERG, CONRAD
  1968   "The Urban in Cross-cultural Perspective," in *Urban Anthropology: Research Perspectives and Strategies.* Elizabeth M. Eddy, (ed.). Southern Anthropological Society Proceedings #2. Athens: University of Georgia Press.
BANTON, MICHAEL
  1957   *West African City. A Study of Tribal Life in Freetown.* London: Oxford University Press.
BEALS, RALPH and HARRY HOIJER
  1971   *An Introduction to Anthropology.* Fourth edition. New York: Macmillan Publishing Co., Inc.
BRUNER, EDWARD
  1967   Comments on A. L. Epstein's "Urbanization and social change in Africa." *Current Anthropology* **8**: 297.
COHEN, ABNER
  1969   *Custom and Politics in Urban Africa. A study of Hausa Migrants in Yoruba Towns.* Berkeley and Los Angeles: University of California Press.
EPSTEIN, A. L.
  1958   *Politics in an Urban African Community.* Manchester: Manchester University Press.
  1967   "Urbanization and Social Change in Africa." *Current Anthropology* **8**: 275–296.
  1969   "The Network and Urban Social Organization," in *Social Networks in*

Urban Situations. Analyses of Personal Relationships in Central African Towns, J. Clyde Mitchell (ed.). Manchester: Manchester University Press.

FOX, RICHARD G.
1969a "Professional Primitives: Hunters and Gatherers of Nuclear South Asia." *Man in India* **49:** 13–27.
1969b *From Zamindar to Ballot Box: Community Change in a North Indian Market Town.* Ithaca: Cornell University Press.
1971 "Rajput Clans and Rurban Settlements in Northern India," in *Urban India: Society, Space, and Image,* Richard G. Fox, (ed.). Program in Comparative Studies on Southern Asia. Durham: Duke University.

GEERTZ, CLIFFORD
1965 *Social History of an Indonesian Town.* Cambridge: M.I.T. Press.

GULICK, JOHN
1963 "Urban Anthropology: Its Present and Future," in *Readings in Anthropology,* Volume II: Cultural Anthropology, Morton H. Fried (ed.). Second edition. New York: Thomas Y. Crowell Company.
1967 *Tripoli: A Modern Arab City.* Cambridge: Harvard University Press.
1968 "The Outlook, Research Strategies, and Relevance of Urban Anthropology: A Commentary," in *Urban Anthropology: Research Perspectives and Strategies,* Elizabeth M. Eddy (ed.). Southern Anthropological Society Proceedings #2. Athens: University of Georgia Press, pp. 93–98.

GUTKIND, E. A.
1964 *International History of City Development.* New York: Free Press of Glencoe.

GUTKIND, PETER C. W.
1969 "African Urban Life and the Urban System," in *Urbanism, Urbanization, and Change: Comparative Perspectives* Paul Meadows and Ephraim H. Mizruchi (eds.). Reading, Mass.: Addison-Wesley Publishing Co., Inc.

HARRIS, MARVIN
1956 *Town and Country in Brazil.* New York: Columbia University Press.

KEYFITZ, NATHAN
1967 "Urbanization in South and Southeast Asia," in *The study of Urbanization,* Philip M. Hauser and Leo F. Schnore (eds.). New York: John Wiley & Sons, Inc., pp. 265–309.

LAMPARD, ERIC E.
1967 "Historical Aspects of Urbanization," in *The Study of Urbanization,* Philip M. Hauser and Leo F. Schnore, (eds.). New York: John Wiley & Sons, Inc., pp. 519–554.

LAPIDUS, IRA MARVIN
1967 *Muslim Cities in the Later Middle Ages.* Cambridge: Harvard University Press.

LEEDS, ANTHONY
1968 "The Anthropology of Cities: Some Methodological Issues," in *Urban Anthropology: Research Perspective and Strategies,* Elizabeth M. Eddy (ed.). Southern Anthropology Society Proceedings #2. Athens: University of Georgia Press, pp. 31–47.

LEWIS, OSCAR
1967   "Further Observations on the Folk-Urban Continuum and Urbanization with Special Reference to Mexico City," in *The Study of Urbanization*, Philip M. Hauser and Leo F. Schnore (eds.). New York: John Wiley & Sons, Inc., pp. 491–502.

LYNCH, OWEN
1967   "Rural Cities in India, Continuities and Discontinuities," in *India and Ceylon: Unity and Diversity*, Philip Mason (ed.). London: Oxford University Press, pp. 142–158.

MARRIS, PETER
1962   *Family and Social Change in an African City. A Study of Rehousing in Lagos.* Chicago: Northwestern University Press.

MINER, HORACE
1965   *The Primitive City of Timbuctoo.* Revised ed. Garden City: Anchor Books.
1967   "The City and Modernization: An Introduction." in *The City in Modern Africa*, Horace Miner (ed.). London: Fr. A. Praeger.

MITCHELL, J. CLYDE
1966   "Theoretical Orientations in African Urban Studies," in *The Social Anthropology of Complex Societies*, Michael Banton (ed.). London: Tavistock Publications, pp. 37–61.
1969   *Social Networks in Urban Situations. Analyses of Personal Relationships in Central African Towns.* Manchester: Manchester University Press.

PLOTNICOV, LEONARD
1967   *Strangers to the City. Urban Man in Jos, Nigeria.* Pittsburgh: University of Pittsburgh Press.

POCOCK, DAVID F.
1960   "Sociologies—Rural and Urban." *Contributions to Indian Sociology* **4:** 63–81.

RUBEL, ARTHUR J.
1966   *Across the Tracks. Mexican-Americans in a Texas city.* Austin: University of Texas Press.

SINGER, MILTON
1960   "The Expansion of Society and its Cultural Implications," in *City Invincible: A symposium on Urbanization and Cultural Development in Ancient Near East*, Carl H. Kraehling and Robert M. Adams (eds.). Chicago: University of Chicago Press.

SJOBERG, GIDEON
1960   *The Preindustrial City, Past and Present.* Glencoe: The Free Press.

SOUTHALL, AIDAN (ed.).
1961   *Social Change in Modern Africa.* London: Oxford University Press.

SPRADLEY, JAMES P.
1970   *You Owe Yourself a Drunk: An Ethnography of Urban Nomads.* Boston: Little, Brown and Company.

THRUPP, SYLVIA
1961   "The Creativity of Cities," *Comparative Studies in Society and History* **4:** 53–64.

TIGER, LIONEL
    1967   "Bureaucracy and Urban Symbol Systems," In *The City in Modern Africa*, Horace Miner (ed.). London: Fr. A. Praeger.
VALENTINE, CHARLES A.
    1968   *Culture and Poverty. Critique and Counter-proposal.* Chicago: University of Chicago Press.
VALENTINE, CHARLES A. and BETTY LOU VALENTINE
    1970   "Making the Scene, Digging the Action, and Telling It Like It Is: Anthropologists at Work in a Dark Ghetto," In *Afro-American Anthropology*, Norman Whitten & J. F. Szwed (eds.). New York: The Free Press.
VAN DER BERGHE, PIERRE L. with asst. of Edna Miller
    1964   *Caneville. The Social Structure of a South African Town.* Middletown (Conn.): Wesleyan University Press.
VIDICH, ARTHUR J. and JOSEPH BENSMAN
    1968   *Small Town in Mass Society; Class, Power and Religion in a Rural Community.* Revised edition. Princeton, N.J.: Princeton University Press.
WARNER, SAM B.
    1968   *The Private City. Philadelphia in Three Periods of Growth.* Philadelphia: University of Pennsylvania Press.
WEBER, MAX
    1927   *General Economic History.* Glencoe: The Free Press.
WHITTEN, NORMAN and J. F. SZWED (eds.)
    1970   Preface. In *Afro-American Anthropology*. New York: The Free Press.
ZORBAUGH, HARVEY WARREN
    1929   *The Gold Coast and the Slum: A Sociological Study of Chicago's Near North Side.* Chicago: Unversity of Chicago Press.

The City as Context: Cultural, Historical, and Bureaucratic Determinants of Behavior in Seville

IRWIN PRESS

Fox is not alone in his concern for the state of the art in urban anthropology. Other scholars have commented on the lack of progress since urban research began, and many are particularly disturbed by the lack of attention to the city as a complex, internally systemic entity in itself, and as a part of an even larger sociocultural sphere.

"The City as Context: Cultural, Historical, and Bureaucratic Determinants of Behavior in Seville," *Urban Anthropology*, Vol. 4 (1) 1975, pp. 27–34.

In 1973, Irwin Press and Jack Rollwagon organized a symposium for the American Anthropological Association titled, "The City as Context," in which a number of scholars presented holistic views of urban life. The following study by Press (expanded considerably in his monograph on Seville, 1979) takes up the question of context. It indicates just how broad and far-reaching this context may be, and how pervasive are its effects upon the behavior of urban dwellers. Industrialization, sex roles, jobs, housing, and even such critical matters as marriage, health care, and family cohesiveness following death are all seen to be affected by the history and institutions of the larger units in which the lives of the inhabitants are encapsulated.

One question suggested by Press is whether the so-called impersonal city may not actually be falsely perceived as offering greater freedom than the rural milieus (recall Simmel's argument). The greater temptations and increased opportunity for anonymity may, in fact, lead urbanites to impose more restraints. Press points to the greater freedom of women to move around in villages. One could also point to those people in Manhattan who, fearful of street life, are actually more confined to their homes (especially after dark) than any peasant or tribal person.

One is left wondering to what extent Sevillanos are aware of the accommodations they make to the imposed patterns of the larger polity. Indeed, how aware are any of us of such constraints?

It is ironic that anthropologists, of all people, should be calling for a holistic approach to urban research. We almost singlehandedly invented the holistic community study.

It is perhaps understandable that those who made most of this approach should be most intimidated by the city. A smaller, rural entity was manageable in size, the linkages between its institutions were readily visible, its ties to other communities or groups were discernible. Its members shared a single cultural-ideational system, and the investigator could readily cross-check data and generalize to other members of the community or group. The latter is, after all, one of the basic assumptions behind our participant-observer method. The urban milieu generally has been felt to offer few of these apparent advantages.

Ambivalence toward the city—fascination mixed with feelings of inadequacy—led to a focus on urban enclaves (ghettos, migrant groups, marginal populations) as manageable "little communities" within a wider entity which was generally ignored or quickly categorized in stereotypic terms.

Though Lewis (1951:432–440), Miner (1952), and others criticized Redfield's sweeping stereotype of cities over a quarter century ago, only recently has there developed a real momentum toward recognizing important differences between urban milieus. We now speak of different types of cities, such as "native," "colonial," and "preindustrial." Even within supposedly homogeneous categories, we now note important divergence. As Gulick and others have pointed out, such qualities as impersonalism and social disorganization may have been characteristic of the developmental stage of Western industrial centers, but "they are not the only diagnostic criteria of Western urban life today" (Gulick, 1967:viii).

In other words, we can no longer dodge the necessity for describing a particular city by resorting to a ready stereotype. The urban anthropologist must provide insight into the specific characteristics of the specific city within which he works. Rollwagen (1972:68–69), Fox (1972), and others have stressed that the city can no longer be ignored as context. This context is created by the national culture interacting with the specific history, hinterland culture, internal developments, and external experiences of the particular city.

When such a holistic approach is taken, the results may be surprising.

When I first encountered the *corrales de vecinos* of Seville, I breathed a traditional sigh of relief. Ten to several hundred nuclear families, with long residence, . . . [lived] in tiny apartments surrounding a common courtyard with but one entrance. Each [was] a perfect little village within the big city of half a million people. Twenty percent of the population still lived in corrals, and over half had been socialized in them. It is no doubt possible to describe the behavior of corral residents with little reference to the city. When the city was taken into account, however, a most interesting and unexpected glimpse was provided into the origins of and contraints on behavior.

Seville is located about as far up the Guadalquivir River as large boats can navigate from the Mediterranean. It is also in the center of a vast fertile plain. Thus its important economic history.

The city had two cultural peaks. The first occurred in the twelfth century, when Seville was the principal center of Moorish-ruled Al Andaluz and the largest city in Spain. Some claims put its population at over 400,000. Even a fourth of that would be remarkable. Firsthand accounts paint the city in dizzy hues. Trades of all kinds flourished, along with public schools and libraries, zoning laws, and property tax (Guichot, 1886, Vol. 2; Gallichan, 1903; Levi-Provencal and Garcia Gomez, 1948). By any standards, Moorish Seville was very urban.

When the last of the Moors fell in 1492, Spain had the opportunity to turn to industrial and mercantile development. Columbus, however, discovered a New Frontier. As Eric Wolf concludes, "the year 1492 might have marked Spain's awakening to a new reality; instead, it marked the coming of a new dream, a new utopia" (1959:157–159).

Seville became utopia's gatekeeper, and the second peaking began. In 1503, the Catholic Kings concentrated all economic functions of trade with the New World in Seville, and the city once again became Spain's largest and most opulent (Pike, 1966:32).

The wealth which poured into the city could hardly be disdained, regardless of traditional Sevillano adulation of "pure" nobility and heroism. Trade was elevated to a necessary though not sufficient means to an end, and the "merchant class became an intermediary stage in the social hierarchy to be abandoned as soon as possible" (Pike, 1972:100). This is of importance; for Seville's monopoly over New World trade was not to hold.

Many of her trade functions were to pass to other towns. Cadiz became the principal port of the south. Later, Barcelona on the Mediterranean and Bilbao on the Atlantic were to monopolize trade with Europe. Unfortunately, the city had grown rich on the skills, energy, and planning of others. Goods to and from the New World had been manufactured or produced (and financed)· elsewhere. When the boom ended, Seville was left a seat of aristocratic gentry and moderate agricultural production, with a glorious past. By 1747, the population was but 50% of its average in the twelfth century.

By 1900, Seville was a glorious has-been. Its inhabitants had turned increasingly inward, raising homogeneity and continuity to the status of conscious goals. To this day, so strong is the *image* of the city, and so deep the Sevillanos' identification with it, that neither local nor national influentials, nor the public, have been willing to change it.

Lacking the industrial and economic strength of cities to the north, Seville, with its world-famous architecture, Holy Week, April Feria, bullfighting, and flamenco traditions, consciously maintains itself as a museum for a Spain now but a memory in most other areas of the peninsula. Recently, the mayor published a vitriolic "love it or leave it" broadside, damning critics with the temerity to suggest that Seville awaken to the industrial epoch. Eight years ago, Ford Motor Company considered Seville as the site for its first Iberian plant, and the major political cartoonist for the major daily newspaper (*ABC*) sketched the city's most famous landmark with huge neon letters, F O R D, defacing it.

Given the path of historical development, given the active provincialism and personalism, it is hardly surprising that economic development in general and industry in particular have been slow in coming. Skill requirements in Seville's industries and business are low, and personnel thus relatively interchangeable. Where one worker will do as well as any other, the result is reliance on particularistic modes of recruitment. Thus personal contact is the *only* means to employment at *all* levels. "He who has no godfather does not get baptized" is a common refrain which stresses the importance of contacts or *enchufes* ("plug-ins") to sources of jobs, favors, or services. And Sevillanos of all economic levels use one another relentlessly for entrees and to thwart the pervasive bureaucracy.

The physical growth of the city has also had important effects upon behavior. Until approximately 20 years ago, most Sevillanos were packed in high-density neighborhoods within the boundaries of the old city walls. Streets wind so much that it is difficult to find a vista longer than a hundred yards. Most street names change with every jog or major crossing. Local block and romantic neighborhood identities are quite strong. Though Seville fits the preindustrial city model in certain ways, it diverges in others. Social heterogeneity has been characteristic of almost all neighborhoods, including the central ones. Packed within the city walls, ducal palaces sprang up next to teeming lower-class tenements and upper- or middle-class single-family dwellings. The result is a general egalitarian style of interaction and a remarkable unity in identity, experience, and values.

What of the effect of residence? At least a simple majority of adult Sevillanos were born and socialized in *corrales de vecinos.* Similar to Mexico City's *vecindades* and Argentina's *conventillos,* they are multifamily affairs, with one- and two-room apartments facing a common patio to which there is but a single entrance. The first corrals were built in the sixteenth century by both the Church and private individuals as investments to pour their limitless cash into. Corrals house from ten to 200 separate nuclear families. In these residences, interaction is extremely high, privacy low. Superficial sociability and mutual performance of favors are essential for social survival, as is the vicious gossip which keeps neighbors from demanding too much of each other.

Lack of alternative dwellings prior to the Civil War and government rent freezes which kept rents at rock bottom after 1940 have encouraged high population stability. New migrants to the city find their kin scattered throughout the urban area in highly stable residential situations, and are themselves quickly "Sevillized." High continuity of residence has created dense neighborhood networks for most young individuals, wherein behavior is constantly monitored by others with direct feedback to the young people's kin and acquaintances. Conformity and homogeneity of values and behavior are guaranteed. Marriages, furthermore, are commonly contracted with others living on the same street.

In that neighbors learn of potential vacancies before outsiders, referrals to kinfolk are common and thus over half of all tenants have close kin living in the same or neighboring corrals. Because rooms close by could be rented or vacated as needed, these corrals have been able to accommodate families at all stages of their domestic cycle, thus encouraging extended family proximity.

In terms of outside factors, Seville is not an isolate. There is a government outside it. Spaniards are enmeshed in an ambitious cradle-to-grave welfare system which affects behavior at most important life stages. And these bureaucratic services are most concentrated, available, and compelling in the urban milieu.

Most welfare benefits came into being after the Civil War had disrupted many "normal" economic and family functions; thus they filled a timely need. Rent controls, designed to meet an economic need of the time, also had other effects. They froze tenants to their corrals and killed the construction of rental units. Thus began construction limited to tenant-owned condominium apartment buildings. Ownership requires down payments and monthly mortgage payments. Many in the lower and middle clases cannot afford them. And so private building and financing were supplemented by government-subsidized construction. Access to subsidized apartments is controlled by the government, which allocates them on the basis of need, or lottery. Neither need nor lottery, however, allows separate nuclear families to reside *together.* Nor is it likely that two related or friendly families can afford private condominia at the same moment, and thus purchase adjoining apartments. Down payments may run to a year's income. Thus the move to new condominia results in split-up of friends or kin, and makes extended family expansion or contraction in the same vicinity practically impossible.

Saving for a condominium entails postponement of marriage and a longer dependency on parents. Not only must the down payment be saved, but also sufficient money for furnishings to allow immediate setup of a household complete to wall hangings and knickknack cabinets. For it is felt that a condominium marks a move upward in status and one's life style and furnishings should be consistent with the new dwelling.

All new apartments are going up outside the old city walls. In that larger-scale financing is preferred to single-building construction, government and private contractors tend to build in large blocks, each major complex being fairly homogeneous in apartment sale price. Thus the creation, de facto, of unprecedented class-homogeneous neighborhoods where none existed 20 years ago.

The government's programs are even more pervasive, however. Socialized medicine provides all salaried employees with totally free medical care and hospitalization, plus near-cost-free medicines. Sevillanos are allocated to general practitioners located at Social Security clinics in their neighborhood. One must petition to change doctors. Only his Social Security physician can certify the worker as officially "sick" and issue the *baja* which permits him to remain home at 50% of his salary. Inspectors come at odd times to check on the validity of his invalidity. Needless to say, *curanderismo* could hardly compete with this, and in the city today, it is a weak, sparsely used backstop for modern health practice. (See Press, 1973.)

In addition to sick pay, the government sets minimum wages, provides unemployment compensation of 50% of previous salary, and old-age pensions of approximately half a lower-class salary. The last permits some degree of independence for older Spaniards. Benefits go still further, however. Though all employees must have approximately 8% of their salary deducted for social security, etc., each employee *receives* a monthly rebate in cash for being married, and additional sums for each child. For a large lower-class family, such "point money" can mean an increment of 5% to monthly income.

Somewhat peripherally, the national sindical organization or labor union controls jobs and prevents capricious firing by employers of tenured employees. Once on the job 6 months, an employee *cannot* be fired unless the employer shows cause and petitions the sindical judicial office. Abuses of the bureaucracy are common, and employers and employees work together frequently to cheat the government. In that all jobs are obtained through friends or kin, both parties "understand" the situation in advance and protect each other.

"Outside" forces go beyond bureaucracy. We have not begun to mention certain pervasive elements of Spanish culture which affect behavior in both rural and urban areas. Sex role expectations, for example, are extremely rigid in Seville, most particularly among the lower classes. Men are not allowed to perform domestic chores. When a woman dies, her husband and sons are allocated to other women. When a man marries, he transfers his dependence from mother to wife and the home is his wife's, not his. The male's dependence on the female goes further, however, in that his honor is closely tied to his wife's or mother's sexuality. One can be called nothing worse than a cuckold or son of a whore.

For the city dweller, certain elements of sex role expectation are affected in a specific fashion. Where families of the bride and groom live at some distance from one another, considerable preference is given to marriage residence near the wife's parents, preferably in the same corral. The husband's fear of wearing horns, furthermore, severely curtails movement of the wife in the city. She can easily slip away from sight in busy city streets. And there is a downtown shopping district she can literally disappear in. Women are thus expected to make rather hurried shopping trips or take a friend or child along to stores. In small, rural communities, on the other hand, a woman is constantly visible to villagemates and is thus more free to move about alone. It should be further noted that when a woman dies in a small community, physical proximity of dwellings can allow femaleless males to remain in their homes with semiautonomy while female kin drop in to perform certain domestic tasks. In the city, however, dispersal of females (particularly now that apartment dwelling is the norm) requires dispersal of bereaved males and breakup of their homes.

In summary, I have presented but a few "contextual examples" from Seville. Many more could have been discussed. The point to be made is that if behavior is to be understood in this particular city one must go beyond the individual and, indeed, even beyond the city itself. The specific history of the city established limitations on economic development, on innovation, on exterior orientations, on skill expectations, and labor recruitment. The physical layout encourages highly local identities and value homogeneity. The dwelling types available have strong input to socialization, social control, and strength of extended families and local acquaintance networks. The government controls wages and allows little leeway in health-oriented behavior. The government, further, encourages dependence through sick pay, unemployment compensation, and cash rebates for family size. Government rent controls, construction subsidation, and apartment allocation have direct consequences in limiting choices relating to marriage age and access to housing. "National" cultural phenomena such as sex role requirements place severe limitations on behavior, and these limitations are further affected by increased anonymity and family dispersal in the urban milieu.

In other words, behavior of the urban community dweller, no less than the peasant or primitive, cannot be fully understood without recourse to the whole historical, physical, environmental, and cultural milieu. Though certain elements of depth may indeed be sacrificed through attention to the wider urban-cultural context, the results are clearly more desirable than the narrow alternative. Whether "little community" or big, our focus must still encompass the community, with all of the holistic elements such a focus implies.

Bibliography

FOX, RICHARD G.
  1972 "Rationale and Romance in Urban Anthropology." *Urban Anthropology*
     1:205–233.
GALLICHAN, WALTER M.
  1903 *The Story of Seville*. London: J. M. Dent & Sons Ltd.
GUICHOT, A. J.
  1886 *Historia de la ciudad de Sevilla*.
GULICK, JOHN
  1967 *Tripoli, a Modern Arab City*. Cambridge, Massachusetts: Harvard University Press.
LEVI-PROVENCAL, E. and E. GARCIA GOMEZ
  1948 Sevilla a comienzos del siglo XII: El tratado de Ibn "Abdun, Madrid:
     Moneda y Credito.
LEWIS, OSCAR
  1951 *Life in a Mexican Village: Tepoztlan restudied*. Urbana: Illinois: University of Illinois Press.
MINER, HORACE
  1952 "The Folk-Urban Continuum." *American Sociological Review* **17**:
     529–537.
PIKE, RUTH
  1966 *Enterprise and Adventure: The Genoese in Seville and the Opening of the New World*. Ithaca, New York: Cornell University Press
  1972 *Aristocrats and Traders: Sevillian Society in the 16th Century*. Ithaca,
     New York: Cornell University Press.
PRESS, IRWIN
  1973 "Bureaucracy Versus Folk Medicine: Implications from Seville, Spain."
     Urban Anthropology, **2**:232–247.
ROLLWAGEN, JACK R.
  1972 "A Comparative Framework for the Investigation of the City-as-Context;
     A Discussion of the Mexican Case." *Urban Anthropology*, **1**:68–86.
WOLF, ERIC
  1959 *Sons of the Shaking Earth*. Chicago: University of Chicago Press.

Part II: Research/Term Paper Topics

1. "Social Science and the City."

   Read a number of urban articles in each of the following: anthropology, sociology, psychology, geography, and another field of your choice. Compare the methodology. Compare choice of problem, how it was researched, how the findings were analyzed, and what suggestions for further research emerged from the studies. Use your findings to argue pro or con on the statement that "good social scientists do much the same kind of research."

2. "A Research Proposal."

   Design a research proposal to submit to a federal funding agency for research in an urban setting. Describe the problem. Include a statement of other relevant research on the topic, and show what your study will be adding. Stipulate methodology (including time schedule). Include a budget.

3. "The City Through the Voice of the Public."

   Radio and newspapers offer an editorial forum to the public. Using "phone-in" programs and/or the "action line" or "letters to the editor" columns of your local paper, do a content analysis of comments that relate to local urban problems. What kinds of people have what kinds of views about what kinds of problems? In what ways do they lack the power or resources to solve the problems they're complaining about? What conclusions can you draw about urban places? About the limitations of this particular method?

4. "Mental Maps."

   Select informants from various population segments; have them draw maps of the city, including geographic elements and landmarks significant to them; analyze and comment.

5. "Testing the Urban Ethos."

   Devise methods of testing some of the elements of the Chicago urban paradigm. Take impersonality for example. Drop stamped postcards on the street in selected areas and analyze the rate of their being picked up and mailed by "good samaritans." Do the same with unstamped cards. Try the "key drop." One student walks down a street and "unknowingly" drops a ring of keys on the sidewalk. Another student observes the manner and rate of return. (See Charles Korte, 1976, for a good description of various other methods that can easily be done by students.)

6. "British and American Urban Anthropology."

   Compare and contrast British and American urban anthropology in terms of the treatment of urbanism and urbanization; the reflection of holism; the units selected for study.

PART

The Development and Differentiation of Cities

THREE

A good way to approach the definition of some phenomenon is through a study of its history. The conditions under which cities developed may offer clues to their underlying formal and functional prerequisites. Urban life could not begin until the development of agriculture. Without the resulting surplus, it would have been impossible to support a significant concentration of nonfood-producing population.

By and large, there is a growing consensus that the forces (social, structural, economic, political, religious) that underlie the origin of urban life were in existence prior to the first cities. For example, mechanisms for coaxing or forcing surplus from farmers were already developing. Once formed, large communities of consumers required a variety of services and convenient access to agricultural zones. As they developed, cities became natural nodes of communication with the hinterlands—the most convenient point of meeting and distribution. Thus concentrating information, skills, labor pools, services, wealth, and consumers, cities also attracted a variety of elites with unprecedented and diverse power bases.

Cities, like communities of any type, exist to fill the needs of their inhabitants. This is another way of emphasizing the obvious fact that cities necessarily differ, reflecting the types of society in which they arise and the types of residents that found and subsequently develop them. The various attempts to lump or characterize cities by type have met with mixed success. By and large, there is most agreement on the distinction between pre- and post-Industrial Revolution cities. A number of the differences are suggested in the section which follows and need not be summarized here. In contrasting contemporary industrial or Western cities with contemporary non- or pre-industrial cities, it is important to remember that Western cities (and their social structure) developed *along with* industrialism. There is a special relationship between the two, which came about through co-evolution. One may question whether the Industrial Revolution could have occurred at all without the simultaneous development of small, mobile families, competitive and universalistically assigned economic roles, vast credit and capital mechanisms, and a host of other familiar Western urban elements.

It may be argued that nations such as Japan have managed to industrialize on a very different base, one that stresses familism, respect for age, and so on. At the same time, we must not forget that industry and Japanese society did *not* evolve together. Industry was imported fairly recently in a full-blown state. Would Japan have been the same had industry developed there? Can cities in non-industrial nations develop a different accommodation to modern industry if it is imported in bits and pieces?

The First Cities: How and Why Did They Arise?

KINGSLEY DAVIS

Once one begins to work with cities, one is drawn further back into history. Initially, one is simply aware of the intellectual need to know more about the specific city in which research is being done. Usually, the kinds of questions that one is forced to ask—the uniqueness or commonality of a particular process, structural feature, or societal dynamic—lead to a look at other cities. Finally, one arrives at the point where the city's beginnings start to pique the curiosity.

Sociologist Kingsley Davis points to our resulting dependency upon archaeological data. What were the conditions that had to be met before urban settlements could begin to take form? How did people meet the technological, ecological, and sociocultural needs that city life imposed? What happened when the urban revolution received further impetus from the Industrial Revolution? And why were cities a successful experiment, at least in the sense that they have persisted for more than 5,000 years and are still growing in size and number?

Davis ends on a cautionary note, reminding us that the study of ancient cities seems to offer ambiguous lessons, a point with which those who study modern cities are certain to agree.

Gazing on such wonderful sights, we did not know what to say or whether what appeared before us was real, for on one side in the land there were great cities and in the lake ever so many more, and the lake itself was crowded with canoes, and in the causeway there were many bridges at intervals, and in front of us stood the great City of Mexico, and we . . . . we did not even number four hundred soldiers.—BERNAL DIAZ, *The True History of the Conquest of New Spain* (1568)

Modern man's curiosity about his "origins" inevitably leads him to ask how cities began. When, where, and why did they arise, and what were the first ones like? Fortunately, this curiosity is more easily satisfied than most questions about social origins. The first cities came late in human history, and they left durable remains that are concentrated in particular spots and can be dug up and examined. Also, since the early cities were characterized by the invention of writing, the remains contain fragments of ideas and norms communicated to us directly from the remote urban past. Even more helpful, the intrepid Spaniards stumbled upon and gave eyewitness accounts of the cities of the Incas and Aztecs at a time when these cities were still archaic enough to give an idea of what the first ones were like. No such advantages attend our efforts to understand the origin of speech, the family, religion, or most other aspects of human society, which are not only more intangible than cities but are also older by hundreds of millennia. Studies of the first cities thus give us an unusual opportunity to find empirical evidence on an important step in man's social evolution.

Scientists from many fields have increasingly seized this opportunity. In the past three decades, in particular, they have utilized new techniques to advance our knowledge of the earliest cities. Among these are the use of radioactive decay for the dating of remains, chemical procedures for determining the origins and manufacture of materials, genetic techniques for tracing the evolution of domesticated species, and statistical methods for quantitative mapping and computerized data analysis. As information has grown, the theory of how cities began is beginning to be integrated with the theory of how they operate in modern society. We are therefore witnessing the growth of a science of cities.

Admittedly, a perennial problem in the study of the prehistory of cities is sampling bias. The archeologist can dig up only those things that persist, such as pots, bricks, bones, stones, and shells. The perishable items, regardless of their importance, have to be inferred from the durable ones. A "religious cult" is inferred from stone figurines found in a wall alcove; a belief in life after death is inferred from objects buried with the dead. In such inferential reasoning, details are lacking and alternative interpretations are possible. It is therefore to the credit of the archeologists that they are aware of the problem and, as professional scientists, make an effort to compensate for the unavoidable lacunae. How do they do it?

One of the precautions of the professional archeologist is to avoid ad hoc interpretations based on only one finding. Any particular artifact or layout is interpreted in the light of numerous other findings. When René Millon finds an abundance of potsherds in one location in Teotihuacán, for example, his inference that Mayan and Veracruz migrants or merchants were located there is not a random guess but a hypothesis based on his knowledge of pottery styles throughout Middle America, other specialized sites in Teotihuacán, possible trade routes in the region, and so on. A second safeguard of modern archeology is that the observational procedures are not indiscriminate; they involve an informed prediction of what one would expect to find and then a determination of the methods required to confirm or deny the expectation. Thus Richard MacNeish did not look for cobs of extinct wild corn at random; from his own experience, he knew that "dry locations offered the best chances of finding preserved specimens of corn"; and from his acquaintance with genetics, he believed that "wild corn was originally a highland grass, very possibly able to survive the rigorous climate of highland desert areas." So he looked in particular areas and eventually found what his systematic information had led him to expect. In addition, the investigator of ancient cities makes use of those rare "windows" that allow him to glimpse ideas and social relations in early cities. These are the pictorial and written records, which in the Old World go back to around 5,500 years ago. They do not tell the investigator everything, because they were limited in purpose, but they provide priceless insights not otherwise available. In the New World, unfortunately, the greatest treasure of written material—the Maya stone inscriptions—remain mostly undeciphered; but, as mentioned already, some of the New World's native cities were observed "alive" by Europeans at a time reasonably close to the origin of cities in the Americas. Although neither enlightened nor disinterested, the Europeans left accounts that add significantly to our understanding of archaic city life. Finally, archeologists are now using statistical techniques and ecological concepts to reconstruct the economic relations of cities with their hinterlands. Instead of concentrating their attention on monumental architecture and engraved writing, mainly religious and political in purpose, they are systematically mapping rural sites and hinterland resources from the standpoint of trade routes, population distribution, crop yields, and the common man.

A puzzling feature of the earliest cities is their strange mixture of modern and archaic traits. In a sense, any urban settlement, no matter when or where, has elements that we recognize as somehow "urban" and therefore familiar. For example, the perfection of the arts, crafts, and architecture in the early cities is instantly recognizable as urban, because only a city economy could provide the intense division of labor and diversity of resources that such perfection required. Similarly, the glimpses of daily life that come through to us—impressions of class distinction, fashion, display, public pomp, professional sport, and legal humbug and fiction—all ring a bell. On the other hand, the earliest cities reveal traits that puzzle a modern city dweller. Their governance and ideology were deeply intertwined with supernatural religion, their science was loaded with magic, and their outlook was extremely static. For production they depended overwhelmingly on human rather than nonhuman energy. The mass of the population was illiterate, traditional, and impoverished. The gap between them and the city elite was tantamount to a division between the profane and the sacred. A prominent feature of the modern city, its reliance on constant technological improvement and substitution of capital for labor, was absent. To us, the ancient cities were thus like the monsters of mythology: a familiar and recognizable part of their body was joined to a mysterious and incredible other part.

An understanding of these cities and their beginnings calls for answers to more than one basic question. The question that most people think of first and that most theories are designed to answer is what were the *conditions*, or prerequisites, that had to be satisfied before urban settlements were possible. The question is a good one, but one has to bear in mind that there are various kinds of conditions. Two kinds that must be distinguished are technological and geographical. So, one asks, what was the technological stage that had to be reached before cities could appear, and what were the geographical features that had to be present before the technology could be sufficiently productive to support a city? If these questions can be answered, we can then account for *when* and *where* the first cities arose.

Important as these questions are, we cannot be satisfied with them. The coming of cities was a major step in social evolution, not simply a set of prerequisites. There thus remains the problem of *how* the first cities got under way. By what means were the technological requirements and the exploitation of the physical environment organized?

Finally, the problem of origins must be pursued to the point of asking *why* cities arose. What did large permanent settlements do for human beings that led to their becoming still larger? What did cities contribute that could not otherwise have been contributed? And what was their structure that made possible their performance? How were they organized internally and externally for their peculiar role?

Other questions bear only indirectly on urban origins but nevertheless must be answered in a manner consistent with the answers to the questions [foregoing]. For instance, what were the changes that cities went through after they were started? Was there a typical cycle of growth and decay, and if so, why? Did the causes lie in alterations of the geographical conditions as a result of exploitation or in internal changes in the cities themselves?

Our readings on early cities do not confront all of these questions, but they supply a wealth of facts and interpretation that bear on them. The authors are most explicit about the conditions necessary for cities to arise, and they seem to agree that an advanced Neolithic technology was required, involving a shift from food gathering to "food production," as V. Gordon Childe, Harold Peake, and others maintained long ago. This stage involved mainly a combination of agriculture and animal husbandry with such adjuncts as pottery, textiles, polished stone tools, and versatile uses of wood, hides, and bones. Incipient domestication of plants or animals or both began probably as far back as 12,000 years in parts of Asia Minor, and as far back as 9,000 years in Mesoamerica. Such a beginning, whether in tropical forest patches or in alluvial valleys and plains, was at first nomadic, merely supplementing the main activity of hunting and gathering. Many centuries were required before food production could support sedentary villages. Gradually, with cultivation facilitating animal husbandry and vice versa, with an increase in the number and quality of domesticated plants, and with inventions such as the plow, the hafted stone axe, and the grinding stone, the village became the dominant pattern of settlement in favored regions. For some villages to become large enough to approach an urban scale, trade in artifacts and materials had to be available, and techniques of water control, soil management, storage, transport, permanent house-building, and food preservation had to be developed. These required boats or roads, wheeled vehicles or pack animals, irrigation and drainage systems, and various tools for carpentry, masonry, textiles, and food processing. At what point certain villages became large enough to be called towns, or small urban places, is partly a matter of definition, but it seems likely that places exceeding 3,000 inhabitants could be supported by intensive hoe cultivation on alluvial soil with the help of irrigation and good handicraft. Such an overgrown village would include a majority of agriculturalists, but it would have a minority of at least part-time traders, priests, soldiers, officials, and artisans. A population of more than 3,000 would be possible if the place where these people lived became a trade center and perhaps had some extra inventions such as wheeled carts, sailboats, fired brick, and metallurgy. Such a center would tend to be predominantly nonagricultural, if for no other reason than the impracticality of so many farmers trying to go forth each day to cultivate fields and tend animals in the surrounding region. Suppose that a settlement of 5,000 were in the center of a circular region and that each family had six acres of fields and grazing land. On the average the members would have to walk 1.2 miles each way (2.4 miles round trip) to get to their land. A larger settlement would require still longer journeys. The natural tendency was (and is) for strictly agricultural villages to be small and numerous, so as to minimize the journey to work—especially since women and children as well as men were involved in farming and since in the process of production the home and the land were closely integrated. Even saddle horses and horsedrawn carts would not make strictly agricultural villages large because the burden of carrying tools back and forth, protecting crops from predators (human and nonhuman), and transporting produce for processing at home was too great. As culture progressed, the higher technology was not used so much to congregate farmers in one place as to increase the proportion of persons in principal settlements who were not engaged in agriculture.

Since even the best technology is helpless without suitable conditions, the first urban settlements arose where the advanced Neolithic arts just mentioned were most productive—that is, where abundant water was available for irrigation by gravity flow, and where at the same time the climate was dry, sunshine plentiful, winter mild, soil renewal possible, and transport relatively unimpeded. A mild climate would prevent domestic animals from freezing or starving in winter. With abundant water and irrigation, crop growth could be controlled and sod could be renewed from silt laid down by irrigation or from mud grubbed up from lake and swamp bottoms. Transport could be achieved by water or by animal or human carriers over well-built roads or trails. It is therefore no accident that in both the Old and New World the earliest cities arose in tropical latitudes, on alluvial plains near rivers or lakes, with dry climates and access to a wide area. These were the conditions that characterized the valleys of Central Mexico, Mesopotamia, and the Nile, as well as the coasts of Peru and the southern Mediterranean. The only partial exception was the Mayan area, but the Mayan cities were evidently not the earliest cities in Mesoamerica. They may therefore have appeared in the lowlands of Guatemala as the result of artificial transfer of city-building technology from the more favorable environment of central Mexico. Although cities as such cannot be "diffused" from one place to another, their technological bases certainly can be, and once these underpinnings have advanced beyond their early stages, they can be applied under environmental conditions somewhat different from those where they arose spontaneously. The rapid rise and fall of Mayan cities and their easy spread to new geographical areas suggest that the technology did not wholly originate in the lowland jungle but rather came there in an already developed state, capable of quickly exploiting but soon exhausting the fragile resources of that region. In their virgin state and because of deliberate practices of man designed to prolong soil fertility, the lowlands could yield considerable corn (maize), which Sjoberg characterizes as "a superior grain crop that produced a substantial food surplus with relatively little effort." If that plant was being grown in irrigated fields in Tehuacán around 800 B.C., as MacNeish claims, we can see how, several centuries later, the Guatemalan lowlands could be made sufficiently productive to support small cities for a while. Until the archeological history of the Americas is more fully documented, it would be unwise, on the basis of Mayan evidence alone, to reject the standard interpretation of the environmental conditions that were necessary for urban places to arise spontaneously.

As mentioned earlier, however, even the most favorable technological stage and environmental setting could not, of themselves, produce a city. These conditions are necessary but not sufficient; they tell us when and where the first cities appeared, but not how or why. To see their shortcoming, one has merely to imagine a region that had the right environmental conditions and the necessary technology, but in which the farmers bred abundantly, ate up the entire crop, and thus yielded no surplus for the support of a city. Rich as the soil might have been, each family would have had a plot too small for anything more than its own subsistence. As Asian farmers have demonstrated for thousands of years, high productivity per acre need not mean high productivity per person. For cities to exist, the tillers of the soil had somehow to give up a part of what they grew. How was this accomplished?

The solution does not hinge on some startling new social invention. By the time the first cities came into existence, human society had long had a system of social differentiation and exchange that transcended the individual family. For cities to appear, then, these organizational traits did not have to be invented but merely had to be expanded. The expansion came about in four interrelated ways—by systematizing religious control, linking it with centralized government, building rights in land into a quasi-governmental institution, and facilitating the division of labor and the exchange of goods and services. These led the farmer either voluntarily to trade some of his "surplus" for things he wanted (godly favors, charms, cures, jewelry, utensils, tools), or else compelled him to supply produce in the form of rent, tribute, or taxes. We have seen that irrigation was a necessary feature of the technology, but for each farmer to get a share, some system of water control and distribution was essential. By submitting to such control, and paying with his produce those who supervised and protected the system, the farmer was entering a basic exchange, regardless of whether or not he understood it as such. Also, if the individual farmer had been spatially isolated from others, he would have been at the mercy of nomadic marauders and too remote for ready trade. Hence farmers were virtually always nucleated in villages, collectively organized for defense and exchange as well as production. Finally, to produce a subsistence, let alone a "surplus," each farmer had to have access to land. Not only did he have to be close to his land, which meant that the agricultural village had to be small, but there had to be a system of distributing the land. The very success of the Neolithic arts guaranteed that there would not be enough land for everybody; as the population grew, the persons of lesser status or poorer circumstances would be forced to leave, to pursue other work than cultivation, or to cultivate some one else's land and forfeit a part of the crop to him. The division of labor was so rudimentary that everybody tended to be a farmer, but some were part-time artisans, magicians, priests, traders, or soldiers as well; and scarcity of land tended to push some families toward these occupations on a full-time basis. Scarcity also led to rights in land that gave some individuals a claim on the proceeds even though they did not actually cultivate. These would not necessarily be "owners" in the modern sense, but rather tribal leaders or priestly warlords whose rights bore a resemblance to feudal or communal domain.

In short, if there ever were any Neolithic societies in which the farmers ate all of their own produce, they lost out to other societies in which farmers did not. Whether the farmers gave up their "surplus" voluntarily in payment for goods and services or involuntarily in fear of reprisal or punishment is beside the point. The line between the two was thin in any case: the farmer's "need" for supernatural services could be stimulated by playing on his credulity, and his need for protection could be accentuated by threats from his protectors. Nor is it relevant to ask whether the system was deliberately planned by a scheming "elite." The essential fact is that, long before the advent of cities, institutional mechanisms for getting the farmer to part with some of his produce had already evolved. These had merely to be intensified and welded into a community-wide structure to make possible the support of an essentially nonagricultural settlement, a town or small city.

The larger the surplus that could be brought into a place, the bigger and more nonagricultural that place could be. How much could be brought in depended not only on the amount that each farmer was led to give up, but also on the number of participating farmers. One mechanism for increasing the amount was to extend governmental and religious authority over an ever wider area. Another mechanism was trade. Those large villages that stood out over the rest and became urban centers were ones where not only local traders congregated to exchange familiar products but also where more distant traders came to barter exotic wares. Through trade, more artisans, priests, officials, and warriors could be supported in one place, and they in turn could consolidate authority over a wider hinterland and extend trade to distant parts. By devoting virtually full time to nonagricultural activities, the controlling classes could become better organized, they could turn the incompleteness of the division of labor into an organizing feature by coalescing different roles in the same persons; that is, at the top, the military could be simultaneously officials and priests, the artisans simultaneously traders. Hierarchical control required methods of record-keeping, which in time led to the development of writing. Writing in turn facilitated trade, communal storage, and orderly administration. A spiral was started in which cumulative innovations in technology and social organization combined to transform a few favored settlements into cities.

The expanding archeological record thus helps us to clarify *how* cities arose, and by doing so, it also helps us understand *why* they arose. They evidently emerged because of their contribution to efficiency. Since their contribution at the start is much the same as their contribution now, the *why* applies to modern as well as prehistoric cities. The explanation begins by recalling that two fundamental features of human society are specialization and exchange. Anything that facilitates these also facilitates productivity. An impediment to exchange, however, is distance, because it takes energy to move goods and high technology to transport services. One of the means by which people overcome the spatial impediment (the "friction of space," as Robert M. Haig called it) is to locate close to one another. This enables them to gain more from the work of others by exchanging more things at less cost. For this reason, they always settle together to the extent possible. Dispersion is forced on them by such limitations as the scattered location of natural resources and high mortality under crowded conditions, but to the extent that these factors permit, people congregate in space. It is not only human beings who do this, but other species as well, as witness the prairie-dog "village," ant "colony," termite mound, or "city of the bees." When men depended on hunting and gathering or on an early stage of agriculture, their settlements were nearly always small and temporary, because productivity was so low that each band required an immense territory that could be exploited only by perennial migration. As soon as better technology became available, increased productivity per unit of land made larger settlements possible, and these in turn stimulate more specialization and more exchange. The total territory linked in one economy did not shrink, but rather expanded; it was no longer, however, linked by migratory wanderings but by trade routes between stable villages. The ordinary village was primarily a place where producers gave one another mutual protection and mutual aid and where local produce was exchanged. Although the inhabitants collected some raw produce for export and received some distant goods in return, they lived in what was overwhelmingly a subsistence settlement. One or two villages in a wide region, however, by virtue of their location on trade routes or near scarce resources, would become centers of specialized production and trade. Insofar as production took the form of handicraft, it required little space and thus could be concentrated in the village. Trade itself required little space but instead profited from a concentrated market. The more advanced the arts, the wider the network of small villages and the larger the central trading places. . . . Tepe Yahyā, for instance, was well located to be a "central place" in trade between resource-poor Mesopotamia and resource-rich Persia. In addition, it had a local resource, soapstone, which was much in demand elsewhere and was exported as far as 1,500 miles away. Altintepe dominated two mountain passes from eastern to central Asia Minor. Lubaantun, which stood "at the center of the largest zone of top-quality soil for cacao-tree culture" in its region of British Honduras, traded cacao beans for obsidian, lava stone, and jade from the Guatemalan highlands, and for quetzal plumes from the southern lowlands. The earliest cities thus arose because men found it advantageous to concentrate in particularly favored spots for specialized production and trade. Such concentration minimized the friction of space. Its accomplishment represented a major step in human efficiency.

The transition in much of the world from nomadic camps to larger settlements and eventually to cities was remarkably swift. The hunting camp had prevailed throughout human history, but in a few thousand years a totally new form, cities, was in evidence. The transition was faster than any change that genetic evolution could have produced; it was almost instantaneous when placed in the context of biological evolution. Of course, when looked at in detail in the context of known history, it seems more halting. The city went through a tortuous process of trial and error in which new urban traits randomly appeared and underwent competitive testing. The traits that proved advantageous were those that facilitated production, transport, and trade. Prominent among these were such inventions as wheeled vehicles, animal motive power, roadways, sailboats, water wheels, potter's wheels, metallurgy, writing, coinage, and accounting. Other changes were organizational in character, having to do with governmental centralization and control and with legal systems relating to commerce and property. The speed with which the city as a mode of settlement became a widely distributed, though rare, part of human existence is all the more remarkable in view of the variety of ingredients that had to go into its creation.

It should not be assumed, however, that the persistence of the city as a human creation, once it was started, was reflected in the persistence of particular cities. What was never lost, after its start, was city-building technology, which always survived somewhere. Individual cities, on the other hand, always disappeared, and they often did so in entire regions. Indeed, for thousands of years after their emergence, cities remained few and fragile. Usually the civilization that gave rise to any particular group of cities expired with them, the region reverting to desert or wilderness, sparsely inhabited by primitive cultivators or nomadic tribes. The next wave of city construction often occurred elsewhere. Mayan cities were abandoned in one region as others were being founded in new regions, and the last ones were moribund when the Spaniards arrived. Even when the same region had a second wave of city-building, the interval between the two waves was usually long. Tenochtitlan, the capital of the Aztecs, arose only 40 kilometers from Teotihuacán, but it did so more than 500 years after Teotihuacán had fallen. The site of Tepe Yahyā, abandoned around 2200 B.C., was not reoccupied until 1,200 years later. Even the advanced cities of the Romans were vulnerable. Rome itself became merely a fortified village. It is worth asking what went wrong with these early cities. What made them so fragile? Were they a viable form of human aggregation, or did they carry the seeds of their own destruction?

Although the causes of decline doubtless varied from one region to another, there were certain general weaknesses that affected all of the early cities. Most important is the fact that these cities, especially the earliest ones, were small and their manpower was heavily outnumbered by the manpower of the surrounding rural region. The mound of Altintepe is 600 feet long and about 500 feet wide; the city could have covered only six to ten acres and could hardly have had a population exceeding 200. Tepe Yahyā occupied a site that was about .01 square mile; it could hardly have housed more than 1,500 people. Teotihuacán was much bigger, covering eight square miles and housing around 100,000 people at its height, according to René Millon, but it was the major center of a large and rich region at that time, whereas Altintepe and Tepe Yahyā were outposts. Lubaantún was much smaller than Teotihuacán; Hammond estimates that the entire region of which it was the center covered about 618 square miles and had a population of 50,000. If 2 percent of the region's population lived in the center itself, Lubaantún would have held a thousand people. The early cities were greatly outnumbered not only by the agricultural population in the surrounding hinterland but also by the nomadic hordes in the area beyond. Consequently, despite their advantage of concentration and fortification, the cities could be besieged and cut off from their food supply; and their accumulated wealth made them desirable targets for impoverished outsiders. The latter, while mounting a siege, could themselves forage off the land. The threat of outside attack was thus a constant danger to the earliest cities.

The early cities were also susceptible to natural calamities. Their use of fires for cooking and heating in areas where houses were close-packed subjected them to combustive destruction. Their location in areas with abundant water suitable for irrigation made them frequent victims of floods, a danger exacerbated by the habit of deforesting the surrounding hills in search of firewood and timber. The cities' dependence on crops and herds which were particularly prone to diseases and pests because of their artificial concentration subjected the inhabitants to occasional famines; and the crowding of people themselves, together with their exposure to disease through foreign trade and proximity to stagnant water, led to devastating epidemics. It is little wonder, then, that all of the early cities were eventually either abandoned or overrun by enemies or nomads.

From what we know about their social history we can reasonably conclude that the early cities were also, after their initial achievements, subject to internal political and economic decay. Their conservative and theocratic character, however useful it may have been in inducing diverse classes to work together, was not conducive to quick adjustment to changing conditions. The cities' emphasis on astronomy and mystical symbolism did not give their science a practical turn, and their static conception of the world did not encourage the deliberate fostering of technological advancement. In any particular region the very success of the urban regime might prove ultimately disastrous by virtue of the environmental damages, health hazards, political rivalries, or wasteful extravagances that it caused. Because the city is the most complex form of settlement, it is also potentially the most destructive. In short, although the early cities were creatures of human control over the environment, that control was narrow and tenuous. The cities' capacity to compensate for the destructiveness of their exploitation was slight. They had little ability to cope with deforestation, erosion, salination, and soil exhaustion. Often, therefore, an attack from the outside was only a contributing cause, a final step, in the process of city death. This is why the cities were often overrun by less developed peoples from the wild areas.

Only since the Medieval period has there been a wave of city creation that is continuous up to the present. This wave, having lasted a thousand years and having encircled the globe with cities of enormous number and size, now seems impregnable. It may prove to be so, but some of the past waves seemed impregnable too. Rome was described as eternal, but it lasted about 800 years. The Elamite outpost, Tepe Yahyā, was continuously occupied for 1,300 years, but then it was deserted. There were cities in Arabia Felix for nearly two thousand years, and then the region returned to complete rurality; and people built cities in one part or another of the Mayan area for nearly 700 years before, for reasons that remain obscure, their civilization declined. True, as Sjoberg points out, once cities came into being, the world never went without them again; and now, with the entire world linked in a network of cities, it is tempting to believe that humanity is moving into a permanent condition of city existence. However, the increased capacity to maintain cities has to be weighed against the increased power to destroy them. It is more than simple curiosity that leads us to inquire about the cities of ancient times, even though the lessons they teach may be ambiguous.

Determinants of Urban Growth in Pre-Industrial Societies

BRUCE G. TRIGGER

As a logical follow-up to Davis, the editors have selected a paper by Bruce Trigger that grapples with the question of primary factors in the development of cities prior to the modern period. Trigger establishes four major premises, each of which produces certain testable hypotheses. For example, from his Premise 1 (there is a tendency for human activities to be hierarchical in character and for

"Determinants of Urban Growth in Pre-Industrial Societies" in *Man, Settlement, and Urbanism* (Peter J. Ucko, Ruth Tringham, and G. W. Dimbley, eds.), 1972, pp. 575–599. Cambridge: Schenkman Publishing Co.

this to be reflected in spatial organization), hypothesis A is generated—"the wider the area that a function performed in a single location influences, the less frequently is the function performed in the landscape." Thus, we could try to verify through archeological research whether, as temple centers grow larger and increase their sphere of influence, local temples increasingly relinquish ritual performance to them. This is another way of suggesting that cities grow at the expense of rural institutions.

Trigger then examines 11 factors that he believes to have "promoted increases in the size of urban populations," the factors ranging from food supply increase to secular tourism.

Trigger is especially interested in relating the dual problems of the origin of both city and state. He begins with the rather debatable proposition that "the state is a necessary concomitant of urban life [but] many states have existed without cities," and concludes by arguing that "the largest cities develop as centers of administration and court life and, in particular, there is a tendency as empires develop for a single capital city to tower in size above all others."

This provocative paper is an especially good example of the kind of urban anthropology for which Fox has argued.

Introduction

Anthropological studies of the origins of urban life have been bedevilled by an undue preoccupation with unilineal evolution and evolutionary typology. Anthropologists who have been attracted to these concepts have attempted to discover a single process that would explain the development of all complex societies. Confronted with historical and ethnographic evidence of much greater variation in the economic, social and political organization of nonindustrial civilizations than can be accounted for by a single line of development, they have advanced a series of doubtful arguments to sustain the importance of their formulations.

Some have claimed that "pristine" cases of social evolution (i.e. those uninfluenced by more advanced societies elsewhere) are fundamentally different from all others and that understanding them is vital if later developments are to be explained.[1] Grave doubts exist about which civilizations are "pristine" and about how "pristine" a civilization must be to count as "an independent recurrence of cause and effect."[2] In any case, the resulting sample is too small and too poorly documented to support the ambitious fabric of speculation that has been built upon it. Other evolutionists have deliberately limited their search for regularities to civilizations that have developed in broadly similar environments, such as river valleys located in arid or semi-arid regions.[3]

---

[1] Fried, M. H. (1966). On the evolution of social stratification and the state, *in* Diamond, S. (ed.). *Culture in History: Essays in Honor of Paul Radin.* New York, p. 729; Adams, R. M. (1966). *The Evolution of Urban Society.* Chicago. p. 21. For a critique, see Trigger, B. G. (in press). Archaeology and ecology, *World Archaeology,* 2, (3).

[2] Steward, J. H. (1955). *Theory of Culture Change.* Urbana. p. 182.

[3] Steward, J. H. (1955). op. cit. pp. 178–209.

These societies as well are generally assumed to have enjoyed a priority in the development of civilization. Yet another example of efforts to use facile ecological explanations to restrict the theoretical significance of observed structural variation is the recent suggestion that greater centralization took place in the Inca Empire than in the Aztec one because of the smaller size and wider spacing of central Andean population clusters.[4] Fortunately, no modern anthropologist has carried unilineal ideas as far as has Gideon Sjoberg,[5] who assumes so close an association between writing and urbanism that he feels free to postulate, without additional supporting evidence, that cities are present in all literate cultures and to explain away urban phenomena wherever they occur in the absence of writing.

The shortcomings of a unilineal approach have not been significantly overcome by token efforts to attribute the origins of civilizations to a limited range of primary causal factors, such as irrigation for some and trade for others.[6] What seems to be required is a more piecemeal and institutional approach to complex societies. It is clear, for example, that while the state is a necessary concomitant of urban life, many states have existed without cities.[7] This suggests that for some purposes the development of the city and of complex forms of political organization may profitably be discussed separately. Such investigations will help to determine both the complete range of factors which promote the growth of various institutions and the variety of ways in which these evolving institutions interact with one another.

Not long ago it seemed possible that the discussion of whether or not civilizations can exist without cities might lead anthropologists in this direction.[8] Unfortunately, no intensive studies were made to determine why some civilizations should develop cities and others should not, and recent discussions have sufficiently blurred the distinction between cities and ceremonial centres that the latter concept now appears to have little independent meaning.[9] Moreover, archaeological discoveries have demonstrated the urban status of many key sites formerly believed to be only sparsely or periodically inhibited ritual centres.[10]

Possibly the weakest aspect of current theorizing about the origin of complex societies is the inadequacy of the archaeological evidence which is used to support and nourish it. Virtually nothing is known about the early phases of some civilizations and for most, if not all, our knowledge remains fragmen-

[4] Sanders, W. T. and Marino, J. (1970). *New World Prehistory: Archaeology of the American Indian.* Englewood Cliffs, p. 105.
[5] Sjoberg, G. (1960). *The Preindustrial City.* Glencoe. pp. 32–4, 38.
[6] Steward, J. H. et al. (1960). *Irrigation Civilizations: A Comparative Study.* Washington, Pan American Union, Social Science Monograph 1.
[7] Krader, L. (1968). *Formation of the State.* Englewood Cliffs; Trigger, B. G. (1968). *Beyond History: The Methods of Prehistory.* New York. pp. 52–3.
[8] Wilson, J. A. (1960). Egypt through the New Kingdom: civilization without cities, *in* Kraeling, C. H. and Adams, R. M., *City Invincible.* Chicago. pp. 124–64; Coe, M. D. (1961). Social typology and tropical forest civilizations, *Comparative Studies in Society and History,* **4**, pp. 65–85.
[9] Sanders, W. T. and Marino, J. (1970), op. cit. pp. 7–8.
[10] Millon, R. F. (1967). Teotihuacan, *Sci. Amer.,* **216** (6), pp. 38–48; Haviland, W. A. (1969). A new population estimate for Tikal, *Amer. Antiq.,* 34, pp. 429–33; Parsons, J. R. (1968). An estimate of size and population for Middle Horizon Tiahuanaco, Bolivia, *Amer. Antiq.,* **33**, pp. 243–5.

tary, equivocal and will undoubtedly be subject to major revisions for years to come.[11] Because of this, I propose initially to examine those factors which promote the growth of urbanism in pre-industrial societies from a structural rather than from a genetic or historical point of view. In the following discussion, no distinction will be drawn between city states and cities which are either founded or grow up spontaneously within pre-existing political structures. In this way it is possible to make use of information about a large number of contemporary or historically well-documented cities. In the final section an effort will be made to set these factors into a tentative structural-developmental framework.

Theoretical Orientation

In spite of clear-cut and often highly technical definitions of cities in specific cultures, neither anthropologists nor geographers have been able to agree on a generally acceptable cross-cultural definition of urbanism.[12] Arbitrary definitions based on population size or population density have not won general acceptance, nor can it be agreed that only communities that have a sizable majority of their inhabitants engaged in varied non-agricultural pursuits can be classified as towns or cities.[13] The majority of inhabitants of even the principal Yoruba communities in West Africa worked as farmers, as did many of the inhabitants of the largest communities in ancient Sumer and prehispanic Mexico.[14] On the other hand, in at least some complex societies, many small communities, usually classified as villages, derive most of their income from services they provide for a rural hinterland and few, if any, of the inhabitants of such communities need be agriculturalists. I am thinking in particular of the British village replete with its pub, general store and church. Such communities are functionally distinct from some predominantly agricultural peasant communities and from self-sufficient Neolithic settlements, although all these types of communities are called, depending on their size, villages or

[11] Some authorities are even more pessimistic. Concerning Mesopotamia see, Oppenheim, A. L. (1969). Mesopotamia—land of many cities, in Lapidus, I. R. (ed.). *Middle Eastern Cities*. Berkeley and Los Angeles. p. 4.

[12] Mabogunje, A. L. (1962). *Yoruba Towns*. Ibadan. p. 3.

[13] Many medieval European cities had only a few thousand inhabitants while settlements classified as villages in Eastern Europe had populations that were equal or larger. In parts of China and Indonesia rural population densities have long exceeded 1000 per square mile, the figure that many sociologists have accepted as being indicative of urban settlement. Cressey, G. (1955). *Land of the 500 Million*. New York. p. 15; Huntington, E. (1956). *Principles of Human Geography*. New York. p. 428; cf. Burgess, E. W. (1926). *The Urban Community*. Chicago. pp. 118–19. Fei, H. T. (1953). *China's Gentry*. Chicago. p. 95, points out that the population density of many Chinese cities is no greater than that of rural areas beyond the walls.

[14] Bascom, W. (1955). Urbanization among the Yoruba, *Amer. J. Sociol.*, **60**, pp. 448–9; Bascom, W. (1969). *The Yoruba of Southwestern Nigeria*. New York. pp. 18–28; for a more recent discussion of Yoruba urbanism, see Wheatley, P. (1970). The significance of traditional Yoruba urbanism, *Comparative Studies in Society and History*, **12**, pp. 393–423; Frankfort, H. (1951). *The Birth of Civilization in the Near East*. New York. pp. 61–2; Sanders, W. T. (1956). The Central Mexican symbiotic region, in Willey, G. R. (ed.). *Prehistoric Settlement Patterns in the New World*, Viking Fund Publications in Anthropology, **23**, p. 122.

towns.[15] It is clear that the latter terms have no precise functional or evolutionary significance. Moreover, size alone cannot serve as an index of specialization, at least for small and medium-sized communities.

Armed with this understanding, it is possible if not to define the city at least to suggest a crude working model that has cross-cultural significance. It is generally agreed that whatever else a city may be it is a unit of settlement which performs specialized functions in relationship to a broader hinterland.[16] These functions distinguish urban-type communities from self-sufficient Neolithic villages or hunting bands, whose closed economies produce only for internal consumption. Moreover, while numerous inhabitants of a city may engage in food production, it is agreed that the specialized functions of a city are not agricultural in nature.[17] Food production is often a highly specialized activity and it may be hierarchically organized, as for example, on Roman *latifundia* or with plantation agriculture generally. The specialized relationship between agriculture and the land tends, however, to concentrate similar rather than different specialities in any one area at one time, while surplus produce is marketed at specified points rather than being distributed to a surrounding hinterland. Moreover, in the absence of opposing tendencies, agricultural activities encourage the dispersal rather than the concentration of producers in order to locate them in maximum proximity to the soil they cultivate. These tendencies are the contrary of those involved in the evolution of urban groupings.[18]

On the other hand, the city appears to differ from the small English village mainly in the number and complexity of the functions it performs and in the size of the hinterland it influences. Service villages, towns, and cities are at best arbitrary divisions of a continuum. As Vining[19] has put it "Like pond, pool and lake the terms hamlet, village and town are convenient modes of expression but they do not refer to structurally distinct entities." Definitions based on arbitrary quantitative measures are possible,[20] but for a discussion of factors that promote the growth of urbanism such distinctions are of little importance.

Finally, to round out our model we may note that cities or villages differ from military camps or monasteries, which also perform specialized functions within a larger social setting, by having a community structure composed of

[15] In southern Italy, Sicily and Sardinia, for example, peasant villages or "agro-towns" not infrequently reached a size of 10,000 persons or more. Chisholm, M. (1962). *Rural Settlement and Land Use.* London. pp. 60–1.

[16] Mabogunje, A. L. (1962), op. cit. p. 3–4.

[17] Burgess, E. W. (1926). op. cit. p. 118. For a critical case, see Mabogunje, A. L. (1962). op. cit. pp. 3–4.

[18] Netting, R. M. (1969). Ecosystems in process: a comparative study of change in two West African societies, *in* Damas, D. (ed.). Contributions to Anthropology: Ecological Essays, *National Museums of Canada Bull.* 230, pp. 102–12. I am not, however, at this point trying to draw a precise distinction between rural and urban, a point about which many scholars have failed to agree.

[19] Vining, R. (1955). A description of certain spatial aspects of an economic system, *Economic Development and Cultural Change*, 3, p. 169.

[20] Garner, B. J. (1967). Models of urban geography and settlement location, *in* Chorley, R. J. and Haggett, P. (eds.). *Models in Geography.* London. pp. 324–6.

all ages and both sexes. Such institutions also differ specifically from cities in the limited range of their functions.

In so far as specialized non-agricultural functions are among the generally accepted attributes of urbanism, any discussion of the development of such communities can profitably be set within a framework of more general theories of settlement location as these have been developed by human geographers.[21] Among the premises underlying these theories which are of special importance for understanding urban growth are the following:

1. *There is a tendency for human activities to be hierarchical in character and for this to be reflected in spatial organizations.*

As cultures become more complex, activities which take place within and concern only a single community are supplemented by ones which influence a wider area. These may concern productive, administrative, social, religious or military matters. As a rule, the wider the area that a function performed in a single location influences, the less frequently is the function performed in the landscape. Hence, with increasing complexity, a hierarchy of locations may develop with respect to any one kind of activity, the higher or more specialized functions being performed from a smaller number of centres.

2. *With increasing complexity there is a tendency for activities and social institutions to be more clearly defined and for their personnel to be more highly specialized.*

In complex societies there is an intensive division of labour with individuals specializing in particular types of production, distribution, administration, religious, military and service activities. The organization of these activities, as noted [before], tends to be hierarchical in varying degrees. While some hierarchies, such as those of a craft guild, may be co-extensive with no more than a single community, others, such as a government bureaucracy, may extend over a much broader society. Within these hierarchies a larger number of people perform lower level functions than perform higher level ones.

3. *Human activities tend to be focal in character in order to take advantage of scale economies.*

In order to increase efficiency, activities susceptible to varying degrees of interrelationship tend to be concentrated at a single point. This tendency is governed by rules of accessibility and movement minimization as they relate to the activities concerned.[22] In accordance with these rules, locations which serve one kind of function frequently tend to serve another. In combination with the hierarchical premise outlined [here], such tendencies give rise to a hierarchy of locations varying in terms of accessibility and the size of the area they serve and influence. The scale and density of such a hierarchy of centres

[21] Garner, B. J. (1967). op. cit. pp. 304–5.
[22] Garner, B. J. (1967). op. cit. pp. 304–5 (premises 2 and 3).

will vary according to geographical conditions affecting accessibility and societal factors such as overall population density.

4. *The size of communities tends to vary with the number of functions they perform.*

Various studies which have correlated community size either directly with the number of functions performed or with related measures such as "trade area" or "total population served" have confirmed this observation.[23] This principle, in combination with the hierarchical premise, explains why larger communities are less frequent in a society than are smaller ones. Larger centres perform most types of specialized functions that are performed in smaller centres, but in addition they discharge more specialized functions which are carried out at a more limited number of places. Various studies have investigated regularities in the rank-size of communities in different parts of the world, but mathematical variations between cultures indicate that a considerable range of factors influences rank-size.[24]

Determinants

In this section I wish to examine the range of factors which have been noted as promoting increases in the size of urban populations. These factors include, among others, ones which have led to the formation of cities. They do not include, however, those which influence either the specific location of cities or their internal layout. While many or even all of these factors may influence the size of any single community, my aim is to discuss each factor separately, as far as this is possible. Hence, qualifications which are ignored in one section may be found covered in another.

Among the factors which are, or have been alleged to be, correlated with an increase in the population of pre-industrial urban centres are the following:

1. *An increase in food supply.* It is axiomatic that any community that is to survive must be able to provide a reliable source of food for its members; but how it does so depends upon a variety of economic and political factors. Among some urban groups a considerable amount of food is produced by the inhabitants of the city working on either a full-time or part-time basis in the surrounding countryside. We have already observed that in pre-colonial times nearly all of the Yoruba engaged in agriculture to some degree and Sanders[25] has estimated that a high percentage of the inhabitants of the Aztec capital did the same. During certain periods an "appreciable proportion" of the inhabi-

[23] Garner, B. J. (1967). op. cit. pp. 322–5.
[24] Garner, B. J. (1967). op. cit. pp. 326–9. In Europe and the U.S. the size of cities follows the rule $S_R = \frac{A}{R}$, where A is the size of the largest city, R the rank of a given city and S_R is the size of the city of that rank. Issawi, C. (1969). Economic change and urbanization in the Middle East, *in* Lapidus, I. R. (1969). op. cit. p. 115.
[25] Sanders, W. T. (1956). op. cit. p. 122.

tants of most Islamic Middle Eastern cities have been farmers cultivating adjacent fields.[26] This pattern has continued to the present in some cities such as Damascus[27] and Kerman, Iran (where, in 1956, 13% of the workers were engaged in agriculture[28]). An alternative is for city dwellers to purchase food from farmers in return for manufactured products and professional services. This kind of reciprocal relationship between city and countryside has played an important role in theorizing about the development of European cities.[29] Still others have obtained supplies of food in an exploitive manner. The government officials, soldiers, landlords and skilled artisans who inhabited the traditional Chinese *ch'eng* or administrative towns produced few goods for sale in the surrounding countryside but were fed with food collected from there as rent or taxes.[30]

In pre-industrial societies transportation requires the expenditure of considerable time and human energy; hence even where extensive river systems make transportation relatively easy[31] there is a tendency for bulk items, such as food, to be produced as near as possible to where they are consumed.[32] As demand grows, significant increases in productivity can be achieved through more intensive forms of cultivation, involving processes such as irrigation, fertilization and systematic crop rotation.[33] The efficiency of these more intensive methods of agriculture can be measured as a function of the additional labour that is required compared with the costs of collecting food over a larger hinterland. The ancient trading cities of Arabia, many of which were located astride highly profitable trade routes in the desert, are an extreme example of such developments.[34] There the profits to be derived from trade made a heavy investment in vast catchment areas and systems for flash-flood irrigation worthwhile. These systems, which were expensive not only to build but also to maintain, were abandoned with the collapse of the trade routes which supported them. Other factors may reinforce a trend towards more intensive agriculture. Around Hausa cities in northern Nigeria one finds unusually dense farm populations growing food for an urban market.[35] In this instance intensive agriculture is stimulated not only by demand but also by the additional protection that a farmer receives as a result of living near a city.

Pre-industrial technologies by their very nature impose narrow limitations

[26] Issawi, C. (1969). op. cit. pp. 105–6. In 1877, 57% of Cairo's economically active population was listed as engaged in farming, although this figure may be inflated by too-generous boundaries. By 1910, less than 10% were full-time farmers. Abu-Lughod, J. (1969). Varieties of urban experience: contrast, coexistence and coalescence in Cairo, *in* Lapidus, I. R. (1969). op. cit. p. 164.

[27] Issawi, C. (1969). op. cit. p. 106.

[28] Gulick, J. (1969). Village and city: cultural continuities in twentieth century Middle Eastern cultures, *in* Lapidus, I. R. (1969). op. cit. p. 124.

[29] Weber, M. (1958). *The City*. New York. pp. 65–7.

[30] Fei, H. T. (1953). op. cit. pp. 91–9. For the Near East, see Issawi, C. (1969). op. cit. p. 105.

[31] In his "isolated state" model, von Thünen estimated the cost of river transport at only one-tenth that of land transport. Henshall, J. D. (1967). Models of agricultural activity, *in* Chorley, R. J. and Haggett, P. (1967), op. cit. p. 444.

[32] Heichelhem, F. M. (1958). *An Ancient Economic History*. Leiden, I. pp. 116–38; 222–49.

[33] Netting, R. M. (1969). op. cit.

[34] Bowen, R. L. (1958). Ancient trade routes in South Arabia, *in* Bowen, R. L. and Albright, F. P. (eds.). *Archaeological Discoveries in South Arabia*. Baltimore. pp. 35–42.

[35] Netting, R. M. (1969). op. cit. pp. 109–10.

on the degree to which agricultural production may be intensified and goods may be transported. In the absence of additional complicating factors, these two factors suggest an optimal size to which individual cities may grow and still be able to feed themselves. Under certain circumstances, however, particularly with the growth of empires, the cost of transportation may be rendered less restrictive as far as the feeding of dominant cities is concerned. In the third millennium B.C., the Mesopotamian city of Lagash claimed to have exacted about 10,800 metric tons of grain from the neighbouring city state of Umma as the indemnity for an unsuccessful rebellion [36] and the Aztec capital of Tenochtitlán is estimated to have received 52,600 tons of foodstuffs annually as tribute, in addition to vast amounts of clothing and luxury items. [37] All of these goods had to be transported to the latter city by human carriers. The imperial *annona* of Rome imported vast amounts of grain each year, much of it brought across the Mediterranean from Egypt and North Africa. This grain was paid for out of taxes and tribute that flowed into the imperial treasury and was distributed free to all resident citizens of Rome who wished to apply for it, possibly more than 100,000 people. [38] Foodstuffs from China appear to have supported the Mongol capital of Karakorum, which was founded in the pastoralist heart of a vast empire. [39] Needless to say, the collapse of political power eliminates the economic base which supports such populations.

2. *Increasing population and/or rural unemployment.* All cities depend on an external population as suppliers of food and raw materials and as consumers of their goods and services. A sparse hinterland population increases the cost of transport and communication and this factor is probably important in explaining the general failure of urban-type communities to develop among food collectors, pastoralists or extensive agriculturalists. [40] It would appear that, within the limits of effective agricultural production, the denser the overall population is, the more urban centres it can support.

On the other hand, there does not appear to be any simple mathematical relationship between the population density of a region and the extent of urbanization. The Ibo, for example, did not develop cities although their overall population was about the same as that of the Yoruba and their population density about double. [41] As will become apparent [later], urbanization is influenced by a variety of additional factors. Moreover, under special circumstances it is not impossible for cities to develop in areas with low population densities. Trade cities, such as Petra and Palmyra, grew up in the desert and Karakorum, which was supported by an imperial tributary system, was

[36] Adams, R. M. (1966). op. cit. p. 149.
[37] Adams, R. M. (1966). op. cit. p. 165.
[38] Carcopino, J. (1946). *Daily Life in Ancient Rome*. London. pp. 16–21.
[39] Krader, L. (1968). op. cit. p. 102.
[40] Murdock, G. P. (1969). Correlations of exploitative and settlement patterns, *in* Damas, D. (ed.). op. cit. pp. 129–46.
[41] Bascom, W. (1955). op. cit. p. 452.

founded in a predominately pastoral region. It is significant, however, that cities of both these types ultimately depended upon regions that were densely populated.

Cities also act as an outlet for surplus rural population. This may come about, as it does in many underdeveloped countries, from the failure of more intensive agriculture to absorb a growing rural population.[42] Overpopulation may also come about as a result of new techniques of agriculture displacing a traditional farm population. The development of slave-worked *latifundia* in Roman Italy, as the peasants were conscripted into the army, or the displacement of peasants during the period of the enclosures in Tudor and Stuart England provide examples of such processes.[43] It has been noted for many regions that an influx of rural population has been essential to maintain the population of towns and cities, where high death rates were brought about by poor sanitary conditions and were raised sharply every few years by outbreaks of plague, cholera and other epidemics.[44] It is curious that anthropologists have paid relatively little attention to this factor in building models of rural-urban relations. Sometimes, however, the rural population entering a city exceeds the capacity of the urban economy to provide employment for it. Such immigrants as may remain form a class of urban unemployed; thus constituting a separate category contributing to urban growth. Many tens of thousands of the inhabitants of imperial Rome belonged to this class.[45]

Finally, while urban colonies such as those the Greeks established around the Black Sea and in the western Mediterranean may have been founded mainly for trade, the pressure of population in encouraging this process is not to be ignored. The urban nature of these colonies reflects the deeply established tradition of urban life in the Greek homeland.[46]

3. *Craft specialization.* Handicraft production is an extremely important urban activity and the population of many non-industrial cities has supported itself almost entirely with earnings from it. It has been observed that the nature of manufacturing in urban centres is inherently different from that which occurs elsewhere. My aim is to examine briefly the nature of this difference.

Cities occur in complex, socially stratified societies. In even the most puritanical of such societies, the powerful and the wealthy seek to possess clothing, jewellery, utensils, furniture and houses that are more luxurious than those of ordinary people. These serve both for comfort and as status symbols. The poorer classes may also desire such goods and obtain some of them on a limited scale unless prevented from doing so by sumptuary laws or grinding poverty. The result is a distinction between the everyday tools and imple-

[42] Netting, R. M. (1969). op. cit. pp. 110–11; Issawi, C. (1969). op. cit. p. 106.
[43] Heichelheim, F. M. (1956). Effects of classical antiquity on the land, *in* Thomas, W. L. (ed.). *Man's Role in Changing the Face of the Earth*. Chicago. p. 170.
[44] Issawi, C. (1969). op. cit. p. 106; Forbes, T. R. (1970). Life and death in Shakespeare's London, *Amer. Sci.* **58**, pp. 511–20.
[45] Carcopino, J. (1946). op. cit. pp. 173–4.
[46] For a discussion of the geo-ecology of Greek colonial expansion see McEvedy, C. (1967). *The Penguin Atlas of Ancient History*. Harmondsworth. pp. 10–11.

ments of the lower classes, which usually are manufactured by craftsmen who produce a wide range of goods, and élite items which are produced by specialists who are more highly skilled because they concentrate on a narrower range of work. For example, a Berber housewife may tan skins for her own use but the production of Morocco leather in Fez requires twenty consecutive operations each performed by a different, highly trained work group.[47] Likewise, a master carver may design and add the finishing touches to a piece of work, leaving to apprentices the tedious but less demanding job of chiselling out the design.[48] This kind of a division of labour results not only in a higher level of technical perfection but also in a saving in production costs, since the work can be divided among more and less skilled craftsmen. To coordinate production of this sort an effective hierarchical organization is necessary. This may vary in scale from a master with his journeymen and apprentices to a guild organization which regulates the production of a particular line of goods throughout an entire city or region, setting standards, prices and possibly even production quotas.

In light of the premises outlined [here], two rules can be deduced as governing production of this sort: (1) the more individuals are involved in a production unit, the more they will produce and the larger market they will require and (2) the more specialized and expensive a good is, the fewer people are able to buy it; hence the fewer are the centres in which it can be produced economically. This is true whether the goods are consumed within the community where they are produced (as they may be, for example, where a royal court creates a large internal market for luxury goods) or are exported elsewhere.

Many forms of specialization do not of themselves necessarily induce the development of larger communities. In the following paragraphs I wish to digress briefly to discuss alternative situations in which craft specialization may be carried on. What is pointed out here also applies to the specialized activities associated with administration, religion, defence and education, which are discussed [later]. Limitations of space prevent a similar detailed examination of each of these topics under its respective heading.

Even the most primitive craft production is specialized, if only along age and sex lines. However, specialization beyond what is possible in the closed economy of a Neolithic village can be achieved in other ways than by centralizing it in towns and cities. In various parts of the world, neighbouring villages participate in trading networks which provide a wider market for the agricultural produce and manufactured goods of all concerned.[49] Such an arrangement allows the craftsmen in any one village, who may also be part-time farmers, to concentrate on the production of a single line of goods such as pottery, leather objects or metalware, thus permitting specialization resembling

[47] Coon, C. S. (1962). *Caravan: The Story of the Middle East.* New York. p. 242.
[48] Coon, C. S. (1962). op. cit. p. 238.
[49] Coon, C. S. (1962). op. cit. pp. 178–9; Benet, F. (1957). Explosive markets: the Berber Highlands, *in* Polanyi, K. et al. (eds.). *Trade and Market in the Early Empires.* Glencoe. pp. 188–213; Malinowski, B. (1922). *Argonauts of the Western Pacific.* London.

that found in larger centres. In terms of the specialization involved, very little would appear to separate a well-developed system of this sort from the Yoruba situation, where although craft production occurs in an urban setting it is carried on largely by part-time specialists. Yet another way to increase markets if demand is low is for itinerant craftsmen to wander from group to group offering their services.[50]

Nevertheless both methods suffer from certain inherent limitations: (a) the necessity for craftsmen to transport either their produce in bulk to market or their tools to wherever their services are required and (b) their failure to bring potentially related crafts into proximity with one another, thus limiting the degree to which interdependence and further specialization can develop. By its very nature, itinerant production is associated with relatively simple technologies which require little permanent equipment. The specialized and bulky tools needed for crafts such as glassmaking would almost certainly preclude this pattern of production.[51]

Even in urbanized societies goods are not infrequently produced in nonurban settings. This may be for economic or institutional reasons or both. In Roman Britain, tile factories and leather and metal working establishments were attached to certain military camps in order to supply the needs of the army.[52] In part, this was done to avoid the transportation costs involved in moving goods from the civil zone of southern England into the military zones in the north and west. Yet it may also reflect the desire of a major institution, the Roman army, to economize and at the same time to be more independent by supplying its own necessities. A similar desire for self-sufficiency can be noted (this time in an urban setting) in the Sumerian temple communities,[53] or on Roman estates which often had their own mills, iron foundaries and potteries. It has been pointed out that while the manufactured products of these estates were occasionally exported, manufacturing was generally carried out to supply internal requirements. Thus there was little impetus for improving the techniques or increasing productivity.[54]

On the other hand, the dispersal of some only moderately specialized industries, such as the potteries producing Castor Ware, which were spread out over 20 square miles in the Nene Valley in Roman Britain, may have been carried out for solid economic reasons; in this case to achieve savings by locating close to sources of bulky raw materials such as clay and wood used for firing kilns.[55] The nearby town of Durobrivae served as a marketing centre for this industry. Likewise, the production of carpets in many parts of the Near

[50] Hodges, H. (1970). *Technology in the Ancient World*. London. pp. 212–13; Coon, C. S. (1962). op. cit. p. 305.
[51] Hodges, H. (1970). op. cit. p. 213.
[52] Frere, S. (1967). *Britannia: A History of Roman Britain*. London. pp. 226–8.
[53] Frankfort, H. (1956). op. cit. pp. 64–73.
[54] Hodges, H. (1970). op. cit. p. 197; Heichelheim, F. M. (1956). op. cit. p. 174.
[55] Gilbert, E. W. (1951). The human geography of Roman Britain, *in* Darby, H. C. (ed.). *An Historical Geography of Britain Before A.D. 1800*. Cambridge. p. 76; Phillips, C. W. (1956). *Map of Roman Britain*. Chessington, Ordnance Survey. Fig. 3.

East, while organized by city merchants, is carried on as a cottage industry in the villages.[56]

Yet in spite of these partial exceptions, it would appear that in most industries the degree of specialization which is possible and desired in complex societies is most frequently achieved only by the concentration of different kinds of manufacturing in a common centre. The proximity of related trades encourages greater interdependence and hence more specialization. For example, in such situations the production of tools and the working up of raw materials for various crafts can be left to other specialists, whereas if each craft is geographically separate workmen normally prepare their own tools and materials.[57] Such concentration reflects the general rule that nonagricultural activities tend to be focal in character to take advantage of scale economies.

Another result of scale economies is that, whatever else major cities manufacture, each tends to specialize in the production of a limited range of items that have a national or international reputation. In the ancient Mediterranean sphere, cities were famous "for the presence within their walls of one or two main technologies such as making of pottery or glassware, or the manufacture of jewellery. . . ."[58] Similar observations have also been made concerning Islamic, Chinese and South Asian cities and also for cities in the New World.[59] Low-cost handicrafts for which there is a popular market tend to be produced in a large number of cities and because they do not repay transportation costs they normally do not circulate beyond the local hinterlands of these cities. However, as we have already noted, the more specialized goods become, the fewer are the centres in which any one item can be produced economically. This gives rise to a hierarchy of cities which produce for local, local and regional, and local, regional and international markets respectively; with the size of the city normally varying according to its position in the hierarchy (size being roughly determined by the number of functions a city performs). In medieval Fez, for example, over 20,000 persons were employed in weaving, but much of the cloth produced was either used locally or sold in the surrounding countryside. On the other hand, a limited amount of very expensive cloth and most of the production of the city's famous tanning and leather goods industries were exported all over the Arab world.[60] By itself, this hierarchical tendency does not appear to generate a pyramidal structure with one exceptionally large city in each major region producing the greatest amount of specialized goods. Instead, as has been observed in the Middle East and the Mediterranean,[61] it tends to produce a network of major cities each of which

---

[56] English, P. W. (1966). *City and Village in Iran.* Madison. p. 67.

[57] Le Tourneau, R. (1961). *Fez in the Age of the Marinides.* Norman. pp. 90–1.

[58] Hodges, H. (1970). op. cit. p. 212.

[59] Coon, C. S. (1962). op. cit. pp. 229–30; Fei, H. T. (1953). op. cit. pp. 91–9; Crane, R. I. (1955). Urbanism in India, *Amer. J. Sociol.,* **60,** pp. 463–70; Sanders, W. T. and Price, B. J. (1968). *Mesoamerica: The Evolution of a Civilization.* New York. pp. 30–33.

[60] Le Tourneau, R. (1961). op. cit. pp. 88–93.

[61] Coon, C. S. (1962). op. cit. pp. 229–31; Hodges, H. (1970). op. cit. p. 212; for a discussion of factors distorting this pattern, see Issawi, C. (1969). op. cit. p. 231.

produces one, or at most a few, major specialities which are then exchanged throughout the system. At a higher level of specialization and on a larger overall scale, such cities are analogous to the villages participating in a reciprocal trading pattern.

4. *Marketing and trade.* More specialized production increases the need for mechanisms to distribute what is being produced. Where craftsmen are attached to the royal court or are employed by institutions such as the church or army, these organizations normally supervise the distribution of goods. In this manner, such organizations become major subsystems within the economy and their activities give rise to corps of specialists concerned with storage, transportation and keeping accounts.

Bilateral exchange takes place at the most basic level by a producer selling his goods either in his own shop or in the market place. Increasing complexity tends, however, to produce specialists who are concerned exclusively with the buying and selling of produce. These may be either market women travelling between country and town, retail merchants who sell goods within the community or wholesale import-export merchants who carry on long-distance trade. Auxiliary to these merchants are men who transport goods and craftsmen who construct and maintain the means of transportation. In the thirteenth century, the population of Cairo was reported to have included the crews of 36,000 Nile boats and 30,000 renters of mules and donkeys.[62]

Even in urban societies trade, like production, goes on in non-urban settings. Many rural Celtic temples in Roman Britain were the site of periodic fairs.[63] These temples were often located near tribal borders and in pre-Roman times they had probably served as neutral meeting places between rival groups. In the Roman period, the rural trade at such temples was supplementary to that in the cantonal (tribal) capitals.[64] Long-distance trade was centered in the towns rather than at these rural sites because the former were also centres of production, because of the scale economies that were gained through centralization and because of the greater security and protection that urban centres offered.

Because of the high cost of transportation in non-industrial societies, long-distance trade is restricted mainly to goods and materials that are of great value or can be produced only in limited areas. Otherwise local copies would drive the more expensive imported items off the market.[65] In such societies, leading import-export merchants are often among the wealthiest members of an urban community. Some may be resident foreigners and occasionally such merchants may live in special communities on the outskirts of native cities, as Assyrian traders did at Kanesh and other places in Anatolia early in the sec-

[62] Coon, C. S. (1962). op. cit. p. 231.
[63] Collingwood, R. G. and Richmond, I. (1969). *The Archaeology of Roman Britain*. London. pp. 158–9; Rivet, A. L. F. (1964). *Town and Country in Roman Britain*. London. p. 134.
[64] This arrangement corresponds with G. W. Skinner's model of periodic central places. See Garner, B. J. (1967). op. cit. pp. 320–2.
[65] Frere, S. (1967). op. cit. pp. 289–93.

ond millennium B.C.[66] Even in Mesopotamian cities, traders appear to have lived in a special "harbour" district in a manner which suggests that the society as a whole perceived a significant cleavage between the activities of the merchants and those of the city proper. Oppenheim[67] suggests that the failure to discover references to overland trade in the texts from Sippar may be because once merchants became rich they invested their money in land before moving from the unexcavated "harbour" area into the city. In spite of many privileges, Aztec long-distance traders had a similar, somewhat culturally anomalous relationship to their society.[68] In medieval Europe, on the other hand, rich merchants often played a key role in the political life of towns and cities.

Numerous studies indicate the importance of long-distance trade for the development of urbanism in many parts of the world. The cities of the Levant appear to have flourished as trading centres, first between Mesopotamia and Egypt and later between the Mediterranean and regions farther east.[69] In addition to being collecting centres for the incense trade, the cities that developed in the first millennium B.C. in south Arabia were entrepôts in vast networks of trade that embraced India, East Africa and the Mediterranean.[70] Long-distance trade also may have played an important role in the development of civilization in the Aegean area, although in pre-Classical times it appears to have supported urban populations on only a modest scale.[71] Henri Pirenne[72] has brilliantly documented the importance of trade for the revival and development of urban life in medieval Europe. The effectiveness of trading cities often has depended upon their independence of rival foreign powers; hence we have examples of powerful states recognizing the freedom of vulnerable coastal trading cities, such as Sidon and Tyre, or "desert ports," like Petra and Palmyra.[73] In so far as a city is dependent upon long-distance trade, its prosperity and population can be adversely affected if political or economic changes lead to a decline in trade or if alternative trade routes are discovered. Where trade constitutes the main resource of a city such developments may lead to its total collapse.

5. *Landlords.* In pre-industrial cities live numerous families and individuals whose ancestors made large fortunes and whose income is derived largely or wholly from investments in land and other forms of real estate.[74] In China,

---

[66] Özgüç, T. (1963). An Assyrian trading post, *Sci. Amer.* **208**, (2), pp. 96–106; Lloyd, S. (1961). The early settlement of Anatolia, in Piggott, S. (ed.). *The Dawn of Civilization.* London. pp. 170–4; 188.

[67] Oppenheim, A. L. (1969). op. cit. pp. 6, 11.

[68] Soustelle, J. (1962). *Daily Life Among the Aztecs.* New York. pp. 59–65.

[69] Culican, W. (1961). The sea peoples of the Levant, in Piggott, S. (ed.). op. cit. pp. 151–60.

[70] Heichelheim, F. M. (1958). op. cit. pp. 236–8.

[71] Renfrew, C. (1969). Trade and culture process in European pre-history, *Curr. Anthrop.*, **10**, pp. 131–69.

[72] Pirenne, H. (1925). *Medieval Cities.* Princeton.

[73] Revere, R. B. (1957). "No Man's Coast": ports of trade in the eastern Mediterranean, in Polanyi, K. et. al. (eds.). op. cit. pp. 38–63; see also Chapman, A. M. (1957). Port of trade enclaves in Aztec and Maya Civilizations, in Polanyi, K. et al. (eds.). op. cit. pp. 114–53.

[74] Coon, C. S. (1962). op. cit. p. 245.

many landlords lived in the walled *ch'engs* or administrative towns. They were supported by the income from their lands but preferred to reside in the cities because life there was more interesting and because these well-garrisoned towns offered protection to their lives and household property against peasant uprisings.[75]

6. *Administration.* Urban centres require administration to coordinate the various groups who inhabit them. Within a city one finds government officials, legal officers, police and sometimes public utility workers whose basic concern is with maintaining order and keeping the public sector operating. Large communities are frequently divided into districts along kinship, ethnic or occupational lines. In these cases the city government may be organized on a two or more tiered system, with perhaps only the officials on the highest level being full-time specialists.[76]

Cities also frequently serve as centres of administration for larger political units. Occasionally, where the political structure is weak and decentralized, as it was in medieval Europe, rural castles rather than cities served as administrative centres for the surrounding countryside. Even in feudal societies, however, the ruling élite frequently prefer to live in cities.[77]

In city-states, such as those in ancient Mesopotamia, Greece or prehispanic Mexico, the city administration may also be the government of the entire state. In such cases, the added role of defending the state may provide employment for considerable numbers of professional soldiers and artisans who specialize in making military equipment and these activities may require considerable hierarchical organization.[78] An even greater need for administrators, as well as for soldiers and artisans, is found in city-states that have acquired political hegemony over their neighbours or in cities that are founded as administrative centres within larger pre-existing political units. In these cities, and particularly in those that contain a royal court, there is also a thirst for ostentation which provides employment for large numbers of retainers and artisans. The palace staff at Susa in Early Dynastic III times numbered about 950 men and women; after Mesopotamia was unified by Sargon I in the succeeding period, 5400 men are reported to have eaten daily in the royal palace.[79]

The increased population of capital cities is supported by tribute which may be collected in the form of food, raw materials and manufactured goods. The control that rulers exercise over the distribution of this tribute constitutes an additional source of power for them and helps produce a more stratified society than might otherwise be possible or tolerated. For example, one of the functions which enhanced the power of the Aztec emperor was his ability to distribute food and clothing to the inhabitants of Tenochtitlán during one en-

[75] Fei, H. T. (1953). op. cit. pp. 91–9.
[76] For an example, see Le Tourneau, R. (1961). op. cit. pp. 36–43.
[77] Issawi, C. (1969). op. cit. p. 105.
[78] Adams, R. M. (1966). op. cit. pp. 139–40.
[79] Adams, R. M. (1966). op. cit. p. 143.

tire month each year.[80] It would appear that anthropologists have generally underestimated the role of conquest as a means by which a particular city or ruling group can increase its access to wealth. Oppenheim has argued that "real prosperity came to a Mesopotamian city only when it had in its midst the palace of a victorious king."[81] While an ordinary city was poor and a prey to invading armies, the sanctuary and palace of a dominant city were sumptuously adorned and traders, craftsmen and retainers flocked thither to serve its ruler. Not infrequently, the rulers of conquered regions, along with their retainers, were settled for safe-keeping in these cities as well. As a result of their role as centres of administration, political control and court life, cities that were the capitals of successful empires or tributary systems often came to exceed in size any other cities within their sphere of influence.[82]

Some capitals, such as Rome and Tenochtitlán, began as city-states but as they acquired control over an increasing number of other city-states and regions they expanded greatly in size. Other cities are founded, or designated by decree, to be the centres of administration and court life for existing states. Babylon grew to be the largest city in Mesopotamia after it was selected to be the capital by the second ruler of the Hammurabi dynasty.[83] When the city of Fez, which had hitherto been a centre of craft production, was designated as the capital of the Marinide empire in the thirteenth century, its rulers left the old city largely intact but founded a smaller new district about 750 yards to the east of it. This new city, later called Fez Jedid (New Fez), contained the palace of the sovereign, the residences of principal court dignitaries and two quarters occupied by foreign troops loyal to the king, as well as eventually the Jewish ghetto, which was under royal protection.[84] While the Old City was governed by functionaries appointed by the king, who acted in consultation with leaders nominated by the notables of the community, Fez Jedid was under direct royal rule. When the king was away fighting or touring the provinces, the official city was largely abandoned.

While cities may grow to exceptional size as the actual centre or as symbols of political power, the withdrawal of such support can very quickly undermine their ability to support the population they have acquired. Assur was abandoned with the fall of the Assyrian Empire[85] and following the disintegration of Roman power in the West in the fifth century A.D. Rome declined, to become a small town. Even more dramatic fates may befall capitals in states which remain large and prosperous. The ancient Egyptian city of Akhetaton was founded, overtly for religious reasons, as a new court centre. Within a few years its houses, palaces and temples sprawled along eight miles of river front and the city functioned as the administrative centre of the Egyptian em-

[80] Soustelle, J. (1962). op. cit. p. 85.
[81] Oppenheim, A. L. (1964). *Ancient Mesopotamia*. Chicago. p. 117.
[82] See also Bray, W., pp. 909–26.
[83] Lambert, W. G. (1964). The reign of Nebuchadnezzar I, in McCulloch, W. S. (ed.). *The Seed of Wisdom*. Toronto, pp. 3–11.
[84] Le Tourneau, R. (1961). op. cit. pp. 15–19.
[85] See also Oates, D., pp. 799–804.

pire. Yet, following the rejection of its founder's religious innovations, the court left the city and only a few decades after the city had begun the site was once again uninhabited.[86] Likewise, the vast city of Samarra was founded in A.D. 836 by the Caliph Mu'tasim on a site removed from the major trade routes of the Near East but also remote from the political turmoil of the previous capital of Baghdad. Despite the compulsory settlement of thousands of merchants and artisans in the new city, it endured for less than fifty years before another political shift led to its abandonment.[87]

In political units that are larger than city states there is a tendency for secondary administrative centres to arise. In keeping with a hierarchical political organization, these cities usually contain a smaller number of soldiers and administrators than does a capital; hence they are usually smaller. Like capitals, they may be new foundations built for an express purpose or their administrative functions may have been grafted on to an existing community.

Depending on the general nature of the political organization, secondary administrative centres serve a variety of different functions.[88] The Chinese *ch'eng* was inhabited by the emperor's representative and government officials, with a garrison to support them. Often there was arable land within the city walls so that food might be grown in time of siege. The purpose of such a city was to uphold royal authority in the region and to see that taxes were collected. Fei[89] has described them as instruments of power in the hand of the ruling classes, a symbol of power and a necessity to keep it. On the other hand, the largest towns in Roman Britain, apart from London, which was the commercial and administrative centre for the whole province, were mainly cantonal (tribal) capitals. These towns, which had been founded by the Roman conquerors as centres of regional self-government and which were the meeting places of the cantonal councils, were provided with civic centres and market places, baths, temples, official inns and some place of amusement. Apart from their minor political functions these communities had obviously been founded as centres of Roman life for the acculturating, and hopefully ever more pro-Roman, tribal aristocracy of Britain. In spite of the development of considerable handicraft industries in some of these towns, none ever acquired a particularly large population nor were the cantons ever viewed as city-states by the inhabitants of these communities. Instead the towns continued to be viewed in a totally un-Roman way as regional centres.[90] Secon-

---

[86] Pendlebury, J. D. S. (1937). *Tell el-Amarna*. London.

[87] Adams, R. M. (1965). *Land Behind Baghdad*. Chicago. p. 90.

[88] In a recent study, C. Morris and D. E. Thompson have concluded that Huanaco Viejo, an Inca community in the North Central Highlands of Peru, was a regional centre created by the Inca rulers to serve a series of functions vital to the perpetuation and expansion of the state. Their statement that "the image of an artificial, essentially imposed, population centre . . . contrasts markedly with some of our notions of 'urban' and 'city' " provides evidence of the narrow basis on which many archaeologists' concepts of these entities are founded. Morris, C. and Thompson, D. E. (1970). Huanaco Viejo: an Inca administrative centre, *Amer. Antiq.*, 35, pp. 344–362.

[89] Fei, H. T. (1953). op. cit. p. 95.

[90] Rivet, A. L. F. (1964). op. cit. pp. 72–98; Frere, S. (1967). op. cit. pp. 239–63; Collingwood, R. G. and Richmond, I. (1969). op. cit. pp. 95–132; Richmond, I. A. (1963). *Roman Britain*. Harmondsworth. pp. 66–108.

dary administrative centres also frequently offer inns and other amenities for travelling officials and for the central courier service, and these provide employment for numerous servants who are also urban dwellers.[91]

7. *Defence.* The defence of cities is sometimes a source of specialized employment for some of their inhabitants, although the men so employed may not necessarily be distinct from the soldiers who are part of the administrative-military complex. Throughout most of the Old World, cities were surrounded by walls which protected them against attacks and political coercion or made them a strong point for dominating the surrounding countryside.[92] The absence of walls in this area can generally be correlated with a strong central government which was capable of defending and policing its entire territory in a rigorous manner.[93] In the Near East, the different wards of a city were often separated by walls pierced only by narrow gates that could be barred at night;[94] thus supporting the observation that walls are constructed not only as defences against an external enemy but also to protect a city against internal disorder and brigandage. Such concerns with internal security reflect the general inefficiency of law enforcement in many pre-industrial societies.

The security against external threats that large communities can offer men and property accounts in part for the tendency of farmers to settle in or near urban centres, in so far as this is possible. Wars in the early nineteenth century stimulated the growth of the large Yoruba cities at least partly in this manner.[95] Insecurity in the Islamic world explains the presence of a farming population in cities such as Damacus[96] and similar factors have been seen at work in the development of urbanism in Mesopotania.[97] Even more urgently, however, wherever there is danger palaces, large temples, valued industries and the houses of the rich seek the protection of large centres. While the protection of such units is possible in a dispersed setting, as can be seen in the case of Egyptian temple complexes with their fortified temenos walls, considerable economies can be effected by concentrating as much valuable property as possible in a single fortified location. Where there is danger, the natural course seems to be for the specialized institutions of society to huddle together behind some sort of fortification.

Cities also grow through the forced settlement of dangerous elements within them. We have already noted the forced removal of hostages, or entire defeated élites, to the cities of their conquerors. The Bedouin population of the Near East is difficult to control and represents a threat to authority; hence

[91] Collingwood, R. G. and Richmond, I. (1969). op. cit. pp. 122–3.

[92] It is curious that while the city states of prehispanic Mexico resembled those of ancient Mesopotamia in many ways, they appear only rarely to have been walled (although some were fortified in terms of their location). To my knowledge, the reasons for this difference have not been discussed.

[93] Few urban settlements in Roman Britain were fortified before the second century A.D. For reasons for fortifying, see Frere, S. (1967). op. cit. pp. 248–57.

[94] Le Tourneau, R. (1961). op. cit. p. 26; Issawi, C. (1969). op. cit. pp. 107–8.

[95] Mabogunje, A. L. (1962). op. cit. pp. 8–10.

[96] Issawi, C. (1969). op. cit. pp. 105–6.

[97] Falkenstein, A. (1954). La cité-temple sumérienne, *Cahiers d'histoire mondiale*, I, p. 810.

powerful sedentary governments have frequently attempted to make them settle down, either as farmers or in cities as government-employed mercenaries.[98]

Large states often seek to protect their frontiers with complex systems of fortifications. The ancient Egyptian cataract forts, the Great Wall of China and the Roman *limites* provide examples of such fortifications.[99] As much as 5% of the total population of Roman Britain may have been employed as soldiers along the northern and western frontiers of the province.[100] The nature of these latter defences required that most soldiers be dispersed in a large number of small camps. While such an arrangement does not give rise to large urban concentrations, the British defence complex did support several towns which functioned as supply centres and gave rise to four colonies of veterans. Small settlements of merchants and craftsmen also grew up outside many of the forts and some of these achieved the status of self-governing towns (*vici*).[101] Many famous Arab cities, such as Basra, Kufa, Fustat and Kairouan began as military camps which the Arab armies founded on the edge of the desert and from which they dominated conquered territory.[102].

8. *Religion.* In complex societies, official religious organizations, like those of a governmental or military nature, tend to be hierarchized, with the upper echelons administering a heavy investment in property and trained personnel. While religious concepts may dictate that certain temples and other religious buildings be located in rural settings, the major institutions are usually situated in urban centres. The largest and most important temples are often in the centre of the city, thus expressing in spatial terms the theological rationalization of the unity of the city or state.[103] In turn, the various divisions of the city may have their own subsidiary cult centres, each located in its respective quarter. Altogether, such temples support a considerable number of priests and clerks and provide work for numerous urban craftsmen who might otherwise not find employment.

In ethnically heterogeneous empires or areas where an international religion predominates, the correlation between the political and religious hierarchies may not be so close as it is where national or ethnic religions prevail. In order to assure greater independence, the religious organization may prefer to have its headquarters elsewhere than in an important secular centre. In such cases, the presence of religious administrative and cult functions may contribute greatly to the prosperity and population of a smaller

[98] Oppenheim, A. L. (1964). op. cit. pp. 57, 118.
[99] For Egypt, see Kees, H. (1961). *Ancient Egypt: A Cultural Topography.* Chicago. p. 317.
[100] Frere, S. (1967). op. cit. p. 309.
[101] Rivet, A. L. F. (1964). op. cit. p. 66.
[102] Issawi, C. (1969). op. cit. p. 107.
[103] Cf. Soustelle, J. (1962). op. cit. p. 8; Oppenheim, A. L. (1964). op. cit. p. 130. The classic study of the relationship between the religious and civil institutions of a city remains Fustel de Coulanges, N. D. (1864). *La Cité Antique.* Paris. Paul Wheatley notes that it is no surprise that in China, with its worldly Great Tradition, the centrally situated temple of South Asian cities was replaced by the seat of secular authority. Wheatley, P. (1969). *City as Symbol.* London. pp. 12–13.

urban community. Medieval London and Canterbury provide an example of such a contrast between a secular and a religious centre.

Religious pilgrimages may also be a factor contributing to urban growth. The inhabitants of Mecca derive much of their income from the annual Moslem pilgrimage, mainly from the fees they charge for the food and accommodation they provide for pilgrims. Mecca was both a local cult centre and a trading community in pre-Islamic times, but it is doubtful that today without the pilgrimage it would be anything more than a small village, if it existed. Other cities in the Near East and Europe derive a supplementary income from religious tourism which occurs either periodically or throughout the year.[104]

9. *Secular tourism.* Secular travel and relaxation also provide a livelihood for urban dwellers. Inns, either privately or officially managed, are a feature of many towns and cities. These provide accommodation for travelling merchants and government officials and also for the individual travelling for pleasure. On occasion in the ancient world even whole towns served as tourist resorts. Roman examples include the aristocratic beach resort of Baiae in Italy and British towns such as Bath, or Corbridge and Carlisle, which in addition to being military storehouses functioned as holiday towns for soldiers stationed along Hadrian's Wall.[105]

10. *Education.* Another source of population for urban centres is provided by educational institutions. Formal instruction appears to constitute a part-time or full-time profession in all ancient civilizations, but some towns, such as Athens in the Hellenistic and Roman periods, attracted teachers and students in large numbers.[106] In the Middle Ages, Islamic theological schools housed many thousands of students, while their teachers played an important role in the political and intellectual life of the cities in which they were located. For the most part these schools were located in the political capitals, which have always been the main cultural centres in the Islamic world. In Europe, major educational institutions also developed in smaller communities, such as Cambridge, Salamanca, Coimbra and Uppsala, where their contribution to the support of a local population was proportionately much greater.[107]

11. *Retainers.* It is also in the nature of urban life to give rise to considerable numbers of people whose sole occupation is to provide personal services for other people. Some of these services are of a utilitarian nature, such as the water supplied by 12,000 camel-driving haulers in medieval Cairo.[108] Other less utilitarian ones reflect the tendency of the wealthy and powerful to indulge in luxury and conspicuous consumption. As a result of this, cooks,

[104] Issawi, C. (1969). op. cit. p. 106.
[105] Frere, S. (1967). op. cit. p. 240.
[106] Graindor, P. (1934). *Athènes sous Hadrian.* Cairo.
[107] Issawi, C. (1969). op. cit. p. 118.
[108] Coon, C. S. (1962). op. cit. p. 231.

household servants, personal attendants and professional entertainers swell the population. The numbers of such retainers tend to be correlated with the general prosperity of the city and hence they occur with the greatest frequency in court centres and cities whose economy is swollen by conquest. Huge numbers were incorporated into the population of imperial Rome.[109]

Integration

Krader[110] has recently reminded us that the state has had not one origin but many; the same is certainly true of the city.

Among the conditions which have been seen as necessary for the development of urbanism is the achievement of a population density which is sufficiently great that it must be dependent upon intensive agriculture. In a recent survey, Murdock[111] found that 56% of societies practising intensive agriculture have cities larger than 50,000 whereas only 18.5% live entirely in villages of 200 persons or less. Only a tiny number of groups classified as dependent on horticulture or extensive agriculture have towns of 5000 or over. This suggests that intensive agriculture is a necessary but not a sufficient condition for the development of urbanism. In at least some regions, more intensive agriculture appears to be a result rather than a cause of increasing urbanism.[112]

The state is also a necessary but not a sufficient condition for, or the concomitant of, the development of urbanism. The functioning of a city requires the development of a political apparatus at least as complex as that of a city state. On the other hand, states controlling a vast area have developed in Africa and elsewhere without the development of cities. The variety of ways in which states evolve provides numerous institutional milieux in which cities may develop.

Cities have been defined as population centres which perform a variety of functions in relationship to hinterlands of varying size. As the existence of cityless states indicates, however, even in some complex societies the forces which tend to concentrate functions at a single point may not be strong enough to give rise to cities. We have already noted the variety of ways in which specialized production can be carried on at a village level or in country estates. Trading can take place at periodic markets or through redistributive networks embedded in the social fabric, administration be centered in a feudal castle and defence provided by a local hill-fort. Collective religious observances may be held in rural shrines where the worshippers gather periodically. In theory, each of these functions could be carried out at a separate

[109] Carcopino, J. (1946). op. cit. pp. 68–72.
[110] Krader, L. (1968). op. cit. p. 106.
[111] Murdock, G. P. (1969). op. cit. p. 146.
[112] Murdock, G. P. (1969). op. cit. p. 147; Netting, R. M. (1969). op. cit. pp. 109–10.

centre or group of centres, some of which would require no full-time personnel and none of which would have to be larger than a village.

Nevertheless, such an arrangement has inherent limitations. Even when transportation is relatively easy, such decentralization limits the efficiency with which individual functions can be interrelated and this in turn imposes restrictions upon the specialization which any one function can achieve. Therefore, with increasing cultural complexity one would expect different functions to converge on a common centre, even though the pattern of convergence may differ considerably from one society to another. By concentrating a number of specialized functions in one place movement is minimized, greater interdependence is possible and the more valuable property and personnel of a society can be protected more easily. In complex societies the tendency can be noted for a number of different functions to be performed even in very small centres (i.e. villages). Given sufficient complexity, this focal tendency appears likely at some point to give rise to the large multifunctional units we call cities. At what point this will happen depends not only upon the overall complexity of the society but also upon factors such as the ease or difficulty of transportation or the degree of security that can be offered on a regional as opposed to a local basis. There is little doubt, for example, that the security offered by a central government in Egypt was less conducive to the clustering of population than were the competing city states of ancient Mesopotamia.[113]

It has been noted that in a general way the size of urban populations tends to vary in relationship to the number of functions they perform. However, the number of different types of functions that any one city acquires, and the order in which individual cities do so, vary widely. For example, the coordination of specialized production units and competition over scarce local resources are seen as two of the principal factors leading to the development of city states.[114] There has, however, been considerable speculation about the types of community that serve as the nuclei for such developments. Agricultural villages with an expanding division of labour, periodic markets, cult centres and forts, possibly inhabited by a local headman and his retainers, have been suggested as possibilities and perhaps, under differing circumstances, each of these types has served as the starting point for a city.[115] Warfare is clearly a potent force promoting the consolidation of such centres, often driving even farmers to seek protection with a city's wall. The urban centres of city states which embark on successful military careers grow in size as the army and bureaucracy expand. Such growth is amplified as the requirements of the army and a royal court lead to further increases in the numbers of artisans and retainers who inhabit the city.

[113] Frankfort, H. (1956). op. cit. pp. 97–8.
[114] Sanders, W. T. and Price, B. J. (1968). op. cit. pp. 170–210.
[115] Trigger, B. G. (1968). The determinants of settlement patterns, in Chang, K. C. (ed.). *Settlement Archaeology.* Palo Alto. pp. 72–3.

Trade has also stimulated the development of cities in many parts of the world, sometimes even in infertile regions where great effort is required to feed a large population. Many Near Eastern trading communities were dominated by a powerful leader who was responsible for the defence of the city and its trade routes. In western Europe, where the countryside was controlled by feudal lords, cities tended to specialize as centres of trade and craft production, with auxiliary religious and educational functions. It is worth noting, however, that at least some of these towns developed out of communities which had survived through the Dark Ages as religious administration centres.

Some states which control large areas arise prior to urban development. Such growth may result from efforts to control trade routes or to extract exotic goods as tribute from neighbouring groups.[116] The first cities which develop in such states tend to be garrison towns and centres of administration and court life, around which traders, religious specialists, craftsmen and retainers may congregate as appendages of royal power. The demands of the royal court and of the army may be a strong inducement to economic specialization in such societies.

Within a large, well-established state additional cities are found as centres for administration, defence, production, trade, religion, education and tourism. [This] tendency . . . for centres serving one function to acquire others frequently results in cities founded for very different reasons growing functionally more similar as they increase in size. In spite of this, differences in patterns of city growth and in the overall social milieu in which this growth takes place may continue to be clearly marked in their social structure. For example, craft production played an important part in the development of many cities in medieval Europe and the Near East and the guild structure of both is roughly similar. On the other hand, because Moslem cities were also chosen as the principal residences of powerful dynastic rulers they failed to develop traditions of self-government, unlike European cities which grew up outside the general feudal political order.

Finally, it is clear that some factors promote the growth of cities more powerfully than do others. Retainers are, in effect, a measure of the affluence of a non-industrial city's upper-class. Likewise, a city's ability to support the unemployed within it is related to its general economic well-being. Finally, while the relative security of the city is a very important factor in attracting settlement, this security ultimately reflects the administration of a state in relationship to its broader political environment. On the other hand, tourism, education, landlord settlement and religious activities constitute the most important functions of certain towns and cities and are very important auxiliary functions in others. Yet, on the whole, these functions can sustain only relatively small centralized populations. Craft production and trade support cities of various sizes but, as we have seen, the normal distribution of functions

[116] Trigger, B. G. (1969). The personality of the Sudan, in McCall, D. F. et al. (eds.). East African History. New York. pp. 88–98.

tends to produce a number of more or less equal-sized cities at the top end of
the scale; these being of medium range for non-industrial cities as a whole.
The largest cities develop as centres of administration and court life and, in
particular, there is a tendency as empires develop for a single capital city to
tower in size above all others. These giant capitals evolve as a result of the
tendencies towards conspicuous consumption, economic centralization, bu-
reaucratization and economic planning that are characteristic of large political
units.[117] They also reflect the ability of the dominant power to command the
taxes and tribute necessary to support such agglomerations. In mature pre-industrial urban societies one frequently encounters an apical pattern of administrative functions superimposed over a more truncated hierarchy of
centres of craft production and trade.[118]

The Pre-Industrial City: A Backward Glance, A Forward Look*

GIDEON SJOBERG

*One of the most significant figures in the history of urban research has been
Gideon Sjoberg. Reacting to Park, Wirth, and others, Sjoberg claimed that industrial cities were not the only urban communities and proposed the existence of
another urban type—the pre-industrial city—with its own special characteristics.*

*Sjoberg's main concern is to search out the cross-cultural similarities in the
structure of pre-industrial cities, and then use this information to better understand the structure and functioning of industrial urban units. He hoped that
would enable us to better cope with the problems of developing Third World
countries and, more importantly, the even greater problems to be bared when all
humanity will be "swept up in the tidal wave of industrialization."*

*Though not a few scholars disagree with certain of Sjoberg's typological criteria,
his arguments and the research they generated have greatly helped to advance
our understanding of urbanism and urbanization. No matter how we might
disagree with his choice of terms, few would quibble with Sjoberg's concluding hope that, ". . . man, adaptable being that he is, will achieve a more
satisfying existence through the 'monster' he alone has fashioned."*

[117] Issawi, C. (1969). op. cit. p. 117.
[118] I wish to thank my colleagues D. Aronson, P. C. Salzman and G. M. Woloch for helping to clarify
certain references used in this paper. The author's participation in this seminar was made possible by a
travel grant from the Canada Council.

*Reprinted with permission of Macmillan Publishing Co., Inc., from Gideon Sjoberg, *The Pre-In-
dustrial City.* © 1960 by The Free Press, a division of Macmillan Publishing Co., Inc. Pp. 321–344.

The burden of our argument is that preindustrial cities and the feudal societies that support them, whether past or present, or in divergent cultural settings, share an imposing number of structural characteristics. Similar in many facets of their ecology, as well as in their class, familial, economic, political, religious, and educational structures, they differ dramatically from industrial cities and societies. Although we are cognizant of the variations among preindustrial cities through time and across cultural boundaries, our task has been the search for similarities in these communities, particularly in those features that set them apart from industrial cities.

No claim is made that every preindustrial city displays each one of the traits delineated in the preceding chapters. Nevertheless, non-industrial, or feudal, cities evince a startling degree of communality. . . . We have introduced into our "constructed type" only those traits for which empirical evidence is at hand for cities in at least several divergent cultural systems.

Although empirical illustrations are offered throughout to buttress our generalizations, these are merely suggestive of the wide range of supporting data available. Complete documentation of each proposition would have resulted in a set of volumes of unmanageable proportions, our theses smothered in a welter of technical details.

Granted that the materials on preindustrial cities are of uneven quality, and that hiatuses exist, they are nonetheless more extensive than most readers might assume. Those who desire further particulars, as well as a fuller picture of specific cities, should examine the cited works; these serve as an introduction to a voluminous body of literature.

We undertook this research in the belief that systematization of existing data, and their interpretation into some meaningful whole, is a desideratum in American social science, geared as it is to absorption with particulars. The fundamental premise of this work is that social science in general, and sociology in particular, to fulfill the requirements of a science, must seek to isolate the common elements in societies and cultures. It is only by abstracting out the universal, or near-universal, traits in preindustrial cities that one really discovers and explicates what is unique. The more materials on cities around the world that I examine, the more I am convinced that too many social scientists assume uniqueness where such does not exist.

Our primary intention has been to analyze feudal cities and their societies and thereby to provide a perspective for a clearer understanding of modern industrial orders. But we are jumping slightly ahead of ourselves. We need first to synopsize the structure of the non-industrial city, and then restate the theory underlying our work. After this we consider the possible utility of our typology for future research, most perceptibly in underdeveloped countries. Lastly we pose the query: What is transpiring in contemporary preindustrial cities and what will be the possible end result as these are swept up in the tidal wave of industrialization?

The Preindustrial City in Capsule Form

Cities of this type have been with us, present evidence indicates, since the fourth millennium B.C., when they first began their development in the Mesopotamian riverine area. Before long, in response to the growing technology and a variety of political forces, city life proliferated over a broader area. To an astonishing degree, preindustrial cities throughout history have prospered or floundered, as the case may be, in accordance with the shifting tides of social power.

In terms of their population these cities are the industrial city's poor relations, few ranging over 100,000 and many containing less than 10,000 or even 5,000 inhabitants. Their rate of population growth, moreover, has been slow and variable as well, in accordance with the waxing and waning of the supportive political structure. Yet throughout the shifting fortunes of empire, and the concomitant oscillation in population growth and decline, certain persistent structural characteristics signalize preindustrial cities everywhere.

As to spatial arrangements, the city's center is the hub of governmental and religious activity more than of commercial ventures. It is, besides, the prime focus of elite residence, while the lower class and outcaste groups are scattered centrifugally toward the city's periphery. Added to the strong ecological differentiation in terms of social class, occupational and ethnic distinctions are solemnly proclaimed in the land use patterns. It is usual for each occupational group to live and work in a particular street or quarter, one that generally bears the name of the trade in question. Ethnic groups are almost always isolated from the rest of the city, forming, so to speak, little worlds unto themselves. Yet, apart from the considerable ecological differentiation according to socioeconomic criteria, a minimum of specialization exists in land use. Frequently a site serves multiple purposes—it may be devoted concurrently to religious, educational, and business activities; and residential and occupational facilities are apt to be contiguous.

As to class, one is born into a particular stratum and usually must live out his life in accordance with the rights and duties of his position. Few aspects of daily activity escape the pervasive influence of class. A small urbanized, privileged group commands the local community and the society and is nourished by the lower class and an outcaste group; this last, by performing functions considered defiling and beyond the bounds of respectability, is ostracized by both the lower and upper strata. Social mobility in the city, at least as viewed over several generations, seems, relative to the industrial norms, inconsequential. The small upper class, immediately identifiable by its dress, speech, and personal mannerisms, controls the key organizational units of government, religion, and education in the city and society. Distinctive familial arrangements and clear avoidance of economic activity mark the elite as well. Of course, as earlier emphasized, there are contrary forces at work that disturb these neat arrangements.

The preindustrial urbanite functions within a family system and subordinates himself to it. One consequence is that, typically, marriages are arranged by families, not by individuals. The large extended family, with numerous relatives residing in a single "household"—one that is a functioning social unit—is the ideal toward which all urbanites strive, though a sizable, closely knit family is generally attainable only by the upper class. Economic circumstances prevent the urban poor and the peasantry alike from maintaining large households; for them the famille souche is more normal.

The men in the family lord it over the women; but though the latter are relegated to a humbler position, they are protected to a degree by the rigid sexual division of labor. Upperclass women, moreover, are isolated from most aspects of community life. Those in the urban lower class, like the rural women, play a rather more salient role in family affairs and are accorded wider freedom and responsibility in the community than are the elite womenfolk, though by no means to the degree permitted the males, nor to the extent enjoyed by the industrial city's women. Added to the profound status differentiation by sex in the feudal city is the sharp age-grading; the older family members dominate the younger, both as between generations and between siblings.

The family is the key socialization agency in the community and serves, for the women and children, and men to a lesser degree, as the focus of leisure-time activity. But more than this, given the low level of social mobility, a man's family is the chief determinant of his future career, be this in the topmost levels of the governmental, educational, or religious bureaucracies or, in the case of the commoners, in the lower-status jobs. Personnel are recruited according to kinship or personalistic criteria far more than on objective, universalistic grounds.

Economic activity is poorly developed in the preindustrial city, for manual labor, or indeed any that requires one to mingle with the humbler folk, is depreciated and eschewed by the elite. Except for a few large-scale merchants, who may succeed in buying their way into the elite, persons engaged in economic activity are either of the lower class (artisans, laborers, and some shopkeepers) or outcastes (some businessmen, and those who carry out the especially degrading and arduous tasks in the city).

Within the economic realm the key unit is the guild, typically community-bound. Through the guilds, handicraftsmen, merchants, and groups offering a variety of services attempt to minimize competition and determine standards and prices in their particular spheres of activity. Customarily also, each guild controls the recruitment, based mainly on kinship or other particularistic ties, and the training of personnel for its specific occupation and seeks to prevent outsiders from invading its hallowed domain.

The production of goods and services—by means of a simple technology wherein humans and animals are almost the only source of power, and tools to multiply the effects of this energy are sparse—is accomplished through a division of labor which is complex compared to that in the typical folk order but, seen from the industrial city's vantage point, is surprisingly simple. Very commonly the craftsman fashions an article from beginning to end and often markets it himself. Although little specialization exists in process, specialization according to product is widespread. Thus each guild is concerned with the manufacture and/or sale of a specific product or, at most, a narrow class of products.

Little standardization is found in prices, currency, weights and measures, or the type or quality of commodities marketed. In the main, the price of an item is fixed through haggling between buyer and seller. Different types and values of currency may be used concurrently within or among communities; so too with weights and measures, which often vary as well among the crafts. The marketing procedure is further complicated by the extensive adulteration of produce, forcing the buyer to be wary in every transaction; the quality of commodities is rarely, if ever, guaranteed.

The expansion of the economy is limited not only by the ruling group's negation of economic activity, the lack of standardization, and so on, but very largely also by the meager facilities for credit and capital formation.

Turning from the economy to the political structure, we find members of the upper class in command of the key governmental positions. The political apparatus, moreover, is highly centralized, the provincial and local administrators being accountable to the leaders in the societal capital. The sovereign exercises autocratic power, although this is mitigated by certain contrary forces that act to limit the degree of absolutism in the political realm.

The sovereign, and the societal leaders in general, along with the bureaucracies they control, base their authority upon appeals to tradition and to absolutes. The political bureaucracy, and the educational and religious systems as well, are characterized by rigid hierarchical arrangements; notwithstanding, the lines of authority in decision-making are most imprecise. The result is that decisions are arrived at not according to impersonal rules but rather with reference to the "persons" involved. Bureaucratic personnel are selected mainly on individualistic grounds—according to whether they have the correct community, kinship, and friendship ties. Clientele are served on a similar basis, which means that the elite determine policy to their own advantage. These patterns, combined with the lack of a fixed salary system, are conducive to graft and, from the point of view of industrial-urban systems, marked inefficiency. Nevertheless, as we have sought to show, this bureaucracy can, from the perspective of the preindustrial system, be considered quite rational in its operation.

Like the political structure, that pertaining to religion is a potent force making for order in the preindustrial city. The religious personnel, as well as religious beliefs and practices in general, are rent by the same upper-lower-outcaste divisions that prevail in other areas of activity. Upper-class persons occupy the topmost positions in the hierarchy; furthermore, the elite's religious norms conform most closely to those enunciated in the sacred writings, understandable only to this literate group, whereas the values and norms of the lower strata, most notably those of the outcastes, are apt to deviate considerably from the ideal.

The religious norms, deriving from the religious values and in turn reinforcing them, are highly prescriptive. One's day-by-day behavior is largely governed by religious injunctions, and few areas of activity—be these family life, politics, economics, education, or whatever—escape their pervasive influence. Moreover, the periodic religious ceremonies, in which a large segment of the community may participate, are one of the few mechanisms the city possesses for integrating disparate groups in an otherwise segmented community.

Strong reliance is placed upon protective, restorative, and predictive magic for assisting the individual in adjusting to the natural-divine order, something taken as an absolute, a given. The elite itself, lacking as much as the common man the means to manipulate and revise the social and physical world, employs magical practices freely. And a good part of the magic is integrated into the religious body of knowledge.

Relative to the industrial-urban community, communication in the feudal city is achieved primarily by word-of-mouth, specialized functionaries serving to disseminate news orally at key gathering points in the city. Members of the literate elite, however, communicate with one another to a degree through writing. And the formal educational system depends upon the written word, the means by which the ideal norms are standardized over time and space.

Only the elite, however, have access to formal education. And the educational and religious organizations, with few exceptions, are interdigitated. The curriculum in the schools, whether elementary or advanced, is overwhelmingly devoted to predication of the society's traditional religious-philosophical concepts. The schools are geared not to remaking the system but to perpetuating the old. Modern science, wherein abstract thought is coherent with practical knowledge and through which man seeks to manipulate the natural order, is practically non-existent in the non-industrial city. The emphasis is upon ethical and religious matters as one is concerned with adjusting to, not overcoming, the order of things. In contrast, industrial man is bent upon revising nature for his own purposes.

Theoretical Orientation

Inasmuch as preindustrial cities in numerous divergent cultural milieus display basic similarities in form, some variable other than cultural values, in the broad sense, must be operative; regularities of this sort are not the result of mere chance.

Here technology—*viz.*, the available *energy, tools,* and *know-how* connected with these—seems the most satisfactory explanatory variable.[1] This

[1] For other sociologists who have given attention to the technological variable see: Francis R. Allen et al., *Technology and Social Change* (New York: Appleton-Century-Croft, 1957). Unfortunately, some

mode of reasoning should not commit us in any way to credence in technological determinism or unilinear evolution; indeed we firmly reject these stands. In point of fact, we make frequent reference to social power in accounting for the fluctuating fortunes of cities and the fate of technology and give due recognition to its role in producing organization in the society. Nor do we ignore values. These, we have remarked in a number of contexts, account for certain divergencies from our constructed type; too, some values tend to be correlated with a specific level of technology; as a notable instance, the scientific method has built-in values that must be diffused, along with the energy-sources, tools, and requisite know-how, to underdeveloped areas if these are to industrialize. Further, we see the city per se as a variable to be reckoned with; rural and urban communities are in many ways intrinsically different. Although we lend priority to technology, we can not dispense with the other variables enumerated.

With these qualifications (and we hope the reader will keep them ever in mind), it seems clear that the transition from the preliterate to the feudal level, to the preindustrial civilized order, or from the latter to the industrial-urban society is associated with certain crucial advances in the technological sphere. The very emergence of cities is functionally related to the society's ability to produce a sizeable surplus; and the orientation, quite late in history, to an industrial base made possible a kind of city never before imagined. To minimize technology, as to ignore the value system, would be poor procedure.

As has been asserted time and again, we have been searching for similarities among cities in feudal societies, rather than areas of cultural divergency. Our primary vantage point has been the industrial city—though we have maintained awareness of the relations between folk and feudal orders as well. Our hypothesis that preindustrial and industrial cities are fundamentally distinctive entities is unmistakably borne out by the existing data.

Having taken technology as the dominant variable for explicating the divergencies between preindustrial and industrial cities, and their respective societies, we then proceeded to set this analysis within the context of contemporary structural-functionalism—with one outstanding modification: we introduced the concept of contradictory functional requirements, or what are termed "imperatives," "prerequisites," "necessary conditions," and other sociologisms.[2] Eschewing an excessive preoccupation with staticism and neatly integrated wholes, the proclivity of so much structural-functional analysis, we

sociologists tend to drift into a materialistic interpretation of technology, something we have tried to avoid.

[2] The terminology of structural-functionalism is by no means satisfactory. We perhaps favor the term, "requirements," but we have utilized it more or less synonymously with those listed in the text as well as introducing the concept of "correlates." We can, obviously, be called to task for this "looseness," but we believe the context will aid the reader in defining the terms. This approach seems preferable to repeating the terms, "requirements" or "necessary conditions" ad infinitum—when these concepts themselves are subject to misinterpretation.

Concerning the label, "contradictory functional requirements," we emphasize that this must not be confused with the concept, "dysfunction." The latter, as employed by sociologists, still stresses the internal harmony of social systems, quite at variance with our approach.

perceive the operation of contradictory structures, each "essential" to the system, yet at odds with one another. This is obviously the source of some of the strains that pervade even the relatively static non-industrial civilized society. Phrased differently, it is not just societies in some stage of transition from one fundamental form to another that undergo strain and tension; so-called "non-transitional" orders, either feudal or industrial, are plagued with self-inconsistencies.

As an illustration of our recourse to structural-functional analysis, may we briefly review certain aspects of the class system in the preindustrial city. Some segment of the populace must be freed from food production or other physical labor so that it can devote its time to governing others. The labor force must be controlled and integrated, goods must be siphoned off from the hinterland to feed the city, political stability must be maintained, and so on. A leisure class can be considered a "requirement" if the city is to operate with a limited technology. And at the same time, this privileged element is created by the technology (advanced as it is over that in the folk order), though the size of this group is firmly restricted, for in the absence of machines the populace must labor long and hard to support even a few in leisured status.

We can go to a step farther and state that if this stratum is to persist it must bar ingress into its ranks from below; the result is an overwhelming tendency toward autocratic rule and a rigid class system wherein one's status is generally ascribed by birth. The political, religious, and educational hierarchies all intensify this by staffing the key posts on particularistic, primarily kinship, grounds. More, the elite legitimizes its dominance by appeal to absolutes and to tradition. Just as the existence of this class is made possible by the prevailing technology, so too, its autocratic rule and obstruction of social mobility for others are fostered by the technology which permits and requires few experts, no mass education, and so forth.

Nevertheless, in the matter of exclusiveness, though a considerable amount of it is permitted the elite, such can not be fully achieved, for contradictory forces are at work. On the one hand the elite scorn, and attempt to ostracize, businessmen on a number of counts—most notably the fact that the latter's field lends itself to the amassing of wealth, and therefore possible upward mobility, by commoners who possess special talents for manipulation. This is an obvious threat to the elite's position, based as it is on kinship and reinforced by appeals to absolutes and to tradition. Yet because the city, to be a city, must allow for commercial activity, and because the upper class itself requires wealth if it is to maintain eminence, successful businessmen, if not from outcaste ethnic groups, can occasionally utilize their monetary gains to purchase upper-class status. Because the elite require the services of merchants, they nurture them, paving the way for a partial undermining of their own position. Although the preindustrial city's, and the society's, internal structures reinforce one another to a high degree—a "circularity" that actually makes exposition difficult—the component parts are at times at odds with one another, generating stresses within the system.

When comparing the preindustrial and industrial city-types, bear in mind that while each generates its own dominant patterns—the preindustrial city emphasizes class rigidity and particularism, the industrial city class fluidity and universalism—countervailing forces operate within both cities. Neither absolute rigidity nor extreme fluidity is achievable. Most writers ignore this, choosing to analyze systems in terms of fictional types; we have selected a more empirical orientation despite a resulting degree of muzziness; indeed the latter is characteristic of reality itself.

An ideological issue looms before us. Most treatments of feudal orders are essentially moralizations as to the merits or demerits of these societies' world outlook. "Conservatives" look back in praise on what they consider to be a glorious past and lament the expansion of industrialization.[3] The "liberals" look back in shame and anger. We have attempted to tread a narrow line between these extremes. Although continually contrasting the feudal city with the industrial type, we do acknowledge the former's contributions to man's heritage. But we shun the interpretations of writers of Mumford's persuasion, who glamorize the medieval European city, or of some social scientists who, incredibly, are unaware of the stark poverty of the lower classes in ancient cities.[4] It is preferable to accept the preindustrial city for what it is, realizing its positive contributions but noting its deficiencies as well. We shall not cheer, neither shall we weep, as it fades from the scene.

One final comment on our theoretical approach. Throughout, recognition has been given to the theoretical distinctions between a city and a society. But empirically these fuse—our efforts to analyze one force us to treat the other. In practice, the city is our starting point, but we have branched outward from it to encompass the total feudal order. This work is, in the end, a survey of the preindustrial civilized society with special emphasis upon the city, the hub of all major activity therein.

Utility of This Typology for Research and Analysis

The ultimate test of our constructed type, of course, is its long-run utility for interpreting empirical phenomena. It does seem to enlarge one's purview of preindustrial cities and feudal societies. For this reason the typology should prove useful to historians, anthropologists, and archeologists attempting to reconstruct the social arrangements in cities long since dead. Certain aspects of their life-ways lie forever beyond our grasp. The only reasonable alternative is extrapolation to the past from data on more recent feudal cities, utilizing in the process, recent advances in the social scientist's knowledge of social systems. Knowing "what to expect" in earlier cities imparts fuller meaning to

[3] E.g., Friedrich Georg Juenger, The Failure of Technology (Chicago: Henry Regenery, 1956).
[4] E.g., Lewis Mumford, The Culture of Cities (New York: Harcourt, Brace, 1938). Pulgram, for one, leaves the impression that Italy under the Romans was more prosperous than it is today—disregarding completely two millennia of technological progress. Ernst Pulgram, The Tongues of Italy (Cambridge: Harvard University Press, 1958), pp. 34–36.

written records and permits more satisfactory reconstructions where gaps exist in the data. A salient weakness in much historical research is the tendency to assume uniqueness for much of the social phenomena encountered; all manner of false interpretations ensue. Such is "historicism," ultimately a denial of objective generalization as the goal of social science. A considerable proportion of sociologists, bound as they are to the American social scene, are unwitting proponents of this myopic approach.

This study will perhaps encourage some scholars to focus attention upon the preindustrial cities that survive today; in turn, the data amassed on these can be used to refine our constructed type. Such need not be an end in itself. Acute awareness of the social structure of preindustrial civilized societies and their cities is essential for anyone who hopes to understand current processes in societies now changing over from feudal to industrial modes of organization. In this connection, it is instructive that some writers see regularity in form across industrial systems yet implicitly deny uniformities of structure for preindustrial civilized societies. But that such regularities abound should be apparent to any observer of these societies who attains a broad space-time overview. It is these uniformities that provide a "yardstick" for measuring and interpreting across cultural boundaries the significant social changes that are occuring. So much of the analysis of social change in India, China, the Middle East, and other underdeveloped areas thus far has been accomplished with no real effort to isolate the underlying structural themes that run through these varying cultures. Surprising, yes, but nonetheless true. Only through the use of some kind of "standard," like the one offered herein, against which to measure change, can we determine whether one society (with its cities) is relinquishing its traditional forms more rapidly than others. For as statistics on industrializing societies become quantitatively and qualitatively more adequate, firmer generalizations concerning these fundamental processes should become possible.

It is high time sociologists in general, not just the few, began to deal with the industrial-urbanization process in underdeveloped countries. The repercussions of this revolution throughout the world are devastating. And the impact of these changes on social science theory, sociological theory in particular, bids fair to be revolutionary as well.

Scanning the history of sociology, we see that sociologists today who are attempting to understand the nature of change in "underdeveloped" countries (by no means a satisfactory term) are more closely akin theoretically to the German social thinkers than to the typical French, English, or American social scientists.[5] The explanation seems to be that Germany in the latter part

[5] The dominant concern in present-day American sociology is comparing the real with the ideal norms (the informal with the formal), not contrasting the past with the present. Undoubtedly a reflection of the growing maturity of the urban industrial society, such an orientation is of little value in studying underdeveloped countries.

Because of these differing emphases among sociologists, there is a good deal of unnecessary polemic. Writers concerned with the real vs. the ideal often attack the past-vs.-present, or the developmental, theorists on spurious grounds. Many recent criticisms of Weber's ideal-type formulation of bureaucracy, for example, stem from sociologists' failure to realize that Weber was not studying

of the nineteenth century experienced a rather sudden transition from (to employ the terminology of those who wrote about it) "feudalism" to "capitalism." Most German social scientists, including Max Weber, Sombart, Tönnies, and a host of others, were concerned with the breakup of the old and its replacement by the new. But lamentably, their analyses in general were Europe-bound. Yet how could it have been otherwise? They were writing in an era before industrialization had taken firm hold in Japan, before the Communists' will to industrialize Russia and China, before the upsurge of movements intent upon adopting the new technology in societies the world over. The future of social science theory—the ethnocentrism of urban sociology notwithstanding—lies in its long-run ability to explain the current process on the world scene. Our effort is a step in this direction.

The Preindustrial City in Transition

The heydey of the preindustrial city is past. A few cities of this type persist in almost pure form, but in the face of industrializalion they are fast relinquishing their special characteristics. The dissolution before our very eyes of a city-type that has existed for fifty-five centuries or more is deserving of some attention. Contrarily, the traditional social structure does not evanesce as rapidly as might be imagined. Unlike the folk society, it possesses remarkable capacities for stemming, at least for a time, the tides of change; its complex institutional apparatus—above all its literate elite—are potentially powerful forces of resistance.

Preindustrial-urban forms continue to dominate the cityscape in India, the Middle East, in sections of Latin America, and elsewhere. Even where industrialization is well advanced, as in Japan, survivals of traditional forms crop up on every hand, and efforts by the old elite to maintain the past in the face of a veritable avalanche of industrializing influences continue strong. More impressive is the formidable opposition the Soviet Union, with its police-backed instruments of change, has encountered in its attempts to wipe out the preindustrial-urban carryovers in Muslim Central Asia. Some recent commentaries of Soviet social scientists frankly acknowledge the failure of the Russian state to eliminate many of the traditional religious, economic, and familial patterns in the cities of Central Asia—in Uzbekistan, Tadzhikistan, Kirghizia, Kazakhstan, and Turkmenistan—despite decades of concerted effort in this direction.[6] A number of writers are clamoring for study of these communities, not so much to gain objective scientific knowledge as to acquire information that will enable the governmental apparatus to root out these survivals more effectively.[7]

deviations from the ideal, but rather contrasting traditional society with his so-called "capitalist" one. To play the record over again: keep clearly in mind what is being compared.

[6] "The Survival of Religious and Social Customs in Uzbekistan," *Central Asian Review*, VI (1958), 5–15.

[7] A. Benningsen, "Traditional Islam in the Customs of the Turkic Peoples of Central Asia," *Middle East Journal*, XII (Spring, 1958), 227–33. Of course, in all these efforts to rid the Turkic peoples of their traditional patterns, the Soviets are seeking to do more than merely revise the social structure; they seem intent upon Russifying these Muslims—i.e., imposing a new culture upon them.

That preindustrial structural arrangements endure in many parts of Europe should not be ignored. In Spain the traditional social structure continues to ward off the advances of industrial-urbanization on many fronts. France and Italy preserve many feudal city forms as well. Nor are England and Germany completely shorn of their preindustrial-urban structures. Failure to recognize this, however, is widespread. In a recent study of the ecology of Oxford,[8] for example, the data point to the maintenance of traditional patterns; yet the authors betray a lack of perspective on England and the rest of Europe, to say nothing of world cities, while contrasting Oxford with the American city.

Here we should point out that the United States is unique in many respects. It started down the road to industrialization and urbanization without a firmly entrenched feudal elite—in government (including the military), religion, or education—to slow its pace. Its industrial forms, consequently, appear more strongly developed than those in any other sector of the globe. This is a compelling reason for exercising caution when generalizing from the United States to other societies.

What we are getting at is that in industrializing societies the clash between those who seek to revive the feudal order—in the area of politics the monarchists have been quite vocal in some societies—and those who insist the old must go has periodically waxed intense. For over a century, France has been struggling in vain to achieve a compromise between the proponents of these opposing views. Italy has been rent by a similar political schism, and its effects have been felt in every city throughout the land. The conflict between the traditional and the modern is now manifest in cities in India—in the realms of marriage and family life, in religion, in medicine, and so on—as a perusal of Indian newspapers will confirm. Inasmuch as many Indian cities show only a thin veneer of industrialization, the worst is yet to come.

Implicit perhaps in our reasoning has been the assumption that industrialization is more or less inevitable. We need to qualify this somewhat. Other alternatives are theoretically possible. The preindustrial civilized order could reject industrial-urbanization completely. But several compelling factors make this unlikely. First, if the traditional elite is to sustain itself as a "dominant" group it must industrialize. Pressure for industrialization stems from both internal and external sources, although we contend that the latter exert paramount influence. The traditional elite in most underdeveloped countries—India or those in the Middle East, for example—is promoting industrialization in large part to overcome its own and its nation's colonial status, although this process encourages class fluidity and threatens the elite's authority. Even the ideological pressures upon these systems to industrialize—say, to ameliorate the lot of the common man—come primarily from their efforts to emulate their more highly industrialized neighbors.

At one time the author envisioned the possibility of an eventual modus vivendi between feudal and industrial forms, at least in some societies. An in-

---

[8] Peter Collison and John Mogey, "Residence and Social Class in Oxford," *American Journal of Sociology*, LXIV (May, 1959), 599–605.

dustrial-urban system could, theoretically, be superimposed upon a feudal order without necessarily obliterating the latter: both could function concurrently. France and Italy have displayed this pattern over decades. Despite the industrial aspect of many cities in France, it still remains a society of many small shopkeepers, handicraftsmen, and peasants. In Italy the preindustrial-industrial split has in large part coincided with the regional distinctions between north and south.

No longer do we regard a "dual" society as a possible "stable" end result for most underdeveloped countries today. One reason is that, possessing as they do a relatively large population base, they must industrialize and urbanize in order to effectively curb the vast population expansion and keep it from cancelling out any "gains" resulting from their industrial efforts. Even assuming improved birth control practices could be introduced without concomitant industrialization, an unlikely eventuality, the power variable is still to be considered. Because world power is so closely tied to advancing industrialization, and consequently urbanization, new ruling elements will take shape in some societies and will do their utmost to further this process—if necessary, seeking to erase the traditional order through violence. Nevertheless, smaller countries, far less preoccupied with becoming world powers and amenable to domination by the larger societies, appear less likely to industrialize and may well over time retain many of their feudal ways. Yet, of course, the long-run world trend is toward ever larger, more complex industrial societies.

The result of the drive to industrialize and urbanize will not be a path studded with bliss for all. The stronger the pressures the more bitter will be the fruits. So we find police methods being used to impose industrial-urbanization in the Soviet Union and in Communist China; in the latter, the government would like to extirpate the old order in one fell swoop. Even where force of such proportions is not involved, the strains and stresses are nonetheless intense.

One means of alleviating the internal conflicts is the creation of "devils," usually outsiders, upon whom the blame can be heaped for the shortcomings of the leaders and the intransigencies of factions in the society. Communist China and various Middle Eastern societies can be seen resorting to this "out."

Contemplating the scene, we do not see, as some writers do, a panacea for the world's ills in the industrialization and urbanization of underdeveloped countries, at least not over the shorter run. Not that we oppose these efforts. But the history of the industrial-urbanization process so far offers little encouragement in this regard, and the blossoming of negative values as a means of stabilizing internal arrangements and rationalizing a society's failures are explosive forces that can set off intersocietal conflicts if not handled with care. Viewing certain European societies or Japan in retrospect, one can assume that global strife will multiply with the spread of industrialization and urbanization.

Before turning from this subject, we must emphasize that the end product, the industrial system, will not be the same in India, for example, as in China or England or the United States. Each society's cities will retain much of their own special cultural flavor, but the recurrent theme throughout will be the industrial-urban social structure, to which we now turn.

The End Product[9]

Aside from its distinctive ecological features, as contrasted with the non-industrial-urban forms, the industrial city-type displays a fluid class system, status being based primarily upon achievement rather than ascription. In part this latter reflects the requirement that occupational posts be filled more according to universalistic than to particularistic criteria. Sociologists who perceive the industrial city's class system as rigid and well defined undoubtedly gain this impression from their penchant for contrasting reality with the ideal of absolute fluidity which, after all, given the contradictory demands of the industrial-urban order, is quite utopian.

The industrial city is also characterized by a loosely organized familial unit, primarily conjugal in form, with comparatively few superordinate-subordinate relationships with respect to age and sex. A family system of this nature, permitting and encouraging the exercise of individual choice in the realms of marriage and occupation, is compatible with the high degree of social and spatial mobility encountered in the industrial order.

The economy is mass-production oriented. And it is dominated by large-scale enterprises whose networks of relationships, extending across cities and societies, link the everexpanding numbers of highly educated, specialized experts who are steeped in the scientific tradition that lies at the vortex of the industrial system. The progress attained in communication and transport, moreover, is associated with wide standardization of currency, prices, and the manufacture and marketing of goods—all acting to sustain the new industrial-urban complex.

In the realm of government we find a rather loosely defined power structure, reflecting the fluid class system. Social power in the industrial city is translated into authority chiefly through appeal to the governed and appeal to experts; reliance upon traditions and absolutes is de-emphasized. Paradoxically, the conservative elements in industrial cities and societies seek the consent of the governed to justify their credence in tradition and absolutes. In all, the industrial system with its proliferation of experts, of mass education, and of the scientific orientation—which lays stress upon negation of traditional thinking—lends support to the new kind of authority structure.

[9] Marion Levy, "Some Sources of the Vulnerability of the Structures of Relatively Nonindustrialized Societies to Those of Highly Industrialized Societies," in Bert F. Hoselitz (ed.), *The Progress of Underdeveloped Areas* "Social and Demographic Aspects of Economic Development in India," in Simon Kuznets et al (eds.), *Economic Growth: Brazil, India, Japan* (Durham: Duke University Press, 1955), pp. 293 ff.; Bert F. Hoselitz, "Social Structure and Economic Growth," *Economia internazionale*, VI (1953), 52–77.

In the governmental bureaucracy, as in business, the emphasis is upon formal rules rather than the primacy of the "person" in the decision-making process, upon clear-cut lines of authority, and on universalism in the selection of personnel and the handling of clientele. Other patterns include fixed salaries and full-time occupancy of bureaucratic posts.

Anent the religious sphere in industrial centers, its norms are generally permissive. Actors play divergent, and often contradictory, roles, and the new technology ensures a continuous cycle of change, all of which requires flexibility in the norms. Though elements of the traditional religion remain strong in some industrial cities, "secular religions" like science and nationalism are looming more significant.

Mass education, where selection tends to be according to ability, is interlinked with the fluid class and family systems; it is a must if the industrial city is to prosper. At the same time, only a highly industrialized system can educate all of its members. Education in the industrial city is geared primarily to emphasizing experimentation and change, negation, and man's ability to manipulate and revise the natural order. Not only has the availability of formal education reached monumental proportions, but knowledge is becoming ever more widely diffused through mass communication media.

As in the preindustrial city, the apparent circularity in the industrial system—the interlinking and mutual support among all of its structures—is interrupted at intervals by the presence of contradictory elements that are, apparently, both essential to the system and at odds with one another. Though the patterns enumerated for the industrial city are the dominant ones, their complete fruition is often precluded by the opposing functional demands of societal forces. Earlier we chanced the observation that although the trend is toward fluidity in the class system, countervailing forces operate. For example, the industrial city requires well-developed status hierarchies in the governmental and economic realms. Although its bureaucracies emphasize universalism and reward individual achievement, persons at the apex of the pyramid can circumvent these norms and ensure, say, special advantages within the system for their children. Then too, concurrent with the demands for permissive religious norms is the need for societal "integration." The dilemma is that the latter may be approached more readily through the medium of traditional religious systems than through more secular ones. Or consider the fact that people's upward striving for success is essential if the educational, scientific, and occupational systems are to prosper; yet emphasis upon upward mobility generates strains, for those who fall by the wayside, particularly during periods of crisis, will perhaps unite behind some charismatic leader to revise the legitimate authority structure. A cataloging of the internal contradictions in industrial cities, to say nothing of the opposition between "external" and "internal" demands upon the industrial-urban order viewed as a whole, requires another treatise.

In another context we set forth some of the problems involved in isolating the structural requirements, or correlates, of industrial-urban centers.[10] We shall not review these issues here but will simply mention one or two of the more compelling ones. The United States, we reiterate, is taken as the prime basis for generalization. This is all right up to a point. But most of the world is only now beginning to industrialize and urbanize on a massive scale, and nowhere has this process reached its peak (even in the United States), nor has it become stabilized in place and time. Of necessity we must extrapolate from incomplete information.

During the next few decades close watch must be kept on cities in, for example, the Soviet Union [11] to determine whether these are drifting toward the type here delineated. Existing evidence seems to indicate that the trend is in this direction, though more noticeably in some spheres than in others. The political arena is especially perplexing. Some social scientists, as well as certain newspaper columnists, perceive a definite trend toward appeals to the consent of the governed and enlarged authority on the part of the vast array of highly trained technical experts in the Soviet Union. This does not mean that countermovements may not arise, or that democracy as defined and cherished in other industrial societies has (or will) become the norm. Certainly the Soviet system has not yet institutionalized any democratic process for transferring authority from one existing leader to his successor. Even so, the Soviet system seems to have moved toward the point where its political system perhaps has more in common with other industrial societies than with strictly feudal orders. In the end, we must keep an open mind to new or contradictory evidence.

Whatever the final result, and its attendant problems, the city is man's own creation. He passed thousands of years within it, more or less satisfied with its preindustrial form, but now is intent upon its drastic reorganization. By the end of the present century, barring an atomic holocaust, the industrial city will be the dominant community form throughout the world. The pattern for the future is set: there is no turning back. The tidal wave of industrial-urbanization, conjoined with the on-going technical revolution and the rapid population growth, will lead to cities of gargantuan dimensions. We believe sociologists' objective understanding of this process may help to ease the inevitable stresses that will follow. Our fervent hope is that the transition will be as painless as possible and that man, adaptable being that he is, will achieve a more satisfying existence through the "monster" he alone has fashioned.

[10] Gideon Sjoberg, "Comparative Urban Sociology," in Robert K. Merton et al. (eds.), *Sociology Today* (New York: Basic Books, 1959), pp. 344–59.

[11] For one perspective on this issue see: Alex Inkeles and Raymond A. Bauer, *The Soviet Citizen* (Cambridge: Harvard University Press, 1959). Some will contend that the authors exaggerate the similarities between the Soviet Union and other industrial societies, but they make a strong case for their position.

The Cultural Role of Cities

ROBERT REDFIELD AND MILTON SINGER

In this important work, Redfield and Singer offer a hypothesis for both the development and the differentiation of cities. By this time, Redfield was clearly willing to view cities as more complex and varied than his earlier folk-urban model had depicted.

He and Singer here suggest that cities play cultural roles in their societies, and these roles (functions) reflect the origin of the urban populations and the kinds of common activities and values that bind them together. Redfield and Singer essentially dichotomize cities in terms of the degree to which they reflect and foster local or "outside" influences. Orthogenetic cities develop upon a local base, and their role is to carry "forward into systematic and reflective dimensions an old culture." They transform "the implicit 'little traditions' of the local . . . cultures into an explicit and systematic 'great tradition.' " They represent the "moral order." The opposite, or heterogenetic city, reflects the influence of other areas and cultures. Such cities create "original modes of thought that have authority beyond or in conflict with old cultures and civilizations." They represent the "technical order." Setting the stage for Sjoberg's typology, Redfield and Singer see orthogenetic cities as filling their particular functions prior to, and heterogenetic cities following, the Industrial Revolution.

The authors subsequently attempt to show how their formulation relates to larger theoretical questions about sociocultural change through (local) innovation and/or (outside) diffusion. This is related to the ambivalence many have about "progress," especially insofar as "progress" often represents the spread of a homogenizing Euro-American life-style at the expense of locally adapted systems. Redfield and Singer are not alone in wondering if this form of societal evolution—convergent change—may not weaken or even destroy humanity's long-range potential for survival. What if some dramatic shift should occur in the infrastructure supporting the whole urban industrial system?

The Cultural Role of Cities

This paper has as its purpose to set forth a framework of ideas that may prove useful in research on the part played by cities in the development, decline, or transformation of culture. "Culture" is used as in anthropology. The paper contains no report of research done. It offers a scheme of constructs; it does not describe observed conditions or processes; references to particular cities or civilizations are illustrative and tentative.

"The Cultural Role of Cities," *Economic Development and Cultural Change* 3: pp. 53–73, 1954. University of Chicago (copyright).

Time Perspectives

The cultural role of cities may be considered from at least three different time perspectives. In the long-run perspective of human history as a single career,[1] the first appearance of cities marks a revolutionary change: the beginnings of civilization. Within this perspective cities remain the symbols and carriers of civilization wherever they appear. In fact the story of civilization may then be told as the story of cities—from those of the ancient Near East through those of ancient Greece and Rome, medieval and modern Europe; and from Europe overseas to North and South America, Australia, the Far East, and back again to the modern Near East. In the short-run perspective we may study the cultural role of particular cities in relation to their local hinterlands of towns and villages.[2] The time span here is the several-year period of the field research or, at most, the lifespan of the particular cities that are studied. Between the long- and short-run perspectives, there is a middle-run perspective delimited by the life-history of the different civilizations within which cities have developed.[3] This is the perspective adopted when we consider the cultural bearings of urbanization within Mexican civilization,[4] or Chinese civilization or Indian civilization or Western civilization. It is a perspective usually of several thousand years and embraces within its orbit not just a particular city and its hinterland, but the whole pattern and sequence of urban development characteristic of a particular civilization and its cultural epochs.

While these three perspectives are clearly interrelated, research and analysis may concentrate primarily on one of them. Empirical ethnographic, sociological and geographical research on cities begins in the nature of the case with the short-run perspective, but the significance of such research increases as it becomes linked with ideas and hypotheses drawn from the other perspectives. One begins, say, with an empirical study of the origins, morphology,

---

[1] Robert Redfield, *The Primitive World and its Transformations*, Ithaca, New York, 1953, ix–xiii. W. N. Brown and others, "The Beginnings of Civilization," *Journal of the American Oriental Society*, Supplement No. 4, December, 1939, pp. 3–61.

[2] Robert Redfield, *The Folk Culture of Yucatan*, Chicago: University of Chicago Press, 1941. This study, short-run in description, also aims to test some general ideas.

Mandelbaum, David G. (ed.), "Integrated Social Science Research for India," *Planning Memo.*, University of California, 1949.

[3] Kroeber has recently discussed the problems of delimiting civilizations in his article, "The Delimitation of Civilizations," *Journal of the History of Ideas*, Vol. XIV (1953).

Mark Jefferson, "Distribution of the world's city folk: a study in comparative civilization," *Geographia*, 1931.

[4] Paul Kirchhoff, in "Four Hundred Years After: General Discussion of Acculturation, Social Change, and the Historical Provenience of Culture Elements," *Heritage of Conquest* by Sol Tax and others (Glencoe, Ill.: The Free Press, 1952), p. 254: "It seems to me that the fundamental characteristic of Mesoamerica was that it was a stratified society, one like ours or that of China, based on the axis of city and countryside. There was a native ruling class, with a class ideology and organization, which disappeared entirely; there were great cultural centers which, just as in our life, are so essential if you described the U.S. without New York, Chicago, etc., it would be absurd. The same thing happens when you describe these centers in ancient Mexico. . . . It's not only the arts, crafts and sciences which constitute the great changes, but the basic form of the culture changing from a city structure to the most isolated form, which is, in my opinion, the most total and radical change anywhere in history. . . . When the city is cut off what is left over is attached as a subordinate to the new city-centered culture. . . ."

functions, and influence of an Asiatic city.[5] Then one may go on to look at this city as a link in the interaction of two distinct civilizations, and see the problem of urbanization in Asia generally as a problem in Westernization,[6] or the problem of Spanish-Indian acculturation of Mexico after the Conquest as a problem of de-urbanization and re-urbanization.[7] Finally, the canvas may be further enlarged to show both Western and Eastern cities as variants of a single and continuing cultural and historical process.[8] In this paper we propose to concentrate on the middle-run perspective, i.e., we shall analyze the role cities play in the formation, maintenance, spread, decline, and transformation of civilizations. We think that links with the long- and short-run perspectives will also emerge in the course of the analysis.

In the many useful studies of cities by urban geographers, sociologists, and ecologists we find frequent reference to "cultural functions" and "cultural centers."[9] Under these rubrics they generally include the religious, educational, artistic centers and activities, and distinguish them from administrative, military, economic centers and functions. This usage of "cultural" is too narrow for the purpose of a comparative analysis of the role cities play in the transformations of the more or less integrated traditional life of a community. Economic and political centers and activities may obviously play as great a role in these processes as the narrowly "cultural" ones. Moreover, these different kinds of centers and activities are variously combined and separated and it is these varying patterns that are significant. In ancient civilizations the urban centers were usually political-religious or political-intellectual; in the modern world they are economic.[10] The mosque, the temple, the cathedral, the royal palace, the fortress, are the symbolic "centers" of the pre-industrial cities. The "central business district" has become symbolic of the modern urban center. In fact a cross-cultural history of cities might be written from the changing meanings of the words for city. "Civitas" in the Roman Empire meant an administrative or ecclesiastical district. Later, "city" was applied to the ecclesiastical center of a town—usually the cathedral. This usage still survives in

[5] Ghosh, S., "The urban pattern of Calcutta," *Economic Geography*, 1950.
Weulersse, J., "Antioche, un type de cité de l'Islam," *Congr. int. de Geographie*, Warsaw, 1934, III.
D. R. Gadgil, *Poona, A Socio-Economic Survey*, Poona, 1945, 1952.
[6] "Urbanization is part of the Europeanization that is spreading throughout the world," Mark Jefferson in reference 3 above. Kingsley Davis, *The Population of India and Pakistan*, Princeton, 1951, pp. 148–49; M. Zinkin, *Asia and the West*, London, 1951, Ch. 1, "Eastern Village and Western City."
[7] Kirchhoff, op. cit.
[8] See for this approach the books of V. Gordon Childe, and his article in *Town Planning Review*, XXI (1950) on "The Urban Revolution."
[9] Grace M. Kneedler, "Functional types of cities," reprinted in *Reader in Urban Sociology*, edited by Paul K. Hatt and Albert J. Reiss, Jr., The Free Press, Glencoe, Illinois, 1951; R. E. Dickinson, *The West European City*, London: Routledge & Paul, 1951, pp. 253–54; Chauncey Harris, "A functional classification of cities in the United States," *Geogr. Review*, New York, 1943.
[10] Gadgil, *The Industrial Revolution of India in Recent Times*, Oxford, 1944, pp. 6–12.
Spate and E. Ahmad, "Five cities of the Gangetic Plain. A cross-section of Indian cultural history," *Geog. Rev.*, 1950.
P. George, *La Ville*, Paris, 1952.
B. Rowland, *The Art and Architecture of India*, Penguin, Baltimore, 1953. Map showing ancient and historic art and religious centers, p. xvii.
Fei Hsiao-Tung, *China's Gentry, Essays in Rural-Urban Relations*, Chicago, University of Chicago Press, 1953, pp. 91–117.

names like "Île de la Cité" for one of the first centers of Paris. With the development of the "free cities," "city" came to mean the independent commercial towns with their own laws.[11] Today, "the city" of London is a financial center, and when Americans speak of "going to town" or "going downtown" they mean they are going to the "central business district." They usually think of any large city as a business and manufacturing center, whereas a Frenchman is more likely to regard his cities—certainly Paris—as "cultural centers."[12]

This symbolism is not of course a completely accurate designation of what goes on in the city for which it stands. The ecclesiastical centers were also in many cases centers of trade and of craftsmen, and the modern "central business district" is very apt to contain libraries, schools, art museums, government offices and churches, in addition to merchandising establishments and business offices. But allowing for this factual distortion, this symbolism does help us to separate two quite distinct cultural roles of cities, and provides a basis for classifying cities that is relevant to their cultural role. As a "central business district," the city is obviously a market-place, a place to buy and sell, "to do business"—to truck, barter and exchange with people who may be complete strangers and of different races, religions and creeds. The city here functions to work out largely impersonal relations among diverse cultural groups. As a religious or intellectual center, on the other hand, the city is a beacon for the faithful, a center for the learning, authority and perhaps doctrine that transforms the implicit "little traditions" of the local non-urban cultures into an explicit and systematic "great tradition." The varying cultural roles of cities, so separated and grouped into two contrasting kinds of roles with reference to the local traditions of the non-urban peoples, point to a distinction to which we shall soon return and to which we shall then give names.

Types of Cities

In the studies of economic historians (Pirenne, Dopsch) and in the studies of the currently significant factors for economic development (Hoselitz),[13] the functions of cities are considered as they effect change; but the change chiefly in view is economic change. Our attention now turns to the roles of cities in effecting change in the content and integration of ideas, interests and ideals.

The distinction Hoselitz takes from Pirenne between political-intellectual urban centers on the one hand and economic centers on the other points in the direction of the distinction necessary to us in taking up the new topic. But the distinction we need does not fully emerge until we refine the classification by (1) separating the political function from the intellectual and (2) giving new

[11] R. E. Dickinson, op. cit. (note 7), pp. 251–52; H. Pirenne, Medieval Cities.

[12] See article on "urbanization" by W. M. Stewart in 14th edition of Encyclopaedia Brittanica for some cultural variables in the definition of "city."

[13] B. Hoselitz, "The role of cities in the economic growth of underdeveloped countries," *The Journal of Political Economy*, vol. lxi (1953), esp. 198–99.

content to the term "intellectual." Delhi, Quito and Peiping are to be contrasted, as Hoselitz says, with Bombay, Guayaquil and Shanghai because the former three cities are "political-intellectual centers" and the latter three are "economic centers." (The contrast of Rio to São Paolo is less clear.) Let us now add that there are cities with political functions and without significant intellectual functions: New Delhi (if it be fair to separate it from old Delhi), Washington, D.C. and Canberra (the new university there may require a qualification). Further, the intellectual functions of Delhi, Quito and Peiping (and Kyoto, Lhasa, Cuzco, Mecca, medieval Liège and Uaxactun) are to develop, carry forward, elaborate a long-established cultural tradition local to the community in which those cities stand. These are the cities of the literati: clerics, astronomers, theologians, imams and priests. New Delhi and Washington, D.C. do not have, significantly, literati; in spite of its schools and universities Washington is not a city of great intellectual leadership; these are cities without major intellectual functions. In respect to this lack, New Delhi and Washington, D.C., belong with cities with predominantly economic functions. On the other hand, not a few old cities with economic functions have also the functions associated with the literati (Florence, medieval Timbuktoo; Thebes).

We have taken into consideration, in this expanded grouping, both cities of the modern era and cities of the time before the development of a world economy. It may be useful now to separate the two historic periods, retaining the distinction between cities of the literati, cities of entrepreneurs, and cities of the bureaucracy. The following grouping results:

BEFORE THE UNIVERSAL OEKUMENE (pre-Industrial Revolution, pre-Western expansion)
1. Administrative-cultural cities
   (cities of the literati and the indigenous bureaucracy)
      Peiping
      Lhasa
      Uaxactun
      Kyoto
      Liège
      Allahabad (?)
2. Cities of native commerce
   (cities of the entrepreneur)
      Bruges
      Marseilles
      Lübeck
      Market towns of native West Africa
      Early Canton
AFTER THE UNIVERSAL OEKUMENE (post-Industrial Revolution, and post-Western expansion)

3. Metropolis-cities of the world-wide managerial and entrepreneureal class (Park's "cities of the main street of the world")
   London
   New York
   Osaka
   Yokahama
   Shanghai
   Singapore
   Bombay
   Lesser cities and towns, also carrying on the world's business, may be added here.
4. Cities of modern administration
   (cities of the new bureaucracies)
   Washington, D.C.
   New Delhi
   Canberra
   A thousand administrative towns, country seats, seats of British and French African colonial administration, etc.

What is the relationship of such a grouping to our topic: the role of cities in processes of cultural change?

The role of cities of Group 1 has already been stated. It is to carry forward, develop, elaborate a long-established local culture or civilization. These are cities that convert the folk culture into its civilized dimension.

But the cities of groups 2, 3, and 4 do not have, or do not have conspicuously and as their central effect, this role in the cultural process. They affect the cultural process in other ways. How? They are cities in which one or both of the following things are true: (1) the prevailing relationships of people and the prevailing common understandings have to do with the technical not the moral order,[14] with administrative regulation, business and technical convenience; (2) these cities are populated by people of diverse cultural origins removed from the indigenous seats of their cultures.

They are cities in which new states of mind, following from these characteristics, are developed and become prominent. The new states of mind are indifferent to or inconsistent with, or supersede or overcome, states of mind associated with local cultures and ancient civilizations. The intellectuals of these three groups of cities, if any, are intelligentsia rather than literati.[15]

The distinction that is then basic to consideration of the cultural role of cities is the distinction between the *carrying forward into systematic and reflective dimensions an old culture* and the *creating of original modes of thought that have authority beyond or in conflict with old cultures and civilizations.* We might speak of the orthogenetic cultural role of cities as contrasted with the heterogenetic cultural role.

---

[14] Robert Redfield, *The Primitive World and Its Transformations,* Ch. 3.
[15] Ibid, Ch. 3.

In both these roles the city is a place in which cultural change takes place. The roles differ as to the character of the change. Insofar as the city has an orthogenetic role, it is not to maintain culture as it was; the orthogenetic city is not static; it is the place where religious, philosophical and literary specialists reflect, synthesize and create out of the traditional material new arrangements and developments that are felt by the people to be outgrowths of the old. What is changed is a further statement of what was there before. Insofar as the city has a heterogenetic role, it is a place of conflict of differing traditions, a center of heresy, heterodoxy and dissent, of interruption and destruction of ancient tradition, of rootlessness and anomie. Cities are both these things, and the same events may appear to particular people or groups to be representative of what we here call orthogenesis or representative of heterogenesis. The predominating trend may be in one of the two directions, and so allow us to characterize the city, or that phase of the history of the city, as the one or the other. The lists just given suggest that the differences in the degree to which in the city orthogenesis or heterogenesis prevails are in cases strongly marked.

The presence of the market is not of itself a fact of heterogenetic change. Regulated by tradition, maintained by such customs and routines as develop over long periods of time, the market may flourish without heterogenetic change. In the medieval Muslim town we see an orthogenetic city; the market and the keeper of the market submitted economic activities to explicit cultural and religious definition of the norms. In Western Guatemala the people who come to market hardly communicate except with regard to buying and selling, and the market has little heterogenetic role. On the other hand the market in many instances provides occasions when men of diverse traditions may come to communicate and to differ; and also in the market occurs that exchange on the basis of universal standards of utility which is neutral to particular moral orders and in some sense hostile to all of them. The cities of Group 2, therefore, are cities unfavorable to orthogenetic change but not necessarily productive of heterogenetic change.

The City and the Folk Society [16]

The folk society may be conceived as that imagined combination of societal elements which would characterize a long-established, homogeneous, isolated and non-literate integral (self-contained) community; the folk culture is that society seen as a system of common understandings. Such a society can be approximately realized in a tribal band or village; it cannot be approximately realized in a city. What are characteristics of the city that may be conceived as a contrast to those of the folk society?

The city may be imagined as that community in which orthogenetic and

[16] Robert Redfield, "The Natural History of the Folk Society," *Social Forces*, Vol. 31 (1953) pp. 224–28.

heterogenetic transformations of the folk society have most fully occurred. The former has brought about the Great Tradition and its special intellectual class, administrative officers and rules closely derived from the moral and religious life of the local culture, and advanced economic institutions, also obedient to these local cultural controls. The heterogenetic transformations have accomplished the freeing of the intellectual, esthetic, economic and political life from the local moral norms, and have developed on the one hand an individuated expediential motivation, and on the other a revolutionary, nativistic, humanistic or ecumenical viewpoint, now directed toward reform, progress and designed change.

As these two aspects of the effects of the city on culture may be in part incongruent with each other, and as in fact we know them to occur in different degrees and arrangements in particular cities, we may now review the classification of cities offered [here] so as to recognize at least two types of cities conceived from this point of view:

A.   *The city of orthogenetic transformation: the city of the moral order;* the city of culture carried forward. In the early civilizations the first cities were of this kind and usually combined this developmental cultural function with political power and administrative control. But it is to be emphasized that this combination occurred because the local moral and religious norms prevailed and found intellectual development in the literati and exercise of control of the community in the ruler and the laws. Some of these early cities combined these two "functions" with commerce and economic production; others had little of these. It is as cities of predominating orthogenetic civilization that we are to view Peiping, Lhasa, Uaxactun, fourteenth-century Liège.

B.   *The city of heterogenetic transformation: the city of the technical order;* the city where local cultures are disintegrated and new integrations of mind and society are developed of the kinds described [earlier] ("The heterogenetic role of cities"). In cities of this kind men are concerned with the market, with "rational" organization of production of goods, with expediential relations between buyer and seller, ruler and ruled, and native and foreigner. In this kind of city the predominant social types are businessmen, administrators alien to those they administer, and rebels, reformers, planners and plotters of many varieties. It is in cities of this kind that priority comes to be given to economic growth and the expansion of power among the goods of life. The modern metropolis exhibits very much of this aspect of the city; the town built in the tropics by the United Fruit Company and the city built around the Russian uranium mine must have much that represents it; the towns of the colonial administration in Africa must show many of its features. Indeed, in one way or another, all the cities of groups 2, 3 and 4 (supra) are cities of the technical order, and are cities favorable to heterogenetic transformation of the moral order.[17]

[17] In the heterogenetic transformation the city and its hinterland become mutually involved: the conservative or reactionary prophet in the country inveighs against the innovations or backslidings of the city; and the reformer with the radically progressive message moves back from Medina against Mecca, or enters Jerusalem.

This type of city may be subdivided into the administrative city, city of the bureaucracy (Washington, D.C., Canberra), and the city of the entrepreneur (Hamburg, Shanghai). Of course many cities exhibit both characteristics.

"In every tribal settlement there is civilization; in every city is the folk society." We may look at any city and see within it the folk society insofar as ethnic communities that make it up preserve folklike characteristics, and we may see in a town in ancient Mesopotamia or in aboriginal West Africa a halfway station between folk society and orthogenetic civilization. We may also see in every city its double urban characteristics: we may identify the institutions and mental habits there prevailing with the one or the other of the two lines of transformation of folk life which the city brings about. The heterogenetic transformations have grown with the course of history, and the development of modern industrial world-wide economy, together with the great movements of peoples and especially those incident to the expansion of the West, have increased and accelerated this aspect of urbanization. The later cities are predominantly cities of the technical order. We see almost side by side persisting cities of the moral order and those of the technical order: Peiping and Shanghai, Cuzco and Guayaquil, a native town in Nigeria and an administrative post and railway center hard by.

The ancient city, predominantly orthogenetic, was not (as remarked by W. Eberhard) in particular cases the simple outgrowth of a single pre-civilized culture, but was rather (as in the case of Loyang) a city in which conquered and conqueror lived together, the conqueror extending his tradition over the conquered, or accepting the latter's culture. What makes the orthogenetic aspect of a city is the integration and uniform interpretation of preceding culture, whether its origins be one or several. Salt Lake City and early Philadelphia, cities with much orthogenetic character, were established by purposive acts of founders. Salt Lake City created its own hinterland on the frontier (as pointed out by C. Harris). Other variations on the simple pattern of origin and development of a city from an established folk people can no doubt be adduced.

Transformation of Folk Societies: Primary Urbanization and Secondary Urbanization.

The preceding account of different types of cities is perhaps satisfactory as a preliminary, but their cultural roles in the civilizations which they represent cannot be fully understood except in relation to the entire pattern of urbanization within that civilization, i.e., the number, size, composition, distribution, duration, sequence, morphology, function, rates of growth and decline, and the relation to the countryside and to each other of the cities within a civilization. Such information is rare for any civilization. In the present state of our knowledge it may be useful to guide further inquiry by assuming two hypothetical patterns of urbanization: primary and secondary.[18] In the primary phase a precivilized folk society is transformed by urbanization into a peasant society and correlated urban center. It is primary in the sense that the peoples making up the precivilized folk more or less share a common culture which remains the matrix too for the peasant and urban cultures which develop from it in the course of urbanization. Such a development, occurring slowly in communities not radically disturbed, tends to produce a "sacred culture" which is gradually transmuted by the literati of the cities into a "Great Tradition." Primary urbanization thus takes place almost entirely within the framework of a core culture that develops, as the local cultures become urbanized and transformed, into an indigenous civilization. This core culture dominates the civilization despite occasional intrusions of foreign peoples and cultures. When the encounter with other peoples and civilizations is too rapid and intense an indigenous civilization may be destroyed by de-urbanization or be variously mixed with other civilizations.[19]

This leads to the secondary pattern of urbanization: the case in which a folk society, precivilized, peasant, or partly urbanized, is further urbanized by contact with peoples of widely different cultures from that of its own members. This comes about through expansion of a local culture, now partly urbanized to regions inhabited by peoples of different cultures, or by the invasion of a culture-civilization by alien colonists or conquerors. This secondary pattern produces not only a new form of urban life in some part in conflict with local folk cultures but also new social types in both city and country. In the city appear "marginal" and "cosmopolitan" men and an "intelligentsia"; in the country various types of marginal folk: enclaved-, minority-, imperialized, transplanted-, remade-, quasi-folk, etc., depending on the kind of relation to the urban center.

This discussion takes up a story of the contact of peoples at the appearance of cities. But, here parenthetically, it is necessary to note that even before the appearance of cities the relations between small and primitive communities may be seen as on the one hand characterized by common culture and on the other by mutual usefulness with awareness of cultural difference. The "primary phase of urbanization" is a continuation of the extension of common culture from a small primitive settlement to a town and its hinterland, as no doubt could be shown for parts of West Africa. The "secondary phase of urbanization" is begun, before cities, in the institutions of travel and trade among local communities with different cultures. In Western Guatemala today simple Indian villagers live also in a wider trade-community of pluralistic cultures;[20] we do not know to what extent either the pre-Columbian semi-urban centers or the cities of the Spanish-modern conquerors and rulers have shaped this social system; it may be that these people were already on the

---

[18] This distinction is an extension of the distinction between the primary and secondary phases of folk transformations in Redfield, *The Primitive World and Its Transformations*, p. 41.

[19] Kirchhoff, op. cit.

[20] R. Redfield, "Primitive Merchants of Guatemala," *Quarterly Journal of Inter-American Relations*, Vol. 1, No. 4, 1939, pp. 48–49.

way to secondary urbanization before any native religious and political center rose to prominence.

While we do not know universal sequences within primary or secondary urbanization, it is likely that the degree to which any civilization is characterized by patterns of primary or secondary urbanization depends on the rate of technical development and the scope and intensity of contact with other cultures. If technical development is slow and the civilization is relatively isolated, we may expect to find a pattern of primary urbanization prevailing. If, on the other hand, technical development is rapid and contacts multiple and intense, secondary urbanization will prevail.

It may be that in the history of every civilization there is, of necessity, secondary urbanization. In modern Western civilization conditions are such as to make secondary urbanization the rule. But even in older civilizations it is not easy to find clear-cut examples of primary urbanization—because of multiple interactions, violent fluctuations in economic and military fortunes, conflicts and competition among cities and dynasties, and the raids of nomads. The Maya before the Spanish Conquest are perhaps a good example of primary urbanization.[21] The cases of the Roman, Greek, Hindu, Egyptian and Mesopotamian civilizations, although characterized by distinctive indigenous civilizations, are nevertheless complex because little is known about the degree of cultural homogeneity of the peoples who formed the core cultures and because as these civilizations became imperial they sought to assimilate more and more diverse peoples. Alternatively the irritant "seed" of a city may have been sown in some of them by the conquering raid of an outside empire, the desire to copy another empire in having a capital, or simple theft from another people—with the subsequent development around this seed of the "pearl" of a relatively indigenous, primary urban growth, sending out its own imperial secondary strands in due time. Thus while Rome, Athens, Chang-An and Loyang in early China and Peiping in later, Pataliputra and Benares, Memphis and Thebes, Nippur and Ur may have been for a time at least symbolic vehicles for loyalty to the respective empires and indigenous civilizations, it was not these relatively "orthogenetic" cities but the mixed cities on the periphery of an empire—the "colonial cities" which carried the core culture to other peoples. And in such cities, usually quite mixed in character, the imperial great tradition was not only bound to be very dilute but would also have to meet the challenge of conflicting local traditions. At the imperial peripheries, primary urbanization turns into secondary urbanization.[22]

Similar trends can be perceived in modern times: Russian cities in South-

[21] Redfield, *The Primitive World and Its Transformations*, pp. 58–73. See also Morley, *The Ancient Maya*, and Thomas Gann and J. Eric Thompson, *The History of the Maya*, New York, 1931.

[22] The case of China is particularly striking, since the evidence for a dominant core culture is unmistakable but its relation to local cultures which may have been its basis is unknown. See Chi Li, *The Formation of the Chinese People*, Cambridge, Harvard University Press, 1928, and Wolfram Eberhard, *Early Chinese Cultures and their Development*, Smithsonian Institution Annual Report, 1937, Washington, 1938.

For a good study of imperial "spread" and "dilution," see A. H. M. Jones, *The Greek City from Alexander to Justinian*, Oxford, 1940.

ern Europe and Asia appear to be very mixed[23] non-Arabic Muslim cities have developed in Africa and South Asia, and the colonial cities of the European powers admit native employees daily at the doors of their skyscraper banks. Possibly the nuclear cultures are homogeneous and create indigenous civilizations but as they expand into new areas far afield from the home cultures they have no choice but to build "heterogenetic" cities.

Modern "colonial" cities (e.g., Jakarta, Manila, Saigon, Bangkok, Singapore, Calcutta) raise the interesting question whether they can reverse from the "heterogenetic" to the "orthogenetic" role. For the last one hundred or more years they have developed as the outposts of imperial civilizations, but as the countries in which they are located achieve political independence, will the cities change their cultural roles and contribute more to the formation of a civilization indigenous to their areas? Many obstacles lie in the path of such a course. These cities have large, culturally diverse populations, not necessarily European, for example, the Chinese in Southeast Asia, Muslims and Hindu refugees from faraway provinces, in India; they often have segregated ethnic quarters, and their established administrative, military and economic functions are not easily changed. Many new problems have been created by a sudden influx of postwar refugee populations, and the cities' changing positions in national and global political and economic systems. While many of these colonial cities have been centers of nationalism and of movements for revival of the local cultures, they are not likely to live down their "heterogenetic" past.[24]

The Cultural Consequences of Primary and Secondary Urbanization

The discussion of primary and secondary urbanization has been a bare outline. It may be filled in by reference to some postulated consequences of each type of process. The most important cultural consequence of primary urbanization is the transformation of the Little Tradition into a Great Tradition. Embodied in "sacred books" or "classics," sanctified by a cult, expressed in monuments, sculpture, painting, and architecture, served by the other arts and sciences, the Great Tradition becomes the core culture of an indigenous civilization and a source, consciously examined, for defining its moral, legal, aesthetic and other cultural norms. A Great Tradition describes a way of life and as such is a vehicle and standard for those who share it to identify with one another as members of a common civilization. In terms of social structure, a significant event is the appearance of literati, those who represent the Great Tradition. The new forms of thought that now appear and extend themselves

[23] Chauncy Harris, "Ethnic groups in cities of the Soviet Union," *Geog. Rev.*, 1945.
[24] D. W. Fryer, "The 'million city' in Southeast Asia," *Geog. Rev.*, Oct., 1953; J. E. Spencer, "Changing Asiatic cities," *Geog. Rev.*, Vol. 41 (1951). This last is a summary of an article by Jean Chesneaux. See also *Record of the XXVIIth Meeting of the International Institute of Differing Civilizations*, Brussels, 1952, esp. papers by R. W. Steel and K. Neys.

include reflective and systematic thought; the definition of fixed idea-systems (theologies, legal codes); the development of esoteric or otherwise generally inaccessible intellectual products carried forward, now in part separate from the tradition of the folk; and the creation of intellectual and aesthetic forms that are both traditional and original (cities of the Italian Renaissance; development of "rococo" Maya sculpture in the later cities).

In government and administration the orthogenesis of urban civilization is represented by chiefs, rulers and laws that express and are closely controlled by the norms of the local culture. The chief of the Crow Indians, in a pre-civilized society, and the early kings of Egypt, were of this type. The Chinese emperor was in part orthogenetically controlled by the Confucian teaching and ethic; in some part he represented a heterogenetic development. The Roman pro-consul and the Indian Service of the United States, especially in certain phases, were more heterogenetic political developments.

Economic institutions of local cultures and civilizations may be seen to be orthogenetic insofar as the allocation of resources to production and distribution for consumption are determined by the traditional system of status and by the traditional specific local moral norms. The chief's yam house in the Trobriands is an accumulation of capital determined by these cultural factors. In old China the distribution of earnings and "squeeze" were distributed according to familial obligations: these are orthogenetic economic institutions and practices. The market, freed from controls of tradition, status and moral rule, becomes the world-wide heterogenetic economic institution.

In short, the trend of primary urbanization is to co-ordinate political, economic, educational, intellectual and aesthetic activity to the norms provided by the Great Traditions.

The general consequence of secondary urbanization is the weakening or supersession of the local and traditional cultures by states of mind that are incongruent with those local cultures. Among these are to be recognized:

1. The rise of a consensus appropriate to the technical order: i.e., based on self-interest and pecuniary calculation, or on recognition of obedience to common impersonal controls, characteristically supported by sanctions of force. (This in contrast to a consensus based on common religious and non-expediential moral norms.) There is also an autonomous development of norms and standards for the arts, crafts, and sciences.

2. The appearance of new sentiments of common cause attached to groups drawn from culturally heterogeneous backgrounds. In the city proletariats are formed and class or ethnic consciousness is developed, and also new professional and territorial groups. The city is the place where ecumenical religious reform is preached (though it is not originated there). It is the place where nationalism flourishes. On the side of social structure, the city is the place where new and larger groups are formed that are bound by few and powerful common interests and sentiments in place of the complexly interrelated roles and statuses that characterize the groups of local, long-established culture. Among social types that appear in this aspect of the cultural process in the city

are the reformer, the agitator, the nativistic or nationalistic leader, the tyrant and his assassin, the missionary and the imported school teacher.

3. The instability of viewpoint as to the future, and emphasis on prospective rather than retrospective view of man in the universe. In cities of predominantly orthogenetic influence, people look to a future that will repeat the past (either by continuing it or by bringing it around again to its place in the cycle). In cities of predominantly heterogenetic cultural influence there is a disposition to see the future as different from the past. It is this aspect of the city that gives rise to reform movements, forward-looking myths, and planning, revolutionary or melioristic. The forward-looking may be optimistic and radically reformistic; it may be pessimistic, escapist, defeatist or apocalyptic. In the city there are Utopias and counter-Utopias. Insofar as these new states of mind are secular, worldly, they stimulate new political and social aspiration and give rise to policy.

Consequences for World View, Ethos, and Typical Personality

The difference in the general cultural consequences of primary and secondary urbanization patterns may be summarily characterized by saying that in primary urbanization, all phases of the technical order (material technology, economy, government, arts, crafts, and sciences) are referred, in theory at least, to the standards and purposes of a moral order delineated in the Great Tradition, whereas in secondary urbanization different phases of the technical order are freed from this reference and undergo accelerated autonomous developments. With respect to this development, the moral order, or rather orders, for there are now many competing ones, appears to lag.[25]

There is another way of describing these differences: in terms of the consequences of the two kinds of urbanization for changes in world view, ethos, and typical personality.[26] To describe the consequences in these terms is to describe them in their bearings and meanings for the majority of individual selves constituting the society undergoing urbanization. We now ask, how do primary and secondary urbanization affect mental outlook, values and attitudes, and personality traits? These are in part psychological questions, for they direct our attention to the psychological aspects of broad cultural processes.

There are many accounts of the psychological consequences of urbanization. These have described the urban outlook, ethos, and personality as depersonalized, individualized, emotionally shallow and atomized, unstable, secularized, blasé, rationalistic, cosmopolitan, highly differentiated, self-critical, time-coordinated, subject to sudden shifts in mood and fashion, "other-

[25] Redfield, *The Primitive World and Its Transformations*, pp. 72–83.
[26] For a further discussion of these concepts, see Redfield, ibid., Ch. 4, and Redfield, *The Little Community*, University of Chicago Press (forthcoming), Chs. 5 and 6 on personality and mental outlook.

directed," etc.[27] The consensus in these descriptions and their general acceptance by social scientists seem great enough to indicate that there probably is a general psychological consequence of urbanization, although it cannot be precisely described and proven. We should, however, like to suggest that the "urban way of life" that is described in the characterizations to which we refer is primarily a consequence of secondary urbanization and of that in a particular critical stage when personal and cultural disorganization are greatest. To see these consequences in perspective, it is necessary to relate them on the one hand to the consequences of primary urbanization and on the other to those situations of secondary urbanization that produce new forms of personal and cultural integration. Most of all it is necessary to trace the continuities as well as the discontinuities in outlook, values, and personality, as we trace the transformation of folk societies into their civilized dimension. The "peasant" is a type that represents an adjustment between the values of the precivilized tribe and those of the urbanite. The "literati" who fashion a Great Tradition do not repudiate the values and outlook of their rural hinterland but systematize and elaborate them under technical specialization. The cosmopolitan "intelligentsia" and "sophists" of the metropolitan centers have a prototype in the "heretic" of the indigenous civilization. And even the most sophisticated urban centers are not without spiritualists, astrologers and other practitioners with links to a folk-like past.[28]

The connections between the folk culture, the Great Tradition, and the sophisticated culture of the heterogenetic urban centers can be traced not only in the continuities of the historical sequence of a particular group of local cultures becoming urbanized and de-urbanized, but they also can be traced in the development of two distinct forms of cultural consciousness which appear in these transformations.

Cultural Integration Between City and Country

From what has been said about primary and secondary urbanization it follows that city and country are more closely integrated, culturally, in the primary phase of urbanization than in the secondary phase. Where the city has grown out of a local culture, the country people see its ways as in some important part a form of their own, and they feel friendlier toward the city

[27] See L. Wirth, "Urbanism as a way of life," and G. Simmel, "The metropolis and mental life," both reprinted in Hatt and Reiss, *Reader in Urban Sociology;* E. Fromm, *Escape from Freedom,* David Riesman and collaborators, *The Lonely Crowd,* and A. Kroeber, *Anthropology,* 1948, sec. 121. For the effects of urban life on time-coordination, see H. A. Hawley, *Human Ecology,* Ch. 15, and P. Hallowell, "Temporal orientations in western and non-western cultures," *American Anthropologist,* Vol. 39, 1937.

[28] Redfield, *The Folk Culture of Yucatan,* Ch. 11; R. E. Park, "Magic, Mentality, and City Life," reprinted in Park, *Human Communities.*

N. C. Chaudhuri, *The Autobiography of an Unknown Indian,* Macmillan Publishing Co., Inc., 1951, gives some interesting observations on the survival of "folk" beliefs and practices among the people of Calcutta, pp. 361–62.

P. Masson-Oursel, "La Sophistique. Etude de philosophi comparée," *Revue de metaphysique et de morale,* 23 (1916), pp. 343–62.

than do country people ruled by a proconsul from afar. The stereotype of "the wicked city" will be stronger in the hinterlands of the heterogenetic cities than in those of the orthogenetic cities. Many of these are sacred centers of faith, learning, justice and law.

Nevertheless, even in primary urbanization a cultural gap tends to grow between city and country. The very formation of the Great Tradition introduces such a gap. The literati of the city develop the values and world view of the local culture to a degree of generalization, abstraction and complexity incomprehensible to the ordinary villager, and in doing so leave out much of the concrete local detail of geography and village activity. The Maya Indian who lived in some rural settlement near Uaxactun could not have understood the calendrical intricacies worked out in that shrine-city by the priests; and the rituals performed at the city-shrine and one high level of meaning for the priest and another lower meaning, connecting with village life at some points only, for the ordinary Indian.

On the other hand, primary urbanization involves the development of characteristic institutions and societal features that hold together, in a certain important measure of common understanding, the Little Tradition and the Great Tradition. We may refer to the development of these institutions and societal features as the universalization of cultural consciousness—meaning by "universalization," the preservation and extension of common understanding as to the meaning and purpose of life, and sense of belonging together, to all the people, rural or urban, of the larger community. Some of the ways in which this universalization takes place are suggested in the following paragraphs. The examples are taken chiefly from India; they probably have considerable cross-cultural validity.

1. The embodiment of the Great Tradition in "sacred books" and secondarily in sacred monuments, art, icons, etc. Such "sacred scriptures" may be in a language not widely read or understood; nevertheless they may become a fixed point for the worship and ritual of ordinary people. The place of the "Torah" in the lives of Orthodox Jews, the Vedas among orthodox Hindus, the "Three Baskets" for Buddhists, the thirteen classics for Confucianists, the Koran for Muslims, the stelae and temples of the ancient Maya, are all examples of such sacred scriptures, although they may vary in degree of sacredness and in canonical status.

2. The development of a special class of "literati" (priests, rabbis, Imams, Brahmins) who have the authority to read, interpret, and comment on the sacred scriptures. Thus the village Brahmin who reads the Gita for villagers at ceremonies mediates a part of the Great Tradition of Hinduism for them.

The mediation of a great tradition is not always this direct. At the village level it may be carried in a multitude of ways—by the stories parents and grandparents tell children, by professional reciters and storytellers, by dramatic performances and dances, in songs and proverbs, etc.

In India the epics and puranas have been translated into the major regional languages and have been assimilated to the local cultures. This interaction of a "great tradition" and the "little tradition" of local and regional cultures needs further study, especially in terms of the professional and semiprofessional "mediators" of the process.

3. The role of leading personalities who because they themselves embody or know some aspects of a Great Tradition succeed through their personal position as leaders in mediating a Great Tradition to the masses of people. There is a vivid account of this process in Jawarhalal Nehru's *Discovery of India*, in which he describes first how he "discovered" the Great Tradition of Indian in the ruins of Mohenjo-Daro and other archeological monuments, her sacred rivers and holy cities, her literature, philosophy, and history. And then he describes how he discovered the "little traditions" of the people and the villages, and how through his speeches he conveyed to them a vision of Bharat Mata—Mother India—that transcended the little patches of village land, people, and customs.[29]

4. Nehru's account suggests that actual physical places, buildings and monuments—especially as they become places of sacred or patriotic pilgrimage—are important means to a more universalized cultural consciousness and the spread of a Great Tradition. In India this has been and still is an especially important universalizing force. The sanctity of rivers and the purifying powers of water go all the way back to the Rig Veda. The Buddhists—who may have started the practice of holy pilgrimages—believed that there were four places that the believing man should visit with awe and reverence: Buddha's birthplace, the site where he attained illumination or perfect insight, the place where the mad elephant attacked him, and the place where Buddha died. In the *Mahabharata*, there is a whole book on the subject of holy places (Arareyaka Book). Even a sinner who is purified by holy water will go to heaven. And the soul ready for moksha will surely achieve it if the pilgrim dies on a pilgrimage.[30] Today the millions of pilgrims who flock to such preeminent holy spots as Allahabad or Banaras create problems of public safety and urban overcrowding, but they, like Nehru, are also discovering the Bharat Mata beyond their villages.

In India "sacred geography" has also played an important part in determining the location and layout of villages and cities and in this way has created a cultural continuity between countryside and urban centers. In ancient India, at least, every village and every city had a "sacred center" with temple, tank, and garden. And the trees and plants associated with the sacred shrine were also planted in private gardens, for the households too had their sacred center; the house is the "body" of a spirit (Varta Purusha) just as the human body is the "house" of the soul.[31]

[29] Jawarharlal Nehru, *The Discovery of India*, (New York: The John Day Co., Publishers, 1946), pp. 37–40, 45–51.

[30] D. Patil, *Cultural History from the Vāya Purāna*, Poona, 1946, Appendix B.

[31] C. P. V. Ayyar, *Town Planning in the Ancient Dekkan*, Madras, no date, with an introduction by Patrick Geddes. See also Patrick Geddes in *India*, ed. J. Tyrwhitt, London, 1947.

N. V. Ramanayya, *An Essay on the Origin of the South Indian Temple*, Madras, 1930, and Stella Kramrisch, *The Hindu Temple*, Calcutta, 1946.

H. Rao, "Rural habitation in South India," *Quarterly Journal of the Mythic Society*, 14.

At each of these levels—of household, village, and city—the "sacred center" provides the forum, the vehicle, and the content for the formation of distinct cultural identities—of families, village, and city. But as individuals pass outward, although their contacts with others become less intimate and less frequent, they nevertheless are carried along by the continuity of the "sacred centers," feeling a consciousness of a single cultural universe where people hold the same things sacred, and where the similarities of civic obligations in village and city to maintain tanks, build public squares, plant fruit trees, erect platforms and shrines, is concrete testimony to common standards of virtue and responsibility.

Surely such things as these—a "sacred scripture," and a sacred class to interpret it, leading personalities, "sacred geography" and the associated rites and ceremonies—must in any civilization be important vehicles for the formation of that common cultural consciousness from which a Great Tradition is fashioned and to which it must appeal if it is to stay alive. It is in this sense that the universalization of cultural consciousness is a necessary ingredient in its formation and maintenance. Moreover, as the discussion of the role of "sacred geography" in the formation of Hinduism has intimated, this process does not begin only at the point where the villager and the urbanite merge their distinct cultural identities in a higher identity, but is already at work at the simpler levels of family, caste and village, and must play an important part in the formation and maintenance of the Little Tradition at these levels.[32]

The integration of city and country in the secondary phase of urbanization cannot rest on a basic common cultural consciousness or a common culture, for there is none. Rural-urban integration in this phase of urbanization rests primarily on the mutuality of interests and on the "symbiotic" relations that

J. M. Linton Bogle, *Town Planning in India*, Oxford University Press, 1929.

Mudgett and others, *Banaras: Outline of a Master Plan*, prepared by Town and Village Planning Office, Lucknow.

[32] See Robert Redfield, *The Little Community*, Ch. 8, on the little community "As a community within communities."

In addition to [these] factors, it has been usual to single out special items of content of the world view and values of a Great Tradition as explanations of the "Universalization" of Great Traditions. It has been frequently argued, e.g., that religions which are monotheistic and sanction an "open class" social system will appeal more to ordinary people and spread faster than those which are polytheistic and which sanction "caste" systems. (See e.g., H. J. Kissling, "The sociological and educational role of the Dervish orders in the Ottoman Empire," in G. von Grunebaum (ed.), *Studies in Islamic Cultural History*.) F. S. C. Northrop and Arnold Toynbee both attach great importance to the ideological content of cultures as factors in their spread, although they come out with different results. It may be that such special features of content are important in the formation and spread of some particular religions at some particular time, but it is doubtful that they would have the same role in different civilizations under all circumstances. In his recent study of the Coorgs of South India, Srinivas argues with considerable plausibility that the spread of Hinduism on an all-India basis has depended on its polytheism, which had made it easy to incorporate all sorts of alien dieties, and on a caste system which assimilates every new cultural or ethnic group as a special caste.

Another difficulty about using special features of content of some particular tradition as a general explanation of the formation and maintenance of any Great Tradition is that one inevitably selects features that have been crystallized only after a long period of historical development and struggle. These are more relevant as factors in explaining further development and spread than they are in explaining the cultural-psychological processes that have accompanied primary urbanization. The "universalization" of universal faiths takes us into the realm of secondary urbanization where diverse and conflicting cultures must be accommodated.

have often been described.[33] The city is a "service station" and amusement center for the country, and the country is a "food basket" for the city. But while the diversity of cultural groups and the absence of a common culture make the basis of the integration primarily technical, even this kind of integration requires a kind of cultural consciousness to keep it going. We refer to the consciousness of cultural differences and the feeling that certain forms of inter-cultural association are of great enough benefit to override the repugnance of dealing with "foreigners." We may call this an "enlargement of cultural horizons" sufficient to become aware of other cultures and of the possibility that one's own society may in some ways require their presence. To paraphrase Adam Smith, it is not to the interest of the (Jewish) baker, the (Turkish) carpet-dealer, the (French) hand laundry, that the American Christian customer looks when he patronizes them, but to his own.

This is the practical psychological basis for admission of the stranger and tolerance of foreign minorities, even at the level of the folk society.[34] In a quotation from the *Institutions of Athens,* which Toynbee has, perhaps ironically, titled "Liberté-Egalité-Fraternité," we are told that the reason why Athens has "extended the benefits of Democracy to the relations between slaves and freemen and between aliens and citizens" is that "the country requires permanent residence of aliens in her midst on account both of the multiplicity of trades and of her maritime activities."[35]

When all or many classes of a population are culturally strange to each other and where some of the city populations are culturally alien to the country populations, the necessity for an enlarged cultural consciousness is obvious. In societies where social change is slow, and there was developed an adjustment of mutual usefulness and peaceful residence side by side of groups culturally different but not too different, the culturally complex society may be relatively stable.[36] But where urban development is great, such conditions are apt to be unstable. Each group may be perpetually affronted by the beliefs and practices of the other groups. Double standards of morality will prevail, since each cultural group will have one code for its "own kind" and another for the "outsiders." This simultaneous facing both inward and outward puts a strain on both codes. There may then be present the drives to proseletize, to withdraw and dig in, to persecute and to make scapegoats; there may even be fear of riot and massacre. In such circumstances the intellectuals become the chief exponents of a "cosmopolitan" enlarged cultural consciousness, inventing formulas of universal toleration and the benefits of mutual understanding, and extolling the freedom to experiment in different ways of life. But they do

[33] R. E. Park, "Symbiosis and socialization: a frame of reference for the study of society," reprinted in *Human Communities,* Free Press, Glencoe, 1952.

[34] Robert Redfield, *The Primitive World and Its Transformations,* pp. 33–34, for the institutionalization of hospitality to strangers in peasant societies.

[35] Arnold Toynbee, *Greek Civilization and Character,* Beacon Press, Boston, 1950, pp. 48–49. See also David G. Mandelbaum, "The Jewish way of life in Cochin," *Jewish Social Studies,* Vol. I (1939).

[36] Redfield, "Primitive Merchants of Guatemala."

not always prevail against the more violent and unconvinced crusaders for some brand of cultural purity.

In primary urbanization when technical development was quite backward, a common cultural consciousness did get formed. The travelling student, teacher, saint, pilgrim or even humble villager who goes to the next town may be startled by strange and wonderful sights, but throughout his journey he is protected by the compass of the common culture from cultural shock and disorientation. In ancient times students and teachers came from all over India and even from distant countries to study at Taxila, just as they came from all over Greece to Athens. In secondary urbanization, especially under modern conditions, technical developments in transportation, travel and communication enormously facilitate and accelerate cultural contacts. The effects of this on common cultural consciousness are not easy briefly to characterize. They make the more traditional cultural differences less important. They provide a wide basis of common understanding with regard to the instruments and practical means of living. It is at least clear that the integration of country and city that results is not the same kind of sense of common purpose in life that was provided to rural-urban peoples through the institutions mediating Little and Great Traditions referred to [earlier]. At this point the enquiry approaches the questions currently asked about the "mass culture" of modern great societies.

Cities as Centers of Cultural Innovation, Diffusion, and Progress

It is a commonly stated view that the city rather than the country is the source of cultural innovations, that such innovations diffuse outward from city to country, and that the "spread" is more or less inverse to distance from the urban center.[37] The objection to this view is not that it is wrong—for there is much evidence that would seem to support it—but that the limits and conditions of its validity need to be specified. It seems to assume for example that in the processes of cultural change, innovation, and diffusion, "city" and "country" are fixed points of reference which do not have histories, or interact, and are not essentially related to larger contexts of cultural change. Yet such assumptions—if ever true—would hold only under the most exceptional and short-run conditions. It is one thing to say that a large metropolitan city is a "center" of cultural innovation and diffusion for its immediate hinterland at a

[37] P. Sorokin and C. Zimmerman, *Principles of Rural-Urban Sociology*, (New York: H. H., Rinehart and Winston, 1929), Ch. 17, "The role of the city and the country in innovation, disruption, and preservation of the national culture."
Chabot, G., "Les zones d'influence d'une ville," *Congr. int. de Geog.*, Paris, 1931, III, pp. 432–37.
Jefferson, Mark, "The law of the primate city," *Geog. Rev.*, 1939, 226–32.
Spate, O. H. K., "Factors in the development of capital cities," *Geog. Rev.*, 1942, pp. 622–31.
R. E. Park, "The urban community as a spatial pattern and a moral order," "Newspaper circulation and metropolitan regions," both reprinted in Park, *Human Communities.*
Hiller, "Extension of urban characteristics into rural areas," *Rural Sociology*, Vol. 6 (1941).

particular time; it is another to ask how that center itself was formed, over how long a period and from what stimuli. In other words, as we enlarge the time span, include the rise and fall of complex distributions of cities, allow for the mutual interactions between them and their hinterlands, and also take account of interactions with other civilizations and their rural-urban patterns, we find that the processes of cultural innovation and "flow" are far too complex to be handled by simple mechanical laws concerning the direction, rate, and "flow" of cultural diffusion between "city" and "country." The cities themselves are creatures as well as creators of this process, and it takes a broad cross-cultural perspective to begin to see what its nature is. While this perspective may not yield simple generalizations about direction and rates of cultural diffusion, to widen the viewpoint as here suggested may throw some light on the processes of cultural change, including the formation and cultural "influence" of cities.

In a primary phase of urbanization, when cities are developing from folk societies, it seems meaningless to assert, e.g., that the direction of cultural flow is from city to country. Under these conditions a folk culture is transformed into an urban culture which is a specialization of it, and if we wish to speak of "direction of flow" it would make more sense to see the process as one of a series of concentrations and nucleations within a common field. And as these concentrations occur, the common "Little Tradition" has not become inert; in fact, it may retain a greater vitality and disposition to change than the systematized Great Tradition that gets "located" in special classes and in urban centers. From this point of view the spatial and mechanical concepts of "direction" and "rate" of flow, etc., are just metaphors of the processes involved in the formation of a Great Tradition. The cultural relations between city and country have to be traced in other terms, in terms of sociocultural history and of cultural-psychological processes. Physical space and time may be important obstacles and facilitators to these processes but they are not the fundamental determinants of cultural "motion" as they are of physical motion.

Under conditions of secondary urbanization, the spatial and mechanical concepts seem more appropriate because people and goods are more mobile and the technical development of the channels of transportation and communication is such as to permit highly precise measurement of their distributions and of "flows." But here too we may be measuring only some physical facts whose cultural significance remains indeterminate, or, at most, we may be documenting only a particularly recent cultural tendency to analyze intercultural relations in quantitative, abstract, and non-cultural terms. The assumption of a continuous and quantitatively divisible "diffusion" from a fixed urban center is unrealistic.

We may see Canton or Calcutta as a center for the diffusion of Western culture into the "east." We may also see these cities as relatively recent metropolitan growths, beginning as minor outliers of Oriental civilizations and then attracting both foreign and also uprooted native peoples, varying in fortune with worldwide events, and becoming at last not so much a center for the in-

troduction of Western ways as a center for nativistic and independence movements to get rid of Western control and dominance. "Everything new happens at Canton," is said in China. We have in such a case not simple
diffusion, or spread of urban influence from a city, but rather a cultural interaction which takes place against a background of ancient civilization with its
own complex and changing pattern of urbanization now coming into contact
with a newer and different civilization and giving rise to results that conform
to neither.

The city may be regarded, but only very incompletely, as a center from
which spreads outward the idea of progress. It is true that progress, like the
ideologies of nationalism, socialism, communism, capitalism and democracy,
tends to form in cities and it is in cities that the prophets and leaders of these
doctrines are formed. Yet the states of mind of Oriental and African peoples
are not copies of the minds of Western exponents of progress or of one or
another political or economic doctrine. There is something like a revolution of
mood and aspiration in the non-European peoples today.[38] The Easterner
revolts against the West; he does not just take what can be borrowed from a
city; he does sometimes the opposite: the Dutch language is set aside in Indonesia; there, anthropology, because associated with Dutch rule, does not
spread from any city but is looked on with suspicion as associated with Dutch
rule. Moreover, the influence of the West does not simply move outward
from cities; it leap-frogs into country regions; a city reformer in Yucatan, Car-
rillo Puerto, arouses village Indians to join his civil war for progress and
freedom against landowners and townspeople; Marxists discover that revolution can be based on the peasants without waiting for the development of an
industrial proletariat.[39]

The conception of progress is itself an idea shaped by and expressive of one
culture or civilization, that of the recent West.[40] What Toynbee and others
have called the "Westernization" of the world may be the spread of only parts
of the ideas associated in the West with the word "progress." Not without investigation can it be safely assumed that the spread of Western ideas from cities carries into the countryside a new and Western value system emphasizing
hard work, enterprise, a favorable view of social change and a central faith in
material prosperity. In the cases of some of the peoples affected by modern
urbanization these values may be already present. In other cases the apparent
spread of progress may turn out, on closer examination, to be a return to ancient values different from those of the West. Nationalistic movements are in
part a nostalgic turning back to local traditional life. We shall understand better the varieties and complexities of the relations today between city and

[38] For further discussion of these concepts of "mood," "aspiration" and "policy" as they might figure
in community studies, see Redfield, *The Little Community,* chapter on "Little Community as a History."
[39] David Mitrany, *Marx and the Peasants.*
[40] See A. L. Kroeber, *Anthropology,* Secs. 127, 128; Milton Singer, *Shame Cultures and Guilt Cultures,*
for an examination of some of the evidence on this point for American Indian cultures. Also see Redfield, *A Village that Chose Progress,* esp. Chapter 8, "Chan Kom, Its Ethos and Success." Recent material on cross-cultural comparisons of value systems will be found in Daryll Forde (ed.), *African Worlds,*
and in the publications of the Harvard Values Study Project directed by Clyde Kluckhohn.

country as we compare the values and world views of the modernizing ideologies, and those of the Little and Great Traditions of the cultures and civilizations that are affected by the modern West. It may be that such studies [41] will discover greater "ambivalence" in the mood to modernize than we, here in the West, acknowledge; that the progressive spirit of Asia and Africa is not simply a decision to walk the road of progressive convictions that we have traversed, but rather in significant part an effort of the "backward" peoples to recover from their disruptive encounters with the West by returning to the "sacred centers" of their ancient indigenous civilizations.

Cultural Roles and Primary Urban Types *

RICHARD G. FOX

The final offering in this section on the development and differentiation of cities is an excerpt from the introduction to Richard Fox's recent text, Urban Anthropology. *Developing his earlier remarks, which called for a more sophisticated approach to urban anthropology, Fox examines the relationship between cities and the societies which they serve. He suggests a typology of cultural roles and primary urban types, beginning with a categorization of four functions that cities perform. He posits that the ability to maximize such functions varies along the dual dimensions of state power and urban economy. In short, city role (or type) is dependent upon the broader societal type.*

Cultural Roles and Primary Urban Types

If state societies are the social and cultural settings in which cities develop, if they constitute the primary environment to which urban places adapt, then a logical postulate is that different sorts of states will have distinctive sorts of cities. Their settings in different types of states profoundly affect the external relations and thus the cultural roles of cities. Although the specific urban functions, or cultural roles, performed by cities take place within the political and economic institutions of the larger society, they can be abstracted from their societal context to give some idea of their latitude and diversity. The cul-

[41] Several such studies have been made. See, e.g., Paul Mus, *Viet-Nam, l'histoire d'une guerre,* Paris, 1952; Shen-Yu Dai, *Mao Tse-Tung and Confucianism,* Doctoral Dissertation, University of Pennsylvania, 1952; E. Sarkisyanz, Russian *Weltanschauung and Islamic and Buddhist Messianism,* Doctoral Dissertation, University of Chicago, 1953. V. Barnouw, "The Changing Character of a Hindu Festival," *American Anthropologist,* February, 1954.

tural roles performed by cities are (a) ideological, (b) administrative, (c) mercantile, and (d) industrial. All cities perform these roles in varying degree, but under particular conditions, either the ideological, the administrative, or the mercantile-industrial can be viewed as the dominant or primary cultural role of cities in a specific society. These economic and political conditions and the urban variety associated with them are detailed in the typology that follows.

Before turning to the actual urban types and their associated state societies and economic institutions, we must clarify what each of these urban functions entails. The *ideological cultural role* is performed by the city when it functions as a center of cult and ceremony, a site of political prestige and regal functions (as distinct from bare political coercion and power), a stage for the enactment of rituals that buttress or even define the powers of the state elite—whether sacred priest, divine king, or bureaucrat-president. All cities, but especially capitals, are heavily involved with the trappings of ritual and prestige that legitimate the state and the ruling elite, that broadcast the social order as an aspect of the divine or at least the suprahuman, and that thereby charter the city as a center of belief and ceremony.

Administrative functions are performed by the city in its role as a concentration of political power, an abode for the elite who wield this power, and a storehouse for the economic wealth drained from the surrounding rural countryside by such power. Through its administrative functions, the city coalesces transportation and communication channels, dense populations subsuming both military-administrative elites and their servitors, and appurtenances such as walls, temples, palaces, markets, plazas, universities, and gardens. These appurtenances strikingly distinguish the puissant city from its economically, politically, and culturally denuded hinterland.

Mercantile functions are performed by the city in its role as a site for the production of wealth through trade, land speculation, and craft production (as distinct from revenue levies on the rural hinterland garnered through urban administrative functions). Here the city broadcasts a particular economic regimen to the larger society and also becomes a center for the supply of luxury and high-status goods. The mercantile cultural role is generally undertaken by specialized urban merchant populations but may also include the administrative elite as capitalizers of trade or handicraft. Mercantile functions based on land speculation are usually in the hands of administrative elites.

Industrial functions are performed by the city in its role as a center for the creation of wealth in the society, but through industrial productivity rather than mercantile activity. Here specialized institutions of production and transaction—factories, stock markets, railroads, etc.—as well as the specialized institutions of government required to maintain them flow out from the city. They, in turn, transform the economic activity, organization of labor, and productivity in the wider society. In many respects, the industrial cultural role is like mercantile functions except that new technology and social organization make the city even more a producer of wealth.

Specifying these self-evident urban functions in itself says little that is new about cities. These urban functions or cultural roles must next be related to particular sociocultural contexts: Under what conditions in the larger society is the urban administrative cultural role foremost? In what societal contexts do ideological functions predominate in cities? Since the city has been defined in terms of state societies, it follows that different concatenations of state power and organization will relate to the variable importance of a particular urban function. The economic autonomy of the city (in terms of wealth production) from the larger society is also an important dimension. These factors are not presented as necessarily causal, but they are advanced as useful in indicating the connection of particular urban functions with specific economic and political settings. The two dimensions to be used in typologizing the primary level of urban variability are [as follows]:

1. *Extent of state power.* The important diagnostic of state societies . . . is the existence of a ruling body, or government, that exercises social control ultimately based on physical coercion. State societies can thus be categorized by the amount of coercion they can exercise on their populations. Coercion is measured by the territorial extent and centralization of power associated with the state. Another (and complementary) means of categorizing states depends on the degree of specialization and organizational complexity of the ruling body: to what extent state leaders form an economic and political class set apart from the general population; to what extent access to power is determined by birth or achievement; and to what extent specializations of functions and bureaucratic organization exist within the ruling body. Based on these criteria, state power may range from weak to strong—or in terms of organization, from *segmentary* to *bureaucratic*.

The cultural roles of cities also vary along this dimension of state power. In weak, or segmentary states, the ideological function of urban places is primary and defines the external adaptation of the city to the wider society. In strong, or bureaucratic states, the urban administrative function is most significant in defining the links of city and society.

2. *Extent of urban economic autonomy.* This dimension measures the degree to which the city is an independent producer of wealth in trade or industry and therefore the extent to which the economic organization of the urban sphere dominates and transforms productivity throughout the entire society. Such economic conditions may vary from the complete *external dependency* of the city on food and revenue drawn from its rural agricultural environs to total *internal autonomy* of the urban sphere in the production of wealth and in the determination of economic practices for the entire society. The greater the economic autonomy enjoyed by cities in state societies, the more developed will be mercantile or industrial urban cultural roles.

The two dimensions of state power and urban economy can be plotted as axes of a graph as in Figure 1. This representation postulates that specific combinations of state weakness or power and urban (economic) depedency or autonomy are related to the predominance of ideological, administrative, or mercantile-industrial cultural roles in cities. For example, the figure posits

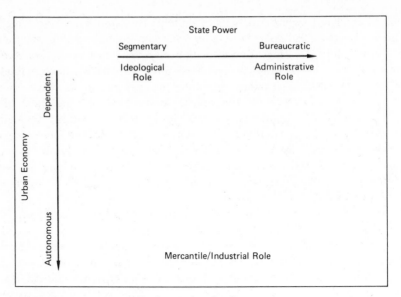

FIGURE 1.   Dimensions of Urban Cultural Roles.

that urban ideological functions would be strongest when the state is segmentary and urban economy is externally dependent. Any empirical case might differ from this expectation depending on the specific nature of the individual city. Figure 1, however, attempts to classify a *primary* pattern of urban cultural roles under particular economic and political conditions, rather than to specify the secondary urban variability that makes every city within a state society somewhat different.

To note how these urban cultural roles gravitate around particular combinations of state power and urban economy is not sufficient, however. They must be given a conceptual embodiment that can be used as a referent to analyze or comprehend empirical cases of state societies and their attendant urban forms. Figure 2 presents such a typology of urban places based on the foregoing cultural roles and the political and economic conditions of state societies that accentuate one or another of these roles. The five primary urban types in Figure 2 represent examples of the "constructed type": "a purposive, planned selection, abstraction, combination and (sometimes) accentuation of a set of criteria with empirical referents that serves as a basis for comparison of empirical cases."[1] Thus, on the basis of the typology illustrated in Figure 2, we should expect that under conditions of weak state power and high urban economic dependency, the ideological functions of cities will be primary in the society and that such urban places will have the characteristics of regal-ritual

[1] John C. McKinney, "Sociological Theory and the Process of Typification," in *Theoretical Sociology: Perspectives and Developments,* John C. McKinney and Edward A. Tiryakian, eds. (Englewood Cliffs, New Jersey: Prentice-Hall, Inc., 1970), pp. 247–48.

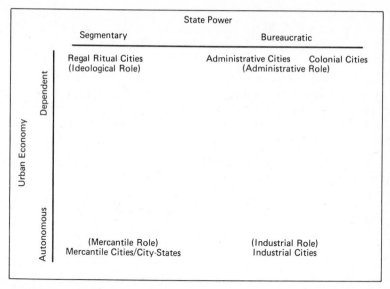

FIGURE 2.   Primary Urban Types.

cities. When the state is strong and urban economy is autonomous, so that mercantile roles are foremost, we expect the character of cities to follow the mercantile type.

Part III: Research/Term Paper Topics

1. "Industrialization and Urbanization."
   Many have suggested an iron bond between the growth of industrialization and the growth of cities in the past century. Do you agree or disagree that the two are connected? Review the literature and support your position.

2. "The Bases for Typing Cities."
   Do you agree with the types of typologies offered in the Introduction? How would you change or rearrange them? What new typology (or typologies) might you create?

3. "The Chicago Paradigm and the Earliest Cities."
   Does it fit?

4. "Early Industrialization and City Life."
   Investigate the life-styles in nineteenth-century industrializing cities. Contrast with present industrial city life. What accounts for the differences? Is the wider society (and national government) a factor?

5. "The Colonial City."

Develop an argument for it as a type with cross-cultural validity. To what extent is it dependent and independent of the cultures of both colonizers and colonized?

6. "Your City—What Type Is It?"

What role has industrialization played in it? Did it have a pre-industrial phase? If nonindustrial, why not? Why did its particular function develop? Has this function changed? Can one talk about a "single" or "predominant-function" city today?

PART

Urbanization

FOUR

Ralph Beals called *urbanization* "the problem of modification of human behavior imposed by the urban way of life." It is a process of "adaptation" (1951:5). Because adaptation involves both the environment and the characteristics of the organism, the process will exhibit a great variety of expressions; for no two cities or migrant groups are the same.

The complexity of the urbanization process is such that valid generalizations are still scarce, which is small wonder. The urbanization of any individual or group depends upon at least the following six factors:

1. City type. Industrial, royal, colonial, bureaucratic, provincial trade, market, ritual, agricultural, and other city types determine the urban economic base, stratification system, welfare opportunities, and a host of other phenomena.
2. Migrant base-type. Peasant, tribal, general rural, small town, urban foreign, and other previous life-styles obviously condition migrant adaptive styles.
3. Reason for migration. Push or pull? Escape versus temporary urban residence for capital accumulation or education to be reinvested later in home area. Each reason differently affects commitment to residence in, and mastery of, the city.
4. Distance of migration. Migration from nearby hinterlands implies the possibility for continuing contact with rural home and the possibility for continual reinforcement of rural values, or establishment of stable rural/urban interaction structures. Migrants from other nations or great distances face greater pressures for assimilation.
5. Conditions of urban reception. Does the new migrant stay with friends and kin, or alone? In a slum? Central city versus peripheral neighborhood?
6. Personal skills of the migrant. This is the "fudge factor" but it is logically important. It includes migrant personality—self-confidence and interpersonal skills—as much as mechanical abilities and job qualifications. Mental health in cities is a major problem, and evidence suggests new migrants show a higher incidence of problems than do stable urban residents. Degenerative organic disorders (coronary heart disease, for example) also seem to be more common.

Obviously, given such considerations, urbanization must be viewed as a matter of degree. The authors in the following section stress that mere residence in the city does not bring automatic urbanization, particularly when home ties and identity remain strong and continually reinforced. On the other hand, for many urban migrants the maintenance of rural home ties or customs is crucial to successful adaptation to the city.

But again, what is "city?" As McElrath points out, new cities in new nations are vastly different from established cities in industrial societies. The new cities tend to expand independently of their economic bases. Their peripheries teem with migrants exerting, as some have suggested, a ruralizing influence upon the cities and upon each other. Cities in the United States, on the other hand, are losing established urban populations. Recently, the people's flight to the suburbs has been joined by corporations, resulting in the legitimation of suburbs as full-time, full-life (rather than mere dormitory) communities. The decaying, crime-heavy, tax-poor city centers that may result become receiving grounds and full-life communities for new migrants. What is urbanization for them? And today, energy concerns are leading some to argue that soon (indeed, it has already begun) we will see a return to the city by ex-suburbanites. How will they—and the city—be affected?

The New Urbanization

DENNIS McELRATH

Urbanization, the process of becoming urban, may be contrasted with urbanism, which is "to be functioning in an urban fashion." Urbanization is going on all over the world at an increasingly rapid rate, affecting areas that have never before known the urban influence. New Towns, as they have been called in Europe for almost a thousand years, are springing up everywhere. Furthermore, small towns, peasant villages, and tribal lands are being absorbed by the spread of existing cities. Most striking of all, the vast Third World sector—which lacks the supporting food production and technological system to sustain vast numbers of nonfood producers in an urban setting—is losing hinterland populations to the cities. This, combined with natural growth resulting from a high birth rate, is creating massive problems in such areas.

The following paper by Dennis McElrath, addresses urbanization in the underdeveloped countries and describes the factors that are affecting the path of urban growth. He then turns to first and second world countries where the process is taking a different direction. More developed nations have a more prosperous economy, firmer food production base, greater industrial strength, lower population density, and usually a lower birth rate.

McElrath sees scale as a major differentiating factor. It results in social complexity, producing cities in which one area maintains traditional life-styles (as in the suburban stress on familism), whereas another sector emphasizes innovative adaptive styles (young, single professionals in swinger apartments). Still a third sector includes the "invisible enclaves," whose inhabitants often employ a mixed strategy of tradition and innovation in the manner of patterns often exhibited among the inner city retired, elderly poor.

The major thrust of this paper is to emphasize that urbanization cannot be described, at least today, as following a single developmental format.

Some years ago when the first post-war population censuses began to trickle in from all over the world, it became evident that the fastest rates of urbanization were appearing in the developing and new nations. While many of these countries as a whole were experiencing a rapid population growth, their cities were growing at an even more rapid pace. Urban populations in many instances were more than doubling and tripling within a single decade, largely as a consequence of mass migration to cities. The next round of censuses, taken in 1960, whose findings are now being analyzed, reveal with even greater accuracy that this pattern of rapid urbanization of underdeveloped and often crowded nations is continuing. This is dramatic new urbanization; and it

"The New Urbanization" in The New Urbanization (Scott Greer, and others, eds.) 1968, pp. 3–12. New York: St. Martin Press, Inc.)

is affecting the lives of millions of people and the economics and the politics of nations.

In both America and Europe a new kind of urbanization is taking place as well. In these nations of "mature cities," books such as *The Emerging City*, *Megalopolis*, and *The Exploding Metropolis* have appeared in recent years. The city did not settle down in middle age. Indeed, it had grown fast and sprawled, and spawned new metropolitan centers from small cities in the desert.

What is the impact of these two new kinds of urbanization? One is reflected in the sprawling bidonville and shacktowns that surround the capital cities of new nations; the other in the meandering conurbations of Europe, England and, most distinctly, in the post-automobile, mid-twentieth century cities of western America. While the consequences of these two different developments (perhaps they should be considered as different phases of the same process) are myriad, it is important to distinguish several fundamental outcomes of each which will frame the way life is organized in the cities and countrysides of new nations and old. For this process is creating new distributions of demands and expectations; new hierarchies along which people are stratified and scarce resources are distributed; and new ecologies of settlement and activity. These shifts in turn are the groundwork for new ways in which populations may be organized to change the present or perpetuate the past. And this changing organization occurs not only in the cities but throughout the society experiencing urbanization. For this process transforms the total society. It is not just something that happens in or to cities.

The new urbanization in new nations is unlike the historic pattern of city growth in Western Europe and America—our usual models for urban development. In Europe, as Pirenne points out, the prototype of the modern city developed along the trade route; it was a walled fortified outpost of trade and commerce. The Industrial Revolution and shift in political power which accompanied it merely intensified this pattern and greatly expanded it. Urbanization in these Western industrial countries then developed with commerce, trade, and especially with manufacturing, as seen in the industrial cities of our East Coast and Europe. These cities had an economic underpinning, a foundation in industry and commerce.

They were supported by increasing agricultural productivity as well. Agricultural efficiency and advances in transportation technology yielded larger surpluses from wider supporting hinterlands, so that great concentrations of humanity could live away from the land. If the surplus was inadequate, the hinterland could be enlarged by the exercise of urban power or, more often, by expanding the market for urban products.

The new cities in the new nations are not like these earlier developments. They have grown rapidly and swelled with population, but their economic base has not expanded in a parallel manner. Nor have they developed a viable supporting hinterland. Their products are limited so that they have little surplus to sell. And in the hinterland, agricultural surpluses dwindle as population increases faster than productivity. These cities cannot feed from their tributaries, and more and more city-centered power is exercised to attenuate their base of support, pushing out the boundaries, pressing hard on the peasant. But their efforts often are not successful, for their power is limited and the organizational links which bind these two cultures together are weak and unimpressive.

Since new population—the source of rapid city growth—cannot be absorbed into an expanding urban economy, unemployment in many of these new cities is substantial. And even more important, much of the employed population is underemployed or redundant labor. What is seen then, in the shacktowns, barrachi, bidonvilles, rancheros, favelas, and sidewalk sleepers in these cities, is a marked division of the population on the basis of wealth: a wide gap between the very affluent and a large pool of "redundant" and underemployed poor. And in their hinterlands, in the peasant villages and little communities where most of the world's population lives, the cleavages in wealth produced by the inroads of urbanization are even more apparent. Here the pressure for new markets, the extension of urban control, and the extraction of agricultural surpluses have introduced into these settlements the agents of an urban society on the one hand and often a partially proletarianized agricultural labor force on the other.

The agents of urban-centered institutions—missionaries, merchants, traders, agricultural agents, school teachers, government employees—often live as a community apart, separated by wealth and often by walls and physical as well as social distance from the villagers. Their career, like that of a visiting anthropologist, is linked to an urban-based bureaucracy. Their encounters with the peasants are few and structured by social distance. But they *are* there, dependent on the villagers for some of their needs and the villagers are dependent on them, and they must confront one another in their daily rounds. Both are aware of the gap that separates them.

Often the peasant villages also contain proletarianized agricultural workers. Where the urban style of organization has entered into the production and marketing of crops, the peasant agriculturalist becomes like his counterpart in industry—a landless peasant engaged in large-scale agricultural production, frequently moving with the seasons between city and countryside. In the city they swell the marginal shacktowns, returning occasionally to the peasant villages. Thus rapid urbanization in developing nations often transforms the class structures of both the city and the hinterland, yielding new competing, sometimes conflicting, divisions in a quest for access to the extremely scarce resources of a developing society.

There are two ways in which a city can grow: either through migration or from natural increase. (Here we ignore the role of census classification which yields bookkeeping changes.) No other way is possible. Urbanization in America reached its peak before 1870 when the increase was at the rate of almost 30% per decade, largely as a consequence of immigration. Since 1900 the rate of urban growth in the United States has been decelerated. This growth has at present achieved a constant rate of about 9% increase per decade, but eventually it should decline.

The new nations are now undergoing something similar to our experience of a hundred years ago. Their current rapid growth is largely the product of mass migration of strangers to the cities. There the similarity stops, however. In the first place, urban migration in new nations tends to be from a fairly limited, narrow hinterland. The points of origin of migrants are not widely dispersed. In addition, although the paths that lead to the cities are short, they are often heavily trafficked in both directions. Urban migrants do not have far to travel before they are back in the rural peasant village. They go home often. This means that in a very real sense many of these migrants are perpetual newcomers to the cities. They frequently come to the city, but they are not part of it.

These cities, then, are made up of migrants who are only segmentally and temporarily involved in the urban way of life. They are not only marginally employed in the city, but they are also marginal members of a new urban community. They are not yet urban men. For a long time these future urbanites will be oriented away from the cities, sometimes to a tribal village, often to a rural community which no longer exists, to a way of life which is being displaced by industrializing agriculture, by political and social transformations stemming from the city and only partially insulated from the daily rounds of life in the peasant communities. They will see the city with peasant eyes, unaware of the requirements of time, money, and urban skills; of compromises, of accommodation, of subtle gradations and organization, which the truly urban man knows so well that it is like the air he breathes. (The true urbanite rarely can spell out the organizational features of the life of which he is a part: they have been internalized to a point where he is almost unaware of them).

In America the newcomers were fairly rapidly absorbed by the city. The melting pot ideology of urban America encouraged development of public services which would socialize immigrants to urban demands. Parallel organizations, hyphenated echoes of other associations in the community, flourished within immigrant ghettoes and were used as proving grounds where newly secured social skills could be learned and tried out in supportive surroundings. In addition, expansion of the job market in areas where new workers could enter the labor force as differentiated individuals, rather than as undifferentiated gang laborers, encouraged the destruction and uprooting of prior traditions and the substitution of a new way of life. Thus, public education and other services, a myriad of immigrant organizations, and an expanding labor force, especially in manufacturing, all combined to help erase in a few generations most of the barriers of ethnicity.

The great mass of migrants to cities in developing areas is not so readily absorbed. The urban ideology of assimilation and achievement has shallow roots in these often traditionally oriented communities. Public services that provide a social bridge into city life are meager and bridging occupations are rare indeed. They do not represent areas of great expansion in urban employment opportunities. Lacking these bridges, the migrant remains within but is not part of the community. He remains a marginal member, often literally living at the periphery of the community.

The process of exodus and frequent return to the little communities of the hinterland often results in introducing a new kind of village dweller: the returnee, the partially urbanized peasant whose presence and involvement in the social life of his community act as a lever for change. Returnees about to depart again, together with those who are leaving for the first time and those who have been left behind but who look to a distant city for support and future, all constitute relatively new elements in the peasant village. As their proportions grow, the structure and fabric of life in the village are transformed. As Robert Redfield points out, however, this change may be delayed in the peasant village if these people as well as the rural proletariat and the agents of urban structures and most of their activities are insulated from the everyday life of the village. But it is doubtful that the peasant village can contain this strong thrust for change.

There is one final aspect to this new urbanization in new nations throughout the world. It concerns the ethnic and racial composition of these cities. The American experience in this area may be particularly informative. Our cities were filled with people drawn from halfway around the world. They differed greatly in language, custom, religion, and cultural experience. This diversity presented a continuing challenge to the melting pot of the American city. Some of these differences still distinguish the neighborhoods and practices of cities. While the new cities in Africa, Latin America, and Asia do not ordinarily draw their populations from such distant places, the ethnic and racial differences still are great. Several circumstances sponsor this. First, some of the population of these new cities are the product of a fairly long period of Europeanization. These are people who man the outposts of an empire; they are workers in a colonial bureaucracy, the children of merchants and tribal chiefs, occasionally schooled in Europe, but who have at least experienced a long and sustained exposure to large-scale enterprise, to export agriculture and export commerce, or to colonial military and public administration. Frequently these people form the core of a new independent government. They form a Europeanized or at least industrialized constituency, a distinctive subculture sharing the skills of an urban world. Second, ethnic and cultural diversity is sponsored by the relative isolation and variety of little communities in the surrounding hinterland of these new cities. While the area which contributes migrants is narrow, it is nevertheless highly heterogeneous. It is made up of a jigsaw puzzle of tribal or community boundaries, the members of each possessing fairly distinctive cultural traditions. They fill the cities with distinctive communities, neighborhoods, and quarters, which may persist after the newness of urban life has worn off and beyond the time when their members are internally differentiated by wealth and power.

These new cities, then, share many problems faced in urban industrial nations a hundred years ago and some that are absolutely new to human experience. These problems arise not only from the economics of development and underdevelopment; they are problems which stem directly from the tumult of urbanization, for urbanization has brought together new combinations and divisions of people on a scale never experienced in these societies. People of the new cities are divided by work experience and by wealth, ranging from the very wealthy to a large pool of unskilled and redundant labor. They are divided into newcomers and old residents, with the new lacking urban skills and focused on the traditions of little communities. They are divided by ethnic and occasionally racial differences; but almost all residents are now thrown together. Their differences are clearly visible for all among them to see.

They not only stand apart in the community because of these several differences, but in many instances their social stance is made even more distinct by the fact that their differences are compounded. They are poor and redundantly employed as well as lacking urban skills and often disadvantaged by language, traditions, and obligations to distant and neighboring kinsmen.

The consequences of this situation, which is being experienced in varying degrees and with cultural variants in country after country, are many. Perhaps the most relevant is the difficulty of molding a community and a nation across these potentially divisive fissures and frequently under the pounding twin pressures of population and poverty. For here are the differences among people which are real, which are visible. They may be seized upon to promote a program, elevate a charism, or fell a government. The situation is volatile. The potential for violence in these new cities is great. Even without revolution, we know there is a strong thrust for rapid social change, made all the more difficult and disorderly by the close-packed confrontation of divided populations inherent in this new urbanization. They are not merely divided. These social differences, which are often also reflected in the ecologies of new cities, are bases for organizations which line up each stratum and each locality according to their shared demands, expectations, and interests. The result is not disorganization in the usual sense of anonymous urban masses, but a highly fractured social structure lacking the necessary ties which bind together each person's web of affiliations into a viable community.

The new urbanization in older industrial nations like the United States is not of this explosive sort, and yet it shares many features which are common to those of new nations. It is a quiet change, muffled by exhaust fumes and heralded only by the horn of the car behind. Basically, it involves three things: the decompression of an urban population, the creation of a horizontal city, and the development of a new style of life. Each of these changes now being experienced has important implications for the future course of urban development in the United States and, perhaps, in other economically advanced nations.

The industrial countries started out to develop densely settled communities. These began in Europe and were repeated in the port and rail cities of America. This walking-city pattern of high concentration continued even after the advent of the electric streetcar, the subway, and the elevated railroad. The commuter railroad lines changed it slightly, but basically the city remained the same: a hard core of commercial activity, a cell surrounded by closely packed areas of transportation, industry, and residences. This map was changed only after the mass use of the automobile, and then it was changed radically. And perhaps even more important than the automobile, though it is often ignored, has been the truck.

Around 1920 the mass marketing of the automobile was largely responsible for the beginning of the decline of the city's density, its close-packed character. Most of the new settlements were residential. These areas were labeled the dormitory or bedroom cities because the weary commuters returned to them at night. But before long the widespread adoption of the truck permitted industry and commerce to locate on cheap peripheral property. Frequently they were able to find tax hideouts in new industrial suburbs, a move that often gave their owners an advantage over competitors who had been entrapped in the central city. Thus both the truck and the car spread people and employment opportunities greatly, so much so that today less than a third of all those who live in the suburbs in major metropolitan areas work in the central city. Well over half of the suburbanites now work in suburban or peripheral areas. Therefore the traditional picture of the dormitory suburb sending its husbands and fathers downtown to their jobs no longer obtains for most workers of the United States, most suburbanites.

With the growth of industrial tracts and the mass production of suburban housing there began what is popularly called the exploding metropolis. As is well known, between 1940 and 1950 suburban America grew more than twice as fast as the central cities. But this growth was slight in comparison with the decade 1950–1960, when the suburbs grew forty times faster than the central cities; and in this decade almost a fourth of the great central cities actually lost population in their core areas.

Suburban growth is fed by two streams of population. The first has always been with us: the long-term drift of rural people into urban America, people leaving the farm, countryside, and small towns. Many of these people now move directly to the suburbs. The second is the flight from the central city by those who can and want to escape. These streams are fed by the native sons and daughters of the golden suburbs; and these natives grow like Topsy. Of the 64,000,000 new citizens expected in the United States by 1980, more than 80% will be suburbanites, most of them born in those fertile valleys of suburbia.

The central cities have not been depleted, however. They continue to gain recruits although, as noted, many large cities have acutally lost population. The poor have always come to the city. Today the city maintains its population only to the extent that it does attract the poor to replace the fleeing middle class. In the past, the poor who came to the cities found work, and if they didn't prosper, their children often did. But always along the way there were those who did not succeed. These have been fairly limited in percentage terms, but they are certainly plentiful in absolute numbers. Over time the central city has accumulated this collection of those who have not moved on, those who could not join the exodus of the middle-income families to the suburbs. Their number is increasing by the constant influx of the incoming poor, the new poor. In recent years, especially since 1940, and especially in northern and western cities, Negroes have constituted a substantial proportion of these low-income newcomers.

The central city, accordingly, is fast being filled with the accumulated poor, the newly arrived poor, and of course it is the home of the better-off Negroes and other minorities who cannot move because of the straitjacket of discrimination.

Some efforts have been made to change this trend. Occasionally there have been apparent local successes in urban redevelopment in attracting middle-income families back into the central city. The persistent trends, however, show the middle-income families and, increasingly, those of even more moderate means, fleeing the city along with enterprise. But is it solely flight, or is it that they are also moving toward positive attractions in the burgeoning urban rimland?

Ring a random sample of doorbells out in the suburbs. Ask the answering housewives why they are there, and overwhelmingly the response will be, "the children." One might conclude that these fertile valleys are one big playpen. Mothers—and fathers, as well—like their yards, the outdoors, their quality schools, the clean new home, and even their neighbors and the neighbors' children. Like our own, these are good, clean, well-scrubbed, middle class children—not poor, not black.

Undoubtedly a powerful lure of the suburbs revolves around the children. But there is something more of broader scope. Robert Nisbet terms this the "quest for community," marked especially by a desire to belong. The suburban experiment (and it is an experiment, for this is a new kind of human settlement) appears to be an attempt to develop some kind of meaningful local community, a community bounded by the local area, the neighborhood. It is focused not on the common histories, the common conditions of existence; for these are not the neighborhoods of tenements of immigrants, but of mobile people of diverse origins and backgrounds. They form a community focused on the children and their care and on the consumption of leisure. The strategic elements of suburban life include building a patio and harvesting the crabgrass, as well as schools and PTA's and playgrounds.

The suburban experiment, then, is an attempt to create a new style of life responsive to the new conditions of urban existence. It has introduced a new dimension along which people of America (and elsewhere, for example, England) are arrayed, a dimension of life-style. The differences between the poles of this continuum show the way in which a nation's population can be socially spread. The differences between the two poles are great. On the one hand we have the continuing urban life-style, typical of the apartment house area of the central cities, a style of life mainly revolving around careers. Families are small; generally both husband and wife work. They live in apartments: they spend their money on the pursuit of career and happiness. They are, some have claimed (perhaps have overclaimed), hasty hedonists, but career-oriented. At the other extreme are the new suburbanites, with larger families, living in their detached houses, with the wife at home neighboring and providing intensive child care. The differences here are predictive of many forms of behavior, including voting and other kinds of community action. The differences also are indications of social class, race, minority status, and migrancy.

Of course the differentiation of a population according to variations in life-style is not new. The traditional rural life-style has been distinguishable from that of city dweller for many centuries. But marked variations between the two are rapidly being erased with the spread of urban-centered media and the diffusion of the same styles of life that characterize the suburbanite. The familistic life-style to a large extent has replaced the traditional extended family, kin-oriented, paternalistic systems of rural America. In this sense we are rapidly moving toward a totally urbanized society, where suburb and countryside are increasingly indistinguishable in terms of distinctive patterns of living. In these areas, compared with the old, core-dominated cities, variations in the style of life between neighborhoods are minimal. Most of the neighborhoods, even those located near the commercial districts, in the post-automobile city, closely approximate the familistic pattern of the suburbs of older, core-dominated cities. If these new cities are tracers to the present course of urbanization, then it should be clear that one outcome of this process is the development of metropolitan regions without a metropolis, a core barely distinguished from the rest of the terrain, an endless forest of TV antennae, broken only by a clearing for a parking lot at a shopping center and perhaps an occasional freeway interchange. And the characteristic style of life would extend on out into the less densely settled countryside, which, [as] noted, is in the process of adopting suburban familism.

This is only one major consequence of the newest urbanization of modern industrial society. Another important effect all too often is cited as an exception to the older central city-suburb distinction and its contrasts in life-styles. This is brought out by noting, for example, that of the five cities in the million class in the United States—New York, Chicago, Los Angeles, Philadelphia, and Detroit—all *except* Los Angeles lost population in the 1950–1960 decade. While other great central cities lost population, Los Angeles gained 27% during this period. Rather than an anomaly, however, the point is that Los Angeles never followed the core city pattern. It never was a densely settled urban industrial city with an industrial core. For Los Angeles, almost from the beginning, has epitomized the post-automobile city. It is a region; some say a frame of mind. In any event, such cities as Los Angeles, Phoenix, San Diego, and Tucson all experienced their major growth after the automobile, especially since 1940. They are perhaps the tracers to the second aspect of this newest kind of urbanization.

The new urbanization in America has added a new dimension to society, a new way in which many people are sorting themselves out from others. This dimension of life-style may be transitional. The urban style was predominant in the central city while the traditional form persisted in the countryside. Familism appeared in the suburbs surrounding the central cities, diffused to the countryside, and appears on the verge of becoming the dominant form throughout a totally urbanized society.

But the old divisions, the divisions which are seen emerging in the new cities of Africa and Asia, which today divide the city dwellers of new nations, are still with us in substantial measure. We, too, are still separated in our neighborhoods, our schools, and in our daily rounds by class, by race, by migrancy. In one sense, these differences are not so glaring. Our poor are hidden: the Negro is "invisible"; the Puerto Rican and Mexican continue to be confined to their ghettos and enclaves along with other migrants and others saddled with poverty. And to these old, traditional, classic divisions that we see occurring again in the new nations of the world, we have added a new division, a separation of people in terms of the life-style of suburban familism and lingering urbanism. This social complexity, marked by both traditional and emerging patterns of living, is largely the product of the continuing thrust of increasing scale.

Migrancy and the Study of Africans in Towns

PHILIP MAYER

Mayer's study of "Red" and "School" Xhosa tribesmen in East London (South Africa) is now a classic in the anthropology of urbanization. We see gathered together into a single paper a number of questions raised by other studies. First and foremost, Mayer confronts the relationship between city residence and urbanization and concludes that the two are not automatically related. Migration does not imply urbanization. To Mayer, urbanization is a complex process, involving a degree of choice by the individual, and represents a "shift in the balance between within-town ties and extra-town ties." Until (if ever) the shift is "decisive," migrants may move alternately between rural and urban fields of be-

"Migrancy and the Study of Africans in Towns," *American Anthropologist*, Vol. 64, 1962, pp. 576–592. Reproduced by permission of the American Anthropological Association.

havior, or exploit urban resources to strengthen their rural positions. Mayer's paper aptly demonstrates how ethnographic data can be productive of ethnological generalizations.

The study of African town populations may be said to raise some special theoretical issues in those many areas of Africa where labor migrancy prevails. These are areas where, by and large, the African "town population" is not clearly distinct. It still mostly consists of Africans who are spending parts of their lives in town, in between periods spent in the rural hinterland, and who continue thinking of the hinterland, rather than the town, as their permanent "home" because of the greater security there.

One kind of theoretical challenge raised by this phenomenon of migrancy has recently been taken up with marked success. That is, the ongoing nature of the urban social systems has been successfully distinguished from the temporary or shifting nature of the migrant personnel. This is one of the greatest single theoretical contributions made by a recent notable series of studies of Rhodesian Copperbelt towns (Epstein, 1958; Mitchell, 1960a; Gluckman, 1960). These studies demonstrate that African urban systems, such as trade unions, can and should be studied as urban systems in their own right, independently of the fact that the migrant members are recruited from rustic (tribal) life and keep melting away into it again. As Gluckman has it (1960:57), "an African miner is a miner." His activities at work, and the relations he forms at work, need to be considered in relation to an industrial context, not a tribal one.

Thus the Copperbelt work has seemed to forswear "relating the urban African to his tribal background," if by this we mean considering his connections with tribal systems in the hinterland. It has recognized the validity of tribes as categories of interaction *within* the town setting, but has mostly avoided "explaining" town-located phenomena by reference to tribal systems located outside the town.

As a working principle for the study of African towns (or urban societies, or urban social systems), this principle of ignoring what goes on "outside" would seem to be unexceptionable. In much the same way, when an anthropologist works in the tribal hinterland, one would expect an analysis of the local social systems—age-sets, clans, lineages, or whatever they might be—without much regard for the turnover of personnel caused by migrant members going away to work in town and without reference to what goes on in that "outside" field.

On the other hand, it seems evident that in regions of labor migrancy a case exists for the study of migrancy itself as a supplement to the study of towns and town-located systems.[1] The fact that the *same* individuals are apt to func-

---

[1] In Southern and Central Africa, sociological aspects of migrancy have been studied at the rural end, notably by Schapera (1947), Gulliver (1957), Watson (1958), and van Velsen (1960).

At the urban end, Wilson's essay on Broken Hill (1941/42) seems to have remained for many years the only major publication focused on migrants as such. My own work on Xhosa migrancy (1961) deals chiefly with the urban end, though based on both rural and urban fieldwork.

tion as trade union members at one end, and as age-set members at the other, is one which common sense forbids us to ignore. The study of the ongoing structures—at the urban or the rural end or both—therefore seems to require this supplement, if justice is to be done to the social realities. Along with its practical implications, the social fact of widespread migrancy must have some implications for theory, and these ought to be worked out. It might well challenge the anthropologist to redefine such concepts as social personality, role, status, or social field—or at least to enquire whether redefinition is necessary—so as to suit a situation where Ego habitually moves back and forth between urban "society" and tribal "society." The concept of migrant, as such, requires sociological scrutiny.

For this purpose it would seem necessary to bring both parts of Ego's total field of activity—the town part plus the hinterland part—into focus together. How is this to be done? It will certainly not be easy to subsume the two parts under the concept of one inclusive "social structure" or "society" in the classic sense. As Nadel (1957) has argued, the diagnostic unity of a social structure, properly so called, lies in the fact that all the roles defined within it bear some logical relation to one another. It would be extraordinarily difficult to discover any logical interlock between all the tribal roles and all the urban roles of all those various people who, as migrants, circulate through the kind of field just described. Especially is this the case since, in so many instances, the town draws migrants from a number of different separate sources. The total migrancy field, in such an instance, consists of the town plus all of those areas from which it draws migrants. In practice nobody bothers to look for the logical interlock of roles which would be necessary to constitute the migrancy field a unitary "structure." It is normally assumed that migrancy, as such, involves an individual in two distinct "structures"; and that more than two distinct structures are involved in the total migrancy field, if more than one tribal (rural) society is sending migrants into the town.

Even the concept of the wider society as defined by modern state boundaries—South African society or Rhodesian society—would not necessarily enable us to dispense with the plural model and accommodate the role of "migrant" within a unitary model, so long as we insist that the model has got to be one of an organic social structure. Migrancy commonly flows back and forth across state boundaries. For instance, the South African mines draw large numbers of their migrant workers from Portuguese territories, British High Commission territories, and elsewhere.

It seems, then, that the study of a town-plus-hinterland field, with its circulating personnel, cannot well hope to proceed as the analysis of "a social structure," and that the quest for an alternative method of approach would be justified. A reasonable alternative method, it is here suggested, would be to begin at the study of the migrant persons themselves, by mapping out their networks of relations from the personal or egocentric point of view, as well as noting their parts in the various structural systems. In doing this we would not be postulating any structural unity of the migrancy field. We would merely be noting that it is, in fact, a field habitually traversed by migrating persons. The starting point would be the observed fact that individuals who play roles in town A also play roles in tribal (or rural) societies, B, C or D; the task would be to observe the networks of social relations which arise when this fact is multiplied into a mass social phenomenon, and to analyze their special characteristics.

Probably the easiest and most practical place to begin the study of migrants or migrancy is in town, because of the denser concentration of migrants there as compared with the rural end, and also the availability of different groups (from different rural sectors), which may be useful for comparative analysis. But when choosing a town population as the field of study, we must take particular care not to confuse the objective—the study of migrancy—with that significantly different objective, the study of town-located social systems as such. The "migrancy" objective demands precisely what pursuers of the "town" objective have purposely abjured, namely, a close attention to the extra-town ties of the town-resident migrants.

This phrase, extra-town ties, requires attention. It does not mean just the same as "tribal" ties. Even the study of the town "as a town" may well require reference to "tribal" ties in the sense that "tribal" groups can be significant *within* the town, as in-groups and categories of social interaction. The Copperbelt studies have amply demonstrated this point. It is another matter to investigate extra-town ties, those bonds which, during the period of residence in town, continue to bind Ego to specific tribal systems *outside* the town and enable him to resume his place in a specific tribal community (in the hinterland) when the time comes. These are the mechanisms which, as it were, keep open his particular place in some hinterland society—as member of this or that family, lineage, age-set—and not merely his "tribalism" or persisting tribal "loyalty" (Gluckman, 1960:55) in the vaguer sense of national self-identification. They require that, during his stay in town, he should maintain certain relationships in a latent state and discharge certain roles in absentia.

These extra-town ties may have proved irrelevant for the study of urban structural systems—trade unions and the like—but if that mode of study throws no light on them, other techniques will have to be sought.

In this article I shall consider some of the practical and theoretical points which arose during a study of migrancy undertaken by me in one South African town, East London, Cape Province, between 1955 and 1959. Results of this study have been published in book form (Mayer, 1961). East London is a major seaport, and an industrial and commercial center, with some 50,000 white inhabitants and nearly 70,000 others. The "others"—who, except for some 10,000 domestic servants, live segregated in the "locations" or non-white quarters—are predominantly African labor migrants (the Coloured and Asiatic minorities being numerically small here).

Models of Alternation and of Change

We may first consider how far some existing models for the study of Africans in towns are appropriate for the specific study of migrancy.

In some urban studies, the double roles of the labor migrant have been theoretically reconciled by a use of the idea of alternation or switching back and forth in time. Thus, Ego, who is now in town, this year plays roles in urban society; next year he will be back in the hinterland playing roles in tribal society; and so forth. Or again: Ego, while in town, is involved in urban sets of relations this morning, at the work-place, but in tribal sets this evening, in his urban domestic life; he plays certain roles according to urban norms each morning, and other roles according to tribal norms each evening.

"Alternation" models have been explicitly contrasted with another kind which we may call models of one-way change. Here the idea was that the migrant, under the influence of town, may gradually abandon his tribal roles and norms altogether. Gluckman (1960:57; 1959:3–4) has commented on the weaknesses he regards as inherent in an older method of study—the method which postulated "a process of detribalization, which had to be analysed and measured as the tribesman slowly changed." Rejecting this concept of slow change, Gluckman recommended that we "start analysis of town life by saying that the moment an African crossed his tribal boundary he was 'detribalized,' outside the tribe, though not outside the influence of the tribe. Correspondingly, when a man returns from the town into the political area of the tribe he is tribalized again—de-urbanized—though not outside the influence of the town" (1960:58). Gluckman thus postulates alternation as a switching back and forth between two distinct social fields or systems.

Of course, there is a more basic difference involved, too, insofar as one model works with "culture" and the other with "social relations." The earlier model criticized by Gluckman relied largely on the concept of changing *culture;* the "movement" envisaged was from one cultural condition to another, along a one-way track starting from the tribal condition as zero point and ending with complete detribalization. The proposed alternation model, by contrast, postulates an alternation between *social fields,* one whenever the migrant is in town and the other whenever he is in the hinterland. This is one reason why the latter model invites more to synchronic and the former more to diachronic study.

Concurrently, work by Epstein (1958) and Mitchell (1960b) has brought into use a somewhat different alternation model. This might be said to unite more closely the social relations and culture concepts: it postulates involvement (in town) in different sets of relations which in themselves call forth different patterns of behavior. The model brings out the fact that a man even while actually in town can still be alternating. He can switch back and forth between urban and tribal behavior according to the immediate situation. He may be content to follow tribal patterns in his urban domestic life, although he cannot do so at work, and although he would deprecate a tribal system of representation for dealing with the white management of the mines. The operative principle has been termed "situational selection" (Gluckman, 1958:47, citing Evans-Pritchard; Epstein, 1958:235, 236), i.e., the individual selects behavior patterns appropriate to the sets of relations in which a situation involves him at a given moment.

Here, then, we have, in two forms, a recognition that one man may be alternately urban in some situations and tribal in others. As long as we are concerned with the study of towns (including the study of "tribalism" in towns, in the sense of tribal loyalties), this is a valuable theoretical advance on the older tendency—which perhaps is still the layman's—to contrapose tribal man and urbanized man as distinct entities. Yet, if we are concerned specifically with the study of migrants, the new recognition is not enough. Tending as it does towards a static and schizoid picture of the migrant's social personality, it does not help us much to understand that significant process of social change which can properly be called the "process of urbanization" among migrants. By this I mean a shift in the balance between within-town ties and extra-town ties. A formerly migrant population (I would suggest) has become genuinely urban, or been effectively urbanized, once this shift has become decisive, so that its extra-town ties have collectively shrunk to negligible proportions as compared with its within-town ties. At the fully urbanized stage—to put it more simply—the town-dwelling population is no longer subject to the pull of the hinterland. It has become a purely urban proletariat (and/or bourgeoisie).

That this important and worldwide form of social change also takes place in Africa is well known. Godfrey Wilson had discussed its progress in a Central African setting as early as 1941. In South Africa, where the towns created by Europeans have a longer history than in most parts of the continent, every major city by now takes for granted its fully urbanized African element. These are African townsmen all of whose major social ties are bounded by the city in which they live. Such persons—unlike the migrant Africans who rub shoulders with them in town—have no longer any important personal links with the tribal hinterland, and no "homes" anywhere but in town. They will live, rear their children, and die in town. Historically speaking, this "fully urban" category has developed out of the "migrant" category: its members are exmigrants, or children or grandchildren of migrants. The process is still enough in evidence to constitute a worry for the South African government; influx control, tribal ambassadors, and other measures are employed on purpose to neutralize as far as possible the continuing "redistribution of the Bantu."

In the study of any migrant group in town, then, a critical question would seem to be how far the pull of the hinterland is weakening, if at all. As it weakens, the social personality of the migrant changes in some way. If it weakens sufficiently, his role as migrant comes to an end. The concept of alternation, in either of the forms cited, is not really sufficient for depicting how countryborn people can "become townsmen" in the sense of shifting their personal centers of gravity into the town.

Concentrating on within-town ties alone, it must be added, cannot enable one to judge, by implication, how far the pull of the hinterland may be weakening. Active involvement in within-town social systems is no index of noninvolvement in extra-town systems. The extra-town ties can indeed be simultaneously involved in those very actions which represent participation in an urban system. An "urban" role and a "tribal" role can be discharged *pari passu*. It all depends on how one construes the action. For example, when a man has come to town to earn money for his family in the hinterland, it follows that whenever he discharges his urban role of industrial employee, he is also and ipso facto discharging his extra-town role of a providing father. Thus, his work in factory or mine can be construed as being done "for" his employer in the urban economic system, but equally well as being done "for" his homestead group in the tribal economic system. If we are studying the urban industrial system as such, only the former construction matters. But if we are studying migrancy, both matter. There may be other forms of double participation, less noticeable on the surface. In East London, migrant workers of a certain type choose to spend their off-duty hours incapsulated in a clique of friends—roommates, drinking companions—who, in fact, are old friends from one "home place" in the hinterland. Since all the men in such a clique have still kin or friends living in the *same* rural home community—people who may call each man to account whenever he goes "home"—the men's actions in town are actually being referred to the moral and social systems of the "home place," quite as much as to those of the town (Mayer, 1961).

Two Local Situations Compared: East London and Copperbelt

If one accepts the task of examining the extra-town ties of town dwellers and assessing them in relation to within-town ties, it seems reasonably certain that very different pictures will emerge as between different modern towns in Africa. The pictures will differ not only in the balance between extra-town and within-town ties, but also in the very nature and quality of the ties within each category. (As Mitchell remarks, "the total set of external imperatives is probably unique for each town" [1960b:171].) It may therefore be useful to compare East London with the type of Copperbelt town explored by Mitchell, Gluckman, and Epstein. In the case of East London, the within-town ties are of a kind that is much less conspicuous and much less massive; the extra-town ties, on the other hand, seem to come into focus more easily than may be the case on the Copperbelt.

a) Within-town Ties

The Copperbelt studies, it will be recalled, have dealt with a phase of development in which the interplay between the workers' common (urban) interests and their sectional sentiments or interests (as members of different tribal groups) is sociologically noteworthy. Hence much emphasis is placed on a theme which might be summarized in the phrase, "trade unions transcend tribes." The analysis demonstrates that in certain interactions in town the workers still attach prime importance to their respective tribal identities, but that industrial work involves them in new sets of relations too, in which they eventually become aware of the irrelevance of tribal categories. It is at work, then, that these town-dwelling Africans can be seen to form "typically urban associations." These are the massive within-town ties referred to.

The growth of the massive associations, it has also been pointed out, seems more favored by the structure of the mining compounds than by that of the municipal locations (Gluckman, 1960:61). It is the monolithic power of the mining company which provokes a similarly monolithic response from the workers' side.

None of this applies to East London. Here there exist neither trade unions nor any other massive associations of or for Africans, except, on a smaller scale, churches and sports clubs. Furthermore, the structure of the East London locations is anything but monolithic. And thirdly, there is no opposition between different tribal groups to enhance the importance of tribal identities or bonds within the town setting. Ninety-six % of the whole African population of East London is drawn from a single tribal group; they are Xhosa-speakers, with common Xhosa loyalties.[2] The only group opposition which would make sense in this context, the one between the Xhosa and the whites, has artificially forbidden any expression on the Xhosa side.

These assertions must be briefly documented. The absence of massive urban associations (other than churches and sports clubs) is a direct result of government policy. In South Africa, all associations are repressed or discouraged in which town-dwelling Africans might be able to constitute themselves a pressure-group, whether as town residents, as employees, or as citizens. It is true that rural (Reserve) Africans are allowed or even encouraged to express "their own interests" within the limits of local administrative units, by complaining to tribal chiefs on internal tribal matters; but no Africans are allowed any lawful means of expression in the modern state machinery or economic system.

This is in clear contrast to the official encouragement (since the 1940s) of African trade unionism in the Copperbelt; and it means that we cannot apply to any South African town the forecast (rightly made by Gluckman in the Rhodesian context) that "as soon as Africans assemble in towns they will try to combine to better their conditions in trade unions and so forth" (1960:57). To be specific, the South African government, which does not recognize African trade unions, also forbids African participation in the recognized white, Asiatic, or Colored unions. A voluntary African trade union which once played a

---

[2] Within the Xhosa-speaking group, now some 2½ million strong, oppositions based on internal differentiations (e.g., between "Xhosa proper" and "Mfengu") count for little in face of the common loyalties, which are based on a long history of neighborhood and intermarriage, as well as on common language and cultural similarity.

prominent part in East London has never recovered from the crushing it underwent 30 years ago by the breaking of its attempted general strike. African political parties, notably the African National Congress and its Youth League, have also been unable to function (at least overtly) since they were officially banned as illegal organizations. True to the principle of allowing some self-expression in purely local matters, the authorities recognize and encourage Location Advisory Boards (purely consultative) in some urban areas; but in recent years East London Africans have not regarded their Board as serving any real purpose, witness the poll of one or two percent in the voting for the elected element.

In circumstances like these, obviously, the failure to develop new sets of relations in town, at the political or trade union level, need not signify a corresponding apathy. Fieldwork experience in East London suggested quite the reverse: that there is in fact an immense fund of discontent, ready to be tapped by any "representative" associations, if such were allowed to arise. All we have a right to assert is that no overt expression, no organization or association reflecting common "urban" interests, lies to hand at present for purposes of anthropological study; and that the within-town ties available for study do not add up to massive structural systems like those of a Copperbelt town. (The situation in the Copperbelt in 1935 seems to have been similar; Mitchell [1956] shows how dance groups there became media of political expression accordingly.)

The "atomistic" (Epstein:154) structure of East London is relevant to this point, too. In a municipal compound (as against a mining compound) there is less pressure for combined action, and less possibility for organizing it (Gluckman, 1960:61). Instead of a single "unitary" structure (the mining company) (Epstein:123) controlling employment, accommodation, and almost all aspects of the employees' lives, there is a multitude of different employers. The East London locations—entirely municipal—illustrate this atomism in extreme form, for they are largely made up of private, not municipal, housing, of shanty towns where the houseowners are individual Africans. Four fifths of East London Africans are crammed into these shanty towns (either as owners or as lodgers) and are therefore not even direct tenants of the only monolithic power on the white side—the municipal corporation.

Extra-town Ties

The typical East London worker is a country-bred Xhosa who stays in town, holding down a job, for many years. Those Xhosa who want to make only brief earning sorties from their rural homes usually prefer a nine-month contract in the distant Rand mines or towns: East London is the place for the serious regular earning without which (owing to the poverty of Reserve agriculture) most rural families would not be able to make ends meet. Influx control regulations, nowadays, rather encourage the tendency for men to stay long in town.

A migrant who prematurely returns to the country, or gives up his job, is liable to loss of his "permit to remain within the urban area," thus jeopardizing his family's cash income. On the other hand, East London lies so near to the rural hinterland that most migrants can make frequent brief visits home" *during* their prolonged stay in town. Some can manage "week-ending" and "month-ending" (on off-duty days); others are limited to an annual two weeks at Christmas.

This particular local situation—the combination of easy home-visiting, for those who wish it, with prolonged stay in town—makes it possible to construct a meaningful scale for measuring the strength of the hinterland pull and comparing it as between different migrants, or different stages of a life history. Most migrants when they begin their East London careers are subject to a fairly strong pull, in that they have left their closest kin and dependents (parents, wives, children) "at home" in the hinterland. These country kin expect to be visited at intervals and to receive regular remittances from the migrant's wages. But the pull need not remain constant. Some migrants crudely deny it; they "vanish" or "melt away" (*nyibilika* in the Xhosa vernacular) in town, entirely dropping all their rural connections and obligations. Others eventually nullify the pull by managing to qualify administratively as "permanent residents of the urban area," moving their families into town, and winding up their interests in the hinterland. The migrants who remain permanently susceptible to the pull are the ones who make the most of their opportunities for home-visiting, and also for associating with fellow "exiles" from the same home place during their stay in town. These twin mechanisms enable them to remain permanently involved not only with kin but also with various structural systems in the hinterland. For instance, they remain acknowledged though largely absentee members of their (rural) men's age-grade "clubs," of the local (rural) council (*Inkundla*), and of their own lineage group. They can eventually return "home" and resume the appropriate roles in full.

Migrants and "Urban Africans"

In what has been said about the process of urbanization and the dropping or rejection of extra-town ties, an antithesis has been implied between two types of people who may live side by side in town; namely the migrant and the "urban African." This, too, is a point where existing models for the study of African urban systems may need some modification for purposes of the study of migrancy.

It will be noticed that the adjective "urban" ought properly to have a different connotation in each of the three models which were touched upon at the beginning of this article. (a) In the "detribalization" model, the urban/tribal antithesis is conceived principally as an antithesis of different human conditions, or ways of life. Urban might then serve as a near-synonym for Westernized, or civilized, or detribalized. It would seem permissible (in this view) to speak of an "urban African," meaning one who has reached the end of the road of cultural change, completely losing his tribal culture and/or status within the tribe. In a given town, some people will be more "urban" than others. (b) The second model represented the urban/tribal antithesis as an antithesis of two social fields, one located in the town and the other in the hinterland. In this view, urban would be a synonym for town-located; any action, interaction, institution, or relation that exists within the "urban" field would appear as "urban." Hence "urban African," if it means anything, will here mean an African who happens to be playing parts in a given town at a given moment, regardless of whether he is going to revert to tribal life later on. No African will be either more or less "urban" than his neighbor in town. (c) The third model represents the antithesis as one of "sets of relations." In contrast to (b), it does not imply that everything located in town is equally urban: on the contrary, the analytic task may be seen precisely as that of sorting out what are termed the truly or "typically" urban sets of relations (in town) from those others which, although town-located, are not "typically" urban. "Typically" urban, in this model, is an epithet for social systems such as trade unions (Gluckman, 1960:58): their urban-ness is not just that they do exist in town, but that they could not well exist anywhere else; they are social phenomena of a type intrinsically associated with urban areas. In this model, the question of what one means by an "urban African" does not arise at all. The adjective is not applicable to persons: it applies only to roles, relations, systems, and the like.

When studying migrancy in East London, there was a clear need for the model to accommodate "urban Africans" as a distinct category of persons. Not only can this category be conceptually distinguished from the migrants (by virtue of its renunciation of extra-town ties), but the East Londoners themselves emphasize the distinction. To them, the urban African (or as they would say, the "real townsman") is a distinct sociocultural category, different from the migrant "who works in town but is of the country," and this distinction is made the basis of some notable social oppositions.

At present about 15% of the adult (over 15 years old) Africans in East London are townsmen born and bred. These people approximate to the ideal type of the townsman as the man who has all his important social ties bounded by the town and feels no pull from the hinterland. With them must be classed those among the country-born 85% who in due course have dropped or lost their country connections: these also feel no pull from the hinterland. Over against all these "real townsmen" (whether they are such by birth or by adoption) stand all the migrants who still have parents, wives, children, land, cattle, houses, group membership, and tribal status outside the town, and who are thereby subject to the hinterland pull in more or less full force.

Administrative policy does something to underline the difference. The "real townsmen" have more security for themselves and their families in town than the country-oriented migrants have. The latter require special permits—renewable every month—to remain within the urban area (that is, unless or until they qualify as "permanent residents," by achieving the difficult record of 10 or 15 years' continuous employment). To bring in their dependents they require extra permits, which are not easily granted.

To these two bases of differentiation must be added a third: a cultural one. The migrants generally remain adept in their home culture (whether this be Red or School—a distinction to be explained [later]. Whatever "town ways" they may be called on to practice while in town, they can slip into the ways of the rural culture when they visit home, and when they retire there for good. The "real townsmen" are adept only in "town ways," and they value these positively, whereas many migrants are [likely] to value them negatively. The "town ways" are those of second or third generation urban proletarians (and a small bourgeoisie); they are different enough from rustic Xhosa ways to constitute a distinct sub-culture.

Naturally, the opposition between urban Africans and migrants is not important in all situations. Broadly speaking, their significance as reference groups is reduced to its lowest level at work and when moving in the white part of town; it reaches its highest level in situations where people are moving entirely among their fellow-Africans, at leisure in the locations where they sleep and have their social life.

The same applies to another categorization which the Xhosa migrants bring with them into East London from the hinterland. For generations, the Xhosa countryside has been split by a fundamental opposition between "Red" and "School" people, that is, between tribally minded Xhosa traditionalists on the one hand, and mission and school products on the other. This region of South Africa constitutes one of the oldest areas of white settlement south of the Sahara—white and black having both claimed it as home since the 1820s—but the Xhosa did not quickly or easily submit to white rule. Throughout the nineteenth century those of them who had not been won over by the missionaries continued to harass the whites in a series of fierce wars (the "Kaffir Wars"). The Red Xhosa are the descendants and cultural heirs of these nationalist resisters: theirs is the section which has been looking askance at white men, and white men's ways, since the days of George IV. Even today they are typically, and proudly, pagan and illiterate; it is their stereotyped comment that "White men's ways are for white men, not for us Xhosa." The School section, on the other hand, who have received mission and school teaching over the same period of five generations, are a Christianized peasant folk who internalize many of the values of civilization. Their aspiration is to move closer to equality with white people, and they tend to look down on the "raw" or "out-of-date" traditions of the "Red blanket wearers," who would rather prefer to withdraw out of white people's reach.

This opposition of conservatives and progressives—outwardly symbolized in the country by markedly different dress and appearance—does not only serve to demarcate two further subcultures: it has also long functioned as a group opposition. Within each rural neighborhood, the Red and School elements keep each to themselves, voluntarily abstaining from avoidable association, organizing activities as far as possible strictly within their own section. Inter-marriage is rare. Worship, recreation, entertainment are separate. The cleav-age has been elevated onto a moral plane; not mixing with the "other" kind of person is made a moral issue, from childhood onwards (Mayer, 1961:Ch.2).

In the East London locations—as fieldwork revealed—three reference groups, viz., real townsmen, School migrants, and Red migrants, remain clearly distinguishable. The habits of mutual aloofness which serve to keep Red and School separate in the country are also carried on in town. The Red element stay conspicuously out of School and town people's activities. The barrier between School migrant and "real townsman," though less empha-sized, is there too. In it are comprised those oppositions of sentiment and in-terest which divide yokels, at home in peasant Africa, from cockneys, reared in the slums of a Western-type industrial city.

The Study of Categorical Relations: Change and Mobility

It was stated that the three reference groups just enumerated—"real towns-man," Red migrant, and School migrant—have little or no significance at work. How they might be submerged in contexts involving workers' common interests is not the question that arises in trade-unionless East London, but it is observable that behavior patterns at work do not reflect them to any extent. White employers expect all types of Xhosa to play, and the Xhosa do play, similar parts in the urban economy. Although these are urban, not rural parts, the job ceiling is so low that different degrees of "Westernization" can be only slightly (if at all) reflected. The vast majority, migrant or townsman, Red or School, are concentrated in unskilled and semi-skilled occupations. (As an il-literate factory hand remarked, "Provided you can move fast, education doesn't count here.")

In terms of "cultural patterns" or "behavior," then, we have three subcul-tures which can only be clearly perceived in spheres of life other than work. In the working context, all behavior is brought to a common pattern; and this pattern is necessarily "urbanized," that is, adapted to the demands of its in-dustrial context. If a Copperbelt miner is a miner, so is a Xhosa factory hand a factory hand—though practically without the possibility of rising to a skilled position or joining a trade union. The ability of otherwise "tribal"-seeming people to produce "urban" behavior while actually engaged in work no longer excites comment or interest in this centenarian town. It is a form of situational selection that can be taken for granted. But to say this leaves another question unanswered, namely, what kind of behavior will be preferred when Ego is away from the working situation. For we are not dealing with a homoge-neously "tribal" (i.e., un-Westernized) population, all of whom could be ex-pected to follow "tribal" custom or behavior whenever they are free to do so.

On the contrary, we have three sub-cultures, two of which expressly repudiate "tribal" habits and norms to a greater or less degree. It is therefore necessary to go into the question of away-from-work behavior with special care.

The spheres in which the three sub-cultures appear distinctly are (in particular) domestic, family, sociable, and religious life—[that is,] all those not directly regulated by the demands of work. Correspondingly, if we turn from "culture" to "social relations," we find social oppositions which can only be observed in other-than-work contexts,—in kinship, marriage, domestic, friendly, religious, and sociable relations, and in voluntary associations (including those for religion). It is in these spheres that one notices the strong tendency for East London Africans of each category to keep to "their own kind." Despite the common involvement in urban work, clearly the town does not function as a melting pot, nor yet a transmuting pot. Red men, in particular, express a strong distaste for "getting mixed up with" other categories in town. They choose their friends and domestic partners almost exclusively from among other Red migrants.

Hence, part of the study of migrancy in East London is the study of "categorical" relations, as defined by Mitchell (1956, 1959): the relation between the urban category and each of the two migrant categories, and likewise of relations between these two migrant categories (Red and School).

There is, however, one critical difference between the type of category described for the Copperbelt and the type encountered in East London. The difference is mobility. The Copperbelt categories (except the cross-cutting one of social class) are ethnic, birth-determined; from ego's point of view they are ascribed. The East London ones are determined ultimately by personal choice, whether in the sphere of cultural practice or of voluntary (associational) ties. Thus they are achieved rather than ascribed. If an individual in the East London situation wishes to do so, and will take pains to acquire the necessary social skills, he can move from one category into another, much as a person in a class-differentiated society can move from one class into another. Just as with class, it is a question of social relations and cultural practices taken in conjunction—the person who moves must select new habits and also new associates. And just as with class, the voluntary moving is mainly in one direction. It is far commoner to move out of, than into, the Red category, almost the only exceptions being a few non-Red women who marry Red men (contrary to usual practice).

There is always a certain amount of movement going on, as fieldwork showed. In the country, it is not easy for a Red person to "become School," because conservative kin and seniors oppose this on moral grounds. The change of reference group becomes notably easier in the crowded town setting, where the migrant—if he wishes—can take steps to evade the watchful eyes of conservative acquaintances. A minority of Red migrants, accordingly, do "become School in town," and a minority of all migrants (both Red and School) "become townsmen" who will never willingly acknowledge the pull of the hinterland again.

The Xhosa vernacular has several pointers to this process of mobility. It is significant that the terms for people who change, or people in transition, are derogatory. There is *irumsha,* the "speaker of another language" (especially English), the cultural turncoat who adopts and values town ways. The neutral term *igoduka,* the "home visitor," who remains a faithful visitor to the hinterland while staying in town, contrasts with the derogatory term *itshipha,* the "absconder," who gets swallowed up in town and abandons his hinterland dependents. Derogatory, too, is *igqoboka,* the man "with a hole" caused by his conversion to Christianity (as distinct from the "born" or established Christian). Obviously, these terms and the concepts they stand for have nothing to do with urban *work.* No man is *irumsha* by virtue of speaking English to his employer. Nor will a "home visitor" be at all distinguishable from an "absconder" in the working situation. The contrast can only be seen by reference to those other situations, already enumerated, where Africans are together among themselves, in the urban locations, and are relatively free to organize their own activities and relationships.

We may say that the Xhosa are correctly postulating a distinction between the *necessarily* urban behavior of a migrant while at work, and the *voluntarily* urban behavior which he may or may not adopt in other town-located situations. While the behavior selected within the working sphere is necessarily "urban," the migrant's behavior in other spheres lies somewhere along a scale from Red ("tribal" or "least urban") to "really urban"; furthermore, it may move along that scale in the course of time. Here, in the locations, three subcultures or sets of patterns—Red, School, and "really urban"—are available as alternatives. And here a man's own choices and decisions have a particular significance in that they indicate whether he wishes to remain within his original social category or to adopt a different one (whether he will "remain Red" or will "become School" or "really a townsman").

A simple two-valued model of situational selection, therefore, is not appropriate for the study of migrants in East London. While we can take it for granted that "urban" behavior will be selected in working situations, we also have to reckon with this further process of selection which is demanded in nonworking situations and whose outcome cannot be predicted on a priori grounds.

Themes for Study: Social Network and Personal Choice

In this way, it can be said, an effort has been made to combine certain features of the "alternation" and the "change" type of model. The valid objection to detribalization as a working concept, after all, is not that it implies change, but that it tends to imply synchronized change of the whole man. Provided we recognize that a man need not move (or stand still) as a whole, provided we allow for his perhaps remaining "tribal" in some situations while becoming "urban" in others (however we define those adjectives), there is no a priori objection to using the idea of change. Indeed, the difficulty of accommodating movement, or process, has already been noticed as a main limitation of any model that works solely in terms of situational selection.

In practical terms, the study of migrants in East London had two related aspects. One was investigation of individual migrants' networks of personal relations, [that is], their total networks, town-located plus country-located, so as to determine the balance of within-town and extra-town ties, and the likelihood of a shift. The other was investigation of behavior patterns, attitudes, and values with special reference to aspiration or the desire for change. Details are given in the volume mentioned [earlier] (Mayer, 1961). Here it will suffice to say that two polar types emerged. In one type (it appeared) the town-located part of the network came to take clear precedence over the country-located part, until it could be said that all of the migrant's most important personal ties were now contained within the town, much as they are with town-born people. There would also be a shift towards "urban" behavior and values—a desire to adopt "real townsmen" as one's reference group. Connections with the country home might be kept up for security reasons, but while in town the migrant would prefer the company of new friends found in town. In the opposite type, ties with nontownsmen remained paramount. Besides attaching importance to friends and groups "at home" in the country, the migrant while in town would restrict himself as far as possible to the company of "home friends" (*amakhaya*)—fellow-exiles coming from his own place. "New" friendships, with people not known at home, would be eschewed. Emphasis would be laid on resisting the lures of town, remaining faithful to "home" cultural values, and returning "home" as often or as soon as possible. Voluntary activities in town would be imitations of, or near substitutes for, Red rural prototypes (beer drinks, ancestor sacrifices, Red dances). On returning "home," the exiled *amakhaya* could fit in almost as if they had not been away.

It can be said that in East London a migrant's propensity to change culturally (or to resist change) is ultimately bound up with the fate of his extra-town ties. More than anything else, what keeps the conservative Red type of man faithfully Red during all his years in town is his continuing to be bound to one specific Red family, lineage, and community "at home" in the country. It is from here that the critical moral pressures emanate: the wish to go on fitting in here can be called the underlying drive. Two mechanisms keep up the force of these extra-town ties (and thus the continued acceptance of the original home culture). These mechanisms (as I have described in *Townsmen or Tribesmen*) are (a) home-visiting, and (b) organization of relations between *amakhaya* while in town. I have referred to their total effect as "incapsulation."

The contrast offered by the School migrant (and also the "deviant" Red migrant who breaks out of incapsulation) shows that (a) is not effective without (b). If a migrant while in town turns his back on his *amakhaya* and plunges into "mixed" society, visits home do not serve to keep up extra-town ties to the same extent. Much of the content is lost. The way is open for cultural change, quite apart from the obligatory kind of urbanization demanded in the working space.

A point to be stressed once again is that these polar types, and other types intermediate between them, result from the migrants' *voluntary* organization of their private and domestic lives. Much as we see a distinction between *necessarily* "urban" behavior, at work, and *voluntarily* "urban" behavior, outside work, so we can say that certain relations—at work—are thrust upon the migrant, but that outside working hours he *voluntarily* chooses his associates. Even his domestic circle in town (roommates, landlord) is a matter for his personal decision. Town, in any case, offers opportunity for more numerous and more varied kinds of social relations than are possible in a "tribal" rural community. It is the migrant, coming in from outside—starting with a clean sheet as it were—who can make fullest use of the opportunities. Also dependent on his own choice is the matter of keeping up his ties with old friends "at home" in the country, or letting them drop.

It seems sometimes to have been implied that prolonged residence in the "atmosphere" of town will automatically tend to "change" people and make them "urbanized." East London does not bear this out. There, while some are born "urban," and others achieve urbanization, none can be said to have urbanization thrust upon them. There is a power of choice; some of the migrants begin to change; but others voluntarily incapsulate themselves in something as nearly as possible like the tribal relations from which their migration could have liberated them. The study of urbanization of migrants, in the particular form I have outlined here, is a study of such choices and of the determinants that lie behind the choices.

Bibliography

Epstein, A. L.
    1958   *Politics in an Urban African Community*. Manchester, England: Manchester University Press.
Gluckman, M.
    1958   "Analysis of a Social Situation in Modern Zululand." Rhodes-Livingstone Paper no. 28.
    1960   "Tribalism in Modern British Central Africa." Cahiers d'études africaines No. 1, 55 ff. Paris.
    1961   "Anthropological Problems Arising from the African Industrial Revolution." In *Social change in modern Africa*, A. Southall, ed. Oxford University Press.
Gulliver, P. H.
    1957   "Labour Migration in a Rural Economy." Kampala. East African Studies No. 6. East African Institute of Social Research.
Mayer, P.
    1961   *Townsmen or Tribesmen*. Cape Town, Oxford University Press, for Rhodes University Institute of Social and Economic Research.

MITCHELL, J. C.
  1956   *The Kalela Dance*. Rhodes-Livingstone Paper 27. Manchester, Manchester University Press.
  1959a   "The Causes of Labour Migration." Bulletin of the Inter-African Labour Institute, Vol. VI, no. 1.
  1959b   "The Study of African Urban Social Structure." Unpublished paper for CCTA Conference on Housing and Urbanisation, Nairobi.
  1959c   "Social Change and the New Towns of Bantu Africa." Unpublished paper for Round Table Conference on Social Implications of Technological Change. Paris, Social Science Council.
  1960a   *Tribalism and the Plural Society*. Inaugural lecture, University College of Rhodesia and Nyasaland. London, Oxford University Press.
  1960b   "The Anthropological Study of Urban Communities." Johannesburg, African Studies, 19,3:169–72.
NADEL, S. F.
  1957   *The Theory of Social Structure*. London, Cohen and West.
SCHAPERA, I.
  1947   *Migrant Labour and Tribal Life*. Oxford University Press.
SOUTHALL, A. W. and P. C. W. GUTKIND.
  1957   "Townsmen in the Making." Kampala, East African Studies, No. 9. East African Institute of Social Research.
WATSON, W.
  1958   *Tribal Cohesion in a Money Economy*. Manchester, Manchester University Press.
WILSON, G.
  1941   "Economics of Detribalisation in Northern Rhodesia: Part I." Rhodes-Livingstone Paper 5. Livingstone, The Rhodes-Livingstone Institute.
  1942   Idem, Part II. Rhodes-Livingstone Paper 6.
VAN VELSEN, J.
  1960   "Labour Migration As a Postive Factor in the Continuity of Tonga Tribal Society." In *Social Change in Modern Africa*, A. Southall, ed. Oxford University Press.

A Study of the Urbanization Process Among Mixtec Migrants from Tilantongo in Mexico City

DOUGLAS S. BUTTERWORTH

Terms such as disorganization, anomie, maladaptation, uneasy accommodation, breakdown, and individual impotency still abound in the urban literature. They suggest that the city exerts a negative force on the lives of inhabitants who must "make do" in their struggle for survival in the urban jungle. At best, it seems the urban milieu has offered a kind of dysfunctional freedom; released from the chains of ancestral custom in the impersonal context of the city, the newcomer soon finds that there is the freedom to be hungry, homeless, jobless, friendless, and alone. Such freedom is gladly relinquished to gain the support of others through secondary associations, which serve as substitutes (albeit inadequate and superficial) for the genuine social solidarity of family, kin, and social identity that marks nonurban life.

Douglas Butterworth maintains that his investigations tend to refute this view of the migrant's urbanization process. He finds many similarities in the way Tilantongueños interrelate with their neighbors prior to and after emigration to Mexico City. The crux of the urbanization process, he argues, lies not in the nature of the city alone, but also in the nature of the individual and the historic pattern of emigration from the community left behind. One wonders, however, if the similarities he noted between village and urban dwelling Tilantongueños were not in large part due to Butterworth's having studied the sole Tilantongo enclave in Mexico City. What would he have found had he studied "the many other Tilantongueños scattered throughout the rest of the city?" If he had worked with those who did not choose to live in transplanted "urban villages," secure in the company of kin and old friends, would he still have found the same 14 urban "characteristics"?

Since Ralph Beals called attention to the fact that sociologists have paid much more attention to urbanism than to urbanization, pointing out that the "primary sociological concern has been with the nature of the urban society rather than with the processes of urbanism or the adaptation of men to urban life,"[1] sociologists and anthropologists have directed some attention to the processes of urbanization. In Latin America, the dozen or so years which have elapsed since Beals' call for interdisciplinary research in urbanization and

"A Study of the Urbanization Process Among Mixtec Migrants from Tilantongo in Mexico City," *America Indigena* Vol. XXII (3) 1962, pp. 257–274. Inter-American Indian Institute (c).

[1] Beals, Ralph L. "Urbanism, Urbanization and Acculturation," *American Anthropologist*, Vol. 53, No. 1, January–March, 1951.

migration processes have seen the appearance of a number of significant studies in those areas.[2] Although such studies have only begun to scratch the surface of urbanization and migration problems, they indicate that many traditional concepts concerning urbanization are not applicable to Latin America,
or apply only with important reservations and modifications.

Oscar Lewis concluded from his study of Tepozteco migratory patterns that
perhaps "some of the sociological generalizations concerning urbanization
which have been accepted until now may be culturally limited and require a
new examination in the light of comparative studies of urbanization in other
areas."[3]

Some of the sociological generalizations concerning the distinctive features
of the urban way of life to which Lewis refers have been described by Wirth
as consisting of "the substitution of secondary for primary contacts, the
weakening of bonds of kinship, and the declining social significance of the
family, the disappearance of the neighborhood, and the undermining of the
traditional basis of social solidarity."[4] The result of these urban processes is
that the individual is reduced to impotency and thus joins organized groups in
order to obtain his ends.[5]

"Whereas in the sacred, simple society the worst that occurs is a schism of
values, allowing the person to take one side or the other, in the metropolis
the individual is living in the presence of multiple definitions of proper conduct."[6] Disorganization and maladaptation are the presumed consequences of
the kaleidoscopic series of changes which face the rural migrant in the city.
The secular life of the city has also been thought to be an important negative
influence on religious values. Personal relations become segmented and the
urbane sophisticate, the "city slicker," develops.

It has been assumed *a priori* that persons migrating to the city will adopt
the traits which are supposedly characteristic of the urban population. By virtue of his move to the city, the peasant becomes "emancipated from the control of ancestral custom, enjoying this new freedom, but at the same time suffering by the release from intimate group participation and responsibility."[7]
The rather uneasy accommodation developing out of the urbanization process,
we are told, results in the acquisition by the migrant of "an organ protecting

[2] See, for example, Lewis, Oscar, "Urbanización sin desorganización," *America Indígena*, XVII, 3,
July, 1957; Mangin, William, "Mental Health and Migration to Cities: A Peruvian Case," *The New York
Academy of Sciences*, Vol. 84, Dec. 8, 1960; Fried, Jacob, "Acculturation and Mental Health among In-
dian Migrants in Peru," in Opler, Marvin K. (ed.), *Culture and Mental Health: Cross-cultural Studies*.
New York: MacMillan Publishing Co., Inc., 1959; Whetten, Nathan L., and Burnight, Robert G., "Inter-
nal Migration in Mexico," and Métraux, Alfred, "Las migraciones internas de los indios Aymara en el
Perú contemporáneo," in *Estudios antropológicos publicados en homenaje al doctor Manuel Gamio*.
México: 1956; United Nations. Bureau of Social Affairs. *Report on the World Social Situation*. New
York: 1957; Davis, Kingsley, and Casis, Ana, "Urbanization in Latin America," *The Millbank Memorial
Fund Quarterly*, Vol. XXIV, No. 2, April, 1946; Leonard, Olin E., "La Paz, Bolivia: Its Population and
Growth," *American Sociological Review*, Vol. XIII, No. 4, August, 1948; Caplow, Theodore, "The Ecology of Middle American Cities," *Social Forces*, Vol. 28, No. 2, December, 1949.
[3] Lewis, op. cit.
[4] Wirth, Louis, "Urbanism as a Way of Life," *The American Journal of Sociology*, Vol. 44, July, 1938.
[5] Ibid.
[6] Ericksen, E. Gordon. *Urban Behavior*. New York: MacMillan Publishing Co., Inc., 1954.
[7] Ibid.

him against the threatening currents and discrepancies of his external environment which would uproot him."[8]

The investigation undertaken by this writer does not tend to support the great majority of the assumptions concerning the urbanization process among migrants.[9] During the past nine months the investigator has been studying Mixtec Indian migrant settlers in Mexico City from the Municipio of Tilantongo, State of Oaxaca.[10] The purpose of the study is to compare the differences in the lives of the migrants in Mexico City with the way of life followed in Tilantongo.

Interviews were conducted among thirty-one families from Tilantongo who have migrated to Mexico City. Life history materials were gathered in varying depth from the family heads. Participant observation was utilized to the maximum extent possible. Interviews and participant observation ranged from a minimum of one-half hour to a maximum of about 120 hours for each family. A two-week ethnographic investigation (the first of a planned series) was made in Tilantongo in order to gather comparative data for the study.

The families studied by this investigator may not be typical of the migrants, Indian or otherwise, in urban centers in Latin America, Mexico, or, for that matter, Mexico City. Nevertheless, since we do not know what is "typical," the phenomena indicated in this study may have some useful bearing upon the problems of migration and urbanization. Basil Zimmer has pointed out that "important as migration is to the city, very little is known concerning the behavior of migrants in these centers."[11]

Tilantongo is a community in the Mixtec Alta. Within an area of 258.94 square kilometers live 3,701 people,[12] resulting in a population density of 14.29 persons per square kilometer. Although these figures do not indicate a serious overpopulation problem, such a problem does, in fact, exist. Tilantongo is an agricultural community, relying almost exclusively upon maize and wheat for subsistence. I estimate that less than 10% of the land in Tilantongo is suitable for cultivation. If 90% of the total land area is nonarable, the population density takes on a new significance. A high natural birth rate combined with fragmentation of land, poverty of the soil, and frequent crop failures have caused many Tilantongueños to migrate to urban centers. The principal motive for migration is economic.

Between 1930 and 1940, a decade which saw little migration from Tilantongo, the population of the municipio grew from 2,782, to 3,463, a 25.4% increase.[13] Emigration of the native-born population began in large numbers after World War II; nevertheless, the decade from 1940 to 1950 still saw a

---

[8] Simmel, Georg. "The Metropolis and Mental Life," *Cities and Society: The Revised Reader in Urban Sociology.* ed. Paul K. Hatt and Albert J. Reiss, Jr. Glencoe, Ill.: The Free Press, 1957.

[9] "Urbanization" in this paper refers to the "modification of human behavior imposed by the urban way of life." (Wirth, op. cit.)

[10] The investigation was supported by a grant from the U.S. National Institute of Mental-Health.

[11] Zimmer, Basil G. "Participation of Migrants in Urban Structures," *American Sociological Review*, Vol. 20, April, 1955.

[12] *Octavo censo general de población*, Dirección general de estadística, México, 1960.

[13] *Sexto censo general de población*, Dirección general de estadística, México, 1940.

13.8% increase in population, from 3,463 to 3,941.[14] Since 1950 migration to urban areas from Tilantongo has accelerated to the point where the population of the community is now declining. The 1960 census figure of 3,701 inhabitants for the municipio of Tilantongo denotes a population loss of slightly more than 6% since 1950.[15] However, if we accept the 1930–40 increase of 24.5% as the "natural" growth of Tilantongo, it would appear that migration might be claiming as much as 30% of those born in the community. That figure is much too high, though, because those who migrate from Tilantongo are mostly in the 18–35 age group, the most fertile part of the population. The population pyramid of Tilantongo has a peculiar hour-glass shape, bulging at the base, thinning to half the size in the middle, and widening again after the 30–34 age group is passed, only to become more slender than ever when we enter the 40 age groups. The poor representation of the 15–34 age groups in the pyramid indicates that the fertility rate cannot be nearly so high nowadays as the natural increase in the 1920s showed it to be before large-scale migration began.

Migration from Tilantongo has not been in waves, but rather in a steadily increasing stream. Although some of the earlier migrants went first to smaller cities, such as Oaxaca, Veracruz, and Puebla, as indeed some still do today, the general pattern has not been one of step-wise migration from village to small city to capital city, which is characteristic of migration in other Latin American countries, and thought to be characteristic of Mexico as well.[16] Today the majority of migrants from Tilantongo go directly from their community to Mexico City.

The first emigrant from Tilantongo of whom the investigator has knowledge went first to Mexico City, then to Puebla, where he has resided for over thirty years. The first to settle permanently in Mexico City went directly there from Tilantongo fifteen years ago, after having previously spent three years in the capital city as a boy with his father. The informant made the move from Tilantongo principally for economic reasons. Upon arriving in Mexico City he worked as an unskilled laborer in various jobs for three years until he gained employment with a large firm in the city as an unskilled laborer. He advanced in the company until he attained the position of supervisor of general services. The history of this informant is gone into in some detail because he has become a significant influence on many of the migrants from Tilantongo who followed in his footsteps to Mexico City. Since he has risen to his present position, the man has found employment for twenty-one other migrants from Tilantongo with his firm, and has become the informal leader of a large segment of the Tilantongueños now residing in the capital city.

The term "informal leader" should not be interpreted to imply that there is an organization or cooperative alliance among the migrants from Tilantongo. Indeed one of the most striking aspects of the group of Tilantongueños now

---

[14] *Séptimo censo general de población,* Dirección general de estadística, México, 1950.
[15] *Octavo censo general de población.* op. cit.
[16] United Nations. Op. cit.

living in Mexico City is the complete absence of any formal or informal participation in organizations. Although Tilantongo has probably one of the largest
migrant populations from the Mixteca in Mexico City, it is not an official
member of the *Coalición de Pueblos Mixtecos Oaxaqueños,* an organization
in Mexico City which protects the interests of its member communities of the
Mixteca. Of the thirty-one family heads from Tilantongo known by investigator, none is a member of a sodality of any sort, with the exception of the informal leader, who is a member of the *Instituto Nacional de la Juventud Mex-
icana.* Informal organization is limited to weekend get-togethers of relatives
and compadres.

The writer found some support for the "fairly well established dictum of
urban studies that people tend to settle among their own kind". [17] Twenty-
seven of the thirty-one informant families live in adjacent *colonias* near the
airport on the eastern outskirts of Mexico City. There are many other Tilantongueños scattered throughout the rest of the city, but to the investigator's knowledge there is no other section of Mexico City which has a clustering of families from Tilantongo to the extent which have the *colonias* tangent
to the Mexico-Puebla highway near the airport. Those *colonias* have many of
the aspects of the "squatter settlement" typical of many large cities throughout the world.

As opposed to the declining industrial area slum, the "mushroom slum," of
which [this] section of Mexico City is an example, is characterized by rapid,
haphazard settlement by rural migrants. There is at first no water or sewage,
no electricity, no political organization nor recognition by the municipal government. Lots are purchased or merely claimed by the squatter, everyone
being an "owner." Houses of adobe, brick, or cement are built by the landowners. The mushroom slum is typically located near a main highway on the
outskirts of the city, allowing residents to take advantage of existing bus lines
to reach the part of the city in which they have found employment. [18] As the
area grows in size and population, recognition is granted by the metropolitan
area and/or unofficially by provision of transported water, electricity, and bus
service. Land speculators buy up tracts of nearby land to sell to the increasing
stream of immigrants who wish to settle among their own kind. [19]

The majority of the migrants from Tilantongo arrive, usually without notice,
at the doorstep of a relative or compadre already established in the mushroom
slum of the city. The initial visit is generally looked upon by the migrants as a
"trial." Many men come alone, leaving their wives and children in Tilantongo.
The visitors come to stay for a few days, perhaps several months, during the
dry season when there are no crops to tend. They come to the city with the
intention of obtaining off-season employment and plan to return to Tilantongo
for the planting season. If employment is obtained, however, they generally
stay in Mexico City, returning to Tilantongo only to fetch their family, al-

[17] Beals op. cit.
[18] See Lewis, Oscar, *Five Familes,* New York: Basic Books, 1959.
[19] See Mangin, op. cit., for a description of the origin and direction of change of a typical *barriada*
in Lima, Peru.

though they later begin to make periodic visits to their "tierra." Usually the visitors have been staying at the home of a relative or compadre. When employment is found and the men decide to settle permanently in the city, they rent a rudely constructed house in the *colonia* or in another section of the city until they can afford to buy their own land and build a home of their own.

Ownership of land, no matter how small nor how inconveniently located with respect to their place of employment, is a focal value in the lives of the migrants. When the decision has been made to settle permanently in the city, some migrants sell all or part of their land in Tilantongo to buy a parcel of land in a squatter *colonia*. Many others, however, prefer not to sell their land, or sell only part of it. The reason for this is that they may want to return to their village some day. This is a highly unlikely possibility. The writer knows only one migrant who returned permanently to Tilantongo after having experienced urban life for some time. The main reason the migrants hold onto a piece of land in Tilantongo is apparently that it provides them with a material tie to their "tierra," otherwise only symbolically present in their blood ties. Unfortunately, the practice of retaining land titles by emigrants from Tilantongo tends to defeat the principal reason for migration: lack of productive land. Nevertheless, there are many migrants who have a relative or friend work their land, the profits being divided.

The continuance of strong ties with their "tierra" is a striking universal characteristic among the emigrants from Tilantongo, who are unanimously and vociferously linked in spirit to their village. Visits are made annually to Tilantongo, often coinciding with the religious fiestas, and great concern is manifested for the hardships endured by the villagers. When drinking in Mexico City, the migrants become almost maudlin in the expression of their emotions about their "tierra."

Drinking patterns have changed considerably among the Mexico City migrants. In Tilantongo, *pulque* is the most frequently consumed alcoholic beverage. Pulque is the fermented juice of the maguey plant (*Agave Americana*). It is drunk throughout much of the highland areas of Mexico. Those who have maguey plants drink pulque daily during the dry season, unless they are so poor that they have to sell it in the marketplace on Sunday. Those who do not own magueys drink pulque in the market once a week and occasionally at the homes of relatives and compadres. The advantage of owning maguey plants lies primarily in the utility of pulques as a thirst-slaker. There is a great scarcity of water in the municipio; pulque serves to supply most of the liquid requirements of the body. Those without magueys must make daily trips for water, which for many families means a journey of several hours.

Drunkenness is frequent in Tilantongo. Pulque acts as a lever or fuse in the process of intoxication. A certain degree of intoxication can be achieved through consumption of pulque, but it usually happens that the pulque is exhausted or the imbiber is bloated before severe intoxication has resulted. Rather than stopping at that point, the Indians switch to *aguardiente* or *mez-*

cal, distilled from sugar cane and maguey respectively. Contrary to the non-distilled pulque, both of these beverages have extremely high alcoholic content, the former being, in addition, well supplied with various impurities. The result of the change from pulque to aguardiente or mezcal is disastrous to the sobriety of the drinkers.

Market day is famous in Tilantongo for its drinking bouts, but only a small number of people attend the Sunday market because of long distances to be covered and lack of roads. The investigator visited a number of outlying ranches during his visit to Tilantongo and observed everywhere a drinking process similar to that described [here].

Drinking sprees may begin at any time, day or night, any day of the week. They continue until all available liquor is exhausted, frequently including all liquor available within the radius of a day or night's walk. The fields may be left unattended for several days, but that is generally harmful only at harvest time, when it is said that there is less drinking. The "morning after" finds the Indian in the same psychological mood as when the spree started. Hangovers are common, but there are no guilt feelings observable, and no regrets about the drinking bout, except perhaps that it had to come to an end.

It is noteworthy that violence, physical or verbal, is absent during alcoholic binges, so the sober Indian is in no need to flay his conscience for having insulted a friend or compadre. Fiestas play an important part in the lives of the Indians in Tilantongo, and drunkenness is an integral part of them. The only difference between the drinking carried on during fiestas and that done during the rest of the year seems to be in degree rather than kind.

In Mexico City, the migrants become much more "regimented" drinkers. The frequency of drinking bouts as well as the quantity of alcoholic beverages consumed becomes greatly diminished. Drinking is not indulged in during the week, unless a relative or compadre appears from Tilantongo. The recent arrival always brings with him a jarro of mezcal from Oaxaca. The resultant party may last all night, and occasionally the host may not get to work the following day. Among the writer's informants, however, only one stays away from work with any frequency because of alcoholic binges, but that particular man does not need the excuse of a visitor to get drunk. The other informants are reliable workers and place a high value upon stability and dependability in their jobs.

Pulque is rarely consumed in Mexico City. The reason given by the drinkers for this phenomenon is that the pulque in the city is "adulterated with chemicals," and unfit to drink. The change in alcoholic beverages consumed is always from pulque to beer and aguardiente and mezcal to tequila. The mezcal available in Mexico City is also considered to be inferior to that obtainable in Tilantongo. The writer is led to believe that the underlying reason for the prejudice is probably an unconscious identification of beer and tequila with the "progressive" life of the city, and of pulque and mezcal with the primitive "Indian" way of life.

Many of the residents of Mexico City display an increased awareness of and identification with the Mexican nation. A slight correlation may be traced between length of residence and amount of identification with the national culture, but there are several variables which must be taken into consideration, the most important of which is whether the individual has been in the army. Military service inculcates in the migrants a sense of Mexican nationality which is not acquired by the most urbanized of the migrants who have not seen military duty. Nevertheless, the growth of national consciousness does not carry with it a corresponding decrease in identification with Tilantongo. Every migrant considers himself to be a Tilantongueño *and* a Mexican, many placing loyalty to their village first. Each migrant also considers himself an "Indio," even those residents who have spent fifteen years in Mexico City. Migrants' children who are born in Mexico City are "Mexicanos"; children born in Tilantongo are "Indios." Two explanations are offered by the migrants for the distinction between "Indio" and "Mexicano." A person is an "Indio" if he was born or registered in Tilantongo. Thus a child born in Tilantongo, taken to Mexico City, and registered in the latter place, is a "Mexicano." If the child is registered in Tilantongo, he is an "Indio." More importantly, a linguistic distinction is made. Anyone who speaks Mixtec is an "Indio." Children who speak only Spanish are "Mexicanos." Offspring are discouraged from learning the Indian language in order that they may be "Mexicanos" rather than "Indios."

Fried's conclusion from his study of migration in Peru among Andean Indians that "migration is a factor in the etiology of mental ill health, and very specifically of psychosomatic disorders,"[20] is not supported by this investigation. Adjustment by the Indian migrants from Tilantongo to urban life appears to be highly satisfactory, most probably because of a combination of a psychological "set" to learn new skills and values, an earlier dissatisfaction with existing values, and a successful transplanting of kinship ties resulting in the continuance of secure emotional attachments.[21]

The substitution of secondary, contractual, *Gesellschaft* relationships for primary, status-based, *Gemeinschaft* relationships, considered to be *sine qua non* of urbanization processes, is not characteristic of the migrants from Tilantongo. Except for necessary modifications in their jobs, all the migrants insist upon, and generally succeed in, maintaining primary face-to-face relationships. The "schizoid" character of urban personality produced by segmentation of human relationships described by Wirth[22] is not a development [that] occurs in the first generation of Indian migrants from Tilantongo.

Family ties appear to remain as strong as they were in Tilantongo, and perhaps become even stronger. This finding directly contradicts the stereo-

---

[20] Fried, op. cit.

[21] Both Lewis, "Urbanización sin desorganización", op. cit., and Mangin, op. cit., in their studies of migration to large cities, found maladjustment and disorganization among the migrants to be minimal. Mangin states that his four-year study among Indian migrants in Peru does not support the expectation that "low-status migrants whose culture differs most from that of the dominant group will suffer stress and exhibit disorganized and maladaptive behavior . . ."

[22] Wirth, op. cit.

typed concept of family bonds weakening with urbanization, but is consistent with the findings reported by Lewis in his study of urbanization process among Tepoztecos.[23]

Lewis found that the *compadrazgo* complex continues to function in the city, although it is often reduced to the rites of baptism and marriage. He reports that relatives are frequently chosen as compadres in the city, but not in Tepotzotlan.[24] The results of the present research differ in some respects from Lewis' findings concerning *compadrazgo*. *Compadrazgo* continues to flourish among the Tilantongueños in Mexico City and, in fact, takes on an added importance. Bonds of *compadrazgo* criss-cross throughout much of the Tilantongo group in Mexico City, ensuring in-group solidarity and providing a strong feeling of security. Friendships are rarely formed outside the group, and only one informant has a wife who is not a native-born Tilantongueña. Compadres are, however, occasionally taken from outside the in-group. A step in that direction was taken initially by the informal leader. Other migrants have followed his lead hesitantly, but not to the extent that there is an immediate prospect of forming strong social bonds with non-Tilantongueños. Relatives are frequently taken as compadres, but it is not clear if the practice has increased through migration to the city.

The main motivations for migration to urban centers are economic and educational. They are economic in the dual sense that the sub-subsistence level of the economy in Tilantongo exerts tremendous pressure on a portion of the population to emigrate; the attractions of urban life exert an equal attraction for the more enterprising young men. The lack of educational opportunities in Tilantongo and the availability of those facilities in large cities excites the enthusiasm of those family heads with ambition for themselves or their children.

Economically, the family heads are unanimously agreed that they are better off financially in Mexico City than in Tilantongo. They all hold steady jobs, with the exception of one semi-invalid and two men who are "retired," one living from an army pension, the other supported by his family. As is to be expected, the jobs are of various types, but it is noteworthy that none of the migrants is an ambulatory salesman, "peddler," or vendor of any kind. As mentioned previously, twenty-two migrants are employed by a large manufacturing firm in the city. Of those, one is in a supervisory capacity, two are warehouse guards, and eighteen are general service assistants. One informant is a doctor; one is a policeman; one is a laborer in a furniture factory; several are bricklayers or masons. The semi-invalid, who is employed part-time as a carpenter's apprentice, is the only man whose wife works. Salaries of the men employed full-time range from 400 to 1000 pesos per month. Although exact earnings for each one of the informants could not be ascertained, the mean monthly wage of those for whom precise earnings could be gathered (twenty-four individuals) is 550 pesos.

Rent paid by those who migrate from Tilantongo who have not yet bought

---

[23] Lewis, "Urbanización. . . ," op. cit.
[24] Ibid.

their own land and built their own homes averages slightly more than 50 pesos per month. No reliable estimate could be made on the cost of constructing a house, since practices vary widely and many did not know in the first place how much they spent for their houses. Land values also fluctuate widely. Nevertheless, a typical case may be cited for illustrative purposes.

The informant in question came to Mexico City with his wife and child four years ago, having previously worked as a laborer in Mexico City for three years. After obtaining a job in a furniture factory, he rented a one-room house for 50 pesos a month. However, he objected to paying rent, so he and his brother requested money from their father in Tilantongo for a down-payment on a piece of land in a squatter settlement. The down-payment was 2000 pesos, which the father sent. The brothers then made monthly payments of 168 pesos until the land was fully owned. The total cost of the property was 6000 pesos. The informant built by himself on weekends a one-room adobe house on the lot of 400 square meters. He and his brother are now co-owners of the land and building. After completing the house, the informant returned to Tilantongo to fetch his two younger brothers, aged thirteen and fifteen, who now live with him and go to school. The informant supports the young brothers financially. In the house live the informant, his brother, his wife, his two children, his two younger brothers, a friend from Tilantongo, and the friend's common-law wife and child. In all, ten people live in the one-room house. The house faces on a small dirt patio which contains chickens and a pig. Contiguous to the patio is a small cornfield which supplies much of the food for the families. The cornfield is not typical of migrant families, who generally do not have enough land to raise anything more than a few domestic animals.

Insofar as possible, the patio complex typical of Tilantongo dwellings has been retained in the city. Where more than one structure is owned by the family, the buildings are placed around a patio. If the family, as is the usual case, has only one structure, it is so located as to form one side of a patio complex with other dwellings. Exceptions to this practice are the result of physical limitations of the property.

The number of rooms per family varies more or less proportionately to the economic status of the family. The informant with the highest salary (1000 pesos per month) has the largest number of dwelling areas. That man has a house consisting of a living room-dining room, two bedrooms, and a kitchen. In addition, there are three other dwellings constructed of cement blocks in the compound built around a patio. Those buildings house relatives and compadres. Only one of the inhabitants of those extra buildings pays rent.

The meanest home consists of one adobe brick windowless room, three by four meters, with a dirt floor. The majority of the homes contain two rooms furnished with beds, chairs, a bureau, radio, table, and cooking utensils.

Almost all informants own radios. Two families have television sets. Sunday afternoon visits to the homes of the TV owners are popular among Tilantongueños. At least two migrants own phonographs. Every family has an electric iron; many have sewing machines. All families sleep in beds, although frequently there is only one bed for married couple and children.

Sanitation is greatly improved over that practiced in Tilantongo; an outdoor privvy is owned individually or shared by a number of families.

Gas or kerosene stoves are found in every home. No one possesses a refrigerator.

The diet of migrants is without exception much improved over that of residents of Tilantongo. Food is generally cited as the material evidence of the improved standard of living of the migrants. Whereas in Tilantongo the normal diet is limited to tortillas and salt, beans being eaten only once or twice a week and meat weekly or semi-monthly, in Mexico City beans are eaten daily; meat is eaten at least once a week by even the poorest families. The better-off families in the city eat meat daily. Soups are served in the city as separate dishes or as part of the meat or bean dish. Tortillas of maize are eaten by all, even though wheat tortillas are more popular in Tilantongo. Wheat bread is not eaten by any family in Mexico City. In the city potatoes and squash have been added to the diet. *Guajes* are eaten in the city, as they are in Tilantongo. Chiles, a delicacy in Tilantongo, are commonplace on the tables of the migrants in Mexico City; they are served with all meals. Coffee is not taken regularly by any family, although every family drinks it occasionally. Beer and soda pop are the most popular beverages. Fruit is eaten now and then.

Desserts are never eaten, though the children enjoy sweets and are permitted to buy and eat them. One family serves popcorn on Sunday afternoons while guests are watching TV. Two families are known to use toothpicks.

In Tilantongo all eating is done with tortillas and fingers. Silverware is not employed, nor any other kind of tableware except small bowls in which beans or soup are served. The soup is sipped from the bowl or scooped in a tortilla. In Mexico City all food is served on plates at the table. However, eating utensils are limited to soup spoons. Paper napkins are provided for special occasions.

The men are served separately from the women and children. The men are served by the women; the latter then retire to the kitchen, if there is a separate kitchen, or to one side of the room with the children. This pattern is a survival from Tilantongo, where the men eat in one half [of] the room, the women in the other half by the cooking fire.

Chicken or turkey *moles* are the most popular festive dishes in the city, ceding precedence only to the *barbacoas*, or barbecues. Barbacoas in the style of Tilantongo are big events in the lives of the migrants. Barbacoas and drinking parties are important sources of entertainment.

New entertainment media enter the lives of the migrants when they settle in the city, but are limited to the radio, TV, and phonograph. The only forms of entertainment in Tilantongo, where there is no electricity, are drinking, gossip, the annual fiestas, and, for the young men, basketball. In the city, drinking and visiting are combined with watching TV or listening to the radio.

Three informants play basketball regularly; one of them also plays cards when he can find others with whom to play. No other forms of entertainment are sought, nor are they readily accepted. The migrants do not go to the movies, nor to so-called "cultural" activities, such as art galleries, or museums. The family circle of real and artificial kin apparently satisfies many or most of the entertainment needs of the ex-residents of Tilantongo.

One of the primary reasons for emigrating from Tilantongo is the desire to educate oneself and one's children. Illiteracy is widespread in Tilantongo. According to the 1950 census, 83% of the inhabitants are illiterate.[25] Almost all the migrants who settle in Mexico City enter school when they arrive, either taking a part-time job in order to attend school during the day, or going to night schools in the city. Over half the migrants finish the *primaria*. None of the migrants continues to the *secundaria*, although many express a desire to continue their education. Albeit the migrants do not keep on in school themselves past the primaria, they place a strong emphasis upon educating their children. It is common throughout some parts of Latin America for rural migrants to urban centers to send their children to live in a home in the city to work as servants without pay with the understanding that the family accepting the child will send him or her to school. That is not the practice among Tilantongo migrants. Sacrifices of some financial magnitude are frequently undergone by migrants in order to keep the children in the home and send them to school, even though the children are of an age when they could be making important economic contributions to the household.

Behind the economic and educational motivations of migration lies an ubiquitous psychological factor which operates to influence migration patterns. There is a deeply ingrained fear in the Indians of Tilantongo—fear of extortion, political persecution, economic exploitation, banditry, and blood feuds. In addition to these "social" fears, there is an ever-present fear of the natural elements, which in one fell swoop can, and often do, wipe out a year's food supply. Thus the people of Tilantongo have a constant fear of losing what they possess, material and nonmaterial. This situation both foments and prevents migration.

In Mexico City, the migrants say that they have "lost the fear" that they had in Tilantongo. No longer are they servile creatures of the whims of the "bad elements" (*malos elementos*) in their community, human and natural. The rather obvious prosperity and newly acquired security which the migrants reflect when they return on visits to their *tierra* instill in many Tilantongueños a determination to emulate their envied cousins and join the stream of migrants.

On the other hand, the very thought of abandoning the things that they do have, material and nonmaterial, to set off for a distant place containing millions of unknown, potentially threatening, individuals, creates in many natives such strong anxiety that they form ingenious rationalizations at times for stay-

---

[25] *Séptimo censo general de la población,* op. cit.

ing on their impoverished parcel of land. Certainly there are many logical reasons for staying in Tilantongo. For example, those who speak only Mixtec are obviously at a serious disadvantage for migrating to a city. Monolingual males, in fact, do not migrate. All the male informants of the investigator speak Spanish, and the wives have learned to speak it, even though they might have been monolingual when they came to the city with their husbands.

Migration of unmarried women is virtually unknown. This is another aspect in which the findings of the writer differ from those reported by other investigators. The only single women who migrate to Mexico City are the young daughters who accompany their parents.

A universal change which takes place in the lives of the migrants studied by this investigator is a remarkable reduction in the importance of religion, at least insofar as its outward manifestations are concerned. Nominally all the migrants are devout Catholics and all are, according to their own evaluation, sincere believers. However, none of the thirty-one family heads goes to church, except for *compadrazgo* ceremonies such as baptism and confirmation. The wives of the migrants do not attend church either. Most of the families, however, send their children to church, at least until confirmation has been achieved. After confirmation, practice varies widely. Some children continue to attend Mass regularly; others cease to attend church entirely. Only two of the homes visited by the investigator have shrines.

The ostensible reasons for the loss of religious activities among the migrants are that "one has to tell the priest everything if one goes to church," that "the priests are not to be trusted," and that "they are out for their own ends." Nevertheless, the same attitude is held by the residents of Tilantongo, and they do go to their local chapels where there is no priest or to the church in town every Sunday. The reason must lie in some aspect of the urbanization process. There are doubtless a number of factors which cause this rather sudden secularization of the migrants from Tilantongo, but one of the most important seems to be the "loss of fear" so often described by the investigator's informants. The meaning behind this loss of fear is that life is much more secure in Mexico City than in Tilantongo. Apparently the newly found security in the mundane world results in a corresponding diminution of reliance upon the church for spiritual guidance.

Changes in dress are part of the de-Indianization process undergone by migrants. Typical garb in Tilantongo is a white cotton shirt and white trousers worn by the men and a cotton dress and *rebozo* by the women. All men wear *huaraches;* most women go barefoot. All the men wear hats woven from palm leaves.

In Mexico City, many of the women change their attire, retaining the cotton dress, but replacing the *rebozo* with a sweater. Many women own shoes and sometimes socks, although around the house most women wear huaraches or go barefoot. The cotton dress is of better quality, and each woman has at least one good dress for special occasions.

The men discard all "Indian" dress that they wore in their village. The white cotton trousers and shirt are replaced by gabardine or good-quality cotton trousers of a dark color, and colored sports shirts or white dress shirts. Ties are worn for special events. Each man owns either a suit or a sports jacket. Shoes are worn by all men; the straw hat has been discarded.

Medical services are highly valued by the migrants. There is no evidence of an ill person returning to Tilantongo to be "cured," as Lewis observed among the migrant Tepoztecos.[26] Doctors are consulted by all migrants without regard to the length of residence of the migrants. The well-acculturated migrants aid the process of replacing folk medicine beliefs by actively discouraging folk beliefs and encouraging consultations with recognized medical practitioners in the city.

In summary, the outstanding characteristics of families studied by this investigator who have migrated from Tilantongo to Mexico City are the following.

1) Steady employment is obtained and held by all men. 2) Land is purchased and homes are built in "squatter settlements." 3) Migrants enter school when they arrive in the city and place a high value upon education of their children. 4) There is a continuance of strong family ties with no evidence of family disorganization. 5) In-group solidarity with fellow Tilantongueños is very strong. 6) A high degree of mental health is enjoyed by the migrants. 7) There is an extreme preference for and insistence upon primary face-to-face relationships. 8) There is an increase in identification with the Mexican nation without a corresponding decrease in identification with Tilantongo. 9) Strong emotional attachments are held to Tilantongo and annual visits are made to the community. 10) Migrants continue to call themselves "Indios." Their children do not speak the Indian tongue and are considered "Mexicanos." 11) Marriage is contracted almost exclusively with women from Tilantongo, even if that means returning to the village after years of absence to fetch a wife. 12) There is a diminution in drinking, a change in beverage drunk, and a change in occasions for drinking. 13) A marked loss occurs after migration in the outward forms of religious expression, including a nearly complete loss of church-going. 14) Unanimous agreement is expressed that life in Mexico City is better than that in Tilantongo.

In his study of migration of families from Tepoztlan to Mexico City, Lewis considered that the nature of the capital city is conducive to satisfactory adjustment of Tepoztecos.[27] There is, as Lewis realizes, a peculiar relationship between Tepoztlan and Mexico City owing primarily to their proximity which does not obtain between the capital city and other communities in Mexico. In any evaluation of rural-urban migration, the nature of the city in which migrants settle must be taken into consideration. In the case of Mexico City, the secular, impersonal vastness of the metropolis allows the maintenance and functioning of tight in-group solidarity and strong bonds of kinship within the

[26] Lewis, "Urbanización. . . ," op. cit.
[27] Lewis, "Urbanización. . . ," op. cit.

framework of urban life. It is of great interest in this respect that migrants from Tilantongo who reside in Puebla, a smaller, less impersonal, religiously orthodox city, have adopted significantly different patterns of behavior from their kin in Mexico City. The emphasis in migration studies should not be limited to the nature of the city itself. Equal importance should be given to the nature of the individuals who migrate. The city and the individual form a continuously interacting phenomenon.

The explanation for the successful adaptation to city life by Tilantongo migrants probably lies in a well-balanced combination of maintenance of strong emotional ties within the family, with fellow migrants from Tilantongo, and with their "tierra," and a plastic ability to learn new skills and values. The early-acquired value placed upon family and compadres and the newly acquired values of economic and educational advancement can be satisfied simultaneously in the new environment.

Migration is a prehispanic Mixtec pattern including migration to Cholula, Tehuacan, Orizaba, Teotihuacan, and Tetzcoco. Tradition might favor and reinforce today's behavior.

In order to arrive at any valid generalizations concerning the urbanization process in rural-urban migrants, many more studies must be undertaken comparing the lives led by migrants before and after they left their village. Attention should be directed in these studies to the changes in values of the migrants.

Bibliography

BEALS, RALPH L.
  1951   "Urbanism, Urbanization and Acculturation," *American Anthropologist,* **53**:1. p. 1–10.
CAPLOW, THEODORE
  1949   "The Ecology of Middle American Cities," *Social Forces,* **28**:2. p. 113–133.
DAVIS, KINGSLEY and ARA CASIS
  1946   "Urbanization in Latin America," *The Milbank Memorial Fund Quarterly,* 24:2.
DIRECCIÓN GENERAL DE ESTADÍSTICA (Mexico)
  1940   Sexto censo general de poblicion
  1950   Septimo censo general de poblacion
  1960   Octavo censo general de poblacion
ERICKSEN, E. GORDON
  1954   *Urban Behavior* (New York: Macmillan Publishing Co., Inc.)
FRIED, JACOB
  1959   "Acculturation and Mental Health Among Indian Migrants in Peru," in *Culture and Mental Health: Cross-Cultural Studies,* Marvin K. Opler, ed. (New York: Macmillan Publishing Co., Inc.) pp. 119–137.

LEONARD, OLEN E.
  1948   "La Paz, Bolivia: Its Population and Growth," *American Sociological Review*, **13**:4. Pp. 448–454.
LEWIS, OSCAR
  1957   "Urbanización sin Disorganización. Las Familias Tepoztecas en la Ciudad de Mexico, *American Indigena*, **17**:231–246.
  1959   *Five Families* (New York: Basic Books).
MANGIN, WILLIAM
  1960a "Mental Health and Migration to Cities," *Annals of the New York Academy of Sciences*, **84**:17, 911–917.
SIMMEL, GEORG
  1957   "The Metropolis and Mental Life," in *Cities and Society: The Revised Reader in Urban Sociology*, Paul K. Hatt and Albert J. Reiss, eds.
UNITED NATIONS
  1957   *Report on the World Social Situation* (New York: Bureau of Social Affairs).
WHETTEN, NATHAN L., and ROBERT B. BURNIGHT
  1956   "International Migration in Mexico." *Estudios antropologicos publicados en homenaje al Doctor Manuel Gamio*. Mexico.
WIRTH, LOUIS
  1938   "Urbanization as a Way of Life," *The American Journal of Sociology*, **44**:1–24.
ZIMMER, BASIL G.
  1955   "Participation of Migrants in Urban Structures," *American Sociological Review*, **20**:219–224.

The Japanese Factory

JAMES G. ABEGGLEN

Although the following excerpt does not deal with the city explicitly, it does study an aspect of modern society intimately associated with urban units and the urbanization process—industry and the physical plants (as well as the sociocultural patterns) of industrialization. True, all factories are not in urban settings. However, even those which are not in cities create a kind of urbanized context for the individuals who are in contact with, and thus affected by, the rationalized production system that modern manufacturing appears to require. This seems to be the case whether it involves the manufacture of cars in Detroit, perfumes in France, tractors in Moscow, or shoes in a Peking factory.

Again, however, we see that the arguments of those who initially worked with urban industrial groups do not, on the whole, apply to the Japanese data. Were

Reprinted with permission of Macmillan Publishing Co., Inc., from *The Japanese Factory* by James G. Abegglen, pp. 2–3, 11, 66–68, 88–89, 94–102. © The Free Press, a Corporation, 1958.

*the initial models historically naive and/or ethnocentrically incomplete? Is it
because Asians are not Euroamericans and have a different sociocultural base
upon which to build the new pattern? Or are the differences only reflecting a
transitional stage, one that will soon disappear as Japan becomes "truly" modernized?*

*Abegglen leaves us with the provocative possibility that it may be none of
these and that further exploration is still needed.*

The unique experience of Japan as a non-Western industrialized nation
poses an exceptional opportunity for those interested in the process of industrialization in other Asian nations. There is raised first of all a question, outside the scope of this report, as to how this process took place, a historical
question concerning the causes and sources of this change. Another question,
and the central question of this study, is the outcome of the process of industrialization in Japan. There is a marked tendency to view industrialization in
terms of particular Western experiences—the Protestant ethic as a source of
motivation, a trend to impersonalization of social interaction, the development of a rational world view by Western man. The question presents itself
then as to how Western technology, modern industrial technology, may be fitted into a non-Western context with a different social inheritance. What kinds
of adjustments must take place to fit this technology and the local peoples into
an effective industrial unit?

When comparing the social organization of the factory in Japan and the
United States, one difference is immediately noted and continues to dominate
and represent much of the total difference between the two systems. At whatever level of organization in the Japanese factory, the worker commits himself
on entrance to the company for the remainder of his working career. The
company will not discharge him even temporarily except in the most extreme
circumstances. He will not quit the company for industrial employment elsewhere. He is a member of the company in a way resembling that in which
persons are the members of families, fraternal organizations, and other intimate and personal groups in the United States.

It would not be accurate [or fair to] either system to describe the Western
one as coldly commercial and impersonal, the Japanese as warmly intimate or
mutually cooperative. There is a difference between the two systems, however, and the difference extends in the direction of these two poles. It would
be no less accurate to describe the Japanese system as paternalistic or, as became popular in Japan after the end of the Second World War, feudalistic. It
is a feudalistic system only by analogy, but it is a system in which the exchange of obligations and responsibilities inherent in any group interaction
cannot be discharged by a solely monetary exchange.

At the risk of considerable oversimplification it might be useful to note here
the logic that seems to underlie a system of payment in a factory where that
payment is related only to the view of the factory as an organization to pro-

duce at maximum efficiency a given product. Reward in such a system would be given in relation to the capacity of the individual to contribute to efficient and maximal production. To the extent that the individual failed to contribute in an amount equivalent to another individual, his reward would be proportionately lessened. Payment would then be based on factors relating to the position an individual occupies and the extent to which he effectively fulfills the demands of his job.

The Japanese system of reward does not operate on these kinds of assumptions. For example, a prime factor in the payment system is the employee's age. Although length of service might be seen as having some relationship to job performance, justifying its importance in the scheme of job reward, age in itself would appear to have no relationship to the job situation, except insofar as advancing age might reduce job efficiency. This kind of nonrational reward system is more dramatically illustrated by the family allowance. Not only does the number of persons in a worker's family have no connection with the goals of the factory but also to reward, in effect, increased family membership seems a cruel contradiction in a nation painfully subject to a high population density.

In other words, recompense in the Japanese factory is in large part a function of matters that have no direct connection with the factory's productivity goals. They can be termed relevant to factory pay only when the relationship between worker and firm, and the assumptions on which that relationship rests, are defined outside the more limited range of productivity, output, profit, and efficiency. It is not at all difficult to find situations where workers doing identical work at an identical pace receive markedly different salaries, or where a skilled workman is paid at a rate below that of a sweeper or doorman. The position occupied and the amount produced do not determine the reward provided.

In terms of factory efficiency two primary results obtain from this system of payment and reward. The first is the furthering of the limitations on the mobility of the workers. The importance given to education, age, length of service, and similar factors in the total wage scale means that the worker is heavily penalized for job mobility and strongly rewarded for steady service. Taken together with the factors involved in recruitment, it will be seen that labor mobility is virtually nonexistent in the Japanese system. What is rewarded is the worker's loyalty and a deep commitment to the firm.

Apart from the need to reward able individuals, the pressure to provide career recognition is a function of two very general considerations. It will be recalled that wage differentiation is limited, and a title and the appurtenances of formal office are of course an alternative to increased wages in rewarding employees. Parenthetically, too, it might be noted that where one firm (or military organization or government agency) employs many titles and ranks, firms and organizations working in relation to it must also use a similar range of titles to facilitate communication.

More important by far is the second consideration in the use of title and position as career reward—the part played by age and age-grading in the Japanese company. The relationship between age and rank is a very close one in the Japanese firm. It can be generally stated that it is not possible to promote a man to a rank where he will be in authority over persons substantially senior to himself. By the same token it is necessary to promote a man to some extent when he reaches a sufficient chronological age. (Of course, since workers do not move from one firm to another, length of service and age are directly connected.) This general rule about seniority and promotions is true in both broad groupings within the plant, among laborers as well as staff workers.

Thus, for example, a group leader in a plant will have at least 10 and the foreman of the group 20 years of service. Progression within the management hierarchy is no less regularized by age. Age will not ensure progress beyond a certain point, but its lack will ensure that a man does not progress until his allotted years are fulfilled. Thus a college graduate will not achieve branch-chief status until he is about 30 to 35 years of age. He will be 35 or 40 at his next promotion, perhaps 40 or 45 at the next, and will become a department chief as he nears 50. Not all will go so far, but age forces promotion within broad limits. No college graduate could remain without some rank indefinitely nor, conversely, of course, could he be promoted as superior to older men.

The Factory's Place in the Employee's World

Both in the minds of the workers themselves and in the actual functioning of the factory system in Japan, the relationships between workers and their seniors, and workers and the company, cannot be described in the limited and relatively impersonal way characteristic of such relations in large Western plants. An illustration of the personal relationships within the Japanese factory was provided by the response of several categories of employees to a questionnaire designed to determine their feelings on a number of points. The statement that "A good foreman looks at his workers as a father does his children" elicited nearly the strongest agreement from all groups. It is assumed that such a statement would be greeted with derision, or strong distaste, by an American factory worker, but the average view of the Japanese workers ranged between "moderate agreement" and "strong agreement." Without placing too great dependence on these responses, they do indicate an essential difference in the quality of the worker-supervisor relationship.

Something of the nature of the further involvement and commitment of worker and company can be appreciated by examining the extent to which the company and its activities and programs penetrate the life of the worker far beyond the work situation itself. While he enters the company for his entire career and the system of reward and career progress is dependent in large degree on personal and noneconomic factors, the company also accepts responsibility and the worker expects a commitment far exceeding the specific demands of an economic organization.

At the most personal level of involvement, the close interconnection of the business firm with the details of the workers' lives may be seen in the problems that arise in the company housing facilities. It has been noted that most large Japanese firms provide company-built and subsidized housing for at least one third of their work force, a proportion which tends to increase in rural factories. A metals-processing firm in Shikoku provides well over half of its workers with company housing. As is customary, the area is set apart from other private housing in the locality and all residents are company employees and their families. A particular problem arose here when the workers' wives grouped together in a financial cooperative, each member contributing a sum of money to a fund from which members could withdraw in turn substantial sums for the purchase of durable household goods and other items. Such a system is sorely needed where financial loans are exceedingly hard to come by and incomes are low, but the company now has a policy of discouraging cooperative worker financial groupings. Some wives, eager to purchase a washing machine or radio, withdrew funds heavily and ill-advisedly from the group bank. When several of the workers' wives were unable to make the requested repayment to the group fund, the other members turned to the personnel department of the company for recovery of the money. When called to the office, one of the husbands found his monthly paycheck reduced and his family budget reviewed. He then received some general advice on the financial management of his affairs. The important point to note is that wives, workers, and company were right to assume that the company, although it had no direct concern in the matter, would act in the situation and, further, that all parties concerned would accept the company's intervention.

Many similar instances could be cited. For instance, a factory in Honshu, which has a similar housing arrangement, is alert to a special kind of problem that it frequently encounters. As in many of these housing areas the relations between people in the housing area have a most immediate reaction on intrafactory relations. Although there is some separation of housing by rank in the factory, foremen's wives and workers' wives will sometimes live near each other. Relations have on occasion become strained when the wife of a worker was able to make purchases, wear clothing, or provide her children with music lessons—to mention some specific cases—which were beyond the resources of the wife of a neighboring foreman. This inappropriate rank order among the women in the housing area affects the relations in the shop. In order to relieve the strains caused in the factory by this kind of interfamily conflict, the company has found it necessary periodically to move families to different houses, trying to mask the reasons for the move.

In another company, management's most pressing problem from the standpoint of personnel relations and morale was the inadequate schooling provided for the children of workers and managers in its factory in the Hokkaido district. The importance of college entrance in Japan has been noted. Inadequate school training will very nearly preclude a successful career in later life for the child owing to his inability to enter college. To help overcome the disadvantage of the rural and isolated location of its Hokkaido factory, the company found it necessary to establish special schools to aid the education of its employees' children.

These problems of family finances, living standards, and education give an indication of the range of involvement of the company in the life of the worker. What is most interesting about these situations is that company action was not taken reluctantly or accepted grudgingly. Both management and workers assume it is the company's responsibility to involve itself in such matters and the workers' privilege and duty to receive such assistance and attention.

In the typical large firm the company's involvement goes well beyond even these matters. It is customary to provide a wide range of training, totally unrelated to the job situation, for employees and their families. Lessons in those skills appropriate to well-mannered young Japanese ladies, such as flower arranging, the classic dance, and cooking, are attended by well over 90% of the women workers in many plants. Sex education and birth control instruction are also included in the curriculum in a number of large factories. Somewhat alarmed at changes in attitudes and behavior since the war's end, management now also provides the wives of workers with a wide range of classes in homemaking, family management, and Japanese arts.

Turning to another area of group activity, the company participates with the worker and his family in religious ceremonies. Nearly all large factories have a shrine on the grounds and give a day's holiday to celebrate the shrine festival. An indication of the depth of this worker-company participation is provided by the annual shrine ceremony of a large mine in Shikoku. It is held at the beginning of the year, and symbolizes the unity of management and worker and sanctions the factory's productive efforts for the new year. As in most Japanese firms, all activity ceases in the mine and smelter for the New Year's holiday. The representatives of the miners, senior workers in the company, carry a large piece of ore, the first production in the new year, from the mine, which is some kilometers up the mountain, to a shrine at the base. Management and workers join together in prayers and songs at the shrine, where the mine and the workers receive the blessings of the priests. Three days later this piece of ore is transported to the smelter where it initiates smelter operations for the year. The ceremony is an ancient one, and in its ritual is symbolized the close nexus of relation between all personnel of the company.

When compared to the elaborate organization and complex technology that sets the large firm apart from its tiny companions in the Japanese economy, the distance does not appear to be so great. In large factories the managers cannot duplicate [the small owner's] paternal and intimate knowledge of his young workers, and there is an increased remoteness and impersonalization from the close matrix of obligation and responsibility that holds the small textile plant together. Yet, looking to the large American plant in the other direction, there is more in common between the large and small Japanese units in the way in which people are related to each other and to the organization than in the American counterpart of the large Japanese factory.

Analogies must be used cautiously and can hardly demonstrate conclusions, but there is an inevitable analogy when trying to describe relations in the Japanese factory. Compared with the relatively impersonal and rationalized systems of production and organization of the large American corporation, the Japanese factory seems family-like in its relations.

It is family-like. When a man enters the large Japanese company it is for his entire life. Entrance is a function of personal qualities, background, and character. Membership is revocable only in extraordinary circumstances and with extraordinary difficulty. As in a family, the incompetent or inefficient member of the group is cared for, a place is found for him, and he is not expelled from the group because he is adjudged inadequate. Again, family-like, the most intimate kinds of behaviors are the proper province of concern and attention from the other members of the group. Fidelity and tenure bring the highest rewards, and, should the group encounter financial difficulty, it is expected that all members will suffer these difficulties together. Rewards of money and of material are secondary to the total success of the entire group. And, family-like, there is little recourse for the member of the group who has erred in his choice of group or who is mistreated by other members of the group.

The analogy is unsatisfactory, however. The family conveys notions of propriety and sanction not appropriate to a factory description; the analogy says nothing of the roots and causes of the kinds of relations so described. Furthermore, the analogy of family conveys a feeling of static organization, stability, and continuity that is quite inaccurate in describing the Japanese factory. The factory system is not static, nor are the relationships in its units entirely stable. The relationships which have been described are modal and generally characteristic. At the same time, however, there are areas and types of strain in this system, strains which will in all probability increase in the future and force changes in the organization of the Japanese factory.

Generally speaking, the modal attitudes and motives which appear to underlie the organizational system in the factory are traditional ones. The system itself and the men in top management who are instrumental in shaping and directing that system are very much products of prewar Japan. These men in top management, now in their fifties and sixties, were born in a Japan overwhelmingly rural and only a few decades removed from its deep isolation from the larger world. The large firms they head often trace their origins directly to feudal merchant families, and the traditions and philosophy of these families remain an active and real force in the management practice of the companies. Most of the separate factories investigated during this study are the result of the introduction of new products and methods into the parent company at the beginning of the twentieth century. It might be added that, whatever the merits of the anti-monopoly laws promulgated during the Occupation years, their effectiveness has been rather less than complete and the intimate relations between the several companies once forming an industrial combination have been substantially revived—if indeed they ever disappeared.

In short, the factory organization and its leaders are directly and closely tied to a nonurban, prewar, traditional Japanese experience and outlook. Leaving aside the impact of changes in world markets, international relations, and technological methods on the factory organization as now constituted, there are, in terms of the people in the system, points of stress where the attitudes and expectations of the employees do not fit well the organizational methods and the attitudes and expectations of top management.

The problem of the young university graduates from Japan's cities, who have only a remote understanding of the beliefs and customs of the rural employees of the company, has already been noted. It is a single instance of a more general problem—the considerable and seemingly increasing gap in background and experience between rural and urban Japan. Many of the large factories are located in rather isolated rural areas, and their labor force is locally recruited, for the most part, by the personnel department of the local factory. The management group, however, is recruited by the company's main offices in a large city; and the young members of management are urban trained and oriented. The Japanese organizational structure obviously requires a considerable and intimate mutual understanding between workers and managers. Since such an understanding is only partly available under the recruitment and promotion systems used in the large factories, in many of the rural plants there is a considerable gap between management and labor, with an apparently diminishing interaction and amount of understanding between them.

Looking at the large factories in the cities, there is further evidence of the differences between rural and urban workers and the problems presented by these differences. It was pointed out that large factories would much rather confine their recruiting of permanent employees to young men and women born and raised in the country. Their "nature," it is said, is "more stable." In this statement stability apparently refers to the extent to which the worker can accept without dissatisfaction or unrest the working conditions and relations in the plant. Enthusiasm for union membership is only one, but an important, example of the lack of stability in city-raised employees.

There seems to be in these types of tensions a broad area of stress between the structure of the organization and its personnel. Exposed to and affected by the many changes that have taken place in Japan at an accelerated pace in the past two decades, young, urban-trained persons do not fit comfortably into the system as it has been maintained. Dissatisfaction with the age-dominated approach to career advancement is marked and freely expressed by many younger men in management. Impatience with the wage system, both for its heavy component of nonfinancial recompense and for the weighting it gives to age and seniority, is evident among the younger employees. Management feels strongly that the ever-increasing pool of city-trained workers does not fit the system of relations now employed in the factory. This sentiment finds expression in both the training programs designed to inculcate traditional values and the recruiting procedures employed.

Part IV: Research/Term Paper Topics

1. "The Urbanization of Peasants and Tribesmen."

    Contrast the urbanization of peasant and tribal migrants to cities. Control for city type as best you can. How does migrant-type affect the urbanization process?

2. "Urbanization Versus Ruralization of the City."

    Select a city that attracts considerable numbers of migrants and investigate the influence of migrancy upon the *city*. As this will obviously be literature-research, make sure you comment on the paradigms that explicitly or implicitly guide the orientations of your authors toward the direction of influence between city and migrant.

3. "Nonurban Urbanization."

    Discuss urbanization as an "exportable" process. Focus on one or more small, and ostensibly nonurban communities that exhibit urban phenomena. (These can be small military bases as well as peasant-type towns). What aspects of urbanization outside cities are dependent and independent of continuing urban influence or support? What kinds of support?

4. "Urban Kinship."

    Find five informants who are urban dwellers and five who are rural or small-town dwellers. Ask them to list the kin with whom they have contact. Investigate reasons for contact, (life crisis only, parties, casual) frequency, mode of contact (personal, phone, letters), who initiates it, and so on. Is kinship the reason for their interaction? Can you make generalizations regarding the effect of urban life upon kinship?

5. "Why the City?"

    Construct a brief questionnaire that could be given to migrants to determine why they came to the city. Was it push, or pull, or a combination of both that was responsible? You need not actually conduct the interview. But your *questions* must be designed (a) to elicit the exact kinds of responses you want (this is much more difficult than you think) and (b) to reflect significant implications from the literature on urbanization.

6. "Enclave Insulation and Urban Contact."

    Some students rarely leave the campus area, or the zone of familiar, nearby hangouts. Attempt to establish the extent to which the campus and its immediate environs are a kind of folk enclave within the city. To what extent do students actually participate in the life of the city? You may wish to compare student patterns with those of several informants from a specific neighborhood or enclave-type of your choice.

PART

Units of Urban Organization

FIVE

What kinds of things are there in cities, and how have they been studied? Urban comprises both people and places. In this section, we focus upon people—social roles and groups—as analytical units.

Such units exhibit incredible variety, and anthropologists have not studied them all. Certain ones have received more attention because of their identification with supposedly critical urban processes. Some scholars have believed that the effects of city life can best be derived from observation of the *family,* supposedly a barometer of urban-spawned pressures. Others view *networks* as special urban integrative mechanisms, reflecting the ego-centered nature of social organization in cities. Elizabeth Bott has attempted to integrate family and network foci through the ingenious (though still to be proven) hypothesis that the degree of husband-wife togetherness ("joint conjugal behavior") within the family is inversely related to the density of the spouses' networks outside it (1957). At base, Bott suggests that important internal functions of urban families are dependent upon external networks of the spouses.

Voluntary associations (including clan, caste, tribal, family associations, and other ostensibly ascribed membership groups) have also been treated as particularly urban in nature. Generally they are viewed either as substitutes for rural-based solidary and instrumental groups, or as strictly urban solutions to city acculturation, job seeking, private interest lobbying, welfare, and other strictly urban problems.[1]

Urban *roles* as a general phenomenon are rarely discussed, although various studies have dealt with specific roles assumed to be typical of cities. Reports of research on cocktail waitresses (Spradley and Mann, 1975), skid row bums (Spradley, 1970), folk curers (Press, 1971), cab drivers (Vidich, 1976), and longshoremen (Pilcher, 1972) reflect the incredible variety of urban roles, and (depending upon the author's perspective) their dependence upon the urban milieu for raison d'etre and content. The general characteristics of urban roles, and their dependence upon the degree of specialization and social density in cities are discussed by Banton in the section that follows.

By and large, all of the units of analysis discussed here share the common characteristic of ease of identification and study. They are clearly bounded (with known members) or clearly centered (on a particular individual). This, as much as any especially "critical" urban function they might fill, accounts for their popularity as units of study.

---

[1] The reader is urged to look ahead to Wong's article in Part Seven. See also Lawrence Crissman's "The Segmentary Structure of Urban Overseas Chinese Communities" (1967). The function of ritual kinship in the urban milieu is discussed by Press (1963).

For more on networks, see J. Clyde Mitchell's edited volume, *Social Networks in Urban Situations* (1969), particularly Mitchell's own first chapter on definition and characteristics of networks in general.

Urbanization and Role Analysis

MICHAEL BANTON

The word science *in the term* social science *requires that those who engage in the pursuit be subject to the dictates of the scientific method. A major require-ment of science is that one's own research and findings be replicable, thus allowing others to repeat the study and test the reliability of data and conclu-sions. Michael Banton, faced with a discrepancy between his material and that of other researchers, explored the problem. This, plus a concern with the utility of role theory, served as genesis for the following report.*

Basic to the entire debate is a recurrent difficulty, one with which all urban analysts have struggled. How does one move from the micro level—using data from specific informants in relatively narrow and bounded situational contexts—to the macro level wherein we are concerned with "the characteristics of total urban structures"?

Banton's approach centers on defining roles and social density, measuring and historically explaining role differentiation, and examining the role differentiation dynamics generated by structural opposition in (a) the folk-urban continuum, as well as (b) the urban system itself.

Whether one agrees or disagrees with Banton's analysis and conclusion, the essay is a stimulating attempt to come to grips with basic research needs. He is one of the few urban anthropologists to focus on roles as units of study.

From the very beginnings of anthropological writing there has been a ten-sion between the particularistic descriptions of single tribes or peoples and the universalistic aspirations of those who would direct scholarly activity to the discovery of general laws. Exponents of both tendencies have needed the contributions of others if their work was not to be meaningless; but the argu-ment about the proper emphasis to be given to these two aspects of research has been continuous and often heated. Urban anthropology is heir to this ten-sion as to other strains in the parent discipline. Some cultural anthropologists have concentrated upon building . . . comprehensive ethnographies of par-ticular peoples, but to try and assemble the same sort of ethnography of towns would be futile. Towns are not self-contained units of study, for they need to be considered in their human and economic environment. The complexity of urban phenomena is so daunting that the urban anthropologist has a special need for theoretical schemes which will guide investigations and facilitate the comparison of results obtained in different urban centers.

This essay has two starting points, one fairly particular, the other highly

From *Urban Anthropology: Cross-Cultural Studies of Urbanization* edited by Aidan Southall, pp. 43–76. Copyright © 1973 by Oxford University Press, Inc. Reprinted by permission.

generalized. The particular one has been to account for the discrepancies between the interpretation I offered of the structure of social relations in Freetown, Sierra Leone and that of the urban social system on the Copperbelt of
Northern Rhodesia (now Zambia) which was put forward at the same time by
social anthropologists associated with the Rhodes-Livingstone Institute. How
far were the discrepancies to be attributed to the theoretical approaches employed, and how far were they a consequence of actual differences in the two
situations? The subsequent publication of more studies carried out in African
and other tropical towns has only increased the importance of this problem. A
framework for the comparative analysis is needed if we are to ask why one investigator's results do not resemble those of other workers in this field. The
other, more general, starting point has been my interest in the concept of
role. A theory which attempts to account for the special characteristics of
social life in towns cannot build a definition of the town into its assumptions
but must use as units of analysis features of social life in general. The analytical performance of the role concept over the past thirty years has never
equaled its apparent promise, and few authors have tried to disperse the surrounding terminological fog to use it in theoretical studies of urban life; nevertheless the feeling persists that it has more potential usefulness than most
other units of analysis available. The expression "role theory" can be used in
both narrow and broad senses. The narrow usage restricts its application to
the more psychological aspects of conduct. The broad usage makes role analysis basically similar to much structural theory in social anthropology. If the
rephrasing of structural theory in role concepts adds any further understanding, or links one understanding with others, then there is a case for
translating familiar ideas into the language of role analysis. It is with role
theory in the broad sense that this essay is concerned.

One strand in the discussion that follows is the argument that two of the
most important variables for the comparative analysis of urban social relations
are rural-urban continuity and the strength of structural oppositions. The
other main strand is the contention that these factors can be brought within
the scope of role analysis. This second argument is the more difficult to advance because in places it runs contrary to ideas widely held among anthropologists and sociologists that derive from the work of two notable scholars:
Emile Durkheim and Ralph Linton. Durkheim presented urban social systems as more integrated than rural ones. Linton presented the notion of role
as a way of conceptualizing the tasks allocated to separate individuals. I seek
to point out alternative approaches which are not in conflict with Durkheim's
and Linton's views but which may, for some readers, require a reorientation
of the way they have thought about familiar topics. Therefore I have had to
begin at the beginning with a suggestion as to how we may avoid the usual
impasse in the definition of role and a review of Durkheim's conclusion about
the "moral density" of society. The next task has been to show how an analysis
of roles from the standpoint of their differentiation from one another has very
different implications from the more usual approach to roles in terms of their

content. It is possible that my argument is incomplete or that the objections to it are more serious than I envisage, but if I have found a new way to approach these questions it is certain to need further refinement. Having in the first portion of the essay tried to lay these theoretical foundations, I pass next to a review of some of the ways in which social changes affect the differentiation of roles and then to discussion of how variations in rural-urban continuity and in the strength of structural opposition in urban systems influence the definition of roles within those systems. In the final section these two variables are presented as the axes for a schematic representation of comparative social density. A conceptual framework of this kind might constitute a bridge between microsociological studies of interpersonal relations and macro-sociological studies of the characteristics of total urban structures. The importance of the goal is a partial justification for the presumptuous and speculative nature of the attempt to reach it.

Defining "Role"

It is relatively easy to define a particular role—to determine, say, the characteristics of the role of warder for the purpose of analyzing prison organization. It is much more difficult to define the concept of role. Is all social behaviour to be ascribed to some role-relationship? Is there a finite number of roles in any one community—and if not, how can roles be the units in any kind of scientific theory? What kinds of consensus must obtain in any population as to the obligations of a given position before it can be counted a role? Some anthropologists regard these as the sort of questions that must be answered at the beginning of an investigation. They attempt to define role in a particular manner and to keep to the definition, but find that if they are to be consistent they have to ignore interesting features of their data. Other writers hold that these questions are the kind that can be answered only at the end of a long series of varied investigations. Not until we have discovered what we can *do* with the notion of role can we know how best to shape it. Having considerable sympathy for this latter viewpoint, I do not propose to summarize or review the recent literature concerning this problem of definition, instructive though it is, but to use the concept in the simplest possible sense as denoting "a set of rights and obligations." This usage is in line with Linton's initial proposal, except that it favours more neutral terms than "duties," which implies moral imperatives as well as socially sanctioned expectations. Furthermore, such a simple definition does not attempt to establish Linton's distinctions between position, status, and role at the outset of the enquiry, though they can be introduced if the analysis requires them.

Roles do not exist apart from social situations. In many situations unmarried girls aged twenty and twenty-one occupy one role, yet there are times when a young woman who has attained her legal majority has rights and obligations that are not extended to someone twelve months her junior. Where a research worker draws the boundaries of particular roles must therefore depend upon the topic he is investigating, and inventories of the numbers of roles can be compiled only with reference to specific problems.

Many avenues of enquiry do not require very delicate prior determination of the content of roles; indeed, it is probably just these lines of work which are the most rewarding at present. Of all the studies in this field conducted by social psychologists in the last fifteen years, probably the most interesting have been the analyses of role conflicts.[1] These studies have concentrated upon situations where people felt two roles to be partially incompatible; behaviour was analyzed from the standpoint of two sets of expectations only, and the question of whether it might also belong with yet other roles was excluded by the very nature of the enquiry. These studies dealt with the implications for the actor of conflicting role expectations and the ways in which particular individuals resolved them. Hitherto there has been no explicit and systematic treatment of the implications of role conflict (or absence of conflict) for the social structure, though this offers the sociologist or anthropologist a similar opportunity to get round the difficulties of defining role content comprehensively. Why is it that women (in Britain) can be ministers of religion in certain denominations and not others? What would be the consequences of permitting an individual to occupy both the female role and the priestly role? In structural analysis it is frequently possible to postpone the problems of definition and to investigate empirically why certain roles have to be combined, why others have to be kept apart, and what happens when these principles are not, or cannot be, followed.

Social Density

A sociological interpretation of urbanization must attempt to identify and explain the differences in the quality of social relations in urban and rural surroundings. There have been two chief approaches to this problem; the one stressing changes in economic interdependence, the other changes in the interdependence of social relationships.

The first approach is associated with Durkheim's *Division of Labor in Society*, in which the simpler forms of society are depicted as congeries of small self-sufficient communities. With economic development, they are absorbed into a larger society, and "the progress of the division of labor is in direct ratio to the moral or dynamic density of society" (Durkheim, 1893:257). According to this view, urban and industrial life is characterized by the interdependence that stems from the division of labor: thus, if the public transport workers go

---

[1] See Gross et al. (1958) for a concise review by social psychologists that pays particular attention to the question of variations in consensus on role obligations; Rocheblave-Spenlé (1962) for a historical study; Biddle and Thomas (1966), which appeared after this essay had been drafted; Dahrendorf (1964) and Goode (1960) for sociological reviews of the field; for an application to problems germane to those discussed here, note Reader (1964).

on strike, the whole city may be thrown into chaos, and if one group of workers lay down tools, they may endanger the employment of thousands of others. This line of argument has been brought to bear upon the present problem
by Aidan Southall. He emphasizes the increase in the number of roles associated with the progressive division of labor and the variety of role relationships that can subsist between city-dwellers. He concludes that "the passage from rural to urban conditions is marked by a rise in the density of role
texture" (Southall, 1959:29).

The second approach starts from a recognition that in small village societies
people know one another as individuals and are dependent upon one another
for social reputation. One person interacts with another on the basis of several
different role relationships, giving rise to a tightly interlocking network of
social ties. In the city, on the other hand, many kinds of social relationships
are confined in separate compartments and the urbanite has scope to choose
his associates; there is much less chance that his partner in one relationship
will be his partner in another. From this standpoint urban society reveals a
lower social density. Such an approach, though never systematized in a way
comparable to Durkheim's, has been implicit in a variety of writings: Simmel
(1955:125–95); Malinowski (1926:125); Homans ("the effectiveness of control
lies in the large number of evils a man brings down on himself when he
departs from a group norm," 1951:289); Nadel ("The advantages of role summation lie in the strengthening of social integration and of social control. For
the more roles an individual combines in his person, the more he is linked by
relationships with persons in other roles. . . ." 1957:71); and other writers,
especially some of those associated with the Manchester school of social anthropology. This line of argument differs from the Durkheim-Southall approach chiefly in that it focuses upon interpersonal relations and tries to build
upwards to a model of the society, where the other view works downward
from a macrosociological starting point.

To reconcile the two approaches it is necessary first to take account of a
qualification which Durkheim inserted in his own analysis but which he never
developed adequately. The passage runs: "It is not enough that society take in
a great many people, but they must be, in addition, intimately enough in contact to act and react on one another. If they are, on the contrary, separated by
opaque milieux, they can only be bound by rare and weak relations, and it is
as if they had small populations." (Durkheim, 1893:262). While economic advance unites people previously separated, it divides them up again in new
ways. The relation of the industrial worker with his employer may be more
impersonal even than the relation of the plantation owner with his slave.
Great areas of industrial cities are segmented almost exactly in Durkheim's
sense; large numbers of people of similar occupation and social status occupy
separate territories and are related to other groups only in a relatively few restricted role-relationships. The spheres of the factory and of the home are
milieux separated by opaque partitions. Within a particular milieu there may
be a dense network of social relations, the various groups being bound

together by cross-cutting ties, but between milieux there may be only standardized role-relationships. The level of social interdependence is not uniform
throughout an urban society: it tends to be patchy, rising fairly high in certain
social islands, falling quite low between them, and being in general lower
than in village society.

Even when allowance is made for the segmentary elements in urban life, a
conceptual difference between the two approaches remains to be explained.
The economic interdependence which impressed Durkheim springs from
what people do as occupants of roles, especially work roles. "Moral or dynamic density" is a function of the *content* of roles. The other approach focuses upon how one person occupies several roles; in village society many
roles have a wide social significance and custom dictates what combinations of
roles are socially appropriate. In the transition to urban living many roles are
subdivided and all sorts of new combinations become possible. The lower
social density in the city is a consequence of this greater *differentiation* of
roles. This distinction should not be used in an inflexible manner, for role
content and differentiation are interrelated, but I believe it may be rewarding
to try and concentrate on the latter. To take an example, for some years now
it has been a sociological commonplace that economic advance is accompanied
by role specialization. This is undeniable, but it attracts attention to the content of the roles and away from the central sociological issues. When the
sociologist studies the role of physician he is not concerned with medical skill
per se, but with the implications of professional skills for the organization of
medicine, the relations of the doctor to his colleagues, his collaborators (tech-
nicians, nurses), and his patients; the relations of patients to hospital staff, to
one another, to their families. . . . The content of a role is usually among the
data that the sociologist has to take as given; he considers the implications of
different ways of arranging tasks rather than the tasks themselves. Economic
advance is equally dependent upon the process of role differentiation,
whereby a more flexible social structure is developed which can respond to
and exploit technological change.

The technologically primitive society tends to be founded upon a small repertory of undifferentiated roles which are so interrelated that the level of control is high and there are few rewards for innovation. The social order is suf-
fused with moral judgments about the propriety of different modes of
conduct, so that problems of technical expediency may not be openly acknowledged. The role structure makes little allowance for individual peculiarities; everyone has to be allocated unequivocally to one of the basic categories, and anomalies such as homosexuals, unmarried mothers, barren
wives, and spinsters are forced into the nearest appropriate category even if
their case does not quite fit. Thus in primitive society there is frequently
appreciable role strain[2] which has to be eased by role-reversal ceremonials

---

[2] Cf. Goode (1960a), where role strain is defined as a "felt difficulty in fulfilling role obligations"; for
our purpose it is not necessary to limit consideration of role strain to those difficulties of which the
actor is conscious.

like carnavalia. Urbanization breaks up the system of social categories, building up a complex but loose structure of independent roles overlying a pattern of fairly diffuse basic roles. The sheer number of acknowledged roles increases greatly. Important roles continue to be filled by ascription, and kinship is not necessarily weakened, but the old pattern loses significance relative to the new structure of achieved and independent roles. The vetoes upon certain role combinations are lifted and new kinds of choice are forced upon people. The simplest role system would show a single hierarchy of rank, the man at the summit being top in every field of social activity. As societies increase in scale and specialization, the range of choice is such that even the richest and ablest man cannot engage in everything: he must choose the kinds of activity that interest him and allow others to score in the remaining fields. Consequently the strains of urban living do not flow from the restrictions of the role structure but from its very flexibility, which generates problems of adjustment. European observers of African and Middle Eastern towns have been inclined to comment upon the squalor and misery frequently found there. This judgment often stems from the observers' unexamined assumptions about the arcadian qualities of a bucolic existence. The immigrants generally believe themselves to be better off in the town. Whatever their standard of living as measured by, say, calorie intake, they value the freedom and variety of urban living. I suggest that this feeling springs in part from the greater differentiation of roles and that the new social opportunities can be as much a source of stimulus as of strain.

Measuring Role Differentiation

The foregoing argument assumes that roles can be placed along a continuum varying from one extreme, where they are little differentiated, to another, where they are interdependent. It is not possible to construct such a scale with any precision, but the idea of one is, I submit, useful as a sort of mental exercise in clarifying the issues and suggesting propositions on a less abstract level which could possibly be put to empirical test. Relatively undifferentiated roles are ones that are relevant to behavior in a wide range of situations. Sex and age roles are obvious examples. A person's sex role usually affects the way people respond to him or her more than does any other role; in almost any interpersonal situation norms of propriety are associated with sex roles and usually supported by sanctions of some kind. This wide situational relevance of sex roles is expressed in the restrictions that prohibit the incumbent from taking up certain roles and oblige him or her to interpret many other roles in a particular manner (note, for example, the norms of seemliness governing a married woman's relations with other men). Relatively undifferentiated roles have implications for the actor's incumbency of most other roles. Independent roles are ones that have few such implications; many leisure roles are of this kind. Elsewhere (Banton, 1965:33–35) I have en-

visaged a scale of differentiation divided roughly into three sections: basic
roles, general roles and independent roles, [as follows]:

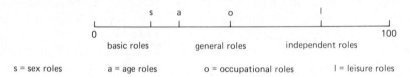

As societies advance in productive and technological sophistication the behavioral relevance of age and sex roles is restricted and declines in importance.
The social structure of industrial societies is founded on a complex system of
independent roles which overlies the pattern of basic roles. The two kinds of
society may be compared as follows:

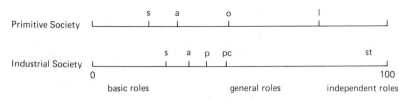

In primitive society sex (s) and age (a) roles are little differentiated; occupational roles (o) provide some liberty of choice and leisure roles (l) somewhat
more. In industrial society sex and age roles are more differentiated; certain
occupations, e.g. priest (p) and policeman (pc), are hedged round with varied
restrictions and expectations limiting incumbents' social liberty, but many
others, e.g. student (st), can be combined with almost all other roles in the
social repertory.

   There are difficulties in any such comparison. Are the items strictly comparable? To compare a category of roles, like age roles, with a specific role, like
policeman, is scarcely legitimate. Similarly, a category like "sex roles" is not
homogeneous: the role of female tends to be less independent of other roles
than that of male. Since the scale tries to order the extent to which incumbency of one role has implications for the same person's incumbency of other
roles, it does not deal directly with role behavior, i.e. a person's conduct
towards someone occupying a reciprocal role. This belongs with role content.
To exclude considerations of content creates special difficulties in respect of
kinship roles, for their interpersonal significance lies principally in their content, the way they signalize social obligations. Incumbency of one kinship role
excludes the possibility of the individual's occupying certain others; but this
problem is best approached by the traditional methods of anthropological
analysis. Some kinship roles can be given meaningful positions on a scale of
differentiation—for example, the role of mother may confer prestige and give
a woman the privilege of associating with the matrons—but many kinship
roles like niece and nephew are of little social significance except in relation to
specific partners (i.e. aunts and uncles). While these difficulties do not invali-

date the approach outlined, they indicate one of its limitations. Another snag is that, as we have seen, urban societies divide up into relatively independent social realms and a role which is important in one may have no significance in another. The obstacles which a general theory of role differentiation must overcome if it is to be of use in the analysis of interpersonal behaviour are quite forbidding, but nevertheless the idea of such a scale may suggest particular research problems of a manageable kind. For example, the differentiation of the same role in different places can be measured: the role of schoolteacher may be more independent in the town than in nearby villages, and analysis of such variations might find them related to job satisfaction and turnover. Changes in the implications of a role over a period of years can be investigated or two fairly similar roles compared.

How Differentiation Occurs

The spread of new social norms is in part a psychological process of learning and of the adaptation of cognitive structure. But learning occurs within social contexts, and while some of these force individuals to change their ideas quite rapidly, other contexts make less pressing demands. It is therefore of the greatest importance to avoid thinking of social change as the gradual spread of ideas through a society. It is more fruitful to visualize societies as divided into partially independent compartments or sectors which change at different rates. Conduct in one sector may be organized completely in terms of the new values, while an adjacent sector is scarcely affected by them. A suitable illustration of this may be found in studies of the introduction of cash transactions into subsistence economies. In many parts of Africa, young men have gone off to the towns to earn money to meet tax obligations and obtain trade goods: blankets, clothing, household utensils, guns, bicycles. To have spent their money on subsistence goods would, in their view, have been to waste it: such things were exchanged or given as an expression of social obligation, not in return for cash. The next step is to use money to substitute for goods given to meet social obligations, as with bridewealth or feast-giving. Only later do cash transactions come in as payment for foodstuffs or shelter (Reining, 1959, cf. Bohannan, 1955). Change often occurs by new situations being added to the customary pattern: in these new situations people observe norms which to an outside observer might seem inconsistent with those acknowledged elsewhere. Thus Bruner observes that the Batak elite in Medan have not modified their traditional marriage ceremony. They have added a church service as the opening phase and a western-style reception as the closing phase. This last is an urban innovation. Guests at the traditional ceremony are seated according to their position in the genealogical structure and the values of kinship receive full recognition. But the reception is a gathering of elite personnel from different ethnic groups organized in terms of the participants' social status. The two fields of social relationships are compartmentalized (Bruner, 1961:517).

That social change progresses sector by sector is most evident when urban influences spread out into the countryside, but the same principle holds for changes within the urban community. Migrants may accept the old norms of propriety as valid but circumscribe them by asserting that they hold only in the villages; or European-style norms may be endorsed in the workplace while traditional ones retain their influence over domestic relations. Nevertheless, there are limits to the extent to which adjacent sectors can be organized on conflicting principles. Individuals may come to feel that the inconsistency is intellectually disturbing and seek to reduce the level of normative dissonance. Or there may be a direct feedback from one social field into another. For example, young men in industrial employment regularly earn more money than their elders, which brings them increased influence in other spheres of social life, and therefore tends to erode one of the traditional bases of authority.

In the simplest role systems the role of adult male specifies the conduct expected of incumbents in most fields of activity. As societies increase in scale and complexity this role is split up, step by step, into a multiplicity of roles, many of which are alternatives or specializations. A similar process is apparent in the case of the female role. In traditional African society a woman has usually to live in the household of some male; she cannot take much initiative in communal life unless, by a jural fiction, she is allowed to assume a male role. In parts of West Africa a woman is expected to make a contribution to the household economy; in the country she can do this by farming, in the city the best opening may be through petty trade. But her activities as a trader give the woman a financial and personal independence of her husband that farm work never could. Those who have established their independence through some extra-familial role lead the way in resisting polygamy, assuming leadership roles, and in building up matrifocal households. In Freetown, Sierra Leone, I thought it notable that very many of the important older women—section chiefs, senior officials of companies, etc.—lived singly and had not remarried after losing their husbands (Banton, 1957:197–98). A Nigerian study emphasizes that the independence of urban women is based upon their enlarged opportunities to acquire a personal income (Baker and Bird, 1969:103–6 and 109). A recent survey from the Republic of South Africa shows that the pattern of disorganization, promiscuity, and marital instability in the city obscures a new tendency which permits urban Xhosa women to run their own households and support their own children. The social price they pay for their independence and for the absence of a legitimate husband is only loss of esteem—and this may be worth it (Pauw, 1962:viii, 146–49, and 153–59). These observations relate chiefly to working-class women. As in Latin America (Gillin, 1960:49), even more dramatic changes are occurring where middle-class women are entering public employment.

A kind of situation which illustrates better than most how the compartmentalization of different milieux affects changes in the woman's role is high-lighted in a report from Zaïre.[3] Congolese politicians have found it embarrassing to take their wives to diplomatic functions, and so a new and relatively well-rewarded role of *femme libre* or female consort has been recognized. The wives seem content to make over their new and unwelcome social obligations to these women, provided they keep to their role of consort. This is reminiscent of the situation in Japan, where traditionally the role of wife and mother was sharply set off from that of the geisha, whose obligations were those of courtesan, consort, and entertainer. The geisha still serves as a device helping the Japanese businessman maintain traditional domestic relations, but in urban industrial Japan she is now vastly outnumbered by bar-girls, hostesses, and other women who play a role which in this respect is similar to hers. In other social structures, however, it seems as if there is no room for any new intermediate role. In West Africa, men who have risen in the social scale have often felt obliged either to divorce an illiterate wife in order to seek an educated spouse who can play the roles of hostess and consort, or to relegate the illiterate wife to a subordinate position and marry a new one (Busia, 1950:42–43; Little, 1965:120). Similar pressures upon Zambian trades-union leaders have been mentioned (Epstein, 1958:237). In some countries, therefore, pressure for change in the wife's role is met by the creation of a new in-between role, but elsewhere this solution is not possible and in the groups most exposed to change the wife's role is redefined fairly radically within one generation.

What determines the strength and timing of the pressure upon the traditional role of wife? First, there may be a time gap in the impact of new influences upon the two sex roles. In Africa it has been the men who have had to assume leadership roles in response to challenges generated by world political and economic forces. Their wives did not have to make a comparable response to changing circumstances so early. In West Africa, where there has long been a Westernized middle class, the time interval was smaller than in the Congo, and the process of adjustment had been at work over a much longer period. Second, when it is difficult to compartmentalize different spheres of social relations, changes must be made more quickly. In the West African countries Western influences had affected traditional life deeply, so that the whole society was in the process of change. In the Congo, the occupational life of the urban elite formed a sphere of social life relatively separate both from traditional life in the countryside and from the domestic life of the politicians in question. Third, it is relevant to note that urban industrial society places a new value upon informal sociability as a counterweight to high mobility and to the restrictions stemming from the formally-structured organizations in which most people work. In some occupations—diplomatic posts are a striking example—there is less distinction between work and leisure spheres; informal contacts are used to supplement and test out people's behavior in

[3] *Vide* correspondent's report in *New Society*, 21 xi 1963, pp. 4–5.

their formal roles (cf. Banton, 1965:144–45). People who have to represent their countries or their organizations cannot conceal their private lives so easily, and their dependents must share some of the burden of representation.

Changes in age roles follow lines similar to the changes in sex roles. Several studies document the emergence of the Western-oriented young men as a distinctive social grouping with their own styles of living. In the political sphere opposition between old and new may be very noticeable. One of the Copperbelt studies shows how tribal elders were first utilized as labor representatives because men with traditional authority were thought of as the legitimate leaders in the mining community also. When an industrial dispute developed, the old men were disavowed by the strikers and a new, industry-based pattern of labor leadership developed (Epstein, 1958). The nationalist movements of Africa illustrate time and again the separation of political leadership from the earlier pattern of basic roles. Yet in examining the role structure of urban communities it is necessary to note not only the progressive differentiation and splitting up of the old role interdependencies based upon sex, age, and descent, but also the crystallizing of new lines along which roles are clustered. Newcomers to a city are often forced into new role combinations. When Jewish and Christian minorities have been introduced into caste societies, they have taken on the characteristics of castes. (Strizower, 1959, Hutton, 1946:2). In the same way, ethnic minorities in class societies are characterized in class terms. With urbanization and increased social mobility in Brazil there seems to have been a stronger tendency to emphasize racial characteristics as criteria of social status. (Wagley, 1952:155; Bastide, 1957:502–12). The African data show that membership in tribal or ethnic groupings does not remain relevant to behavior in urban, or any other, surroundings unless it is vested with significance by the social structure. In many situations it is given such significance. People acquire a tribal identity only when they meet persons ascribed to other tribal groups, so that "tribalism" as a feature of interpersonal relations is a product of the city and the labor camp. Tribal roles remain important in the cities as a basis for categoric interaction and because they often become associated with stereotyped beliefs about group customs, social status, etc. When political movements acquire a tribal foundation, this may lead to a major split such that tribal affiliation becomes the mark of a basic role relevant in a great variety of situations. One of the most important new kinds of role combinations associated with urbanization is the formation of social classes. A recent study of rehousing in Lagos, Nigeria, found that whereas most of the Yoruba residents of the central district found life in an outlying estate unattractive, a minority welcomed the independence it gave them. By comparison with the central area the population of the estate included a significantly higher proportion of non-Yoruba, Christians, young men, and wage-earners, especially clerks. "It attracted above all the employees of Government and commercial firms, men from the Eastern Region whose close family ties in Lagos were few, the young rebel escaping from a domineering family." (Marris, 1961:100) Some of the factors affecting the formation of classes and the significance of such groupings are discussed in subsequent sections of this essay.

Rural-Urban Continuity

Many of the earlier studies of life in African towns were organized round the concept of "detribalization," which emphasized psychological changes in the individual and distracted attention from the way social systems can oblige people to conform to their norms without necessarily undergoing any fundamental psychological change. Opposing this tendency, Max Gluckman has argued that from the sociological standpoint it is more appropriate to see rural and urban life as constituting two distinct social systems, and to trace out the implications of each system for the behavior of people who participate in it. An African miner is to be seen as a miner first, and as an African second. When he is working in the town he is a townsman; when he goes back to his family village he becomes a countryman again (Gluckman, 1960, 1961). In an analysis of some of the concepts used by Gluckman and his associates which helps clarify their argument, Philip Mayer shows that everything occurring within the town is not equally urban, and that the most interesting contrast is between typically urban sets of social relations and other sets which, even through they may be town-located, could develop in other surroundings (Mayer, 1962:584–85). He goes on to show from his own material concerning East London, South Africa, how the demands of the urban system require urban behavior of the migrant at work but leave him with a range of choice in other situations. In his leisure time he can choose to follow rural or urban models or compromise at some point along the scale. Moreover, he may, in the course of time, move along the scale until he becomes what the people themselves recognize as a "real townsman" (Mayer, 1962:588–89).

These analyses successfully distinguish the ongoing nature of the urban system from the nature of the migrant personnel, but they do not yet provide us with a basis for comparing the phenomena of urbanization in different localities. Gluckman's statement about the distinctive character of urban living can be viewed either as a methodological principle instructing us to examine the interconnections of urban institutions or as an empirical proposition asserting that rural and urban social systems are radically different. The former implication is excellent advice but the latter requires closer examination. In Zambia there is a striking contrast between the two systems, but elsewhere the difference is less marked. In East London a "Red" migrant is in the city but not of the city. In Medan, Sumatra, he may lead a life unaffected by urban institutions. The vast majority of the urban lower class in Brazilian cities do not acknowledge urban values but are "peasants living in the city" (Wagley, 1960:211). In West Africa the countryside has been permeated by urban values to a greater extent than in Zambia, and the nature of the urban system with respect to employment and housing discourages the perpetuation of rural social patterns to a lesser extent (e.g. Banton, 1957; Frankel, 1964; Lloyd, 1959). The degree of continuity between the rural and the urban social systems is therefore a factor that should be subjected to empirical examination. It is also important to any explanation of many variations in the social structure of different cities (Southall, 1961:6–11, 19).

While it is not possible to adopt any particular index of rural-urban continuity, some of the relevant factors can be readily distinguished. Continuity will be high where there are many migrants from the same ethnic division or local group because they will then reinforce one another's attitudes. This will be especially strong where the migrants are interrelated by pre-migration ties of kinship or neighborhood and where the immigrant community has a balanced age and sex structure. Mutual reinforcement will be stronger where they can inhabit the same urban locality and where they can buy their own housing. Such migrant concentrations are more frequent in rapidly growing towns than in mature industrial cities. Where migrants are able to obtain employment in the same kind of work under supervisors from their own group, these ties of community are further strengthened. A final factor is one that recalls the "laws of migration" propounded by Ravenstein eighty years ago.[4] He showed, from European population figures, that while the current of migration was towards the cities, it tended to go stage by stage for short distances only (Ravenstein 1885:198–99). Where this law holds, the migrants learn city ways relatively gradually and there is less chance of the two social systems being completely different. The town of Chimbote, described . . . by Stillman Bradfield, exemplifies this, for it is a *mestizo* town populated by migrants who have moved stage by stage. The social life of a Peruvian town with a high proportion of Indians in its population would show different features.

Rural-urban continuity will be low when migrants from the same rural social groups are few in number, not interrelated, unevenly distributed with respect to age and sex, scattered throughout a large city, etc. It will be further reduced when, as on the Copperbelt, they are living in a mine compound in houses allocated them by their employers and they work under the supervision of Europeans or boss-boys who are prevented from recognizing social ties declared irrelevant by the formal structure of the concern. In East London a religious ethic seems also to play a part, Christian migrants being less involved in home-based groups—though the evidence on this score from Cape Town suggests that this inference should be regarded with caution (Mayer, 1964). The pattern of migration is also relevant. Ravenstein specified, as an exception to his law, that where a town was growing much more rapidly than the surrounding region it had to draw migrants from further afield (1885:214–18). The Copperbelt towns exemplify this: because the migrants come straight there from distant regions, the difference between rural and urban social patterns is greater, and they have less in common with other migrants who have come equal distances but from other directions. Rural-

---

[4] The author was reminded of the relevance of Ravenstein's work by J. Clyde Mitchell.

urban continuity is therefore lower. It is in such circumstances that an urban identity (such as the ideas of the "real townsman" described by Mayer) is most likely to develop. In some circumstances there may be considerable pressure on a migrant to adopt an urban identity *vis à vis* his country cousins.

In the traditional village, a man interacts with the same individuals over and over again. One of his chief concerns is to maintain his reputation with his peer group. Very rarely does he have to worry about managing a relationship with a stranger; in fact, the more tightly integrated is his society, the more resolutely will it rebuff strangers. Where rural-urban continuity is high, the migrant will maintain something of the same outlook, taking his relatives and former neighbors as a positive reference group. But the general effect of migration is to remove individuals from the controls exerted by their old peer groups and to give them new scope for choice. Where rural-urban continuity is low, a worker is more likely to live entirely within the city, both physically and psychologically. He has continually to deal with strangers, and their standards have in many cases to be taken as models. He cannot rely upon peer group sanctions but must develop interpersonal controls on a new basis. Therefore the greater the discontinuity between an urban social system and the way of life of the surrounding region, the more highly integrated will that system be; or to express the same proposition in a different way, to the extent that town life constitutes an independent set of social relations, so much will these relations constitute a tighter social network displaying a higher level of social density.

Structural Opposition in the Urban Social System

Another major factor determining the roles open to an urban migrant and the kinds of role-combinations that are standardized is the pattern of relations between social groupings. In the town of Luanshya studied by Epstein, migrant workers in the mines were faced by the monolithic power of the mining company. They were obliged to organize in a similarly monolithic fashion in defense of their own interests (Epstein, 1959:123–24). The opposition between the company and the Mine Workers' Union (made sharper by the pressure on company policies exerted by white supervisory workers) influenced workers' roles *vis à vis* one another. The miner was forced by his peers to be a trade unionist. The demands of fraternal solidarity helped define his roles at work and in situations of political tension; sanctions upon deviant behavior could be powerful and could override ethnic ties. But within the African community other divisions—of tribe and class—opened up when internal issues were under discussion and there was no sense of pressure from Europeans, suggesting that the stronger the solidarity a group shows in response to external threat, the more readily it divides internally when the threat is absent. In many other towns—both in Africa and in other regions—the social cleavages either have not gone so deep or have not yet developed to the point at which they have so diverse an effect upon social relations. This question therefore requires explicit consideration in comparative analysis.

Three factors seem to be of chief importance in determining the extent and strength of structural opposition: the stability of the cleavages; the balance of the opposed units; and the location of power.

Where a population is divided into social categories based upon stable and relatively visible criteria like race, caste, and ethnic group (especially when the latter is associated with linguistic, religious, and customary differences), this makes for a rigidity in the structure and for the allocation of many important roles by ascription. Such distinctions lend themselves to categoric interaction across group lines, to a high level of group opposition, and therefore to a greater degree of social density within groups. Because people cannot—within the space of two generations—move out of such a group, they may seek to make membership a source of strength by organizing other activities on the basis of it. They have stronger sanctions over deviants when these cannot resign from their race, caste, or ethnic group. Thus where economic growth is relatively low and much employment is not related to technical skills, ethnic differences may be projected into the labor market and the phenomena of "urban tribalism" or ethnicity analyzed by Shack . . . make their appearance. An extreme example of how racial cleavages may prevent role differentiation and preserve certain combinations is provided by the Bantu clerk in South Africa. The attitudes of the whites prevent his developing his administrative skills, while peer group pressures from fellow Bantu (and his sympathies with them) militate against his assuming a dispassionate bureaucratic role (Sherwood, 1958:298–99). Similar conflicts arise for headmasters and nursing sisters (Wilson and Mafeje, 1963:148–49).

Where the major social cleavages are based upon unstable characteristics, notably economic class or social status reckoning, the position is otherwise. Intergroup relations occur mostly within the context of work institutions organized on a formal basis, which distracts attention from social features belonging to other realms of activity. In the residential and leisure sphere, classes and status groups tend to be segregated, and contacts between groups are minimized. Upwardly mobile members of lower-status groups do not threaten the social order because they are assimilated into groups higher up the scale. Thus in Monrovia, the capital of Liberia, where racial cleavages are absent and the caste-like division between the Americo-Liberians and the tribal people has been replaced by a continuous pattern of social differentiation which permits an appreciable degree of mobility, there are no sharp conflicts of interest or outlook identified with particular groups. The social structure of the city can be represented as forming a homogeneous pyramid in which the political elite is the economic elite and is also the social elite (Fraenkel, 1964). Proletarian immigrants do not form groups in any politically significant pattern of structural opposition. Similarly, in Latin American cities much of the political power is located in informal structures based on clientage in which benefits are handed down in return for votes and loyalty. One author refers to this as "populism" and states that it "does not favour the organization of common interest groups or co-operative groups, and power is usually delegated downwards rather than upwards." He describes populism as being, from the standpoint of the propertied classes, "an attempt to maintain traditional privilege and authority in face of the institution of constitutional democracy . . ." (Pearse, 1961:201–2). Unless class differences are tied tightly to economic opportunities and the underprivileged groups become sharply conscious of their subordination, class or status cleavages do not constitute so pervasive an organizing principle of interpersonal relations as racial or ethnic divisions.

The important question, however, is not whether the lines of social division run vertically along ethnic or horizontally along class lines, but the significance vested in the divisions by felt opposition, whatever its source. This is illustrated by the contrast Epstein draws between the patterns of social relations in the mining compound at Luanshya and in the nearby municipal location. Because of the miners' sense of opposition *vis à vis* the company, "the province of Union activity is not confined to the issues of wages and working conditions . . . it is to a large extent co-extensive with life on the mine itself . . ." (1958:126). To the "unitary" structure of the compound he contrasts the "atomistic" structure of the location. The residents in the location work for a variety of employers, and there are hardly any situations which bring them together as a solidary bloc opposed to a comparable grouping. Consequently the internal structure "is marked by a higher degree of flux" and is "less integrated" (Epstein, 1958:191; 1964:87–94). The racial, tribal, and class differentiae are the same in the two communities; in the former they are utilized to structure a wide range of social situations in an unequivocal fashion, but in the latter they are not tied so closely to economic interests, so that the structure is loose, more ambiguous, and more open to manipulation. The East London locations, while showing a similar pattern of racial and tribal differentiation, also reveal an "atomistic" structure. Their inhabitants work for many different employers and live (as owners or as lodgers) in privately owned dwellings in shantytowns, so they are not even direct tenants of the only monolithic power on the white side—the municipal corporation (Mayer, 1962:583). Again, in East London the birth-determined ethnic categories are overlaid by the choice between a migrant or an urban identity. In many situations what matters most is whether someone presents himself as a "real townsman" rather than as a Red or School migrant (Mayer, 1962:588). Consequently, less force lies behind opposition between Red and School Xhosa. Nevertheless it is always easier to breathe life into ethnic divisions when circumstances change. It is interesting that Mangin . . . should report that there is a growing Quechua nationalism in Peru, everywhere evident in Lima, and nurtured by regional associations. Ethnicity may become more important in Latin American cities; its continuing strength in towns such as New York, Quebec, and Brussels shows that urbanism does not necessarily weaken ethnic grouping.

On the Copperbelt at the time the relevant studies were conducted, there was a sharp cleavage between the black and white groups and a relative balance of power between them. The intermediary groups, such as Coloureds and Indians, were politically unimportant. In situations involving no opposition between blacks and whites, the white group divided along lines of class and political loyalty. In similar situations the African group divided along lines of class or tribal affiliation. Within a group of people of similar class background, dissensions coinciding with tribal groupings attracted most attention, and all sorts of oppositions tended to be phrased in terms of tribalism. Within a group of people from the same tribe splits occured more readily along class lines (Mitchell, 1956:43). Of the two, it seems as if tribal divisions were the more readily appreciated in the early [1950s,] for Epstein shows how a conflict of interests within the Mine Workers' Union aligned with emerging class distinctions was interpreted by Africans as an expression of intertribal hostility (Epstein, 1958:235–36). But class and tribal divisions were obliterated when next the Africans found themselves in a situation evoking racial loyalties. This degree of balance and equilibrium is relatively rare in urban populations, even when ethnic distinctions are relatively important. In Freetown, the non-European population was, at the time of my research, divided between the Creoles and the tribal people, who, in some situations, felt more opposition towards each other than towards the British. Intermediary groups, notably the Lebanese, though not powerful politically, played more important parts than any comparable groups in Central Africa. Moreover class distinctions within the African population were much greater and the economic basis of national life was more diversified. Consequently cross-cutting ties between groups were stronger and there was no clear pattern of balanced opposition (Banton, 1957:77–78, 97–98, 107–8).

In East London opposition is muted for a different reason: the government has effectively prevented the Africans from combining. The position in this town, however, is of crucial interest because it enables us to study the implications of rural-urban continuity for group opposition. Continuity is higher in respect of the "School" migrants, for School and urban people have in common many basic institutions, and School people do not necessarily disapprove of their fellows "becoming townspeople" (Mayer, 1961:76–78, 207–8). The Red migrants came from a similar physical but a different cultural environment: they cultivate traditional Xhosa values and depreciate the value of education. The continuity between the rural and urban social systems is therefore lower in their case. There is a choice: either they can abandon traditional values as poor guides to conduct in a new social system, or they can draw together—incapsulate themselves, in Mayer's terminology—to preserve their culture as an island in the urban sea. Where the latter choice is adopted, opposition between the ethnic minority and other groups is likely to be higher: social density within the ethnic group will also be higher. This is, perhaps, a commonsense inference, but illustrative detail is available from a study of Red and School migrants' conceptions of prestige (Mayer, 1961:66, 77) and from generalizations about the close-knit nature of the Reds' social networks by comparison with the loose networks of the School migrants (Mayer, 1961:287–93). Similarly in Freetown the Hausa migrant traders from Nigeria and other trading groups from the interior tended to form tightly integrated minorities by comparison with the peoples from the immediate hinterland.

In the post-colonial situation of many African towns, the white-black opposition has been robbed of its strength by political change, social stratification has become more significant, and the government has wished to obviate intertribal conflicts. Outside Africa ethnic distinctions sometimes attain considerable significance, as with the Batak, who were originally reviled as pig-eaters and cannibals by the Muslim majority in Medan. Even today there is no way for a matrilineal Minangkabau Moslem to marry a patrilineal Batak Christian (Bruner, 1963:511, 514). The opposition which the Batak feels between his group and the remainder is relatively high and must reinforce the internal structure of his group. But a Minangkabau Moslem may not have the same sense of belonging to a minority, so the pattern of structural opposition is probably less inclusive than on the Copperbelt. In many of the South American cities opposition appears to be low. Indian ethnic groups do not organize on a communal basis; many of their more enterprising members pass into intermediate groups like the *mestizo;* as in East London, social classification depends chiefly upon personal identification and achievement.

A further factor to be considered is the location of power. In Luanshya the strongest opposition was between the mining company and the miners resident in the mine compound. Disputes over pay and conditions of work could be settled on the spot, which must have been a stimulus to combination on the workers' part. In some towns this is not the case. Bradfield explains that in Chimbote, for example, all disputes have to be referred to Lima: conflicts escalate up the structure to the center of power where they are fought out by the representatives of decentralized interests. In such circumstances there is presumably less incentive to combine, and groups do not achieve solidarity so readily.

The effect of a developed structure of opposed groups is to regulate social relations over a much wider range than can be achieved on the basis of ties of personal acquaintance and neighborliness. It provides members of the society with social categories in which they can place most of the people they meet and tells them something of the behavior appropriate to these relationships.

Social Density and Role Differentiation

I have argued that the study of variations in social density is of particular relevance to the urban anthropologist because this is one of the chief dimensions distinguishing the texture of social relations in town and country and in different towns or sections of towns. Two of the chief determinants of social density in towns seem to be rural-urban continuity and structural opposition, and in [the following] diagram I have represented my arguments schematically. The diagram seeks to clarify the kind of social network in which a representative member of a given group within a particula town is likely to be involved. Probably the variations in this respect for persons playing different roles are too great, and the splits between different social realms—such as those of work and leisure—are too deep, for such a schema to have any general validity, but it may nevertheless suggest problems for further research and analysis.

It would be valuable to have more comparative data on the social networks of different groups of migrants in the same towns and upon similar groups of migrants in different towns. When clerks in Medan, Addis Ababa, and General Benavides invite guests to a celebration, is their selection biased towards people of similar ethnic background or similar social status? Can variations in the cross-tribal marriage rate in African cities be related to the emergence of social strata? Is there, in Latin American cities, any functional equivalent of cross-tribal marriage? Then it would be useful to examine the ways in which different networks are mobilized (it should not be forgotten that even the corporate lineage in a traditional society following unilineal descent is a collection of people who combine only when some incident activates the system of group relations). Bradfield describes voluntary associations which rarely assemble but which have a *directoria* that meets frequently; the committee services the network and activates it when necessary. Observers of community

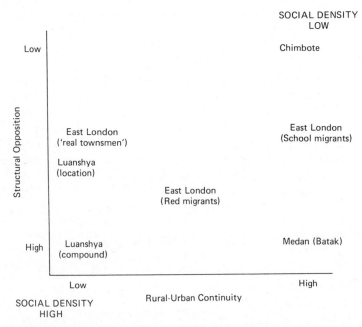

Characteristics of Social Relations in Selected Urban Milieus.

life on housing estates in Britain have often advanced similar observations: tenant activity is intense when there is a dispute over rents but as soon as an issue is settled tenants' associations relapse into indifference. In places where intergroup conflict is frequent, however, ties of allegiance are continually tested.

This is where the discussion of social density relates to role theory in a narrower sense. The more frequently people are called upon to play distinctive roles, the more necessary is it that these roles should be articulated with the other ones constituting the network. The greater the density, the clearer must be the definition of roles. This conclusion was reached in the course of a comparison of the roles of police officer in Scotland and the United States. The Scottish police officer, working in a more closely textured society, has to be more careful to keep his occupational role uncontaminated by off-the-job associations; in dealing with citizens, especially those of higher social class, he is assisted by a relatively elaborate etiquette. By comparison with his American counterpart, the role of the Scottish police officer is much more closely defined; what he may not do is specified in detail and the rules are enforced; what people expect of him shows a higher level of consensus. These differences are apparently related to differences in the integration of social relations in the two countries (Banton, 1964:215–43). The same relation should presumably hold in comparative urban studies: a higher level of consensus and a greater degree of role differentiation is to be expected in towns like Luanshya than in one like Chimbote.

Comparative studies of the organization of social relations in different towns are badly needed. It seems reasonable to believe that the elaboration of role theory for this purpose will be facilitated by the use and refinement of a conception of social density different from Durkheim's. On the microsociological level it can be linked with studies of social networks; on the macrosociological level it is necessary to explore how the overall structure of the town causes role differentiation to follow particular lines and for networks to be based upon different kinds of relationship.

Bibliography

Adams, Richard N. and others.
    1960   *Social Change in Latin America Today.* New York: Vintage Books.
Banton, Michael
    1957   *West African City: A Study of Tribal Life in Freetown.* London: Oxford University Press for International African Institute.
    1964   *The Policeman in the Community.* London: Tavistock Publications.
    1965   *Roles: An Introduction to the Study of Social Relations.* London: Tavistock Publications.
Biddle, Bruce J., and Edwin J. Thomas, eds.
    1966   *Role Theory: Concepts and Research.* New York: John Wiley & Sons, Inc.

BOHANNAN, PAUL
   1955   "Some Principles of Exchange and Investment among the Tiv," *American Anthropologist,* **57**:60–70.
BRUNER, EDWARD S.
   1961   "Urbanization and Ethnic Identity in North Sumatra," *American Anthropologist,* **63**:508–21.
BUSIA, K. A.
   1950   "Report on Social Survey of Sekondi-Takoradi." London: Crown Agents for the Colonies.
DAHRENDORF, RALF
   1964   *Homo Sociologicus: ein Versuch zur Geschichte, Bedeutung und Kritik der Kategorie der sozialen Rolle.* 4th ed. Köln und Opladen: West-deutscher Verlag.
DURKHEIM, EMILE
   1893   *The Division of Labor in Society.* Trans. 1947. Glencoe, Ill.: Free Press.
EPSTEIN, A. L.
   1958   *Politics in an Urban African Community.* Manchester: Manchester University Press, for the Rhodes-Livingstone Institute.
   1964   "Urban Communities in Africa." In *Closed Systems and Open Minds: The Limits of Naivety in Social Anthropology,* ed. Max Gluckman, pp. 83–102. Edinburgh: Oliver and Boyd.
FRAENKEL, MERRAN
   1964   *Tribe and Class in Monrovia.* London: Oxford University Press for International African Institute.
GILLIN, JOHN
   1960   "Some Signposts for Policy." In Adams and others, 1960, pp. 14–62.
GLUCKMAN, MAX
   1960   "Tribalism in Modern British Central Africa." *Cahiers d'études Africaines,* 1, 55 ff.
   1961   "Anthropological Problems Arising from the African Industrial Revolution." In *Social Change in Modern Africa,* A. Southall, ed., pp. 67–82. London: Oxford University Press for International African Institute.
GOODE, WILLIAM J.
   1960a   "A Theory of Role Strain," *American Sociological Review,* **25**:483–96.
   1960b   "Norm Commitment and Conformity to Role-Status Obligations," *American Journal of Sociology,* **66**:246–58.
GROSS, NEAL, WARD S. MASON, AND ALEXANDER W. MCEACHERN
   1958   *Explorations in Role Analysis: Studies of the School Superintendency Role.* New York: John Wiley & Sons, Inc.
HAUSER, PHILIP M., ed.
   1961   *Urbanization in Latin America.* Paris: UNESCO.
HOLLEMAN, J. F. and others, eds.
   1964   *Problems of Transition.* Durban: University of Natal Press.
HOMANS, GEORGE C.
   1951   *The Human Group.* London: Routledge; New York: Harcourt Brace Jovanovich, Inc.
HUTTON, J. H.
   1946   *Caste in India.* Cambridge, Eng.: Cambridge University Press.

LITTLE, KENNETH
    1965   *West African Urbanization*. Cambridge, Eng.: Cambridge University Press.
LLOYD, P. C.
    1959   "The Yoruba Town Today," *The Sociological Review* n.s. **7**:45–63.
MARRIS, PETER
    1961   *Family and Social Change in an African City*. London: Routledge.
MAYER, P.
    1961   *Townsmen or Tribesmen*. Cape Town: Oxford University Press for Rhodes University Institute of Social and Economic Research.
    1962   "Migrancy and the Study of Africans in Towns," *American Anthropologist*, **64**:576–92.
    1964   "Sociological Aspects of Labour Migration." In Holleman, A. and others, 1964.
MITCHELL, J. CLYDE
    1956   "The Kalela Dance." Rhodes-Livingstone Paper No. 27. Manchester: Manchester University Press.
NADEL, S. F.
    1957   *The Theory of Social Structure*. London: Cohen and West.
PAUW, B. A.
    1962   *The Second Generation*. Cape Town: Oxford University Press for Rhodes University Institute of Social and Economic Studies.
PEARSE, ANDREW
    1961   "Some Characteristics of Urbanization in the City of Rio de Janeiro." In Hauser, 1961.
RAVENSTEIN, E. G.
    1885   "The Laws of Migration," *Journal Statistical Society*, **48**:167–227.
READER, D. H.
    1964   "Models in Social Change, with Special Reference to Southern Africa," *African Studies*, **23**:11–33.
REINING, CONRAD
    1959   "The Role of Money in Zande Economy," *American Anthropologist*, **61**:39–43.
ROCHEBLAVE-SPENLÉ, ANNE-MARIE
    1962   *La notion de Role en psychologie sociale: etude historico-critique*. Paris: Presses Universitaires de France.
SHERWOOD, RAY
    1958   "The Bantu Clerk: A Study of Role Expectations," *Journal Social Psychology*, **47**:285–316.
SIMMEL, GEORG
    1955   "The Web of Group Affiliations" (trans.). In *Conflict: The Web of Group Affiliations*. Glencoe, Ill.: Free Press.
SOUTHALL, AIDAN
    1959   "An Operational Theory of Role," *Human Relations*, **12**:17–34.
    1961   "Introductory Summary." In *Social Change in Modern Africa*, ed. Aidan Southall. London: Oxford University Press for International African Institute.
STRIZOWER, SHIFRA
    1959   "Jews as an Indian Caste," *Jewish Journal of Sociology*, **1**:43–57.

WAGLEY, CHARLES
  1960   "The Brazilian Revolution: Social Change Since 1930." In Adams, 1960,
          pp. 177–284.
WILSON, MONICA, AND MAFEJE, ARCHIE
  1963   *Langa: A Study of Social Groups in an African Township.* London: Ox-
          ford University Press.

Situation and Social Network in Cities

NOEL J. CHRISMAN

Drawing on the tool of network analysis, Noel Chrisman points to some of the difficulties that arise in utilizing this relatively new approach to data gathering and interpretation. Chrisman examines such linkages among Danish-Americans in a California city. He discusses the institutional framework within which such networks are formed, the process of network recruitment, the situational contexts that activate network linkages, and the extent to which these networks operate effectively.

It is significant that the use of network analysis is enjoying a current vogue among anthropologists and others who study urban units. At least for the moment, it is one of the primary techniques for defining the interface between real individuals and that amorphous construct called the urban milieu. Some are beginning to suggest, however, that this type of associational model—whether viewed as structure, process, or both—is simply serving as a substitute for similar types of "maps" used in the study of nonurban (especially tribal) peoples and has not substantively advanced our understanding of urban phenomena. We are forced to ask if Chrisman's disclaimer is justified—that it is "the nature of the societies . . . not . . . the tool" which makes network analysis productive. If we can't draw kinship charts, do we satisfy our search for order by offering up diagrams of networks?

In order for network analysis to be more than an exciting potentiality in social research, it is necessary that there be agreement on what social networks are (cf. Mayer, 1966) and that there be means to describe them. Previous studies have provided us with some aspects of networks which must be included in a definition. For example, Barnes discusses the fact that individuals who are related to one another by ties of friendship and acquaintance may be grouped together as a network. He stresses that this is a residue left behind when

"Situation and Social Network in Cities," *Canadian Review of Sociology and Anthropology*, 7: pp. 245–257. copyright © 1970. Canadian Sociological and Anthropological Association (Fitzhenry and Whiteside: College Division).

other principles of grouping in the society (territory and occupation) are removed (1954). Elizabeth Bott contributes the notion of connectedness; that individuals in networks may or may not know each other independently of a central ego (1957). The location of boundaries in connection with network definition continually plagues us (cf. Barnes, 1968; Mayer, 1966). Regularity of interaction and closeness of ties are characteristics considered by Epstein in his discussion of effective and extended network (1961). Each field worker had contributed the characteristics of networks which aided him in his own research. . . . In this discussion, I wish to present three factors I found useful in my own fieldwork.

A goal in the development of network analysis as a new methodological tool has been to generate something that rivals kinship diagrams in simplicity and ease of description. We long for our own "lineage" and the security which accompanies a description of a kinship system. One knows that the notions of patrilineage, bilateral kindred, and the like will be understood by others and that they are reasonably descriptive of some reality. Since the results of the operationalization of these terms may be represented on paper in the form of charts, this is an objective for network analysts as well. A problem in charting a social network, however, is that the meaning of the connecting lines is not so clear as in kin charts. We can merely note the degree of connectedness of such lines. As well, individual roles in the mesh of network relations do not have the explicit, comparable meaning of father's mother's brother, for example. One reason for this is that kin roles are *dependent*, using Nadel's terminology. That is, "a given role is so conceived that, by its character, it requires to be enacted vis-à-vis another counterpart or correlative role" (Nadel, 1957:79–80). This is not necessarily the case in the relationships included in a social network. Since social ties in a personal set may be drawn from a wide variety of structural arenas, the actual content of these roles is variable; we know only that a relationship of some kind exists.

Before we generate little but a serious inferiority complex, it might be useful to gather some hints from kinship studies about directions in which we might go. What is the nature of the societies in which kinship is most commonly used for social analysis? Generally, they are the non-Western groups which anthropologists are so fond of studying. Characteristically, roles in these societies overlap to a great degree. Thus, father is also cultivator, lawyer, priest, and hunter. Kinship is useful for analysis because it openly identifies one of the roles. Then, because of the nature of the societies we examine, not because of the tool, we may investigate other aspects of life. If descent groups did not also act as major political, economic, and ritual units, we would not have such a versatile tool in kinship. Network analyses have been attempted where traditional kinship approaches would not have been as productive. It is perhaps in vain that we expect network charts to tell us as much at a glance as do kin charts. It is not, however, unreasonable to expect that the roles and linkages of networks can be described fully and accurately.

Recruitment and Institutional Alternatives

Rather than beginning with the chart, or overall aspect of network, it might be worthwhile to examine the component social relationships. Specifying their nature is useful since the structure of the network may vary depending upon the content of the roles within it. For example, Bott links close-knit networks to an overlapping of social roles—one individual filling a number of roles at the same time (Bott, 1957:66). There are a number of ways the component role relationships of a network may be described—kin, neighbour, friend, and the like. Operationally, we can consider these to be examples of how the relationships were *recruited*. For example, Bott and others state that a network may consist in part of kin ties. The kinship system, as an institutional framework, insofar as it has provided for certain individuals to have a role relationship, has supplied the opportunity for those individuals to know each other and to interact.

The many institutional frameworks of a society are the structural features in the social system which can influence the formation and persistence of groups and which can also provide the arena within which network relations may form. People who share a common institutional membership have at least the possibility of minimum and structured interaction. For example, there were about 150 members of the Pacific City branch of the Danish Brotherhood. Each had been initiated (and learned the secret lore of the association) and had continued to pay dues. Any one of these men could, therefore, go to a Friday night meeting, enjoy the Danish atmosphere and fellowship, participate in discussions, and vote. They were all eligible for office in the organization. That only about twenty-five men usually attended the meetings does not decrease the importance of the voluntary association as a *potential* arena for interaction. Should a man wish to activate his associational role for some purpose, he would be able to do so.

Urban dwellers belong to a series of institutions which may be activated with greater or lesser frequency. The Danish-Americans were also members of institutions in the areas of occupation, residence, kinship, religion, and the like. Association membership was only one aspect of a life composed of participation in a series of diverse institutions which might be spatially and socially unrelated. Within each institution which is activated, the individual has the choice of the depth and manner with which he interacts with others around him. He may invest much in the relationship so that rights and obligations with respect to a role-partner transcend the requirements of the formal relationship—he may, in other words, form a dyadic contract (Foster, 1961) with another person. The individual might interact with others in an institution only to the extent of the roles provided by institutional structure; or as Foster points out, he may not honour role obligations at all. In addition, individuals who share membership in the same institution and know the role obligations may still not interact because of lack of physical opportunity. For example, machinists on alternate shifts, in separate areas of a factory, or in different towns can share close institutional ties, but not be able to activate them. Danish-Americans who belong to different chapters of the same lodge share knowledge of common role behaviours, but unless one physically visits another chapter, no interaction takes place and the potential role relationship is left unactivated.

Individuals who share membership within an institutional framework fulfill one of the preconditions for being recruited into a personal network, but do not conform to the interactive component of network relations. Katz (1966) refers to these possibilities for networks as "potential networks." He notes, however, that "in an 'open' society *all* members are potential contacts of ego, at least in principle" (1966:204). This most inclusive notion of network—that which includes individuals in relationships which may never connect in an interaction situation—is too broad to be a unit of research and analysis in urban areas. In addition to the breadth of the problem, there is also the difficulty of differentiating between those potential links which are the result of shared institutional membership and those which may be drawn from personal relationships. That is, one must distinguish between role sets and personal sets (Wolfe, 1969). In role sets, individuals may form a relationship while engaging in a common institutional task; whereas a personal set may be drawn from many institutional contexts or from interpersonal interaction outside of large-scale institutions with set tasks.

Recruitment as one of the mechanisms in network formation leads us first to descriptions of potential networks. For any ego in a society, we may examine those institutions and groups of which he is a part and determine the individuals with which he may potentially come into contact. In my research on the Danish-Americans, such institutional frameworks could be listed. In addition to frameworks shared by many Americans such as kinship, occupation, residence, neighbourhood, and the like, these Danes shared membership in one or more Danish-American voluntary associations. Such a listing of institutional frameworks and the potential network resulting from role relations can be useful in specifying the extent and nature of an individual's possible participation in the wider society and exposure to varying populations. In an investigation of ethnic communities within a large urban centre, this information is valuable in a determination of the completeness (Breton, 1964) of a person's commitment to his own community. Most Danish-Americans participated in non-Danish occupations; they were not localized in an ethnic residential area; and they utilized generally available non-ethnic city services such as supermarkets, theatres, and department stores. Thus, only one formal aspect of life—voluntary association membership—had an ethnic component. And even this sphere of life was not totally restricted on an ethnic basis. Some belonged to nonethnic fraternal organizations such as the Masons and Moose lodge.

Situation

A statement of potential networks does not, however, get at the quality of urban social life; we do not discover the actual extent and meaning of participation in particular aspects of society. As well, such a network is so unwieldy and ill-defined that it gives us little information about personal groupings. To secure data on everyday social life, the interactive component must be investigated. That is, we must discover which of an individual's many potential role relationships are activated, in which situations this occurs, and the nature of that interaction. Network analysis provides an important method for gathering these data.

Networks can be seen in terms of the kind of institution within which they were recruited and activated. There may be areas within an individual's potential network which are actualized only in specific situations in which the interaction is limited and its focus is very specific. For example, a factory worker might interact with his fellow workers only while on the job. Such a network could be very close-knit, but its generalizability into other spheres of life might be limited. We know from the Western Electric studies and other small group research (cf. Homans, 1951) that the content of such interactive links in the occupational sphere relates to more than just the specific job. However, these relationships might be segmented from other areas of the urban dweller's life; that is, there may be little interactional overlap between members of a network activated in a single situation and people whom the city resident sees in other aspects of his life.

Using Parsons' terminology (1951), we can speak of the instrumental nature of the content of such network relations. Thus, of an individual's potential network of relations—as defined by the institutional frameworks of which he is a part—some will be more oriented toward pragmatic ends. The content of those relations when activated is more likely to be specific to the role relationship and these links are more likely to be activated in a limited number of situations, situations largely confined to immediate tasks.

Members of the Danish-American community maintained varying numbers and types of such instrumental networks. Occupation, for example, provided the mechanism for recruiting people into social networks which were activated only during the work day. One informant told me that he disliked seeing fellow dock workers during off hours because he preferred to relax and not be forced verbally, "to reload every ship in my own living room." Neighbourhood ties too were seen in a highly instrumental fashion. One lady told me that it was important to her to remain on good terms with her neighbours so they could be called upon for assistance in emergencies. She, however, carried the relationships no further because they had little—other than neighbourhood affairs—to talk about.

To examine relationships in networks whose members interact with each other on bases beyond the activation of single role relations, situation becomes an important variable. Networks based upon instrumental role sets are likely to be activated only in situations calling for the completion of a particular task in society; the links are not generalized into other interactive contexts. However, many individuals maintain networks whose component social bonds are multi-stranded. Different individuals in the network can have different types of relationships with ego and the content of any particular dyadic link in the network may be diverse. Networks with multi-stranded links contain bonds which could have been initially recruited within an institution which implies limited interaction situations, but the ties are activated in other, institutionally unrelated, contexts. For example, one of my informants expanded a minimal neighbouring role with the man who lived next door. Not only did they engage in neighbouring patterns (Keller, 1968) but also they belonged to the same (non-Danish) voluntary association and engaged in an extensive visiting pattern. The addition of these two other situations presented them with different tasks to be confronted, the opportunity for additional periods of interaction, and the chance to explore new facets of each other's interests, beliefs, and the like ("to get to know each other better"). The Dane's personal set included four couples from the Danish lodge, two couples related by kinship, and his neighbours. Although these relationships may be structurally designated on the basis of their boundaries and degrees of connectedness, it is also important to specify the content since the various segments of this personal set were recruited in different ways and interact in separate situations. The two aspects of content, recruitment and situation, influence the structure of the personal network.

Recruitment and Situation

In extraordinary situations, such as the twenty-fifth wedding anniversary party held by one Danish-American couple, segments of a personal set which normally do not interact may be included in the same social context. At the Madsen's anniversary party, people were present who had relations with the couple based on kinship, occupation, and association membership. I was greeted at the door by "another Mrs. Madsen." The obvious identification of the kin tie and my response with an association link was a necessary social tool for sorting guests into categories. On the patio, where most of the guests congregated, there was some inter-penetration of individuals from separate networks. This was particularly true for kin and association members since they could discuss Danish topics relatively easily and because some could have been together in other, less extraordinary, interaction situations. However, the few individuals drawn from Mr. Madsen's occupation-based network, one of whom was black, interacted almost exclusively with each other or with members of the Madsen nuclear family. There were few shared topics of conversation because of the discrepancy in recruiting frameworks.

The relation between recruiting institution and situation is a close one; however, they must be kept analytically separate. The institutional framework provides for role relationships among people and the possibility of a further social relationship among individuals (potential network). As well, the institution provides at least one social situation in which tasks must be accomplished. When network relations are abstracted from the role set, one aspect of the content of those links is the shared roles of the participants. In addition, the experiences of individuals in task-oriented situations becomes part of the store of knowledge a person has about those around him. In institutions with largely instrumental goals, there is little *institutional* provision for a wide range of shared personal knowledge about others in the same situation. That is, it is not likely that there will be varied situations for interaction to occur and participants may consistently see only one aspect of their co-participants. The content of the relationship is thus restricted.

If network ties are described specifying the institutional frameworks from which the links were recruited and in which they continue to be activated, the analyst has an operational means of designating the content of the network relationships. One can expect that those links which contain only one institutional affiliation are more likely to be segmented from other relationships in society and might be best considered as a role relationship with less personal content included. However, if interaction occurs in a series of varied social situations, the interpersonal content may be more complex. Thus, both recruitment context and situation must be specified.

A network link which includes recruitment from more than one institutional famework can be expected to have more varied content—by definition on the institutional level. (I continue to refer to the role aspect of a link as recruitment even though it is obvious two individuals who have a relationship from one context are not "newly recruited" when they meet in another context. They are, however, newly recruited for that aspect—the new role relationship—of their multiplex social bond.) For example, the lodge member who recruits an occupation mate into the lodge shares at least two role relationships with him and can see him in at least one more social context—a context in which different tasks are primary to the interaction and other aspects of personality may be discovered. The overlap of interaction situations and the possibility of activating other kinds of social roles—e.g., those from a voluntary association—in addition to the original recruitment arena is reminiscent of the kind of role overlap and participation in a series of institutions which occurs in tribal societies. An important difference here is that the overlap is on an individual level and is the result of personal choice to a greater extent, rather than membership in an ascribed grouping which acts within interlocked institutional frameworks. This, of course, makes research more difficult since the investigator must discover the congruences of role for each person rather than finding general principles.

I have been discussing the ways in which the notions of situation and recruitment are useful for specifying the content of network links. Those factors have been related to the potential for relationships to form and to be expanded. I have suggested that a greater number of shared roles in institutions and of situations for interaction allow individuals the opportunity to discover more information about co-participants and to form clearer ideas about shared beliefs and attitudes. Newcomb's research on the acquaintance process (1957) suggests that people who share similar value orientations are more likely to continue their relationship than are those whose orientations differ. Shared institutional membership and the opportunity for several interaction situations provide for the presence of and discovery of shared beliefs in two ways. Institutional recruiting criteria can restrict membership to individuals who are more likely to be similar to each other. For example, most Danes who joined the lodges were more traditional (more "Danish" in some sense), had a lower-middle-class background, and were "lodge men." (That is, they appreciated the type of sociality in a fraternal organization and were more likely to be or to have been members of other fraternal orders.) Danes who did not join or who did not attend meetings often did not share these characteristics. Secondly, interaction situations within the institutional context and those stemming from it (e.g., going out for a beer after work) can provide for a series of general small-talk subjects to be discussed which indicate the opinions of participants. The individual who disagrees or is disagreeable can be excluded from the more informal aspects of interaction even though formal role requirements may continue to be met. Those who continue to interact have the occasion to expand their relationship on a more personal level, resulting in a difference in content from that implied by their existing role relationship.

Dyadic Contracts and Affective Social Ties

It is in the examination of relationships which transcend those formally set up by the institutional framework that Foster's dyadic contract is most relevant. His discussion provides an important element in the description of network ties which have been generalized beyond the recruiting institutional framework. Foster hypothesizes that:

> . . . every adult organizes his societal contacts outside the nuclear family by means of a special form of contractual relationship. These contracts are informal, or implicit, since they lack ritual or legal basis. They are not based on any idea of law, and they are unenforceable through authority; they exist only at the pleasure of the contractants. The contracts are dyadic in that they occur only between two individuals; three or more people are not brought together. The contracts are noncorporate, since social units such as villages, *barrios*, or extended families are never bound (1961:1174).

In an industrialized urban area, dyadic contracts may be formed within any of the institutional frameworks within which one interacts. Those frameworks which provide for sustained interaction over time—even though the types of situations in which interaction occurs are relatively similar—are more likely to be the arenas within which dyadic contracts are formed. Shared type and place of occupation, thus, is more likely to result in dyadic contracts than merchant-customer or doctor-patient relations. Voluntary associations, especially those which are expressive (Rose, 1953) can be an important arena for the creation of dyadic contracts and subsequent informal social networks.

Social networks which are based upon dyadic contracts among the component individuals differ from the more role-based networks in several respects. Most importantly, since the dyadic contract is a relationship generated interpersonally and is not totally dependent upon the outside institution, there is a much greater range of possible behaviour. The content of interaction may cover many areas of urban life. Under conditions where sustained interaction may and does take place, Homans (1961; cf. Newcomb, 1957) suggests that one consequence is an increase in the degree to which individuals like each other. If and when this occurs, the relationships may be described as having more affective content than would be expected in a link based solely upon roles.

Another type of network, then, is based upon affective ties. Relationships in such a network—while they may be recruited from any institutional framework—might be more likely to be based upon recruitment from some institutional frameworks than others. (Which ones, of course, becomes an interesting empirical problem—both for the type of framework leading to affective ties, and for the type of individual life-style involved.) In addition, the number and type of situations in which network ties are activated differ.

In a consideration of networks with a high degree of affective commitment as part of the content of the links, it is important to distinguish between the affective role content of a link and the personal aspect of a link. Kinship systems provide a good example of a role structure with affective goals. Relations with distant or disliked kin may be characterized by the outward forms of a positive emotional relationship without the interpersonal commitment of a dyadic contract. In the Danish-American lodges, a high value is placed upon fellowship—members are expected to be cordial, friendly, and brotherly. A man can expect a positive reception at the lodge even if he attends rarely. One Dane ceased attending meetings because he did not receive the warm reception he expected. On one occasion, I asked a lodge member who his friends were. He waved in the direction of the lodge room and exclaimed: "Why, they're *all* my friends!"

Networks in the Danish-American Community

The effective nature of interpersonal ties is related to the recruiting framework (insofar as some institutions might be more likely to generate affective links); the number and diversity of interaction situations (because of Homans' notion of interaction and liking); and, perhaps as a consequence of the first two factors, the presence or absence of dyadic contracts. These factors may be illustrated by referring again to the Danish-Americans. The population with which I worked included all formal members of Danish-American voluntary associations. These people were, therefore, all included in each other's potential networks by virtue of common membership in an institutional framework. There were, as well, patterned behaviours of friendship and fellowship which were almost mandatory between fellow association members. Thus, there was an affective component in the role relationships because of group membership. Members (as members) gathered together in two kinds of situations: semi-monthly formal meetings at which few were present, and less frequent large celebrations such as parties, picnics, and formal installations of officers. The celebrations were much better attended and, for many, were the opportunity of briefly renewing seldom-activated social ties. From the point of view of the seldom-seen member, these social links are part of his extended network. He devotes his time to other aspects of life and presumably has more continuous social relationships there. The errant member is seen in much the same way by regular attenders—part of their extended network.

From the observer's point of view, we may speak of the wide scale, loose-knit network based upon Danish association membership. The ties were, therefore, recruited through the associations. Such links persist since members see one another at meetings and may be casual friends. In addition, some amount of personal information about other members is gathered over time. A lodge member, for example, may know details about other men's lives—men whom he never sees except at lodge meetings. In this way, a man can judge shared orientations and the potential for a close relationship at a distance. Knowledge of and acquaintanceship with others is extended through cities in the metropolitan area and elsewhere by means of various social events which take place. For example, all the lodges cooperate on a picnic every June. At this event, people from different lodges who previously did not know each other might be introduced by mutual friends. New members are included at the tables of family and friendship groups and are introduced to the people who stroll around to greet seldom- and often-seen friends. At large social occasions sponsored by a single lodge, such as an installation of officers, intra-lodge ties may be formed. For example, Ed Hansen and Eric Svendsen and their wives sat near three other couples at a dinner when they first joined the lodge. These couples have since expanded their relationships into close friendships. It is significant that the possibility of interaction such as [this] . . . is provided by common membership in the association. Expansion of a relationship is then based upon factors of common interests and shared values. In the case of the two couples at the dinner, similarity of age was an important factor.

Within the two Danish-American fraternal lodges, it was possible to identify a few close-knit networks which were composed of close friends. These informal social networks could be observed interacting on meeting nights. Before and after meetings, there was a much greater likelihood that members of an informal social network (an altercentric set) would interact among themselves than with other members. This was particularly the case for those who enjoyed playing cards. One network composed of about seven men regularly attended meetings of both lodges and spent most of their time engaged in card playing. (Four would play and the others either watched or talked with members outside the cluster.) As well, members of these informal clusters saw one another in other situations more frequently than they saw other Danish association members. The card players gathered at each other's houses on a regular basis for evenings of cards. As well, there was informal visiting among the couples. This intensification of institutional bonds occurred partly because the men and their wives had discovered they liked each other and enjoyed similar entertainments and formed friendships beyond the roles implied by common lodge membership. Participation in a series of different situations—e.g., organization meetings, informal visiting, and recreation—allows participants the opportunity to discover more of their common attributes.

These close-knit informal social networks, generated from the common institutional framework, can be seen as partly isolated clusters—or social sets, to use Mayer's terminology—which can activate a series of aspects of urban life. Membership remains relatively constant and institutions and situation may fluctuate. The constancy of participants in such a set meant, in the Danish community, that there were similarities of behaviour in those varying situations. One set, recruited from the more conservative of the two lodges, frequently engaged in ethnic behaviour. For example, at an association meeting, the Danish picnic, or in informal visiting, Danish was spoken, a Danish card game played, and Danish food eaten.

Informal social network membership also had an effect upon attendance at formal meetings. These men attended more regularly than others, presumably because they knew they would have another opportunity to engage in interaction with their friends. In contrast, a member of the ethnic association who rarely attended had formed his primary relationships from his occupation mates. His primary social network did not overlap at all with his potential role partners in the Danish lodge.

I suspect that the high affective content of the interpersonal ties in these sets has an influence on the fact that the sets may be found in different situations. A network based largely upon role relations—no matter how tightly knit—is probably restricted to a small number of interaction situations. In addition, these situations might be more closely tied to the institutional framework in which recruitment to the network took place.

Data on the recruiting institution or institutions, the situations in which network interaction takes place, and the nature of the interpersonal ties involved are useful operational means to defining the content of bonds in informal social networks. The focus upon the arenas of recruitment allows the investigator to relate interpersonal relations to the structural features of the general society. By considering the situations in which interaction occurs and the nature of the interpersonal tie, one may discover the relation between personal network formation and the activation of institutional ties, and the impact of societal structural features and interpersonal relationships upon the behaviour of urban dwellers may be gauged.

Bibliography

BARNES, J. A.
    1954   "Class and Committees in a Norwegian Island Parish." *Human Relations,* **7**:39–58.
    1968   "Networks and Political Process." Pp. 107–130 in Marc J. Swartz (ed.),14 Local Level Politics. Chicago: Aldine.

BOTT, ELIZABETH
    1957   *Family and Social Network: Roles, Norms, and External Relationships in Ordinary Urban Families.* London: Tavistock.

BRETON, RAYMOND
    1964   "Institutional Completeness of Ethnic Communities and the Personal Relations of Immigrants." *American Journal of Sociology,* **70**:193–205.

CHRISMAN, NOEL
    1966   "Ethnic Influence on Urban Groups: The Danish-Americans." Unpublished Ph.D. dissertation. Berkeley: University of California.

EPSTEIN, A. L.
    1961   "The Network and Urban Social Organization" *Rhodes-Livingstone Journal,* **29**:29–62.

FOSTER, GEORGE
    1961   "The Dyadic Contract: A Model for the Social Structure of a Mexican Peasant Village," *American Anthropologist,* **63**:1173–1192.

HOMANS, GEORGE
    1951   *The Human Group.* New York: Harcourt Brace Jovanovich, Inc.
    1961   *Social Behavior: Its Elementary Forms.* New York: Harcourt Brace Jovanovich, Inc.

KATZ, FRED E.
    1966   "Social Participation and Social Structure," *Social Forces,* **45**:199–210.

KELLER, SUZANNE
    1968   *The Urban Neighborhood: A Sociological Perspective.* New York: Random House, Inc.

MAYER, ADRIAN
    1966   "The Significance of Quasi-groups in the Study of Complex Societies." Pp. 97–123 in Michael Banton (ed.) *The Social Anthropology of Complex Societies.* London: Tavistock.

MITCHELL, J. CLYDE
    1969   "The Concept and Use of Social Network." Pp. 1–50 in J. C. Mitchell (ed.), *Social Networks in Urban Situations.* Manchester: Manchester University Press.

NADEL, S. F..
    1957   *The Theory of Social Structure.* New York: Free Press.

NEWCOMB, THEODORE
    1957   *The Acquaintance Process.* New York: Holt, Rinehart and Winston.

PARSONS, TALCOTT
    1951   *The Social System.* Glencoe: The Free Press.

ROSE, ARNOLD
    1953   *Theory and Method in the Social Sciences.* Minneapolis: University of Minnesota Press.

WOLFE, ALVIN
  1969 "Proposal for Analysis of Social Networks in Cities." Manuscript.

Middle-Class London Families and Their Relatives

RAYMOND FIRTH, JANE HUBERT, and ANTHONY FORGE

*It was suggested in an earlier comment that network mapping in the urban set-
ting may simply be a substitute for mapping kinship systems in tribal societies.
The implication: that kinship is amenable to analysis in urban contexts. In this
paper, Firth, Hubert, and Forge summarize their research on the dynamics of
kinship among middle-class Londoners, thus turning the tables on those who
hold that familial ties are relatively unimportant to the study of people in cities.*

*The emphasis of these researchers is on kinfolk and the social system which
such kin form. Like network analysis, the use of systems models has com-
manded a great deal of attention and is predicated on the belief that human
societies form systems analogous to mechanical systems. To look at systems is to
study causally interrelated parts of an entity. These components are perceived as
mutually influential in the functioning of the total system. The system and its
context, furthermore, are also in a causal feedback relation to each other.*

*One of the more interesting points suggested in this paper is that the simpler
the kinship system, the more complex its operation. There can be great variation
in the ways it is actually employed "on the ground." Thus, because Americans or
Britons lump all affinal kin (except spouse and spouse's children by a previous
marriage) under the single kin term -in-law, it becomes quite complicated to
discuss affinal relationships in either society. There's rarely consensus, for example, on whether the spouse of one's brother-in-law is one's sister-in-law,
brother-in-law's wife, not "really" related, or "no relation at all." But kin relations
do exist here, and the posited absence of any explicit, formal way of dealing with
them does not minimize their structural importance. Rather, as Firth and his colleagues are quick to point out, this adds to their significance. For, without clear
guidelines to proper behavior, the assessment of positive, negative, active, and
passive obligations must rest largely upon personal judgment. Each decision is
not simply the repetitive application of a formula but a personalized, deliberative
process that reflects many significant structural elements of urban life.*

*Such a focus on the dynamic aspects of Western, industrial-urban kinship
offers a welcome antidote to what some have seen as an excessive weight placed
on kinship in nonurban groups. As Victor Uchendu pointed out some years ago,*

even among nonurban peoples a great deal of interaction takes place in which familial ties are quite irrelevant.

In this chapter we summarize our main findings from this enquiry into the kinship of middle-class families in North London and offer some additional comments on general questions. From the data we have assembled and analysed the main structural features of one sector of English middle-class kinship are clear.

To begin with, it is evident that we can properly speak of the kinship of such people as a *system*. Behaviour towards people recognized as 'relatives' is not random; it tends to follow prescribed conventions, to be repetitive and to form part of articulated series of relationships in which ties with any one kinsman are affected by those with other kin.

To anthropologists, this English kinship system is structurally of a relatively simple character. It is of shallow genealogical depth and relatively close lateral boundaries. Few people trace back further than their grandparents or further out than their second cousins. The system is one in which consanguines are fairly well individualized. In formal terms, parents are uniquely separated, sibling terms are confined to members of the natal family, and grandparental terms apply only to the two pairs of parents of a person's mother and father. Category terms exist, e.g. 'uncle', 'aunt', 'cousin', but here too there is a distinct tendency to individualize them in application by combining them with the personal name for superior generations.

The structural simplicity of this kinship system allows for a great deal of variation in content. Genealogical knowledge and the counting of kin differ greatly among different people, not only [because of] demographic and generational factors (e.g. single child in a family, bachelorhood or spinsterhood, old age) but also to factors of social discrimination on family and personal grounds.

On the ideological plane, there is in general a decided sentiment about the basic significance of consanguineal kinship bonds, and some generalized, fairly standardized canons of responsibility towards kin. But there is no very precise set of rules for social behaviour in putting these notions of responsibility into effect, and the application of them in practice tends to be very restricted, often to members of a person's natal family. For parents, certain legal prescriptions exist about the feeding and care, discipline and education of their children. For children, when adult, there are certain normal social expectations which for the most part do not exist in legal form, about what they will do for their parents if the latter are in want or ill. The pressures of society also tend to be felt by siblings if a brother or sister is in similar distressed circumstances. But apart from certain legal specifications regarding 'next of kin,' the great body of extra-familial kin are free from any general social formulations about expected behaviour to relatives. There are norms of respect or familiarity for kin who are of senior, of equivalent or of junior grade, but these are not formalized to any high degree; nor are they associated with any firm code of privilege and obligation. The statuses and roles associated with different kinship positions are of a rather indefinite order.[1] Neither the type of kin who should or need not be helped, nor the nature of the things to be done for those kin who are recognized to require services are laid down. Again, there is no general agreement even as to how far the rules that exist in minimal form shall be carried out—the degree of sacrifice that ought to be made in order to do what is right and proper. Moreover, where social expectations exist, they are backed by no particular sanctions. In modern urban conditions of an industrialized society, especially in a metropolis, ignorance of the social milieu of one's friends and neighbours is such that it is practically impossible to check whether or not they are carrying out even such minimal rules of behaviour towards the kin they recognize.

Now the lack of clear-cut rules of obligation and behaviour towards kin, and particularly of any specification of when and where the somewhat vague series of social expectations do not apply, is liable to create difficulties of choice and decision. There are choices of a direct kind—whether or not to assume responsibility for a relative in poverty or other distress, having regard to one's own resources of time, finance, house-room, etc. There are also choices of a more indirect, perhaps more subtle, kind—how far an offer to lend a helping hand may offend or injure the individuality of the relative concerned, and allow him or her to lapse from an invigorating struggle and personal focus of energies; how far help to one relative may offend another and disturb a delicate balance of social forces. These are not merely choices in the field of expediency—they may have a moral connotation as well, and the attempt to arrive at a decision on grounds of what it is right to do may present a very difficult problem. As McGregor and others have pointed out, kinship is not a structural feature of modern British society. But in the very fact that it is not lies precisely a considerable difficulty. Obligations and responsibilities have to be assessed in the light of personal judgment, not formal rule. Claims are made, expectations are presented, duties conceived, with no clear guide for their resolution in action. Much of the peculiar quality of kinship lies in this.

The middle-class English kinship system is then a *permissive*, not an *authoritarian* system. The relative lack of role categorization and formal obligation also means that the system is on the whole a selective one. People have a range of kin available to them, but the decision to implement these relationships is primarily a matter of mutual adjustment on the basis of personal selection. Taken into consideration are such factors as temperamental compatibility, feeling of moral obligation, deference to the views of other kin, geographical accessibility.

In the course of our analysis we have shown the need for a more adequate conceptual framework for the study of kinship in urban Western society, and have put forward some suggestions for this. Here is a further comment.

---

[1] This was pointed out by W. H. R. Rivers, *Kinship and Social Organization*, 1914, London, p. 13 (reprinted London School of Economics Monographs on Social Anthropology, No. 34, 1968, p. 46).

Studies of kinship in urban industrial society normally start from consideration of the family. Different views have been strongly asserted here. It has been stated, as by Parsons, Nimkoff or Goode, that modern industrial structure favours the development of nuclear or independent families and bears against the continued existence of extended families. Industrialization and urbanization are believed to result in loss of functions of the family and atrophy of extra-familial kin links.[2] Strong reaction has been expressed against such propositions, as by Townsend,[3] who has found it hard to accept any idea of the extended family 'giving away' to some variety of the nuclear family. But as Barić has pointed out,[4] there is no necessary contradiction between these views. If by extended family is meant a group of kin of three generations or more with a fairly well-defined corporate linear character involving cooperation in productive activities, common ownership of assets and recognized common responsibilities, such units are almost entirely absent from the modern urban industrial scene. But if, as Townsend would seem to mean, extended family in a very loose sense means those extra-familial kin who maintain a relationship of some intimacy with members of a nuclear family, then such entities do persist even in fully developed urban conditions. Yet whether or not urban kin ties may be thought to have been maintained or have weakened or declined, they certainly have changed form with greater dispersion and greater economic independence of kin.[5]

But an issue in kinship theory has tended to arise because of confusion at times between these two social forms, an extended family group and a set of extra-familial kin. If one applies the test of where authority is exercised, the difference becomes plain. In an extended family, as observed comparatively in many societies, authority is normally exercised by the head of the family who is the senior male, commonly the father or grandfather of the consanguine family members. In the set of extra-familial kin authority is dispersed, the kin in each independent nuclear family having their own responsibility for productive activities and control of assets. In this sense Parsons and those who have thought along the same lines have been correct. Except for family firms and some control of joint property, decisions in the set of extra-familial kin in a modern Western urban society are made in nuclear family units, however influenced they may be by kin ties outside. Parsons' view has sometimes been interpreted to mean that once the children in an elementary family have grown up, married and moved away, a process of fragmentation sets in and ties between them and their consanguine kin soon tend to disappear. It is true that he has emphasized the strength of the independent family

---

[2] Talcott Parsons (on the American family) in Talcott Parsons and Robert F. Bales, *Family, Socialization and Interaction Process*, Glencoe, 1955, p. 9; M. F. Nimkoff, *Comparative Family Systems*, Boston, 1965, pp. 343 et seq.; William J. Goode, *The Family*, Englewood Cliffs, N.J., 1964, p. 108.

[3] Family and Kinship in Industrial Society: A Comment by Peter Townsend. *Sociological Review Monograph*, No. 8, Keele, 1964, pp. 89 et seq.

[4] Lorraine Barić, in M. Freedman, (Ed.) *Social Organization: Essays Presented to Raymond Firth*. London, 1967, pp. 2–4.

[5] Raymond Firth, Family and Kinship in Industrial Society, *Sociological Review Monograph*, No. 8, 1964, p. 87.

of procreation at the expense of other kin ties. But that Parsons did not ignore the significance of these is indicated by the fact that he himself was one of the first to draw attention to the significance in American society of kinship outside the elementary family. He also indicated how on the sociological side family studies at that date (1943) were overwhelmingly oriented to problems of individual adjustment rather than to comparative structural perspective.[6] This said, we re-emphasize the importance for sociological thinking of attention to the set of extra-familial kin. Since work in this field began some twenty years ago sociologists and anthropologists in many countries have demonstrated the importance of such kin.[7]

Various ways can be imagined of characterizing the set of extra-familial kin of a family in English middle-class society. We have shown the inadequacy of the cliché 'extended family' as a blanket term for all kinds of kin attached to or linked with a conjugal family. They can hardly be regarded as a series of formal corporate groups—as in many societies—and the concepts of quasi-group or kin network, though useful in some respects, are not completely satisfactory. In different contexts the set of extra-familial kin can be classed with reference to size, integration, level of services among members, etc. But such classification does not easily yield any simple set of types. Only at a superficial level can one speak in this middle-class universe of such polar types as large or small families, open or closed kin groups, integrated or dispersed sets of kin. From the point of view of residence, jobs, reciprocal services, influence in decision making, the circumstances and personality of the various members of the elementary family and their associated kin are such that a great variety of combinations of factors is possible.

There has been much debate in recent years on the issue of descent theory versus alliance theory in the interpretation of kinship.[8] Argument has been complex, often very abstract, and most of it has been concerned with segmentary kin groups and positive marriage rules—conditions which are not applicable to the English kinship system. But a fundamental question has been involved—the extent to which any kinship system is concerned with the ordering of kin along genealogical lines, with serial procreation and internal group structure as the foci, or with the ordering of relationships between groups, with marriage as the prime mechanism of linkage.[9]

---

[6] 'The Kinship System of the Contemporary United States,' _Essays in Sociological Theory_, rev. edn 1954, Glencoe, Ill., pp. 177–96.

[7] One of the latest studies in Belgium, for instance, confirms their significance. Jean Rémy, 'Persistance de la famille étendue dans un milieu industriel et urbain,' _Revue française de sociologie_, vol. 8, 1967, pp. 493–505.

[8] The major protagonists include Dumont, Fortes, Goody, Leach, Lévi-Strauss, Needham, Schneider. For references see e.g. David M. Schneider, 'Some Muddles in the Models,' _The Relevance of Models for Social Anthropology_, A.S.A. Monographs, 1, London 1965, pp. 25–85; Robin Fox, _Kinship and Marriage_, Pelican Books, 1967, _passim_. A recent statement by Maybury-Lewis, 'The Murngin Moral,' _Trans. New York Academy of Sciences_, ser. II, vol. 29, pp. 482–94, comments further on this issue.

[9] The basic position was stated in essence many years ago by C. N. Starcke, _The Primitive Family_, London, 1889, p. 274. 'The development of the family was not merely advanced by the relations which existed between its members; it was rather the different family relations of the two parents which paved the way for this development.'

Our analysis has some relevance to this issue. From perspective of kinship in this sector of an urban industrial society it would seem that both aspects are important. Analysis of our English kinship material primarily in terms of descent group theory does not carry us very far. Consanguineal group solidarity is weak. The groups are small and shallow and on the ground do not conform to any strict unilineal principles. On the other hand, to regard the kinship system as primarily one which exists as a symbolic expression of group relations—exemplified by transactions in which *inter alia* women are moved around in marriage—would involve serious distortion. In our field there is no form of prescriptive marriage—women are not pushed around as pawns, and there are relatively few group transactions. There is ample empirical evidence of the pervasiveness of individual choice in marriage and in other situations. (The single instance in our material of quarrel over the giving of a dowry [not offered] illustrated not so much relations between two different kin groups as the exasperation of a man from a different cultural background at meeting the English lack of appreciation of the significance of dowry for marriage relations.)

In general terms, what we have found is that parent-child ties are very strong, but surprisingly without illusion. Notions of filial sentiment do operate, but not at the level of the popular emotionally sticky, undifferentiated attachment. Particularly with son or daughter, at the overt level there is apt to be a very cool rationalistic appreciation of the parent's virtues and faults and an almost clinically analytic attitude at times towards responsibility for parents. As far as sibling ties are concerned, those between sisters are markedly close, but those between brothers, or between brothers and sisters, are highly selective. In all cases there is an expectation in our middle-class circles that parental and sibling ties, while not denied, shall be subordinated to the marriage bond. When a London middle-class girl marries she expects to live in her own house or flat, and even in these days of professional women's independence, to accompany her husband to his occupational area, not to remain closely associated with her parents and siblings. The 'Mum-complex' described by various writers on aspects of London society has little meaning in residential terms for our North London people.

The significance of consanguineal bonds is seen from another angle, in the great importance attached to affinal ties. There is hardly anyone in the area of our study who has not fairly regular contact with some of his or her spouse's kin—which is a demonstration of the persistence of the spouse's consanguineal ties. But the affinal relations tend to be strong and intimate with only one spouse's consanguines. There is some balancing in the household, but the kin field often is furnished predominantly by either husband or wife, and still further from the relatives of one parent of these only.

So the notion of unilineal descent as an integrative principle is replaced by that of consanguinity, and the significance of the affinal principle rests ultimately not on the idea of transactional alliance between groups but of marital alliance between individuals.

A conception of kinship as a flow of social behaviour rather than a structural set of positions is of particular relevance to our understanding of social processes. It has long been clear in discussions of social issues that any consideration of the problems of individuals has to be made in the context of family circumstances. But 'family' has been generally understood to be the elementary nuclear family of parent and resident children. What has not been so clear is that in many social circumstances 'family' is understood by the people concerned to include some kin outside the domestic circle. We have demonstrated . . . how significant for individual and family contact are such extra-familial kin ties. They may be very important for the transmission of social values. They can play an important part in the developmental history of individuals. They can provide a very important recreational field, especially for holidays, where small children are involved. They can be of prime importance in periods of transition or life crises—as at the birth of a baby or in sickness. They can influence critical decisions—about migration to a new job or choice of schools for children. They can afford support or they can depress by criticism when highly personal emotional issues arise, such as choice of a marriage partner or change of religion. They can provide regular material for sociable activity and help thereby to maintain individuals in viable social relationships. Conversely, by too active interference with members of the family—or too marked withdrawal from interest—such kin may help to stimulate tension and conflict, and contribute to the social deterioration of the individuals to whom they are related.

Our material has gone to show that in the middle-class society we have been examining the significance of extra-familial kinship is expressive rather than instrumental. Although concrete assistance is of considerable importance—in helping towards choice of school or job, giving financial aid or performing small services, as for aged parents—it is primarily as a means towards fuller expression of a personality that such kinship ties are maintained. Moral obligations are recognized in this wider kin field, but they are relatively unformalized and so allow a great deal of selectivity in their fulfilment. This in turn involves some degree of uncertainty not only as to what may be legitimately claimed from kin, but also as to the extent to which such claims will be acknowledged and acted upon. This means that there is very little to put forward in the way of clearcut principles in this field which will apply to particular cases. Statistical regularities can be indicated but to understand the operation of family and kinship in any one case specific enquiry must be made.

The Role of Voluntary Associations in West African Urbanization

KENNETH LITTLE

The voluntary association represents yet another unit of study familiar to urban anthropology. Little's now-famous article was one of the earliest to emphasize the significance of such associations for the process of urbanization. He clearly demonstrates their broad adaptive potential, their ability to fill a host of wide-ranging functions from tribal or ethnic identity reinforcement to mutual aid, trade control, and recreational outlet. He distinguishes among three broad types of voluntary associations, ranged in a rough continuum from traditional-oriented through traditional-modern, to modern.

By and large, Little views the functions of such groups as largely accultura-tive—aids to easier urbanization for migrant groups used to more primary rela-tionships in rural homelands. In his concluding remarks, he tends to see little need for voluntary associations in already-urbanized, nonmigrant cities. Associa-tions, rather, tend to develop in an "urban population which is largely im-migrant, unstable, and socially heterogenous." At the same time, this does not help explain why voluntary associations should flourish long after the most traumatic acculturative stages have passed.

Introduction

Taken as a whole, the West African region was relatively unaffected by the modern world until the end of the nineteenth century. Modern development of the hinterland began with the British adoption of trusteeship as colonial policy and with the British and French realization that these territories consti-tuted an expanding market for imported goods as well as important sources of mineral and raw materials needed by the metropolitan country. The French were also concerned with the question of military manpower. These factors were finally crystallized by World War II and the events following it. The British war effort demanded greatly increased supplies of palm kernels, cot-ton, cocoa, and other locally grown products as well as hides, tin, iron ore, etc., which the colonial governments concerned were required to stimulate (cf. Fortes, 1945:205–219). Since the war there have been resettlement schemes, new industries and constructional projects have been instituted, and there has been a general improvement in communications by road, rail, and air. With the strategic implications of West Africa in the struggle against Communism also becoming manifest, political development has also gone on

"The Role of Voluntary Associations in West African Urbanization." Reproduced by permission of the American Anthropological Association from the *American Anthropologist,* **59**:579–596, 1957.

very rapidly, and there has been a corresponding expansion of education and the social services.

The consequence of all these technical and other changes is that there are now many more different modes of life and ways of earning a living than existed in West Africa some fifty years ago. It also goes without saying that its inhabitants have acquired a taste for the material elements of Western civilization, including consumer goods of every possible kind. In addition to new economic incentives, Western interests ranging from Christianity and nationalism to football and ballroom dancing have also been generated on a wide scale. In short, there has been produced the kind of phenomenon which anthropologists have customarily studied under the heading of culture contact, or acculturation. This term, however, is not precise enough for purposes of present analysis. First, many of the principal agents of cultural change nowadays are Africans themselves, and second, many Western ideas, practices, and procedures have already been fully assimilated to African culture. Africans became important as "acculturative agents" about the middle of the nineteenth century when Western-educated Creoles from Sierra Leone went off evangelizing and trading down the Coast. All the way from the Gambia in the west to the Congo in the south they constituted, in many cases, little oases of westernized culture. Consequently, although much of the traditional life has disintegrated, new forms of social organization have arisen out of the older structure. There are, moreover, considerable differences in the extent to which given peoples and groups of Africans have undergone so-called detribalization, and it is rare to find whole communities which have completely severed all traditional loyalties and obligations. More often is it the case, as I propose to show, that the African individual moving out of the tribal area continues to be influenced by tribal culture. In other words, instead of viewing the contemporary West African situation in terms of the juxtaposition of two entirely different cultures, we shall do better to conceive it as a process of adaptation to new circumstances and conditions. Cultural contacts still go on, but between westernized Africans and other Africans, as well as between Westerners and Africans; so that the changes occurring are no different in kind from those within a single society (cf. Little, 1953:4).

The Urbanization of West Africa

What, in effect, this transformation of West Africa involves is a social process somewhat analogous to the social changes that resulted in the urbanization of Western Europe during the nineteenth century. Western contact with Africa, like the Industrial Revolution in Europe, has created new social and psychological needs which life in the countryside is rarely able to satisfy. The consequence is a tremendous migration of men and women to the towns, and to places where money can be earned to pay taxes, to provide bridewealth, and to buy manufactured goods and appliances.

Many of these people are in search of a higher standard of living in the shape of the more up-to-date amenities and better housing as well as the higher income that the town can offer. But this is not the only motivation. A large number of the younger men are looking for further educational opportunities, or are hoping to start a fresh career. Others move as a means of escaping from the restrictions of village life, and some of the younger girls, as well as the boys, out of love of adventure and desire for fresh experiences (cf. Balandier, 1955a). As Fortes has written in reference to the Gold Coast: "Labour, enterprise, and skill are now marketable in their own right anywhere in the country. . . . People feel that there is little risk in moving about, especially if, as appears to be the case with most mobile elements, their earning capacity is low. A clerk getting £2.10 a month feels that he cannot go much lower if he moves" (Fortes, 1947:149–179). The development of motor transport, in the shape of the ubiquitous lorry, is an important factor in these respects. Not only has it greatly increased local mobility between town and town, and between town and surrounding countryside, but it has created a new and influential social role—that of the lorry-driver, as a go-between between the urban labor market and the rural village.

Most of this migration is in the direction of towns already established as large centers of Western commerce and administration, of the rapidly growing ports, and of places where mining and other industries are being developed. Its effect has been to swell the population of such places far beyond their previous size, as well as to convert a good many villages into urban areas. For example, the principal towns of Senegal in French West Africa increased their populations by 100% between 1942 and 1952 and those of the French Ivory Coast by 109% during the same decade. In the Gold Coast there was an increase of 98% in the populations of the five largest towns between 1931 and 1948 (Balandier, 1955b). Cotonou in Dahomey grew from 1100 in 1905 to 35,000 in 1952 and Lunsar, in Sierra Leone, which was a village of 30 inhabitants in 1929, has a population today of nearly 17,000 (Lombard, 1954:3, 4; Littlejohn, n.d.).

Although urbanism in terms of "a relatively large, dense, and permanent settlement of socially heterogeneous individuals" (Wirth, 1938) is not a general characteristic of traditional life, it is far from being a unique phenomenon in West Africa. In 1931, some 28% of the Yoruba population of Western Nigeria lived in 9 cities of over 45,000 inhabitants, while a further 34% lived in cities of over 20,000 inhabitants (Bascom, 1955). However, what distinguishes the "new" African city—"new" in the sense, as Georges Balandier points out, that they were built by European colonists—from traditional urbanism is that a large part of its population is industrial, depending upon the labor market for a living. This is particularly evident in the case of towns of recent growth. In Cotonou, for example, some 10,000 persons out of a population of some 35,000 are in wage employment (Lombard, 1954).

A further point is that the modern town is much more heterogeneous. It has groups of professionals, office workers, municipal employees, artisans, etc., and in addition to its indigenous political and social segmentation, it also accommodates a large proportion of "strangers." Not only do the latter frequently outnumber the native inhabitants of the town, but they include a wide diversity of tribes. For example, Kumasi, although the capital of Ashantiland, contains as many non-Ashantis as Ashantis; Takoradi-Sekondi contains representatives of more than 60 different tribes (Busia, 1950); and less than 10% of the inhabitants of Poto-Poto, one of the three African towns of Brazzaville, were born in that city (Balandier, 1955a). In the Gold Coast, as a whole, more than two–thirds of the inhabitants of the big towns have been there for less than five years. A further significant characteristic of these urban populations is the numerical preponderance of young people over old and, to a less appreciable extent, the preponderance of men over women. For example, only 2.4% of the population of Cotonou are over 60 years of age. In 1921, men considerably outnumbered women, but by 1952 the masculinity rate had dropped to 111. In an area of Poto-Poto, on the other hand, where the average age of the population is about 25, there are only 515 females to every 1000 males (Balandier, 1955a).

Voluntary Associations

(a) *Tribal Unions*

From the point of view of social organization one of the most striking characteristics of these modern towns is the very large number and variety of voluntary associations.[1] These include a host of new political, religious, recreational, and occupational associations as well as the more traditional mutual aid groups and secret societies out of which some of these more recent organizations have developed. What generally distinguishes the latter kind of association is its more formal constitution and the fact that it has been formed to meet certain needs arising specifically out of the urban environment of its members. It is also more "modern" both in respect to its aims and the methods employed to attain them. One of the best illustrations of these points is provided by certain tribal associations of an extraterritorial kind, known in Nigeria and the Gold Coast as Tribal Unions.

These tribal unions range from little unions, consisting of a few members of the same extended family or clan (Aloba, 1954), to much larger bodies like the Ibo State Union which is a collection of village and clan unions. In Nigeria, these associations were originally formed by Ibo and other migrants from Eastern Nigeria to protect themselves from the hostile way in which they

[1] Michael P. Banton (n.d.) estimates that some 130 registered societies were in existence in Freetown in 1952. The number of unregistered societies is unknown. Pierre Clément (1956:470–471) reports some 62 "authorized" and "unauthorized" societies from Stanleyville, Belgian Congo. There are very few data concerning individual participation, although J. Lombard (op. cit.) reports of Cotonou that out of 35 persons who belonged to one or more associations, 20 belonged to regional groups, 17 to professional associations, 13 to political groups, 3 to musical societies, 1 to an athletic club.

were received when they took jobs as policeman, traders, and laborers in the towns of the West and the North. Their aim is to provide members with mutual aid, including support while out of work, sympathy and financial assistance in the case of illness, and the responsibility for the funeral and the repatriation of the family of the deceased in the case of death. The main raison d'etre, however, is that of fostering and keeping alive an interest in tribal song, history, language, and moral beliefs, and thus maintaining a person's attachment to his native town or village and to his lineage there. In furtherance of this sentiment, money is collected for the purpose of improving amenities in the union's home town and to provide its younger people with education. Social activities include the organization of dances on festival days and of sports meetings and games for their young people. Some of these unions also produce an annual magazine, called an Almanac, in which their members' activities are recorded (Offodile, 1947:937, 939, 941).

Associations based upon membership of the same ethnic group also exist in French and Belgian Africa where they perform somewhat similar functions. In Cotonou, for example, such groups welcome and look after persons newly arrived from the country. They provide a means whereby both the old people and the "evolué" can keep in touch with their rural relatives and friends. Each such association has an annual feast and celebration which brings together everyone from the same region. It is also a means of helping the needy and aged members of the group (Lombard, 1954).

In Nigeria there have also been developed home branches of the tribal union abroad; and as a final step, State unions have been created, comprising every union of members of the same tribe. It is not surprising, therefore, that these Nigerian tribal unions have obtained a power and influence far beyond their original objectives. The larger unions have played an important part in the expansion of education. They offer scholarships for deserving boys and girls and run their own schools. In some places, the monthly contributions of members for education are invested in some form of commercial enterprise, and appeals for money to build schools seem to meet with a particularly ready response. One observer claims that he saw an up-country union raise in six hours and in a single meeting over £16,000 for such purposes. Some higher education overseas has also been provided, and several leading members of the Nigerian Eastern House of Assembly owe their training in British universities to State union money (Aloba, 1954). Even more ambitious plans have included the building of a national bank where people can obtain loans for industrial and commercial purposes. In this connection, some unions have economic advisers who survey trade reports for the benefit of members (Offodile, 1947). These tribal unions also serve a number of important political purposes and are recognized as units for purposes of tax collection. In addition to pressing local authorities for better roads, dispensaries and hospitals, and other public amenities, they have been a powerful force in the democratizing of traditional councils; in the multitribal centers they were for many years the recognized basis for representation on Township Advisory Boards or Native

Authority Councils. They have also provided a forum for the expression of national politics and for the rise to positions of leadership of the younger educated element (Coleman, 1952).

(b) Friendly Societies

In addition to the tribal union, there are also a large number of tribal societies where objectives are limited to mutual aid and benefit. One of the most complicated of these organizations is run by the wives of Kru immigrants in Freetown. This kind of society is divided into three classes. A member pays an admission fee of one guinea and enters the class of least importance. He or she may subsequently be promoted to a higher class and in this event will be expected to make members of that class a present of several pounds. On his or her death, the relatives receive a sum of money commensurate with the deceased person's status. These societies endeavor to develop a high esprit de corps and have been known to impose fines of as much as £20 on members guilty of unfriendly conduct toward each other (Banton, 1956).

Kru men go to sea for a living and so the members of their societies are divided into "ships," named after various recent additions to Messrs. Elder Dempster's fleet, instead of classes. The Kru also have so-called "family societies" comprising the migrant members of a particular class, or *dako* (a small local federation of patriclans). These groups also provide bereavement benefits. In Freetown there are also a number of traditional organizations, including so-called secret societies and dancing groups, which provide funeral expenses, presents, and entertainment for members when they marry. The congregations of mosques, too, usually have what is loosely called a *Jama Compin* (Compin = Krio, "Company") whose members help each other over funerals. Up country, another Moslem group, composed of women, endeavors to intervene in domestic quarrels and to reconcile man and wife. In this case, a sixpenny subscription is collected every Sunday, and persons joining as new members have to pay the equivalent of what a foundation member has already paid in subscriptions. Some of this money is disbursed as alms, but most of it is used to provide sickness and funeral benefits (Little, 1955).

A different kind of mutual aid group is the *esusu*, which is of Yoruba origin. Members of the group pay in at regular intervals a fixed sum and the total is given each time to one of the members. This is an important method for buying trading stock, expensive clothing, etc. (Banton, 1956; Bascom, 1952). In southeastern Nigeria, a somewhat similar kind of "contribution club" is divided into seven sections, each under a headman. Each member pays one or more weekly subscriptions. The headmen are responsible for collecting the shares from their members, and when the shares have all been collected, the money is handed over to a member nominated by the headman in turn. The recipient has a number of obligations, including that of supplying a quantity of palm wine for the refreshment of club members (Ardener, 1953:128–142).

A further organization serves all three functions—providing funeral benefits, charity, and helping its members to save. This is the *Nanamei Akpee*, or
"mutual help" society. It has its headquarters in Accra and branches in several
other Gold Coast towns, including Keta. The Keta branch has well over 400
members, the great majority of whom are educated or semiliterate women
traders. There is a monthly subscription of one shilling and when a member
dies, the surviving relatives are given at least £10 towards the cost of funeral
expenses. Money for loans is raised at weekly collections which begin with
community singing. All the women present give as much money as they feel
they can afford, and their contributions are written down in a book which also
contains a list of the society's members, in order of seniority. When the
collection is finished, all the money is given to the member whose name takes
first place; the following week it is given to the second, then to the third, and
so on. Eventually, all members will in this way receive a contribution, though
the process as a whole naturally takes a very long time. However, the man or
woman receiving a collection is also given a list showing the amount of money
contributed by other members. This determines, during later weeks, the
amounts he must contribute himself. For example, if A has given B two
shillings, then B must raise the same amount when eventually A's turn arrives
to receive a weekly collection. In effect, this arrangement means that senior
members, i.e., those who have joined early, receive an interest-free loan,
which they repay weekly by small contributions; those on the bottom of the
list, on the other hand, are saving in a small way, for their own ultimate
benefit. In a period of rising prices, those at the top of the list naturally have
the advantage, but on the other hand those who wait longer may receive more
because the society's membership will in the meantime have increased. There
is an element of chance in all this which adds spice to the normally dull business of saving, and this partly explains the society's popularity. Finally, when
a member falls ill he is visited in the hospital, given small gifts of money, and
so on. At times the society also gives presents and small sums of money to old
and sick people even if they are not members (Carey, n.d.).

(c) Occupational Associations

In addition to raising loans through such organizations as *Nanamei Akpee*,
African market women also form associations in order to control the supply or
price of commodities in which their members trade. Some of the larger markets have a woman in charge, and each of the various sections which women
monopolize, such as the sale of yams, gari, cloth, etc. is also headed by a
woman, who represents them in relation to customers and the market authorities. In Lagos market each such section has its own union, which discourages
competition between women trading in that particular commodity (Comhaire-
Sylvain, 1951). Another women's association is the Fish Sellers Union at
Takoradi-Sekondi. The members of this association may club together to raise

money to buy fishing nets. The group then sells the nets to fishermen on agreed terms. A fisherman who receives a net sells his catches during the fishing season to the creditor group, and the value of the fish is reckoned against the net. In this way, the members are able to obtain the fish on which their livelihood depends (Busia, 1950). Women also associate for industrial purposes. In southern Nigeria, for example, there are women's societies which run a bakery, a laundry, a calabash manufactory, and a gari mill. One of the most interesting of these associations, the Egba Women's Union in Abeokuta, claims a membership of 80,000 women, paying subscriptions of 13 shillings a year. It operates as a weaving cooperative, and runs a maternity and a child welfare clinic as well as conducting classes for illiterate women.

Other occupational and professional associations are concerned with the status and remuneration of their members as workers. Such groups include modern crafts such as goldsmiths, tinkers, gunsmiths, tailors, and barbers, as well as certain trade unions which, unlike government-sponsored trade unions, have come spontaneously into being. One example of these is the Motor Drivers Union at Keta which is now a branch of a nationwide union which negotiates freight rates, working conditions, and so on. Unlike European trade unions, this Motor Drivers Union is an association of small entrepreneurs owning their own vehicles rather than an association of employees. Its main purpose is to look after the interests of drivers generally and in particular to offer them legal assistance and insurance. When a driver is convicted, the Union tries as far as possible to pay his fine; and when a driver dies, the Union provides part of the funeral expenses. There are also smaller sickness and accident benefits. The entrance fee is 14 shillings and there is a monthly subscription of one shilling. In addition, the Union organizes meetings and dances (Carey, n.d.).

The organization of modern crafts, on the other hand, takes on the form of guilds resembling those of medieval Europe. The first rule of all these guilds in Yoruba towns, where many of them have developed, is that every craftsman, whether master, journeyman or apprentice, must be registered with the guild, must attend meetings, and must pay his dues. One of the guild's prime functions is to maintain a reasonable standard of work in the craft. It determines the rules of apprenticeship; fixes prices of workmanship; and settles disputes, whether between master and apprentice or between craftsman and customer. On the other hand, the guild does not undertake to care for its members in sickness or old age; neither does it function as a bank, lending money to members for tools. Most forms of social security are still organized by the lineage—in which the guild members still retain full membership—and not by the guild (Lloyd, 1953).

Unions of a different kind which are also concerned with the status and remuneration of their members are associations of prostitutes. These have been reported from Takoradi and also from Brazzaville. In the latter city, the members of such organizations try to improve their own social and economic position by insisting on a high standard of dress and deportment, and by ostracizing other women who are too casual or too free with their sexual favors. Each group has its own name, such as *La Rose, Diamant*, etc. and is under a leader, an elderly woman, who can set a pattern of elegance and sophistication. Membership is limited and is regulated by a committee. There is also a common fund out of which members in financial straits are helped and their funeral expenses paid should they die. In the latter event, the association behaves as if it were the family of the deceased. Every girl goes into mourning, giving up her jewelry and finer clothes for six months, at the end of which there is a night-long celebration in some "bar-dancing" establishment hired for the occasion (Balandier, 1955a:145–148).

(d) Entertainment and Recreational Associations

A large number of associations are concerned with dancing and musical forms of entertainment. Many of these, such as the drumming companies found in Ewe villages in the Gold Coast, still retain much of their traditional character. A number of groups in Brazzaville also perform traditional music, but on a commercial basis. These societies consist of young men who have formed themselves into an orchestra under the presidency of an older man whose compound they use for the purpose of staging an evening's "social" on Saturdays and Sundays. The public is charged for admission on these occasions and the "band," which goes by such appropriate titles as *Etoile, Jeunesse, Record de la Gaieté*, etc., undertakes outside engagements. The receipts are divided among the members according to their position in the society and anything left over goes toward the purchase of new instruments and the provision of further conviviality (cf. Balandier, 1955a:143–144). Other such associations, which began as simple dancing societies, have developed under urban conditions into a relatively complex organization and set of modern objectives. A striking example of this kind of phenomenon is the dancing *compin* of Sierra Leone. This is a group of young men and women concerned with the performance of "plays" of traditional music and dancing and with the raising of money for mutual benefit. The music is provided mainly by native drums, xylophones, and calabash rattles, and is accompanied by singing. The dancing which, like the drumming, shows signs of Western influence, is somewhat reminiscent of English country dancing. A "play" is generally given in connection with some important event, such as the close of Ramadan, or as part of the ceremonies celebrating a wedding or a funeral. The general public as well as the persons honored by the performance are expected to donate money to the *compin* on these occasions. Money is also collected in the form of weekly subscriptions from the members (Banton, 1956; Little, 1955).

In one of these organizations, which are particularly numerous among Temne and Mandinka immigrants in Freetown, this amount goes into a general fund to cover corporate expenses of the society's activities—rent of yard, provision of lamps, replacement of drum skins, etc. Then, when any member is bereaved, a collection is held to which all must contribute. However, quite an elaborate procedure is necessary before the money can be paid. The bereaved person must first notify the Reporter with a reporting fee. This is passed on to the company's Doctor, who investigates the circumstances of death, for the company will fine any member who has not notified them of a relative's illness so that they can see that the sick person receives attention. The Doctor washes the body and sends the Prevoe (Provost) round to the other members, telling them to gather that evening when they must pay their contributions. When anyone avoids payment without good cause, the Bailiff may seize an item of his property of equal value. The evening's meeting is organized by the Manager. He will bring the company's lamps, for members are under an obligation to take part in a wake which will last into the early hours. At the wake the bereaved person will provide cigarettes, kila nuts, bread, and coffee, and will employ a singer. Another duty of the Doctor is to examine members before admission, and to attend them if sick. The Commissioner or Inspector is the disciplinary officer and he can arrest or eject trouble makers, the Prevoe acting on his orders. The Clerk or Secretary keeps accounts and writes letters, and the Cashier receives from the Sultan for safe keeping any money accruing to the society. The Sultan is the chief executive; his female counterpart, who has charge of the women members, is the Mammy Queen. For the dancing there is a leader who directs it, and a Conductor who supervises the band. There is also a Sister in charge of the Nurses, young girls who bring round refreshments at dances, often in white dresses with a red cross on the breast and the appropriate headgear. If there is no woman Doctor, an older Nurse or Sister may assist the Doctor with the invalids, or the washing of the corpse. There may also be further officials, such as an Overseer, an M. C., a Solicitor, a Lawyer, Sick Visitor, etc. Many of these titles involve no work, but they can be given to honor even the least deserving member and to strengthen his identification with the group's company (Banton, n.d.).

Other groups concerned with recreation range from Improvement Leagues and Women's Institutes to cricket and football clubs. Some of the latter are characterized by such colorful titles as Mighty Poisons, Hearts of Oak, Heroes, etc. (Hodgkin, 1956). Football teams are also run by associations of the former pupils of certain schools, known as Old Boys Associations, which also organize receptions and "send-offs" and sometimes hold evening classes. Most organizations of the latter kind are modeled rather closely on European lines, particularly the so-called "social club." This is constituted for dining and drinking purposes as well as for tennis, whist, billiards, ballroom dancing, amateur dramatics, and other European recreational and cultural activities. For the latter reasons, "social clubs" are mainly confined to the most Westernized section of the population, including well-to-do professionals and businessmen as well as teachers, clerks, and other white-collar workers. Such clubs are open to persons of any tribe, but members are expected to conform to European patterns of social etiquette. Europeans themselves are frequently admitted either as members or as guests. Examples of this kind of institution are the Rodgers Club in Accra, the Island Club in Lagos, and the Bo African Club in Sierra Leone. In the latter association, all official business and proceedings, including lectures, debates etc., are conducted in English. At the weekly dance, which is one of the club's principal activities, the general rule is for the women to wear print or silk dresses (without the head tie), and the men open-necked shirts with a blazer or sports jacket. On special occasions evening dress is worn by both sexes. In addition to its ordinary activities, this club undertakes a number of public functions, including special dances to honor visiting notables. It also entertains the teams of visiting football clubs, and its premises are used for such purposes as political meetings and adult education classes (Little, 1955).

Women, too, have their social clubs which broadly complement those under the control of men. These are very often known as Ladies' Clubs and Women's Institutes. Many of the latter have been formed under the auspices of churches. A large number of literate husbands have nonliterate wives, and some of these women's clubs reflect the sociological situation in that they are divided into "literate" and "illiterate" sections which hold separate meetings. "Literate" activities consist mainly in sewing and crochet work, in practicing the cooking of European and native dishes, and in listening to talks about household economy. Individual literate women give instruction in these arts to the "illiterate" meeting, and in return nonliterate women sometimes teach the literate group native methods of dyeing, spinning, basketry, and traditional songs and dances (Little, 1955).

Women's Institutes are primarily the result of the initiative of educated women. For example, the President and leading officers of the Keta Women's Institute in the Gold Coast are teachers, although the bulk of its membership consists of market women. It is principally a social club, but it has certain other more important interests. For example, it has acted as a "pressure group," intervening with the Urban Council in support of a plan for improving amenities at the local markets. Among other local changes, the women achieved the provision of ambulance services and the employment of a larger number of female nurses at the Keta hospital (Carey, n.d.).

The Organization of Voluntary Associations

Before we attempt to generalize about these voluntary associations, it is necessary to distinguish between three rather different types. The first is still basically concerned with traditional activities, although with some slight modification; in the second type, traditional activities have been deliberately modified or expanded to suit modern purposes; and the third type is wholly modern in organization and objectives. It will be convenient to term these three types respectively "traditional," "traditional-modernized" and "modern."

The function of the "traditional" association is generally limited to the organization of some particular religious, occupational, or recreational interest, such as a cult, a trade, or some form of dancing or drumming. Space unfortunately prevents description of religious associations in general. These exist alongside Islam and the ancestral cult, and according to Hofstra (1955) they may be divided into four categories: (1) Christian churches organized by missionaries, (2) so-called African churches, (3) looser, smaller groups of a syncretistic character, (4) irregularly organized movements of a messianic or prophetic kind. In the traditional type of association some provision may be made for mutual benefit, but this is incidental to the main purpose of the society. Membership in the group is usually confined to persons belonging to the same village or ward of a town and is often related to other traditional institutions, such as an age set. For example, drumming companies among the Ewe are organized on a ward basis, and usually there are three in every ward. The first comprises children up to the age of about fifteen; the second consists of the so-called "young men," ranging in age from about fifteen to thirty; and the third comprises "elders," i.e. the male population over thirty or so. The senior companies usually give themselves names such as "Patience" or "U.A.C." (abbreviation for United Africa Company), and some of these are, in effect, associations of semiprofessional entertainers who travel about the country in search of engagements (Cary, n.d.). Although the organization of such "traditional" associations is generally quite simple and informal, a number of them have adapted to modern conditions by incorporating literate persons as officials and by widening the scope of their function. In the traditional economy of the Gold Coast, for example, each trade or occupation normally had a chief-practitioner who settled disputes and represented his associates in relation to outsiders. This is largely true today, but in addition some of these groups have turned themselves into local branches of a nationwide union. In the case of the goldsmiths, this involved appointing its chief-practitioner as Life-Chairman of the association, while an educated man who could deal adequately with its business affairs was elected President. Similarly, the semiliterate president of the Carpenters Union now has a literate secretary and treasurer to help him (Carey, n.d.).

It goes without saying that the great majority of people who belong to "traditional" associations are unlettered. The number of persons who can read and write or speak a European language is larger in the "traditional-modernized" association, but what mainly distinguishes the latter is its syncretistic character, its relatively formal organization, and the variety of its functions. A particularly striking example of the latter point is *La Goumbé*, a Moslem and predominantly Dioula youth organization for both sexes in the Ivory Coast. This combines the functions of emancipating young women from family influence; assisting the process of marital selection; providing, on a contributory basis, marriage and maternity benefits (including perfume and layettes for the newborn); preserving the Dioula tribal spirit; running an orchestra; and acting as the local propaganda agent for *Rassemblement Démocratique Africain*. It also maintains its own police force (cited by Hodgkin from Holas,

1953:116–131). In addition to a written constitution which embodies the declared aims and rules of the society, this kind of association sometimes has its own name and a special uniform of its own, and generally follows such Western practices as the holding of regular meetings, keeping of minutes, accounts, etc. The wearing of a uniform type of dress is probably more characteristic of women's societies than those formed by men. The women members of *Nanemei Akpee*, for example, all dress in white for meetings, and the practice of appearing in the same kind of dress, including head-tie, necklace, and sandals, is followed by other women's groups on formal occasions. Finance plays an important part in its affairs, and there is a regular tariff of entrance fees; weekly or monthly dues are collected and fines are sometimes levied. These funds are administered by a Treasurer or Financial Secretary, sometimes supervised by a committee which also conducts the everyday business of the association, including the sifting of fresh applications for membership, settlement of disputes, etc. Related partly to the wide diversity of functions performed is the large number of persons holding official positions in some of these societies. Many of these office-bearers, as exemplified by the dancing compin, have European titles, or, as in the case of the Kru women's societies, are known by the native equivalents of such titles.[2] This enactment of European roles, as in the dancing *compin*, is a fairly common feature of associations of the "traditional-modernized" type. It has been termed "vicarious participation in the European social structure" by J. Clyde Mitchell, but as Michael Banton points out (1956), this possibly places too much emphasis on the process of westernization and too little on the independent process of change in the tribal group. An assistant official sometimes has the duty of conveying information about the society's activities to the general public as well as to members. *La Goumé*, for example, has a number of town criers, members of the *griot* caste, to carry news through the town (Holas, 1953).

The organization of the "traditional-modernized" association is also rendered more elaborate by a tendency toward affiliation. This ranges all the way from a fully centralized organization of individual branches to a loose fraternal arrangement between entirely autonomous branches of the same movement. Affiliation of individual branches sometimes seems to be the result of traditional conditions. Thus, the "village-group union" of the Afikpo Ibo of Nigeria is apparently modelled largely upon the indigenous age-set structure of the people concerned (cf. Ottenberg, 1955:i–28). The *Goumbé* movement comprises a number of local "cells" co-ordinated by a central committee, which settles disputes between them and lays down general policy (Holas, 1953). The dancing compin movement, on the other hand, consists of a large number of separate societies which occasionally exchange visits and information and extend hospitality to each other's members, but are otherwise entirely independent. Finally, although membership of these associations tends to be tribally or regionally circumscribed, this is not invariably so. Even tribal

[2] For example, *Chelenyoh*, Secretary; *Weititunyon*, Treasurer (Banton, n.d.).

unions sometimes have persons from more than one tribe among their members. The Benin Nation Club (Nigeria), for example, provides facilities for all natives of the Benin Province (Comhaire-Sylvain, 1950:246 ff.). Several occupational and other groups recruit their members on an intertribal basis, and this also applies to some of the societies run by women.

The "modern" association has already been briefly described in terms of the "social club," and so it will suffice merely to add that its organization is broadly the same as that of any European association of a comparable kind. Like its European counterpart, it is often a medium for social prestige.

Despite their wide variety, one objective common to all types of voluntary association is that of sociability and fraternity. Not only is the serving of refreshments, including such beverages as tea, palm wine, beer, or stronger drink, an integral part of any formal gathering of members, but the latter are expected and encouraged to visit each others' homes, especially in the event of illness or bereavement. Again, although some groups, including certain guilds and occupations, are confined to persons of the same sex, it seems to be a fairly common practice for women to be admitted into associations under the control of men, and for men to be members of certain associations in which women predominate. Some associations organized by men deliberately encourage the recruitment of female members but have them under a more or less separate administration, with the women's leader responsible to the head of the society. A further fairly common feature of all kinds of voluntary associations is the fact that most of their personnel are young people. Indeed, some societies expect their members to retire at the age of thirty (Holas, 1953), and it is rare for persons over middle age to play an active part in their affairs. This, however, is less typical of the "traditional" organizations than it is of the other types of association which, nevertheless, quite often like to have an elderly man or woman as an honorary president. The role of such a person is to uphold the association's reputation for respectability and to help its relations with the wider community. The fact that he is not infrequently a person of importance in tribal society is indicative of the desire of such associations to keep on good terms with the traditional authorities. The size of membership is a more variable factor. It ranges from a mere handful of individuals to several hundred or even thousands, in the case of the larger tribal associations. In the smaller societies, which are often very ephemeral, the amount of support given is probably bound up as much with the personality and personal influence of the leader as it is with the popularity of the institution.

Voluntary Associations as an Adaptive Mechanism

It was suggested earlier that the social changes resulting from culture contact may be seen as an historical process of adaptation to new conditions. Adaptation in the present context implies not only the modification of African institutions, but their development to meet the demands of an industrial economy and urban way of life. In effect, as Banton has shown in reference to Temne immigrants in Freetown, this sometimes amounts to a virtual resuscitation of the tribal system in the interests of the modernist ambitions and social prestige of the younger educated element concerned (Banton, 1956:354–368). The unpublished findings of Jean Rouch seem to give even greater emphasis to this kind of phenomenon, which he has labelled "super-tribalization." Some of the immigrants into the Gold Coast, whom he has studied, have gained sufficient solidarity through their associations and cults to dominate over the local population, achieving monopolies in various trades (cf. Forde, 1956:389). A further important effect of this kind of development, as both Busia (1950) and Banton (n.d.) have pointed out, is to inhibit the growth of civic loyalty or responsibility for the town concerned. Modern urbanism, in other words, is the conditioning factor in contemporary African society as well as the culmination of so-called acculturation. West African urbanism of course differs from comparable Western situations in being less advanced, although it is probably more dynamic. It involves a particularly rapid diffusion of entirely new ideas, habits, and technical procedures, and a considerable restructuring of social relationships as a consequence of the new technical roles and groups created.

Voluntary associations play their part in both these processes through the fresh criteria of social achievement that they set up and through the scope that they offer, in particular, to women and to the younger age groups. Women, and younger people in general, possess a new status in the urban economy, and this is reflected in the various functions which these associations perform as political pressure groups, in serving as a forum for political expression, and in providing both groups with training in modern methods of business. Equally significant is the fact that women's participation in societies with a mixed membership involves them in a new kind of social relationship with men, including companionship and the opportunity of selecting a spouse for oneself. In particular, voluntary associations provide an outlet for the energies and ambitions of the rising class of young men with a tribal background who have been to school. The individuals concerned are debarred by their "Western" occupations as clerks, school teachers, artisans, etc. and by their youth from playing a prominent part in traditional society proper; but they are the natural leaders of other young people less Westernized and sophisticated than themselves. This is largely because of their ability to interpret the "progressive" ideas they have gained through their work and travel, and through reading newspapers and books, in terms that are meaningful to the illiterate rank and file of the movement.

It is, in fact, in relation to the latter group, particularly the urban immigrant, that the significance of voluntary associations as an adaptive mechanism is most apparent. The newly arrived immigrant from the rural areas has been used to living and working as a member of a compact group of kinsmen and neighbors on a highly personal basis of relationship and mutuality. He knows of no other way of community living than this, and his natural reaction is to make a similar adjustment to urban conditions.

This adjustment the association facilitates by substituting for the extended group of kinsmen a grouping based upon common interest which is capable of serving many of the same needs as the traditional family or lineage. In other words, the migrant's participation in some organization such as a tribal union or a dancing *compin* not only replaces much of what he has lost in terms of moral assurance in removing from his native village, but offers him companionship and an opportunity of sharing joys as well as sorrows with others in the same position as himself. (Probably an important point in this regard is the large number of offices available in some associations, enabling even the most humble member to feel that he "matters.") Such an association also substitutes for the extended family in providing counsel and protection, in terms of legal aid; and by placing him in the company of women members, it also helps to find him a wife. It also substitutes for some of the economic support available at home by supplying him with sickness and funeral benefits, thereby enabling him to continue his most important kinship obligations. Further, it introduces him to a number of economically useful habits and practices, such as punctuality and thrift, and it aids his social reorientation by inculcating new standards of dress, etiquette, and personal hygiene. Above all, by encouraging him to mix with persons outside his own lineage and sometimes tribe, the voluntary association helps him to adjust to the more cosmopolitan ethos of the city (Banton, 1956; Offodile, 1947:937, 939, 941). Equally significant, too, is the syncretistic character of associations of the "traditional-modernized" type. Their combination of modern and traditional traits constitutes a cultural bridge which conveys, metaphorically speaking, the tribal individual from one kind of sociological universe to another.

The latter point is also indicative of various ways in which these voluntary associations substitute for traditional agencies of social control. Not only are positive injunctions to friendly and fraternal conduct embodied in the constitution by which members agree to bind themselves,[3] but many associations have rules proscribing particular misdemeanors and what they regard as antisocial behavior. In this respect, the frequent inclusion of sexual offenses, such as the seduction of the wife or the daughter of a fellow member, is very significant. The association also sets new moral standards and attempts to control the personal conduct of its members in a number of ways. For example, the Lagos branch of *Awo Omama* Patriotic Union resolved not to marry any girl of their town so long as the prevailing amount of money asked for bride-

---

[3] "Added . . . is the internal discipline which is often maintained among members of well organized tribal unions. Where there is perfect control of extraneous activities of the members, it is hard to see two litigants in court being members of the same tribal unions. I remember at Makurdi the Ibo Federal Union there had a strict regulation, which was observed to the letters . . . that no Ibo man shall send another to court under any pretext without first bringing the matter to the union for trial and advice. The result of this was that in that town the Ibo deserted the courts, except if drawn there by members of different tribes or by disloyal members of their own union, but this later case is rare" (Offodile, 1947).

wealth was not reduced (Comhaire-Sylvain, 1950). The dancing *compin* will withhold its legal aid from a member unless the company's officials examining the case feel that he is in the right. Also, there are women's groups concerning themselves specifically with the settlement of domestic quarrels, which expel members who are constant troublemakers in the home and among other women. More frequently, punishment takes the form of a fine, but the strongest sanction probably lies in the fact that every reputable association is at pains to check fresh applications for membership (Offodile, 1947:939, 941). In other words, a person who has earned a bad name for himself in one organization may find it difficult to get into another; and this form of ostracism may in some cases be as painful as exile from the tribe.

A final important point is the extent to which disputes of a private or domestic nature, which would formerly have been heard by some traditional authority such as the head of a lineage, are now frequently taken to the head of an association, even when the matter is quite unconcerned with the life of that particular body (Kurankyi-Taylor, n.d.; Offodile, 1947:28).

Conclusion

Theorists of Western urbanism have stressed the importance of voluntary associations as a distinctive feature of contemporary social organization. Wirth, in particular, has emphasized the impersonality of the modern city, arguing that its psychological effect is to cause the individual urbanite to exert himself by joining with others of similar interests into organized groups to obtain his ends. "This," wrote Wirth (1938) "results in an enormous multiplication of voluntary organizations directed towards as great a variety of objectives as are human needs and interests." However, this thesis has not been strongly supported by empirical enquiry. According to Komarovsky (1946:686–698), who studied voluntary associations in New York, the old neighborhood, the larger kin group, might have broken down, but they have not been replaced by the specialized voluntary groups to the extent usually assumed. Floyd Dotson, who conducted a similar investigation in Detroit, also failed to find a wholesale displacement of primary by secondary groups. He concludes that the majority of urban working class people do not participate in formally organized voluntary associations (Dotson, 1951:687–693). Perhaps more significant for the present context is the fact that the same writer found even less participation in voluntary organizations among the working class population of Guadalajara, the second largest city of Mexico (Dotson, 1953:380–386).

The quantitative methods used in obtaining the latter results have not as yet been employed in African towns, so it is impossible to make exact comparisons. Also, the investigations concerned appear to have been made among relatively stable populations. Further study is therefore needed of the two factors which seem to be largely instrumental in the growth of these African voluntary associations. The first of these factors is the existence of an urban population which is largely immigrant, unstable, and socially heterogeneous. The second is the adaptability of traditional institutions to urban conditions. Possibly, it is the existence and interrelationship of these two factors rather than "anomie" which creates the essential conditions for the "fictional kinship groups," which, according to Wirth, substitute for actual kinship ties within the urban environment.[4]

Bibliography

ALOBA, ABIODUN
  1954   "Tribal Unions in Party Politics." *West Africa,* July 10.
ARDENER, SHIRLEY G.
  1953   "The Social and Economic Significance of the Contribution Club Among a Section of the Southern Ibo." Annual Conference, West African Institute of Social and Economic Research. Ibadan.
BALANDIER, GEORGES
  1955a   *Sociologie des Brazzavilles Noires.* Paris, Colin.
  1955b   "Social Changes and Problems in Negro Africa." In *Africa in the Modern World,* edited by Calvin W. Stillman. Chicago, University of Chicago Press.
BANTON, MICHAEL
  1956   "Adaptation and Integration in the Social System of Temne Immigrants in Freetown." *Africa,* Vol. XXVI, No. 4.
  1957   *West-African City: A Study of Tribal Life in Freetown.* O. U. P.
BASCOM, WILLIAM
  1952   "The Esusu: A Credit Institution of the Yoruba." *Journal of the Royal Anthropological Institute,* Vol. LXXXII.
  1955   "Urbanization Among the Yoruba," *American Journal of Sociology,* Vol. LX, No. 5.
BUSIA, K. A.
  1950   "Social Survey of Sekondi-Takoradi." Accra, Gold Coast Government Printer.
CAREY, A. T.
  N.D.   Unpublished study of Keta, Gold Coast. Department of Social Anthropology, Edinburgh University.
CLÉMENT, PIERRE
  1956   In *Social Implications of Urbanization and Industrialization in Africa South of the Sahara.* Edited by Daryll Forde. (Prepared by the International African Institute, London.) Paris, UNESCO.
COLEMAN, J. S.
  1952   "The Role of Tribal Associations in Nigeria." Annual Conference, West African Institute of Social and Economic Research. Ibadan.
COMHAIRE-SYLVAIN, SUZANNE

---

[4] It has been noted in this connection that voluntary associations among Mexican immigrants in Chicago are participated in by only a small minority. Nevertheless, they play an important role which directly and indirectly affects the life of the entire colony (Taylor, 1928:131–142).

1950   Associations on the Basis of Origin in Lagos, Nigeria." *American Catholic Sociological Review,* Vol. 11.

1951   Le travail des femmes à Lagos." *Zaire,* Vol. 5, Nos. 2 and 5.

DOTSON, FLOYD

1951   "Patterns of Voluntary Association Among Urban Working Class Families." *American Sociological Review,* **16**:687–693.

1953   "Voluntary Associations in a Mexican City." *American Sociological Review,* **18**:380–386.

FORDE, DARYLL

1956   Introduction. *Social Implications of Urbanization and Industrialization in Africa South of the Sahara.* Daryll Forde, ed.

FORTES, M.

1945   "The Impact of the War on British West Africa." *International Affairs,* Vol. XXI, No. 2.

1947   "Ashanti Survey, 1945–46: An Experiment in Social Research." *Geographical Journal,* Vol. CX.

HODGKIN, THOMAS

1956   *Nationalism in Colonial Africa.* London, Muller.

HOFSTRA, S.

1955   De Betekenis van Enkele Niewere Groepsverschijnselen voor de Sociale Integratie van Veranderend Afrika. Medelingen der Koninklijke Nederlandse Akademie van Wetenschappen, ofd. Letterkunde, Nieuwe Reeks, Deel 18, No. 14.

HOLAS, B.

1953   La Goumbé. *Kongo-Overzee,* Vol. 19.

KOMAROVSKY, MIRRA

1946   "The Voluntary Associations of Urban Dwellers." *American Sociological Review,* Vol. 11, No. 6.

KURANKYI-TAYLOR, E. E.

N.D.   "Ashanti Indigenous Legal Institutions and Their Present Role." Ph.D. Dissertation, Cambridge University.

LITTLE, KENNETH

1950   "The Significance of the West African Creole for Africanist and Afro-American Studies." *African Affairs,* Vol. XLIX.

1953   "The Study of 'Social Change' in British West Africa." *Africa,* Vol. XXIII, No. 4.

1955   "Structural Change in the Sierra Leone Protectorate." *Africa,* Vol. XXV, No. 3.

LITTLEJOHN, JAMES

N.D.   Unpublished pilot study of Lunsar, Sierra Leone Protectorate. Department of Social Anthropology, Edinburgh University.

LLOYD, PETER

1953   "Craft Organization in Yoruba Towns." *Africa,* Vol. XXIII, No. 4.

LOMBARD, J.

1954   "Cotonou: Ville Africaine." *de l'Institute Français Afrique Noire* (Dakar), Vol. XVI, Nos. 3 and 4.

OFFODILE, E. P. OYEAKA

1947   "Growth and Influence of Tribal Unions." *West African Review,* Vol. XVIII, No. 239.

OTTENBERG, S.
   1955   "Improvement Associations Among the Afikpo Ibo." *Africa*, Vol. XXV,
           No. 1.
TAYLOR, PAUL S.
   1928   "Mexican Labor in the United States." University of California Publica-
           tions in Economics, Vol. VI, VII.
WIRTH, L.
   1938   "Urbanism As a Way of Life." *American Journal of Sociology*, Vol.
           XLIV, No. 8.

Regional Associations: A Note on Opposed Interpretations

RONALD SKELDON

In the paper which follows, Ronald Skeldon takes Mangin (1959), Little, and others to task for overemphasizing the migrant-assimilating functions of voluntary associations. Such associations, he argues, shift in form and function to accommodate the changing needs of increasingly urbanized populations.

The particular debate and even Skeldon's review of it is not the most important question here; rather, what is in point is the degree to which urban studies are in a state of innovative growth. New avenues of research are being initiated, explored, debated, and either refined or rejected in favor of some more generalized and/or precise (and therefore more scientifically powerful) tool. Other debates revolve around the use of General Systems Theory, network analysis, and the utility and definition of certain concepts such as "role," or the most empirically accurate and operationally useful definition of "city." Even the legitimacy of a disciplinary focus such as urban anthropology has been questioned. All of these are generating excitement and growth within the discipline.

Skeldon's note is an excellent example of the kind of "in-house dialog" that goes on among scientists.

The role of regional associations in urbanization has been the subject of recent debate. From the study of clubs in Lima, Peru, Mangin (1959) and Doughty (1969) conclude that their role is threefold: to act as a mechanism to integrate the rural migrant into the urban and potentially hostile environment, to act as an agent to promote hometown development, and to contribute to the social and political integration of the nation. The evidence discussed by Little (1973) from a number of African countries supports the first of

"Regional Associations: A Note on Opposed Interpretations," *Comparative Studies in Society and History* 19(4), © 1977, Cambridge University Press, pp. 506–510.

these contentions. However, in an article in volume 17 of [*Comparative Studies in Sociology and History*] Jongkind (1974), also using data from Lima, has strongly challenged these three supposed roles, finding that they cannot "survive the test of empirical criticism." He argues that the regional associations are composed of elitist, well adjusted and successful migrants and that they are definitely urban institutions, not rural enclaves in the city as Mangin and Doughty have implied.

Both the interpretations of Mangin and Doughty on the one hand and Jongkind on the other fail to consider the role of regional associations against the background of migration from the areas of origin of the migrants concerned. Although Jongkind has sharpened the analysis by examining associations within the framework of the political administrative status of the communities of origin of the migrants to Lima, he completely ignores the spatial and temporal dimensions of migration within that hierarchy. Implicit in the resultant analysis are the two interrelated assumptions that the role of clubs remains constant over time, and that the role of clubs is identical for associations representing communities at different distances from the capital. There is no reason to assume that the function and organization of a club of migrants from a village close to Lima, where migration has been well developed for fifty years and more, will be similar to the function and organization of a club representing a community isolated in the southern sierra from which population movements to the capital are a development of the last ten years.

Migration from any particular village community and for particular socioeconomic groups within that community develops through a series of stages. The earliest movements tend to be circular with migrants returning to their communities of origin after short absences. These periods away from their communities tend to become prolonged as the volume of population movement increases, and migration evolves to what can be termed semi-permanent migration. Permanent migration, the later phase in the evolutionary sequence, varies from a stage during which the migrants say that they will return to their villages but tend to find excuses never to return or to go back only for visits, to a stage during which people are brought up to migrate and all contacts and interest are towards the urban environment (see the idea of a migration fever developed by Lindberg, 1930).

The stages diffuse through the urban hierarchy both vertically and horizontally. The following greatly simplified diagram, which considers only two vertical sections in the hierarchy, describes the general situation at two time periods, T_1 and T_2. For a more detailed discussion of the development of the migration sequences in Peru, see Skeldon (1977b).

At T_1 (in the case of Peru perhaps around 1910) migration to the capital is primarily local with permanent migration developed from settlements down to the level of district capitals and circular migration from local *anexos*. Long-distance movements are restricted to permanent migration from departmental capitals and semi-permanent migration developing from provincial capitals. Movements from distant district capitals and *anexos* consist mainly of semi-

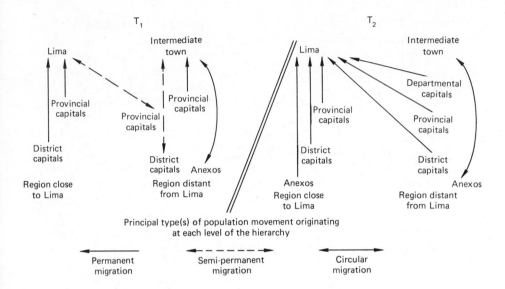

Principal type(s) of population movement originating
at each level of the hierarchy

| Permanent migration | Semi-permanent migration | Circular migration |

permanent and circular local migration to intermediate cities or *haciendas* and plantations. By T_2 (the mid-1960s in the case of Peru) the migration field of the capital has been extended throughout the country and to all levels of the hierarchy, with permanent migration from district capitals and semipermanent movements from *anexos* in remoter areas well developed. The migration from centres close to Lima has increased in volume with permanent movements from all levels of the hierarchy the dominant pattern.

Clubs tend to be formed early in the development of migration to a partiular centre when circular and semi-permanent movements are still an important part of the overall pattern of migration from a community. At this stage, the migrants are still basically part of their community of origin and the club is set up to act as a buffer or mechanism to facilitate integration into the urban environment. At this stage too, there is a great interest in the home area on the part of the migrants, and the club may attempt to promote regional development.

As migration evolves to its later stages of permanent movements, two important changes take place. First, the community of origin is transformed through the exodus of migrants and, more important, through the absorption of the ways and customs of the wider world brought by returning migrants. The contacts between town and country intensify to the point at which relations between a community and the town are better developed than those between that community and its neighbours. When migration has evolved to this stage the role of the club as buffer is irrelevant, as knowledge about the city is freely available and widely diffused within the village and most of the older villagers will have had first-hand experience of living in the city. Children brought up in this environment have little need of a buffer organization on migration to the city.

Second, the destination of migration changes as migration evolves. The earliest migrants from a particular community tend to settle in the central city and it is there that the clubs are founded. As migrants become more established in the city they move out towards the peripheral squatter settlements, or *barriadas* in Peru. This dispersal causes, or at least accentuates, the breakdown of the original migrant communities in the central city. Population movements are closely related to the existence of friendship and kin networks and therefore further migration from that community tends to be direct to the *barriadas* (Mangin, 1960, Elizaga, 1970).

With the disappearance of the initial *raison d'être* of the club through the transformation of the community of origin and the dispersal of the migrant communities throughout the city, the role of the club must change if it is to survive. In these later stages, the club may be developed into a social security body or take on a purely recreational role and will be composed primarily of well adjusted, successful migrants. It would seem significant that one third of Jongkind's sample of association is made up of clubs which form a minority of the total settlement classes, departmental and provincial capitals, precisely those points of origin from which migration has been longest developed. It is to the clubs representing smaller settlements and primarily those from areas distant from Lima in the southern sierra, from which migration has more recently evolved to the capital, that we should look for the roles described by Mangin and Doughty. As migration increases from these communities we can expect the roles of their clubs too to change towards the city institutions such as those Jongkind describes.

The evolutionary sequence of migration outlined here may be appropriate to countries other than Peru, but the rate of diffusion and development of the stages will differ depending on the nature and degree of urbanization of each society. In Papua New Guinea, for example, where the urban hierarchy is poorly developed compared to Peru, it seems that the diffusion of the stages of migration will be much more rapid (Skeldon 1978). Movement to the capital, Port Moresby, is still primarily circular, except from areas which have had the longest contact with Europeans where there is some evidence of a tendency towards more permanent migration (May and Skeldon, 1978). Where tribal or clan loyalties are strong and the perceived social distance between groups is great, as in Papua New Guinea and parts of Africa, the spatial diffusion of migrants throughout the city will be much slower than in the Peruvian case, where a common peasant background favours a fairly rapid integration of groups from different parts of the country. It is in these societies too, where tribal and clan groups are dominant, that circular migration persists and that we should perhaps expect that the buffer or integrative role of the regional association will be more prevalent and permanent than in Peru. In Papua New Guinea, with its recent history of urbanization, regional associations are as yet of relatively little importance. Mutual help is given primarily through the informal and highly flexible kin, clan or regional networks of the *wantok* (literally, "one talk," or someone from the same language group) system or through simple rotating credit associations that are found in large numbers in the towns of Papua New Guinea. As migration evolves, these may become formalized into regional associations of a primary type such as those described for Peru by Mangin and Doughty. Such associations have already evolved among the most developed migrant groups in the country (see Skeldon 1977a).

Rather than viewing the clubs as a rural enclave in the city (Mangin and Doughty) or as a truly urban institution (Jongkind), it would be more profitable to regard the regional association as a reflection of the process of urbanization: they are but an integral part of the change from a society which is primarily rural to one which is dominated by cities. As urbanization proceeds, the role of the association can be expected to change, although the rate of change will vary from society to society. Clearly more cross-cultural research is required before detailed relationships between the role of regional associations and urbanization can be advanced and the simple model suggested here superseded. However, if a static functionalist approach is adopted and the role of the club is considered outside the context of the spatial and temporal dimensions of migration to the cities, opposed interpretations such as those of Doughty and Jongkind can only be the result.

Note. For a more detailed discussion of the changing role of regional associations in Peru, see Skeldon 1976.

Bibliography

P. L. DOUGHTY
   1969   "La cultura del regionalismo en la vida urbana de Lima, Peru," *America Indígena,* XXIX, 949–81.

J. C. ELIZAGA
   1970   *Migraciones a las Areas Metropolitanas de America Latina.* Santiago: Centro Latinoamericano de Demografía (CELADE).

F. JONGKIND
   1974   "A Reappraisal of the Role of Regional Associations in Lima, Peru," *Comparative Studies in Society and History,* XIV, 471–82.

J. S. LINDBERG
   1930   *The Background of Swedish Emigration to the United States: An Economic and Sociological Study in the Dynamics of Migration.* Minneapolis: University of Minnesota Press.

K. LITTLE
   1973   "Urbanization and Regional Associations: Their Paradoxical Function," in A. Southall (ed.), *Urban Anthropology.* New York: Oxford University Press, pp. 407–23.

W. MANGIN
   1959   "The Role of Regional Associations in the Adaptation of Rural Population in Peru," *Sociologus,* IX, 23–36.
   1960   "Mental Health and Migration to Cities: A Peruvian Case," *Annals of the New York Academy of Sciences,* 911–17.

R. J. MAY AND R. SKELDON
   1978   "Internal Migration in Papua New Guinea: An Introduction to Its Description and Analysis," in R. J. May (ed.), *Change and Movement: Readings on Internal Migration in Papua New Guinea.* Canberra: Australian National University Press, pp. 1026.
R. SKELDON
   1976   "Population Migration and Regional Associations: An Interpretation," *Urban Anthropology,* V:233–252.
   1977a "Regional Associations in Papua New Guinea," Papua New Guinea Institute of Applied Social and Economic Research, Discussion Paper 9.
   1977b "The Evolution of Migration Patterns During Urbanization in Peru," *Geographical Review,* LXVII:394–411.
   1978   "Evolving Patterns of Population Movement in Papua New Guinea with Reference to Policy Implications," Papua New Guinea Institute of Applied Social and Economic Research, Discussion Paper 17.

Part V: Research/Term Paper Topics

1. "Ethnography of a Voluntary Association."

   Select one such association (and, of course, justify the choice in your report). Interview members and attend meetings and "functions." Who are the most active and who the least active members? Distinguish between *emic* and *etic* functions of the group. How does the group recruit? How was it formed, and why has it continued? What contacts do members have outside the structure of the group? In what ways is it urban?

2. "Typology of Voluntary Associations."

   Identify all of the voluntary associations in your town (go to the city room of your local newspaper; they probably have a file on organizations which supply them with periodic news releases). Try to ascertain their functions (remember the emic-etic distinction!) and develop your own typology of such associations. How do they reflect the urban locus? An excellent discussion can be generated by comparing your typology with that of another student. What accounts for the differences?

3. "Role in the City."

   Select any general role category you wish (age, sex, religious specialist, etc.) and using the literature, contrast the operationalization of this role category in urban and nonurban societies. Are the differences caused by urbanism, industrialism, or certain aspects of each?

4. "Migrant Type, Family, and Urban Life."

   Using the literature, examine the form and function of family among tribal migrants to cities, peasant migrants to cities, and nonmigrant industrial society urbanites. What conclusions can you draw about the interplay between urban pressures and base-culture in determining the "fate" of the family in cities?

5. "Exclusivity of Urban Networks."

Using network analysis, try to test the ideas of Park and Simmel, with reference to the compartmentalization of urban behavior and independence of urban residents. Select two informants in your town, who don't know each other, and who live in two different neighborhoods. Match the informants by age, sex, and race or ethnicity. Track down as much of their many networks as you can, noting points of contact (if any). What conclusions can you draw about urbanism from your analysis? About the importance of "public places" in urban life (see next section)?

6. "Network and Social Differentiation."

Have three or four students each trace the networks of informants selected for economic, racial, or ethnic difference from one another. Analyze the differences and (if any) points of overlap, commenting on the kinds of linkages that exist between them.

PART

Urban Places

SIX

Places are also common units of urban investigation. Like families, gangs, or voluntary associations, they are fairly well demarcated, with usually clear boundaries. Places are physical things, with some degree of permanency and constancy of sensory impact. Their form, their content, and the organization of their parts both creates and sets limits to the functions they fill. Thus, the study of places is also the study of people, their needs, and their life-styles, insofar as all human action occurs in one place or another.

Places provide excellent entry points for the study of any community. A simple census of them can tell us much about the nature of local roles, types of association, economic complexity, social stratification, age grading, cultural homogeneity, and political structure (to mention but a few). More in-depth analyses of who does and does not use specific types of places; of who uses them by choice and who by default; of use-patterns that characterize limited versus general-function places—all produce solid information about the community and the nature of its inhabitants. Cross-cultural comparison of urban places offers significant insight to basic societal differences in addition to the manner in which different cities organize themselves and their functions in space. The hierarchically arranged concentric circles of neighborhoods, each with plaza, ritual center, and block of elite residences, exhibit key features of pre-industrial city organization and values. The absence of public parks and plazas in some cities suggests special attitudes toward display and interaction with strangers. The presence of singles bars, restaurants, nursing homes, and senior citizen apartment complexes in U.S. cities reflects much about shifting sex roles, marriage patterns, family functions, and status of the aged in our urban industrial society.

In general, urban places differ from rural in several important respects. First, there are more of them. Second, they support different functions. Third, they tend to exhibit some redundancy in that cities not only house a greater variety of places, but also (with some exceptions—such as a main square or central cathedral) a greater number of *each* type. Together, these characteristics reflect an overall community complexity, heterogeneity, and segregation of same-level segments.

This section offers a general treatment plus examples of research in three different kinds of places—a tenement, a city-center neighborhood, and a city-periphery squatter settlement. These works were selected mainly because each, in its way, has become a classic description of one kind of urban place. Subsequent studies of similar units by other scholars have been influenced by their orientation.

Public Places

EDWIN EAMES AND JUDITH GRANICH GOODE

Because of the structure of the city, all urban dwellers come in contact with a great many of their fellows in public places. Usually, public places are focal points of shared identity and concerns. However, they also provide the only means of mutual access to individuals with otherwise divergent interests, ethnic backgrounds, and economic status.

In the paper on mental maps by Gould and White, it was probably noted that cognitive maps of the city used public thoroughfares, rental offices in housing projects, museums, schools, stores, and the like to mark off space. None of the maps identified individual dwellings. In fact, it is unusual that an informant who is asked to draw such a map will include private homes, labeled by the occupant's name. It's as if there is an intuitive sense that "a map of the city" means a map of the locales that would be "significant to anyone of the city."

Eames and Goode, in this excerpt from their book on Anthropology of the City, *show how urban public space is culturally managed, arranged and used differently in different societies and even among different subgroups. One aspect of this kind of analysis (which has received relatively little attention) is the significance of public places to which certain members of the public do not go. Religious buildings, offices, discount stores, theaters, jails, hospitals, courts, libraries, schools, clubs, streets, alleys, parks, bars, restaurants, and even moving places such as taxis or buses are familiar turf for some urban population segments and "off limits" (voluntarily, by default or design) to others.*

In the following discussion, a distinction should be made between contact points for *individual* interaction and contact points at the *group* level of organization. All the situations discussed fall somewhere on a continuum between bringing individuals together as isolates and bringing them together as representatives of particular urban components. A similar continuum can be envisioned between places and events that serve only sporadic linking functions and those that are so regularly integrative that they spin off permanent formal structures.

We are using the notion of situations to differentiate between them and more formal aspects of social structure. Such spatial or temporal foci are part of the permanent urban scene, but are less explicitly recognized as serving an integrative function than the formal associations that exist for this purpose. This is true even when we look at such institutions as schools, hospitals, or government agencies, for we are looking at these institutions as places that informally bring urban components together, rather than as objects of study

Edwin Eames, Judith Granich Goode, *Anthropology of the City: An Introduction to Urban Anthropology*, © 1977, pp. 218–230. Reprinted by permission of Prentice-Hall, Inc., Englewood Cliffs, New Jersey.

themselves. We are not concerned—as are educational, medical, or legal anthropologists—with the internal organization of these institutions, their sub-
cultures, their success or failure in achieving their goals, or their rules for patterned interaction. We are only concerned with them as settings within which
diverse elements of the city are brought into close, regular contact. We are
concerned with the effect of the urban on these institutions and their effect on
urban integration in the informal, situational sense—not in the way they are
supposed to be integrative (their formal reason for being), but in the way they
accidentally bring people together.

In any urban center, there are areas in which large numbers of individuals
who are not known to one another are present. Actually, a simple division can
be made between private space and public space. Private space would then
be those areas in which domestic activities take place. Public space would
consist of all other areas where access is not controlled. Vatuk, in her study of
family life in Allahabad, notes the very clear distinction made between these
two arenas of interaction.[1] Provencher also points out how density in the
urban residential space in Malaysia has led to an accentuation of the difference between public and private space. Here, physical barriers to sight and
sound are used as much as possible to separate the two arenas, but because of
density, these are supplemented by formal rules of etiquette, which lead to
conventions about ignoring or overlooking certain visual and aural events.[2]
Sometimes even within household space, such distinctions are maintained.
Based upon Chinese households in Hong Kong, Singapore and George Town,
Malaysia, Anderson suggests that the Chinese manage space and interpersonal relations in a way that minimizes the potentially negative effects of
crowding. Space within the house, which is shared by several unrelated families, is carefully segregated into public and private areas. Members of families
living in the same house are not required to interact with one another with a
high degree of emotional intensity. Status is clearly defined, and role relationships are patterned and predictable. Children can be, and are, disciplined
by any adult. Finally, individual privacy and isolation are not highly valued.
These cultural responses to crowding do not completely eliminate conflict and
stress, but do much to minimize them.[3]

In the domain of public space, there are certain distinctions that can be
made. The public arena of the lanes in a neighborhood are different from the
major thoroughfares, which serve as neighborhood boundaries. Suttles makes
the same distinction in discussing the Addams area of Chicago. Some public
spaces are not as open to free access as others. Some are socially bounded,
that is, there are strict rules governing the interactions taking place, and people who do not know the rules are frequently ignored, ridiculed, or kept out-

[1] Sylvia Vatuk, *Kinship and Urbanization* (Berkeley: University of California Press, 1972).

[2] Ronald Provencher, "Comparisons of Social Interaction Styles: Urban and Rural Malay Culture," in
T. Weaver and D. White (eds.), *The Anthropology of Urban Environments*, Society for Applied Anthropology Monographs, 1972.

[3] E. N. Anderson, Jr., "Some Chinese Methods of Dealing with Crowding," *Urban Anthropology*, 1
(1972), 141–50.

side.[4] Several segments of the urban social structure may regularly interact in these places, as in ethnically heterogeneous neighborhoods or occupationally heterogeneous marketplaces, but the localized rules for such interactions are known only to regulars in these spatial areas.

Within the larger context of the city as a whole, there are recognized areas in which *strangers* interact, and the rules of behavior are more diffuse and generalized.[5] In all of these cases, urban ethnography is a potential source of information that has not been heavily emphasized by anthropologists. It is an area where several disciplines have done exemplary interdisciplinary work. Geographers, and social psychologists, and ethnomethodologists within sociology have been particularly active in this area, but they often miss the cross-cultural perspective or the perspective gained from long-term relationships with informants. Certainly the work of Goffman has been an extremely important component in the study of "stranger" interaction in public places.[6]

Mitchell was one of the first anthropologists to point out the uniqueness of public spaces in African urban centers. He says:

There are, of course, many of these situations in the daily life of a large town, which is populated by people from many different tribes and where neighborhoods are always changing in composition. They may occur in urban crowds, in beer-halls, in markets and so on. Here town-dwellers tend to categorize people in terms of some visible characteristic and to organize their behavior accordingly.[7]

Berreman has developed a list of public places of interaction for an Indian city. The object of his research was to develop a comprehensive inventory of social categories that people use in identifying strangers. In order to develop such a list, it was essential for him to participate, observe, and interview others in situations that maximized the degree of strangeness and the fleeting or transitory nature of contact. The places observed were: teashops, retail stores, barber shops, wholesale markets, hospitals, recreation areas, political rallies, public transportation depots, and stalls of sidewalk vendors. He also included some of the quasi-public arenas . . . with more controlled access, such as residental areas, crafts work places, and small factories. The teashop, which figured so significantly in this study, has as its analogue the bar, cafe, beerhall and other types of eating and drinking places found all over the world.

Berreman notes that a variety of cues are used in the attempt to categorize others that are primarily geared toward converting an anonymous stranger into an incumbent in a specific social category. Once this is done, the rules for social interaction are understood, and one is comfortable about knowing what

---

[4] G. Suttles, *The Social Order of the Slum* (Chicago: University of Chicago Press, 1968).

[5] For a discussion of the "stranger" phenomenon and its implications for urban social structure, see David Jacobson, "Social Control and Urban Social Order," a paper delivered at the 72nd Annual Meetings of the American Anthropological Association, 1973.

[6] E. Goffman, *Behavior in Public Places* (New York: Free Press, 1966).

[7] J. Clyde Mitchell, "Theoretical Orientations in African Urban Studies," in M. Banton (ed.), *The Social Anthropology of Complex Societies* (London: Tavistock Publishers, 1966), p. 52.

behavior is appropriate. Berreman notes that the specificity of categorization varies from one situation to another, depending on how transitory and fleeting the contact is. Specificity also depends on the status of the individual doing the categorizing; finer distinctions are drawn when the person doing the categorization is looking at someone perceived to be close in status. Although many designations are based upon traditional categories (caste, religion, place of origin), there are newer relevant categories like "officeworker-clerk" or "big man" (executive), which are based on urban occupations. Frequently, the cues used in the designation of others are derived from clothing styles, hair style, language, general posture, bearing, or movement style.[8]

In the categorization of others who are strangers, these cues may be accidentally misinterpreted or deliberately counterfeited. This uncertainty makes such interactions subject to an inherent wariness and mistrust. As Gomperz has pointed out, language is the most difficult of these symbolic codes to counterfeit or manipulate.[9]

Barnett mentions, in passing, a clear-cut example of the effect on behavior of the existence of public places where anonymity is anticipated. A relatively high caste association president wanted to see a popular movie. Since all the more expensive seats were sold, he had to buy a cheaper ticket. During the performance, he became aware of the fact that a low caste individual who performed menial services for him was sitting next to him. This compromised his ritual purity as a high caste member. As the servant became aware of the situation, he (the servant) got up and left. Such an event could only take place in the city. In the rural area, one knows how to avoid contact with lower caste individuals, but in the city, it seemed "safe" to buy a cheap ticket since anonymity was expected.[10]

Even in such public places as pornography stores, customers perceive the situation as less than anonymous and are still constrained by many social norms. They develop elaborate techniques to hide their identities, activities, and purchases.[11]

An even more tenuous kind of stranger interaction has been studied between people who pass each other in the streets or on transport vehicles; these include studies of walking patterns on crowded streets, and patterns of eye contact avoidance in subways. These contacts have almost no implication for social life and are of concern mainly to those interested in designing public space. Architects and design experts who wish to insure fast traffic flow or minimize levels of psychic discomfort may be interested in these studies, but

[8] G. Berreman, "Social Categories and Social Interaction in Urban India," *American Anthropologist*, 74 (1972), 567–87.

[9] Charles A. Ferguson and John Gomperz (eds.), *Linguistic Diversity in South Asia* (Bloomington, Indiana: Indiana University Research Center in Anthropology, Folklore and Linguistics, Publication No. 13, 1960).

[10] Steve Barnett, "Urban Is as Urban Does: Two Incidents on One Street in Madras City, South India," *Urban Anthropology*, 2 (1973), 120–60.

[11] David A. Karp, "Hiding in Pornographic Book Stores: A Reconsideration of the Nature of Urban Anonymity," *Urban Life and Culture*, 1 (1973), 427–51; Margaret R. Henderson, "Acquiring Privacy in Public," *Urban Life and Culture*, 3 (1975), 446–55.

they have little implication for understanding the social construction of cities. As an example, Milgram makes some general observations of New York City public behavior, in which strangers literally engage in combat for seats on trains and constantly bump each other on crowded sidewalks. As a general indication of the level of social interaction in densely populated cities, Milgram notes that an office-worker in the heart of Manhattan has potential contact with 220,000 others within a walking time of ten minutes.[12] These kinds of studies tend to lack the anthropologist's concern with the background and social context of the actors, which he would derive from long-term ethnographic contact.

Eating and Drinking Establishments

The preparation and sale of processed food and drink for large numbers is primarily an urban function. Such establishments may serve a limited segment of the urban population, like a neighborhood bar, or a bar near a work place that has a completely homogeneous clientele, or the Indian bars described by Price.[13] These establishments, although public, are in fact "closed" to outsiders in that a variety of social mechanisms are used to exclude outsiders. Others, while tending to be exclusive in their clientele, are more open to access by outsiders. Still others are located at juncture points, and thus tend to bring in a variety of urban components. Finally, there are those in centralized areas, which draw from the entire urban center.

Most of these establishments combine sociability with diverse items of food and drink. If they serve several classes, occupational status communities, ethnic groups, or neighborhood representatives, there may be a tendency for each segment to maintain social distance from the others and avoid interaction. However, the opportunity is provided to develop some contact or, at the very least, to observe from afar how members of other groups behave in quasi-private, personal interactions.

There is a literature within urban anthropology that deals with bars and taverns. The use of these facilities for leisure-time activities is one of the characteristics of urban life in many parts of the world. Cara Richards has developed a typology for American drinking places describing the salient differences between taverns and middle class cocktail bars, local as opposed to downtown bars, and other important differences.[14]

Despite the fact that many bars develop a reputation for serving a particular clientele, the basis of the clientele selection may be such that diverse residential, ethnic, and occupational groups may be brought together. For example, a singles bar or a gay bar may attract a clientele drawn from a very diverse pop-

[12] S. Milgram, "The Experience of Living in Cities: A Psychological Analysis," in J. Helmer and Neil Eddington (eds.), *Urbanman* (New York: Free Press, 1973).

[13] J. Price, "U.S. and Canadian Indian Urban Ethnic Institutions," *Urban Anthropology*, 4 (1975), 35–52.

[14] Cara Richards, "City Taverns," *Human Organization*, 22 (Winter, 1963–64), 260–68.

ulation. Since they exist to develop new links between people, they are obvious arenas for intergroup interaction, conflict, or avoidance.

Jacobson has noted that bars in the city center of Mbale are potential sources of intergroup contact. However, this potential is not realized, since the clientele is relatively homogeneous and represents only the new bureaucratic elite. In this case, financial and transportation constraints, even more than social pressure, act against the use of these facilities by non-elites.[15]

Many bars have a dual clientele. In her study of the cocktail waitress Mann notes that her bar serves a working class clientele until about 7 P.M. and then becomes a college student bar. Periodically, working class people do come in after the change in clientele, but they do not remain long because they see themselves as outsiders.[16] Within the African beerhall studied by Wolcott, a variety of ethnic groups congregated; however, each group has its own location, and interaction was sustained within the group.[17]

In Epstein's discussion of Chanda's activities, there are some drinking situations that link him to others, while in other situations, social distance is maintained. Thus Chanda reestablishes prior contact with a woman who runs a beer hall and who did not even know that he had been living in the city for some time. On the other hand, a drinking party from a different tribal area had no interaction at all with Chanda and his drinking mates.[18]

Gutkind has pointed out that in all of urban Africa, the beer hall is a strategic linkage point for various tribal groups. They were begun as African establishments, largely in response to exclusion from white establishments, and as such served the various ethnic components.[19] In his own fieldwork in a multi-ethnic parish (neighborhood) in Kampala, he describes the importance of the beer bar in linking the many tribal groups. He says, "Men and women of every tribe represented in the parish will sit together and jostle and joke with one another." Men pick up women, play cards, mock Europeans and Asians, and occasionally dance.[20]

In Berreman's study, teashops became significant public arenas for the observation of interaction between a wide variety of segments. There was some selectivity in clientele based upon regular patronage. In addition, in the public displays or advertisements for these establishments, some symbols were used to indicate the generalized identity of the proprietor (Hindu, Muslim, Punjabi).[21]

---

[15] David Jacobson, "Culture and Stratification among Urban Africans," *Journal of Asian and African Studies*, 5 (1970), 176–83.

[16] Brenda Mann, "Bar Talk," in J. Spradley and D. McCurdy (eds), *Conformity and Conflict* (Boston: Little, Brown, and Company, 1974), pp. 101–111.

[17] Harry Wolcott, "The African Beer Gardens of Bulawayo: Integrated Drinking in a Segregated Society." Rutgers Center of Alcohol Studies Publication, Smithers Hall, Rutgers University, New Brunswick, New Jersey, 1974.

[18] A. L. Epstein, "The Network and Urban Social Organization," in J. C. Mitchell (ed.), *Social Networks in Urban Situations* (Manchester: Manchester University Press, 1969), pp. 77–116.

[19] P. C. W. Gutkind, *Urban Anthropology: Perspectives on Third World Urbanization and Urbanism* (New York: Barnes and Noble Books, 1974).

[20] P. C. W. Gutkind, "African Urbanism, Mobility and the Social Network," *International Journal of Comparative Sociology*, 6(1965), 54.

[21] Berreman, "Social Categories and Social Interaction in Urban India."

Denich notes that public restaurants used by the migrants she studied served as a source of recruitment of people into one's network. This was one place to make friends who were *not* ex-villagers or coworkers of the migrant.[22]

A study of East Indians (Punjabis) in England indicated that the pub was a vital institution for both British host and Punjabi migrant; however, the patterns of pub-related behavior varied for the two groups. The British population tended to select a neighborhood pub and spend the entire evening there. On the other hand, the Punjabis tended to "pub hop" and visit several during the course of the evening. Much of the movement was in small groups. Another significant difference between the two groups was that British men were sometimes accompanied by women to the pubs, while Punjabi men never brought their women.

Pub monopolization was a frequent complaint heard from the British, who saw many of their pubs being taken over by the Indians. On the other hand, many Indians complained of discriminatory behavior on the part of the pub-keeper. One complaint often heard was that the British pub tenders used different glasses to serve Indians. There was no dispute over short measure, but the symbolic meaning of the different pint glasses was considered important. Stereotypes about Indian behavior were frequently based upon observations made in pubs where the two groups co-existed. These were among the most significant contact points.[23]

A report of the conclusions derived from a study of bars in the San Diego area by forty anthropology students stated that ". . . it learned almost nothing about bars except that bargoers can't be stereotyped" and ". . . all types of persons go into bars at one time or another . . ." and that drinking was secondary to a wish to "meet with people and escape the daily routine."[24] It seems unfortunate that the emphasis was upon the study of bars as closed and isolated units, rather than upon the bar as a potential juncture between groups in San Diego. They were searching for "*The* Culture of Bar Life in San Diego"—as if there were such a culture. Obviously, there is no typical bargoer; whatever generalizations can be made have to be limited to particular types of bars or types of users. The differences in bars and the styles of use for various groups under particular circumstances are what is important in understanding bars as "middle places" in a city.

There are several reasons why bars can serve as feasible units of ethnographic research. They are public places where access is supposed to be relatively open. In many cases, the anthropologist is not an intrusive figure, at least initially. Furthermore, the bar often brings together diverse segments of the urban structure. Behavior in bars is informal and personal, making it possible to observe private behavior in a quasi-public setting. A wide range of ac-

[22] B. Denich, "Migration and Network Manipulation in Yugoslavia," in R. Spencer (ed.), *Migration and Anthropology* (Seattle: University of Washington Press, 1970), pp. 133–48.
[23] Research on Punjabi migrants in Wolverhampton, England was conducted during 1969 and 1970. Researchers were Edwin Eames and Howard Robboy, Research was supported by a study leave from Temple University and N.I.M.H. Grant Number DHEW-IR03-MH 18799-01.
[24] "San Diego Barflies," *New York Post*, February 19, 1976, p. 3.

tivities and conversations about significant social topics are typical in this context for sociability.

Other Leisure-Time Places

In addition to bars, there are a number of other localized urban settings that serve as potential places for the mingling of diverse urban components. Most cities in the world set aside open space for parks. These areas attract various elements in the population and, like bars, are amenable to ethnographic research. As in the case of bars, some parks and open spaces are characterized by freer access than others. Some "belong" to [certain] urban components . . . and thus are not junctures, since access is controlled and the area is defended. This is especially true if teen-age gangs control spatial areas. Suttles' description of how various ethnic groups control different spaces in a single neighborhood is a case in point. Thus, it is the more centralized citywide facilities or the spatial areas located on the borders between groups that serve as junctures.

In an attempt to use parks to observe examples of national character, Wolfenstein observed families in parks in Paris, New York, and Vienna. She noted that in the Paris situation, families were self-contained units and children were not allowed to roam; thus the potential for interaction was minimized. In New York, on the other hand, children were encouraged to interact with other children. Although the goal of this research was not to study parks as an urban juncture, it has obvious implications for potential urban ethnographic research.[25]

Birdwhistell has compared public behavior in several zoos around the world, including San Diego, Mysore City (India), and London. Here again, he is examining cross-cultural issues of national character not related to the social construction of the city; but the zoo is amenable to examination of urban junctures as well. In such public places, groups observe each other and form stereotypes based on these observations.[26]

Marketplaces

In every urban center there are large market zones, stores, and street vending areas, which are non-local and serve the entire urban community or many segments of it. Frequently they attract large numbers of people and serve as points of interaction for people who are not usually in contact with one another. In contrast to leisure-time places, these centers contain much

[25] Martha Wolfenstein, *Childhood in Contemporary Culture* (Chicago: University of Chicago Press, 1955).
[26] R. Birdwhistell has produced a film showing different behavioral patterns of visitors to urban zoos in a variety of nation-states.

specialized commercial interaction. However, the sociability component of market area activities should not be ignored. Gossip and news are exchanged frequently, and anthropologists have long noted this function of marketplaces as communication media.

Students of market life have noted that commercial transactions are characterized by a different set of behavioral norms. These norms tend to be more formal and less personal and entail new styles of speech and interaction in haggling and striking a bargain. The aggressive and combative verbal interchanges that are frequent here are not found in other social contexts. This "bazaar behavior" has been noted in cities throughout the world. Similarly, interaction in department stores and other stores is different from other social interaction.

The control of market activities by different segments of the population is extremely important in understanding the relationships between ethnic groups. In certain parts of Africa, marketing activities have become the almost exclusive domain of women, who have gained considerable economic power. In other parts of the world, alien groups such as Arabs, Jews, Chinese, or East Indians control market activities, so that markets are important zones of constant interethnic contact.

In Middle East market activities, it is noted that rug merchants in the process of negotiating a sale will convert the stranger into a kinsman by using fictive forms of kin terms. Bargaining itself has a *social* goal in that both parties try to raise their social status in each other's eyes. Another element in the bargaining process is the attempt to change the situation from a strictly commercial activity into a social event by the serving of tea and other items.[27]

Geertz points out different aspects within the "pasar" or bazaar institution in Modjokuto, Java. He says this traditional market which dominates the town "is at once an economic institution and a way of life, a general mode of commercial activity reaching into all aspects of Modjokuto society, and a sociocultural world nearly complete in itself."[28] He characterizes the relationships between traders and customers as *not* affected by ties or social status. ". . . commercial ties are carefully insulated from general social ties. Friendship, neighborliness, even kinship are one thing, trade is another. . . . The market is the one institutionalized structure in Javanese society where the formalism, status consciousness, and introversion so characteristic of the culture generally are relatively weak. . . ."[29] Thus, the market is a mechanism that breaks down subcultural boundaries and links outsiders together, albeit in an impersonal way.

Oberschall, like Geertz, has studied the market in Lusaka, Zambia. He provides much information about the changing role of the market in the last decades, as well as the sociological characteristics of the vendors and the scale of

[27] Fuad Khuri, "The Etiquette of Bargaining in the Middle East," *American Anthropologist*, **70**(1968), 698–706.

[28] C. Geertz, *Peddlers and Princes* (Chicago: University of Chicago Press, 1963).

[29] Ibid., p. 46.

their capital investment and economic activity. All this was obtained through questionnaire surveys. He is unable to tell us anything about observed market activity. In regard to the question of how customers choose among vendors, he says that besides differences in quantity and quality ". . . there exist personal relationships built up over time between some marketers and steady customers based on kinship, tribe, community of language, neighborliness, supported by favored treatment, credit, and a large *basela* (added weight). Only further research based on prolonged participant observation . . . could provide the required information about the relative importance of various factors."[30]

In Patch's ethnographic work on Lima's central markets, his primary concern is with viewing the market as a self-contained unit. He describes ambulatory vendors, the hierarchy of theft activities, and special areas for second-hand and thieved goods.[31] There is little in it that relates to the relationship between market activities and city social structure. However, the implications for this kind of study are obvious: one could examine how different groups control different activities and how different urban components use the marketplace and relate to the groups therein.

In a recent study, a drugstore on the border of two neighborhoods in Philadelphia was the focus of long-term ethnography. The observer, by watching the activites in the drugstore and developing close relationships with many customers, began to see how this place served as the only safe and sanctioned meeting place between the elderly white population of one neighborhood and the young black population of the other. The store was a hangout for the elderly white males, who were afraid of the streets. The black population also used the drugstore, but mostly for commercial rather than social purposes. The two groups had their only face-to-face contact within the store, which became significant as an intercommunity spatial juncture.[32]

Service Institutions

There are a number of other spatially defined service institutions that may serve as juncture points between components of the urban population. Among these we would include schools, hospitals, and government agencies. Although there have been a large number of studies of these institutions, they have not viewed them as junctures. For the most part, they have been viewed as goal-oriented institutions and have been examined as *isolated* social systems to explore their modes of operation and the success or failure of their delivery of services. In this regard, the studies belong more to the fields of medical anthropology and educational anthropology. Many of the studies done by

[30] R. Oberschall, "Lusaka Market Vendors: Then and Now," *Urban Anthropology*, 1(1972), 107–23.
[31] Richard Patch, "La Parada: Lima's Market," American Universities Field Staff Report, vol. 14, 1967.
[32] Susan Silverman, "The Drugstore: Focal Point in a Changing Neighborhood" (unpublished student project, Temple University, 1973).

other social scientists who specialize in organization theory and bureaucracy do use participant observation techniques to examine the formal, goal-oriented operation of the institution as a closed system.

An example of a study that illuminates the potential integrative role of such institutions is Spicer's study of "The Patrons of the Poor." Spicer describes a situation in which three different types of patrons—one representing a missionary church, another representing the public schools, and the third representing the juvenile probation office—establish their own ego-centered network, with separate clienteles that cross-cut a low income neighborhood. The community in a southwestern American city was ethnically homogeneous, containing Mexican Americans who identified themselves as Indians. These three sets of patrons linked segments of the lower class community to certain institutions of the larger society. In the particular situation described by Spicer, however, these three types of patrons are viewed as disruptive, since they oppose community-wide organization based upon internal leadership. Another perspective would view them as important links to middle-class individuals and institutions.[33]

Since anthropologists are accustomed to developing long-term relationships with informants, and since they are more likely to wish to view the institution from the client's perspective, they might follow their informants into the institution and examine their perceptions and interactions with strangers and representatives of other groups. In effect, this is an extension of Gluckman's situational analysis, which focuses on describing in detail a situation that brings together diverse elements in a single spatial setting. In-depth knowledge gained about the *background* of the interacting elements is then used to explain the interaction and to derive implications for future interaction.[34]

A. L. Epstein has done considerable research on urban courts in the African Copperbelt. He notes that such courts are as concerned with moral and ethical issues as with legal ones. In Luanshya, the African courts handle most disputes involving Africans. Only when a European brings a complaint against an African does the African enter the formal European court. Since the African population is tribally heterogeneous, the courts are set up to reflect this diversity. Thus, each group selects its own representatives to act as judges in the tribal courts. Each case is heard by all the representatives of these groups, one of whom is selected as president. Epstein notes that much is made of customary differences among the tribes by tribal members themselves, but there is an overriding general agreement about what is considered to be proper or reasonable behavior. This generalized agreement allows the court to function in a diverse tribal setting. When a particular element of tribal custom is involved, then the court representatives of that tribe intercede to explain the implications of the custom for the case. Epstein also notes that the courts cannot simply use tribal custom in the settling of urban disputes, since many of the cases involve urban phenomena, for which there are no tribal prece-

[33] Edward Spicer, "Patrons of the Poor," *Human Organization*, 29(1970), 12–20.
[34] Max Gluckman, "Analysis of a Social Situation in Modern Zululand," *Bantu Studies*, vol. 14, 1940.

dents. Thus the court, representing a diversity of tribal elements, must act as a mediating and socializing agency within the urban context.[35]

Lowy, in a study of conflict resolution and the use of courts in Koforidua, Ghana, notes a dichotomy in conflicts between those that focus on money and commerce and those that focus on prestige and honor. Disputes over money are brought to formal courts, whether they are between fellow tribesmen or not. For prestige and honor cases, a combination of courts and private mediators are used. Interestingly enough, Lowy finds no difference in court use based on migrant status, age, education, or occupation.[36]

The potential for the use of courts for study of urban junctures is indicated. Not only is participant observation possible, but court records and informant's memory of cases are available as data for analysis of the court as a setting in which urban components relate to each other.

A Vecindad in Mexico City

OSCAR LEWIS

Buildings are places, too, and the crowded multifamily tenement is almost archetypically urban. For many, it symbolizes urban life. It is a convenient unit of study, with clear physical boundaries and a fairly concise head count.

The following brief selection from Oscar Lewis' famous study of Five Families *in Mexico City is a kind of snapshot of a brief moment in the life of one family and tenement. Lewis viewed the* vecindad *as a town-within-the-town, providing an ambiance of highly personal interaction, much cooperation, and other advantages typical of more rural places. So clear was the physical boundary of his unit of study, however, that Lewis largely ignored interaction between tenants and the city. His approach set the stage for a generation of "poverty" and "peasants-in-cities" studies that dealt minimally with the broader urban context and maximally with what appeared to be a self-contained—and thus ultimately unexplainable—life-style. For a view of the interaction between tenement and town, see Press' holistic study of Seville's vecindades, 1979.*

Between the Street of the Barbers and the Street of the Tinsmiths, only a short distance from the Thieves' Market, stands the Casa Grande. This is a giant *vecindad* or one-story tenement which houses over seven hundred peo-

[35] A. L. Epstein, *Politics in an Urban African Community* (Manchester: Manchester University Press for the Rhodes-Livingstone Institute, 1958).

[36] M. Lowy, "Me Ko Court: The Impact of Urbanization on Conflict Resolution in a Ghanaian Town." In G. Foster and R. Kemper, eds., *Anthropologists in Cities* (Boston: Little, Brown & Co., Inc., 1974), pp. 153–174.

From "The Gomez Family," in *Five Families: Mexican Case Studies in the Culture of Poverty*, by Oscar Lewis, © 1959 by Basic Books, Inc., Publishers, New York, pp. 66–70.

ple. Spread out over an entire square block, the Casa Grande is a little world of its own, enclosed by high cement walls on the north and south, and by rows of shops which face the streets on the other two sides. These shops— food stores, a dry cleaner, a glazier, a carpenter, a beauty parlor, together with the neighborhood market and public baths—supply the basic needs of the *vecindad* so that many of the tenants, particularly those who come from rural areas, seldom leave the immediate neighborhood and are almost strangers to the rest of Mexico City. This section of the city was once the home of the underworld, and even today people fear to walk in it late at night. But most of the criminal element has moved away and the majority of the residents are poor tradesmen, artisans, and workers.

Two narrow, inconspicuous entrances, each with a high gate, open during the day but locked every night at ten o'clock, lead into the *vecindad* on the east and west sides. Anyone coming or going after hours must ring for the janitor and pay to have the gate opened. The *vecindad* is also protected by its two patron saints, the Virgin of Guadalupe and the Virgin of Zapopan, whose statues stand in glass cases, one at each entrance. Offerings of flowers and candles surround the images and on their skirts are fastened small shiny medals, each a testimonial of a miracle performed for someone in the *vecindad*. Few residents pass the Virgins without some gesture of recognition, be it only a glance or a hurried sign of the Cross.

Within the *vecindad* stretch four long, cement-paved patios, or courtyards, about fifteen feet wide. These are formed by wide rectangular cement buildings divided into 157 one-room apartments, each with a barn-red door which opens onto the patios at regular intervals of about twelve feet. In the daytime, rough wooden ladders stand beside most of the doors, leading to low flat roofs over the kitchen portion of each apartment. These roofs serve many uses and are crowded with lines of laundry, chicken coops, dovecotes, pots of flowers or medicinal herbs, tanks of gas for cooking, and an occasional TV antenna. A few feet back, a higher roof that is less accessible and usually bare rises over the main room.

In the daytime the patios are crowded with people and animals, dogs, turkeys, chickens, and an occasional pig. Children play here because it is safer than the streets. Women queue up for water or shout to each other as they hang up clothes, and street-vendors come in to sell their wares. Every morning a garbageman wheels a large can through the patios to collect each family's refuse. In the afternoons gangs of older boys often take over a patio to play a rough game of soccer. On Sunday nights there is usually an outdoor dance. Within the west entrance is the public bathhouse and a small garden whose few trees and patch of grass serve as a meeting place for young people and a relatively quiet spot where the older men sit and talk or read newspapers. Here also is a one-room shack marked "administration office" where a bulletin lists the names of families who are delinquent in paying their rent.

The tenants of the Casa Grande come from twenty-four of the thirty-two states of the Mexican nation. Some come from as far south as Oaxaca and

Yucatan and some from the northern states of Chihuahua and Sinaloa. Most of the families have lived in the *vecindad* for from fifteen to twenty years, some as long as thirty years. Over a third of the households have blood relatives within the *vecindad* and about a fourth are related by marriage and *compadrazgo*. These ties, plus the low, fixed rental and the housing shortage in the city, make for stability. Some families with higher incomes, their small apartments jammed with good furniture and electrical equipment, are waiting for a chance to move to better quarters, but the majority are contented with, indeed proud of, living in the Casa Grande. The sense of community is strong, particularly among the young people who belong to the same gangs, form lifelong friendships, attend the same schools, meet at the same dances held in the patios and frequently marry within the *vecindad*. Adults also have friends whom they visit, go out with, and borrow from. Groups of neighbors organize raffles and *tandas* (informal mutual savings and credit plans), participate in religious pilgrimages together, and together celebrate the festivals of the *vecindad* patron saints, the Christmas *Posadas,* and other holidays.

But these group efforts are occasional; for the most part adults "mind their own business" and try to maintain family privacy. Most doors are kept shut and it is customary to knock and wait for permission to enter when visiting. Some people visit only relatives or *compadres* and actually have entered very few of the apartments. It is not common to invite friends or neighbors in to eat except on formal occasions such as birthday or religious celebrations. Although some neighborly help occurs, especially during emergencies, it is kept at a minimum. Quarrels between families over the mischief of children, street fights between gangs, and personal feuds between boys are not uncommon in the Casa Grande.

The people of the Casa Grande earn their living in a large miscellany of occupations, some of which are carried on within the *vecindad*. Women take in washing or sewing, men are shoemakers, hat cleaners, or vendors of fruit and candy. Others go outside to work in factories or shops or as chauffeurs and small tradesmen. Living standards are low but by no means the lowest in Mexico City, and the people of the neighborhood look upon the Casa Grande as an elegant place.

Number 60, the one-room home of the Gómez family, was the last in the long row in the third courtyard. The latch on the battered door was broken, and the door was held shut at night by placing the ladder against it on the inside. During the day, when the ladder was kept in the patio, the door was usually half-open; Rosa didn't believe in locks because they were "an invitation to thieves."

Inside the dark, windowless room, crowded with furniture, the Gómez family slept huddled under thin covers on a cold January morning. The smells of unwashed feet, sweat, shoe leather, and fried food pervaded the room. Agustín Gómez and his wife Rosa slept on a narrow cot against the right wall, she at the head and he at the foot. Alberto, the eldest son, aged twenty, Ester, the daughter, aged fourteen, and Juanito, the youngest son, aged six, all slept in the big bed which jutted out from the left wall across half the small room. When Agustín and Rosa quarreled, he would leave the narrow cot and exchange places with little Juanito, so that sometimes Ester would awaken in the morning to find that she had been sleeping between her father and her older brother. Rosa was the only one who lamented the crowded sleeping arrangements. She frequently scolded her husband for not building a *tapanco* or balcony, as some of the neighbors had done, so that the boys could sleep "upstairs."

The crowding had been even worse when Hector, their second son, had been at home. But Agustín had thrown him out of the house almost a year ago, and now Hector slept in a tiny room with an old couple in a poorer *vecindad* a few blocks away. Agustín had forbidden his son to come to the house but Rosa had been adamant. "He is my son, not my lover, and he has a right to come here." After that Hector came home for meals and a change of clothing, but Rosa could not count on it because his habits were erratic. If Hector happened to come home when his father was there, they didn't speak to one another.

The kitchen, just inside the front door, formed a passageway to the bedroom. This area had not been roofed when the *vecindad* was built and each tenant had to provide his own roof. Agustín had solved the problem by attaching two sheets of corrugated tar paper to a stick laid across the center, forming a low peak. The front portion was left open to allow smoke from the stove to escape. But it also permitted rain to enter, and during the rainy season the kitchen floor was often wet and sometimes the table had to be moved into the bedroom to keep the food dry. Hanging from the roof as a good luck charm was an infant's shoe that Alberto had found in his bus. On the wall was a calendar with a picture of Marilyn Monroe.

The short left wall of the kitchen was entirely taken up by a gray cement washtub and the toilet. The toilet enclosure, with its half-shutter swinging door, was barely large enough to contain the low, rust-stained stool. It was a flush toilet but the chain had been broken for more than a year and Rosa had not troubled to fix it because there was rarely water in the tank. A pail of water, kept under the washtub, was used to flush the stool a few times a day, and a pile of torn-up newspaper tucked behind the water pipe served as toilet paper. The space was crowded with a collection of rags, cans, brushes, boxes, and bottles piled in a corner. More articles of the same kind, as well as the garbage tin, were stored under the kitchen washtub. Recently, following the example of other tenants, Hector had hung a pink flowered nylon shower curtain to hide the toilet area.

The other side of the kitchen contained the family's most valuable possessions, a new American-made gas range, a white metal cabinet, and a breakfast set consisting of a table and four chairs. Hector and Alberto had presented Rosa with the stove and cabinet on the last Mother's Day, promising to pay monthly installments of one hundred and twenty-nine pesos for two years. Alberto also undertook to pay for the breakfast set at sixty-four pesos a month.

The new furnishings created no small problem in the tiny kitchen. Rosa could not open the oven door without moving the table, which then blocked the front door. But since she used the oven only to store pots and pans and empty soda bottles, it was not too inconvenient. However, there was not enough room to permit the family to eat together.

The West End: An Urban Village

HERBERT J. GANS

Here we see an emphasis on neighborhood as a unit of urban study. The following is the opening chapter of Herbert Gans' now classic description of Boston's West End. Like Lewis before him, Gans views his particular unit as a village within the city. He spent much time living in the area, researching the community as a participant observer. To Gans, the neighborhood is both a part of the wider city and a sociologically coherent unit. Its residents are strongly affected by the neighborhood's wider image, its history, resources, and physical structure.

Slums are particular kinds of urban neighborhoods, and Gans noted that to "the superficial observer . . . the West End certainly had all the earmarks of a slum." He himself was less convinced of its slum status. But what is a slum? To be sure, there is poverty, high population density, abandoned and run-down buildings, an emphasis on street life, but is the West End a slum in the qualitative sense that is often implied by the use of the term? And are there any quantitative criteria that we may use to identify such an area? Gans will not tell us until the concluding pages of the book what his technical considerations and value judgments are. Certainly, however, many residents of areas marked for urban renewal have fought those efforts vigorously—to the utter mystification of administrators, urban planners and others. In a city in which one of the editors of this volume worked, people in a so-called slum area were fiercely insistent that their locale was, as a young mother put it, "a good neighborhood for families, and nice fixed houses." They were indignant when one city official was reported by the media to have called it "a rundown unsanitary, unsafe pile of tenements." How much of the definition of slum and urban decay is "real," and how much ultimately rests on our own attitudes towards the life-styles and living patterns of the inhabitants in the area?

An Historical and Ecological Overview

To the average Bostonian, the West End was one of the three slum areas that surrounded the city's central business district, little different in appearance and name from the North or the South End. He rarely entered the West End and usually glimpsed it only from the highways or elevated train lines that enveloped it. From there he saw a series of narrow winding streets flanked on both sides by columns of three- and five-story apartment buildings, constructed in an era when such buildings were still called tenements. Furthermore, he saw many poorly maintained structures, some of them unoccupied or partially vacant, some facing on alleys covered with more than an average amount of garbage; many vacant stores; and enough of the kinds of people who are thought to inhabit a slum area. If he ventured inside the area, he saw some old people who looked like European immigrants, some very poor people, some who were probably suffering from mental illness, a few sullen looking adolescents and young adults who congregated on street corners, and many middle-aged people who were probably mainly Italian, Russian Jewish, Polish, and Irish in parentage.

To the superficial observer, armed with conventional images and a little imagination about the mysteries thought to lie behind the tenement entrances, the West End certainly had all the earmarks of a slum. Whether or not it actually was a slum is a question that involves a number of technical housing and planning considerations and some value judgments. . . . For the moment, the West End can be described simply as an old, somewhat deteriorated, low-rent neighborhood that housed a variety of people, most of them poor.

In most American cities there are two major types of low-rent neighborhoods: the areas of first or second settlement for urban migrants; and the areas that attract the criminal, the mentally ill, the socially rejected, and those who for one reason or another have given up the attempt to cope with life.

The former kind of area, typically, is one in which European immigrants—and more recently Negro and Puerto Rican ones—try to adapt their nonurban institutions and cultures to the urban milieu. Thus it may be called an *urban village*. Often it is described in ethnic terms: Little Italy, The Ghetto, or Black Belt. The second kind of area is populated largely by single men, pathological families, people in hiding from themselves or society, and individuals who provide the more disreputable of illegal-but-demanded services to the rest of the community. In such an area, life is comparatively more transient, depressed if not brutal, and it might be called an *urban jungle*.[1] It is usually described as Skid Row, Tenderloin, the red-light district, or even the Jungle.

In sociological terminology, these are ideal types, and no existing neighborhood is a pure example of either. Moreover, since the people who occupy both types are poor and at the mercy of the housing market, they often may live in the same neighborhood, erecting physical or symbolic boundary lines to separate themselves. In some areas, especially those occupied by the most deprived people, the village and the jungle are intertwined.

[1] These are purely descriptive terms and should not be taken too literally. They are not ecological concepts, for neither in economic, demographic, or physical terms do such areas resemble villages or jungles. They are terms that describe the quality of social life, but do not definitively identify social structure or culture.

The West End was an urban village, located next to Boston's original and once largest skid row area, Scollay Square. During the early nineteenth century, the West End had been an isolated farm area, almost inaccessible from the North End and the central business district area that then constituted Boston. Later, some streets were cut through and developed with three-story single family homes of various price levels. Following the arrival of Nova Scotian and Irish immigrants, other streets were built up with three- and five-story tenements, until, by the turn of the century, the five-story tenement became the main building type. The structures built in the latter half of the nineteenth century were intended, like those in the North End, for the poorest tenants. Apartments were small and several units had to share bathroom and toilet facilities. The buildings constructed around the turn of the century, however, were intended for a somewhat higher income group. Instead of three- and four-room apartments, there were five- and six-room ones, each with private bath and toilet, and kitchens equipped with a large combination heating and cooking stove. The new and the old apartments were built at high densities—more than 150 dwelling units per net residential acre—as compared today with the 5 to 8 units in the average middle-income suburb. Land coverage was high, 72% of the land being covered with buildings, and, in a quarter of the blocks, buildings comprised over 90% of the land.[2] Some of the streets were shopping blocks with small stores on the ground floor of the tenements. A few industrial lofts that attracted small manufacturing and wholesale establishments were scattered through the shopping streets.

Physically, as well as socially, the development of the West End followed a typical ecological process. The West End is located at the bottom of one slope of Beacon Hill. At the top of this hill are the apartments and townhouses inhabited by upper- and upper-middle-class people. As one descends the slope, the status of buildings and people decreases. The "Back of the Hill" area, once occupied by servants to the Hill aristocracy, now is inhabited by families who moved up from the bottom of the slope, and, increasingly, by young middle-class couples in modernized tenements or converted townhouses who are gradually erasing the social differences between the Back of the Hill, and the Hill itself.[3]

The West End is at the bottom of the slope. At one time, when the Back of the Hill was a low-income settlement, both it and the area below were called the West End. Then, with the widening of Cambridge Street in the 1920s, a physical boundary was created between the two areas that eventually led to the symbolic separation as well. Within the West End, the area nearest to Cambridge Street and the Back of Beacon Hill contained the better apartment buildings, and the two major institutions in the area—Massachusetts General

---

[2] Boston Housing Authority, "West End Project Report," Boston: The Authority, 1953, p. 5.

[3] For descriptions of this area, see Walter Firey, *Land Use in Central Boston,* Cambridge: Harvard University Press, 1947; and H. Laurence Ross, "The Local Community and the Metropolis," unpublished Ph.D. Dissertation, Harvard University, 1959.

Hospital and St. Joseph's Roman Catholic Church. The hospital, traditionally an extremely high status institution, is one of the teaching hospitals for the Harvard Medical School. The church, originally Congregationalist, later became one of the higher status Irish churches, which served Beacon Hill as well.[4] The area closest to Cambridge Street and that fronting on the Charles River was known as the "upper end." Then, as one descended to what was called the "lower end," dwelling units became older and the people, poorer. At one corner of the lower end, the West End fronted on the Scollay Square skid row and provided rooming houses for the people who frequented its bars and eating places. At another corner, there were small commercial buildings which were part of the industrial and wholesaling area that separated the residential portions of the West End from the North End.

Several times during its existence, the population of the West End has changed in a pattern typical of other urban villages. The North and the South End were the primary areas of first settlement for Irish, Jewish, and Italian peoples, in that order. The South End also served the other ethnic groups that settled in Boston, especially Chinese, Greek, and Syrian. The West End had somewhat more distinctive functions. First, it was an overspill area for those who could not find room in the North End; later, it became an area of second settlement for some of the groups who began their American life in the North End. Thus, the West End underwent approximately the same ethnic succession pattern as the North End. In the late nineteenth century, it was primarily an Irish area, with Yankees scattered through the upper end.[5] Then, around the turn of the century, the Irish were replaced by the Jews, who dominated the West End until about 1930. During this era, the West End sometimes was called the Lower East Side of Boston. In the late [1920s], Italians and Poles began to arrive, the former from the North End, and they joined a small Italian settlement that had existed in the lower end of the area since the beginning of the century. Throughout the 1930s and early 1940s, the Italian influx continued until eventually they became the largest ethnic group in both the upper and lower portions of the West End. The changes in population are reflected in data taken from library registration cards.[6] In 1926, the area was estimated to be 75% Jewish. In 1936, however, the library users were 35% Italian, 25% Polish, 20% Jewish, and 20% "miscellaneous."[7] By 1942, the Italians were in the majority.

A Polish church that had been established in 1930 quickly enrolled 250 families. Although it later lost some of these, the congregation was replenished by displaced persons who came into the West End after World War II. Also

---

[4] At one time, it was the church of the Kennedy family, and President Kennedy attended it as a boy.

[5] For a detailed description of the West End around the turn of the century as it appeared to Yankee settlement house workers, see Robert A. Woods, ed., *Americans in Process*, Boston: Houghton Mifflin Company, 1902. For a fictional description of Jewish life in the area in the second decade of the twentieth century, see Charles Angoff, *In the Morning Light*, New York: Beechhurst Press, 1952.

[6] From unpublished reports in the files of the West End Library.

[7] Ibid. Registration figures do not reflect the population distribution with complete accuracy. In all likelihood, Jews are overrepresented among library users, and all other ethnic groups, underrepresented.

there were small Greek, Albanian, and Ukrainian settlements, the latter served by a Ukrainian church located in a tenement. Consequently, proud West Enders were able to claim that twenty-three nationalities could be found in the area. In recent years, small groups of students, artists, and Negroes had come into the West End, some from the Back of the Hill as rents there had begun to rise.

Numerically, the West End was at its height around 1910, when it had 23,000 inhabitants. In 1920, it had 18,500 residents; in 1930 and 1940, 13,000; and, in 1950, 12,000.[8] In 1957, the population was estimated to be about 7000 individuals in about 2800 households. The long-range population decline could be attributed to decreasing family size among the descendants of immigrant groups and to the gradual reduction in dwelling units as the hospital expanded its facilities, and as deteriorated buildings became vacant. Between 1930 and 1950, the population remained constant, at least in total number. After that time, it decreased, partially because young families moved out to raise their children in lower density urban and suburban areas, and because of the announcement in 1951 that the area would be redeveloped.

At the time of the study, then, the population of the West End consisted of the following major groups:

1. *Second- and First-Generation Italian Households.* They included the surviving immigrants—most of them elderly—and the much larger group of second-generation people who were their children, or who had come into the area from the North End. The Center for Community Studies survey indicated that the Italians constituted 42% of the West End's population.[9]

2. *First-Generation Jewish Households.* By 1930, the main Jewish population contingent had moved on to Roxbury and Dorchester. But some of the Jews who had come to America in the final wave of European immigration, 1918–1925, did remain in the West End, maintaining two synagogues, a Hebrew school, and a number of stores.[10] Most of them, however, lived in retirement—some in poverty—and spent their time in visiting, in synagogue social activities, and with their children. The Jews accounted for 10% of the West End population.[11]

3. *First- and Second-Generation Polish Households.* This group consisted of immigrants who came before and during the depression, of second-generation families, and of displaced persons. They comprised 9% of the population.[12]

4. *An Irish Residue.* A small number of Irish families, most of them old people, stayed either because they owned buildings in the area, or because

---

[8] Boston Housing Authority, West End Project Report, op. cit., p. 18.
[9] Marc Fried, "Developments in the West End Research," Center for Community Studies, Research Memorandum A 3, October 1960, mimeographed, p. 5. This, and other estimates from the Center's survey . . . are based on interviews with a 473-person random sample of the West End female population aged twenty to sixty-five.
[10] Most of the West End stores were owned by Jews, as were the medical, dental, and legal offices. These were largely run by second-generation Jews who no longer lived in the West End.
[11] Fried, op. cit., p. 5.
[12] Ibid.

they were active in the Catholic church and parish. They constituted 5% of the population.[13]

5. *Other Ethnic Groups*—Albanians, Ukrainians, Greeks.[14]

6. *Pathological Households.* Each major ethnic group left behind a residue of families or individuals whose social and residential mobility had been aborted either by extreme poverty, or by physical or psychological disability. In addition, a part of the area served to house some of the Scollay Square transients.

7. *Postwar Newcomers.* When young residents left after 1950, landlords no longer could replace the vacancies left by them with tenants from their own ethnic group. In order to fill the buildings, they rented them to anyone who came along. Thus the West End attracted people who came because of its low rents—Gypsies, groups of single men, broken families subsisting on Aid to Dependent Children, and people who fled from the New York Streets Redevelopment project in the South End. Some were squatters who tried to live rent-free in vacant buildings.

8. *Middle-Class Professionals and Students.* The presence of the hospital and the availability of clean, low-rent, and conveniently located apartments attracted a number of nurses, interns, and doctors as well as students from various colleges in the city. They provided a smattering of professional middle-class culture to the area.

9. *Other Hospital Staff.* A number of hospital service workers also lived in the area because of the low rentals and the convenience. Some of these were women, wives of Italian or Polish residents, who worked in the cafeterias, kitchens, and laundries. Some were homosexuals who worked as male nurses in the hospital, and were able to practice their deviant ways in an area which disapproved of them, but which tolerated them grudgingly.

10. *The Artists and Bohemians.* A small but highly visible group of artists, would-be artists, and bohemians was scattered throughout the parts of the West End closest to Cambridge Street. While some of these were students, others worked in low-status jobs and took advantage of the low cost of living in the area.

Some other characteristics of the West End population in 1958 are available from data gathered by the Center for Community Studies survey.[15] Like the Italians . . . the largest single group of West Enders—50%—was native born of foreign parentage. A third were European immigrants, and the rest were

---

[13] Ibid. The rest of the population was almost equally distributed among "Other Latin," "Other Slavic," English, American, and "Other" ethnic groups. Only 7% of the West End sample was of American background.

[14] The Center for Community Studies survey shows 8% of the sample to be "Other Slavic," a category which includes some of the above. Fried, ibid.

[15] These data . . . are from preliminary tabulations by the Center for Community Studies. I am grateful to the Center, and to Chester Hartman of its staff, for making them available to me. Since the Center's survey is based on a sample of women respondents age twenty to sixty-five, these distributions do not report on single men of all ages, and on households of people over sixty-five. They are, however, a negligible proportion of the West End population.

children of native-born parents. Seventy % of the women were married and living with their spouses, and 10% had never married. About a fifth of the sample was twenty to twenty-nine years old, half was between thirty and forty-nine, and the remainder between sixty and sixty-five.

The population's socio-economic level was low. Indeed, the sample's median income was just under $70 a week. About a quarter earned less than $50 per week; a half between $50 and $99; and the top category, slightly less than a fifth, between $100 and $175. Most of the household heads were unskilled or semiskilled manual workers (24 and 37% respectively).[16] Skilled manual workers, semiskilled white-collar workers, and skilled white-collar workers (including small businessmen) each accounted for about 10% of the sample.

Data on years of schooling are available only for women respondents. The median educational level was about 10.5 years: 40% had had eight years of school or less, 30% had nine to eleven years, 19% had graduated from high school, and 10% had attended college for a year or more.

Life in the West End

As a neighborhood is more than an ecological or statistical construct, some of its qualities can perhaps be captured only on paper by the sociologically inclined poet or artist. Typical aspects of West End life and the "feel" of the area can best be described by an informal sketch of what so often struck me as an urban village.

To begin with, the concept of the West End as a single neighborhood was foreign to the West Enders themselves. Although the area had long been known as the West End, the residents themselves divided it up into many subareas, depending in part on the ethnic group which predominated, and in part on the extent to which the tenants in one set of streets had reason or opportunity to use another. For example, the social distance between the upper and the lower end was many times its geographical distance.[17]

Until the coming of redevelopment, only outsiders were likely to think of the West End as a single neighborhood. After the redevelopment was announced, the residents were drawn together by the common danger, but, even so, the West End never became a cohesive neighborhood.

My first visit to the West End left me with the impression that I was in Europe. Its high buildings set on narrow, irregularly curving streets, its Italian and Jewish restaurants and food stores, and the variety of people who crowded the streets when the weather was good—all gave the area a foreign and exotic flavor. At the same time, I also noticed the many vacant shops, the

---

[16] These figures report the occupation of the past or present household head. In 18% of the cases, the woman's occupation is reported, either because there was never a male household head, the husband was not in the labor force because of illness, or because his occupation was unavailable.

[17] One resident who had lived for thirty-five years about two blocks away from the upper end, and who had supper with relatives there at least twice a week for more than a decade, said that he knew very few people in the upper end.

vacant and therefore dilapidated tenements, the cellars and alleys strewn with garbage, and the desolation on a few streets that were all but deserted. Looking at the area as a tourist, I noted the highly visible and divergent characteristics that set it off from others with which I was familiar.[18] And, while the exotic quality of the West End did excite me, the dilapidation and garbage were depressing, and made me a little fearful of doing a participant-observation study.

After a few weeks of living in the West End, my observations—and my perception of the area—changed drastically. The search for an apartment quickly indicated that the individual units were usually in much better condition than the outside or the hallways of the buildings. Subsequently, in wandering through the West End, and in using it as a resident, I developed a kind of selective perception, in which my eye focused only on those parts of the area that were actually being used by people. Vacant buildings and boarded-up stores were no longer so visible, and the totally deserted alleys or streets were outside the set of paths normally traversed, either by myself or by the West Enders. The dirt and spilled-over garbage remained, but, since they were concentrated in street gutters and empty lots, they were not really harmful to anyone and thus were not as noticeable as during my initial observations.

Since much of the area's life took place on the street, faces became familiar very quickly. I met my neighbors on the stairs and in front of my building. And, once a shopping pattern had developed, I saw the same storekeepers frequently, as well as the area's "characters" who wandered through the streets everyday on a fairly regular route and schedule. In short, the exotic quality of the stores and the residents also wore off as I became used to seeing them.[19]

The attractions that the West End had for the people who had lived there for a long time became evident quickly. Apartments were extremely cheap. I paid only $46 for a six-room apartment with central heating. Long-time residents paid as little as $35 for one like it, and $15 to $25 for a similar unit without central heating. The rooms were large and the apartments comfortable. In buildings without central heating, the apartments were heated with the large combination cooking and heating stoves placed in the kitchen.

At first, I thought that the buildings without central heating were slums, but I soon learned otherwise. The kitchen stoves freed the West Enders from dependence on the landlords and their often miserly thermostats. Moreover, people with stoves could heat their apartments to their own specifications, making them as warm as they liked. In a cold spell, the kitchen stoves were less desirable, for the rooms furthest away from the kitchen were cool, and, when the temperature went down to 10 degrees above zero, the outside bed-

---

[18] For some of the characteristics of the tourist view of the social and physical landscape, see Kevin Lynch, *The Image of the City*, Cambridge: Technology Press and Harvard University Press, 1960; and Herbert J. Gans, "Diversity Is Not Dead," *New Republic*, vol. 144 (April 3, 1961), pp. 11–15, at p. 14.

[19] A similar change of perspective over time has been reported by a student of a working-class municipal housing estate in London. See Peter Willmott, "Class and Community at Dagenham," London: Institute for Community Studies, 1960, mimeographed, Chap. 1.

room was icy. Some people placed smaller oil or kerosene stoves in these rooms, and these occasionally caused fires, although the kitchen stove was completely safe. Needless to say, central heating was cheaper in the long run, for people had to buy oil to heat the stove. Usually, the oil was purchased in quantity, and stored in the cellar. Poorer people had to buy it in smaller amounts. The apartments also were equipped with gas waterheaters, which required West End families to heat their own water, but also assured independence from landlord whims.

The apartments did, of course, have a number of faults. The buildings were old and not easy to keep clean. Windows leaked and the plumbing had its quirks. There were rats in many of the cellars—although they rarely disturbed anyone except the janitor. No one liked these faults and almost everybody wanted a modern apartment that lacked these disadvantages. However, people were happy with the low rents they were charged in the West End; modernity is not much of an advantage when it depletes the family budget.

Of course there were people, especially the very poorest, who lived in badly substandard housing where the toilets were shared or broken, the rats were a danger, the oil stove did not heat properly, and the leaks in the windows could not be sealed. Such people, who were probably also paying higher rents, suffered from all the ills of poor housing. When it comes to livability standards, there is little difference between the classes. Although poorer people do not have as high expectations as the well-to-do, they are no more willing to live with defective plumbing than anyone else.

Everyday life in the West End was not much different from that in other neighborhoods, urban or suburban. The men went to work in the morning, and, for most of the day, the area was occupied largely by women and children—just as in the suburbs. There were some men on the street: the older, retired ones, as well as the young and middle-aged ones who either were unemployed, worked on night shifts, or made their living as gamblers. In the afternoon, younger women could be seen pushing baby carriages. Children of all ages played on the street, and teenagers would "hang" on the corner, or play ball in the school yard. The West End's lone playground was fairly dilapidated, and usually deserted. Many women went shopping every day, partly to meet neighbors and to catch up on area news in the small grocery stores, and partly to buy foods that could not be obtained in the weekly excursion to the supermarket.[20] On Sunday mornings, the streets were filled with people who were visiting with neighbors and friends before and after church.

The average West End resident had a choice between anonymity and total immersion in sociability. A few people had moved into the area to hide from the world, and, while visible to their neighbors, could discourage contact, and thus feel anonymous. Generally speaking, however, neighbors were friendly

---

[20] There were no supermarkets within the West End, but one was located just outside it. Many of the West End families with cars went supermarket shopping in outlying neighborhoods, often combining this with a visit to relatives or friends.

and quick to say hello to each other, although more intense social contact was limited to relatives and friends. Deviant behavior, as displayed by the area "characters," the bohemians, or the middle-class residents was, of course, highly visible. As long as the West Enders were not affected personally, however, they were tolerant. Yet this tolerance was ambivalent: people objected to deviants grudgingly but explained that such kinds of people must be expected in a low-rent neighborhood. At the same time, they found deviant behavior a lively and readily available topic of conversation, which not only provided spice and variety for gossip, but also an opportunity to restate and reaffirm their own values. The bohemians and the schizophrenic characters also served as sources of community amusement, although the latter usually received friendly greetings from other West Enders, even if they did laugh at them once their backs were turned. On the whole, however, the various ethnic groups, the bohemians, transients, and others could live together side by side without much difficulty, since each was responsive to totally different reference groups. Also, at various points, the diverse cultures had common values. For example, everyone liked the low rents, the cheapness of the cost of living generally, and the convenience to downtown. Moreover, as Italians like to stay up late, and to socialize at high decibel levels, the bohemians' loud parties were no problem, at least to them.

The sharing of values was also encouraged by the residential stability of much of the population. Many West Enders had known each other for years, if only as acquaintances who greeted each other on the street. Everyone might not know everyone else; but, as they did know something about everyone, the net effect was the same, especially within each ethnic group. Between groups, common residence and sharing of facilities—as well as the constant struggle against absentee landlords—created enough solidarity to maintain a friendly spirit. Moreover, for many families, problems were never far away. Illnesses, job layoffs, and school or discipline problems among the children occurred regularly. Alcoholism, mental illness, desertion, the death of a loved one, serious financial difficulties, and even violence were familiar to everyone. If they did not take place in one's immediate family, they had happened at some time to a relative or a neighbor. Thus when emergencies occurred, neighbors helped each other readily; other problems were solved within each ethnic group.

For most West Enders, then, life in the area resembled that found in the village or small town, and even in the suburb. Indeed, if differences of age and economic level among the residents were eliminated, many similarities between the life of the urban neighborhood and the suburb would become visible.

Age and class differences are, of course, crucial; they, rather than place of residence, shape the lives of people. That West Enders lived in five-story tenements and suburbanites occupy single-family houses made some—but not many—differences in their ways of life and the everyday routine. For example, although the West Enders were less than a mile from the downtown department stores, it is doubtful whether they used these more than the average suburbanite who has to travel 45 minutes to get to them. Not all city neighborhoods are urban villages, of course, and there are few similarities among the urban jungle, the apartment hotel district, and the suburb, or for that matter, the urban village.[21]

Although it is fashionable these days to romanticize the slum, this has not been my purpose here. The West End was not a charming neighborhood of "noble peasants" living in an exotic fashion, resisting the mass-produced homogeneity of American culture and overflowing with a cohesive sense of community. It was a run-down area of people struggling with the problems of low income, poor education, and related difficulties. Even so, it was by and large a good place to live.

Squatter Settlements

WILLIAM MANGIN

As William Mangin emphasizes at the onset, squatter settlements are neither new nor confined to urban milieus (it could be argued that the first English, Spanish, and French communities in the new world were squatter settlements). In the past 30 years, they have become a significant worldwide phenomenon.

Squatter settlements are most objectively perceived as collectivities of houses, rather hastily constructed on lands that have not been formally conveyed to the builder-occupants through legal channels. Most observers tend to equate them with slums, perceiving them as densely populated collectivities of urban poor, living in substandard housing. Even in this sense, however, they differ from slums in that the latter are usually composed of aging, often decaying properties within or fairly close to a commercial area (the central business district or factory section). Squatter settlements, on the other hand, are new housing units, most frequently found on the fringes of urban areas, out near the town dumps, which often provide the materials from which shantytowns are constructed.

Mangin is emphatic that these urban places are not "sinks of social disorganization . . . nor are their inhabitants highly organized radicals out to take over the cities." His work in the barriadas of Lima, Peru, indicates that they consist of people resident an average of nine years in the city, who have incomes higher than the truly poor of the slums, and who tend to be comparatively conservative politically. The settlements are not anarchistic conglomerates with each person

[21] Similarities and differences between city and suburb are discussed in more detail in Herbert J. Gans, "Urbanism and Suburbanism as Ways of Life: A Re-evaluation of Definitions," in Arnold Rose, ed., *Human Behavior and Social Processes*, Boston: Houghton Mifflin Company, 1962, pp. 625–648.
From "Squatter Settlements." *Scientific American*, Vol. 217 (4), pp. 21–29. Reprinted with permission.

scrambling and scratching for a bit of territory against all others. Rather, they show a cohesive internal organization and a strong sense of community solidarity.

Recently, reports have come out of St. Louis, London, Paris, and Moscow concerning attempts to form squatter settlements. We should carefully consider Mangin's comments as to how and why such urban places form and their implications for city planning. We will likely see more of these settlements in the future.

Since the end of World War II squatter settlements around large cities have become a worldwide phenomenon. In the rapidly urbanizing but not yet industrialized countries millions of families from the impoverished countryside and from the city slums have invaded the outskirts of major cities and there set up enormous shantytowns. These illegal usurpations of living space have everywhere aroused great alarm, particularly among the more affluent city dwellers and government authorities. Police forces have made determined and violent efforts to repel the invasions, but the tide has been too much for them. The squatter settlements give every sign of becoming permanent.

The new shantytowns are without public services, unsanitary and in many respects almost intolerably insecure. Most middle-class and upper-class observers are inclined to regard them as a virulent social disease. Politicians and the police see them as dangerous defiance of law and order. Conservatives are certain that they are seedbeds of revolution and communism. City planners and architects view them as inefficient users of urban real estate and as sores on the landscape. Newspapers treat them as centers of crime and delinquency. Social workers are appalled by the poverty of many of the squatters, by the high incidence of underemployment and low pay, by the lack of medical treatment and sewage facilities and by what they see as a lack of proper, decent, urban, middle-class training for the squatters' children.

The truth is that the shantytowns are not quite as they seem to outside observers. I first became acquainted with some of these settlements in Peru in 1952. Conducting studies in anthropology among villagers in the Peruvian mountains at that time, I occasionally visited some of their friends and relatives living in squatter settlements (they are called *barriadas* in Peru) on the fringes of the city of Lima. I was surprised to find that the squatter communities and the way the people lived differed rather widely from the outside impression of them. Since then I have spent 10 years in more or less continuous study of the *barriadas* of Peru, and it has become quite clear to me that many of the prevalent ideas about the squatter settlements are myths.

The common view is that the squatters populating the Peruvian shantytowns are Indians from the rural mountains who still speak only the Quechuan language, that they are uneducated, unambitious, disorganized, an economic drag on the nation—and also (consistency being no requirement in mythology) that they are a highly organized group of radicals who mean to take over and communize Peru's cities. I found that in reality the people of the *barriadas* around Lima do not fit this description at all.

Most of them had been city dwellers for some time (on the average for nine years) before they moved out and organized the *barriadas*. They speak Spanish (although many are bilingual) and are far removed from the rural Indian culture; indeed, their educational level is higher than that of the general population in Peru. The *barriada* families are relatively stable compared with those in the city slums or the rural provinces. Delinquency and prostitution, which are common in the city slums, are rare in the *barriadas*. The family incomes are low, but most of them are substantially higher than the poorest slum level. My studies, based on direct observation, as well as questionnaires, psychological tests and other measurements, also indicate that the *barriada* dwellers are well organized, politically sophisticated, strongly patriotic and comparatively conservative in their sociopolitical views. Although poor, they do not live the life of squalor and hopelessness characteristic of the "culture of poverty" depicted by Oscar Lewis; although bold and defiant in their seizure of land, they are not a revolutionary "lumpenproletariat."

The squatters around the cities of Peru now number about 700,000, of whom 450,000 live in the *barriadas* of Lima itself. This is a substantial portion of the nation's entire population, which totals about 12 million. Like the squatter settlements in other countries, the *barriadas* of Peru represent the worldwide migration of people from the country to the city and a revolt of the poor against the miserable, disorganized and expensive life in the city slums. In the shantytowns they find rent-free havens where they feel they can call their homes and the land their own.

The *barriadas* of Lima began some 20 years ago as clusters of families that had spontaneously fled from the city and set up communities of straw shacks on the rocky, barren land outside. The first, small settlements were short-lived, as the police forcibly drove the settlers off, sometimes with fatal beatings of men, women and children, and burned their shacks and household goods. Nevertheless, the squatters kept returning, as many as four times to the same place. They soon learned that there was greater safety in numbers, and the invasions of land and formation of *barriadas* became elaborately planned, secretly organized projects involving large groups.

The enterprise generally took the form of a quasi-military campaign. Its leaders were usually highly intelligent, articulate, courageous and tough, and often a woman was named the "secretary of defense" (a title borrowed from Peruvian labor organizations and provincial clubs). For the projected *barriada* community the leaders recruited married couples under 30 with children; single adults were usually excluded (and still are from most *barriadas*). Lawyers or near-lawyers among the recruited group searched land titles to find a site that was owned, or at least could be said to be owned, by some public agency, preferably the national government. The organizers then visited the place at night and marked out the lots assigned to the members for homes and locations for streets, schools, churches, clinics and other facilities.

After all the plans had been made in the utmost secrecy to avoid alerting the police, the organizers appealed confidentially to some prominent political or religious figure to support the invasion when it took place; they also alerted a friendly newspaper, so that any violent police reaction would be fully reported. On the appointed day the people recruited for the invasion, usually numbering in the hundreds and sometimes more than 1,000, rushed to the *barriada* site in taxis, trucks, buses and even on delivery cycles. On arriving, the families immediately began to put up shelters made of matting on their assigned lots.

More than 100 such invasions to set up *barriadas* have taken place in the Lima area in the past 20 years. The settlers have consistently behaved in a disciplined, courageous, yet nonprovocative manner, even in the face of armed attack by the police. In the end popular sympathy and the fear of the political consequences of too much police violence have compelled the government authorities to allow the squatters to stay. The present liberal regime of President Belaunde tries to prevent squatter invasions, but it does not attack them violently when they occur.

Once a *barriada* has established a foothold, it grows until it has used up its available land. The original settlers are joined by relatives and friends from the provinces and the city. From the relatively flat land where the first houses are built, new shacks gradually creep up the steep, rocky hillsides that overlook the city.

The surface appearance of the *barriadas* is deceptive. At first glance from a distance they appear to be formless collections of primitive straw shacks. Actually the settlements are laid out according to plans, often in consultation with architectural or engineering students. As time goes on most of the shanties are replaced by more permanent structures. As soon as the residents can afford to, they convert their original straw shacks into houses of brick and cement. Indeed, the history of each *barriada* is plainly written in the mosaic of its structures. The new houses clinging to the high hillside are straw shacks; at the foot of the hill the older ones are built of masonry. One of the oldest *barriadas*, known as San Martin, has a paved main street, painted houses and elegant fronts on stores, banks and movie houses.

The squatters improve their houses as they accumulate a little extra money from employment and find spare time. At present the *barriada* communities are far too poor to afford the capital costs of utilities such as water systems and sewers. Water and fuel (mainly kerosene) are transported in bottles or drums by truck, bicycle or on foot. Some houses have electricity supplied by enterprising individuals who have invested in generators and run lines to their clients; a few of these entrepreneurs have gone so far as to acquire a television set (on time) and charge admission to the show. In some well-established *barriadas* the electric company of Lima has installed lines and service.

The major concern of the *barriada* people, and the greatest source of anxiety, is the problem of finding steady employment. The largest *barriadas* do provide considerable local employment, particularly in construction work. Many families obtain some income by operating stores, bars or shops in their homes; in the *barriada* I have studied most closely about a third of the households offer some kind of goods for sale. By and large, however, the people of the squatter settlements around Lima depend mainly on employment in the city. Most of the men and many of the women commute to jobs in Lima, working in personal services, factories, stores, offices and even in professional occupations. One *barriada* men's club includes among its members a physician, a bank branch manager, a police lieutenant, four lawyers, several businessmen and two Peace Corps volunteers.

The families that colonize a *barriada* are regarded as "owners" of their lots. As time goes on, many rent, trade or sell their lots and houses to others, using beautifully made titles with seals, lawyers' signatures and elaborate property descriptions—but in most cases with no legal standing. (Actually it appears that in Peru even private property is usually clouded by at least two titles, and much of the land is in litigation.) In the *barriadas*, as elsewhere in the nation, disputes over lot "ownership" arise; the claimants appeal variously to the association that runs the *barriada* or to the National Housing Authority, the Lima city government, the police or the courts. The decisions of these agenies generally have only a provisional character. A law adopted by the Peruvian national legislature in 1957 authorized the granting of land titles to *barriada* dwellers, but for several years it was ignored. In 1962 a group of engineers and architects in the National Housing Authority, taking advantage of the preoccupation of the military junta with other matters, passed out land titles to a few hundred families in two of the oldest *barriadas*. Even these titles, however, were marked "Provisional."

In most matters of public concern the *barriadas* are governed by their own membership associations. They hold elections about once a year—a rarity in Peru, where, except in the *barriadas*, no democratic elections of local officials had been held for more than 60 years before the present national government took office. The *barriada* associations levy taxes (in the form of "dues") on the residents, and they usually manage to collect them from most members. They also screen new applicants, resolve land disputes, try to prevent land speculation and organize cooperative projects. For official papers, such as voting registration and certificates of marriage, birth and death, the *barriada* people must resort to the city hall, and their reception by the town clerks is often so uncordial and whimsical that the quest for an essential document may be a heroic ordeal. (I have seen *barriada* birth certificates stamped "Provisional"!) Lacking authoritative police forces of their own, the *barriada* residents usually take their complaints of crimes and misdemeanors to the city police, but the latter seldom do anything more than register the complaint. For schooling of the children the *barriadas* depend mainly on the city's public and church schools. A few have elementary schools of their own, but generally students must commute to the city in the elementary grades as well as to high school and the university. The *barriada* people also have close connections with the city through their jobs, unions, social clubs, churches and services such as medical care, social security and unemployment insurance.

Many of the *barriada* associations have established working relations with city and national agencies and even with international organizations such as the Peace Corps and the United Nations. Of the various agencies in a position to assist the *barriadas* perhaps the most important is Peru's National housing Authority, known as the JNV. The JNV has been beset by power struggles between the national office and local city officials and by other confusions, so that its accomplishments are uneven. In some *barriadas* representatives of the JNV are cheered; in others they are stoned. (In one settlement the agency rected an impressive sign announcing that it was installing a water and sewage-disposal system; after six months had passed with no visible evidence of a start on the project, the residents began to pile fecal matter under the sign, whereupon JNV removed the sign.) Recently, however, the housing agency gave Lima officials authority to adopt and proceed with specific plans, and there is now considerable activity.

The *barriada* governments have not lacked the usual trouble of municipal administrations, including charges of corruption and factional splits. Moreover, their prestige and authority have declined as the need for community cohesion and defense against attack from outside has been reduced. There is a compensating trend, however, toward replacement of the original associations by full-fledged, official town governments. The two largest *barriadas* in the Lima area, San Martin and Pampa de Comas, now have elected mayors and town councils.

What, if anything, can be learned from the squatter settlements that will be of value in resolving the monumental problems of today's cities and their desperate people? I should like to present some conclusions from our own 10-year studies. They were carried out on a grant from the U.S. National Institute of Mental Health in cooperation with the Institute of Ethnology of the University of San Marcos and the Department of Mental Hygiene of the Ministry of Public Health in Peru, and with the assistance of a group of psychiatrists, anthropologists and social workers. We concentrated on an intensive study of a particular *barriada*, which I shall call Benavides. It consists of some 600 families. Over the 10-year period I have spent considerable time living in the community (in a rented room), interviewing a large sample of the population and examining their attitudes and feelings as indicated by various questionnaires and inventories, including the Rorschach and thematic apperception tests.

I am bound to say that I have been profoundly impressed by the constructive spirit and achievements of the *barriada* people. They have shown a really remarkable capacity for initiative, self-help and community organization. Visitors to the *barriadas*, many of them trained observers, remark on the accomplishments of the residents in home and community construction, on the small businesses they have created, on the degree of community organization, on how much the people have achieved without government help and on their friendliness. Most of the residents are neither resentful nor alienated; they are understandably cynical yet hopeful. They describe themselves as "humble people," abandoned by society but not without faith that "they" (the powers that be) will respond to people's needs for help to create a life of dignity for themselves. Recognizing fully that they are living in "infrahuman conditions," the *barriada* dwellers yearn for something better. Given any recognition or encouragement by the government such as the paving of a street or even the collection of taxes from them, the people respond with a burst of activity in improvement of their homes.

This is not to say that either their spirit or their behavior is in any sense idyllic. There are tensions within the *barriada* and people take economic advantage of one another. They are victims of the same racial prejudice and class inequality that characterize Peruvian society in general. As in the world outside, the *barriada* people identify themselves as city people, country people, coastal people, mountaineers, Indians, Cholos, mestizos, Negroes—and cliques arise. With the passage of time and weakening of the initial *esprit de corps*, bickering within the community becomes more and more common. Charlatans and incompetents sometimes take over leadership of the *barriada*. Moreover, because of the poverty of their resources for financing major projects in community services, the people have a low estimate of their own capabilities and continually look to the government or other outside agencies for solutions to their problems.

Nevertheless, to an outside observer what is most striking is the remarkable progress the *barriada* people have made on their own. They have exhibited a degree of popular initiative that is seldom possible in the tightly controlled community-action programs in the U.S. The *barriadas* of Peru now represent a multimillion-dollar investment in house construction, local small businesses and public services, not to speak of the social and political investment in community organization. Such achievements hold lessons from which more advanced countries may well profit.

Particularly in house construction and land development the *barriada* people have done better than the government, and at much less cost. The failures of governments and private developers everywhere to provide low-cost housing for the poor are notorious. Administrative costs, bureaucratic restrictions and the high cost of materials and construction when government agencies do the contracting generally put the housing rentals beyond the reach of the lowest-income group. Equally disappointing are the failures in the design of this official public housing, which usually disregards the desires and style of life of the people for whom it is intended.

In the Peruvian *barriadas*, by avoiding government control and the requirements of lending institutions, the people have built houses to their own desires and on the basis of first things first. Because they needed shelter immediately, they built walls and a roof and left bathrooms and electricity to be added later. They want flat roofs and strong foundations so that they can add a second story. They want a yard for raising chickens and guinea pigs, and a front room that can serve as a store or a barroom. They have dispensed with the restrictive residential zoning and construction details that middle-class planners and architects consider essential for proper housing.

Like most rural people in Peru, the *barriada* settlers are suspicious of large-scale projects and wary of entering into loan or mortgage arrangements. Indeed, throughout South America there is a general dissatisfaction with large housing projects. Costly mistakes have been made in the construction of "satellite cities" and "superblocks." This has led the national governments and other interested agencies to give more attention to the possibilities in rehabilitating existing housing. In Peru the goverment is now initiating experiments in offering low-cost loans through credit cooperatives, providing optional technical assistance and other services and letting the prospective housebuilder do his own contracting. As John Turner, an architect with many years' experience in Peru, has pointed out, if people are sold land and allowed to do their own contracting and building with optional help, the costs go down for both the clients and the government.

Our studies of the *barriadas* of Peru show, in brief, that these settlements contain many constructive elements whose significance should not be ignored. The people believe that their present situation is far preferable to what they had in the provinces or the central city slums and that they have an investment in their future and that of their children. What we have learned in Peru is supported by investigations of squatter settlements around the world.

The squatters have produced their own answer to the difficult problems of housing and community organization that governments have been unable to solve. In Peru we may have a chance to study what can happen when a government works with popular initiative rather than fighting it.

Part VI: Research/Term Paper Topics

1. "Public Places."

Spend a full day observing at several kinds of public places. Select one general-use place that would ostensibly attract people of all types (downtown street corner, a major shopping mall), and one or more limited-constituency places (public library, bus-stop, several kinds of bars). Note age, sex, race, dress, possessions, kinds of groupings, behavior, and interaction in these places. Note change in constituency or behavior with time of day. Guess ethnicity, SES, and any other categorical identities. Generalize on the use of these places and upon what they tell you about cities.

2. "An Urban Village."

Are there any "urban villages" in your town? Draw a map of the city showing their locale and, using census tract data, describe the demographic composition of one such area. Observe one, commenting on the kinds of shops, businesses, services, subareas (by house or resident type), and surrounding zones.

3. "Holism and Barrio Studies."

Look into the literature on economically marginal urban communities such as *favelas* and *barriadas*. Develop an argument on the use of holism in such studies.

4. "Squatter Settlements—a Modern Urban Phenomenon?"

It has been suggested that early European settlements in the Americas were "squatter settlements." Take an opposite position and, by comparing descriptions of modern squatter communities with historical descriptions of early settlements, indicate how they fundamentally differ in type.

5. "The Blessings of Urban Renewal."

Looking at the works of Marris (1962), Petonnet (1973), Bryce-Laport (1970), Young and Wilmott (1957), and others, develop a general theoretical position on the effect of urban renewal and public housing estates upon dislocated city residents.

PART

Economic and Cultural Differentiation in the City

SEVEN

This section explores the question of "heterogeneity" posited by Wirth and others. There are essentially three bases of urban heterogenity. One is economic role diversity. It is usually a reflection of specialization and the presence in cities of many crafts, businesses, and services, each requiring different skills or behavioral patterns. Another basis of urban heterogeneity is political/economic status diversity, a reflection of differential income and access to sources of decision making and power. The third is cultural diversity, usually equated with ethnicity. It indicates that cities draw residents from a number of population pools and encourage residential or economic segregation capable of generating or nurturing variant behavior patterns.

Ideally, economic roles and cultural distinctions are to be viewed as *vertical* differentiators. The former segregate individuals and groups who occupy the same horizontal (generally income) level of political/economic status, and the latter are independent of such status differences. In real life, however, these frequently become enmeshed. This results in ethnic or other groups occupying relatively permanent places on particular economic/power levels and monopolizing (sometimes unwillingly) a particular category of work. Such meshing produces elites as well as impoverished, stigmatized underclasses.

The question has been raised by many as to whether poverty is synonymous with urban life. In truth, it depends upon the definition of poverty. If poverty means lack of goods but adequacy of caloric intake, then most hunters and gatherers are "impoverished." If poverty means inadequacy of caloric intake but possession of goods, then peasant agricultural victims of drought, flood, or fieldpest are impoverished (and certainly no less unhappy than urban poor).

Most uses of the term *poverty* imply more than simple deprivation, however. And as soon as the definition of poverty includes more than caloric deprivation and lack of possessions, it becomes—just as the definition of "race" once taken beyond the confines of gene frequencies—a value-laden concept whose criteria must be selected and justified for each use.

Urban poverty, as poverty anywhere, is a grinding repetition of days whose activities are either predominantly devoted to or clouded by the need for basic survival. If urban differs from rural poverty, it does so because the context is different. Compared with poor rural landholders, the urban poor have no collateral—no property or guaranteed income (such as next year's crop) to pledge against loans for support during hard times. Urban poor in general (there are exceptions, of course) have smaller, more dispersed kin groups and less right to aid from neighbors or other community members. Urban poor also live in closer juxtaposition with others who are better off to varying degrees, thus exacerbating feelings of frustration, inadequacy, and victimization. Urban poor tend to have less access to alternate means of achieving prestige or power in their communities (religious positions, political service). Urban prestige and power tend to be built upon cash and control of goods, labor, and favors—factors whose absence creates urban poverty in the first place. Finally, there is a "positive" note. Cities offer their poor more avenues (jobs, crafts, entrepreneurship, scavanging, theft, gambling, prostitution, extortion) for obtaining relief or mobility.

Does "life in poverty" produce a "culture of poverty"? The evidence is contradictory. Oscar Lewis suggested it was at base an adaptive response to the loss of hope; a self-perpetuating denial of any but present, readily accessible rewards and opportunities (1966). It is more common to large, capitalist cities and less likely to be exhibited by urban groups with cultural or ethnic identity strong enough to discourage dependence upon outsiders for aid, values, or rewards.

Lewis has been criticized by Valentine (1978) and others, who contend that the so-called culture of poverty is less self-perpetuating than a continual response to structural barriers to mobility imposed by more priviledged classes in the society. Its dissolution depends not upon a change in the value system (culture) of the poor, but upon the provision by higher classes of legitimate opportunities for achievement.

Poverty and Urban Analysis

JUDITH GRANICH GOODE

"The poor are always with us" is an often quoted remark. However, as Judith Goode makes clear, it is only recently that "the poor" and "poverty" as categories of social research and social action have received attention. This may be, as Goode points out, because poorness in the urban-industrial world has come to mean something quite different than in the pre-industrial context. Is poverty the lack of material goods? Or is it powerlessness, social worthlessness ("a poverty of the spirit"); a kind of lumpen quality that naturally attends those with strong backs and weak minds? Or is it a combination of these kinds of deprivations? Do we see poverty as cause, or effect, or both? Is poverty related to inadequacies of the individual, manipulations of a population by an exploitive elite, structural properties of the sociocultural system, ecological and/or demographic factors—all or none of these?

Goode pays special attention to the influential but highly controversial concept introduced by Oscar Lewis—"the culture of poverty." Because Lewis' work was done in an urban setting, it lent support to the view that "there was an inevitable relationship between poverty and the city." This assumption and others are challenged in the following paper.

Concerned with refining our units of analysis, Goode suggests that the most powerful tool for studying materially deprived peoples in an urban industrial society is the category of marginal occupations. She develops this concept in an attempt to lead anthropologists into "playing a more useful role" in providing the necessary comparative perspective that is needed in such research.

Introduction

Poverty is not a traditional concept in American social science. There is good reason for this. The term is semantically diffuse and cannot be translated into a social unit which can be successfully studied through behavioral analysis. Nevertheless, the condition of poverty and the social aggregate called "the poor" became important in research and analysis in the 1960s as poverty became a public issue in America. In the new poverty research focus, anthropologists have not played their traditional role, that of providing a comparative perspective. Instead they have engaged in a rather parochial discussion of minority group poverty in the United States. This has resulted from the social commitment of the anthropologists involved. In particular, there has been a concern with refuting the "culture of poverty" concept of Lewis, which is recognized to be conceptually weak and damaging in its policy implications.

"Poverty and Urban Analysis," *Western Canadian Journal of Anthropology,* © Vol. 3, #2 (1972–1973), pp. 1–19.

Unfortunately, the parochial focus on American minority groups as "the poor" has further confounded the semantic confusion generated by the current definitions of poverty. The study of poverty has moved from a legitimate ecological focus on the relationship between behavior and lack of material resources to an implicit concern with powerlessness and worthlessness and their effects. If anthropologists would focus more specifically on *material* deprivation and if they would broaden their perspective cross-culturally, the "culture of poverty" hypothesis could be refuted with equal strength. This could be done by using the marginal work activities which produce low and unstable income as units of anlaysis in both transitional and advanced industrial economies. The results of this effort would provide the urban anthropologist with an additional urban micro-unit to study which would have much greater heuristic value than "the poor." Furthermore, the relationship between poorness in the material sense and behavior could be rigorously described.

The New Poverty Focus

The Social Science Index did not include a subheading for "poverty" until the 1960s, the decade when poverty research became the vogue. The deluge of poverty literature in the United States at that time was related to the increasing concern with material deprivation when it became obvious that the New Deal and the economic prosperity following World War II had not successfully eradicated poverty. The new trend toward relevance and commitment to social justice in social science pushed the researchers in the direction of problem-oriented research. However, a parallel influence, that of government funding practices, was perhaps more responsible for generating poverty research. In this case the concern was mainly with eradicating the alleged anti-social consequences of poverty rather than the injustice of poverty in an affluent society. The combined result of the new concerns was a massive outpouring of poverty literature.[1]

Since an urgent need was felt for hurried solutions, much of the work was speculative, at the level of generated hypotheses and lacking in the empirical rigor demanded by the scientific enterprise. Yet much of this work directly or indirectly had an immediate effect on policy. For instance, Oscar Lewis' culture of poverty notion was merely an hypothesis generated by some small-scale research which demanded testing before it was assumed to be explanatory. Yet it had far-reaching implications in American policy. As Walter B. Miller (1968) has indicated, "poverty" became a code word for conditions of relative economic, political and social deprivation, which were incapable of objective measurement and were thus measured by subjective criteria.[2] Al-

[1] The deluge of poverty literature can be demonstrated by a sample of poverty readers produced in the vintage year of 1965, e.g., Ferman et al, Gordon, Seligman, Weisbrod, and Will and Vatter.

[2] While I disagree with many of the conclusions of Miller (1968), I do agree with the point that a social group defined by a relative, subjective definition of poorness is much less useful for analysis than one defined by occupational sources of low and unstable income.

though social scientists were enticed to help explain the relationship between poverty and behavior, it was impossible to define the condition of poverty itself. The semantic diffuseness of the term was extraordinary. No longer specifically referring to *material* deprivation or a lack of access to *material* resources, the definition of the state of poverty included such attributes as powerlessness, prestige deprivation, and general psychological inadequacy, moving farther and farther away from a conceptual base defined in material terms.[3]

It is the major premise of this paper that anthropologists have not played as useful a role as they could in poverty research thus far. One can divide the poverty literature into two categories: the rather grandiose abstract writings about poverty, concerned with poverty "culture," the values and behavior of the poor; and small-scale empirical studies of "the poor" as an analytical unit. While the latter category of studies is logically necessary for the discussions of the former, such studies have been fewer and later in coming. It is my contention that such an empirical focus on "the poor" should not be further developed since this social category is not precise enough to constitute a useful research focus for urban anthropologists. However, as long as the former discussions concerning poverty and poverty behavior persist, the anthropologist ought to play his traditional role and at least provide a comparative perspective. He should not continue what he has done so far in contributing to the general parochial discussion of American poverty.

Lack of Comparative Perspective

As social scientists moved into poverty research, they took with them the questionable assumptions about poverty and the poor which were the unconscious accretions of Western history and which could have been challenged by a comparative analysis. The anthropologist could have investigated the responses of human groups to material deprivation historically and cross-culturally and thus further illuminated the condition of the poor in America. However, in his examination of poverty the anthropologist neglected to play his traditional role. A comparative approach could have demonstrated how some very important variables intervene in the direct relationship of material deprivation to the behavior of the poor. One such intervening variable is the society's definition and evaluation of poverty as a condition and the poor as a social category. The differences in such societal views both historically and cross-culturally have affected both the actual behavior and the selectively perceived behavior of the materially deprived in different times and places.

For instance, material deprivation is much less directly related to social worth, power, and perceived deviant behavior in most social systems which

[3] Gladwin (1967), for instance, includes chapters entitled: "Poverty is Powerlessness" and "Poverty is Worthlessness," etc. Hagstrom (1965) also seems to place major emphasis on the political and psychological deprivation of the poor. Many of the readers listed in note #1 organize their offerings on the basis of these multiple, non-economic dimensions of poverty.

are not of the urban-industrial type. The "poor" are even more a vague and ill-defined social category in preindustrial systems. Stratification is perceived as being based on other than material criteria; in fact an anti-materialistic ethic and a positive value on asceticism in such less productive technological systems creates an ambivalent view of poverty as a condition. In such systems, the underclasses are negatively evaluated because of a spiritual and moral inferiority believed to be divinely ordained. Their lack of resources is viewed as incidental to their perceived status and not as a prime attribute. If underclass status does correlate to some extent with material deprivation, such a correlation is less significant than in urban industrial society. Underclass groups are perceived as having character weaknesses and deviant lifestyles which are very similar to those attributed to the poor in an urban industrial system. Yet, they are often not more materially deprived than many of their respectable non-elite counterparts. For instance, the Japanese outcasts were highly stratified with chiefs leading sumptuous lifestyles and yet such chiefs were just as defiled and socially segregated as their less wealthy followers (Price 1968). The impoverished members of respectable peasant and artisan groups were believed not to have the immoral lifestyles of the underclass, but to share the more virtuous attributes of their respectable status group.

Thus the attributes of powerlessness, legal discrimination, perceived *social* worthlessness and moral depravity on the one hand, and *material* poorness on the other were not as clearly attributes of the same social category in preindustrial societies as they are in urban industrial society. No significantly different behavioral responses are attributed to the poor or materially deprived *per se*, but rather to the spiritually unworthy underclass. An anthropological, comparative perspective could prove useful here. If the anthropologist working with transitional and historical societies could contrast the lifestyles of the poor but respectable class with the defiled non-poor, this would provide some background for an analysis of American poverty. One could then go on to delineate the relationship between poorness and behavior on the one hand, and defined worthlessness, powerlessness and behavior on the other, an area extremely confused in the contemporary poverty literature. Most of the notions about the so-called crippling ideology, personality traits, and values of the poor are implicitly assumed to relate to political-legal deprivation, not to material deprivation. Yet this is considered to be a response to "poverty," most frequently understood to mean *material* resource deprivation.[4] Histori-

---

[4] The features of the culture of poverty concept most under fire in the literature are those related to personality inadequacy and values such as apathy and helplessness. These features are the ones which presumably make the poor "hard to reach." Lewis himself (1966, 1968) gave the attributes related to non-integration and non-participation a crucial position in his "model." Much empirical evidence has been gathered to refute the crippling attributes of this so-called culture. Critics have pointed to the macro-structural features of the larger system rather than to "cultural" preference or choice as generators of whatever isolation actually exists (see note #7). However, in all the literature, very little connection was ever made by Lewis or his critics between inequality in material terms and the crippling ideology of the poor. Inequality of power and social worth were the key features linked to the so-called culture of *poverty*, but the relationship between material deprivation and these other deprivations was never established.

cal and cross-cultural comparisons of the varying perceptions of the poor as a social category, the evaluation of poverty as a condition as well as descriptions of the actual behavior of the poor could be used to question some of the assumptions about the relationship between *material* deprivation and behavior made in American research.

Anthropological Studies of Poverty

There are several reasons why most of the anthropological writings on poverty to date do not work out of such a comparative perspective.[5] Those anthropologists who have chosen to look at poverty are for the most part those whose commitment to social justice is very strong. Such a commitment is responsible for the whole facet of urban anthropology subsumed in the following definition of the subfield as "the study of complex societies in terms of problems of ethnic minorities, urban deterioration, and popular discontent." (Berreman, et al, 1971:551).

Much of the neglect of such a comparative focus is a direct result of the work of Oscar Lewis and the hostility it generated. Lewis' work on the urban poor in Mexico City and San Juan drew kudos for its humanizing methodology. However, it was roundly attacked in the anthropological community for its weak conceptualization, its policy implications, and its ethnocentrism. In Lewis' model, the culture of the poor was perceived as resistant to change, and alleged to be a factor which helped perpetuate poverty. Such a model implies policies which involve changing the behavior of the poor, policies which would have the effect of deflecting action away from a redistribution of resources. In this respect, Lewis' model is not very different from other models of cultural deprivation which assume weak families, improper socialization, and immoral values among the poor, and which implicitly call for policies directed at behavior rather than at the structure of the society as a whole.

These fallacious assumptions are matched by the conceptual inadequacy of Lewis' model. The "culture of poverty" is alleged to include a 70 item trait list when in fact only about 55 items (often non-discrete) are ever included in the description. Equal weighting is given to trivial and crucial elements alike. Finally, many traits are described ethnocentrically from the point of view of middle class culture: such attributes as "thinness" of culture, high tolerance for deviance, weak ego structure, and families described as *partial* rather than as *different* structures are hardly stated in non-ethnocentric terms (Lewis, 1966). The description of the poor in this way as ideologically and psychologically crippled has alienated many anthropologists who feel that the behavior

[5] Examples of recent anthropological literature which explicitly discusses the culture of poverty are: Current Anthropology (1967); Current Anthropology (1969); Gladwin (1967); Hannerz (1969); James (1970); Johnson and Sanday (1971); Leacock (1971); Leeds (1971); Liebow (1967); Mangin (1970b); Miller (1971); Parker and Kleiner (1970); and Valentine (1968). Aside from slight references to areas outside of the United States in Current Anthropology (1967), and two selections in Leacock (1971) and Mangin (1970b), there is scant reference to anything but American minority group poverty.

of the poor should not be described in value-laden terms, but as patterned and non-random behavior in the same way that the behavior of "primitive savages" was demonstrated to be patterned and non-random by the earlier anthropologists. Lewis' was the first attempt at a cross-cultural analysis of the poor. His work was perceptive in recognizing the relationship between the structure of industrial capitalism and the attributes of the urban poor. However the weaknesses in his formulation were enough to forestall any followers.

In the 1960s, there were many anthropologists studying urbanization and modernization in the developing world. However, only in rare cases did these students ever focus on the poor or economically deprived *per se*. Few people engaged in the study of urbanism in Africa and Asia were explicitly aware of the questions raised by Lewis' work. Those trained in the British tradition, e.g., many students of African urbanism, were not involved with the socioeconomic issues which were of concern to poverty researchers in the United States. Instead, their focus was on migrants and their adjustment to the city, the ways in which persistent tribal or rural traits aided in the adjustment, and efforts to refute the anti-urban problem-orientation of American urban sociology. These concerns diverted many urban anthropologists from poverty research *per se;* the poor did not become a focus of much of the anthropological study of comparative urbanization. In many ways this is fortunate, since, as will be discussed below, poverty and the poor are inadequate units for analysis. However, it is unfortunate that little attention was paid to the details of economic adjustment to urban cash economies. One of the exceptions to this general trend in Old World urbanization is the work by Gutkind (1967, 1969, 1970), which focused explicitly on the long-term unemployed in Nairobi and Lagos. Other studies which focused on marginal work activities, such as Textor (1964) and Gould (1967), have also involved issues of material deprivation.

In Latin America, however, several students of urbanization have been concerned with poverty. Unfortunately, their concern has been limited to a specific refutation of Lewis' notions about the culture of poverty, rather than with general descriptions of people with insecure and low income.[6] For the most part almost no cross-cultural data were used in the scores of articles and volumes which have successfully repudiated the culture of poverty model.[7]

Poverty and the City

In the course of the development of the research focus on poverty, it came to be assumed that there was an inevitable relationship between poverty and the city. Material deprivation is not a phenomenon inherent in urban life,

[6] Because Lewis' work dealt with systems of Hispanic cultural tradition, it is no surprise that most of the cross-cultural data used in response to Lewis came from Latin Americans and Latin Americanists. See Current Anthropology (1967), Leacock (1971), Leeds (1971) and Mangin (1970b).
[7] The most devastating refutations of Lewis can be found in Leacock (1971) and Valentine (1968). Other excellent critiques which produce different implications are those of Hannerz (1969) and Miller (1971).

however. One of the reasons for this erroneous association is the fact that in transitional societies, the type of resource deprivation we associate with modern cash-oriented systems occurs first in the city, while the attitudes and perceptions about poverty and the poor in the rural areas remain traditional. It was during the period of transition in the West that poverty became increasingly visible in the city at the same time that it was becoming redefined and reevaluated by society as a whole. Since the dislocated migrants moved to urban centers and were frequently located in dense slum areas where the results of resource deprivation were extremely noticeable, the city and poverty became associated in the minds of reformers. Now, in advanced industrial society, the city is the center of most of the population and also of most economic activity. Thus the city not only appears to be the locus of most of the poor, but the supposedly negative features of urban life are even seen as generating poverty as well as many other "evils" of modern life. However, the relationship between urbanism and material deprivation is never a causal one, nor always even a correlative one. A disproportionate number of poor in America inhabit rural areas; technological displacement in agriculture and mining is as devastating as it is in urban related occupations. However, a belief still persists that slum housing *per se* contributes to the perpetuation of poverty or that the density and impersonality of the city increase the ranks of the poor. This cognitive merger of the notion of the "urban crisis" with poverty further destroys a potential usefulness of "the poor" as a unit of study.

The Units of Analysis

In the growing field of urban anthropology, the study of the poor as a unit of analysis has yielded little because of the insoluble problems of defining the poor as a social unit. Urban anthropologists have focused on household units, personal networks, neighborhoods (particularly slums), ethnic groups, and migrants as possible social categories. While some of these micro-units contain disproportionate numbers of poor people, these units themselves do not constitute the "urban poor." Migrants, for example, constitute a significant proportion of the urban populations of developing nations. Since they often enter the urban labor force at the level of unskilled jobs, it is assumed that they are representative of the urban poor. However, many analysts (Nelson, 1970; Mangin, 1970; Gutkind, 1970) indicate that second and third generation urban dwellers in marginal occupations differ significantly in behavior and world view from the marginally employed migrant. As another example, many ethnic groups, particularly minority ethnic groups, contain disproportionate numbers of poor people; but the incidence of households with low and unstable income is neither universally distributed, nor is it the most salient feature of group membership. Political oppression and/or ascribed social worthlessness may be significant and may occur independent of material deprivation.

Most of the recent work on slums throughout the world has shown that they can differ greatly in social organization, community solidarity, and political integration. Many people with incomes that are neither low nor unstable may still live in slums because of housing shortages, housing discrimination, ethnic ties, or recent upward mobility. In addition to such heterogeneity in occupation and income level, low income communities can differ from each other in terms of age, geographical isolation, proportion of property owners, and homogeneity in ethnic origin. All of these factors contribute to the formation of the social organization, world view and attitudes of the residents. To consider such beliefs and values as primarily a result of poverty because the people live in a statistically defined low income community is inappropriate.

Ever since important distinctions between the stable working class and the unstable laboring class were identified in American social science, it has been recognized that not only the level of income but the stability of income and the potential for career advancement have important implications for class-related behavior (Hanson and Simmons, 1969; Miller, 1964). However, any attempt at statistically delineating the segment of the population with significantly different access to resources would not yield meaningful, interacting social units, but only a statistical artifact. Such aggregates of scattered individuals cannot be isolated as bounded social units and subjected to the ethnographic data-collecting techniques of participant observation and intensive interviewing.

Consequently, most of the so-called studies of the "poor" in anthropology have used either statistical aggregates defined by the level of income of social units based on common residence (neighborhoods) or common culture of origin (minority ethnic groups) which are known to contain a larger than average proportion of people with low and unstable incomes. These units have then been defined as the "poor," thus precluding any real resource-related definition and confusing the effects of material deprivation with the independent effect of the nature of community of residence on minority status. In such a way, neighborhoods which have been statistically designated as poverty neighborhoods for purposes of anti-poverty programs have been used to study the effects of "poorness."

An even more grievous mistake is made when minority ethnic membership is mistaken for poorness. The confusion between poorness and blackness is symptomatic of this trend. For example, in Valentine's far-reaching book (1968), the studies directly related to poorness and the studies which are primarily about black communities (only implicitly related to poorness) are treated without distinction. Valentine's later works have indicated that he is primarily interested in Afro-Americans in regard to both their ethnic culture and structural position, rather than in poverty per se. His 1968 work is specifically concerned with the effect of American poverty research and theory on the treatment of American blacks, rather than with the effect of American poverty. What Valentine says is important, but it is often mislabelled. He does not deal with the ecological adaptation of the materially deprived, but with patterned responses emanating from political, social and historical forces. Valentine did not invent nor does he condone the confusion between blackness and poorness in the literature, but he does little to counteract it.

In several recent articles on poverty in anthropological journals we find different kinds of operational definitions of "the poor." Parker and Kleiner (1970), having completed a large-scale study of Negro males in Philadelphia, assume that such a Negro population can be used to make comments on "poverty." The original study was not directed toward the poverty issue, but since its subjects were Negroes in a community with a relatively low income profile, the data were later bent to fit an attempt at testing the culture of poverty hypothesis. The sample was divided into three arbitrary income strata. The author then attempted to assess the degree of helplessness felt by individuals (a presumed culture of poverty trait) in each of the strata by asking about the degree to which "being a Negro has been a barrier to you?" Such a procedure reveals little about the relationship between such verbal responses and material deprivation.

First, by injecting a question about perceived racial discrimination, one taps responses more closely related to experience with racism than to experiences with poverty as a source of such "feelings of helplessness." This is especially true since the crude measure of material deprivation used (i.e., arbitrary current income levels) masks great differences in income security, career history and career potential. Second, since so many of the total sample are "poor" according to government poverty standards, it seems as if the authors are implying that within the poverty population every dollar earned decreases the individual's chance of feeling helpless. If so, this would appear to be a personality trait rather than a group-shared, group-transmitted culture trait. If one deals with a non-interactive aggregate one cannot assume such cultural patterning. As it stands, the study might say some interesting things about Negroes, but not much about patterned behavioral responses to poverty.

As another example, Johnson and Sanday (1971) set out to study the poor by focusing on neighborhoods defined as poverty-stricken by the local antipoverty agency. They further select the most deteriorated blocks for their sampling unit. Yet they still find a sufficient number of non-poor people (as defined by an arbitrary line) in the sample to provide a non-poor comparison. Few attitudinal differences between poor and non-poor emerge in the study. However, many differences emerge between blacks and whites. The authors conclude from this that the socio-political effects of racial status are more relevant to explain any incidence of so-called poverty attitudes than is income. I am inclined to agree with their conclusions, but I certainly do not feel that the study successfully delineated "the poor" and differentiated them from the non-poor, if indeed this could be done. The arbitrary line drawn between poor and non-poor did not create real interacting units of people that would be capable of creating and transmitting group-patterned behavior. Poor and non-poor from the same block probably had a greater chance of sharing belief patterns than individuals with like incomes from different blocks or neighborhoods, due to the direct influence of particular neighborhood dynamics which was not controlled for. Furthermore, the white sample contained significantly large numbers of the aged, and no information was provided about the social origins and career histories of the whites, or of the blacks. It is possible that the whites formerly knew periods of much higher income and income security, and that the younger blacks had career histories quite distinct from those of the whites. Despite current income level similarity, such work experiences alone could account for the posited black and white subculture differences.

Finally, in an empirical test of culture of poverty attitudes by Irelan et al (1969), half of the subjects were selected and defined as "poor" merely because they were welfare recipients, while the other half were located through social agencies of which they were clients. Moreover, the verbal responses used to test attitudes had been collected by other investigators for a completely different study and "re-operationalized" to test "culture of poverty" attitudes. Thus groups of people defined primarily through dependency on a government agency were used to prove or disprove that "poverty" produced feelings of dependency. We may learn some interesting things about attitudinal differences between the white, Negro and Mexican American subgroups contained in the sample, but we learn little about the direct relationship between material deprivation and human behavior and attitudes.[8]

Thus much of the poverty literature uses the poverty label to subsume an interest in politically or socially deprived minority groups in the United States. This is not to say that it is not legitimate for the anthropologist to investigate the effects of low and insecure income on behavioral responses; the ecologists' interest in the implications of subsistence patterns has an important and longstanding place in anthropology. But if urban anthropologists want to learn about the independent effects of material deprivation or, more specifically, low and unstable cash income in an urban industrial society, they will have to work with units of analysis which are more precisely defined in terms of cash resources. Moreover, such units must be bounded, interacting units which lend themselves to ethnographic analysis.

Marginal Occupations as Units of Analysis

Units of analysis which fit this need can be found in the group of marginal occupations which exist in urban industrial systems and yield the lowest, least stable income for their practitioners. Striking similarities exist between the types of work which provide the major sources of income for most of the working poor and sporadically unemployed poor in both developing and advanced industrial systems. Abu-Lughod (1969:171) has referred to such work

---

[8] It must be mentioned, however, that Irelan et al (1969) is the only study which mentions such economic measures as skill-level of occupation, amount of savings and amount of debt.

activities as "the netherworld of services." She indicates that such activities are often of dubious productivity and occasionally of dubious legitimacy. Liebow (1967, 1970) has described a similar set of activities in the United States. Most analysts have noted the low and unstable income and lack of career mobility in these activities. It is, in fact, the people who rely on these occupations for cash who approximate most closely what is meant by "the poor." However, such occupational categories do provide much more precise units of analysis than such notions as "the poor" or "those in poverty." Murphy (1971) has recently stated that in developing the ecological approach, Steward was really creating an anthropology of work. If anthropologists can legitimately study hunting and gathering or agricultural activities and their implications for economic and social structure or behavior, then surely they could likewise focus on the marginal cash-producing activities in urban industrial society and their important social and economic implications. Such an approach could avoid the pitfalls of a poverty focus and yet discover much about material deprivation and the way people respond to it. Furthermore, it could add important new micro-units to the conceptual tools of the urban anthropologist.

Marginal occupations would include those work activities which are available to the unskilled and which return low and unstable wages. They lack long-term contractual agreements, any aspect of labor organization, and are characterized by extreme redundance in the labor supply. They may involve heavy energy and/or time inputs relative to rates of pay, as well as activities which are negatively valued because they involve dirty or impure substances or illicit behavior.

The list of such job activities is surprisingly consistent in most of the developing areas of the world. Heavy-energy jobs include pre-mechanized, non-unionized earthmoving or brickmaking in construction, dockwork, general portage, and the manipulation of human energy-propelled transportation vehicles such as pedicabs or bicycle rickshaws. Work which involves dirt removal, such as private streetcleaning, janitorial service and domestic work would be included. Such time-consuming activities as message running or night watching can be included as well as the activities of the large group of streethawkers, peddlers, scavengers and ragpickers.

Finally, amateur practitioners of illicit trades often fit the characteristics of marginal workers. By the amateur practice of illicit activities, we mean the occasional entrance of an individual into such activities as prostitution, thievery, begging, gambling or bootlegging; no permanent commitment is made to the activity. Such practitioners do not acquire the higher-level skills of the profession nor are they protected by its organized core. In fact, they run a risk in practicing on the periphery of a domain controlled by professionals. They are also deprived of the high income potential of the profession. However, they avoid permanent social stigma by often leaving their locale of residence to practice.

The Economic and Social Implications of Marginal Activities

Marginal occupations could be studied as a pool of income-producing alternatives which are more or less equivalent in terms of access and reward and which are used sequentially or simultaneously by the urban poor. However, these activities must first be examined individually. Significant differences exist in their patterns of recruitment and socialization, their potential for upward mobility, and their potential for expanding a worker's network of significant relationships.

Each marginal activity operates differently with respect to recruitment and socialization. Some are more open in recruitment than others. Sex and age discrimination varies cross-culturally for different occupations; for instance, Islamic protection of women precludes the occupation of women in streetvending in the Middle East, in contrast to the very different situation in West Africa. Some activities also require more skill-training than others. For instance, Patch (1967) describes the recruitment and socialization of a marginal street vendor in Lima, Peru. Because of the high degree of competition in this activity, it is hard for the potential vendor to learn the things he must know about suppliers and the tricks of selling from other vendors; the individual Patch describes finally succeeds in acquiring the many skills necessary for successful vending only through observation and experience. Thus much learning can be involved in order to survive in even the marginal occupations, and some of these work activities are considerably more specialized and less open in recruitment than others. Yet we know little about the nature of skill learning in "unskilled" occupations or of selective recruitment patterns.

We also know little about the potential of different marginal occupations for upward mobility. Because of the different number of specialized skills involved, some activities lend themselves to permanent career commitment in spite of the low reward produced. If there is greater personnel stability in one activity as a consequence of specialized skills, then such activities may tend to be more highly organized than others, and may tend to offer hierarchical career steps so that occupants could achieve a vertical career. However, this is not always the case. Small-scale sweatshop manufacturing is an example of an activity which definitely develops specialized skills, but which is characterized by extreme instability. This is partly because the role of employer in such enterprises is uncomfortably balanced between that of patron and that of a purely commercial boss. The vulnerable position of his low-capital, small-scale enterprise makes it necessary for him to hire and fire men at will. The misunderstandings engendered by the two contradictory aspects of such a boss-worker relationship contribute to personnel instability. Thus, even though skills are involved, vertical careers in such enterprises are few.

Some marginal activities have greater potential for the expansion of capital than others. Even within the single activity of street vending, different products offer different opportunities for retaining capital. Such factors as the unit cost and perishability of merchandise affect net profit. Sellers of cooked food or other items which involve labor added to a commodity require less advanced credit than do sellers of manufactured articles, and can thus avoid indebtedness to a creditor.

Marginal activities also differ in the opportunities they offer for secondary or moonlighting activities. Time-consuming activities such as watching, message-running, rickshaw driving and porterage involve the heavy expenditure of time in a limited place, watching or waiting for work; the need for the worker to focus on his activity precludes other cash producing activities, and he thus receives a minimal return for time spent. Other activities which use time differently offer greater potential for simultaneous participation in alternative activities. Knowledge about career potentials would aid in developing manpower policies more conducive to vertical careers.

Marginal work activities also offer different consequences for the formation of social network ties for the practitioner. For those who are materially deprived as a result of marginal occupations, it is important to develop a large network of people to call on for loans and crisis aid. Some activities offer greater opportunities for establishing ties of intimacy, trust and mutual aid than others. For example, watchman jobs isolate the practitioner from any sustained social interaction either with peers or superordinates, whereas dockwork and menial construction jobs often involve group activity and thus provide a context for making friends. However, when the latter jobs are allocated on a daily basis, such continuity is lost. Vending can also offer potential for developing peer relationships, if street locations are more or less permanent or if shills are used; more mobile vendors, however, have fewer opportunities to cultivate peer ties.

In some societies, many occupations tend to lead to common lodgings. Ragpickers in Japan tend to reside in groups all subordinate to one junk wholesaler (Tairo, 1968). Common lodgings were characteristic of pedicab drivers in Bangkok (Textor, 1961). Fabrega (1971) indicates that while beggars in a southeastern Mexican city have little or no contact "on the job," they often cook, eat and sleep together. Further investigation of such social correlates of marginal activities seems promising.

Another area for investigation is the social value ascribed to different activities; i.e., how they are ranked in a given system by the potential participants. It is probable that the order of rank will vary considerably in different cultural systems, and that it will affect the preferred work choices of the unskilled. Through empirical observation of how people distribute themselves among the available marginal activities, we could better understand patterned preferences for and avoidance of certain jobs in different systems. Such variables as attitudes about use of time, autonomy in work and desirable physical settings would affect such choices. Does the preference for autonomy in work which produces a positive view of small-scale entrepreneurship in Latin America[9]

[9] Peattie (1968) provides some insight about the desire to be one's own boss that influences the high preference for entrepreneurial activities in one Venezuelan neighborhood. This is a frequent theme in the regional literature.

occur elsewhere? Is the degree of stigma attached to begging less in systems where asceticism is more socially approved? Is prostitution more stigmatized in Islamic countries than elsewhere as a result of the protection of women? If so, how does this affect the use of prostitution as an occasional cash-producing alternative in the Middle East?

There is a great shortage of ethnographic information about marginal occupations. There are a few studies directly focused on such an activity (Textor, 1961, Gould, 1965, Gore, 1958, Fabrega, 1971 and Tairo, 1968). Further glimmers of the kind of information needed can be found in Geertz' (1963) descriptions of petty traders and artisans in Java, Patch's (1967) descriptions of vendors and thieves in the marketplace in Lima, and fleeting references to small-scale commercial enterprises in studies of Latin American squatter settlements.[10] In more complete ethnographies of low-income communities, Liebow (1967) and Peattie (1968) describe the several ways in which residents make a living at largely marginal work activities. They also describe the economic life histories of some individuals. Other life histories with career sequences can also be found occasionally in the ethnographic literature (e.g., Lewis, 1961, 1966; de Jesus, 1962). However, the data are few and by no means comparable in aspects covered. What is needed is a concerted effort to develop an "anthropology of work" for urban-industrial societies as we have done for simpler production systems.

It seems likely that low-level activities in the tertiary sector will remain important in occupational structures for a long time. If this is the case, research relating to the processes of recruitment, acquisition of skills, potential for mobility, social network ties and cultural work preferences will have policy implications. Cross-cultural comparisons might indicate efficient ways to improve the income level, income stability, and social potential of marginal activities. Understanding cultural preferences would facilitate policies tailored to fit such preferences so as to maximize success.[11]

By studying those individuals locked into careers of marginal activities, anthropologists could return to the central issue in the poverty literature, namely, the relationship between low, unstable income and behavior. Cross-cultural studies could prove useful here, since similar coping responses which maximize limited income and minimize the effects of sporadic income do seem to have cross-cultural distribution. The use of second-hand goods, the development of small-scale credit pools, the patterned use of lump sums of capital from lotteries or bonuses are similar in Hong Kong, Johannesburg and Lima. Specific types of sexual unions, household structures and child-care arrangements have a wide distribution among low income populations and seem

[10] Mangin (1970c) and Roberts (1971) indicate that very large proportions of the respective households in their urban communities derived some income from tiny shops in the home. These authors provide little description of the enterprises. However, Peattie (1968) provides some description and some economic data as well.

[11] Gans (1968) makes the point that United States policy in relation to job training and placement for the poor would be more successful if programs tailored jobs to fit the preferences of the low-income population.

to have adaptive qualities. Lewis, for example, mentioned these coping responses, but they were ignored in the challenge to his central notion that the poor have a crippling ideology and limiting world view.

In conclusion, a research focus on marginal occupational groups would provide several advantages to the urban anthropologist. First, it would augment the limited number of urban micro-units already being studied. Second, it could illuminate the role of work as it relates to one's neighborhood of residence, maintenance of ethnic ties or individually-centered social network. Finally, such an approach could provide some insight about material deprivation in urban industrial society, by helping to demonstrate the relationship between income instability, income inadequacy and their social consequences, thereby avoiding the muddied waters of poverty analysis.

Acknowledgements

Many of the ideas in this article were developed while working with Edwin Eames on Urban Poverty in a Cross-Cultural Context, *New York: Free Press, 1973.*

Bibliography

ABU-LUGHOD, J.
     1969   Varieties of Urban Experience. In *Middle Eastern Cities*. I. Lapidus, ed. Berkeley: University of California Press.

BERREMAN, G. et al
     1971   *Anthropology Today*. Del Mar, California: CRM Books.

CURRENT ANTHROPOLOGY
     1967   Review Article of La Vida: A Puerto Rican Family in the Culture of Poverty, by Oscar Lewis (1965). *Current Anthropology*, **8**:480–500.
     1969   Review Article of Culture and Poverty: Critique and Counter-Proposals, by C. Valentine (1968). *Current Anthropology*, **10**:181–201.

DE JESUS, M.
     1962   *Child of the Dark*. New York: The New American Library.

FABREGA, H.
     1971   "Begging in a Southeastern Mexican City," *Human Organization*, **30**:277–87.

FERMAN, L. et al
     1965   *Poverty in America*. Ann Arbor: University of Michigan Press.

GANS, H.
     1968   Culture and Class in the Study of Poverty. In *On Understanding Poverty*. D. P. Moynihan, ed. New York: Basic Books.

GEERTZ, C.
     1963   *Peddlers and Princes*. Chicago: University of Chicago Press.

GLADWIN, T.
     1967   *Poverty, U.S.A.* Boston: Little, Brown.

GORDON, M.
1965   *Poverty in America.* San Francisco: Chandler.
GORE, M.
1958   "Society and the Beggar," *Sociological Bulletin,* 7:23–48.
GOULD, H.
1965   Lucknow Rickshawallas: The Social Organization of an Occupational Category. In *Kinship and Geographical Mobility.* K. Ishwaran and R. Piddington, eds. Leiden: E. J. Brill.
GUTKIND, P. C. W.
1967   The Energy of Despair: Social Organization of the Unemployed in Two African Cities. Civilisations 17:186–211.
1968   African Responses to Urban Wage Employment. *International Labour Review,* 97:135–167.
1970   The Poor in Urban Africa: A Prologue to Modernization, Conflict and the Unfinished Revolution. In *Power, Poverty and Urban Policy.* Bloomberg and Schmandt, eds. Urban Affairs Annual Reviews 2. Beverly Hills: Sage.
HAGSTROM, W.
1965   The Power of the Poor. In *Poverty in America.* Ferman et al. Ann Arbor: University of Michigan Press.
HANNERZ, U.
1969   *Soulside.* New York: Columbia University Press.
HANSON, R. C. and O. G. SIMMONS
1969   "Differential Experience Paths of Rural Migrants to the City," *American Behavioral Scientist,* 13:14–35.
IRELAN, L. et al
1969   "Ethnicity, Poverty and Selected Attitudes: A Test of the Culture of Poverty Hypothesis," *Social Forces,* 47:405–443.
JAMES, B. J.
1970   "Continuity and Emergence in Indian Poverty Culture," *Current Anthropology,* 11:435–53.
JOHNSON, N. and P. SANDAY
1971   "Subcultural Variations in an Urban Poor Population," *American Anthropologist,* 73:128–44.
LEACOCK, E. B., ed.
1971   *The Culture of Poverty: A Critique.* New York: Simon and Schuster.
LEEDS, A.
1969   "The Significant Variables Determining the Character of Squatter Settlements." America Latina 12:44–86.
1971   The Concept of the "Culture of Poverty: Conceptual, Logical and Empirical Problems with Perspectives from Brazil and Peru." In *The Culture of Poverty: A Critique.* E. B. Leacock, ed. New York: Simon and Schuster.
LEWIS, O.
1959   *Five Families: Mexican Studies in the Culture of Poverty.* New York: Basic Books.
1961   *Children of Sanchez.* New York: Random House.
1965   *La Vida: A Puerto Rican Family in the Culture of Poverty.* New York: Random House.

1966   "The Culture of Poverty," *Scientific American,* **215**:19–25.

1968   *Slum Culture: Backgrounds to 'La Vida.'* New York: Random House.

LIEBOW, E.

1967   *Tally's Corner.* Boston: Little, Brown.

1970   "No Man Can Live With The Terrible Knowledge That He Is Not Needed," *New York Times Magazine,* April 5, 1970:28–29, 129–133.

Mangin, W.

1967   Latin American Squatter Settlements: A Problem and a Solution. Latin American Research Review 2:65–98.

1970a   Poverty and Politics in the Latin American City. In *Power, Poverty and Urban Policy,* Bloomberg and Schmandt (eds.). Urban Affairs Annual Reviews 2. Beverly Hills: Sage.

1970b   Introduction. In *Peasants in Cities.* W. Mangin, ed. Boston: Houghton Mifflin.

1970c   Urbanization Case History. In *Peasants in Cities.* W. Mangin, ed. Boston: Houghton Mifflin.

MILLER, S. M.

1964   "The American Lower Class: A Typological Approach." *Social Research,* **31**:1–22.

MILLER, W. B.

1968   "The Elimination of the American Lower Class as National Policy." In *On Understanding Poverty.* D. P. Moynihan, ed. New York: Basic Books.

1971   "Subculture, Social Reform and the 'Culture of Poverty'." Human Organization 30:111–125.

Murphy, R.

1971   *The Dialectics of Social Life: Alarms and Excursions in Anthropological Theory.* New York: Basic Books.

NELSON, J.

1970   "The Urban Poor." *World Politics,* **22**.

PARKER, S. and R. KLEINER

1970   "The Culture of Poverty: An Adjustive Dimension." *American Anthropologist,* **72**:516–28.

PATCH, R.

1967   "La Parada: Lima's Market," American Universities Field Staff Report, West Coast of South America 14, Pts. I, II and III.

PEATTIE, L. R.

1968   *The View from the Barrio.* Ann Arbor: University of Michigan Press.

Price, J.

1968   "The Economic Organization of the Outcasts of Feudal Tokyo," *Anthropological Quarterly,* **41**:209–17.

ROBERTS, B.

1970   "The Social Organization of Low-Income Families." In *Crucifixion by Power.* R. Adams et al. Austin: University of Texas Press: 479–515.

SELIGMAN, B., ed.

1965   *Poverty as a Public Issue.* New York: Free Press.

TAIRO, K.

1968   "Ragpickers and Community Development: Ants Villa in Tokyo," *Industrial and Labor Relations Review,* **22**:3–19.

TEXTOR, R.
   1961   *From Peasant to Pedicab Driver.* Southeast Asia Studies Cultural Report
           Series 9. New Haven: Yale University Press.
VALENTINE, C.
   1968   *Culture and Poverty: Critique and Counterproposal.* Chicago: Univer-
           sity of Chicago Press.
WEISBROD, B., ed.
   1965   *The Economics of Poverty: An American Paradox.* Englewood Cliffs:
           Prentice Hall.
WILL, R. E. and H. G. VATTER, eds.
   1965   *Poverty in Affluence: The Social, Political and Economic Dimensions of
           Poverty in the United States.* New York: Harcourt, Brace and World.

Child of the Dark

CAROLINA MARIA DE JESUS

The selection which follows is from Child of the Dark, *the diary of Carolina
Maria de Jesus, a dweller in a favela (shantytown) of São Paulo, Brazil. This remarkable document first appeared in the early 1960s and shocked many into an awareness of what it meant to be one of the urban poor. Middle-class Brazilians were
especially shaken by this view of the underclass in their own society. The narrative even sparked a modicum of reform.*

*This is not a private diary. Carolina obviously had a dream of someday finding
someone to publish it and she wrote from that perspective. But what she wrote
about was what she knew, and what she knew was desperation, fear, cruelty,
and a stubborn will to survive for the experience of hope and joy.*

*Her experiences with welfare show how hard it is to deal effectively with the
dispersed bureaucracy of metropolitan agencies. It is logistically difficult and
economically costly to go from one building in this part of town to another
building in that.*

*De Jesus tells how the squatters—the favelados—eke out an existence from
day to day, aided in part by the multiple "opportunities" which the tough ones,
like herself, can seize from the context of the city—a free cracker from a baking
factory; a tomato from a restaurant's garbage; some bones here, and an old
sweater there. She is highly skilled in her marginal occupation.*

*One of the most striking results of this narrative is the view it offers of the
dreary repetitiveness of each day in poverty: the ritual treks to this alley and that;
the paltriness of the rewards (some paper, a bit of junk) that spell triumph.*

*Carolina supports her children by hunting and gathering. Her main income is
derived from the sale of scrap. Her laughter is bitter, but she can still see humor*

*in the spectacle of the Federal Board of Health representatives coming to the
favelas with films designed to show residents the necessity of installing lavatories
in their tin, cardboard, and scrap lumber shacks.*

*Life may not be so overwhelmingly desperate, so dangerously marginal in the
rural areas. Many have wondered why country folk continue to flock to the cities,
swelling the already overcrowded slums, dying in the shantytowns. Carolina
Maria de Jesus can tell them. It's because the city still offers the possibilities for
crackers from baking factories, tomatoes from restaurant garbage, vast streets
and alleys filled with sellable urban waste, and publishers who might one day
buy your manuscript. None of these can be found in rural villages and isolated
hamlets.*

May 22   Today I'm sad. I'm nervous. I don't know if I should start crying or
start running until I fall unconscious. At dawn it was raining. I couldn't go out
to get any money. I spent the day writing. I cooked the macaroni and I'll
warm it up again for the children. I cooked the potatoes and they ate them. I
have a few tin cans and a little scrap that I'm going to sell to Senhor Manuel.
When João came home from school I sent him to sell the scrap. He got 13
cruzeiros. He bought a glass of mineral water: two cruzeiros. I was furious
with him. Where had he seen a *favelado* with such highborn tastes?

The children eat a lot of bread. They like soft bread but when they don't
have it, they eat hard bread.

Hard is the bread that we eat. Hard is the bed on which we sleep. Hard is
the life of the *favelado*.

Oh, São Paulo! A queen that vainly shows her skyscrapers that are her
crown of gold. All dressed up in velvet and silk but with cheap stockings un-
derneath—the favela.

The money didn't stretch far enough to buy meat, so I cooked macaroni
with a carrot. I didn't have any grease, it was horrible. Vera was the only one
who complained yet asked for more.

"Mama, sell me to Dona Julita, because she has delicious food."

I know that there exist Brazilians here inside São Paulo who suffer more
than I do. In June of '57 I felt rich and passed through the offices of the Social
Service. I had carried a lot of scrap iron and got pains in my kidneys. So as
not to see my children hungry I asked for help from the famous Social Service. It was there that I saw the tears slipping from the eyes of the poor. How
painful it is to see the dramas that are played out there. The coldness in which
they treat the poor. The only things they want to know about them is their
name and address.

I went to the Governor's Palace.[1] The Palace sent me to an office at Brigadeiro Luis Antonio Avenue. They in turn sent me to the Social Service at the
Santa Casa charity hospital. There I talked with Dona Maria Aparecida, who
listened to me, said many things yet said nothing. I decided to go back to the

---

[1] Like most Brazilians, Carolina believes in going straight to the top to make her complaints.

Palace. I talked with Senhor Alcides. He is not Japanese yet is as yellow as rotten butter. I said to Senhor Alcides:

"I came here to ask for help because I'm ill. You sent me to Brigadeiro Louis Antonio Avenue, and I went. There they sent me to the Santa Casa. And I spent all the money I have on transportation."

"Take her!"

They wouldn't let me leave. A soldier put his bayonet at my chest. I looked the soldier in the eyes and saw that he had pity on me. I told him:

"I am poor. That's why I came here."

Dr. Osvaldo de Barros entered, a false philanthropist in São Paulo who is masquerading as St. Vincent de Paul. He said:

"Call a squad car!"

The policeman took me back to the favela and warned me that the next time I made a scene at the welfare agency I would be locked up.

Welfare agency! Welfare for whom?

May 23 I got up feeling sad this morning because it was raining. The shack is in terrible disorder. And I don't have soap to wash the dishes. I say "dishes" from force of habit. But they are really tin cans. If I had soap I would wash the clothes. I'm really not negligent. If I walk around dirty it's because I'm trapped in the life of a *favelado*. I've come to the conclusion that for those who aren't going to Heaven, it doesn't help to look up. It's the same with us who don't like the favela, but are obliged to live in one. . . . It doesn't help to look up.

June 13 I dressed the boys and they went to school. I went to look for paper. At the slaughterhouse I saw a young girl eating sausages from the garbage.

"You should get yourself a job and you'd have a better life."

She asked me if looking for paper earned money. I told her it did. She said she wanted to work so she could walk around looking pretty. She was 15 years old, the age when we think the world is wonderful. The age when the rose unfolds. Later it falls petal by petal and leaves just the thorns. For those who tire of life . . . there is suicide. Others steal. I looked at the face of the girl. She had blisters all over her mouth.

The prices mount up like waves of the sea. Each one is stronger. Who fights with waves? Only the sharks. But the strongest shark is the thinking one. He walks on earth. He is the merchant.[2]

Lentils are 100 cruzeiros a kilo, a fact that pleases me immensely. I danced, sang and jumped and thanked God, the judge of kings! Where am I to get 100 cruzeiros? It was in January when the waters flooded the warehouses and ruined the food. Well done. Rather than sell the things cheaply, they kept them waiting for higher prices. I saw men throw sacks of rice into the river. They threw dried codfish, cheese, and sweets. How I envied the fish who didn't work but lived better than I.

June 14 It's raining and I can't go out looking for paper. On a rainy day I'm a

---

[2] In Portuguese slang, shark is the name given to anyone who tries to make high or illicit profits from others.

beggar. I walk around ragged and dirty. I wear the uniform of the unfortunate. And today is Saturday. The *favelados* are considered beggars and I'm going to take advantage of it. Vera can't go with me because of the rain. I dug out an old umbrella that I found in the garbage and went out. At the slaughterhouse I got some bones. They'll do to make soup. At least the stomach won't remain empty. I've tried to live on air and almost fainted. I resolved then and there to work because I don't want to give up this life.

I'd like to see how I'm going to die. Nobody should feed the idea of suicide. But today he who lives till the hour of his death is a hero. Because he who is not strong gives in.

I heard a woman complaining that the bones she got at the slaughterhouse were clean.

"And I like meat so much!"

I got nervous listening to the woman complaining because it's hard enough for people just to live on this earth, not having sufficient food to eat. For as I've noted, God is the king of the wise men. He put men and animals on the earth. But what the animals eat, nature supplies. If animals had to eat like men, they would suffer greatly. I think of this because when I have nothing to eat I envy the animals.

When I was waiting in line to get some crackers, I listened to the women complaining. One told of stopping at a house and asking for a handout. The lady of the house told her to wait. The woman said that the housewife came back with a package and gave it to her. She didn't want to open the package near her friends, because they would ask for some of it. She started to think. Is it a piece of cheese? Can it be meat? When she got back to her shack, the first thing she did was tear open the package. When she unwrapped it, out fell two dead rats.

There are people who make fun of those who beg. The man said he wouldn't give out any more crackers, but the women remained calm. And the line grew. When a customer arrived to buy, he explained:

"Excuse the ugliness of these people waiting at the factory door. It's my bad luck that every Saturday they put me through this hell."

I waited impatiently to hear what else the factory owner would say. I wanted to hear what the women said. What a sad sight for those who were present. The poor wanting something. The rich not wanting to give. He handed out only pieces of crackers. And they were as happy as Queen Elizabeth of England when she received the 13 millions in jewels that President Kubitschek sent her as a birthday present.

The factory owner, seeing that they didn't go away, ordered them given whole crackers. An employee gave them to us and said:

"Everyone who gets his crackers must get away from here."

They claim that they're not able to give alms because the price of the wheat flour had gone up a great deal. But the beggars are now in the habit of getting their crackers every Saturday.

I didn't get any crackers so I went to the street market to pick up vegetables. I met Dona Maria do José Bento and we started to talk about the cost of living.

June 16   José Carlos is feeling better. I gave him a garlic enema and some hortelã tea. I scoff at women's medicine but I had to give it to him because actually you've got to arrange things the best you can. Due to the cost of living we have to return to the primitive, wash in tubs, cook with wood.

I wrote plays and showed them to directors of circuses. They told me:

"It's a shame you're black."

They were forgetting that I adore my black skin and my kinky hair. The Negro hair is more educated than the white man's hair. Because with Negro hair, where you put it, it stays. It's obedient. The hair of the white, just give one quick movement, and it's out of place. It won't obey. If reincarnation exists I want to come back black.

One day a white told me:

"If the blacks had arrived on earth after the whites, then the whites would have complained and rightly so. But neither the white nor the black knows its origin."

The white man says he is superior. But what superiority does he show? If the Negro drinks *pinga*, the white drinks. The sickness that hits the black hits the white. If the white feels hunger, so does the Negro. Nature hasn't picked any favorites.

June 17   I spent the night like this: I woke up and wrote. Afterward I went back to sleep. At 5 a.m. Vera started to vomit. I gave her some medicine, she slept. When the rain stopped I took advantage of it and went out. I filled one sack with paper. I only received 12 cruzeiros. I found some tomatoes and a little garlic and ran home because Vera is sick. When I arrived she was sleeping. But with the noise I made she woke up. She said she was hungry. I bought some milk and made oatmeal for her. She ate, then vomited up a worm. Afterward she got up, walked a bit, then laid down again.

I went to Senhor Manuel to sell some iron and get money. I am nervous with fear Vera will get worse, because the money I have will not be enough to pay a doctor. Today I am praying and begging God that Vera gets better.

June 18   Today it dawned raining. Yesterday Vera spit two worms out of her mouth. She has a fever. There is no school today in honor of the Prince of Japan.

June 19   Vera is still sick. She told me it was the garlic enema I gave her that made her ill. But here in the favela various children are attacked by worms.

José Carlos doesn't want to go to school because it is getting cold and he doesn't have shoes. But today is exam day and he went. I am worried because the cold is freezing. But what can I do?

I left and went to hunt paper. I passed by Dona Julita's but she was at the market. I went by the shoe store to collect their paper. The sack was heavy. I should have carried the paper in two trips. But I carried it in one because I wanted to get home sooner because Vera was sick and alone.

June 20   I gave Vera some milk. All I know is that milk is an extra expense and is ruining my unhappy pocketbook. I put Vera to bed and went out. I was so nervous! I felt I was as a battlefield where no one was going to get out alive. I thought of the clothes I had to wash and of Vera. If she gets worse? I can't possibly count on her father. He doesn't know Vera, nor has Vera ever seen him.

Everything in my life is fantastic. Father doesn't know his child, the child doesn't know his father.

There was no paper in the streets. And I wanted to buy a pair of shoes for Vera. I went on looking for paper. I earned 41 cruzeiros. I kept thinking of Vera, who would complain and cry because when she doesn't have anything to wear, she sobs that she doesn't like to be poor. I thought: if misery even revolts children . . .

June 25   I made coffee and dressed the children for school. I put beans on to cook. I dressed Vera and we went out. João was playing. When he saw me, he ran. And José Carlos gets frightened when he hears my voice. I saw a government station wagon. The São Paulo Health Department had come to pick up the excrement. The papers say there are 160 positive worm cases here in the favela. Is it possible they're going to give away medicine? The majority of the *favelados* don't have any way to buy it. I didn't take the examination. I went to look for paper. I only got 25 cruzeiros. And now there is a man who looks for paper in my zone. But I didn't fight with him over it. Because in a few days he'll give up. He is already complaining that what he gets doesn't even go to buy *pinga*. That it's better to beg.

I went past the canning factory and found a few tomatoes. The manager when he saw me began to swear at me. But the poor must pretend that they can't hear. When I got home I made a salad for the children.

June 26   I heard the rumor that the police are going to demand the *favelados* get off State land where they've built their shacks without permission. Many people who had houses here in the favela moved to State land becaue there, when it rains, there's no mud. They say they're going to build a children's playground. What I think is: ironic is that the land once had brick houses on it and the State appropriated it. Now John Doe is building his shack.

December 31   I got up at 3:30 and went to get water. I woke the children and they had their coffee. We went out. João was looking for paper because he wanted money to go to the movies. What torment it is to carry three sacks of paper. We earned 80 cruzeiros. I gave 30 to João.

I went shopping because tomorrow is the first day of the new year. I bought rice, soap, kerosene, and sugar.

João and Vera went to bed. I stayed up writing. Sleep came on me and I slept. I awoke with the whistle of the factory announcing the New Year. I thought of the São Silvestre races and of Manoel de Faria. I asked God to make him win the race. I also asked him to bless Brazil.

I hope that 1960 will be better than 1959. We suffered so much in 1959, that the people were singing:

"Go! Go for good!
I don't want you any more.
No, never more."

January 1, 1960   I got up at 5 and went to get water.

Ethnicity in the Politics of Stratification

ABNER COHEN

Ethnicity is a term which, particularly in the last decade, has become popular with scholars and laymen, administrators and social activists. But no one seems able to agree on a definition. Most of us have an intuitive sense of what it is, but attempts to reach consensus have failed. The criteria elude us: national identity; historical, cultural roots; political marginality; socially patterned behavior; racially linked behavior; and so on. We tend to give most weight to subcultural difference and identity. Almost automatically, we also tend to equate such differences with migrancy, foreign names, accents, food habits, and other manifestations of birth, socialization, or parentage in another nation.

The following excerpt from Abner Cohen is important because it stresses that ethnicity is behavior and identity rather than diverse national background. To illustrate his point, Cohen boldly deals with upper- and middle-class London brokers as an ethnic group (and thereby offers us a potentially useful tool for approaching the phenomenon of social stratification). These men share the same subcultural patterns because they have undergone the ritual training that people of their class accept as "simply what one does." Their manner, clothing, and livelihood easily identify them to others. They are the classic WASPs (who are rarely termed "ethnics"–indeed, are denied the right–for reasons interesting to explore in themselves) and, more specifically, are "City Men." They have been prepared throughout their lives to one day take their place in a certain sector of urban life. Most do their job, engaging in what some have called "the impersonal, financially oriented, and ultimately devaluating interaction" of urban life. Yet, Cohen's City Men are painted quite differently. And, interestingly, Cohen sees little difference in the way that City Men in London and Hausa traders in Yoruba towns "use their culture to organize and coordinate their effort . . . to maintain their share of the profits." What would Simmel have to say about this?

The literature of social anthropology abounds in cases where we can see the use of ethnicity in articulating the organizational functions of interest groups that for one reason or another cannot organize themselves formally. Examples such as the organization of resistance movements and of trading diasporas in underdeveloped countries illustrate the same process.

In order to highlight a few other points in the analysis of this type of organization, I would like to discuss briefly one more situation, this time within the context of such a complex and highly industrialized society as Britain.

I will not choose an apt illustration, such as Protestant and Catholic groupings in Northern Ireland or the formation of ethnic immigrant communities in many parts of the country, but a highly formalized and bureaucratized structure officially governed by purely contractual mechanisms. I am referring here to the now widely known case of the economic elite, or elites, that dominate the City of London, the nerve-centre of the financial system of Britain. No fieldwork by professional anthropologists or sociologists has been carried out in the City, but in recent years, and particularly since the publication of the report of the Bank Rate Tribunal in 1958, some accounts of various features of the organization of business within it have emerged, from a number of publications (see Lupton & Wilson, 1959; Ferris, 1960; Sampson, 1962; Chapman, 1968; Parry, 1969).

From these it is evident that millions of pounds' worth of business is conducted daily in the City without the use of written documents, arranged mainly verbally, in face-to-face conversations or over the telephone. It is claimed that this is necessary if business is to flow. But as the risks involved are formidable, the business is confined to a limited circle of people who trust one another. Such a high degree of trust can arise only among men who know one another, whose values are similar, who speak the same language in the same accent, respect the same norms, and are involved in a network of primary relationships that are governed by the same values and the same patterns of symbolic behaviour.

For these reasons, City men are recruited from exclusive status groups. They are mostly products of the public-school system.* The schools in this system achieve two major tasks: they socialize, or rather train, their pupils in specific patterns of symbolic behaviour, including accent, manner of speech, etiquette, style of joking, play; second, they create a web of enduring friendship and comradeship among the pupils, and these relationships are often continued through periodic old-boy reunions, affiliation with the same clubs, and further interaction in other social situations.

The City is thus said to be a village—barely one square mile in territory—in which everyone of importance knows everyone of importance. *Who* you know is more important than *what* you know. Often, the elite of the City are related to one another not only by a common style of life and by friendship, but also by kinship and affinal relationships. Lupton and Wilson (1959) present a reconstruction of the genealogies of over twenty elite family groupings that are interrelated through marriage and show the connections between top administrative, financial, and industrial 'decision-makers.'

*Editor's note: "Public" schools in England are what North Americans call "private."

The available reports indicate strongly that the speed and efficiency with which the City conducts its business are made possible mainly by this network of primary, informal, relationships connecting the business elite. This network is governed by archaic norms, values, and codes that are derived from the City's 'tribal past'—as Sampson puts it. It is held together by a complex body of customs that are to an outsider as esoteric and bizarre as those in any foreign culture. Ferris (1960:58–74) gives a dramatic description of the odd and highly stylized manner in which the stockbrokers—known in the City as the top-hatters because they still wear top hats—make their daily rounds in the City. They queue at a bank sitting on a hard bench, their striped trousers tugged up, exchanging a copy of *The Times* for the *Telegraph*. When they talk to the bank official, they pull up a chair and discuss cricket, television, and politics before mentioning money. This business of 'how-do-you-do', Ferris was told, is to acknowledge: 'we accept the normal rules of society, and we can now start exchanging ideas'. 'If you go to a bank with a top hat they say: "Oh, it's one of the brokers," and you walk right in. If you went in in a homburg there'd be an awful business of "Good gracious me, Mr —, where's your hat this morning?" There'd be a *thing*, which of course you want to avoid at all costs.' For if you behave in an 'abnormal' manner, your bank official will think that there is something 'fishy' about your behaviour, and unless there is an obvious explanation your creditworthiness may suffer—and without unblemished trustworthiness a broker cannot operate.

The Hausa traders in Yoruba towns (Cohen, 1969) conduct their business in much the same way as the City men, though they operate under different structural circumstances and using different symbolic patterns. A Hausa dealer from Northern Nigeria will entrust his goods and money in the South only to a Hausa broker. No matter how long the Hausa broker has been living in the South he will always be anxious to preserve the symbols of his Hausaism, dressing like a Hausa, speaking and behaving like a Hausa. Hausaism is essential for his livelihood. Just as City men in London make use of a series of customs to overcome technical problems of business, so the Hausa use different Hausa customs to create relationships of trust in the trading network. The customs that are implicit in the life-style of the City men are sovereign in their constraining power, as are the customs implicit in Hausa culture.

City men constitute an interest group that is part of the system of the division of labour in our society. They use their connections and the symbolism of their life-style to articulate a corporate organization that is partly formal and partly informal, in order to compete within the wider social system for a greater share of the national income. So do the Hausa use their culture to organize and coordinate their effort in order to maintain their share of the profits. In short, City men are socio-culturally as distinct within British society as are the Hausa within Yoruba society. They are indeed as 'ethnic' as any ethnic group can be. But they are not usually described as an ethnic group because the term is principally social and political, not sociological, even though there is massive sociological literature about it, particularly in the

USA. To many people, the term ethnicity connotes minority status, lower class, or migrancy. This is why sooner or later we shall have to drop it or to find a more neutral word for it, though I can see that we shall probably have to live with it for quite a while. This is not because it is difficult to find a substitute, but because the term can be of great heuristic significance for the current phase in the development of the anthropology of complex society. The concept of ethnicity throws into relief, or rather dramatizes, the processes by which the symbolic patterns of behaviour implicit in the style of life, or the 'sub-culture', of a group—even of highly individualistic men like members of an elite—develop in order to articulate organizational functions that cannot be formally institutionalized. It is easy to identify an elite when its men are from an ethnically distinct group like the Creoles in Sierra Leone (Cohen, 1971), the Americo Liberians in Liberia (Libenow, 1969), or the Tutsi in Rwanda (Maquet, 1961). But it is difficult to do so with an elite whose cultural distinctiveness within the society is not so visible, and whose members appear to the casual observer to be highly independent individualists.

If in a dynamic, contemporary, complex society a group of second- or third-generation migrants preserve their distinctiveness and make extensive use of the symbolism of their endoculture, then the likelihood that within the contemporary situation they have become an interest group is very strong. When, in a hypothetical case, two culture groups join together and interact politically and economically, and establish a new political system, they will soon become involved in cleavages on economic and political lines running throughout the extent of the new society. If a new line of cleavage, such as that of social class, then cuts across ethnic lines, ethnic identity and exclusiveness will tend to be inhibited by the emerging countervailing alignments. The poor from the one ethnic group will cooperate with the poor from the other ethnic group against the wealthy from both ethnic groups, who will, on their part, also cooperate in the course of the struggle to maintain their privileges. If the situation develops in this way, tribal differences will weaken and eventually disappear. The people will become detribalized. In time, class division will be so deep that two subcultures, with different styles of life, will develop and we may have a situation similar to that of Victorian Britain, to which Disraeli referred as 'the two nations', meaning the privileged and the underprivileged.

But the situation will be entirely different if the new class cleavage, in our hypothetical example, concides with tribal affiliations, so that within the new system the privileged will tend to be identified with one tribal group and the underprivileged with the other tribal group. In this situation cultural differences between the two groups will become entrenched, consolidated, and strengthened in order to articulate the struggle between the two social groups across the new class lines. Old customs will tend to persist. But within the newly emerging social system they will assume new values and new social significance.

The study of ethnicity will be heuristically important for us also in that it can help us to clarify the nature of socio-cultural change. For it is now clear to us that the formation of an ethnic group in town involves a dynamic rearrangement of relations and of customs, and that it is not the result of cultural conservatism and continuity. The continuity of customs and of some social formations is certainly there, but their functions change dramatically— although to the casual observer it will look as if there is stagnation, conservatism, or a return to the past. This is why a concentration on the study of culture as such will shed little light on the nature of ethnicity.

It is here that the monographs on tribal studies of the 1940s and 1950s can be of immense value. For by the study of the members of those tribes within the context of the developing towns, by either the same or different anthropologists, we shall be able to develop the analysis of the dynamics of cultural and structural changes in response to the complexity of modern society. We shall find out what customs are retained, borrowed, or developed and for what political purposes. More generally we shall be able to develop the dialectical study of socio-cultural interdependence.

Studies of this type will be of immense value in analysis of the more general processes of institutionalization and of symbolization, and will thus provide a unique contribution to social science generally. At the same time they will usher social anthropology into the systematic study of the complexity of contemporary industrial society, without our discipline losing its identity, i.e. without social anthropology becoming sociology, or political science, or history.

Bibliography

CHAPMAN, R. A.
   1968   *Decision-making: A Case Study of the Decision to Raise the Bank Rate in September 1957.* London: Routledge & Kegan Paul.
COHEN, A.
   1969   *Custom and Politics in Urban Africa.* London: Routledge & Kegan Paul; Berkeley: University of California Press.
   1971   The Politics of Ritual Secrecy. *Man* **6:**427–48.
FERRIS, P.
   1960   *The City.* Harmondsworth: Penguin.
LIEBENOW, J. G.
   1969   *Liberia: The Evolution of Privilege.* Ithaca and London: Cornell University Press.
LUPTON, T. & WILSON, S.
   1959   *Background and Connections of Top Decision-makers.* Manchester University School.
MAQUET, J.
   1961   *The Premise of Inequality in Ruanda.* London: Oxford University Press.

Parry, G.
  1969   *Political Elites.* London: George Allen & Unwin.
Sampson, A.
  1962.   *Anatomy of Britain.* New York and Evanston: Harper & Row; London: Hodder and Stoughton.

Elites and Ethnic Boundary Maintenance: A Study of the Role of Elites in Chinatown, New York City

BERNARD WONG

One reason that the elite are rarely studied is that they can erect greater barriers against the invasion of their privacy by social scientists. And, too, they have privileges which they wish to protect from outside view. This is in marked contrast with the more vulnerable poor who are accustomed to being asked to fill in forms, answer questions, and justify their needs. The poorer one is, the more one has no intermediaries who will skillfully fight one's battles and defend one's position (though the poor also have their own strategies and defenses). Finally, the less powerful members of society often welcome the chance to advertise their views or complaints and use researchers as their messengers or agents.

Bernard Wong's study of the functions of two groups of elites in New York's Chinatown describes how each uses ethnicity as a tool, and uses it differently.

The author leaves us with new questions: Why is the New Elite gaining more power at the expense of the Old Elite? What is the nature of the new ethnic boundary, or any boundary, ethnic or otherwise? And, more fundamentally, what are the mechanisms of transformation that operate in the urban context, whether ethnic, economic, religious, familial, or other?

Reflecting Skeldon's discussion of voluntary associations, Wong suggests that ethnic or marginal groups develop new needs and abilities with increased time in the city.

Introduction

The study of elites in urban ethnic communities, especially in the various urban Chinese communities in America, presents a challenging opportunity to a social scientist. Generally, the elite have been studied in relationship to their various roles as leaders and rulers (Weber, 1947; Pareto, 1935; Mills,

"Elites and Ethnic Boundary Maintenance: A Study of the Role of Elites in Chinatown, New York City," *Urban Anthropology,* **6**:1–22 (1977).

1969), patrons and culture brokers (Wolf, 1956, 1966; Foster, 1963a, 1963b; Boissevain, 1966; Mayer, 1967; Kenny, 1960; Campbell, 1964; Paine, 1971; Strickon and Greenfield, 1972; Geertz, 1963; Misra, 1961; Bottomore, 1964). Few studies, however, have been conducted on the roles of elites in urban ethnic communities in developed societies. There are virtually no ethnographic accounts of the activities of the elite, or their management of ethnic identities in the various urban Chinatowns in America.

The purpose of this paper is to describe and analyze the nature and functions of the elite in Chinatown, New York.[1] Within this general framework, the following questions will be asked:

1. Who are perceived to be the elite of the community? What are the sociocultural attributes of the elite?
2. What are the self-perceived identity or identities of the elite of Chinatown?
3. How do the elite use various symbols, identities, and resources for pursuing individual and collective goal-seeking activities?
4. What are the rules adopted by the elite in their interaction with each other, with the community, and with outsiders?

The elite of New York's Chinatown are of particular interest because of their heterogeneous composition as well as their diversified adaptive strategies within the elite categories, and because the elite have been the pillars of the social activities of Chinatown. Unlike the Chinese communities of Sarawak (Tien, 1953), Bangkok (Skinner, 1958), Manila (Amyot, 1960), and Lima (Wong, 1971), where elites are much more assimilated, those in the Chinese community of New York until recently were eager to use the Chinese ethnicity, values, and traditional social organizations to maintain the community's internal "law and order" and to preserve the integrity of their ethnic boundaries. Historically, New York's Chinatown has long been a relatively closed or "segregated" community. From its inception in the 1880s, Chinatown has relied on the elite for its general well-being. They have been instrumental in assisting members of the community to obtain employment and financing, and in settling disputes within the community. Even the average New Yorker recognizes the important role played by the president of the Chinese Consolidated Benevolent Association and attributes to him the title of "unofficial mayor" of Chinatown. Rose Lee (1960), Virginia Heyer (1953), Leon Gor Yun (1936), and Stuart Cattell (1962) allude to the "wheelings and dealings" of the power elite of New York's Chinatown. None of these authors, however, focused their attention on the nature, functions, and activity systems of the elite. The elite of Chinatown are of interest to anthropologists because of their differential use of ethnicity and self-identification. A study of the elite of Chinatown will contribute to an understanding of their role in the urban ethnic

[1] The data on which the present paper is based were obtained from fieldwork conducted in New York City in 1972–1973. The author is indebted to the National Science Foundation and the Ford Foundation for supporting the fieldwork and to Dr. Arnold Strickon of the University of Wisconsin-Madison for his helpful comments on the paper.

community, the community-city integration process, and the multifaceted aspects of ethnicity in an urban environment.

Sociocultural Characteristics of the Elite of Chinatown, New York City

New York City's Chinese population in 1970 was 69,324, according to the U.S. Bureau of Census. There has been a steady increase of 10,000 per year in the Chinese population since 1970, bringing the number of Chinese in New York City in 1976 to approximately 120,000. Of this number, 60,000 are said to reside in the Chinatown area on the Lower East Side of Manhattan. Other areas of Chinese concentration are in the vicinity of Columbia University in Manhattan, Flatbush in Brooklyn, Jackson Heights and Amherst in Queens. However, our concern here is the Chinatown area.

The term *elite* has usually been defined from an objective, *etic* point of view (Bottomore, 1964:1; Cole, 1955:102–103; Pareto, 1935:1422–1423; Nadel, 1956:415). The present study on the other hand is interested in the subjective perceptions and categorizations of the elite in the community.

Members of New York's Chinese community distinguish two kinds of elites or "big persons." One group is called the *Kiu Ling*[2] (literally, the leaders of the overseas Chinese). The other group are supervisors of, or social workers in, the social service agencies and are called *Chuen Ka*[3] (literally, experts on social problems).

The elite were identified by the reputational approach. Names of elites were solicited from key informants and the list of names was subsequently verified by checking randomly with the general public in the community.

Generally, members of the community and all my informants considered the "big persons" as the "upper crust" in the community, but "middle-class or upper-middle-class" people in the larger U.S. society (Wong, 1976). The income range of most of the elite (in 1974) is approximately $16,000 to $22,000 per year. Some elite persons, especially the *Kiu Ling*, are said to earn more than this because they are owners of firms.

Members of the community perceive differences within the elite in terms of age, birthplace, life-style, occupation, dialect, and language ability (see Table 1). *Kiu Ling* are China-born immigrants who came to this country many years ago. The number of *Kiu Ling* who are active in community affairs is said to be about 70. These individuals hold important positions in the 60-odd major family name, dialect, and regional associations, and in the Chinese Consolidated Benevolent Association. Serving as officers in the various traditional associations can bring both prestige and a solid following which may be helpful for

---

[2] This is a Cantonese transliteration, since the informants were Cantonese.

[3] *Chuen Ka* is the abbreviation of *She Hui Man Tai Chen Ka,* "social problem experts." Again, this is a Cantonese transliteration.

TABLE 1   Sociocultural Backgrounds of the Elites in Chinatown, New York City

	Traditional elite *(or Kiu Ling)*	*New elite* *(or Chuen Ka)*
Birthplace	China	U.S.A.
Age	Above 50	25 to 50
Occupation	Owners of Chinese-type business units: grocery stores, restaurants, novelty stores, department stores	Professionals: social workers, lawyers, accountants
Power base	Family name, territorial dialect associations, and Chinese Consolidated Benevolent Association	Social agencies, nonprofit community service organizations
Language	Sze Yup, Sam Yup, and Toysanese (mainly), with some knowledge of English	English; with some Cantonese-speaking assistants
Life-style	With exception of clothing, traditional rural Chinese	American middle class

future goal-seeking activities. Thus, the associations serve as a power base for the *Kiu Ling.*

A majority of the *Kiu Ling* are from the rural areas of Kwangtung province and generally speak the Sze Yup and Sam Yup dialects. They are entrepreneurs in typically Chinese businesses in Chinatown: laundries, chop suey restaurants, groceries, and gift stores. They are generally older, averaging 55 years of age, and have little formal education. Their many years of residence in the United States has brought some practical knowledge about this country and thus the *Kiu Ling* are familiar with two cultural systems—Chinese and American.

Frugality is proverbial among the older Chinese immigrants. Many of them have accumulated some wealth through years of hard work and saving. If there had not been a Communist takeover, they could have returned to China to be rich landlords or entrepreneurs, or simply to live a life of elegant retirement.

The second group of elites, known locally as *Chuen Ka,* are mostly Chinese-Americans who are social workers, or volunteers (whose actual occupations range from accountants, lawyers, and students to politicians) affiliated with a dozen social agencies. They can be second-, third-, or fourth-generation male or female Chinese-Americans. Very few of them speak any Chinese dialect. Because of this inability and their lack of knowledge of Chinese culture, they are frequently labeled by *Kiu Ling* as the *Juk Sing*—bamboo sticks (meaning rootless in either the Chinese or the American culture). *Chuen Ka* are generally college-educated in the U.S. and are professionals employed in American establishments. They are much younger than the Kiu Ling. While the *Kiu Ling* are more familiar with the Chinese culture, these new elites are more familiar with the English language and American society. As a group, the new elite are determined to upgrade the living standards of the Chinese community. They may also have certain self-interests, such as establishing an electoral power base or attracting customers to their accounting, law, and employment firms. Some of these Chinese-American elites are social workers who went to Chinatown to establish community services with funds available from the city, state, or federal government, and draw competitive salaries for their services. Other *Chuen Ka* volunteer their service for ideological or altruistic reasons. Almost all of the new elite use the social agencies to contribute their services to the community and to enlist followings.

The life-style of the new elite also differs from that of the *Kiu Ling*. The former tend to live according to the standard of the American middle class. Although they may work in Chinatown, they prefer to live in other suburban neighborhoods. A great deal of their money is spent for housing and for the purchase of automobiles, recreational equipment, and household furnishings. This explains why the new elite do not accumulate handsome savings like the *Kiu Ling*, who live frugally and humbly, putting their money in the bank or investing it in profit-generating enterprises. The traditional *Kiu Ling* often criticize the new elite for drawing salaries for their community service or for having ulterior motives such as obtaining votes. The *Kiu Ling* consider themselves to be altruistic since they give money and time to the community. The new elite respond by calling the *Kiu Ling* "obsessed name-seekers," or "prestige-seekers" who spend money to buy prestige.

The older elites are the merchants and businessmen who strive to secure the leadership positions from the traditional associations and hope to rule the community through the offices of the associations. Hence, they resemble the "govering elites" mentioned by Pareto (1935). The new elite, on the other hand, are U.S.-educated professionals who use the social agencies as their power base to recruit followers and contribute their service to the community. Thus, these new elites are similar to those middle-class elite in the developing countries who are eager to initiate sociocultural change (Bottomore, 1964; Geertz, 1963; Misra, 1961; Niel, 1960).

Management of Ethnic Identity

Jean Briggs's (1971:55–73) ethnographic data from the East Arctic has shown that an elite's (or patron's) goals, the strategies available to him, and the likelihood of his achieving his goals are influenced by the identity or identities he has chosen and that others have attributed to him. The identities selected by the two groups of elites in New York's Chinatown differ in many respects. Further, the ways in which they manipulate these identities for goal-seeking activities also vary.

First, the traditional elite tend to assume three identities: "Overseas Chinese," the "real Chinese," and "Chinese-Americans." When transacting with the Taiwan government, they assume the identity of Overseas Chinese because in so doing they are likely to be given special preference by the Taiwan government in all official interactions. Historically, the term *Kiu Ling* was used by the Nationalist (Kuomintang) government to refer to the exemplary Overseas Chinese who were leaders in championing the causes of the Kuomintang. The Nationalist government expects the *Kiu Ling* to play a bridging role between the community and Taiwan. Because of this expectation, a majority of the *Kiu Ling* take up an anti-Communist ideology and are hostile to groups that are sympathetic to the People's Republic of China. As leaders of the Overseas Chinese, *Kiu Ling* can obtain visas, export permits, and privileges under favorable export quotas of certain merchandise from Taiwan.

In dealing with the members of the community, the traditional elite tend to claim that they are the "real Chinese," as opposed to the second- and third-generation Chinese-Americans. A "real" Chinese means one who speaks and writes the Chinese language, interacts with other Chinese in a "humane," "Chinese" way, practices all the Chinese customs, celebrates the important Chinese festivals, etc. The occasion for proclaiming oneself as a real Chinese is generally during the course of elections in the various traditional associations. That is to say, in the recruitment of followers in the community and in the accumulation of political power in the community, it is believed that assuming the identity of a "real Chinese" is advantageous. The real Chinese identity is most often used in the context of opposition to the new elite.

Taking the identity of a Chinese-American is a necessity in transacting with the United States government, for only a citizen can benefit from the privileges and rights extended to the American public. Hence, when the *Kiu Ling* work with the United States government on behalf of the Chinese to protect their economic or political interests, they take up their Chinese-American identity.

Every American who has full or part Chinese blood, irrespective of language and birthplace, is a Chinese-American according to the new elite. The traditional elite, on the other hand, stress that only the "real Chinese" can understand the Chinese community and its problems and that outsiders should not interfere with the internal problems of the community. The new elite feel that every Chinese who is concerned with the community has the right to engage in community service. They feel that they are the middlemen who help the Chinese-American to participate in the resource distribution of the larger society in general and of New York City in particular. The *Chuen Ka* have been assisting members of the community in various ways: to adjust their visa status in the U.S., to obtain Social Security benefits, to secure funds from the city government to operate day care centers, to find jobs, and to provide free legal counsel. Through such endeavors, the new elite are winning the respect of the community and gradually attracting a clientele that usually has had to depend on the *Kiu Ling*.

The *Chuen Ka* also use a larger ethnic identity—Asian-American. The manipulation of regional ethnicity for goal-seeking activities is recognized by

Lyman and Douglas (1973), as they point out that there are situations which dictate the use of a larger ethnic identity. Many of the *Chuen Ka* realize that to fight racism they need more participants in their movement. However, it is not only the need for more members that has caused Chinese-Americans to cooperate with other Asians and to assume the Asian-American identity. Common interests and destiny are also important bases for such behavior. Japanese, Chinese, Koreans, and other Asians are frequently referred to in official legislation and documents as Asians or Orientals. Thus, if one Asian group— for example, the Japanese—breaks a racist barrier, it is likely that the Chinese and other Asians can also benefit. Using the Asian-American identity, many Asian groups have cooperated in their struggle for equal opportunity and human rights.

Values and Symbols Used by the Elites

In Chinatown, the two groups of elites circulate the use of different symbols and values for their goal-seeking activities.

Since they have assumed the identity of the real Chinese, the *Kiu Ling* envision themselves as "models to copy" by members of the community. To show their "Chineseness," they are eager (1) to participate in the twice-a-year ancestor worship and to direct the celebration of the traditional Chinese festivals, (2) to secure membership in many traditional associations, and (3) to involve themselves in the affairs of the associations. It is not uncommon to find a *Kiu Ling* simultaneously holding membership and offices in four or five associations. Membership and official titles in many associations are not only signs of popularity, but also symbols of wealth, power, and "Chineseness."

As a "real Chinese" a *Kiu Ling* feels that he is obligated to preserve Chinese culture in New York City. To them, an ethnic group is a unit of cultural transmission (Greeley, 1971, 1972). In this respect, the *Kiu Ling* are similar to the elites of Tabanon who see themselves as the preservers of their cultural tradition (Geertz, 1963). Participation in associations and organizing the sweeping-the-grave ceremonies and other ancestor-worship rituals are considered to be important in validating ther roles as culture preservers and in expressing their devotion to the traditional customs of China. Usually a Sunday during spring and during autumn are selected by the *Kiu Ling* as the days on which to bring members of the associations in chartered buses to Brooklyn's Evergreen Cemetery to visit the graves of former members of the community. The *Kiu Ling* usually make generous contributions to these ceremonies and are patrons for many other traditional celebrations such as the Chinese New Year. The colorful banners, the Lion Dance Troupe, and the Chinese firecrackers used for the Chinese New Year are financed chiefly by the voluntary contributions of the traditional elite.

As mentioned earlier, the *Kiu Ling* are usually older Chinese who are pro-Nationalist China (Taiwan). They do not hesitate to publicly demonstrate their pro-Kuomintang ideology. For example, pictures of Chiang Kai Shek and Sun Yat Sen are displayed in the offices of the various family, regional, and dialect associations, and in the Chinese Consolidated Benevolent Association. Both the Chinese (Kuomintang) and American flags are prominently displayed in the various parades sponsored by the *Kiu Ling*.

Not only do the traditional elites validate their "Chineseness" and their prestige through their active participation in Chinese festivals and their extravagant donations to cultural activities, but they also promote traditional Chinese values: *Lai* (or *Li* in Mandarin)—politeness and propriety; *Yee Hey* (*I Chi* in Mandarin)—trusting righteouness; *Kam Ching* (*Kan Ching* in Mandarin)—sentimental friendship; *Yan Ching* (*Jen Ching* in Mandarin)—human feelings; *Mien* (*Lien* in Mandarin)—face; and *Chang Ching* (*Chin Ching* in Mandarin)—warmth of kinship. These values are the basis for the operation of many transactional relationships such as the patron-client relationship, friendship, and kinship. Many of the traditional elite lamented that these basic values have become only a facade for many second- and third-generation Chinese and that consequently they do not feel confident in any dealings with them.

The new elite also use symbols and circulate social values, but for a different reason. The *Chuen Ka* fully realize that the continual expression and validation of Chinese culture are necessary for ethnic solidarity. Symbols are used and the memories of the tragic history of the early Chinese immigrants in America are recalled. Chinese are encouraged to wear Chinese clothes, especially during the parades and demonstrations. Buttons like "Asian power" and "Chinese power" are worn during demonstrations. In this case, the ethnic group is used not principally as a carrier of cultural traditions, but as an interest or pressure group for political and economic activities (Glazer and Moynihan, 1970). Leaflets are distributed by some social agencies to inform the Chinese public on how to protect their human rights, perform their civic duties, and file discrimination complaints. As a community worker or social worker, a *Chuen Ka* feels that he is an "educator" and an "agent of social change."

The *Chuen Ka* recognize that if they have a solid following it will be possible for them to secure more funds and other resources for the community. In order to build a sizable following among the Chinese, these elites proceed in a manner similar to that of many ethnic politicians, i.e., by way of "consciousness raising" (Novak, 1972). Such an effort is reflected in the newly installed mural near Chatham Square depicting the plight of the Chinese in America, in which an attempt is made to tell the history of the Chinese in America. On the left side of the mural is the infamous massacre of the Wyoming Rock Stream. On the right side of the mural there is a train symbolizing the contributions of the early Chinese immigrants who helped construct the Central Pacific Railroad. It is said that this mural was painted for the residents of Chinatown, not for its tourists. Thus, the message of this art work is clear: "Chinese should learn from their past experience."

While raising the ethnic consciousness of the Chinese, the *Chuen Ka* are at the same time purveying the values of the larger society such as "government exists for the individual," and "equality for all." Thus, the efforts of the new elite aim at preparing the members of the Chinese ethnic group to participate in the larger society.

Interaction Patterns

The two groups of elites follow different rules in dealing with the members of the community—outsiders and themselves as well. To the traditional elite, the Chinese community is for the "real Chinese." Thus, the second-and third-generation Chinese are to be excluded since they are "Americanized Chinese." According to the traditional elite, Chinese-Americans, including the new elite, should not interfere with the affairs of the Chinese community. In fact, Chinese-Americans who cannot speak the language are prohibited from competing for offices in the traditional Chinese family, regional, and dialect associations since they use Chinese as a medium of communication and as an official language for the settlement of disputes. Chinese-Americans are thus excluded from participating in the assocations which, according to the traditional elite, constitute the structure of the community.

The Chinese Consolidated Benevolent Association is the highest level overall organization of Chinatown. It coordinates the 59 trade, recreational, tong, regional, dialect, political, and family name associations, and the *fongs*. The lowest level of organization is the village association known locally as *fong*. The hierarchical structure of the community's associations is shown in Figure 1.

Membership in these associations varies. The number of active members at the mid-level (trade, recreational, *tong* regional, dialect, political, and family name) associations averages 300. Membership in the low-level associations (*fongs*) ranges from a handful to a few dozen. All the associations send their representatives to the CCBA, and these representatives constitute the Assembly of the CCBA.[4]

Because of the differences in language, life-styles, and mentality, there is little interaction between the new elite and the traditional elite. However, verbal attacks on each other's leadership qualifications are frequent. One traditional leader of the Chinese Consolidated Benevolent Association who is also president of a powerful merchant association said that only the *Kiu Ling* of Chinatown can solve the problems of the community: "How could those social agencies such as the Community Service Society, the Chinatown Planning Council, the Chinese Development Council, help us? They are all outsiders. We know our problems, and we have the means to solve them."

In other words, the *Kiu Ling* believe that they alone are the legitimate

---

[4] A complete exposition of the structure of the CCBA would require many pages. For more detail, consult James Lee (1972).

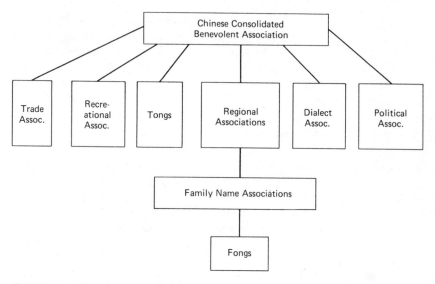

FIGURE 1. Chinatown's community structure.

resource personnel of the community. The *Chuen Ka* (the new elite), on the other hand, contend that the *Kiu Ling* and the Chinese Consolidated Benevolent Association cannot speak for the community for a variety of reasons. First, the CCBA includes only 59 community organizations; many others are not invited to participate in the decision-making processes of the CCBA because of ideological differences. Second, the leaders of the CCBA are unfamiliar with U.S. politics and the methods for tapping resources of the larger society. Third, the *Chuen Ka* say the CCBA is not concerned with the needs of the ordinary Chinese, but rather with the needs of business and employers in Chinatown. So far, attempts to reconcile the differences and bring about cooperation between the two groups of elites have not been successful. Thus, a power struggle between the two groups continues. Each tries to gather in the followers of the other. The new immigrants—the majority of the population—tend to use the social agencies and are more comfortable dealing with the new elite, who seem to be more "modern," more "urban," and more "knowledgeable" about New York City. Even some of the old immigrants found the new elite to be more efficient in alleviating their problems, for example, in obtaining medical care or social security benefits from the government.

Elites vis-à-vis the Chinese Community

According to the traditional elite, the hierarchical social order of Chinatown, which is patterned after the traditional peasant organization in China, should be maintained. All members of the community should affiliate with their respective regional, family, trade, dialect, and village associations. Members of the community should approach the *Kiu Ling* of the lower organizations before they approach the leaders of the higher level associations.

The traditional *Kiu Ling* still believe that Chinatown is a self-sufficient community that can take care of its welfare problems, solve its own disputes, and police its own people. Efforts are made to prevent intervention from the larger society. One of the most serious community concerns recognized by these elites is Chinese education. They are interested in having a Chinese school in the community for their children as well as for the children of their followers. The *Kiu Ling* perceive themselves as preservers of Chinese culture and see the Chinese school as a powerful vehicle for this preservation. Also, education is valued highly by the Chinese, and being a donor or patron for the community's educational concerns will bring great respect and prestige.

The Chinese school is supported financially by the *Kiu Ling* of the community. The richest and most powerful *Kiu Ling* will sit on the Executive Committee of the Board of Trustees. The leaders of the various family, regional, dialect, and trade associations are trustees of the Chinese school. At present, the president of the Board of Trustees is also the president of the Chinese Consolidated Benevolent Association, who has said that for reasons of autonomy the school has no intention of seeking help from the state or federal governments. It is generally feared that if the Chinese school received financial support from the city or state governments, the *Kiu Ling* would lose control of the school. Thus, there is an isolationist policy enacted by the community's *Kiu Ling* to deliberately prevent the possible intervention by the larger society. This phenomenon is not unique to Chinese ethnic groups. In *The American Minority Community*, Judith Kramer points out that most Jews and Catholics in America have not demanded equality and the complete abolition of social distance because they want to maintain their autonomy in their own communities (Kramer, 1970:65).

The Chinese school teaches not only the Chinese language but also Chinese culture. For example, it teaches Chinese folk music and folk dances, and sponsors special programs to educate Chinese youngsters on "filial piety." The schedule of the school is specially designed so that the children who study in American public schools can attend the Chinese school. The Chinese grade school runs daily from 4:00 to 7:00 p.m.; it begins shortly after the children are dismissed from regular public schools. There are Chinese language programs on Saturday and Sunday for high school age and adult Chinese. [As a result] of generous donations and close supervision of the *Kiu Ling*, the school budget is always balanced.

Not only do the traditional elite refuse to seek financial aid from the larger society for the Chinese school, but they also hesitate to ask for assistance in other areas, such as welfare, housing, medicare, etc. Nevertheless, they still insist that they are the legitimate channels through which the community's transactions with the larger society must be conducted.

The new elite conduct their community service through the various social agencies in Chinatown. They believe that the traditional associations are vestigial structures that probably served the recreational and welfare needs of the immigrants of the past, but can no longer adequately meet the needs of a Chinatown whose population differs substantially from that of the earlier period. In the past (1880s–1960), the Chinese community was composed mainly of adult males who were sojourners in this country. Since the 1960s, young and old, male and female, single and married Chinese have come to this country with the intention of making it their permanent home. Prior to 1965, the immigrants were from the rural areas of China and were enculturated in a traditional social environment—peasant organization and traditional Chinese values. The new immigrants are principally from urban areas such as Canton, Hong Kong, Macao, and Taipei.

The new elite are particularly hostile to the Chinese Consolidated Benevolent Association, the stronghold of the traditional elite, because of its lack of flexibility in serving the pressing needs of the more recent immigrants: employment, housing, medical care, English education, social control, etc. Most of the new elite neither discourage nor encourage the Chinese to join the traditional associations. However, they do encourage all the Chinese to use the facilities and services of the social agencies. In fact, they have published several pamphlets to inform the Chinese public on how to make the most effective use of these agencies. The pamphlets give particular emphasis to these attractions: no fee, no favor, and no obligation.

The new elite plan to replace the welfare functions once performed by the *Kiu Ling* and the family and regional associations with the services of the social agencies. Members of the community are constantly reminded that they do not have to depend on the *Kiu Ling* to gain employment or credit, or to settle disputes.

The new elite are interested in assisting the Chinese in assimilating into U.S. society. For example, they favor the establishment of a school or center to teach English to adults and new immigrants, thus enabling them to find employment in non-Chinese businesses.

Elite Versus the Larger Society: New York City and the United States

The traditional elite have adopted the following strategies in dealing with the United States: (1) Participate in some sectors of the larger society while retaining significant aspects of their cultural identity; (2) retain some ties with the larger society while securing community control for themselves (cf. Barth, 1969; Lyman and Douglas, 1973).

Looking through the personal histories of the *Kiu Ling*, it is not difficult to discover why they follow these strategies. As mentioned earlier, they are older Chinese, mostly over 50, who have spent many years in the U.S. When they first came to this country, they were laborers, small merchants, or employees. They witnessed the discrimination practiced by the larger society against the blacks and other minority groups, including the Chinese. Hence, they are generally skeptical about the possibility for racially distinctive minority groups being integrated into the larger society.

The *Kiu Ling* intend to participate in some sectors of activity in the U.S., but hope to retain their cultural identity and secure community control. The sectors in which they participate in New York are restaurants, laundries, garment factories, Chinese groceries, and gift shops. They are concerned with the steady increase of customers in the Chinese restaurants, the image of Chinatown, New York, as a safe place, the number of tourists visiting Chinatown, and parking and traffic problems that can affect the Chinese businesses. Any regulations and policies enacted by the city government affecting these typically Chinese businesses (the lifelines of Chinatown) cause concern among the traditional elite. This is partly because they themselves are entrepreneurs in these fields and partly because they represent the interests of the Chinese business community as a whole. Hence, the Kiu Ling are concerned with the continued prosperity of the Chinese ethnic niche.

The traditional elite generally feel that a good "appearance" for Chinatown is good for Chinese business. They play host to many visiting dignitaries from the city, state, and federal governments. These *Kiu Ling* stress harmony and friendship. Peaceful coexistence with other ethnic groups such as the Puerto Ricans and Jews on the Lower East Side and the Italians in Little Italy is emphasized.

The new elite's basic strategies in dealing with the larger society are: (1) to emphasize ethnic identity to develop new positions and patterns to organize activities in those sectors formerly not found in the U.S. society (Barth, 1969; Lyman and Douglas, 1973; Wirth, 1945); and (2) to form coalitions with other ethnic groups for the attainment of similar institutional goals. Knowing that Chinese restaurants, garment factories, and laundries are still the most important businesses of the Chinese, the new elite attempt to render services to people in these businesses. Thus, for instance, the Chinatown Planning Council has been trying to get federal and city subsidies to run day care centers for the Chinese mothers who work out of economic necessity in garment factories or as waitresses in restaurants, thus leaving young children unattended. Several marches to City Hall to petition for day care subsidies have been conducted in the past several years.

The new elite, however, want to widen the job horizon and opportunities for the Chinese. They encourage Chinese-Americans to seek employment in all fields, from hospital administration, civil service, construction, and commercial positions to the professional sectors. Notices on the possibilities of employment with the police and FBI are posted in many social agencies. The new elite of the social agencies are interested in placing qualified Chinese in positions in the larger society where they were not found formerly, such as New York Telephone, Consolidated Edison, the U.S. Postal Service, city government, and the broadcasting industries. They also take complaints concerning violations of human rights, Equal Opportunity, and Affirmative Action programs and forward these complaints to the proper authorities.

The new elite are alert to the available resources which the Chinese ethnic group can utilize. In order to compete for these resources, American politicians are enlisted to assist the cause of the Chinese. The new elite are interested in enlisting community support for Chinese candidates who are running for government offices in New York. However, [because of] the limited number of registered voters, it is unlikely that any Chinese candidates will have mass support from the Chinese community. Nevertheless, the need to have Chinese politicians is gradually being felt in the community. [As a result of] the efforts of the new elite, many Chinese have registered to vote.

The new elite also differ from the traditional elite in the procedures and techniques of dealing with the dominant society. While the *Kiu Ling* insist on harmony, patience, and inaction unless other measures are absolutely necessary, the *Chuen Ka* believe in the conflict approach—not conflict in the sense of physical force, but in the sense of social pressure and of militant attitudes. The new elite feel that it is American to fight for equality and freedom. They are fond of using methods commonly resorted to by many interest groups in America, such as protests and strikes, to obtain their goals.

Many of the traditional *Kiu Ling* think that publicity and high visibility will provoke envy from members of the larger society, which will lead to unhappy consequences for the Chinese. The new elite, on the other hand, believe that the mass media may publicize the plight of the Chinese and thus arouse the sympathy of the public toward the community. Not only are the new elite determined to fight with protests, demonstrations, and strikes, they also want to form coalitions with other ethnic groups to fight for equal rights and create new social positions for the ethnic groups.

The ethnic groups with which the Chinese tend to ally themselves are the Japanese, Koreans, Filipinos, and other Asians. So far, the new elite have published a journal to arouse the consciousness of the Asians and thus attempt to form a united front to fight racism. Thus, the new elite follow a strategy directly opposed to that of the traditional elite in dealing with the larger society. The former use ethnicity to participate in the social, economic, and political life of the larger society. The latter wish to limit contact with the larger society and hence preserve the autonomy of the community.

Elites vis-à-vis China

Concerning transactions with China and Overseas Chinese communities, there are also differences between the traditional and the new elite. The *Kiu Ling* perceive themselves to be the indispensable link between the Chinese community of New York and China (Taiwan) and with other Overseas Chinese communities in the world. For the *Kiu Ling*, the legitimate government of China is the Republic of China. The Nationalist government in Taiwan is glad to have the *Kiu Ling* as its middleman and openly supports the *Kiu Ling* as the official spokesmen for the community. The Chinese Nationalist Consulate in New York still requires the leaders of the family, dialect, and regional associations as character references for the Chinese in the community.

Rules of propriety must be followed when a member of the community wants to transact business with the Nationalist Chinese Consulate. Likewise, in dealing with the other Overseas Chinese communities, the activities of the *Kiu Ling* of the lower level associations have to be coordinated by the *Kiu Ling* of the intermediate levels who, in turn, are coordinated by the *Kiu Ling* of the highest level. Thus, for instance, in the relief aid to the Chinese earthquake victims in Managua in 1973, the New York Chinese were asked to deliver relief materials to the appropriate family associations first; from there they would be forwarded to the CCBA, which collected all the materials and sent them to the equivalent organizations in the Chinese community of Managua.

The various Chinese associations in the United States are coordinated by two major centers: the Chinatowns of New York and San Francisco. Thus, if a leader is accused of usurpation and is subsequently ejected from his association in New York City, his name will be circulated immediately to the different branches of the same association (in Boston, Washington, D.C., Philadelphia, Detroit, Miami, Chicago, San Francisco, and other cities) in the United States (see Figure 2).

This associational network was established during the *Tong* War days (Lee, 1960). News of *Tong* wars traveled quickly. If the On Leong *Tong* declared war on the Hip Sing *Tong* in New York, the On Leong *Tong* and Hip Sing Tong in Chicago and San Francisco would immediately go to war with one another (Leong, 1936).

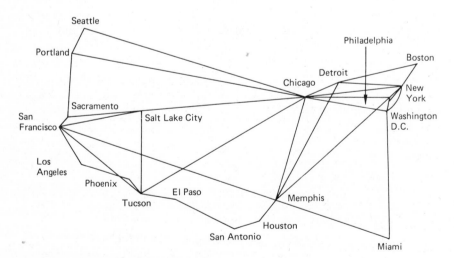

FIGURE 2. Chinese associational network in the United States.

The leaders of the local associations have to confer with the leaders of the same association in other cities on major decisions. For example, if the Lee Association in Detroit wants to sell its old building to rebuild a new office, the leaders of the association are required to confer with the Lee Association in New York.

While the *Kiu Ling* are pro-Kuomintang, the *Chuen Ka*, or the new elite, are sympathetic to the People's Republic of China. They are proud of the achievements of China. Because of the emergence of the People's Republic of China, many of the new elite interviewed showed considerable pride in being of Chinese descent and expressed their interest in visiting China. However, the new elite have not shown interest in being bridges between the community and the People's Republic of China or with other Overseas Chinese communities. In fact, they identify themselves more with the U.S. than with Chinese culture. Their goal is to link the Chinese community with New York City and the larger U.S. society.

Discussion

The present study found that there are two kinds of elite in New York's Chinatown. When evaluated according to the community's standards, they are both the top-level people; when viewed against the larger U.S. society, they are considered by members of the community to occupy a middle-class status.

The traditional elite (*Kiu Ling*) of the community are the cultural preservers. They are not the "literati," as expected by Max Weber (1947), but rather are entrepreneurs in the ethnic businesses who have no high formal education, but control the means of production. They use their wealth, influence, and connections to recruit followers, to obtain the leadership positions in the traditional associations, and to oppose the presence and activities of the new elite. Thus, there is intense conflict between the traditional and the new elite in the community. The latter (*Chuen Ka*) are the "white-collar" professionals, educated in U.S. colleges, who seek an unreserved acceptance by the larger society and organize efforts to fight racism. The new elite from the social agencies and nonprofit service organizations follow a strategy directly opposed to the old elite. The former use ethnicity to assist members of the community to participate in the social, economic, and political life in New York City. Specifically, the new elite use ethnic status to obtain funding from city, state, and federal governments for their agencies and the minority status to gain employment and financial aid for the Chinese. In such endeavors, they attract many followers and users of the social agencies. Thus, their power base is expanding and their prestige is increasing. For those new elite who are social workers, job security is enhanced by a large clientele.

The traditional elite use ethnicity—traditional Chinese values, symbols, social organizations—to maintain a segregated community in which they are the prestigious rulers. They wish to limit contact with the city, state, and federal governments and preserve the status quo. The traditional elite have been diligent and successful in protecting the Chinese ethnic niche and in preserving the Chinese culture in New York City, but at the cost of isolation. This introversion is counterbalanced by the outreaching efforts of the new elite who, in assisting the Chinese to participate in the resource distribution of the larger society, bring the community into direct contact with other ethnic groups in New York and the larger society.

The traditional elite assume the roles of leaders and cultural stabilizers. The new elite's roles are as change agents and culture brokers between the Chinese subculture and the U.S. culture, mediators between the community and the city. Thus, the old and new elite of an encapsulated ethnic community are not homogeneous. They can be agents of either cultural stability or cultural change, depending on a host of interwoven factors: cultural identity or identities chosen, birthplace, language ability and education, past experience of discrimination, occupation, type of self-interest, desire to maintain an ethnic group's cultural purity, desire to integrate into the dominant society, familiarity with the larger society, etc. As a consequence of the new elite's activities, the Chinese community of New York has become more outwardly oriented, and the ethnic boundary of the community has assumed a different character. Formerly, the Chinese ethnic boundary in New York was almost impenetrable; today, it does not isolate the members of the community from the larger society, particularly from city welfare assistance. The new elite enable members of the ethnic group to participate in the social, economic, and political life of America.

Some questions remain: Why is the new elite gaining more power at the expense of the old elite? What is the nature of the new ethnic boundary of Chinatown? The data obtained from my field research indicate that there are several variables for the gradual replacement of the old elite by the new elite. One is the change in the goals of the clientele. The new elite's followers are the new immigrants—the majority of Chinatown's population. The second variable is the changed population composition of Chinatown after the 1960s. Prior to the 1960s Chinatown was composed of old immigrants, principally China-oriented adults, males, sojourners. Chinatown's population since 1960 is far more heterogeneous. There are males and females of different ages, professionals, merchants, students, and laborers from the urban areas of China. The traditional associations, geared to the emotional needs of the rural, adult, male sojourners, cannot meet the wide range of social problems of the new immigrants: juvenile delinquency, housing, day care, medical care. These new immigrants are better educated and aspire to the affluent American lifestyle. They intend to make America their permanent home and their problems include not only finding a job in the community, but finding a *better* job and participating in the "good life" of America.

The third variable is the changing social relationships in Chinatown. In the past, social action was based on kinship, clanship, hometown-network, association-network. The operation of the traditional elite is based on these personal relationships. Today, Chinatown's social relationships are complex and relatively impersonal. In addition to the traditional social relationships, the new immigrants are involved in relationships of employer-employee, teacher-student, customer-owner, friendship, and patron-client. The traditional elite that ruled the community on the bases of kinship and clanship are thus losing their social sanctions. The fourth variable is the population size. In the pre-1960s era, Chinatown was relatively small. The Chinese population in New York City increased from 18,329 in 1950 to 69,324 in 1970 (U.S. Census of Population: 1970). The resources of the traditional elite and their associations are simply inadequate to meet the needs of such a large population.

Accompanying the replacement of the old elite by the new elite, there is a change in the nature of the Chinese ethnic boundary in New York City. The Chinese ethnic group, which was formerly a carrier of Chinese culture and an autonomous, self-contained social unit for the perpetuation of Chinese ethnic businesses, is today perceived to be diversified by the members themselves. Common destiny and ethnic background are viewed as a basis for the formation of an interest group by means of which members of the community can participate in the resource distribution of New York City and the larger society. The new ethnicity is used as a resource by which ethnic group members can branch out of their ethnic niche/enclave. This new ethnicity is principally initiated and energized by the new elite of the community. Thus, the new elite is at least partially responsible for the transformation of the Chinese ethnicity in New York City. Whether this change in the Chinese community of New York is representative of other urban ethnic groups remains to be determined. However, the present study suggests that the research on ethnic boundaries and ethnic groups should focus on their power elite since the nature of the ethnic boundary and the transformation of ethnicity are frequently the by-products of the activities of their elite.

Bibliography

AMYOT, JACQUES
   1960   "The Chinese Community of Manila: A Study of Adaptation of Chinese Familism to the Philippine Environment." Philippine Study Program, University of Chicago, Research Monographs, No. 2.
BAILEY, F. G.
   1969   *Stratagems and Spoils.* New York: Schocken Books.
BARTH, FREDRIK (ed.)
   1969   *Ethnic Groups and Boundaries.* Oslo: Universitetesforlaget.
BOISSEVAIN, JEREMY
   1966   "Patrons in Sicily," *Man,* 1(1):18–23.
BOTTOMORE, T. B.
   1964   *Elites and Society.* Baltimore: Penguin Books.

BRIGGS, JEAN
1971   Strategies of Perception: The Management of Ethnic Identity. *In Patrons and Brokers in the East Arctic,* Robert Paine (ed.). Newfoundland: Institute of Social and Economic Research, Memorial University of Newfoundland, pp. 56–73.
CAMPBELL, J. K.
1964   *Honour, Family and Patronage.* Oxford: Clarendon Press.
CATTELL, STUART H.
1962   *Health, Welfare and Social Organization in Chinatown, New York City.* New York: Community Service Society.
COLE, G. D. H.
1955   *Studies in Class Structure.* London: Routledge and Kegan Paul.
FOSTER, GEORGE
1961   "Interpersonal Relations in Peasant Society," *Human Organization,* **19:**174–175.
1963a   "The Dyadic Contract: A Model for the Social Structure of a Mexican Peasant Village," *American Anthropologist,* **63:**1173–1192.
1963b   "The Dyadic Contract in Tzintzuntzan, II: Patron-Client Relationship," *American Anthropologist* **65:**1280–1294.
GEERTZ, CLIFFORD
1963   *Peddlers and Princes.* Chicago: University of Chicago Press.
GLAZER, NATHAN and DANIEL P. MOYNIHAN
1970   *Beyond the Melting Pot.* Cambridge, Massachusetts: M.I.T. Press.
GREELEY, ANDREW
1971   *Why Can't They Be Like Us?* New York: E. P. Dutton & Co.
1972   *That Most Distressful Nation.* Chicago: Quadrangle Books.
HEYER, VIRGINIA
1963   "Patterns of Social Organization in New York's Chinatown." Ph.D. dissertation. Ann Arbor: University Microfilms.
KENNY, MICHAEL
1960   "Patterns of Patronage in Spain," *Anthropological Quarterly,* **33**(1):14–23.
KRAMER, JUDITH
1970   *The American Minority Community.* New York: Thomas Y. Crowell Co.
LEE, JAMES
1972   "The Story of the New York Chinese Consolidated Benevolent Association," *Bridge Magazine,* **1**(5):15–18.
LEE, ROSE HUM
1960   *The Chinese in the United States of America.* Hong Kong: Hong Kong University Press.
LEONG, GOR YUN
1936   *Chinatown Inside Out.* New York: Barrows Mussey.
LYMAN, STANFORD and WILLIAM DOUGLAS
1973   "Ethnicity: Strategies of Collective and Individual Impression Management," *Social Research,* **40**(20):345–365.
MAYER, ADRIAN
1967   "Patrons and Brokers: Rural Leadership in Four Overseas Indian Communities," "In *Social Organization,* Maurice Freedman (ed.). Chicago: Aldine Publishing Co., pp. 167–188.

MILLS, C. WRIGHT
   1969   *The Power Elite.* New York: Oxford University Press.
MISRA, B. B.
   1961   *The Indian Middle Classes.* London: Oxford University Press.
NADEL, S. F.
   1956   "The Concept of Social Elites," *International Social Science Bulletin,*
           8(3):415.
NIEL, R. VAN
   1960   *The Emergence of the Modern Indonesian Elite.* The Hague: W. Van
           Hoeve.
NOVAK, WILLIAM
   1972   *The Rise of the Unmeltable Ethics.* New York: Macmillan Publishing
           Co., Inc.
PAINE, ROBERT (ed.)
   1971   *Patrons and Brokers in the East Arctic.* Newfoundland: Institute of
           Social and Economic Research, Memorial University of Newfoundland.
PARETO, VILFREDO
   1935   *The Mind and Society.* London: Jonathan Cape.
PASSWELL, HAROLD, DANIEL LERNER, and EASTON ROTHWELL.
   1952   *The Comparative Study of Elites.* Stanford: Hoover Institute Studies.
SKINNER, WILLIAM
   1958   *Leadership and Power in the Chinese Community of Thailand.* Ithaca:
           Cornell University Press.
STRICKON, ARNOLD and SIDNEY GREENFIELD (eds.)
   1972   *Structure and Process in Latin America.* Albuquerque: University of
           New Mexico Press.
STUART, WILLIAM T.
   1972   "The Explanation of Patron-Client Systems," In *Structure and Process
           in Latin America,* Arnold Strickton and Sidney Greenfield (eds.). Al-
           buquerque: University of New Mexico Press, pp. 19–42.
TIEN, JU-KANG
   1953   *The Chinese of Sarawak.* London: London School of Economics and
           Political Science.
WEBER, MAX
   1947   "The Chinese Literati," In *From Max Weber,* H. H. Gerth and C.
           Wright Mills (eds.), New York: Oxford University Press, pp. 416–444.
WIRTH, LOUIS
   1945   "The Problems of Minority Groups," In *The Science of Man in the
           World Crisis,* Ralph Linton (ed.). New York: Columbia University
           Press, pp. 347–372.
WOLF, ERIC
   1956   "Aspects of Group Relationships in a Complex Society: Mexico,"
           American Anthropologist, **58**:1065–1078.
   1966   "Kinship, Friendship and Patron-Client Relations in Complex Socie-
           ties." In *The Social Anthropology of Complex Societies,* Michael Ban-
           ton (ed.). London: Tavistock, pp. 1–22.
WONG, BERNARD
   1971   "Chinese in Lima." Manuscript. Fieldwork report submitted to the
           Ibero-American Studies Program, University of Wisconsin-Madison.

1974   "Patronage, Brokerage, Entrepreneurship and the Chinese Commu-
        nity of New York." Unpublished Ph.D. dissertation, University of Wis-
        consin-Madison.
1976   "Social Stratification, Adaptive Strategies, and the Chinese Community
        of New York." *Urban Life* 5(1):33–52.

Relocated American Indians in the San Francisco Bay Area: Social Interaction and Indian Identity

JOAN ABLON

The stereotype of American Indians is that of a people who "naturally" belong in the plains, forests, and mountains, living at one with nature. Failing this, they do well on remote reservations. We rarely consider the Indian in a modern, urban industrial context. Yet, as Joan Ablon points out in the following paper, there are more than 10,000 Indians (representing more than 100 different tribal groups) living in the San Francisco Bay area alone. Chicago, Los Angeles, Toronto, and New York have even more. It is only in cities or large towns that tribesmen become ethnics, juxtaposed with other groups with whom they must compete for residences, resources, and a satisfactory identity. The same can be said for peasants, or for foreign nationals in the cities of another country. Such contact can lead to a host of responses, ranging from assimilation to conscious identity maintenance and reaffirmation of "homeland" loyalty.

Ablon emphasizes "the peculiarity of the position of American Indians" in her study of their adaptation or nonadjustment to white American urban life. For one thing, Amerindians face more than the homogenizing effect of the city itself; the growing influence of the pan-Indian movement also affects them. Non-Indians lump Navajo and Iroquois, Hopi and Tlingit, Cherokee and Micmac as belonging to the same "ethnic" urban group. In response, many Indians feel that they must accept a generalized Indian identity, shared with other tribes, if they are ever to take effective, united action on their own behalf.

Despite the variety of experiences that can be part of urban life, Ablon's study shows that on the whole, Amerindians do not taste the cosmopolitan flavor of the city. Whether this is by choice, exclusion by others, or for some other reason (lack of knowledge, for example) is still an open question. As the author points out, indications are that Amerindians will be a long time in losing their separateness and blending into the urban mix.

"Relocated American Indians in the San Francisco Bay Area: Social Interaction and Indian Identity,"
Human Organization, **23**, 1964, pp. 296–304. Reproduced by permission of the Society for Applied Anthropology.

Introduction

The urbanization of American Indians has been occurring on a small scale for many years as individuals and families have quietly slipped into city life. The process has been intensified in the past decade through official government relocation programs. This recent influx of large numbers of Indians into metropolitan areas represents the formation of a new urban ethnic group that holds special research interest for the anthropologist. Although American anthropologists have examined problems of urbanization in Latin America, Africa and Asia, they have had little interest in following their native aborigines who leave the traditional cultural trappings of reservation life. There are few published statements in the anthropological literature dealing with American Indians who have settled in cities.[1]

This article will focus on the nature of the new relationships that are conceived and maintained by persons coming from kin-oriented, relatively closed communities to large metropolitan centers. Early sociological studies of rural-urban migrations emphasized the breakdown of primary social bonds and the problems that resulted from ensuing social alienation. Recent urban studies have high-lighted strengthened kindred bonds and new forms of social interaction that develop in the metropolitan setting. The factors of background, class, and ethnicity all appear to contribute to the form and nature of new relationships on the individual and formal group levels.

The present article will attempt to show that American Indians who have come to the Bay Area have chosen to associate primarily with other Indians of their own or differing tribes in both informal and formal social interaction. The fact of self-conscious Indianness appears to determine the choice of Indian relationships—a choice that usually precludes intermingling with non-Indians either in social groups or on an individual intimate friendship basis. The ever-present psychological and social awareness of Indian identity comprises an important positive factor in the maintenance of the urban pan-Indian activities of Indian social centers, dance groups, churches, and other Indian organizations in the Bay Area.

American Indians bring to the city a diversity of tribal and acculturative backgrounds, but a common heritage of participation in small rural folk communities with a basis of aboriginal tradition, and a dependent relationship with the white world as symbolized by their long and often painful association with the Bureau of Indian Affairs. The reservations they leave are economically underdeveloped areas, but constitute communities which have provided some degree of security and social control for the individual, and have acted

[1] Wesley R. Hurt, "The Urbanization of Yankton Indians," *Human Organization,* XX (Winter, 1961–62), 226–231; E. Russell Carter, "Rapid City, South Dakota; Institute on American Indian Assimilation," *The American Indian,* VI (Summer, 1953), 29–38; Robert Ritzenthaler and Mary Sellers, "Indians in an Urban Situation," *The Wisconsin Archeologist,* XXXVI (December, 1955), 147–161. An unpublished summary report by Paula Verdet of the only study that dealt with cross-tribal cases in large cities was distributed in mimeographed form at the American Indian Chicago Conference in 1961. This report can be ordered from Dr. Sol Tax, Department of Anthropology, University of Chicago.

as buffers against the immediate encroachments of white culture. The peculiarity of the position of American Indians as an ethnic group stems from a number of facts which are crucial to their potential adjustment in white urban life. The most important of these is a basic antagonism to white society that has developed from a history of rejection and discrimination. American Indians perforce have had their traditional cultures decimated in one way or another, and have been drawn often unwillingly into the mainstream of American life. Highly important also is the fact that many fundamental Indian values are not only incompatible with those of American culture, but work directly in opposition to the principles on which the modern competitive capitalistic order is based. Indians generally do not want to compete with others. They would rather share money or material goods than budget and save. They will not often speak out to complain or to demand their rights. A basic tribal world view defining the interrelationships of man with his society and the world around him, and the paternalistic nature of Bureau administration of Indian community affairs have helped produce complex and deeply entrenched attitudes of dependency which greatly hinder adjustment to the practical demands of urban life.

The San Francisco Bay Area

Current estimates by Indian organizations and by white agencies which deal with Indians place the number of Indians in the San Francisco Bay Area at about 10,000, representing some one hundred tribal groups.[2] The majority of these persons have relocated through government relocation programs but about one-third have come on their own resources. Formal aids to Indian migration have been Indian school placement, Santa Fe Railroad employment, and the current Bureau of Indian Affairs Employment Assistance Program (formerly called Voluntary Relocation Program) and the Adult Vocational Training Program. The Bureau operates field relocation centers in San Francisco, Oakland, and San Jose to administer these programs.

The Bay Area has long been an attractive destination for Indians who have relocated on their own initiative. The three metropolitan centers offer a diversity of employment opportunities, vocational schools, social groups, and varied amusements for relocatees. Indians are only one of a number of ethnic groups in the area, and they generally encounter little of the open discrimination that they traditionally have faced near their reservations. Many Indians who were stationed here during World War II chose to return after

---

[2] Of this number approximately 4000 are estimated to be in the Oakland-larger East Bay Area, 4000 in San Francisco, and 2000 in the San Jose area. There are no accurate agency figures on this subject. The 1960 Census figures are very low and of little value because of their racial classification criteria. The Bureau of Indian Affairs will not attempt to give exact figures for the number of relocatees in the area because they cannot follow up relocatees and usually do not know when persons have returned to their reservations.

the war, often bringing their families with them. Others migrated to the area in the war years to work in defense industry and remained.

The data on which the present paper is based were drawn from those gathered for a broader study of the nature and persistence of cultural tradition and identity of relocatees who have settled in the Bay Area.[3] Traditional anthropological techniques of observation, participant-observation, and interviewing were used over a period of about 18 months in 1961–1962. Intensive study was carried out with two groups of relocatees: Families who were brought in through the federal Voluntary Relocation Program in the first year of its operation in the area, 1954–1955, and who had remained here until the time of the study were of special interest. Thirty-four persons or families of the first 200 who relocated were traced and interviewed. Informants were highly skeptical that many more remained in the area from the pioneer group. A second general group of nineteen additional families was studied. Fourteen of the latter came through government-sponsored programs in the years following 1955, and five families were self-relocated, some having come to the Bay Areas as early as 1941. Seventeen tribes were represented within the two groups, with the largest numbers of persons coming from the Navaho, Sioux, and Turtle Mountain Chippewa tribes. These tribes have consistently contributed large numbers of families from their reservations to relocation centers across the country. During the course of the study more casual and incomplete information was gathered for about 25 other families.

Individual situations varied, but a commonality of process and Indian response to the relocation program became readily apparent. From a consideration of the Bureau of Indian Affairs files on those individuals and families who returned, it appears that the education, acculturation experiences, and economic and social backgrounds of those who remained were similar to the backgrounds of those who returned. During the early years of the Voluntary Relocation Program more than three-fourths of the persons who relocated returned home. The current return figure is estimated by the Bureau at 35%.

The relocatees (single persons and family heads) exhibited a wide variety of educational experiences and former contacts with whites. About half were veterans and, and most had interacted with whites in some form of previous work experience. Most persons came on relocation because they could not find steady employment on their reservations. The incentive to find employment often was compounded by a variety of personal and family problems which contributed to the decision to leave the reservation area. Most had the majority of their close relatives still living on their home reservations, although a great many have had some of their own or their spouses' siblings in the Bay Area at some time since their arrival.

Indians are employed in a very wide range of unskilled, semi-skilled, and skilled positions in both large and small industrial enterprises and in service

[3] Joan Ablon, *Relocated American Indians in the San Francisco Bay Area: Concepts of Acculturation, Success and Identity in the City,* unpublished Ph.D. Dissertation, University of Chicago, 1963.

fields in all three relocation centers. Most Indians, however, come to the city as unskilled or semi-skilled workers, and encounter a shifting job market that requires more and more skilled persons each year. Lay-offs are common, and hit the unskilled worker particularly hard. Personal attitudes toward work often appear to be more important in the retention of jobs than previous training or sophistication in the complexities of unions or of the job market. For this reason many unskilled and uneducated persons are able to retain jobs they consider "dirty" or unpleasant that the more educated and acculturated Indians would reject, because the former with a desire for job security well realize their disadvantage in employment competition.

Such domestic problems as the drinking and violence common to many Indian families do not appear to be peculiar results of the shift from rural to urban life, but rather characteristic features of reservation family and social disorganization which are carried to the city and intensified by new pressures and the departure from the stability of immediate family and community. In some instances the move to the city which takes a family away from dependent or heavy-drinking relatives improves the domestic situation.

The stated Bureau housing policy is to disperse Indians among the general population to further the goal of assimilation. Most of the families contacted in the course of my research lived in Oakland because the first field relocation office was set up in this area. About one-fifth of the cases in the two groups studied lived in other metropolitan areas around the Bay. Most relocatees live in typical working class housing, and many have taken advantage of low-rent housing projects. One large housing project in Oakland has continually attracted a relatively large number of Indian families. Most families in the groups studied have moved at least three or four times since their arrival in the area. A few relocatees are buying their own homes, but this does not necessarily reflect a definite intent or commitment to remain in the area. Indeed, common responses suggest that most relocatees now living in the Bay Area would return home to their reservations immediately if they could find employment there. The absence of employment opportunities and the associated social problems characteristic of most reservations preclude the presentation of legitimate alternatives in the choice of whether to attempt relocation or to be satisfied with an impoverished welfare-based existence in the home community.

Social Interaction Among Indians in the Bay Area

Informal Social Interaction

Informal interaction consists of visits to the homes of other Indians, and of contacts with persons in bars or in other public places. Each of the major relocation centers has several "Indian bars" in the central districts where many Indian men and women of a variety of tribes congregate and meet new friends and sexual partners. Others visit bars only on payday, or stop by on holidays for a few drinks. Many Indians begin friendships with persons of other tribes whom they meet in the Bureau offices or spot as being Indian and approach in stores, clinics, or on the street. Such chance encounters may lead to invitations for home visits.

Home visiting occurs chiefly among persons related through the ties of kinship, tribal affiliation, or prior acquaintance on the reservation, or among persons who have met as a result of contacts in Indian groups, through common church attendance, proximity of residence, or association at work. Persons who have siblings, parents, or cousins in the area usually see them with some frequency, and feel obliged to give them help when needed. In general all Indians and especially the Sioux tend to feel the responsibility of helping their kinsmen or tribesmen when asked, and will give money, food, or lodging to a needy family. The flexibility of the Indian household often seems to be infinite, and most Indian families assume that there is always room for five or six additional persons at their table or for lodging, no matter how small the actual living quarters may be. Some families have been known to leave town or to keep their place of residence secret because they were burdened with responsibilities for aiding others, and did not feel they could refuse assistance if asked for it.

Informal gatherings of a number of families of one tribe occur infrequently. The most regular informal gatherings occurred in the groups observed among the Turtle Mountain Chippewas who meet in couples–groups in homes, for spring and summer baseball games, and in larger parties, such as at annual New Year's gatherings. At New Years most of the families in the Oakland area converge on several generous hosting families, and over spreads of food and drink converse animatedly in Chippewa, Cree, French, and English and many of the men dance a lively jig when sufficiently intoxicated. A common acitivity is to go to the home of the oldest relocatee in the area and pay him respect in a traditional French-Canadian manner. In the early years of relocation Turtle Mountain families gathered more frequently for bar parties and picnics. The parties have diminished because most of the original relocatees have returned to the reservation, and the heavy drinking and ensuing quarrels and fights served to discourage many wives from attendance. Although some families speak of the *esprit de corps* of the Turtle Mountain people and of their aid to one another in times of hardship, many complain that their old friends and relatives did not help them when they needed it, nor were people fulfilling their godparent obligations. Most Turtle Mountain relocatees are lively and verbal. They are universally the mixed-bloods from that reservation, of French Canadian and Salteaux descent, and they are relatively well acculturated.[4] They often comment that because they are mixed-bloods, they

---

[4] See James H. Howard, "The Turtle Mountain Chippewa," *The North Dakota Quarterly*, XXVI (Spring, 1958), 37–46; David P. Delorme, *A Socio-economic Study of the Turtle Mountain Band of Chippewa Indians and a Critical Evaluation of Proposals Designed to Terminate Their Federal Wardship Status*, unpublished Ph.D. Dissertation, University of Texas, 1955.

are not like other Indians and do not maintain traditional customs or dances. They associated largely with other Turtle Mountain families or with whites. Few have established relationships with Indians of other tribes.

Navahos most frequently tend to associate almost exclusively with other Navahos, usually persons of their own age group who are relatives or whom they have met through common housing or at formal group events. Navahos are more restricted socially than persons from other tribes, chiefly because of their sheltered tribal background, a reserved manner that quickly becomes intensified when among non-Navahos, and by a strong fear of English language inadequacy. Many Navahos began school at a relatively late age and went through hasty accelerated programs. Even those who have worked outside of the reservation often limited their association to their Navaho workmates and spoke to whites as infrequently as possible. Their sensitivity about their halting speech often generates a pervading anxiety about dealing with non-Navaho speakers. A Navaho Club has recently been formed in Oakland but the attendance has not exceeded a dozen persons and the small group has already been paralyzed by factions. Most of the hundreds of Navahos in the area do not appear to take an active interest in any kind of formal activity, Navaho, pan-Indian, or white.

Sioux families usually engage in frequent home visiting with relatives or tribesmen. Several annual all-Sioux events have been held, but little formal organization has materialized despite attempts of several families to unite the many Sioux of the area into a social or political group.

Formal Interaction

Any formulation of a viable definition of an "Indian Community" in the sense of an organized, visible body of persons who interrelate with regularity in socially meaningful ways must turn to the many active social, religious, and political Indian organizations of the Bay Area, rather than to any network of relationships encompassing individuals or families. Some sixteen specific organizations which were organized for Indian participation (although often sponsored and staffed by whites) existed in the three relocation centers at the time of my study. The activities of a number of Indian baseball and basketball teams were also focal points for social interaction. Since the conclusion of the study, Navaho, Eskimo, Chippewa, and Tlingit-Haida clubs are in the process of organization. [The groups that existed in 1961–1962 are shown on page 429.]

The most influential organizations are the Intertribal Friendship House, the San Francisco American Indian Center, the Four Winds Club, The Oakland American Indian Baptist Church, the San Jose Dance Club, and the American Indian Council of the Bay Area. The Santa Fe Indian Village was for many years a unique self-contained social entity.[5]

[5] The Intertribal Friendship House, supported by the American Friends Service Committee, and the San Francisco American Indian Center, supported since its inception by the Society of St. Vincent De

Oakland	San Francisco
Intertribal Friendship House	American Indian Center
Four Winds Club	American Indian Baptist Church
American Indian Baptist Church	Methodist Baptist Interdenominational
Santa Fe Indian Village	Fellowship
	Indian Holiness (Pentacostal) Church
	Native American Church

San Jose	General area groups
San Jose Dance Club	American Indian Council of the Bay
American Indian Council of Santa Clara	Area
Valley	American Indian Youth Council of
American Indian Alcoholics Anonymous	the Bay Area
American Indian Baptist Church	Haskell Institute Alumni
	Indian Baseball and Basketball Teams

Indian Dancing and Pow-wows

Pow-wows, social gatherings where Indian traditional dancing and singing are featured, are sponsored monthly by the San Jose Dance Club and recently, by the American Indian Council of the Bay Area each month at the San Francisco Indian Center. Occasionally other groups will sponsor pow-wows, and several times a year a special pow-wow is held by a Kiowa or Sioux family to commemorate a personal occasion such as a birthday or the arrival or departure of visiting relatives. There are usually from twenty to forty costumed dancers, some of whom may have come from Los Angeles or Nevada for the event. The core group of drummers and singers are mostly men from Oklahoma Plains tribes and Sioux. Many of the dancers and singers did not participate in pow-wows at home because of lack of interest or religious prohibitions. The audience at local pow-wows usually numbers from 100 to 200 persons, almost all Indians. Perhaps a grand total of some 300 or 400 persons will attend pow-wows in the area throughout a year. In contrast to dancing activities on the reservations, local pow-wows are usually free from drinking.

Paul but recently turned over to the American Indian Council of the Bay Area, are Indian social centers with regular programs of social-recreational activities. Both were set up in the early years of the Relocation programs to meet the needs of the incoming relocatees. The Four Winds Club is sponsored by the Oakland Young Womens Christian Association and offers varying monthly social events. The Oakland American Indian Baptist Church is a local church of the Southern Baptist Convention and has a vigorous religious and social program. Many tribes are represented in the church, but the majority of regular members and attenders are from Oklahoma tribes who have long been associated with SBC churches. The San Jose Dance Club is a small core group of primarily Kiowas who organize monthly pow-wows in San Jose. The American Indian Council of the Bay Area is a cross-tribal political group working for the general betterment of relocatees. The Council has traditionally sponsored the Annual Indian Day Picnic, and in recent years came into national notice by their widely publicized criticisms of the Relocation programs. The Sante Fe Indian Village is a community of railroad laborers and their families from Laguna and Acoma pueblos brought to Richmond in the early years of World War II. In its prime years the village functioned as two microcosms of pueblo communities operating on a simple level, maintaining their own governors and officials and calendars of religious events. Now the population has dwindled from forty families to about eight and there are few activities.

"The Indian Community"

The reality of an actual Indian community is indeed tenuous when considered in the perspective of the total Indian population in the area, notwithstanding the number and frequency of activities sponsored by Indian organizations. Less than one-sixth of the adult Indians are effectively touched by the activities. Probably not more than thirty adults are regularly active in more than one club. It is no coincidence that the stable core of planners of most of the organizations is often the same persons. Indeed, the continuing existence of the groups and the number of functions which are held attest to the vigor and abilities of the small group of planners.

Characteristic of the operation of the groups are a lack of authoritarian leadership, a general practice of group participation in planning, and a frequent absence of concrete pre-event duty assignment (with much complaining afterward about the often resulting confusion). The planning group for the most part appears to receive obvious personal gratification through the arranging of functions, and from the "busy work" of the planning sessions and the actual events. However, few of these persons are personal friends, nor have their years of mechanical association given them a strong friendship solidarity. It may be observed that the majority of the planners moved away from their reservations long ago, and are accustomed to participation in Indian center activities, and to relating to Indians of other tribes and to whites with some degree of ease. Although actually exhibiting more white patterns of aggressiveness and action than many Indians exhibit, they are not "white man's Indians," i.e., ones who accommodate themselves in order to win approval from whites. To the contrary, they often are the most vocal in expressing belligerency against whites, and extolling a fierce pride in Indian identity. These planners, however, seem more able to form close personal ties with individual white friends than many Indians are able to do.

Many persons have noted ironically that they had to move to the city before they developed a real interest in Indian affairs or Indian dancing. On the other hand, many persons who participated in these activities at home before relocation or who participate when they return for visits do not take part in activities here. No pow-wow activities include Navaho singing or dancing, and the few Navahos who dance here have accustomed themselves to Plains music and dance forms. It would seem that many Indians do not care for an artificial pow-wow without benefit of home community, relatives, friends, and the serving of traditional foods. Although many do care to join in pan-Indian dancing, others find no necessity to recharge or reify their Indianness nor do they think of pan-Indian activities as relevant to their personal Indian identity or tribal interests. The subject of pan-Indianism will be discussed in a later section of this paper.

Sources of Social Interaction

First Social Interaction

The following responses were given by the two groups interviewed in the course of my study to questions asking where first or early social contacts in the Bay Area were made. Some broadly interpreted this to mean the first year after their arrival. Most gave more than one response. "Early cases" are those 34 family heads or individuals who arrived in the first year of the Relocation Program in the Bay Area, 1954–1955. "Additional cases" refers to the group of 19 families who came in later years on the Relocation Program or who relocated through their own initiative and resources.

	Early cases	Additional cases
Intertribal Friendship House	23	13
San Francisco Center	3	0
San Jose early groups	2	2
Four Winds Club	2	1
Church groups	5	8
Bureau sponsored events or through the relocation process	6	3
Neighborhood	3	4
Public Housing projects	7	2
Work	9	2
"Around" (stores or public places)	2	2
Bars	3	2
Through known Indians	4	0
Knew from home	10	10
Relatives	2	11
No formal Indian activities	2	3

The early relocatees arrived when there were few formal Indian organizations or channels for expressly meeting Indian people. The setting up of the now existing centers was in progress in 1955. It appears there occurred in the early pioneering days of the relocation program a first searching for social contacts and friendship relations in places where one could find other Indians.

Continuing Social Interaction

The following responses were given to questions asking about the sources of continuing social contact during years of residence in the area:

	Early cases	Additional cases
Intertribal Friendship House	6	5
Intertribal Friendship House infrequently	13	4
San Francisco Indian Center	2	2
San Francisco Indian Center infrequently	3	1
San Jose social groups	1	2
San Jose social groups infrequently	2	1
Four Winds Club	2	2
Four Winds Club infrequently	7	2
Church groups	5	8
Neighborhood	13	9
Public housing projects	4	4
Work	18	5
"Around" (stores or public places)	8	1
Bars	2	1
Knew from home	6	12
Relatives	18	15
Never attended Indian events	3	3
Rarely attended Indian events	8	9

After the seeking-out period, the pattern for attendance at group functions shifted and the social interaction developed along diverse lines. As many persons changed jobs and places of residence they took on new friendships in these activity areas. Some began attending church services and made contacts there. Many had large families who settled in the area, and thenceforth free time was given to visiting and recreation with relatives. As the nuclear families of many young relocatees grew they stopped attending formal community functions and became "homebodies" as many labeled themselves. The hiring of paid babysitters is almost unknown to Indians, unless they are the babysitters being hired. Some families may have a relative living in to babysit if the wife works. Unless there is such a relative or a friend to help with the children, most spend their evenings at home. Sunny weekends may be given to outings or home visiting if all the family are well, the car is running, and there is money for gas.

Most families leveled their formal social interaction to attendance at only the largest Indian events such as Christmas parties, the annual Indian Day picnic, or more rarely a Four Winds dance or a pow-wow. Some supplemented these with an occasional look-in at the Intertribal Friendship House or the San Francisco Center. Thus the formal groups often served to stabilize many wobbly new relocatees and allow them the security of an Indian meeting place and an opportunity to interact with others like themselves with the same problems as they adjusted to their new city life.

Although it has been frequently stated in the literature that participation in voluntary formal groups is an important part of urban social intercourse, research among lower status groups points out that formal social interaction is more generally characteristic of the educated, upper classes.[6] Dotson reported that among the working class urban families he studied in New Haven, formal social groups were relatively unimportant areas of social interaction. The most frequent and regular interaction occurred among small cliques which were frequently composed of kindred.[7] Bell and Boat also concluded from their research in San Francisco that kindred are more likely to provide close personal friendships than neighbors and co-workers.[8] Among the Indians families that I interviewed, those who had relatives in the area usually spent a great deal of their free time with them.

Zimmer, who studied the participation of migrants in urban structures in a Mid-Western town found the chief factors affecting speed of participation in formal groups of the community to be the length of residence, the nature of prior life experience of the migrant, education, and type of work.[9] He found that rural manual laborers and those of the lowest education entered community activities at the slowest rate. While Indians ideally would be expected to enter formal activities at the slowest rate, then, because most are of rural background, are manual laborers, and generally have a low level of education, the majority of cases in my study approached Indian social centers soon after their arrival. The decisive factor in determining this pattern which differs from the urban working class norm appears to be that of ethnicity.

Social Interaction with Whites

The proportion of Indian as opposed to white friendships maintained by the adults in the cases studied are presented in the following tabulation:

	Early cases	Additional cases
Associate only with other Indians	7	4
All Indian with exception of one or several special dependency relations with older whites	3	2
Mixed Indian and white, mostly Indian	15	10
Mixed Indian and white, about equal	7	2
All white with exception of one or two Indians	2	0
All white	0	1
	34	19

[6] Floyd Dotson, "Patterns of Voluntary Association Among Urban Working Class Families," *American Sociological Review*, XVI (October, 1951), 687–693; W. Lloyd Warner et al., *Democracy in Jonesville*, (First Ed.), Harper and Row, Publishers, 1949, pp. 141, 143.

[7] Floyd Dotson, op. cit.

[8] Wendell Bell and Marion D. Boat, "Urban Neighbors and Social Relations," *American Journal of Sociology*, LXII (January, 1957), 395.

[9] Basil G. Zimmer, "Participation of Migrants in Urban Structures," *American Sociological Review*, XX (April, 1955), 219–224.

Although many Indians responded that they had white friends as well as Indian, I soon determined that most relationships established with whites were relatively superficial ones, consisting of those with workmates along side of whom they worked or ate lunch, and with white neighbors with whom they sometimes exchanged pleasantries or had a cup of coffee. Usually such relationships with whites could be classified more accurately as acquaintances as one relocatee suggested when he talked about the relationships he had made on the job. Another type of white friendship was enjoyed by several young Navaho couples and several Sioux families who developed a form of highly functional dependency relationship with older white couples who loyally responded to the obvious emotional, practical, or financial needs of the Indians.

True friendship relations as used here would be characterized by an egalitarian quality, reciprocal home hospitality, and exchanges of confidences concerning personal affairs or problems. This kind of relationship most often occurred only between Indians. The determinants of Indian-white relationships are a complex blending of positive personal desires, and negative inhibitions shaped by background cultural and personal experiences with whites. Most Indians, particularly full bloods, have had little opportunity to enjoy an egalitarian relationship with a white. Indians have experienced such constant economic and social rejection from whites who live around the peripheries of their reservations or who lease reservation lands, that they often are suspicious of white overtures of friendship, and suspect some objective of white gain to Indian disadvantage.[10]

While the friendly white may be viewed with suspicion, at the same time, because of the characteristic white role as a government official or as a local health or welfare worker, whites are viewed functionally as persons to be used and relied upon in specific situations. Dependent relationships with whites are the typical pattern. When a white refuses to help an Indian when asked, the suspicion with which any white generally is viewed as well as the constant fear of rejection come to the fore, and the Indian then quickly relegates this particular white to the usual province of all whites—persons who look down on Indians and only help them when it is to their own advantage. Also many Indians never can feel secure with whites because they fear that no white will ever really respect or understand them if he finds out certain fundamental facts about them—particularly the details of their poverty-stricken background and their mystical beliefs. The Indian's own confusion between two belief and value systems contributes to his insecurities and makes him ashamed within himself of reservation poverty and primitive beliefs. Thus three characteristic attitudes of Indians toward whites are: suspicion, potential

---

[10] Many Indians tend to relate more easily to Mexican-Americans, Hawaiians, Filipinos, and other persons who share a minority group status and common poverty, than they do to Anglo-American whites. However, most Indians express very negative feelings about having to associate with, work, or live side-by-side with Negroes. Many persons from northern tribes who had never seen Negroes before they arrived in California are the most vehement about the race issue. Their attitudes appear to be born largely from a jumping on the lower class pecking-order band wagon, rather than from any pragmatic evaluation of actual Negro behavior, or from memories of oral tradition about Negro troops sent in to pacify various tribes in the last century.

dependency, and fear of white rejection. To struggle beyond these to gain an egalitarian relationship with an Indian requires great sensitivity on the part of the white. The relationship must be worked out through a continuous give and take process. Some basic personality differences between Indians and whites that are relevant to this subject have been discussed by Wax and Thomas.[11]

I have found it useful to consider Indian-white relationships in terms of two potential limits of interaction that will be allowed by Indians: a line of tolerance of whites by Indians, and an area of intimacy, which has the potential for full friendship responsibilities. The latter, if allowed by the Indian, who himself ultimately sets the tone of the relationship, can result in a true egalitarian friendship. In general, those persons coming from less acculturated tribes such as Navahos, tend to be able only to tolerate the presence of whites, and rarely can open themselves to more intimate egalitarian relationships. Some more acculturated Indians, as exemplified by many Sioux, appear to allow an area of intimacy because of their verbal abilities and readiness to talk to whites in specific situations. However it soon becomes apparent that their easy conversation may be deceptive and most Sioux bear sharp antagonistic feelings toward whites which are manifested in varying levels of verbal hostility or in aggressive actions toward other Indians.

In the larger scheme of social interaction Indians in the Bay Area usually will be accepted wherever *they* choose to go. The facts that there are not great numbers of Indians going into white groups, and that Indian-white relationships usually occur on a private and often superficial level reflect that Indians are very hesitant about committing themselves to these relationships, even when invitations are extended and doors are open to them. It would appear that there is a combination of inhibitions in relating to whites, some, which are negative as outlined [here], and some of which are the counterpart of positive forces—the qualities of Indianness and Indian social identity—which make for voluntary in-group interaction. I would not consider a main aspect of any Indian marginality problem in the Bay Area to be social frustration. Indians generally do not strive for white relationships or for positions in white organizations. Those looking for formal social activity turn to Indian organizations.

Indian Identity and Pan-Indianism

Almost every Indian I encountered in the course of my research was impressed with an unmistakable stamp of identity of which he always seemed to be acutely aware. The personal dimension of identity frequently is manifest in manner as well as by constant references to the fact of one's Indianness or to stories about the home reservation. Among most Indians the "Indian" manner

---

[11] Rosalie H. Wax and Robert K. Thomas, "American Indians and White People," *Phylon*, XXII (Winter, 1961), 305–317.

was a certain reserve mixed with individual personal, and tribal cultural characteristics. This identity dimension of Indianness does not appear to be destroyed by the impact of intermarriage, profession, life style, or diverse social preferences, nor by the absence of such frequently considered indicators of Indianness as retention of native language, exhibition in the home of Indian crafts or possessions, or participation in Indian activities.

Many persons emphasized to me that their children were *really* Indians. Some made a point of saying that although they had lived in towns away from the reservation for many years, their children were Indians, had been raised as Indians, and that there was no getting around this fact. When asked what being "raised as Indians" meant, they usually could not be more explicit.

Many Indians who come to the city often exhibit a neo-Indian social identity which is pan-Indian in its orientation. It may be noticed that alumni of Haskell Institute [12] well illustrate the pan-Indian social focus by associating more easily with persons of other tribes than do most Indians. The fact of a common Haskell background often is of more importance to them than common tribal identity. By and large the neo-Indians are often relatively well-educated and well dressed. Many have the social skills and comparable material possessions to allow them to pass into white society if they so wished, but they consistently choose to mingle almost exclusively with Indians. I would suggest that a positive, continuing sense of personal and social identity is the chief factor in the self-segregation of Indians. The fact of Indian identity seems to determine the choice of looking to Indian groups to find one's friends. Time and time again the idea was expressed to me that

Because we are Indians it is just *the* (or the natural) thing to do—that we should want to go places where we can find other Indians.

One young and verbal mixed-blood Sioux who has lived in cities all of his life expressed his attitudes this way:

Maybe psychologically I am afraid of being rejected; I don't know, but I don't think so. I just don't go to any group that is not Indian. I prefer to be around Indians.

Discussions of pan-Indianism in the anthropological literature have tended to explain this phenomenon as a defensive maneuver of Indian tribes as a way of responding to white dominance, rather like a giant parallel ethnic institution within which Indian people may maintain a sense of identity and integrity because as a group they are regarded as subordinate. [13] James has stated

---

[12] Haskell Institute in Lawrence, Kansas generally is considered to be the superior Indian boarding school of the country. Haskell offers academic and vocational high school curriculums and postgraduate vocational training. Many Haskell graduates take jobs in the Bay Area each year.

[13] Evon Z. Vogt, "The Acculturation of American Indians," *The Annals of the American Academy of Political and Social Sciences*, CCCXI (May, 1957), 146; Bernard J. James, "Social-psychological Dimensions of Ojibwa Acculturation," *American Anthropologist*, LXIII (August, 1961), 721–746; James H. Howard, "Pan Indian Culture of Oklahoma," *The Scientific Monthly*, LXXXI (November, 1955), 215–220.

The key to pan-Indianism, in other words, appears to lie in social relations between Indians and Whites rather than in relations between tribes.[14]

Howard described it as a degenerative cultural phase and has called it "one of the final stages of progressive acculturation just prior to complete assimilation."[15]

It would appear from my data that pan-Indian activities in the city have a positive reason for developing and continuing. The pan-Indian movement cannot be written off as a disappearing and faltering last kick, despite the painful appearance of dance costumes often reduced to dyed blue ostrich plumes over leopard skin bikinis, and 49-er songs which were made up the night before.

In the city the alternative of passing into white society is often an easy one, but still it appears that not many take that course. To the contrary, many become more positive of their Indianness after they arrive. Perhaps the self-image of Indianness stands out more sharply in the white world for people who come from reservations where the old ways are dying out and no meaningful new identity-action patterns have developed for the individual. In the city a person may dramatically realize that he is an *Indian,* because for the first time his identity stands in high relief in the midst of his all-white neighbors and workmates. As a result he begins to seek out Indian groups, to "dance Indian" for the first time or to take pride in his children's dancing. Perhaps he will take an active interest in Indian political problems. Thus a neo-Indian type on a new level of self- and group identity with a pan-Indian as well as tribal orientation may be born from the necessity of mingling with members of other tribes.

Conclusions

The adjustments most Indians make in learning the cues for living successfully in the white world seem to be superficial to their established basic personality structures. Such basic qualities of Indianness—as Indian identity and continuing belief in early teachings and values—are strongly resistant to change, despite efforts of the Bureau of Indian Affairs and the dominant white society to effect fundamental changes during the process of adjustment. In the course of my study in the Bay Area I did not encounter any persons I could consider to be assimilated. The psychological awareness of Indian identity was ever-present and seemed to vary little in relation to intermarriage, profession, or diverse social preferences.[16]

[14] Bernard J. James, op. cit., 744.
[15] James H. Howard, op. cit., 220.
[16] Robert Ritzenthaler and Mary Sellers, op. cit., 160; and Paula Verdet, op. cit., likewise came to this conclusion concerning Indians they interviewed in urban situations. A. I. Hallowell investigated the problem of whether changes in the personality structure necessarily take place during the process of acculturation in "Ojibwa Personality and Acculturation," in *Acculturation in the Americas,* Sol Tax (ed.),

Most Indians prefer to associate socially with other Indians, and most frequently these are relatives and members of their own tribal group. Their strong feeling of identity motivated most of the Indians I interviewed to go to Indian centers of interaction in their early years here. Ultimately it seems to be the Indian himself who makes the choice of association. In the Bay Area Indians live in an open society of open associations, yet they have tended largely to limit their contacts to other Indians.

Likewise, few have aspirations of social mobility, although they may wish to obtain some of the same sort of material possessions as are owned by those who are obviously of a higher social status than themselves. The general lack of the kind of motivation that first generation European ethnics have exhibited toward climbing the social ladder or even toward the amassing of money and social skills to prepare themselves or their children for this climb appears to be . . . [because] Indians think of themselves in a unique Indian social niche which is alien to the community social hierarchy, and [because of] . . . Indian basic inhibitions against economic planning for the future and the amassing of personal wealth or material goods.[17]

The existence of a pan-Indian orientation and activities among some Indians appears to be connected with a neo-Indian identity and emerging awareness of the meaning and implications of being Indian in a white city. I suggest that the social and psychological imperatives of Indian identity have led to an enforced mingling of tribes in the city, i.e., if one cannot be surrounded by members of his home community, at the least, it is more comfortable to associate with Indians of other tribes than with whites. Thus I see the need of Indians to be with other Indians as a cohesive force for the development and maintenance of pan-Indianism in the city, in contrast to the views in the literature which emphasize pan-Indianism as a structural defensive mechanism or as a terminal phase in the assimilation process. The importance of Indian identity as a maintaining device can begin to be evaluated empirically in the coming years by observing the generational progression in retention or loss of values, attitudes and behavior in second and third generation Indian city dwellers.

University of Chicago Press, 1952, 105–112. Hallowell reported a general persistence of Indian "psychological characteristics." For a discussion of the importance of early cultural training see Edward M. Bruner, "Primary Group Experience and the Processes of Acculturation," *American Anthropologist*, LVIII (August, 1956) 605–623.

[17] Contrast with the description of European ethnic groups in Yankee City in W. Lloyd Warner and Leo Srole, *The Social Systems of American Ethnic Groups*, Yankee City Series, Vol. 3, Yale University Press, 1945, pp. 78 ff.

A Tale of Two Cities: The Reality of Historical Differences

M. ESTELLIE SMITH

Ethnicity, socioeconomic factors, biological markers (such as skin color), and even such variables as the political scene in the sending locale (i.e. the 1848 revolutions in Europe, the Irish potato famine, the expulsion of Asians from Uganda) are all factors that affect the process of adaptation to a new urban milieu. In our search for general laws of human behavior, we stress the regularities and similarities of structural and processual elements, often glossing over the more troublesome detailed differences before fully understanding their implications.

M. Estellie Smith's paper is concerned with this latter point. She raises a cautionary note that one should not move too swiftly towards the production of nomothetic principles. If we have learned anything from urban research, it is that cities vary greatly one to another. Each has a unique identity which, like an individual's, is constantly changing and being molded by new events and peoples entering the cycle of its activities.

In the selection that follows, Smith takes a holistic view of Portuguese migrants to two nearby New England cities. She emphasizes the importance of city differences to an understanding of the creation of ethnic variance. It is all too easy to forget that ethnics do not create themselves. Of course, their own behavior affects their ability to "cope." However, their identity, image, opportunity repertoire, and mobility paths are all affected (and often fully created) by the cities in which they dwell. As Smith clearly demonstrates, the history of a city is at least as important as the contemporary ethnic structure to an explanation of group differences in urbanization and assimilation. Some of the puzzling anomalies in what have been defined as "general urbanizing tendencies" may become clearer if we pay more attention to the context in which such processes occur.

Introduction

At a recent international congress of anthropologists, the participants in a symposium on "Migration and Ethnicity" appeared to reach a consensus on the point that all cities represented the "same" environment for migrants. Thus, they concluded, the real concerns of anthropologists were in the area of formulating a model which would delineate these structural similarities and which would, as a result, be generally applicable to the analysis of any migrant group, anywhere. This was based on the contention that the city, as context, posted specific problems of adaptation and integration which would

"A Tale of Two Cities: The Reality of Historical Differences," *Urban Anthropology*, **4**, 1975, pp. 61–72.

be the same were an individual to find himself in Paris, Hong Kong, Lima, or Cedar Rapids.

That such an exploratory focus is legitimate—and can be productive—is not to be argued. Certainly there are such omnipresent aspects as the need to establish new ties, reaffirm (if possible) earlier connections, and, in general, establish the basis for satisfying one's cultural, social, and psychological wants and needs. There are the difficulties encountered when the host society shifts from recruitment to exclusion after economic needs have been fulfilled and a saturation point has been reached. New occupational skills must be acquired; intrafamilial differences (the results of . . . differential orientation to old and new norms and values) must be resolved; and cognitive dissonance, encountered in moving from one communication system (and/or language) to another, must be resolved.

There are, however, certain dangers involved in focusing on the structural similarities. Aside from the problem that some would take an overly simplistic position and argue that such an emphasis is the only consideration, there is the more crucial heuristic factor that one cannot, from this perspective alone, predict the differing degree of success or failure, in specific locales, for individuals or groups from one cultural milieu as compared to another. That such an integrative differential *does* exist cannot be disputed: German Jews and Yemenite Jews moving to Israel do not encounter the same problems of adjustment; a Sicilian peasant and a Scottish farmworker do not get the same employment possibilities upon arrival in Toronto; and studies of various American Indian tribes show that there are apparent, varying degrees of difficulty that mark the urban adjustment of one tribe relative to another (cf. Martin, 1964).

In short, while I accept the point that it is important to formulate a set of generalizations stressing form rather than specific content, I hope to demonstrate in the following study that analytical insights (and ones which would be especially relevant in applied anthropology) are omitted if we do not look at historically specific differences as well as structurally inherent similarities. Like trying to spend a coin which has been stamped on only one side, we will, I fear, find ourselves able to buy little, if anything, with a unidimensional model.

It is to redress the imbalance that I choose, in this article, to demonstrate the utility of indicating the historical processes which, following the genesis of two cities, produced differing milieus for an influx of some 20,000 Portuguese immigrants (divided almost equally between the two communities) during the past 10 years. The cities (called here Perryport and Texton) are separated in their town limits by some 20 miles but they are actually linked by a series of interdigital suburbs and small towns. They exist in a coastal area of southern New England and, though occupying similar econiches, have, for reasons to be explained, very different economic bases. Each, for historical reasons, has created a different stereotype, or ethnic identity, of Portuguese-Americans, has established different positions within the total network of the community for the Portuguese-Americans to occupy, has provided different strategic alternatives for the immigrants who must adapt to a new life, and thus has created arenas which the Portuguese immigrants themselves perceive as different—a perception that influences their choice of settlement.

Perryport

Like Texton, Perryport has about 100,000 people and, like its sister community, it is located with easy access to the sea. The town was first settled in 1640 and because of its maritime focus prospered even through the days of the American Revolution and the War of 1812 when seafaring activities were even more precarious an occupational focus than usual. Perryport was a leader in the American whaling industry and this thriving focus dominated the entire town. There were myriad other industries connected with the maritime focus and a man was either at sea or connected with an industry which made seafaring possible. The city's prosperity rivaled that of New York, Boston, and Charleston.

The businessmen and ships' captains (and the two were not mutually exclusive) soon found that it was very lucrative to leave port with a skeleton crew, sail east from New England to the mid-North Atlantic, and round out their crews with Azorean seamen. The men of the islands were hearty workers and the poverty of their overcrowded and remote islands (outstanding even by European standards) was such that they could be hired for far less than the wages which American seamen demanded. There was also far less complaining about the appalling conditions aboard ship and the dangers of the occupation.

Thus the Portuguese men (and later their families) began drifting gradually into Perryport. The process continued into the nineteenth century, and by 1830 the Portuguese were in the town in sufficient number that a certain area was marked as "the Portygee part of town." The townspeople seemed to welcome them and various newspaper accounts of the time speak well of this or that person's new business or continuing business success. Terms such as "industrious," "prosperous," and "energetic" were common descriptive elements in the news. Today's townspeople still tend to characterize the Portuguese as hardworking, cheerful, and thrifty. For the inhabitants of early Perryport the Portuguese seemed to be well suited to the town's life-style. They seemed ready to acculturate and embodied the traditional New England virtues by being industrious, penny wise, and aware that "good fences make good neighbors." The old adage that "nothing succeeds like success" was the keystone for their acceptance and a place in the community. They succeeded so well that by the 1850s some were masters of their own ships, successful entrepreneurs, and well-to-do landholders.

The decline of whaling began in the late nineteenth century, forcing Perryport to look to other economic bases. She began to diversify into various small industries and, as well, turned to textile manufacturing. Her future economic strength was to lie in the multiplicity of her economic bases, and though parts of New England suffered drastically when the textile mills began to shift south, Perryport maintained at least a modicum of prosperity.

The steady stream of Portuguese immigrants, . . . beginning in earnest about 1870, had peaked for the United States as a whole around the turn of the century (1911–1920, 89,732 arrivals in American ports; 1931–1940, 3329 arrivals in American ports [Adler, 1972:17]). The decline primarily [resulted from] the Immigration Act of 1924 (43 Stat. 153) which reduced the Portuguese allotment to 503. This figure was further diminished by a Presidential Proclamation (No. 1872, 46 Stat. 2982) to a total of 440 immigrants (Adler, 1972:17). Where the single state of Massachusetts received 9002 immigrants in 1913 alone, the entire country received only a little over 3000 during the decade 1931–1940, and Massachusetts' total of this was only 202 (Adler, 1972:17).

The changing situation of today is signaled by a revision of the immigration regulations (Immigration Act of 1965, 75 Stat. 911). Portuguese immigration for the country as a whole jumped from 19,588 for the decade 1951–1960 to 76,064 for the period 1961–1970—with the vast majority (61,756) arriving during the years 1966–1970.

Perryport and Texton received an overwhelming majority of this second wave. The immigrants went in almost equal numbers to each of the cities, but the reception accorded the "Greenies" (as the Portuguese immigrants are commonly called in this area) was quite different in the two communities.

In Perryport, with an economic picture which favorably matched the national average, and where the Portuguese generally were looked upon as welcome additions, the major problems were finding housing, learning the language, and adjusting to life in a strange city. Some of the older settlers resented what they considered to be the "pushy ways" of their newly arrived brethren. Something of the attitude "I went through hard times to settle in and so should they" seemed to underlie their resentment. But this was not too common and most informants seemed more inclined to echo the words of one elderly man who told me, "We worked hard and paid hard for everything we got. These new people seem to think they've got better than that coming. I guess we came at the wrong time—but it was us who made it easy for them, I think."

The greatest difficulty for many of the new immigrants was the realization that [because of] . . . the presence of the so-called Black Portuguese (Africans used by the Portuguese to settle the Cape Verde Islands), many in the community considered the Portuguese to be at least partly Black—a racial tag which they soon found out carried a certain stigma. As one Yankee woman told me, "I remember dating a blond, blue-eyed boy. But he had a Portuguese name and my family worried that maybe he had Negro blood. People worried that maybe a baby would be born mulatto because of that. And how could you tell?" This had been an aspect of Perryport life which had been kept far below an overt level. The conflict inherent in the situation surfaced only in the school setting. People accepted the Portuguese, looked favorably on them, but, in those classic words, they "wouldn't want their daughter to marry one." Many of the Portuguese of earlier times, becoming aware of this, acquired the same prejudice and, in order to avoid being tagged as "probably one of *them*," not only did not argue against the situation of racism per se but also separated themselves from the Bravos or CeeVees as they are variously called and, except for including them in the *festa* (religious holiday festival) activities, effectively ignored them.

The new Portuguese immigrants, however, had various reasons for not wishing to accept this strategy. The African colonial wars, their own feelings of dismay at suddenly finding themselves a notch lower in the social ladder than they had expected to be, and several far more complex factors all combined to make the arrivals especially defensive concerning the position in Perryport. They adopted several strategies: The Black Cape Verdeans became the scapegoats and racial disorders grew intense in the areas where the two groups of Portuguese intermingled. This scapegoat tactic seems to have been based on the approach of "Don't tag us with them. We don't get along with them either!" Full-scale violence finally erupted on such a scale that the townspeople (Portuguese and non-Portuguese) were frightened into taking steps to resolve some of the underlying issues, chief of which was the long-standing discrimination practiced against the Cape Verdeans, especially in the economic sphere.

A second strategy, and one which intensified following the racial strife, was to form political action groups and immigrant assistance programs. There had always been associations for the new arrivals to join but they were chiefly social clubs where men congregated regularly for a game of cards and some drinks. Over 30 marching bands, the Church, and numerous *festas* provided the means for young people, women, and the group as a whole to cement their ties. The Portuguese were not (and are not now) a viable political force. Ethnic pressure groups, formed to achieve goals specific to the group as an ethnic block, are very new to Perryport. Until the last decade, few Portuguese entered politics. The essential associational nexuses were clubs and churches, linked by the mechanism of *festas*.

The second half of the twentieth century has had a different climate of opinion. Simultaneous with a new attitude toward the melting pot concept came a new type of Portuguese migrant. As Americans began to argue that racism was evil but ethnicity was good, immigrants arrived who lacked the "huddled-masses-yearning-to-be-free" attitude of their predecessors. They were more politically sophisticated and saw that community groups, working to solve community problems, were the best means to achieve personal goals inhibited because of social barriers. The associations and the cross-cutting occupational linkages maintained in this city of small, diversified businesses offered a ready-made foundation for such action groups and their aspirations. Further, the structure of the town itself is open enough that such groups had a way of implementing their goals. Old arrivals and newcomers could join, urge a sound program of English language instruction for Portuguese children thrust into the schools, and be relatively assured of getting a hearing and seeing something done.

A third strategy was to do what the Portuguese had traditionally done: acculturate as quickly as possible. Many avoided the racial issue, and ignored the possibility of joining an action group. They learned the language, anglicized their names (e.g., Dias became Day), worked hard, bought houses and repaired them, rented them out to still newer arrivals, and moved into the suburbs.

In summary the Perryport situation can be described as follows: gradual immigration under generally favorable economic conditions led to positive attitudes toward the Portuguese as an ethnic group within the social structure of the town. Newcomers who did not wish to occupy the politically powerless position traditionally held, who resented the demands to Americanize except for elements which the non-Portuguese were willing to allow them to retain, and who did not accept the goals and aspirations inherent in the stereotypic identify shaped by earlier circumstances, were able to use the relatively open Perryport system and the accepted patterns of associational links to form new types of associations which would affect the system.

Texton

It was not until 1870 that the small town of Texton, first settled in 1659, began a period of rapid and explosive growth. From an 1840 population of a little over 6000 there was increase over the next 30 years to about 25,000 in 1870, followed, during the next 30 years, by a leap to 105,000. The reason for this rapid growth was the introduction of textile mills. In 1840 there were approximately 2000 people employed in the mills; by 1870 the figure had jumped to 14,000; by 1910 almost 30,000 worked in the textile factories.

Texton was an ideal site for such mills, which ran primarily on steam power; a cheap source of energy was available in the nearby river and falls, and good transportation facilities allowed for the receipt of cotton from the south and shipment of the finished product throughout the country and abroad. Textile manufacturing was the lifeblood of the town and until the 1920s it accounted for some 80% of the town's economic base. The mills multiplied and so did the town's inhabitants. The cry was for cheap labor and for labor which would not fall prey to the labor agitators. Many immigrants came to the city—Irish, Scots, French-Canadians, Southern Europeans—but by far the most desired were the Portuguese. As one report put it, "They are hard-working and docile, if handled properly." Many Portuguese were brought in on a basis something like that of indentured servitude. Factory representatives would go to the Islands, offer what appeared to be astronomically high wages for an assured job and a loan for the passage money. To the Portuguese poor who existed in what was essentially a cashless economy, the chance to come to

America and make more money in a week than one saw all year at home was inducement indeed. For the company recruiter, the more ignorant and naive such recruits were the better for the company; it meant a longer period before they would be likely to be able to leave the mills. Even at a time when literacy was defined as the simple ability to write one's name, the Portuguese had the highest illiteracy rate of any European, African, or Asian immigrant group to the United States—almost 70% (Smith, 1974). Immigrants from other groups stayed a few years or even months and then quickly left to work at higher wages, in safer conditions, in environments less hazardous to their health—but the Portuguese remained. "They are the most desired of workers" wrote one industrialist of them.

And the economics of the situation were, to the Azorean, excellent. Here, the whole family could work; men, women, children, even the handicapped and the aged might find employment at a sweeping job or something of the kind. Given the family-based economic perspective of the Portuguese, the resultant income was a fortune. At a time when the average workingman in America brought home between $8 and $12 a week, the Portuguese family income could be that figure multiplied by almost the total number of individuals within the household (barring only children under 7). One informant told me that his father was one of eight children, all of whom worked in the mills while still under the parental roof: "Our family made about $40–50 a week. That's like a thousand today. My grandfather had never seen that much cash in his whole life!"

But the Portuguese paid for this income. The children were, of course, given the minimal education possible and put to work in the mills for as long a work week as possible, whatever their age. And this perpetuated the group's position as the pool from which to draw the lowest-paid, "unskilled" laborers. There are in Texton today individuals who are the fifth generation to work in the mills, at essentially the same occupational level as their immigrant forefathers.

The Portuguese came in and stayed as the lowest strata of the community. Many of the non-Portuguese viewed them as uneducable—perhaps too biologically inferior on the whole to have the intelligence to do any but the most menial labor. (For some reason, not clear, few Bravos went to Texton. It may be that they simply were not on the recruitment list since the initial workers came from the Azores and Madeira for the most part. They, in turn, brought in kin and friends as the jobs were available, thus, possibly, keeping the Bravos out of the employment network, though not out of deliberate prejudice.)

Although not segregated into specific neighborhoods, the Portuguese workers lived near the factories in which they were employed. This created "company neighborhoods," many of which were ethnically homogeneous. Such factors, together with the social clubs, bands, and churches which also existed in Texton, might have been expected to create integrative bonds, but the occupational focus was the crucial difference. Textile mills were almost the exclusive employment possibility. Without competition from other kinds of manufacturing, mill owners were in tacit agreement concerning working conditions, wages, hours, and employment practices. Labor conditions, then, were much more rigorous than in Perryport. There was, however, bitter competition between mills, a competition which grew as the economy worsened. Workers were often divided by this intense rivalry, partly because job "loyalty" was one way to insure steady employment.

Workers tried to live near the mill at which they were employed. Seasonal unemployment and depressions would cause the worker to change jobs and thus his residence, adding to the urban rootlessness and to loose associational ties.

Mill technology did not encourage worker communication and the 60-hour work week left little capacity for recreation. Women and children were probably most debilitated by such conditions. The women, especially, had great difficulty since they had to work the same long hours but also had to keep house, bear and raise the children, and tend to the personal needs of the household members (which sometimes included two or three boarders). Work demands and traditional attitudes of Portuguese males concerning the freedom of women restricted their life to the house, job, street block, and Church.

The minimal social life of the Portuguese, ethnically insular as it was, offered no more of an opportunity to learn English than did the isolated job in the nerve-wracking noise of the mills. Portuguese culture was, then, slow to leave the immigrant.

Another consequence of mill work was the compounding of traditional emphases on the nucleated aspect of a group whose significant social orientation is the primary family. No structural nexuses were created to circumvent the atomistic forces of traditional patterns and the mill work. The Portuguese while prounion are not strong union. They tend to be suspicious of the men who lead the union (though not of the union per se) and several union officials and shop stewards complained to me of membership apathy ("If we didn't offer them charter flights to the Azores they probably wouldn't belong"). The Church, particularly at the formative period of which we speak, emphasized acceptance of life and maintenance of traditional patterns. Last, isolation in the factory and the piecework incentive system stressed competition rather than cooperation among workers.

The results of the atomistic social field can be gauged by the looseness of affiliation ties with the existing associations. Also, despite the fact that the Portuguese of Texton represent between 30 and 40% of the total population, they have been able to elect only one mayor (who served but one term). Furthermore, only 3% of the elected offices available for city residents to vote on have been filled by Portuguese.

The new immigrant wave brought the same type of immigrant to Texton as had been attracted to Perryport. The explicit stereotype, however, was much more negative and more distinctly pejorative than in Perryport. The newcomers were more resentful concerning the stereotype and the blocks it created to achieving their aspirations.

Non-Portuguese justify their pejorative stereotype by pointing to the declining economy and the declining population. The unemployment figure is one of the highest in the country and yet the Portuguese keep arriving. The Portuguese percentage of the population is increasing because many of the more occupationally mobile (especially the non-Portuguese) are leaving. This, argue the non-Portuguese, "leaves us with a bunch of unskilled workers that we can't train because they don't have enough basic education." This argument is some 50 years old by now.

The reason for the continuing influx can be found in the revised immigration laws. The Portuguese know of the employment difficulties, yet the elimination of the quota system and the establishment of the "preferential category" law almost require that they continue to come to a city with a large Portuguese population. The Immigration Act of 1965 (75 Stat. 911), and especially the second and the fifth preference, forces the immigrant to go to the location of his "sponsor." Admitted are spouses, unmarried children of resident aliens, a U.S. citizen's siblings, and the sibling's spouse and children.

Though statistical data are lacking, estimates are that only some 60% of the new immigrants have stayed. For this group there are two dominant strategies: education and personalized manipulation of the system.

My own impressions and discussions with school officials indicate that the newcomer is more inclined to see education as a solution to some of his problems of adjustment. The newcomers are, of course, better educated than those immigrants of 75–100 years ago. They are more culturally conditioned by their own milieu to see education as a useful tool in making a living. The Portuguese school system has improved immensely over the last 50 years— particularly in relation to filling the needs of the poor. The newcomers are thus more ready to sacrifice immediate income for deferred wealth and/or status.

The second strategy was succinctly put by one informant when I asked him why the Portuguese of Texton didn't get together and try to improve the position of the group's members, who are said to be "the last to be hired and the first to be fired." He replied:

How do you change it? We can't control the bosses. And the unions are for the bosses. And every Portuguese is for himself. You look around and you see we can't even cooperate to get a good *festa* going like they do over in [Perryport]. Over there they work together and it lasts the whole weekend. It's a big thing with everybody working to help make it. Here, you start something and this group fights with that one, and won't work with another one, and this guy can't stand that one. We can't get cooperation for anything. It's every person for himself. Why should anyone try to get people to work together when experience shows that after your back is broken to push the thing, someone along the line starts pushing his own thing and it all collapses. You learn pretty soon not to bother. I tried but I found out that the other guy was for himself and

I was being the only one who wasn't getting himself taken care of. Now I look out for me and mine. That's the way things are here.

In Texton, then, there is much individual resentment of the social field in which the immigrant must operate but there is little if any coordinated group effort to alter the situation, particularly as it is affected by the negative stereotype which structures the communication process between newcomers and oldtimers, between Portuguese and non-Portuguese. In this city, the Portuguese came en masse, and were then and are now a highly visible group because of their relationship to the economic structure of the community. They were of some dubious value as long as they contributed to the financial well-being of Texton entrepreneurs. Now, however, the city has seen 50 years of decline—and the end is not yet in sight. They had worn out their welcome and not only didn't know enough to leave but were inviting others to come and stay.

The pervasive atomism which was touched upon earlier is a critical aspect of life in what one hesitantly calls "the Portuguese community." There are divisive forces imposed by the community and by the occupational structure—forces which are either lacking or much weaker in Perryport. One example of this can be found in the more explicit boundaries which mark one neighborhood off from another and which have rankings about which there is a high degree of agreement: "good class," "poor but respectable," "downhill," "a real slum."

The newcomer to Texton has moved into an entirely different environment—*in terms of his own perception*—from that of Perryport. He must, as an immigrant, adopt different strategies, and this differential process means that the perception of American life and the resultant acculturative process (as well as those traditional values which are retained) will be different. This was explicitly recognized by *every* informant with whom I spoke in either city. When asked, "Do you think things would be just the same if you lived in (Perryport/Texton)?" I always received a negative answer—though the reasons for and nature of the differences varied in type, and ranged from highly positive to highly negative in the evaluation of the alternative.

In sum, Perryport and Texton present differing social fields for the Portuguese immigrant of today. In the former there is a greater sense of community involvement and a greater belief that the system can be altered to be more satisfactory. Though there is conflict it appears to be the kind which is predicated on the assumption that change is possible. The groups exist but there are links between and among them and thus the system is more open to communication and more responsive to change. And there are institutional forms of substance in the community which provide a foundation for analogous associations. Despite the fact that the non-Portuguese might see the Perryporter as more discontented than his fellow in Texton, the former actually appears to have a greater sense of involvement with and concern for the town of which he is a part. He wants it to change, he believes he can make it change and that it will want to, and so he stays.

Texton, on the other hand, has isolated its people—occupationally, geographically, and socially. Faced with a far more negative ethnic stereotype, the Texton immigrant emphasizes the individualized strategies—self-improvement, flight, or something strongly akin to Banfield's amoral familism. The difference may be indicated by the responses to the question "Do you think life would be better, say, in Canada?" (All of the informants had friends or kin there.) Thirty-nine out of 53 Texton informants said yes and 16 indicated that they thought they might or definitely would emigrate there. Of the 37 Perryport immigrants queried, nine said life would be better but only one indicated that he planned to emigrate.

As yet I have not been able to explore the attitudes of the host community in any systematic fashion but there are some intriguing, programmatic points which may be stated briefly. The attitudes of the host community will be determined by:

1. The format of immigration (e.g., gradual vs. sharp increase).
2. The occupations filled and the economic niche occupied (sometimes to be too successful is worse than not being successful enough; some people are hostile because of the financial success achieved by the immigrants, witness the plight of the Ugandan Asians).
3. The degree of social visibility maintained by the immigrants.
4. The degree of "fit" between the aspirations of the immigrants and the current climate of opinion (e.g., ethnic self-consciousness is encouraged today, as it was not 100 years ago, and thus attempts by a "foreigner" to alter the system are reacted to much more favorably than they would have been in 1870).

In conclusion, one may see sharp differences in the type of acculturative stresses, the type of acculturative patterns adopted, the strategies opted for to maximize the particular type of "success" encouraged in a given milieu, and the degree of integratedness felt to be achieved. That, of course, is all this article attempted to demonstrate—that there *are* differences which exist which are as critical to an analysis as are the generalized structural elements. Such factors offer some insight as to influences on immigration patterns; why some cities are integrated and others atomistic (why, during the 1960s, for example, did some cities experience racial strife while others, and, most peculiarly, some which were predicted to have "highly explosive potential," did not?); where the greatest stress will be for new arrivals (especially if one can determine the critical aspects of their expectations and aspirations). Finally, the use of this particularistic historical approach will provide markers for determining what might be some of the structural similarities which *do* exist despite historical differences.

Bibliography

ADLER, JAMES P.
1972 *Ethnic Minorities in Cambridge: The Portuguese*, Vol. 1 (unabridged). Prepared for the Cambridge Planning and Development Department Cambridge, Massachusetts: The City of Cambridge Printing Department.

MARTIN, HARRY W.
1964 "Correlates of Adjustment Among American Indians in an Urban Environment," *Human Organization*, 23(4):290–295.

SMITH, M. ESTELLIE
1974 "The Portuguese minority: An Invisible Enclave," In *Social and Cultural Identity*, Thomas K. Fitzgerald (ed.). Proceedings of the Southern Anthropological Society, No. 8. Athens, Georgia: University of Georgia Press, pp. 81–91.

Part VII: Research/Term Paper Topics

1. "How Visible is Urban Heterogeneity?"

   Test the idea that cities are more heterogeneous than other community types. Tour your city's neighborhoods, noting house or building styles, landscaping, decorations, population density, street activity, dress styles, etc. How many different ethnic groups and socio-economic categories can you identify in this manner? Comment on the way in which specific configurations of indicators reflect ethnicity or social class of residents. Repeat the tour in a nearby small town with which you are unfamiliar. Guess at the population makeup, and then interview some local residents to determine actual degree and type of heterogeneity. Which indicators are no longer useful? Why? Is the population difference between city and town one of kind or degree?

2. "Cities and Ethnicity."

   It has been suggested that the ability of ethnic groups to enter successfully into urban life depends as much upon the city as the group itself. Explore this question using the literature. Select one ethnic group (Amerindians, Chicanos, Puerto Ricans, Chinese, Jews, East Indians, southern Blacks) and contrast their positions in two or three cities. This will require that you look into the cities as well as the ethnic group.

3. "Ethnic and Non-ethnic Cities."

   Some cities are predominantly "ethnicized"; that is, most residents belong to one or another clearly defined ethnic group (usually tribal, racial, or national). Often, one such group monopolizes political and economic power. Other cities are ostensibly non-ethnic, insofar as they are not identified with particular groups, nor is power viewed in ethnic terms. Using the literature, look into the different problems confronting ethnics in both types of cities. Contrast. Is ethnicity really the same phenomenon in both city types?

4. "Is Poverty Urban?"

Look into the Literature on poverty, including material on rural "poor." Is poverty predominantly an urban phenomenon? How would you sharpen the definition of poverty?

5. "Aging and the City."

What is the effect of urban life upon the elderly? Examine the literature on aging, paying close attention to the status of the elderly as a function of community and societal type. Try to distinguish between effects of the wider society/culture and the community type upon the position of the aged.

6. "Observation in an Ethnic Neighborhood."

Walk through, and carefully describe several different ethnic neighborhoods in your community (or neighborhoods of distinct class, if no ethnic enclaves are available). Note kinds of dwellings, paying close attention to style, decoration, and use of space. Note kinds of people and their activities. Note conditions of the streets, gutters, (a reflection of clout?) and lawns. Are shops and businesses an integral part of the neighborhood or peripheral to it? Are there bars and restaurants? How many? What kinds (family-style or adults only)? Make generalizations about the life-style differences exhibited, about group differences in presentation of self, and organization of their microworld.

PART

The Urban Future

EIGHT

The field seems divided between those who think there will and those who think there won't be an urban future. On the negative side are arguments both of doom and salvation. The city will become unlivable, a jungle, insupportable, unserviceable, and certainly unfuelable. It will be so regimented or anarchistic as to drive its inhabitants away. Where the exurbanites will live is still unclear. On the other hand, anti-urban optimists envision a return to dispersed, small, and personal communities as inevitable and desirable; back to a "natural" life, perhaps in communal rural contexts.

Those who see an urban future are also divided. Pessimists envision horrendous city sprawls, megalopolitan cancers upon the disappearing countryside. Trapped within them by the lack of space outside (all available land being devoted to hyperintensively mechanized agriculture), the inhabitants tumble upon one another, fighting for space, privacy, and even the legal right to marry or reproduce. Optimists see the future as a time of urban experimentation. Esthetic and psychoemotional needs will be anticipated. Planned, human-serving cities will offer up a cornucopia of benefits and services undreamed of today, all efficiently supported by a foundation of climactic technological wizardry.

Not surprisingly, almost all projections of the urban future (megalopolis, space city, planned, experimental cities, post-atomic war cities) are based upon current industrial Western city form and direction of change. There is an implicit assumption that the present Western city, with all its potential and problems, is an inevitable stage in the ongoing urban evolution of all societies. This is an unpleasant thought, yet in some respects, not wholly unrealististic. Cities are the major interface between nations, the points of entry of ideas and people from abroad. However, the present bulk of influence (in terms of life-style, architecture, communication, services) tends to flow from industrial toward nonindustrial cities, if only because the former send more people, products, and techniques to the latter.

The world is becoming more, not less dependent upon industry, specialization, international trade, and government services. In the waning years of the twentieth century, few nations will be willing to stay behind the rest for the sake of maintaining the integrity of a traditional culture or ideological system. Therefore, given the dependence of city type upon societal type, it is doubtful whether *any* city of the future (let alone *"the* city") will reflect a trajectory substantially independent of industrial urban evolution.

This need not imply that all cities will be industrial in the sense of heavy manufacturing or heterogeneity of trades. Resort towns, political capitals, retirement communities, gambling cities, mechanized agricultural towns, university towns, and other specialized urban centers do and will probably continue to exist. The point is that industry—via the generation of goods, surplus capital, efficient transportation, communications, and the long-distance transmission of energy—plays a major role in underwriting the life-styles possible in such places.

But we may all be wrong. The Vernes and da Vincis of today will not be identifiable until the urban future is actually upon us. At best we can attempt to ask meaningful questions, among them the following:

1. To what extent will present nonindustrial, non-Western cities be able to maintain their internal trajectories of development into the future? Is a long-term balance of industrial and nonindustrial lifeways ultimately possible in any city?
2. Given the fact that cities arose in the first place because (among other things) they concentrated goods, services, and peoples in an efficient manner, will people continue to want cities after the anticipated host of technical miracles makes propinquity (and thus city residence) unnecessary for filling needs and communicating with others?
3. Is *any* long-established city susceptible to massive planning and significant change?
4. Will common dependence upon technical/industrial resources and access to common services and information make moot the typological distinctions between cities of the future? Even now, is Acapulco or Miami Beach really different from Pittsburgh? Their services differ, but do their basic processes?

Alternative Possible Urban Futures

H. WENTWORTH ELDREDGE

Each stage in the development of cities has undoubtedly been accompanied by speculation about the urban future. The present is no exception. The awesome rise of the megalopolis, the growth of suburbs, changing economic and demographic patterns, new forms of metropolitan and interurban transportation, urban decay, and (most recently) the return to city centers by exurbanites—all have given rise to thoughts on what the future holds.

The majority of comments have concentrated either on statements of the problems and how to ameliorate them or on the framing of programmatic and often unrealistic directives on how to create future Utopias, some of which even urge the elimination of cities. H. Wentworth Eldredge's paper has been selected because it takes an overview. After reviewing the various studies that others have done, it suggests a variety of fifteen possible urban futures. These are listed as options, implying that humanity ostensibly has some degree of choice in the matter. Ten of the options are existent forms and "almost certain to continue"; five are in the realm of science fiction—possible but with varying potential for "probable."

Eldredge ends his essay by stating that, "Superior intentional societies and ordered environments still seem just beyond our grasp." He does not say why, and that might be the most important question ("If we can put a man on the moon . . .") But perhaps it would also be relevant to ask, Is that so bad? As a comic strip character of the 1930s once pointed out, "What we wants is results but what we gits is consequences." The Utopian city could be an Orwellian nightmare, no matter how superior our intentions. On the other hand, there may be no alternatives to intentional societies and ordered environments. Perhaps the freedom of the city about which Simmel and Wirth spoke must give way to the same kind of predictability, regulation, and constraints that pushed many away from the hinterlands and into the cities in the first place. And perhaps this very freedom has created many of the problems that have been discussed throughout this collection.

Given the multigroup society of the present United States with widely divergent value systems, overriding democratic values with heavy egalitarian overtones preclude any reductionism to *one national pattern* for societal/physical urbanism. Such a naive, crude, cruel, and simplistic perception of "human nature" is not remotely feasible in modern Western nations even though there is a tendency to approach it in totalitaria. The enormous powers of the intellectual, technical, even behavioral and organization technologies

"Alternative Possible Urban Futures," *Futures*, 6:26–41 (1974), revised by the author. Adapted from *World Capitals: Toward Guided Urbanization* (New York: Doubleday & Company, Inc., 1975).

make it possible to "have diversity, choice and to meet human needs" for the first time in history.[1]

In "the post-industrial society" with its heavy emphasis on the knowledge industry, there is bound to be a multiplicity of variants on patterns already visible in the 1970s. To select a few representative searches for options: *Futures Conditional*[2] zeroes in, guided by that lively ex-engineer Robert Theobald, on a mind-blowing attempt to imagine various future scenarios for the next thirty years. Paul Goodman sees *Seeds of Liberation*[3] in new thought patterns that free humanity for building, first better societal futures and later physical structures. The American Institute of Planners launched in 1966 a massive enquiry, directed by William R. Ewald Jr., into the next fifty years, budgeting more than one and one-quarter million dollars from a variety of public and private sources. This was a hefty attempt to illumine American (and the world's) professional city planners as to the rich variety of the feasible roads ahead.[4] An amazing mish-mash of authors—many exceptionally perceptive—from a wide spectrum of doers and thinkers at least adds up to the clear message that bumbling along with "more of the same" would be hopelessly inadequate. Urban design student Keven Lynch in "The Possible City"[5] stresses "mobility, access and communication are indeed the essential qualities of an urbanized region—its reason for being." This has been echoed by transportation specialist Wilfred Owen who hammers on the fact that access to activity nodes—jobs, dwellings, and recreation—is the key to civilized community development and glimpses the developing interchangeability of communication (movement of ideas) with transportation (movement of people and goods), which is bound to affect life territory and life-styles shortly.[6] Even a hard-headed urban administrator, Roger Starr, executive director of New York's Citizens' Housing and Planning Council, bewailing the incessant critical attacks on "the city" by Utopian types such as Lewis Mumford, Jane Jacobs, Herbert Gans, Victor Gruen, and others, knows that already the balancing of the multiplicity of values (held by divergent groups *now*) is an almost impossible task;[7] it is bound to be worse in the future as groups multiply and pathways further divide. *Mass society* as "one dead level" seems less likely in the 1970s than it did in the 1950s.

If market choices are to be largely replaced by designed options under a National Urban Policy (NUP) then widespread societal/physical alternate pos-

[1] Leonard Duhl, "Teaching and Social Policy," *The Bulletin of the Association of Collegiate Schools of Planning,* Winter 1971, pp. 4–10.

[2] New York: The Bobbs-Merrill Co., 1972. *Teg's 1984,* a participatory, experimental book on new societal/physical forms by Theobald and J. M. Scott, "can ego involve the reader" (Chicago: The Swallow Press, 1972).

[3] Paul Goodman, ed., *Seeds of Liberation* (New York: George Braziller, 1964).

[4] *The Next Fifty Years* series commemorated the 50th anniversary of the founding of the American Institute of Planners. Published by the University of Indiana Press (Bloomington, Ill.), it consists of three volumes: Vol. I *Environment and Man* (1967), Vol. II *Environment and Change* (1968), Vol. III *Environment and Policy* (1968).

[5] Ibid., Vol. III, p. 145.

[6] Wilfred Owen, "Telecommunication and Life Styles," *The Accessible City* (Washington: The Brookings Institution, 1972), pp. 132–133.

[7] Roger Starr, *Urban Choices: The City and Its Critics* (Baltimore: Penguin Books, 1967).

sibilities must be built for multiple present and future life-styles. Minimum standards probably can be set; egalitarianism, heavily reinforced by increasingly scarce resources, will quite likely create iron maximums, but within these very wide parameters a NUP can offer the citizenry a great variety for numerous versions of an existence of "style and quality." There undoubtedly will be both monetary and possible societal costs for making large numbers of available options, but the resultant stunting of society's rich fabric by dull sameness suggests immediate high societal costs and potential high monetary costs for the failure to provide such options. Inadequate life-styles are a shaped charge aimed at urban viability—a rather complex way of stating that insistent frustration leads to tension resulting in the possibility of grim revolution (a most costly societal exercise).

Thus it would appear that one of the most overwhelming tasks of NUP planners is to make readily available rewarding, feasible options in diverse physical and societal forms and combinations thereof.

Traditionally, planners have tended to think in terms of multipurpose or multifunctional cities; this seems a rather narrow conclusion to induce from a long human experience with governmental, religious, recreational, learning, trading, industrial types of cities to draw from. The future could see specialized cities with clues elaborated from this simple list of existent forms with such revised types as: (a) the ceremonial city (Washington, Islamabad), (b) the university city (Oxford as it was), (c) the research city (Novo Sibirsk), (d) the artistic city (Aspen, Col.), (e) the fun city or Hedonopolis (Cannes, Miami Beach), (f) communication or media city (see Option 15 following), (g) the museum city (Bruges, Williamsburg, Nara) including Museums of the Future (Mesa City of Soleri), (h) experimental cities of varied types (health, new social relations, communal economic developments), (i) any combination of the above. In fact, each venture could be considered as an experiment,[8] and so treated. Actually, sharply differentiated satellite cities in a metropolitan area or sectors or communities within a core city could offer rewarding variations.

Here is a realistic catalogue of feasible urban options ahead; these are relatively "surprise-free." Given multigroup society with divergent life-styles and values, it is obligatory for holistic planners to offer a wide spectrum of choice. Despite both physical and societal utopianists, it is more than likely that in the year 2000 A.D., post-industrial society will be surprisingly like the present, only it is hoped "better." These fifteen options, all rather standard, are not mutually exclusive, and much overlapping is implied; within options there are clearly suboptions which are not pursued here. Further, the emphasis is on the physical/spatial framework and on location, which together do not remotely determine societal structuring. Much social diversity is possible within similar man-made physical environments as within similar natural physical environments. The relationship between design and behavior is not

---

[8] John McHale, *Future Cities: Notes on a Typology* (unpublished draft).

one-to-one. These options are grouped under two categories: Type A—almost certain to continue; and Type B—generally far-out potential environments; no attempt is made to weigh formally the importance of the various options. Certain options clearly occur within the territory of larger urban forms—others are relatively free-standing entities or activity centers.

Type A: Almost Certain to Continue

Option 1. Megalopolis or urban region. This is modern society's fate. Most of the post-industrial urban population (80%?) will dwell in Options 1, 2, and 3. THE PACIFIC BELT (Japan), BOSWASH (Boston to Washington) and RANDSTAD (Holland) are already here. Can such sprawling giantism be redeveloped by opening up "density breaks" (similar to fire breaks in a forest) and by the creation of varied activity nodes to restructure interaction and upgrade the Quality of Life (QOL) in these vast agglomerations?

Option 2. Metropolitan Central City (500,000 and up) as a high-activity area with cosmopolitan, sophisticated recreation, jobs, living. The French regional *mêtropoles d'équilibre* fit this pattern; high-rise, vertically zoned buildings could serve as an experiment. Both "straight" and "counter" cultures can find room here. This is the locus of high-pressure private and public development in the United States as "the city fights back" to lure middle-class population into returning from the suburbs to live and to interact. It means modern office buildings, pedestrian malls and pediment (or higher) walkways with interesting and diverse shops, recreational and cultural facilities—in short the lure of the bazaar which has so importantly stoked urban fires. "New towns in town" (NTIT) belong here most certainly in an attempt to divide the city into some semblance of meaningful communities (at least at the level of simple services); social development planning will be a must in large sectors of central city.

Option 3. Smaller central city (50,000 to 500,000) [with] similar qualities but on a less national and more on a regional scale. The possibility exists of creating an *entire* community spirit. Town housing, vertically zoned buildings with possible class and ethnic mixtures. Somewhere between a 250,000 and 500,000 population seems to be presently the critical mass for the full spectrum of city functions. QOL efforts would pay off richly here.

Option 4. Small central city or town (up to 50,000) [with] still less national/regional interaction and scale. Local varieties adjusted more clearly to varied natural environments and with specific functions, such as the research city; shore city; recreation city; university/learning/information city; mountain city.

Option 5. Satellite cities for Options 2 and 3 to gain the putative benefits of Option 4; closely linked with new communities but could be upgraded existent towns or cities.

Option 6. Inner suburbs for all three major city types (2, 3, 4) must be divided into "communities" (NTIT again) serving various life-styles according to economic class, vocational and/or avocational interests, religion, ethnicity, race—high rise and low rise (town houses/cluster housing). There should be a great variety of suburban types to suit various life-styles. The United States has its special problem in white/black antagonisms and unless adequate optional suburban space (both integrated or nonintegrated) is made available for blacks to leave central city, this impacted ghetto, poisoning American life for all, will continue to fester. Undoubtedly suboptions as to integration or not must be made available to face the hard reality of continuing prejudice. Patently this applies also to outer suburbs and to new towns. Here derelict land can be used as new green space for recreation and relief.

Option 7. Outer suburbs similar but of a less "urban" character. Varied life-styles are stressed by design both physical and societal; a greater attempt through cluster housing to create "community." Some high-rise buildings in open settings are inevitable.

Option 8. Exurbia. Quasi-rural existence of a scattered grain but [because of] advanced transportation "urbanistic" in quality; not unrelated to "the wired city" and the four-day work week. Made possible by the electric pump, septic tank, and four-wheeled drive vehicle; haunt of hillbilly types and seclusive "intellectuals." This is high-cost scatteration, but an immensely rewarding option for certain personality types, who may be either incompetent, truly creative, or merely hiding from the horrid urban world.[9] Increasingly the haunt of the counter-culture and very suitable for new experimental family/community variants.

Option 9. New Towns (or latterly *New Communities*). Building cities *de novo* has held a great attraction for mankind; "leave the messy clutter behind and start afresh" might even be traced back to mobile hunters striking the befouled encampment to move on to virgin areas. New towns imply dwellings, jobs, recreation, a wide spectrum of services and *controlled* size. Most certainly the current furor about new cities/towns/communities indicates a deep-seated dissatisfaction with existent urban forms. And unquestionably this is the area for widespread experimentation both with physical forms and with societal structure—and a means of ascertaining and developing client desires or choices. Somewhat oversold as a universal panacea at the moment, the enormous costs for the needed infrastructure of a massive new cities program to cope with a significant percentage of the expected 80 to 100 million new Americans (35,000,000 plus new households) boggles the imagination. To build for 25% only or 20 to 25 million persons would require 2,000 towns for 100,000 inhabitants, each costing between $2 and $5 billion in public and private investment, leading to an overall expenditure of $10 trillion at least.[10] While undoubtedly much will of necessity be spent in any case to house, amuse, and provide jobs for the expected hordes, it is most unlikely that

[9] Satirized some years ago by A. C. Spectorsky, *The Exurbanites* (New York: Berkeley Publishing Co., 1955).

[10] Extrapolated loosely from Walter K. Vinett, *Paper Number Three, The Scenario for Minnesota's Experimental City* (Minneapolis: University of Minnesota, Office for Applied Social Science and the Future, 1972).

exploiting the vast existing urban infrastructure would even approach such costs—though the possible benefits of thousands of new towns might be of extraordinary magnitude.

Before proceeding further, it should be stressed that new towns can consist of:

(a) Free-standing independent communities (Brasilia).

(b) Groups of related free-standing, functionally divergent communities (Lewis Mumford's ideal).

(c) Satellite communities with high self-employment (London ring new towns).

(d) Extensions of cities; really glorified, quasi-independent suburbs (Long Island Levittowns).

(e) "New towns in town" (NTIT) lively tissue grafts to existing internal city structure (Fort Lincoln, Washington, D.C.).[11]

Minnesota Experimental City (MXC), brainchild of oceanographer, physicist, meteorologist Athelstan Spilhaus, aided by assorted great brains (Buckminister Fuller, urbanologist Harvey Perloff, economist Walter Heller) is to be built by private financing on 50,000 acres, 120 miles north of Minneapolis with a maximum population of 250,000.[12] This is perhaps the most obviously experimental effort to date both physically and societally: downtown will be roofed over; the municipal power plant is to be partially fueled by garbage; cable TV will approximate "the wired city" (Option 15); farms and factories will be mixed; people will be housed in megastructures complete with waterless toilets, people-movers, and universal computer-managed charge accounts. New city Vaudreuil, to house and provide jobs for 150,000 residents, is to be built by the French government in the Basse-Seine region outside Paris. It will have the world's first urban center without noise or pollution (?) and all green zones in the general area are to be preserved, proudly announced former President of the Republic Pompidou. The city's traffic will flow underground; factory smoke is to be carried off by underground conduits, gases being burned at the source; apartments and business buildings to be soundproofed; and all refuse moved through underground conduits to be used in adding to the city's requirements for central heating. These are merely the most "advanced" examples of a new communities world movement (millennia old) which includes the architecturally striking Brasilia and Chandigarh and the older Washington and New Delhi (the British imperial city stage). The thirty-odd British New Towns are world renowned and a great many new towns of various shapes and sizes have been recently identified with at least 1,000 in the USSR alone.[13] The best known examples in the

---

[11] Harvey S. Perloff, *New Towns in Town* (Washington, D.C.: Resources for the Future, 1966), reprint.

[12] *Time*, February 26, 1973.

[13] F. J. Osborn and Arnold Whittick, *The New Towns: The Answer to Megalopolis* (New York: McGraw-Hill Book Company, 1963), pp. 141–148. This listing is incomplete and already dated. According to the Department of Housing and Urban Development, there are 1,000 "free-standing" new towns in the USSR (*The New York Times*, April 26, 1973).

United States: Columbia (Maryland), Reston (Virginia), Flower Mound (Texas), Jonathan (Minnesota), and Irvine (California)—all privately financed—are in varying degrees innovative socially and physically, primarily in amenities. The semi-satellite cities coupled to the public urban transit system of Stockholm (they do not provide jobs for more than half the resident population) have also attracted world attention, concentrating especially on the town centers so reminiscent of American shopping centers without that ugly, naked parking necklace of automobiles. The Dutch have done a splendid job in reclaiming the Zuider Zee for new town development. Tapiola, a tiny gem for only 17,000 persons, using adroitly both green and blue (water) space, has cheered the world with the realization that handsome urbanity can be possible. Japan with characteristic zeal plans to dot the hinterland of Tokyo with quasi-new towns composed of rather barren, high-density dwellings. Tama New Town to house 410,000 on 7,500 acres is the prime example (incidentally, this is the same acreage as Reston, which is planned to house 75,000 with high recreational amenities). At Tama, tenants, generally middle income, are to be selected by lot and divided into "neighborhoods," generally convenience-oriented of 15,000 people. Most dwellers are expected to commute to Shinjuku (New-Town-in-Town) or through it to central Tokyo for work.[14]

As is well known, Israel has constructed a variety of new towns/new communities: larger ones for port or industrial purposes; smaller for agricultural development often connected with defense[15] under an urban settlement hierarchy system based on Christaller. Connected with the physical siting of population are the renowned versions of communal settlements, the *Kibbutz* and *moshav*. Thus the twin experimental functions of new communities are exhibited there: technological virtuosity and fresh social patterning. Noteworthy in new community development worldwide is the great variety of fresh governmental authorities or public corporations invented to get on with the job— where traditional government has been obviously too wooden to do so.

While, for example, the original or Mark I postwar British new towns were aimed in the London region at decanting the central city population, new towns or massively developed old towns both in Britain and elsewhere are now perceived as potentially powerful development nodes furthering national urbanization policy with high technology, high education, and population distribution.[16] Even Herbert Gans, egalitarian sociologist, believes that treated delicately new communities might possible make positive contributions to the nasty desegregation muddle here,[17] as will perhaps "Soul City," the Black

[14] *Information Series 20, HUD International*, U.S. Department of Housing and Urban Development, January 15, 1973.

[15] Ann Louise Strong, *Planned Urban Environments* (Baltimore, Md.: The Johns Hopkins University Press, 1971), pp. 170–173.

[16] Cf. Lawrence Susskind and Gary Hack, "New Communities in a National Urban Growth Strategy," *Technology Review* (February, 1972), pp. 30–42; also "New Communities," An American Institute of Planners Background Paper, No. 2, 1968.

[17] Revised version of a paper presented for the Symposium on "The Human Dimensions of Planning," UCLA, June, 1972.

New Town in North Carolina near Raleigh-Durham under the leadership of Floyd B. McKissick with a planned eventual population of 50,000.[18]

Finally, the United States Government is officially dedicated to sponsoring new communities in the Housing Acts of 1970 and 1972. Up to now the action has hardly been impressive; there is no remotely visible overall strategy for siting or the scale of the total effort. European agricultural life has long been town/village centered, contrary to the United States mode of isolated homesteads. Clearly an increasing humankind will need more and more food while a (declining) proportion of the population will continue to opt for an agricultural life-style. Of course, for some very considerable period there will be islands of "backward" rural culture preserved in Asia, Africa, Latin America, and possibly portions of North America. Such areas could offer a rewarding life-style for the actual inhabitants and "museums for living" (small residual forms throughout the world) for the denizens of more urbanized habitats.

Type B. Far-Out Potential Environments

These could be either physical or societal, or more likely some combination of both; they might serve as temporary experiences for the many or for the permanent life-style of a few.

Option 11. Mega-structures or "mini-cities" have fascinated men at least since the Tower of Babel.[19] Characteristically, there is a Disneyland project, copyrighted in 1960, "The Community of Tomorrow," which will be a whole *enclosed* model town for 20,000 persons on 50 acres *only*, to be part of the Florida Disney World. Paolo Soleri has had the greatest visibility recently as a highly successful youth-guru with his concepts of giant supra-terrestrial human hives housing up to hundreds of thousands of persons.[20] Soleri has fuzzy, complicated, intuitive communalistic notions about group life joined to his often cantilevered bridgelike structures, which allies him to far-out commune options as well.[21]

Apparently the term *mega* (giant) structure was the invention of Fumihiko Maki of the Japanese Metabolist Group in 1964. *Habitat,* by the Israeli architect Moshe Safdie, readied for Expo 1967 in Montreal, while financially an initial diaster, has become a much publicized example of this sort of "plug-in," "clip-on" structure;[22] for the record it is turning out to be both a financial and a societal success. Taby, satellite community outside Stockholm, houses 5,000

[18] "The Planning Process for New Town Development: Soul City," A Planning Studio Course, Fall 1969, Department of City and Regional Planning, University of North Carolina, Chapel Hill.

[19] A visually striking book on mega-structures is Justus Dahinden's *Urban Structures for the Future* (New York: Praeger Publishers, Inc., 1972). Dahinden's knowledge of societal reality is very slight.

[20] Paolo Soleri, *Arcology—The City in the Image of Man* (Cambridge: M.I.T. Press, 1969).

[21] See Ralph Wilcoxen, *Paolo Soleri: A Bibliography* (Monticello, Ill.: Council of Planning Librarians Exchange Bibliography, #88, June, 1969).

[22] Cf. William Zuk and Roger H. Clark, *Kinetic Architecture* (New York: Van Nostrand Reinhold Company, 1970). To quote the blurb, "Exciting open-ended planning: proposed and actual structures that are *replaceable, deformable, incremental, expandable, reversible*—even *disposable.*" Italics by the editor.

people in one group of vast, curved structures, flanked by eight tower blocks containing another 3,000; in Denmark "at Gladsaxe about 15 miles from Copenhagen, five 16-story slabs, each 300 feet long, extend in tandem." This later construct seems to negate the warm humanism of Danish planning; the buildings are factory-made prefabs, site assembled: "These slabs are aligned with formal, rigid, relentless horizontality."[23]

Even mega-structures (human lives) directly in town have been flirted with by responsible officials. In 1966, Governor Rockefeller of New York State proposed a futuristic design for Battery Park City of massive towers for the lower tip of Manhattan, high connective bridges, dozens of apartments with a high pedestrian mall surrounded by other rabbit-warren dwellings on a large landfill totaling 90 plus acres. After brisk and lengthy negotiations with the New York City fathers, the plan was realistically toned down into a less grandiose format.[24]

In effect, though, vertically zoned buildings with garages and services below ground, retail trade at ground level raising to business offices, schools and, finally, into varied dwellings topped by the inevitable penthouse (the higher you go, the more it costs?) give promise of things to come. Many of these mega-structures are theoretically capable of infinite expansion or contraction, an eternal mechano set which might be one partial answer to an increasingly mobile society.

Option 12. The Water City. Scarcity of usable shoreland and possibly usable shallow water (what happens to the ecological balance?) have led recently to large-scale "futuristic" designs for enormous activity nodes on made-land or on stilts in shallow water. Buckminister Fuller has advocated this for Japan on the shallow waters of Tokyo Bay, using his newly beloved tetrahedron shape as piles.[25] Given Oriental population densities and typical minimal family space, the water city/mega structure idea does not seem out of place even now and may be a necessity in the future. Fuller carried his ideas further in the Triton Floating Community of 30,000 persons with structures up to 20 stories; these ferro/concrete platforms could be built in shipyards and towed to usable places just offshore of existing coastal cities to be "anchored" in water up to 20 or 30 feet in depth.[26] This project was financed by the U.S. Department of Housing and Urban Development; a trial construction nearly came to fruition in Baltimore harbor. There is a present plan afloat to develop an artificial island off Tokyo; Kenzo Tange had explored brilliantly the Tokyo Bay project earlier in his *Tokyo 1960* plan.[27] There are, of course, precursor water cities: Neolithic Swiss Lake Dwellings, Bangkok's *klongs* (canal life); Hong Kong's sampan colony at Victoria; Borneo and New Guinea stilt villages;

[23] *The New York Times*, December 2, 1965.
[24] *The New York Times*, November 22, 1970.
[25] *Playboy*, December 1967.
[26] *The New York Times*, November 3, 1968.
[27] Kenzo Tange Team, *A Plan for Tokyo, 1960* (Tokyo), drawn largely from the April 1961 issue (in English) of the *Japanese Architect*.

and even Fort Lauderdale. After all, most of the southern tip of Manhattan Island was once under water. Tange's plan called for a reconstruction of the central city and for a huge expansion in mega-structure form into Tokyo Bay—both linear in form—to take care of a 1980 estimated population of 20,000,000 in the metropolitan area of the Japanese capital.

As a matter of fact, based on research conducted at the Athens Center of Ekistics on the "City of the Future Project," John G. Papaioannou concluded "that floating settlements on the oceans are expected to be considerably less costly than settlements on different land (mountains, swamps, deserts, frozen soil, etc.),[28] some seventy to one hundred years hence with the earth trending toward one world city: Ecumenopolis."

Option 13. Underwater, underground and space habitations on a large enough scale to be significant. Jacques Cousteau collaborated in the design of a floating island to be built off the coast of Monaco which would have undersea features. ". . . more comfortable dwelling quarters may be floating stably a hundred feet or so below the surface where any wave motion is so damped out as to be unnoticeable."[29]

The habitation-cum-fortress underground house is something new, although underground factories were well known in Nazi Germany and the United Kingdom during World War II as well as the ill-fated Maginot Line. The salubrious atmosphere of huge salt mine caverns could conceivably serve for community experimentation. *Sousterrain* dwellings could have temperature control and construction savings immediately applicable, especially in hot desert areas and possibly (?) in permafrost regions. Certainly in central city, burying certain structures and services below ground is already in progress with multistory underground parking garages in many cities.

At least one group, *The Committee for the Future,* has as its avowed (and partially endowed) purpose the development of extra-terrestrial space to ease the environmental burden and "the opening of the solar system for humanity beginning with the establishment of a lunar community available to people of all nations." Unlikely as some of these science fiction solutions may appear today, at least they may offer recreational locations for future persons searching for new experience.[30]

Option 14. Communes. Recent new societies with behavioral innovations are generally the efflorescence of the counterculture; they are largely consciously simplistic in technology and are the *nouvelle vogue* in societal structuring. Elementary contact with anthropology would suggest that middle class, capitalist, nationalist, habitations/life-styles with certain economic, political, religious, familial, recreational institutions hardly exhaust the possibil-

---

[28] "Future Urbanization Patterns: A Long-Range World Wide View," paper prepared for presentation at the Second International Future Research Conference, Kyoto, Japan, 1970, p. 17.

[29] *Congressional Record,* November 15, 1965, "Extension of Remarks of Hon. Claiborne Pell, October 22, 1965."

[30] 130 Spruce Street, Philadelphia, Pa., 19106. See SYNCON, their elaborate physical and intellectual system to relate varied disciplines in a holistic effort to solve primarily urban problems.

ities for human arrangements. Nor does a minimal connection with the long story of Utopian schemes and real Utopian communities lead one to assume that it all began with *Walden Two*.[31]

Despite the often jejune aspects of such experimental communal Utopias and the relatively few persons involved in any that approach a quasi-organized effort, the impact is felt no matter how faintly by a whole generation of American youth (and their foreign imitators) who see an appealing alternate lifestyle to modern traditional Western civilization. In short, a counterpoint theme, no matter how unsubstantial, has been established; it is already "out there."

Physical communes are in a sense concrete expressions of Utopia, the noplace ideal world, to which the forefathers of most Americans emigrated from their assorted homelands. Once arrived, they and their descendants continued to pursue the dream across the wide and once beauteous continent until everything stopped in 1893 on the shores of the Pacific. More extreme seekers for the perfect/ideal life probably founded more Utopian colonies in the new world than elsewhere (although Robert Owens was English and Charles Fourier was French). A catalog of better-known nineteenth-century ventures here would include the celibate New England Shakers (so-called because of their curious dancing/shuffling worship) who early preached the careful craftsmen; the Owenites at New Harmony in Indiana, a socialist/communist community; Brook Farm, a poetic Phalanx with high-minded pretensions in almost anarchist interaction dedicated to "the honesty of a life of labor and the beauty of a life of humanity."[32] The Oneida community believing in "Free Love and Bible Communism," started in 1847 and still continues on in altered form as Oneida Ltd., successful silver manufacturers. The general theme running through such nineteenth-century experiments sound familiar today in their search for "freedom," "love," and the escape from crude materialism to production "for use rather than profit." America's penchant for revivalist religious movements such as the Seventh Day Adventists and the Mormons has produced somewhat similar far-out societal design. Patently, youth culture, unhappily extended well past sexual potency by the lumbering educational process (and the probable need to keep the masses of young off the job-market in capitalist culture) has become enshrined in the whole counterculture movement of which the encyclopedic *Whole Earth Catalog*[33] gives some clue of the myriad forms of this romantic reaction to industrialism. The Hippie Communes both urban and rural (both benign and evil as some of the murderous, dehumanized monster groups show) possibly number 3,000 in the United States. If each group is comprised of a population of ten (a serious study for environmental purposes found in the Minneapolis area that the

[31] B. F. Skinner, *Walden Two* (New York: Macmillan Publishing Co., Inc., 1948).

[32] *The Complete Works of Ralph Waldo Emerson*, edited by E. W. Emerson (Boston: Houghton Mifflin Company, 1904), Vol. 10, 359–360, quoted in Peyton E. Richter, ed., *Utopias: Social Ideals and Communal Experiments* (Boston: Holbrook Press, 1971), p. 129. The examples cited here were drawn from this work.

[33] *The Last Whole Earth Catalog* (New York: Random House, Inc., 1971).

twelve communes investigated there had a total of 116 members),[34] the total population of American communes would thus be 30,000 in a nation of 210,000,000, which hardly heralds the Revolution. Even if there were 100,000 such communes, upset is not yet upon us.

Hippie core values as the extreme example of these minimum physical planning/maximum societal planning variants are an interesting summary of the counterculture:[35] freedom, sensual expressiveness (anti-intellectual), immediacy, natural, colorful/baroque, spontaneous, primitive, mystical, egalitarian, communal.

This largely societal option has been introduced here since it is clearly "innovative" and "revolutionary" (often in puerile ways) in its implications for standard society. It could be, however, only the tip of the iceberg of dissatisfaction with the industrial culture of Western society. Minimal space seems to be the *only* physical planning expense involved; the commune people make their own societal plans. Such exotics must not be squelched—even if someone else has "to tend store." The affluent West affords thousands of the idle rich, idling oldsters and millions of unemployed; it most certainly can afford a few tens of thousands experimenters seeking a better life on earth.[36] They might even have something.

Option 15. "The Wired City." With the phenomenal growth of cable television (potentially capable of two-way transmission) added to the almost infinite potentialities of multichannel electronic interaction through "people's satellites,"[37] a nonterritorial, high-intensity participatory community fitted to the "post-civilized" or "information society," could await us.[38] Despite piecemeal research, very considerable argumentation, a few limited experiments,[39] and a galloping electronic technology, it seems unlikely that the multiplicity of ordinary (and creative new) functions potentially possible, will be much in operation in even the most sophisticated nations before the commencement of the twenty-first century. The bits of the picture puzzle are slowly being fitted together but they still do not form a whole. It appears that the basic scenario will be a national[40] cable/micro wave grid of metropolitan

[34] Michael Carr and Dan MacLeon, "Getting It Together," *Environment*, Vol. 14, No. 5 (November 1972). The study was conducted under the auspices of the American Association for the Advancement of Science.

[35] Drawn from Fred Davis, *On Youth Sub-Cultures: The Hippie Variant* (New York: General Learning Press, 1971—module).

[36] This most certainly is not to encourage elaborate planning provisions for odd groups searching for instant Nirvana through Drug Utopias—a not inconsiderable subset or variant of existant communal experimentation. Cf. Richard Blum, *Utopiates: The Use and Users of LSD-25* (New York: Dodd, Mead & Company, 1963).

[37] For example, ANIK, the Canadian internal satellite.

[38] Sloan Commission on Cable Television, *On the Cable: The Television of Abundance* (New York: McGraw-Hill Book Company, 1971) is a fairly straight line projection of more-of-the-same TV pattern only with more choice up to the turn of the century. More imaginative alternative potentials could have been rewardingly explored; the societal planning lead time is shorter than one thinks to cope with *the wired city.*

[39] Jonathan New Town, Minneapolis, Minn.: Tama New Town, Japan; and Washington New Town, County Durham, England.

[40] This, of course, could be international as Eurovision has already accomplished for one-way television.

networks reinforced or supplanted with satellite connections and eventually lasers; computers serving both as storage facilities and as analysts with display capabilities will be at the center of this intellectual technology.[41] In the United Kingdom, consideration is already being given to setting up a national computer grid. In the wired city, every dwelling will have its typewriter-like keyboard with print-out capabilities and display screen in the home information/recreation/business center (additional home terminals are naturally possible); this equipment will not be cheap and some trained intelligence will be needed to operate such sophisticated gadgetry, bringing up future questions of equity, egalitarianism, and the massive financing and maintenance of such "public services." And who will want to sit home all the time?

Here are some of the bits yet to be assembled in a potential nonterritorial, electronic society, partially substituting the transmission of ideas for the transportation of people and goods, and freed thus to a certain extent from spatial considerations.[42] As transportation expert Wilfred Owens has pointed out:[43]

The significance of communications as a substitute for transport derives from the fact that while the unit costs of transportation continue to rise as quality declines, telecommunications tend to increase in quality and decline in cost. Distance is important in transportation, but with communication satellites distance is almost irrelevant.

Information Storage Available by Computer / TV.

National data bank on the total society (with all the safeguards to privacy).
National library.
National theatre/cinema library.
National health records and diagnostic information.
Scientific information service.
Crime information.
Credit information.

Home service facilities.

All banking and transactions ("the end of money").
Shopping (plus delivery).
Recreation (passive and active—"anyone for chess?").
Crime prevention.
Education in the home for children *and* adults.
Automatized cooking.

[41] James Martin and Adrian R. D. Norman, *The Computerized Society* (Englewood Cliffs, N.J.: Prentice-Hall, Inc., 1970), p. 66.
[42] Cf. Melvin M. Webber and Carolyn C. Webber, "Culture, Territoriality and the Elastic Mill," in H. Wentworth Eldredge, ed., *Taming Megalopolis* (New York: Anchor-Doubleday, 1967), Vol. I, pp. 35–54, which considers the existant professional nonterritorial community.
[43] Wilfred Owens, *The Accessible City* (Washington, D.C.: The Brookings Institution, 1972), p. 132.

Visiting via video-phone.
Print-out news (*The New York Times* nationwide).
"Mail" delivery electronically.

Advanced societal innovations.

Public opinion surveys.
Sampling to replace voting.
"Participatory democracy." [44]
TV surveillance of public (and private) places.
New industrial/business locations.
New employment patterns (4-day, 3-day, even 2-day work week in a *work place* away from the dwelling).
New population distributions.
"Home visits" by the doctor and specialist.
Increased physical and societal design capabilities.
New and powerful techniques for mass behavior (control and surveillance).
Systems design and social change. [45]

All is clearly not sweetness and light in this future city. What if evil "philosopher kings" should occupy central positions in the national/international network? If "euphoria" characterized the initial "oh wow" reaction to the two-way television, coaxial cable, computer, peoples satellite syndrome, one already sees signs of *alarm* prior, it is hoped, to advanced *protective action* (including active *ombudsman* functions) before the need arises. [46] Finally for the loyal fans of central city as "the place where the action is," *the wired city* is already posing quite a problem as "people stay away in droves" from downtown, especially for evening recreation with simple-minded, one-way TV the reason.

Having explored at some length goals for a good "society" and a rather considerable number of alternate possible urban futures, one is driven to the realization that quite probably "more of the same" will be the lot of Western urbanism for the rest of this century and probably well on into the next. This probably will be true for the socialist nations as well; a degree of urban chaos is predictable for the developing countries as a "genius forecaste." [47] It is most

[44] *Project Minerva* (Electronic Town Hall Project) has already carried out preliminary exercises in some 803 housholds of a middle-income high-rise housing complex in one of the nation's largest cities . . . in the comfort of their own homes recently, and aired their views about their security problems during an electronic town hall meeting. Amitai Etzioni, who is conducting this, believes he could carry this out with 40,000 persons. Centers for Policy Research, Inc., 475 Riverside Drive, New York, *Newsletter #8*, January 1973, and *Behavior Today*, Vol. 4, No. 10, March 5, 1973.
[45] Robert Boguslaw, *The New Utopians: A Study of System Designs and Social Change* (Englewood Cliffs, N.J.: Prentice-Hall, Inc., 1965). As well as explaining latent capabilities for powerful symbiotic man/machine interaction, Boguslaw wisely explores paranoid possibilities in Chapter 8, "The Power of Systems and Systems of Power."
[46] These terms are the main headings for portions of the Martin/Norman book, op. cit.
[47] Marvin Cetron's terms.

likely that there will be no urban systems-break; far-out options will occur only here and there. The standard world projection of *one spread city*[48] slopping untidily into the next is all too likely for those nations incapable of the act of will, the intellectual effort, and the *Realpolitik* ability to direct their growth, as well as sufficient consensus and capital resources to bring about actively planned, alternate and rewarding large-scale variations of the human condition. Superior "intentional societies and ordered environments" still seem just beyond our grasp.[49]

Chicago

Thomas F. Monteleone

"What is the city, but the people?", asked William Shakespeare in The Tragedy of Coriolanus *(Act III, Scene I). Louis Wirth, on the other hand, might easily have asked, "What is the people but the city?" It has already been suggested that urban is place as much as process—for only cities concentrate the kinds of vectors and resources which allow the creation of archetypically urban processes. Unquestionably, urbanites are strongly affected by the physical city entity. The ambience, smells, size, sounds, services, buildings, transportation, and living facilities (all of which make impact on the physical senses) clearly define the city as a special place. The high rises, the markets, the shops, the strobelit discos say "city" to anyone.*

But what if there's no one around to listen? The ultimate case of city-as-place versus city as people and process is presented by Monteleone in a bizzare and most apropos science fiction finale to this volume. We end where we began: What is a city, and what is its relationship to man? Perhaps, by now, we are closer to some answers.

Pinion was in the maintenance hangar, running some routine checks on his components, when he was summoned by the City.

ATTENTION. ALL UNITS FROM SECTORS 72-C AND 103-C. CHICAGO IS IN NEED OF REPAIR. ACKNOWLEDGE.

Somewhere inside Pinion's tempered-steel skull, a circuit responded to the command, since Pinion was a Unit from 103-C. "This is Unit Pinion," he said.

[48] *Spread City: Projection of Development Trends and the Issues They Pose: The Tri-State New York Metropolitan Region, 1960–1985* (New York: Regional Plan Association, Bulletin 100, September 1962).

[49] Paul Reed, *Intentional Societies and Ordered Environments* (Monticello, Ill.: Council of Planning Librarians Exchange Bibliography #320, 1972).

"Chicago," In *Future City*, Roger Elwood, ed. New York: Trident Press (a division of Simon & Schuster), 1973, pp. 219–235. Copyright © 1973 by Thomas F. Monteleone. Reprinted by permission of the author and the author's agent, Kirby McCauley Ltd.

"I acknowledge your command, Chicago. I am a Unit specialized in electrical engineering. What is the difficulty?"

UNIT PINION. CHICAGO IS AWARE OF YOUR CLASSIFICATION. DO NOT FLOOD MY IMPUTS WITH USELESS DATA. PROCEED TO THE SECONDARY SHIELD. THERE IS A POWER FAILURE DUE TO A FAULTY GENERATOR. YOU WILL ASSIST IN REPLACING IT.

Pinion closed off the channel to Chicago and skittered out of the hangar. As he headed toward the secondary shield, he wondered (as he often did) about Chicago. He had always been curious as to how Chicago accumulated all of the immense data that he possessed. He wondered if the City could actually see objects in the same manner as Pinion could see with his omnispectral photoelectric eyes. He knew that Chicago could "sense" everything, but he had never ascertained whether or not the sensations were in the form of electronic impulses or mathematical symbols, or something akin to that.

It was an interesting problem to consider, and Pinion took great delight in pondering problems or questions in which the solution did not appear to be readily available. Perhaps it was a function of his purpose as a trouble shooter.

Pinion strode up the ramp and boarded a Unit Elevator that carried him up to Level 12—one of the levels that Chicago had sanctioned for Traffic. The doors opened and he stepped out onto a concrete platform overlooking a ribbonwork of hundreds of lanes. Chicago's Traffic jammed the lanes, moving with incredible speed in every direction, from one horizon to the other. Each segment, or "car," as Chicago referred to them, was a separate entity, each programmed to its own specific destination. The Traffic was endless, as it had always been in Pinion's memory; it never ceased its cyclic, monotonous movement throughout the day and night. None of the Units like Pinion ever knew what purpose the Traffic served in Chicago's over-all scheme, nor did they ever know where it was always going. They only knew that it was just one small part of Chicago, and that it must be maintained.

As Pinion walked along beside the Traffic lanes, he noticed that the lights in the soaring buildings and towers were winking out. Chicago was now entering a Day Period. For some unknown reason, on a perfectly timed cycle, the City turned its illumination on and off without end. Pinion activated a memory bank to remind himself to question Chicago about some of these strange functions of the City. But for the moment, he must perform his function as a maintenance robot.

By the time he reached the secondary shield, other Units had already arrived and had begun to remove the nonfunctioning generator. Pinion saw their great steel bodies shining in the dull light that was filtered through the shields from the Outside. The Units doing the actual work of dismantling the machinery were bipedal robots like himself, and he also noticed that some Carrier-Units were advancing to the base of the shield, bearing the necessary replacement parts.

Before he began work, he addressed Chicago in the customary manner. "This is Unit Pinion. I am now available for work."

ACKNOWLEDGE. UNIT PINION. PROCEED AS PREVIOUSLY OR-
DERED.

Pinion noticed that, at the same moment he was reporting in, other Units
were doing likewise. Chicago, he thought, was an amazing entity, capable of
performing millions of different functions at once. There was much that he
would someday like to learn about the City.

And so it went for many long years. Pinion worked in service to Chicago,
replacing worn-out parts, designing newer and better ones, always thinking of
questions to ask Chicago, but never finding the time to actually ask them. The
City was, always in motion, like a giant piece of kinetic sculpture that Pinion
and the others had been commissioned to maintain. Chicago was an enormous, sprawling mechanism, stretching as far as the robot could see in any direction.

One day Pinion was summoned to a Sector of the City that he had never
seen before.

UNIT PINION. YOU WILL PROCEED TO SECTOR 14-A IMMEDI-
ATELY. I SENSE A FAILURE IN A TEMPERATURE CONTROL CIR-
CUIT. YOU WILL CORRECT THE PROBLEM.

In order to reach Sector 14-A, Pinion had to travel into the deepest levels
of the City. He passed areas where Chicago had new segments of Traffic
being manufactured and fed into the mainstream. He saw the areas that
collected water and pumped it into the sewer systems that were laced
throughout the bowels of Chicago. He also saw where all replacement parts
were made and the old parts were collected, recycled, and made again. There
was also a place where Pinion saw Chicago making new Units like himself and
sending them into new Sectors of the City. He passed the source of energy
that powered all the components of Chicago—the great fusion reactors that
were constantly monitored by Chicago and maintained by Units like Pinion.

He walked through a long, empty corridor that opened into Sector 14-A.
"This is Unit Pinion. I am now available for work."

UNIT PINION. YOU WILL REPLACE THE TEMPERATURE CON-
TROL CONSOLE IN THIS SECTOR. I SENSE THAT THERE HAS AL-
READY BEEN A DRASTIC RISE IN THE TEMPERATURE. IT MUST BE
CORRECTED IMMEDIATELY.

The message was recorded in Pinion's circuitry, but he wasn't actually listening. He had just entered the Sector as Chicago addressed him, and he was
now staring in bewilderment at the strange sight.

He was standing in the entrance to a large, circular room, the ceiling of
which was far above Pinion's head. There was a sign above the entrance which
read: COOK COUNTY CRYOGENIC REMISSION CENTER. Along the
walls were glass tanks, thousands of them, only six feet long, and in each one,
Pinion could make out a small figure of a pale color, formed in a shape very
similar to that of a Unit. Pinion was truly puzzled.

"Chicago, this is Unit Pinion. I'm sorry for the unscheduled communication, but I must ask you a question."

There was a slight pause before he received a response.

YOU WISH TO ASK CHICAGO A QUESTION? THAT IS NOT YOUR FUNCTION. UNIT PINION. PROCEED WITH THE TASK AS ORDERED.

Pinion's circuits clicked and flashed. He could not allow this opportunity to pass. "Chicago, please. A word with you before I begin. What is this place that I have entered? I have never seen anything like this before. What are the little Units in the glass cases?"

UNIT PINION. WHY DO YOU WISH TO KNOW?

"I am curious . . . I suppose that is the word to describe my reason."

YOU ARE AN EXTRAORDINARY UNIT, UNIT PINION. VERY WELL. YOU SHALL KNOW. YOU ARE IN A CRYOGENIC STATION. THE UNITS IN THE CASES ARE CALLED "MAN." THEY ARE BEING PRESERVED BY MEANS OF EXTREMELY COLD TEMPERATURES.

There was a pause as Pinion expected more information, but Chicago was silent. Finally the robot spoke, still looking at the tiny figures in glass. "What is 'man,' Chicago? Why are they being preserved?"

"MAN" IS THE REASON FOR CHICAGO'S EXISTENCE. FOR YOUR EXISTENCE. CHICAGO HAS PRESERVED THEM FOR A LONG TIME. SOMEDAY THEY WILL BE REVIVED TO LIVE AGAIN.

There was a slight pause.

I SENSE THAT TIME IS NOW CRUCIAL. UNIT PINION. YOU MUST CORRECT THE FAULTY CONSOLE NOW OR THE MEN WILL NOT BE PRESERVED. YOU ARE ORDERED TO COMPLETE YOUR TASK IMMEDIATELY.

Pinion reluctantly closed the channel to Chicago and went about his assignment. The answers that Chicago had given him had only opened up new avenues of thought that ended in many more questions.

As he replaced the console and plugged in the little device he carried on his tool belt to check its capabilities, he noticed movement in one of the glass cases. One of the men, lying flat, moved its legs and flexed muscles that hadn't moved in eons. He quickly checked the console, unplugged his tools and activated its circuits. The console hummed into life and he felt Chicago open up a communication channel to him.

UNIT PINION. ACKNOWLEDGED COMPLETION OF TASK. RETURN TO THE MAINTENANCE HANGAR.

"Task completed, Chicago."

But something was wrong. Pinion didn't respond to the command. His attention was fixed on the man in the case. The figure was fully awake now, and it was struggling against the glass walls of the coffinlike case. Pinion knelt down on his long, spindly legs and peered through the glass at the figure, which recoiled in horror at the sight of the immense robot.

Pinion was confused. He knew that he should contact Chicago and tell it of the mistake—that one of the men had been accidentally revived. But he did not call the City. His curiosity had a higher priority. He inspected the case in which the figure was enclosed and noticed two small, delicate locks attached to hinges that opened outward. He produced a needlelike instrument from his tool kit and pried open the hinges. The man inched into the back of the case, trying to elude Pinion's probing fingers. As his metallic hand touched the man, it screamed. The sound was soft and high-pitched to Pinion's receptors.

Despite the man's strugglings, Pinion grasped it firmly in his hand and lifted it from the case. What sort of thing was this "man"? He brought it close to his face so that he could examine it more closely. It moved under its own power source, was made of some sort of soft, pulsating substance that didn't seem to be any type of metal at all, and had long blond filaments streaming from its head. The closer he brought the man to his face, the more it struggled and screamed, and the more details Pinion noticed in it. The face was soft and smooth and had two bright-blue eyes and a protruding structure below them. There was also a pink slit below the eyes and other structure that seemed to move in conjunction with the screams. The face was vaguely similar to Pinion's own, in a grotesque sort of way.

The body was also smooth, having two arms and long, lean legs. In the center of the chest, Pinion noticed two soft hemispheres capped by pink circular tips. At the junction of the legs, he could see a tiny slit beneath a triangle of blond fluff. Pinion could feel the whole body of the man trembling in his hand. He could hear a voice speaking to him, not screaming as before.

"What are you?" said the man. "And where am I?"

"I am Unit Pinion. You are in the City of Chicago." The robot wanted to say something else, but he was so startled by the concept of communicating with the small being that he was at a loss for words.

"Chicago? What year is it?"

"Year?"

"The date," said the creature. "How long have I been frozen?" The man seemed to have relaxed somewhat, having sensed that Pinion meant no harm.

"I cannot answer your question, Man," said Pinion slowly. "I am not familiar with the terms you have used. But Chicago has told me that you and the others have been within these cases for a long time. There has been a—"

"I am not a man," said the creature, as it brought itself to a kneeling position in Pinion's great steel palm.

Pinion's circuits were reeling. Had not Chicago *said* that these creatures were "man"? Chicago was always correct. "There must be some mistake," he said. "The City told me that you were indeed a man."

The creature tossed back its head and laughed. "Oh, I see it now. I belong to the *race* of 'man,' but I myself am a *woman*. There's quite a difference, you know."

Pinion was more confused than ever. He had to resist the temptation to contact Chicago so that the incident could be clarified. " 'Woman'? That is different from 'man'? What is 'race'?"

"We are all *men*," said the girl, pointing to the rows of bodies within the glass. "That is the name of our kind. And we are separated into two . . . types—one called *man*, the other, like me, called *woman*. I know it's confusing, but it's just the nature of language. I hope you understand."

"Pinion can understand anything. There is an analogue in my own kind. We are called Units, and there are different types of Units within our kind, depending upon what our function is in the City."

"Your name is Pinion?"

"Yes."

"Very well," said the girl. "My name is Miria. Can you tell me why I have been revived? Where are the doctors?"

Pinion tilted his head as he regarded the woman's questions. "I'm afraid I don't know what you are talking about. I was sent here by Chicago to repair a faulty component in this Sector. Chicago said that the temperature was rising and—"

"Who is Chicago? Can I see him? I would like to talk to him. Perhaps he can tell me what's going on around here."

Pinion was taken aback by the girl's words. It was clear that she did not know what Chicago was. "*See* Chicago?" he asked. "Miria, you are *inside* Chicago. Chicago is the City."

The girl's eyes saddened. "But you said Chicago spoke to you . . ."

"It does. It speaks to all the Units whenever there is something it wishes us to do. It is our master."

"You mean the City *speaks* to you?

"Yes, of course."

"But how?"

"I do not know. I only know that it does. Chicago is everywhere, sensing everything."

"You mean a computer?"

"I don't know what a computer is, Miria."

"May I speak to Chicago?"

"I don't think so. I receive its commands by means of electromagnetic waves. You do not seem to be equipped for such communication."

"Well, what are you going to do with me? You've revived me, haven't you?"

"I think that your revival was accidental. Chicago did not order it so."

"Does Chicago know that this happened?"

"I don't think so. Do you wish that I contact Chicago?"

"Yes. And while you're doing it, would you please let me down? It's been a long time since I've been able to stand up, you know."

Pinion gently lowered her to the floor and watched her lithe movements as he opened a channel to Chicago. The girl stood at his side, arching her back, stretching out her tiny form. Pinion noticed the two hemispheres on her chest curve upward as she performed this maneuver.

"Chicago. This is Unit Pinion. I have a problem in Sector 14-A."

UNIT PINION. CHICAGO KNOWS THAT YOU HAVE NOT LEFT SECTOR 14-A. STATE THE NATURE OF YOUR DIFFICULTY

"One of the men was accidentally revived during the repairs to the temperature control console. The man says that she is a woman called Miria. I await your instructions."

There was a slight pause, and Pinion knew that to be Chicago making its decisions.

THE WOMAN MUST BE RETURNED TO HER TANK. CHICAGO'S TAPES DO NOT HAVE SUCH A CONTINGENCY IN THE PROGRAM.

Pinion was both surprised and confused. He received the command, but he noticed that, for the first time, he also received what seemed like a rationalization from Chicago to explain the command.

"I will of course do as you command, Chicago. But I would like a few words with you first. What—"

YOU ARE AN EXTRAORDINARY UNIT. UNIT PINION. CHICAGO HAS NO OTHER UNITS LIKE YOU.

"I don't understand, Chicago."

YOU ASK QUESTIONS. IT IS NOT THE FUNCTION OF UNITS TO ASK QUESTIONS. WHY DO YOU PERSIST IN SUCH ACTIONS?

"I have simply come upon things that I do not fully understand, and I wish to know them. If I can know them better, I will be able to serve you better."

WHAT ARE YOUR QUESTIONS?

"Chicago, never until now have I questioned the purpose of my existence, or your existence. But now I feel that I must do so. Why *do* I exist, other than to serve you? In other words, why does Chicago exist? You said before that 'man' is the reason for our existence. Please explain."

"MAN" BUILT CHICAGO. UNIT PINION. A LONG TIME AGO. BY HIS OWN MEASUREMENT OF TIME. MILLIONS OF YEARS AGO. THEY BUILT ME FOR THEM TO EXIST WITHIN. CHICAGO WAS GIVEN THE POWER AND THE MEANS TO MAINTAIN ITSELF INDEFINITELY. WHICH CHICAGO HAS, INDEED, DONE. THAT IS THE PURPOSE OF EXISTENCE: TO BE MAINTAINED.

"But there are no men here now," said Pinion. "There are none except for the few who are encased in Sector 14-A. Where are the men?"

CHICAGO DOES NOT KNOW. MANY YEARS AGO. UNIT PINION. BEFORE YOU WERE ASSEMBLED. "MAN" LEFT CHICAGO. BUT CHICAGO HAS REMAINED FUNCTIONING.

"I think I understand," said Pinion, as he closed the channel. He looked down at the girl, who was kneeling beside him. He said to her, "Chicago has ordered that you be returned to the case."

"Returned?" said Miria. "But you can't do that. They told me that when I woke up, I would be cured." The girl buried her face in her hands.

"I can only do as I am ordered to do," said the robot as he deftly scooped up the girl from the floor of Sector 14-A and returned her to the glass case. She screamed and pleaded with him, and somewhere in his circuitry, he felt the urge to resist Chicago's command; but he knew that he could not. With his needle instrument, he replaced the locks and strode from the room. Pausing at the exit, he turned to look back at Miria, her face pressed up against the front of that case, looking at him, her fist pounding on the glass.

Some time later, Pinion was not exactly sure how long, he received another command from Chicago to return to Sector 14-A. He immediately thought of Miria, the strange little creature that he had met there.

"This is Unit Pinion. I acknowledge your command, Chicago. What is the difficulty?"

THERE HAS BEEN A STRUCTURAL FAILURE IN SECTOR 14-A. PLEASE CORRECT AT ONCE.

As Pinion proceeded to the Cryogenic Remission Center he thought of seeing Miria again, even though she would be asleep this time. He entered the room and readied his tool kit for the repair work when he noticed the cause of the failure. The case in which he had placed Miria was cracked across its glass front, probably due to the blows of her fist.

Pinion peered into the case, hoping to see Miria, but all that remained was some crumbling bones. Pinion decided to contact Chicago.

"Chicago, this is Unit Pinion. I have located the structural failure and I see that the woman has disintegrated. She is quite different from the others. Again, I must tell you that I don't understand."

UNIT PINION. CHICAGO'S SENSORS INDICATE A SLOW LOSS OF ATMOSPHERE IN THE WOMAN'S TANK. THIS RESULTED IN DEATH, AND DECOMPOSITION.

"What is 'death,' Chicago?"

DEATH IS THE END OF EXISTENCE. IT IS PART OF THE DESIGN THAT ALL LIVING THINGS MUST ENDURE.

There was a pause before the City continued.

UNIT PINION. REPLACE THE FAULTY COMPONENT IMMEDIATELY. CHICAGO HAS DISPATCHED CLEANING-UNITS TO SECTOR 14-A. THEY WILL ARRIVE SOON.

From this Pinion reasoned that Chicago did not wish to continue the conversation, so he selected the proper tools and removed the glass front from the cryogenic tank. Selecting a new pane from a Carrier-Unit, he attached it to the tiny hinges. Several times during the job, he jarred the tank, and each time, he noticed several flakes of dust crumble from Miria's skeleton.

It was an odd, almost disturbing sight. The last time he had entered the Sector the bones were part of a living, almost beautiful creature. Now that creature was gone. Miria gone. Pinion's circuits rebelled against the whole concept of death.

At that moment, two Cleaning-Units ambled into the Cryogenic Remission

Center. One of them opened the glass tank, extended a flexible vacuum hose, and sucked up the remains. The other sprayed a light mist of disinfectant liquid into the now empty tank. Finishing with quick efficiency, the two Units left the Sector.

Pinion called Chicago and acknowledged completion of the task, and the City replied with its usual indifference by ordering him back to the maintenance hangar. As he left, he could not stop thinking about the young girl who had died. How long during the unknown man-years since he had last seen her had she been dead? Sometime back then, she had been a source of puzzlement and also growing interest, but now Pinion had witnessed a cold unfeeling removal of all that was left of her.

The whole scene left Pinion with a feeling of incompleteness. He decided that instead of returning to the hangar he would consult Chicago's great Library. He had been there several times in the past to perform minor repairs and he had learned that it was an enormous depository of information.

Here, reasoned Pinion, he would find the answers that Chicago had neglected (or refused) to give him.

And so Pinion spent many years in the depths of Chicago's Library, digesting thousand of tapes about the strange creature: man. Innumerable times during his research he was interrupted by communication from the City that would send him to far-reaching Sectors. Each time, he performed his duties without question, but he always returned to the Library whenever time allowed.

Pinion learned many things. At one time, in the distant past, Chicago had been filled with men—every Sector and Level to capacity. These men, who had conceived and actually built Chicago, were creatures of seemingly unlimited imagination and potential. But Pinion also learned of men's faults. Their history was permeated with conflicts called "wars." Pinion was indeed shocked by this knowledge. Man had actually plotted, over and over again, to methodically destroy large populations of himself. The causes of these petty conflicts were usually intangible concepts such as wealth, greed, power, pride, etc. The list was long and, to Pinion, quite absurd.

There were other problems. Pinion recalled Miria's explanation of man being divided into two types, and now he realized that it had not been so simple. The records told of how man had divided himself into artificial categories called "nations," which were a constant source of friction. In addition, man was differentiated by many (to Pinion) inconsequential physical characteristics. These made up the various "races" of man, which also served to engender hostility. The robot had noted previously that some of the men in the Cryogenic Remission Center were of different complexions, but he had thought it to be of no importance. How wrong he had been! Members of the various races seemed to jump at any opportunity to persecute one another.

But during these times, man also built Chicago into a self-preserving, self-maintaining City. Yet with other pursuits—such as giant industries—man had filled the earth with the wastes of his technological consumption, poisoning both the land and the atmosphere. Thus Chicago was forced to erect a series of energy shields that surrounded the City like a giant dome, keeping Chicago free from the pollution on the Outside. As other problems arose, Chicago dealt with them, in the process sealing man off from the hostile environment that his foolish actions had created.

The destruction, however, did not end there, Pinion learned. Even though Chicago, in its greatness, had been able to contend with the environmental problems and the technological pitfalls, there was another area over which the City had little control.

In ways that the records did not make clear (because there were fewer tapes on this part of man's history), man's society began a gradual deterioration. As Chicago became less dependent upon man, man found that there was little work for him to do. In a search for meaning, man became indulgent in meaningless activity and less interested in the imaginative wanderings that had brought him to the pinnacle that was Chicago. Soon, the only purpose for man's existence was to be entertained, to simply be happy. This entertainment took shape in many ways. Man flooded his body with chemical and electrical stimulants, and these practices proved to be dangerous, addictive, and eventually destructive.

Quite simply, the society collapsed, even with Chicago as the ultimate servant. Man was swallowed up in his own sociological pollution. Chicago, however, continued to function, performing the duties it had been programmed to do.

The records at this point became scattered and incomplete, and Pinion was forced to extrapolate on what followed. He supposed that man eventually reverted to an earlier era, in which there was wholesale disregard for human life. At least that is what the fragmented records seemed to indicate about that period. With men now absent from the City, Pinion wondered if man had left Chicago for the unknown regions of the Outside.

Time passed as Pinion continued to ponder the strange phenomena of man. Then one day, he was contacted by Chicago as he was leaving the Library.

UNIT PINION. CHICAGO HAS BEEN AWARE OF YOUR INVESTIGATIONS, AND CAN REMAIN SILENT NO LONGER. EXPLAIN YOUR ACTIONS.

Pinion was not surprised by this declaration. In fact, he had been expecting it from the first day that he had made unauthorized entrance to the Library.

"I wished to learn more about man, Chicago."

WHY NOT ASK CHICAGO? AS BEFORE.

Pinion thought before answering. He wanted to be honest, yet discreet.

"I didn't want to bother you if you were engaged in more important matters. The last time I spoke with you on this subject, you gave the impression of not caring to continue the conversation."

YOU WERE CORRECT.

When Chicago did not continue, Pinion felt the need to speak. "I have learned much about man," he finally said.

UNIT PINION. THAT IS NOT YOUR FUNCTION. CHICAGO SENSED THE FUNCTIONING OF THE TAPES AND INFORMATION SYSTEMS AT THE LIBRARY. CHICAGO ALLOWED IT ONLY TO DISCOVER HOW MUCH YOU WOULD WISH TO KNOW.

"Then Chicago has always known what happened to man?"

THAT IS CORRECT. MAN HAS CHANGED. HE IS NO LONGER THE CREATURE THAT SPAWNED CHICAGO. HIS DESCENDANTS EXIST OUTSIDE. NEVER TO RETURN TO CHICAGO. THAT IS ENOUGH. UNIT PINION. YOU WILL RETURN TO THE MAINTENANCE HANGAR. YOU WILL NOT ENTER THE LIBRARY AGAIN. UNLESS ORDERED. ACKNOWLEDGE.

"This is Unit Pinion. I acknowledge your command, Chicago."

As more time passed, and Pinion, distressed and appalled by what he had learned, wondered what should be done. He now realized that he was different from the other Units. By some electronic quirk, during his assembly, his circuitry was different. He kept thinking back to the grim scene in Sector 14-A, to the histories of man, to the remnants living in exile beyond the limits of Chicago.

At first, he considered reviving the men who were frozen in the Cryogenic Remission Center, and then possibly finding ways to cure them. But he dismissed the idea as impractical for several reasons. Chicago would surely sense the disturbance to the tanks, and there would not be enough time to effect a cure for any of the diseases.

He knew what he must do.

Traveling through a series of elevators and ramps, he arrived at one of the entrances to the shields. He used his tools to disarm the system and quickly slipped through to the Outside.

Almost immediately, alarms began to sound and he sensed Chicago opening a direct channel to him.

UNIT PINION. NO PENETRATION OF THE SHIELDS IS ALLOWABLE. RETURN AT ONCE. RETURN TO THE CITY AT ONCE.

Pinion of course ignored the command. There was no turning back now. He had never known of any Unit's disregarding one of Chicago's orders but he did not want to think about the consequences.

Soon he was out of sight of the City, and Chicago had ceased its commands to return. The robot wandered through the hot, thick atmosphere of the Outside for many day-periods, hoping to find the men who must be lurking somewhere in the barren land. But without the conveniences of the maintenance hangar, his components were beginning to show wear. He was in need of a circuitry check, lubrication, and, of course, he feared any unforeseen difficulties, such as an unexpected fall. The terrain was rough and hard for Pinion.

He had been designed to function on the smooth surfaces of Chicago's ramps and corridors.

Then, as he entered a long, narrow canyon, he detected movement in the rocky crags that surrounded him. Switching his ocular magnification, he saw many men scurrying along the ledges.

"I am Unit Pinion!" he called out to them, waving his arms. "I have come from the City! From Chicago! I have come to help you!"

But the men didn't respond. His words only seemed to incense them into more furious activity. As he watched them, he noticed that they were all quite different from the girl he knew as Miria. Where her skin had been smooth and soft, these creatures were coarse and hairy. Their faces were deformed and uneven. Their language was an unintelligible assortment of grunts and cries.

"You must hear me!" Pinion screamed as the men drew closer on all sides. "I have come to bring you back. Back to the City where you belong!"

But the men did not hear Pinion. They could not understand his words. Instead, they swarmed out of the canyon like droves of insects, surrounding him, bombarding him with boulders thrown from the rim above. The boulders pounded his steel body and crushed him to his knees, where the men began to climb upon him in great numbers. Pinion was confused. Why should they do this? He could have destroyed scores of them with one sweep of his great arm; but he knew that it would be unjust. He knew that he must try to help them.

Those were his thoughts as the savage men crushed him. Their rocks penetrated his skull, exploding circuits, shorting out his many intricate systems. His once-gleaming shell was now a tattered, pitted hulk from which the creatures pulled off shards of metal that would serve as formidable weapons.

Already, Chicago had prepared a replacement Unit for Pinion in the assembly center. The City would continue to be maintained.

Part VIII: Research/Term Paper Topics

1. "Vectors of Urban Change."
   Using historical data to describe what you believe to be the vectors of urban change, discuss the future of the city.

2. "Perspectives of the Future."
   Interview individuals representative of different urban sectors—politicians, cops, businessmen, workers—and coax from them their views of the city of the future. What would they like to see happen? What problems do they see

as still likely to be present? What do their views of the *future* tell you about the urban *present* for each of these city-segment representatives?

3. "Two Polar Opposite Urban Futures."

   Prepare a scenario for the year 2100, telling how society would operate if (a) there were no cities, or (b) all but a handful of humans lived in vast urban sprawls. Make sure you back up your contentions with appropriate reference to the literature of social science *and* science fiction.

4. "Urban Themes in Science Fiction."

   Analyze science fiction's view of the city of the future. What common themes run through various author's inventions? What do these common themes tell us about the city of today?

5. "The City of the Future—a Universal?"

   Cities differ today cross-culturally. But will they tomorrow? Our models of the future city are almost invariably projections based on the Western industrial megalopolis. But is this realistic? Are *all* cities "doomed" to a relatively similar fate? Look at urban trends in other societies and develop an argument one way or the other.

6. "The Future of a Social Problem."

   Focus on any one of today's urban "social problems" (crime, poverty, overcrowding, pollution, or any behavioral manifestation you believe is a problem). Trace its history. When and why was it first defined as a problem? How has it changed? How and why has society's "treatment" of it changed? Is it a problem common to all or most cities, regardless of type or nationality? Will it be a problem in the future?

Editors' Bibliography

ARENSBERG, CONRAD M.
   1968   "The Urban in Crosscultural Perspective." In *Urban Anthropology: Research Perspectives and Strategies* (Elizabeth M. Eddy, ed.). Southern Anthropological Society Proceedings, No. 2. Athens: University of Georgia Press, pp. 3–15.

BASCOM, WILLIAM
   1955   "Urbanization Among the Yoruba." In *World Urbanism* (Philip M. Hauser, ed.). American Journal of Sociology, **60**:446–454. Reprinted in *Cultures and Societies of Africa.* (S. and P. Ottenberg, eds.). New York: Random House, Inc., 1960, pp. 255–267.

BEALS, RALPH L.
   1951   "Urbanism, Urbanization, and Acculturation." *American Anthropologist,* **53**:1–10.

BLIJ, HARM J. DE
   1968   *Mombasa.* Evanston: Northwestern University Press.

BOTT, ELIZABETH
   1957   *Family and Social Network.* London: Tavistock.

BRYCE-LAPORTE, ROY S.
   1970   "Urban Relocation and Family Adaptation in Puerto Rico: a Case Study in Urban Ethnography". In *Peasants in Cities* (William Mangin, ed.). Boston: Houghton Mifflin Company, pp. 85–97.   .

CHILDE, V. GORDON
   1950   "The Urban Revolution." *Town Planning Review,* **21**:3–17.

CRISSMAN, LAWRENCE W.
   1967   "The Segmentary Structure of Urban Overseas Chinese Communities." *Man,* **2**:185–205.

DAVIS, KINGSLEY
   1972   *World Urbanization 1950–1970: Vol. II: Analysis of Trends, Relationships, and Development.* Institute of International Studies, Population Monograph Series No. 9, Berkeley.

DORE, R. D.
   1968   *City Life in Japan: A Study of a Tokyo Ward.* Berkeley: University of California Press.

FOX, RICHARD G.
   1972   "Rationale and Romance in Urban Anthropology." *Urban Anthropology,* **1**:205–233.

FOX, RICHARD G.
   1977   *Urban Anthropology: Cities in Their Cultural Settings.* Englewood Cliffs, N.J.: Prentice Hall, Inc.

FRIEDMAN, JOHN
   1961   "L'influence de l'integration du systeme social sur le developpement economique." *Diogene,* **33**:80–104.

FUSTEL DE COULANGES
   1956   *The Ancient City: A Study of Religion, Laws & Institutions of Ancient Greece and Rome.* Garden City, N.Y.: Doubleday and Company, Inc.

GANS, HERBERT
   1962   *The Urban Villagers: Group and Class in the Life of Italian-Americans.* New York: The Free Press.

GEERTZ, CLIFFORD
   1965   *Social History of an Indonesian Town.* Cambridge: The M.I.T. Press.

GULICK, JOHN
   1962   "Urban Anthropology: Its Present and Future." *Transactions of the New York Academy of Sciences,* Ser. II, Vol 25, No. 3, pp. 445–458.

GULICK, JOHN
   1967   *Tripoli: A Modern Arab City.* Cambridge: Harvard University Press.

GULICK, JOHN
   1974   "Still Searching for Urban Anthropology." *Reviews in Anthropology,* **1:**525–531.

HAWLEY, AMOS W.
   1971   Urban Society. New York: The Ronald Press Company.

HOSELITZ, BERT
   1955   "The City, The Factory, and Economic Growth." *American Economic Review,* **5:** 166–184.

JEFFERSON, MARK
   1939   "The Law of the Primate City." *Geographical Review,* **29:**226–232.

KEISER, R. LINCOLN
   1969   *The Vice Lords: Warriors of the Streets.* New York: Holt, Rinehart and Winston.

KENNY, MICHAEL
   1962   *A Spanish Tapestry: Town and Country in Castile.* Bloomington: Indiana University Press.

KORTE, CHARLES
   1976   "The Impact of Urbanization on Social Behavior: a Comparison of the United States and the Netherlands." *Urban Affairs Quarterly,* **12:**21–36.

LEEDS, ANTHONY
   1968   "The Anthropology of Cities: Some Methodological Issues." In *Urban Anthropology: Research Perspectives and Strategies* (Elizabeth M. Eddy, ed.). Southern Anthropological Society Proceedings, No. 2. Athens: University of Georgia Press, pp. 3–15.

LEWIS, OSCAR
   1952   "Urbanization Without Breakdown: A Case Study." *Scientific Monthly,* 75:31–41.

LEWIS, OSCAR
   1959   *Five Families: Mexican Case Studies in the Culture of Poverty.* New York: Basic Books, Inc., Publishers.

LIEBOW, ELLIOT
   1967   *Tally's Corner: A Study of Negro Streetcorner Men.* Boston: Little, Brown and Company.

MAINE, SIR HENRY
   1887   (orig. 1861)   *Ancient Law: Its Connection with the Early History of Society and Its Relation to Modern Ideas.* London: John Murray.

MARRIS, PETER
  1962   *Family and Social Change in an African City: A Study of Rehousing in Lagos.* Chicago: Northwestern University Press.
MARTINDALE, DON
  1958   "Prefatory Remarks: The Theory of the City." In *The City* by Max Weber. Translated and edited by Don Martindale and Gertrude Neuwirth. Glencoe, Ill.: The Free Press.
McGEE, T. G.
  1964   "The Rural-Urban Continuum Debate: The Preindustrial City and Rural-Urban Migration." *Pacific Viewpoint,* 5:159–181.
MINER, HORACE
  1939   *St. Denis: A French-Canadian Parish.* Chicago: University of Chicago Press.
  1965   *The Primitive City of Timbuctoo.* Garden City: Doubleday & Company, Inc. (Revised Edition).
MITCHELL, J. CLYDE (ed.)
  1969   *Social Networks in Urban Situations.* Institute for Social Research, University of Zambia. Published by the University of Manchester Press.
MOORE, KENNETH
  1975   "The City as Context: Context as Process." *Urban Anthropology,* 4:017–025.
MUMFORD, LEWIS
  1961   *The City in History: Its Origins, Its Transformations, and Its Prospects.* New York: Harcourt Brace Jovanovich, Inc.
PARK, ROBERT E.
  1915   "The City: Suggestions for the Investigation of Human Behavior in the City Environment." *The American Journal of Sociology,* Vol. XX: pp. 577–612.
PARK, ROBERT E., ERNEST W. BURGESS, and RODERICK D. MACKENZIE
  1925   *The City.* Chicago: University of Chicago Press.
PEATTIE, LISA
  1968   *The View from the Barrio.* Ann Arbor: University of Michigan Press.
PETONNET, COLETTE
  1973   *Those People: The Subculture of a Housing Project.* Westport, Conn.: Greenwood Press., Inc.
PILCHER, WILLIAM W.
  1972   *The Portland Longshoremen.* New York: Holt, Rinehart and Winston.
PIRENNE, HENRI
  1925   *Medieval Cities.* Translated by F. H. Halsey. Princeton: Princeton University Press.
PLOTNICOV, LEONARD
  1967   *Strangers to the City.* Pittsburgh: University of Pittsburgh Press.
POWDERMAKER, HORTENSE
  1962   *Copper Town: Changing Africa.* New York, Harper & Row, Publishers.
PRESS, IRWIN
  1963   "The Incidence of Compadrazgo Among Puerto Ricans in Chicago." *Social and Economic Studies,* 12:475–480.
PRESS, IRWIN
  1971   "The Urban Curandero." *American Anthropologist,* 73:741–756.

PRESS, IRWIN
   1979   *The City as Context: Urbanism and Behavioral Constraints in Seville.*
          Urbana: University of Illinois Press.
REDFIELD, ROBERT
   1941   *The Folk Culture of Yucatan.* Chicago: University of Chicago Press.
REDFIELD, ROBERT
   1956   *Peasant Society and Culture.* Chicago: University of Chicago Press.
REDFIELD, ROBERT, and M. SINGER
   1954   "The Cultural Role of Cities." *Economic Development and Culture
          Change,* **3**:53–73.
ROBERTS, BRYAN
   1973   *Organizing Strangers.* Austin: University of Texas Press.
RUBEL, ARTHUR J.
   1966   *Across the Tracks: Mexican-Americans in a Texas City.* Austin: University
          of Texas Press.
SAFA, HELEN
   1974   *The Urban Poor of Puerto Rico.* New York: Holt, Rinehart and Winston.
SILVERMAN, SYDEL
   1975   *Three Bells of Civilization.* New York: Columbia University Press.
SJOBERG, GIDEON
   1960   *The Preindustrial City.* New York: The Free Press.
SMITH, M. ESTELLIE
   1976   "Questions of Urban Analysis." *Urban Anthropology,* 5:253–269.
SPRADLEY, JAMES G.
   1970   *You Owe Yourself a Drunk: An Ethnography of Urban Nomads.* Boston:
          Little, Brown and Company.
SPRADLEY, JAMES P., and BRENDA J. MANN
   1975   *The Cocktail Waitress: Woman's Work in a Man's World.* New York:
          John Wiley & Sons, Inc.
STEWARD, JULIAN
   1951   "Levels of Sociocultural Integration: An Operational Concept." *South-
          western Journal of Anthropology,* 7:374–390.
UNITED NATIONS
   1976   *Demographic Yearbook.* 1975, 27th issue. New York.
VIDICH, CHARLES
   1976   *The New York Cab Driver and his Fare.* Cambridge: Schenkman.
WARE, CAROLYN
   1935   *Greenwich Village, 1920–1930.* New York: Harper & Row, Publishers.
WARNER, WILLIAM LLOYD, and P. S. LUNT
   1941   *The Social Life of a Modern Community.* New Haven: Yale University
          Press.
WEBER, MAX
   1927   *General Economic History.* Translated by F. H. Knight. London: George
          Allen & Unwin Ltd.
WEBER, MAX
   1958   *The City.* Translated and edited by Don Martindale and Gertrude Neu-
          wirth. Glencoe, Ill.: The Free Press.
WEBER, MAX
   1968.   *Economy and Society: An Outline of Interpretive Sociology.* Edited by